# Feasting on the Word

# Editorial Board

# Feasting on the Word

## Preaching the
## Revised Common Lectionary

DAVID L. BARTLETT and BARBARA BROWN TAYLOR

*General Editors*

Westminster John Knox Press
LOUISVILLE • LONDON

*Book design by Drew Stevens*
*Cover design by Lisa Buckley*

*First edition*
Published by Westminster John Knox Press
Louisville, Kentucky

This book is printed on acid-free paper that meets the American National Standards Institute Z39.48 standard. ∞

PRINTED IN THE UNITED STATES OF AMERICA

08 09 10 11 12 13 14 15 16 17—10 9 8 7 6 5 4 3 2 1

**Library of Congress Cataloging-in-Publication Data**

Feasting on the Word : preaching the revised common lectionary / David L. Bartlett and Barbara Brown Taylor, genberal editors.
    p. cm.
  Includes index.
  ISBN 978-0-664-23096-8 (v. 1: alk. paper)
  1. Lectionary preaching.   2. Common lectionary (1992)   I. Bartlett, David Lyon, 1941–
II. Taylor, Barbara Brown.
  BV4235.L43F43   2008
  251'.6—dc22                               2007047534

# Contents

# Publisher's Note

*Feasting on the Word: Preaching the Revised Common Lectionary* is an ambitious project that is offered to the Christian church as a resource for preaching and teaching.

The uniqueness of this approach in providing four perspectives on each preaching occasion from the Revised Common Lectionary sets this work apart from other lectionary materials. The theological, pastoral, exegetical, and homiletical dimensions of each biblical passage are explored with the hope that preachers will find much to inform and stimulate their preparations for preaching from this rich "feast" of materials.

This work could not have been undertaken without the deep commitments of those who have devoted countless hours to working on these tasks. Westminster John Knox Press would like to acknowledge the magnificent work of our general editors, David L. Bartlett and Barbara Brown Taylor. They are both gifted preachers with passionate concerns for the quality of preaching. They are also wonderful colleagues who embraced this huge task with vigor, excellence, and unfailing good humor. Our debt of gratitude to Barbara and David is great.

The fine support staff, project manager Joan Murchison and compiler Mary Lynn Darden, enabled all the thousands of "pieces" of the project to come together and form this impressive series. Without their strong competence and abiding persistence, these volumes could not have emerged.

The volume editors for this series are to be thanked as well. They used their superb skills as pastors and professors and ministers to work with writers and help craft their valuable insights into the highly useful entries that comprise this work.

The hundreds of writers who shared their expertise and insights to make this series possible are ones who deserve deep thanks indeed. They come from wide varieties of ministries. But they have given their labors to provide a gift to benefit the whole church and to enrich preaching in our time.

Westminster John Knox would also like to express our appreciation to Columbia Theological Seminary for strong cooperation in enabling this work to begin and proceed. Dean of Faculty and Executive Vice President D. Cameron Murchison welcomed the project from the start and drew together everything we needed. His continuing efforts have been very valuable. President Laura S. Mendenhall has provided splendid help as well. She has made seminary resources and personnel available and encouraged us in this partnership with enthusiasm and all good grace. We thank her.

It is a joy for Westminster John Knox Press to present *Feasting on the Word: Preaching the Revised Common Lectionary* to the church, its preachers, and its teachers. We believe rich resources can assist the church's ministries as the Word is proclaimed. We believe the varieties of insights found in these pages will nourish preachers who will "feast on the Word" and who will share its blessings with those who hear.

Westminster John Knox Press

# Series Introduction

A preacher's work is never done. Teaching, offering pastoral care, leading worship, and administering congregational life are only a few of the responsibilities that can turn preaching into just one more task of pastoral ministry. Yet the Sunday sermon is how the preacher ministers to most of the people most of the time. The majority of those who listen are not in crisis. They live such busy lives that few take part in the church's educational programs. They wish they had more time to reflect on their faith, but they do not. Whether the sermon is five minutes long or forty-five, it is the congregation's one opportunity to hear directly from their pastor about what life in Christ means and why it matters.

*Feasting on the Word* offers pastors focused resources for sermon preparation, written by companions on the way. With four different essays on each of the four biblical texts assigned by the Revised Common Lectionary, this series offers preachers sixteen different ways into the proclamation of God's Word on any given occasion. For each reading, preachers will find brief essays on the exegetical, theological, homiletical, and pastoral challenges of the text. The page layout is unusual. By setting the biblical passage at the top of the page and placing the essays beneath it, we mean to suggest the interdependence of the four approaches without granting priority to any one of them. Some readers may decide to focus on the Gospel passage, for instance, by reading all four essays provided for that text. Others may decide to look for connections between the Hebrew Bible, Psalm, Gospel, and Epistle texts by reading the theological essays on each one.

Wherever they begin, preachers will find what they need in a single volume produced by writers from a wide variety of disciplines and religious traditions. These authors teach in colleges and seminaries. They lead congregations. They write scholarly books as well as columns for the local newspaper. They oversee denominations. In all of these capacities and more, they serve God's Word, joining the preacher in the ongoing challenge of bringing that Word to life.

We offer this print resource for the mainline church in full recognition that we do so in the digital age of the emerging church. Like our page layout, this decision honors the authority of the biblical text, which thrives on the page as well as in the ear. While the twelve volumes of this series follow the pattern of the Revised Common Lectionary, each volume contains an index of biblical passages so that all preachers may make full use of its contents.

We also recognize that this new series appears in a post-9/11, post-Katrina world. For this reason, we provide no shortcuts for those committed to the proclamation of God's Word. Among preachers, there are books known as "Monday books" because they need to be read thoughtfully at least a week ahead of time. There are also "Saturday books," so called because they supply sermon ideas on short notice. The books in this series are not Saturday books. Our aim is to help preachers go deeper, not faster, in a world that is in need of saving words.

A series of this scope calls forth the gifts of a great many people. We are grateful first of all to Jack Keller and Don McKim of Westminster John Knox Press, who conceived this project, and to David Dobson and Jon Berquist, who worked diligently to bring the project to completion. We thank President Laura Mendenhall and Dean Cameron Murchison of Columbia Theological Seminary, who made our participation in this work possible. Our editorial board is a hardworking board, without whose patient labor and good humor this series would not exist. From the start, Joan Murchison has been the brains of the operation, managing details of epic proportions with great human kindness. Mary Lynn Darden, John Schuler, and Dilu Nicholas have supported both her and us with their administrative skills.

We have been honored to work with a multitude of gifted thinkers, writers, and editors. We present these essays as their offering—and ours—to the blessed ministry of preaching.

David L. Bartlett
Barbara Brown Taylor

*Feasting on the Word*

# *Isaiah 64:1-9*

¹O that you would tear open the heavens and come down,
    so that the mountains would quake at your presence—
²as when fire kindles brushwood
    and the fire causes water to boil—
to make your name known to your adversaries,
    so that the nations might tremble at your presence!
³When you did awesome deeds that we did not expect,
    you came down, the mountains quaked at your presence.
⁴From ages past no one has heard,
    no ear has perceived,
no eye has seen any God besides you,
    who works for those who wait for him.
⁵You meet those who gladly do right,
    those who remember you in your ways.
But you were angry, and we sinned;
    because you hid yourself we transgressed.

## Theological Perspective

This passage from Isaiah raises substantial theological questions about the character of God and God's action in the world. These verses, part of a larger lament (63:7–64:12), introduce us to both a baffling God who hides from the people and a redeeming God who is their father and maker.

Following the traditional pattern of the lament, Isaiah begins in 63:7 by recounting "the gracious deeds of the Lord." He recalls the paradigmatic event of divine deliverance—God's rescue of the Israelites from Egypt in the exodus. Yet, given God's visible and spectacular actions in that story, Isaiah finds it all the more troubling that God is not so visibly or powerfully present to postexilic Israel. As chapter 64 opens, Isaiah cries out to God, "O that you would tear open the heavens and come down"—do what you did in the past, bring fire and earthquake, make our enemies tremble! Three times he asks for God's "presence," but God has hidden himself from the people (64:5,7).

The language of God's "hiding" in this passage (echoing 1:15 and 45:15) seems to serve two purposes. First, it disabuses Israel of any notion that God belongs to them or can be contained or controlled by them (they cannot "attempt to take hold of [God]," Isa. 64:7). They must become again "like those not called by your name" (Isa. 63:19), in

## Pastoral Perspective

Advent begins with a prayer of the prophet Isaiah that is both a lament and a plea. The heavens will open and the God of Sinai will come down with righteous power to stun the enemies of Israel with his presence, bringing shock and awe to his adversaries. Even though the people of God have sinned and feel God has hidden God's face from them, they still trust God in their spiritual exile. In spite of all, they know that they are clay and the works of the hand of the Almighty Potter.

Although the details of Israel's situation differ from those of our nation, there is a deep similarity between our existential conditions. We know that our reliance upon our own massive, ruthless political power, rather than the pursuit of justice, has brought us into political disrepute among nations. Our national prayer is a kind of sacrilegious prayer of the prophets; we would depend upon military power alone to make the mountains quake and the nations tremble. Isaiah is not a proponent of a sentimental theology of easy grace. He shows us a God who is angry and silent, one who hides God's face from a people who reject God's righteous ways. For us, the path leading from repentance to redemption involves an appeal to a more universal God than was called upon by Israel. Our task and the healing of the nations depend upon our remembering that we are

<sup>6</sup>We have all become like one who is unclean,
    and all our righteous deeds are like a filthy cloth.
We all fade like a leaf,
    and our iniquities, like the wind, take us away.
<sup>7</sup>There is no one who calls on your name,
    or attempts to take hold of you;
for you have hidden your face from us,
    and have delivered us into the hand of our iniquity.
<sup>8</sup>Yet, O Lord, you are our Father;
    we are the clay, and you are our potter;
    we are all the work of your hand.
<sup>9</sup>Do not be exceedingly angry, O Lord,
    and do not remember iniquity forever.
    Now consider, we are all your people.

## Exegetical Perspective

The passage (63:19b–64:8 in Hebrew) marks the high point of an extended communal lament that begins in 63:7 and concludes at 64:12. The lectionary unfortunately drops 64:10–12. These final verses imbue the passage with a historical specificity, as well as bring it to an explosive climax.

The lection is a cry of "pain seeking understanding." Composed sometime after the Babylonian conquest (586 BCE) but prior to the rebuilding of the temple (515 BCE), the lament reflects Israel's disorientation in the wake of devastating exile. The sanctuary lies in ruins (63:19): "Zion has become a wilderness, Jerusalem a desolation" (64:10b). Although the crisis shook the religious foundation of the community to its core, Israel's response was unabashedly theological: a lament to God punctuated by plaintive questions regarding "where" God is in the face of such calamity (63:11, 15) and "why" (63:17) and building up to direct appeal in chapter 64.

The lament proper begins in 63:7 with a resounding note of praise of God's abundant "steadfast love" (Heb. *hesed*) demonstrated in history by God's "gracious deeds" (63:7). God has chosen a people and in so doing has become their "savior" (63:8). The exodus and the wilderness trek, the events of liberation and guidance, are lifted up as the

## Homiletical Perspective

The season of Advent is a time when the church is reminded to wait and prepare for the coming of the Messiah. Advent is projected from our pulpits as a time of new hope and new birth, when the Christ child is born into our world and ultimately into our hearts. Words of assurance abound amid the promises that God will come again. Yet the voice of Isaiah tells us that God may have forgotten us altogether.

On this first Sunday of Advent, preachers may squirm at the idea of preaching from Isaiah who says, "We have all become like one who is unclean, and all of our righteous deeds are like a filthy cloth" (v. 6). But that is not all. Isaiah also says, "Do not be exceedingly angry, O Lord, and do not remember iniquity forever. Now consider, we are all your people" (v. 9). Isaiah's words may seem too harsh for some preachers who want to focus on overcoming hopelessness by shining the spotlight on the manger. Yet the season of Advent has always held in tension the combination of God's judgment and God's promise.

Isaiah portrays a God in history who does awesome deeds that often surprise God's people. Yet God's people have forgotten to call upon God, who in return has hidden from the people. Isaiah portrays God as up there in some remote place while the people are down here sinning out of control.

# Isaiah 64:1-9

## Theological Perspective

order to be called anew. Second, it symbolizes a withdrawal of protection so that the Israelites will be awakened by the consequences of their sin. God "hides" in order to deconstruct a distorted set of beliefs and practices, thereby opening Israel to receive again (as gift and event) their calling to be God's people. Hiding is a form of divine judgment that ultimately serves divine mercy, a "No" that clears the ground for a more profound "Yes."

But this divine inaction is more than judgment. It tells us something about the way God has chosen to relate to the world. The hidden God of Isaiah 64 is the God who refuses to act powerfully and dramatically to rescue Israel from their distress. The frustration expressed in the opening verses of chapter 64 reflects Isaiah's struggle to reconcile the ancient stories of God's powerful presence with his present experience of God's absence.

Who has not at one time or another wondered the same thing? If in biblical times God intervened in history with "awesome deeds" (64:3), why does God not do so today? Surely there are egregious wrongs that deserve to be righted. Why would God deliver Israel from Egypt but not deliver six million Jews from Hitler's death camps? We read stories about God's spectacular interventions, yet we look in vain for such visible signs of God's involvement in the world today. We want the mountains to quake and the nations to tremble at God's presence. Instead, the sufferings of our day are too often met with divine silence.

Dietrich Bonhoeffer, writing from a German concentration camp in 1944, dared to draw the logical conclusion, "God would have us know that we must live as men who manage our lives without him. The God who is with us is the God who forsakes us (Mark 15.34). The God who lets us live in the world without the working hypothesis of God is the God before whom we stand continually. Before God and with God we live without God. God lets himself be pushed out of the world on to the cross. He is weak and powerless in the world, and that is precisely the way, the only way, in which he is with us and helps us."[1]

For Bonhoeffer this realization did not amount to a denial of faith but to a retrieval of faith in the God of the cross, whose power is suffering, whose omnipotence is vulnerability. What Bonhoeffer discovered was that the hiddenness of God is not a cloak of humility temporarily covering an awesome,

[1] Dietrich Bonhoeffer, *Letters and Papers from Prison* (New York: Macmillan, 1971), 360.

## Pastoral Perspective

all the people of this awesome God: Jews, Christians, Muslims, Hindus, and Buddhists.

It is a strange way to begin this time of Advent. Beginning Advent with weeping and a lament? That is unusual!

And powerful. This is where we need to begin. The coming of Advent jolts the church out of Ordinary Time with the invasive news that it's time to think about fresh possibilities for deliverance and human wholeness. Peace, the peace of shalom/salaam, is at the heart of the promise born at Advent, but it is difficult to arrive there safely and without becoming vulnerable along the way. It is difficult to set out on the journey without repentance and forgiveness. We can feel the tears glistening on our cheeks as we gaze upon Baghdad and Jerusalem, Darfur and Beirut, Tehran and Seoul. We are living in a time of brokenheartedness, a time when most Americans know that we must find ways to make peace in Iraq, but we feel helpless, hopeless, and just plain brokenhearted over the devastation in the Middle East.

I recall a comment that our country has changed over the past years from one that wanted to be good to one that wants to feel good. We see some of this desire every Christmas season as people run from store to store and shopping mall to shopping mall, searching for the things that will bring them and their families some sort of fulfillment and happiness. Peace, the kind of peace that the world is hungering for, will not come from trying to fill ourselves up with material things. We try to stem our hurt and pride by running away from pain and caring only about what is ours. We cannot create peace through selfishness, but by opening ourselves to hope. Hope is what is left when your worst fears have been realized and you are no longer optimistic about the future. Hope is what comes with a broken heart willing to be mended.

"No eye has seen any God besides you," Isaiah pleads, "who works for those who wait" for the forces of hate and evil to be overthrown, the people to be restored, and the house of David to be revived. A righteous branch will emerge to execute justice, hope, and possibility for God's people. Hold on to the promises of God, encourages the prophet, even though the circumstances are bleak and seem nearly impossible. We pray for the hope of Advent: that God will break into the ordinary, bringing the promise of peace, hope, and restored life.

At Advent, God's people summon the courage and the spiritual strength to remember that the holy

paradigmatic examples of God's "great favor" (63:11–14). Such events empowered a people and made for God "a glorious name" (v. 14b). But God's unmediated care was met by rebellion (63:10). God's turnaround is swift: God turns from "savior" to "enemy" vis-à-vis the people, and Israel feels abandoned. The preface to the lection in 63:7–19 acknowledges Israel's sin as sufficient warrant for God's absence, but at the same time refuses to excuse God from withholding compassion (63:15). The stage, then, is set for direct petition.

The lection follows a movement that progresses in fits and starts, specifically with two highly disjunctive sections ("but" in v. 5b and "yet" in v. 8a). It opens with direct appeal to God that recalls an earlier time of God's decisive action (64:1–3) and slides into a profession of faith, an assertion of God's incomparability and care (vv. 4–5a). But as in 63:10, the language abruptly turns toward confession of sin and acknowledgment of God's anger (64:5b–7). In verse 8, however, another faith assertion is made that highlights the relational intimacy between God and the people. The lection concludes as it began, namely, with urgent petition (v. 9).

Content-wise, the lection proceeds with a series of evocative images and bold assertions. Stronger than its parallel in 63:15, the opening verse in chapter 64 calls God to immediate and decisive action, expressed in poignant desperation ("O that . . ."). The petition is cast in the language of theophany, of God's earth-shattering, heaven-shredding presence (cf. Ps. 68:7–8; Hab. 3:3–15). Flaming brush and boiling water connote nature's travail before God's inbreaking presence (Isa. 64:2a). The quaking of the mountains has its parallel in the trembling of the nations (v. 2b). The community fondly recalls when God caused just that by committing actions without precedent ("unexpected") in behalf of a people in crisis (v. 3). God's mighty acts evince an incomparability that is no match theistically: no other god has ever been "seen" (v. 4a). All mighty acts are ascribed to the one God who "works" salvation for those who long ("wait") for God (v. 4b). A pervasive theme through-out Isaiah and the Psalms (e.g., Isa. 8:17; 30:18; 40:31; Ps. 37:7), "waiting for God" is no passive endeavor; it involves painful longing and bold allegiance, in short, a passionate patience. It is a tensive waiting charged with the pathos of lament and conjoined with the joy of remembrance and the anticipation of praise.

But an explosion erupts in the middle of verse 5. The message up to this point is one of mutual intimacy and care between God and Israel: God's

However, Isaiah reminds God that the people are like clay that needs to be molded into the people God wants them to be. Isaiah calls upon God's long-term memory by reminding God that the people should be forgiven of their iniquities because they are all God's people.

The preacher needs to begin by connecting the longing of the people of Israel in Isaiah's time with the longing of the people in the pews today. The preacher will want to know under what conditions Isaiah makes his statements. Obviously, the people of Israel know a lot about waiting for God, but their confidence in God has all but disintegrated. The preacher will recognize that the situation of Israel is very similar to the people who sit in the pew waiting, wanting, and expecting to see the face of God.

A decision will need to be made about how to construct the sermon in the present-day situation without losing the historical biblical perspective. Are we active participants in Isaiah's message? Does the text need to be interpreted from God's perspective or Isaiah's perspective? Is the sermon to be told from an onlooker's perspective, with certain analogies to the birth of Jesus?

The fact is that we *are* onlookers and the Advent season opens us to the need for God to break into our lives. Advent affords us the opportunity to look at how God interacts with humankind from ages past to the present day. Unfortunately, many of us are onlookers from the perspective of the culture in which we live. Hence the sermon message must compete with the prominent and distracting cultural messages of Christmas. Opening the ears of those who cannot wait to shop for Christmas sales requires the preacher to stand alongside the message of Isaiah. Shaping the sermon as a shopper eavesdropping on a conversation Isaiah has with God may be one way to design the sermon.

Such a conversation is not without some assumptions about when and where Isaiah decides to share his concerns with God. The text very clearly illustrates Isaiah's concern for the people of Israel. The text also shares Isaiah's concerns for God and perhaps God's selective memory. Isaiah begins by reminding God of the history and the intimacy God had with the people. From time to time, God even surprised the people of Israel. Flipping through his notes, Isaiah recalls how the mountains used to quake at God's presence.

Isaiah probably takes God by surprise when he hints that it may be God's fault that the people have fallen deeper and deeper into sin and rebellion. His

# Isaiah 64:1-9

## Theological Perspective

powerful glory (a kind of Clark Kent/Superman act), but rather is a reflection of the divine character, a divine determination to relate to the world through the vulnerable path of noncoercive love and suffering service rather than through domination and force.

God's refusal to replicate a Red Sea–type deliverance does not mean that God has abandoned Israel (or the church). Our hope does not rely on God's acting today in the same ways God acted in the ancient stories, but it does rely on God's being the same God yesterday, today, and tomorrow—a God who hears our cries, a God who does not abandon us, a God who will finally redeem all that is lost in a new heaven and new earth (Isa. 65:17). The tradition of biblical lament does not invoke the past as nostalgia, nor does it dismiss the present in despair; rather, it draws on the collective memories of God's people as a source of hope for the future.

Here the images of God as father and potter are helpful. Isaiah refers to God as "father" twice (63:16) in the verses preceding this pericope and again in 64:8 as the lament shifts from confession to plea. In contrast to the hidden God, the image of God as father and potter suggests closeness and personal connection. Yet neither image suggests a God who "would tear open the heavens." Instead they evoke a God whose mode of action looks more like that of the artist or the parent than that of the superhero. God forms and shapes the people as a father over time shapes the character of his children, as a potter lovingly molds her clay. Isaiah calls on Israel to be malleable in the hands of God, and he reminds God to fulfill the task of forming Israel into a people of blessing.

In the season of Advent, Christians imaginatively enter a time of waiting for the Christ child, who comes as God hidden in human form, who comes not to inaugurate an apocalyptic cleansing but to reveal the power of the powerless in his self-giving on the cross. In so doing, he reveals the will of the Father who is eternally, patiently molding and shaping the clay of creation into the New Jerusalem.

SCOTT BADER-SAYE

## Pastoral Perspective

breaks into the daily. In tiny ways, we can open our broken hearts to the healing grace of God, who opens the way to peace. May that peace come upon us as a healing balm, as a mighty winter river, gushing and rushing through the valleys of our prideful fear and our own self-righteous indignation. As a friend has said, this is not a season for passive waiting and watching. It is a season of wailing and weeping, of opening up our lives and our souls with active anticipation and renewed hope. At the church I serve, we even fantasized about building a wailing wall close to the peace pole, a place where we can pray and weep for our broken world and then get up and continue the hope of God, made fresh and new again.

Last December, at the end of a beautiful Advent retreat, all who were there climbed up a hill to a small chapel at a place called Sky Farm. The chapel was dark and quiet and smelled of incense and old wood. We sang, "Let there be peace on earth, and let it begin with me." Each one of us was given a bright candle to carry in the darkened world, in order that we might burn brightly with the hope of the prophets and the courage of the gospel. The holy broke into the ordinary, flooding us with hope for peace and making our hearts strong again, so that we could move into the world with courage and compassion.

And so we do not lose heart; rather, we live with our hearts broken open so that compassion, caring, and God's reckless love can find a way into our hearts and the heart of the world. Make straight in our hearts a highway for the possibility of peace.

PATRICIA E. DE JONG

## Exegetical Perspective

grace has been met with Israel's trusting allegiance. But now the very integrity of that relationship is threatened by sin. Astonishingly, the lament claims that no one party is at fault. While fully acknowledging its sin and fragility (v. 6), the community charges that God too is implicated: "*because* you hid yourself we transgressed" (v. 5b; although this verse is reconstructed from textually corrupted Hebrew) and "*for* you have hidden your face" (v. 7b). Human sin is occasioned, indeed initiated, by divine absence! God cannot afford to wash God's hands of the "filth" that has beset the community. Such a claim, however, is meant not to excuse the community before God, but rather to motivate God to act in redemption. Indeed, punishment in this passage avoids making direct reference to God's punishing hand; rather, it is "the hand of our iniquity" that is fundamental. Punishment is spelled out as the *consequence* of iniquity. Iniquity carries its own power to dissemble and dissolve a community (vv. 6b, 7b). The translation of the Hebrew text of verse 7b is "and [you] have melted us into (or by) the hand of our iniquity." The community confesses a guilt so pervasive that even God is not immune, a guilt that has overtaken both Israel and its God.

But the clincher comes in the final section (vv. 8–9 [12]), which marks a return to the relationship of intimacy explicated in vv. 4–5, but now inscribed with images as poignant and evocative as those employed in the confession. These final verses establish the ties that bind God to God's people. God is "our Father," equated earlier with "our Redeemer from of old" (63:16). To claim God as paternal is to assert God's familial claim upon Israel and Israel's claim upon God, a kinship that necessitates continued recognition and care for Israel. Indeed, Israel was begotten by God in more ways than one. The community is also God's handiwork, pottery, no less, shaped by loving hands (cf. Jer. 18). God would not let a people slide into destruction any more than a father would sacrifice his son or a potter would destroy her prized bowl. The bottom line is that "we are all your people," whether God likes it or not, for the covenantal bond is indissoluble. God, thus, is bound to act.

WILLIAM P. BROWN

## Homiletical Perspective

statement appears to be the-chicken-or-the-egg question. Was it the people who caused God to get angry and hide from the people, or did the absence of God cause the people to do unrighteous things? Isaiah's final assertion is a metaphor that God is the potter and the people are the clay. Isaiah implores God to take responsibility for the clay and mold them into the people of God.

By telling the story, Isaiah seems to be reminding both God and the people of Israel about their history together. God is in charge of the world, and Isaiah does not want the people to forget about God's sovereignty. On the other hand, Isaiah does not want God to forget that the people of God need to be molded into whatever God wants them to be. Isaiah also recognizes that God can easily get angry at the people, but he pleads for God not to hold a grudge forever.

The season of Advent provides every preacher the same opportunity to be as forthright as Isaiah. The words of Isaiah remind us that God is and has been faithful. When the faith community recalls that God is present among them, then perhaps they will also see how God has molded them in the same way the potter molds the clay.

Yet recognizing God's presence may be a daily task, especially given the world in which we live. Like Isaiah, the preacher will need to remind the people when God has been visible in their midst. Waiting with hope that God will be visible once again is the call of Isaiah to God. Watching with eyes to see is the call of Isaiah to the people of faith. To hear the voice of Isaiah is to proclaim that Advent is more than a time to hear promises about God. Advent becomes a season of attentiveness to the presence of God already among us.

DONALD BOOZ

# Psalm 80:1-7, 17-19

[1]Give ear, O Shepherd of Israel,
   you who lead Joseph like a flock!
You who are enthroned upon the cherubim, shine forth
[2]   before Ephraim and Benjamin and Manasseh.
Stir up your might,
   and come to save us!

[3]Restore us, O God;
   let your face shine, that we may be saved.

[4]O LORD God of hosts,
   how long will you be angry with your people's prayers?
[5]You have fed them with the bread of tears,
   and given them tears to drink in full measure.

## Theological Perspective

"Restore us, O God; let your face shine, that we may be saved" (Ps. 80:3). This is a psalm of deep yearning, and thus very appropriate for use in worship on the first Sunday of Advent. Much of the theological substance of this liturgical season is latent in this brief text, and can be brought to mind, pondered, and given voice through its use. As with so much of the Psalms, the language here resonates with relevant passages and themes throughout the Bible—in texts that were part of the psalmists' own heritage and in texts that bear their influence. In this way, the "prayer book of the Bible," as Dietrich Bonhoeffer called the Psalter, helps the Bible itself become the prayer book of the church. Two interrelated theological features may be of particular importance to our reading and interpretation of these verses now.

One of these features has to do with how the community of faith understands its most pressing need before God. A tension is evident in this psalm, as elsewhere in the Psalter, among various understandings of the source of our distress. Two options rise to prominence in this psalm. In one of these, the source of our troubles is "our enemies": other people, who are out to get us. In our prayers, accordingly, we call on God to come and save us from them, or to make us victorious over them. God is invoked as our ally.

## Pastoral Perspective

The people of Psalm 80 are in a world of hurt. They want God to know about it. "Give ear!" (v. 1). They hold God responsible for it. "You make us the scorn of our neighbors; our enemies laugh among themselves" (v. 6). Most of all, they want God to *do* something about it. "Stir up your might, and come to save us!" (v. 2).

This no-holds-barred psalm is an odd source for a pastoral word in Advent. It portrays God as unhearing, heartless, and downright hurtful. Unlike its counterpart in Psalm 23, this Shepherd of Israel did not walk with the people in the valley of the shadows or protect them with rod and staff. God did not prepare a table for them, but fed them with "the bread of tears." In the presence of their enemies, they are the objects of ridicule. Their cup overflows with tears, not blessings.

What pastoral word, much less Advent hope, can be found in such a psalm? What is needed is a profound word, especially in this season. Psalm 80 gives voice to a people's grief and anguish at God's seeming absence. In so doing, it gives them power. As anyone who has experienced loss can affirm, grief both paralyzes and silences us. We feel "at a loss for words" or, in Paul's description, left only with "sighs too deep for words."

This psalm provides the words and, with them, a way out of the despair. Like other biblical laments, it

⁶You make us the scorn of our neighbors;
  our enemies laugh among themselves.
⁷Restore us, O God of hosts;
  let your face shine, that we may be saved. . . .
. . . . . . . . . . . . . . . . . . . . . . . . . . . . . . . . . . . . . . .
¹⁷But let your hand be upon the one at your right hand,
  the one whom you made strong for yourself.
¹⁸Then we will never turn back from you;
  give us life, and we will call on your name.
¹⁹Restore us, O Lᴏʀᴅ God of hosts;
  let your face shine, that we may be saved.

## Exegetical Perspective

Psalm 80 is a communal lament: a prayer for salvation in response to a catastrophe that has befallen the community. It is the sixth in a series of nine psalms of Asaph that open Book III (Pss. 73–89) of the Psalter. First Chronicles reports that Asaph was the chief among those Levites appointed by King David for "the singing of praises to the Lᴏʀᴅ" (16:7). The designation "of Asaph" thus indicates the tradition or style of psalm composition and performance begun by Asaph and continued by his descendants and students.

The mention of the tribes of Ephraim and Manasseh and the half-tribes of Joseph and Benjamin suggests that the psalm refers to some catastrophe that befell the northern kingdom of Israel, perhaps even its utter destruction by the Assyrians in 722 BCE. Refugees who survived the invasion by fleeing south into Judah might have composed it; the Jerusalem temple establishment would later have absorbed the psalm into its worship. Given the massiveness of the fall of the north in the history of God's people, however, anyone who endured a similar catastrophe later could have recalled it as a way of giving voice to their own sorrow, so that a precise date or occasion for the psalm's composition remains elusive.

The lectionary omits verses 8–16, an extended metaphor that succinctly retells the story of the

## Homiletical Perspective

A fruitful area for the preacher to explore in this psalm is the tension between vv.1–2 and vv. 4–6. This tension is the gap between theology and experience. As the psalmist speaks for the people, he recognizes that what they believe and what is happening around them do not cohere.

The people believe at least two broad affirmations about God. God is strong and powerful, represented by God's place "enthroned upon the cherubim." This powerful God is not distant or uncaring, however. God is a Shepherd who takes special interest in and cares for the people. As with all good theology, this poem mixes its metaphors; God is ruler, shepherd, and vinedresser. All of these metaphors speak to God's might and deep involvement with the people.

This belief and trust in God cannot—in the minds of the people and the psalmist who serves as their spokesperson—be reconciled with the crisis hanging over the community. The psalmist interprets the crisis not merely as the absence of God, but as God's active punishment of the people. God is angry. God has fed them tears.

The implicit assumptions behind the psalm's treatment of the divine/human relationship are refreshing and theologically helpful. In contrast to many other scriptural understandings of suffering, this psalm recognizes that suffering and trouble are a

# Psalm 80:1-7, 17-19

## Theological Perspective

Contrasted with this is another understanding, in which the source of our troubles is—to put it briefly—God. What this means, and why this is the case, are other questions, and various other psalms explore various possibilities in this regard, but often—as in this instance—that question is left open. What is clear is that in this psalm the tension is decisively resolved in favor of this second understanding.

The tension between the two approaches is perhaps more evident in the complete psalm than in these selections, and may reflect something of the psalm's redaction history, but in any case there is no doubt as to its resolution. In this, our psalm displays a tendency characteristic of the biblical canon as a whole. Karl Barth put the point memorably in addressing a conference of preachers in 1922: "To suffer in the Bible means to suffer because of *God*; to sin, to sin against *God*; to doubt, to doubt of *God*; to perish, to perish at the hand of *God*."[1] This "monotheizing" dynamic in Scripture, as James Sanders has called it,[2] is evident in such lines as these: "You have fed [your people] with the bread of tears. . . . You make us the scorn of our neighbors; our enemies laugh among themselves" (Ps. 80:5–6). Whatever the more proximate facts of the situation may be, *God* is the ultimate problem with which (or with whom) we need to deal. The enemies (or neighbors; it is worth noting that the two words are in apposition in the parallel construction here) are, along with ourselves, to be seen in a more comprehensive context, and our prayers will take on a different character in consequence of this changed perspective.

The God-problem that becomes the main theme in this psalm might be more clearly identified as the lack of God, or the unavailability of God. But the self-examination or introspection that is a familiar element in many psalms makes no appearance in this one. There is no searching of the heart, no probing of reasons for God's anger or withdrawal or distance, no explicit acknowledgment of fault. There is simply sheer need for God: the pain of absence and the longing for God's presence.

The language in which this longing is expressed points to the second theological feature of particular interest in the season of Advent. It is a language of radiance. The initial "shine forth" (80:1) and the

[1] Karl Barth, "The Need and Promise of Christian Preaching," in *The Word of God and the Word of Man*, trans. Douglas Horton (New York: Harper & Row, 1957), 119.
[2] James A. Sanders, *Canon and Community: A Guide to Canonical Criticism* (Philadelphia: Fortress Press, 1984), 56–60.

## Pastoral Perspective

breaks the silence and validates the reality of the people's suffering. With Job, it cries, "I will speak in the anguish of my spirit" (Job 7:11).

But in contrast to Job, the voice of Psalm 80 increases the power of its anguished words. First, its voice is *communal*. This is not one lone person lamenting his or her fate. It is a whole congregation of Jobs crying out. Its communal voice reminds speaker and listener alike they are not alone.

Second, it is a *bold* voice, not one of weak resignation. Other psalms (e.g., Pss. 5, 55, 84) ask God to "give ear to my sighs." But this "give ear" ends with an exclamation point! Moreover, the psalm contains no confession and hardly a note of repentance (v. 18's "then we will never turn back from" may allude to their having done so in the past). Instead the psalm lays the responsibility for the people's suffering solely at God's feet. "You have fed them with the bread of tears. . . . You make us the scorn of our neighbors" (vv. 5–6).

Its unrepentant tone could seem out of place at the start of Advent's penitential season. But Psalm 80 is an incredible confession, not of sin, but of faith. It confesses the people's trust in a God who is big enough to hear their hurt, strong enough to handle their anger and pain. It also identifies the congregation as a people who, even in their suffering, have the courage to call on the Lord God of hosts to help them.

Third, it is a *liturgical* voice. This bold psalm is to be used in worship. That liturgical context under-scores the legitimacy of the lament. The people do not have to "clean up" their anguish or deny their disappointment in God, even in God's house. The psalm also demonstrates the pastoral power of corporate worship. *Together* the people proclaim what they have experienced, who they trust God to be, and the power of the covenant between God and them.

Fourth, it is a *prophetic* voice. This anguished voice from thousands of years ago can be heard in the voices of our time—the loved one with a diagnosis of MS, the worker whose job has been outsourced, the Katrina evacuee with no place to call home, the victim of senseless war in Iraq or senseless violence in our schools.

Finally, it is a *hopeful* voice. The psalm moves the community beyond disappointment with God to a call to God to act. "Let your hand be upon the one at your right hand"—be it the king or the whole people. That call to action is also expressed in the refrain of verses 3, 7, 19: "Restore us . . . let your face shine, that we may be saved." It reminds them of

## Exegetical Perspective

exodus from Egypt and the settlement into Canaan in terms of a vine that God transplanted. After the vine spread through the land, foreigners stole its fruit, boars ravaged it, and unnamed others cut it and burned it. Consistent with the rest of the lament, the psalmist asks why God has allowed this, calling upon God to look with compassion upon the vine and with wrath toward its destroyers.

If God is a vintner in verses 8–16, the rest of the psalm portrays God through the metaphor of the shepherd-king. The psalm begins by addressing God as the "Shepherd of Israel" who is "enthroned upon the cherubim," a reference to the empty throne in the Holy of Holies in the Jerusalem temple. Verse 2 invokes the corresponding functions of king and shepherd: "Stir up your might, and come to save us!" The flock cries out to the shepherd for rescue. King David, the man after God's own heart (1 Sam. 13:14; Acts 13:22), was both a fearless warrior and a shepherd, and thus provides part of the earthly basis for the metaphor.

Verse 3 introduces a refrain that the psalm repeats in verses 7 and 19, but with each repetition adding a term to the divine name: verse 3 "God" (*'elohim*); verse 7 "God of hosts" (*'elohim tsebaot*); verse 19 "LORD God of hosts" (*yhwh 'elohim tsebaot*). The refrain grows from the generic appellation "God," a term for deity with cognate forms throughout the Semitic languages, to the addition of the honorific "of hosts," to the addition of the proper name unique to Israel's God. Doubtless the expansion of the divine name would have been accompanied by a corresponding crescendo or musical figure with each repetition. The refrain encapsulates the purpose of the psalm, to implore God to restore God's people.

The long form of the divine name reappears in verse 4, a question that introduces the psalmist's complaint. The NRSV's "angry" is an interpretation of a metaphor; the Hebrew asks how long God will "fume" against the prayers of the people. Certainly to "fume" frequently means to be furious, and to show it outwardly. One thinks of cartoon figures with smoke coming out of their ears. It is also possible, however, that the metaphor here conveys divine indifference. Isaiah 6:4 portrays the heavenly temple as filled with smoke. Perhaps our psalmist envisions the prayers of God's people never quite penetrating through a thick haze of divine indifference to the suffering of God's people. The psalmist calls for God to "shine forth" (v. 1), and to "let your face shine, that we may be saved" (vv. 3, 7, 19). This divine light, a symbol of transcendent

## Homiletical Perspective

mystery. At no point within the psalm does the poet assume that the people are suffering because of their sins. This is an especially instructive insight for the contemporary church. Although foolish and reckless behavior can lead to suffering, the church needs to hear that sin and suffering do not always line up in direct correlation. Far too often, trouble, illness, setbacks, depression, and a host of other manifestations of suffering carry guilt as part of the baggage. The terrorist attacks in September of 2001 prompted a number of reprehensible "interpretations" of God's purposes within that event. The psalm is an outcry in response to sustained, community-wide, and confusing misery, originally the Assyrian assault on Samaria. Although contemporary preachers will stop short of blaming God for cruelty, they will give voice to the laments of the community without assuming that the suffering is a deserved punishment for wrongdoing.

In the tension between theology and experience, creative new understandings and growth can occur. The sensitive preacher will explore the specific ways that tension occurs in the congregation. A skillful sermon on this psalm will enable the congregation both to move beyond simplistic theological assertions and to deepen a sense of trust in God in spite of life's pain that erupts unexpectedly and inexplicably. The preacher will want to reflect on how the congregation might express God's power. How might one convey the sense of God's majesty behind the phrase "enthroned upon the cherubim"? What image might work best in a particular congregation? How might the people in a local church understand God's particular interest in them, as expressed in the poem by the metaphors of shepherd and vinedresser (which does not appear in the part of the psalm recommended by the lectionary committee)? In what ways do the members of the congregation experience God as absent, or even as oppressive? Would any member of the congregation dare to express an understanding of God as angry? The members of the congregation may not acknowledge having such sentiments. A careful exploration of this psalm, with its honest ventilation about God's active participation in the suffering of the people, may help the congregation give voice to suppressed frustration at God. Permission to express anger at God can be liberating.

The psalm expects a concrete action from God. The psalmist pleads on behalf of the people for God to intervene in a specific situation. In the earliest form of the psalm, the poet wanted God to intervene

# Psalm 80:1-7, 17-19

## Theological Perspective

repeated "let your face shine" (80:3, 7, 19) are particularly striking. They immediately evoke the Aaronic blessing of Numbers 6:24–26 ("the LORD make his face to shine upon you . . . the LORD lift up his countenance upon you") and carry reminders of the divine radiance that figures so vividly in the Sinai stories—especially that of the transfiguration of the face of Moses by the glory of the Lord, in Exodus 34:29–35.

For Christian readers, the transfiguration accounts in the Synoptic Gospels also come readily to mind—and understandably so, given the close literary and theological connections between the Sinai narrative and the earliest accounts of Christ's transfiguration.[3] The shining face the psalmist seeks is not simply a figure for divine favor; it is more fundamentally a theophany that is being sought, a manifestation of the divine reality that will restore the people to the life that they are meant for. God's energizing radiance brings not only illumination or the assurance of favor, but life itself.

And where does that glory shine forth? Here too the connection with the transfiguration narratives can be a crucial key, just as those narratives themselves are a kind of key to what has been going on (and will continue to go on) in the events of Jesus' life: the enfleshment or becoming human of God, and the restoration of humankind in God.

An important aspect of the transfiguration motif in the Orthodox tradition is its ascetical significance. That is to say, we are unprepared to see the light of God's glory where it is being manifested: in the humility of Jesus. "Our hearts are conditioned by the society in which we live far more than by the Gospel."[4] The reconditioning of our hearts—painful as that process may be—is part of what we rightly pray for, when we pray this psalm in Advent. "Restore us, O God; let your face shine, that we may be saved."

CHARLES M. WOOD

## Pastoral Perspective

God's past faithfulness, when God's countenance did bless them, and it expresses their hope that God has the power to save them now.

As a book about a high school girl's basketball team affirms, "hope is a muscle." In Psalm 80, the congregation builds their muscle of hope and faith with three repetitions of "Restore, shine, save." Each repetition expands the image of God's power. The "O God" of v. 3 becomes "O God of hosts" (v. 7) and finally "O LORD God of hosts" (v. 19).

As often happens in times of loss, hope is mixed with longing for the past. "Restore us" comes from the Hebrew word *shub* ("turn again"), the word Orpah used to tell Ruth and Naomi to go back home. "Let your face shine," recalls Moses' encounter with God on Sinai and his brother Aaron's blessing on the people (Num. 6:24–26). Longing for the "glory days" is not limited to the original community of Psalm 80. Especially at Christmas, our congregations are often filled with people with that same yearning for restoration of a life we once knew, be it the life of our families, relationships, churches, or even nation.

But while we may look back, God always looks ahead. For Christians, the psalm leads not to the past but to the future when God did "give ear." Indeed, the Shepherd of Israel gave much more, namely God's whole self. The Lord God of hosts left the throne of cherubim and joined the rest of us in Psalm 80's congregation, who can also know what it is like to feel that God has forsaken you.

God answered the demand, "Let your face shine that we might be saved," though not as anyone expected. Not in a return to the glory days of the past, but in the light of the Child born in Bethlehem, the light the darkness has never overcome.

TALITHA ARNOLD

---

[3] See John Anthony McGuckin, *The Transfiguration of Christ in Scripture and Tradition* (Lewiston, NY: Edwin Mellen Press, 1986), chap. 1.
[4] Ibid., 141.

power throughout the religions of the ancient Near East, cuts through the smoke, whether of anger or indifference, restoring God's beneficent interest and unleashing power to save.

The complaint continues, conveying grief and suffering through the metaphor of food and drink consisting only of tears (v. 5). The "scorn" of verse 6 relies on a textual variant; rabbis Rozenberg and Zlotowitz translate the line, "You have sown strife with our neighbors."[1] This reading would point toward an attack by enemies, as opposed to a natural catastrophe. In any case, the psalmist sees God, not enemies or nature, as the cause of Israel's suffering. This is not a psalm of confession; the psalmist nowhere mentions the sins of the people. Rather, the psalmist cries out to God for restoration, rescue, and, in verse 16b, the punishment of Israel's enemies. (The first reading for this Sunday, Isa. 64:5–6, connects God's anger with the people's sin.)

After the metaphor of the vine (vv. 8–16), the psalmist calls for God to convey power to the earthly, or possibly messianic, king (v. 17), promises fidelity and faithfulness in return for the gift of life (v. 18), and drives home the request for salvation, invoking the long form of the divine name in the refrain (v. 19).

The metaphor of God as shepherd-king lays the foundation for the messianic expectation that Jesus invokes. Whereas Psalm 80 anticipates that God will act by conveying divine power upon the Davidic king, the one at God's right hand (v. 17), Jesus points toward the ultimate rescue, the consummation of history, "'the Son of Man coming in clouds' with great power and glory" (Mark 13:26). Jesus identifies himself with the shepherd in Mark 14:27, and in 14:62 Jesus declares to the council that he is the one "seated at the right hand of the Power."

PAUL D. BRASSEY

in the Assyrian crisis. As the final form of the poem evolved, it was reworked in other situations, but usually with a specific outcome in mind. How can we speak of God acting in the individual and community crises of the contemporary congregation? How do we hope God will act? How might we tell if God's face is shining in our midst? Would the difference be in our circumstances or within us? Certainly we can hope and pray for God's intervention in specific situations. We can pray for the capacity to trust when situations do not change. That the psalm was written initially for one situation in Samaria and then reworked for subsequent situations indicates that God's intervention never settles the matter. New trouble, new suffering break out afresh. In lamentation the people and their leaders maintain a dialogue with God. That dialogue is always better than giving up on God.

The season of Advent is marked by anticipation, which presupposes a sense of longing. This psalm gives expression to the longing of an ancient people for God to act. The opening stanza calls for God to do four things: give ear, shine forth, stir up might, and save. The preacher can proclaim how God has done these things in the birth of Jesus, where God did not act in the way this psalmist would have expected. God did not end political and military oppression. God's might was expressed in the vulnerability of a baby who grew up to die at the hands of the oppressors. The first advent sustains us until the second advent, when God will establish the dominion in its fullness. The birth of Jesus the Christ shows God's response to this psalm. God has given ear, has shone forth, has stirred up might, and has brought salvation. God's answer to this psalm sustains us until God acts fully for salvation. We are freed from the assumption that all suffering represents punishment and anger from God. We can trust that God will continue to lead us as a shepherd and tend us as a vinedresser until the time when all of creation recognizes God as the one enthroned on the cherubim.

CHARLES L. AARON JR.

---

[1]Martin S. Rozenberg and Bernard M. Zlotowitz, *The Book of Psalms: A New Translation and Commentary* (Northvale, NJ: Jason Aronson, 1999), 499.

# 1 Corinthians 1:3-9

[3]Grace to you and peace from God our Father and the Lord Jesus Christ.
[4] I give thanks to my God always for you because of the grace of God that has been given you in Christ Jesus, [5]for in every way you have been enriched in him, in speech and knowledge of every kind— [6]just as the testimony of Christ has been strengthened among you— [7]so that you are not lacking in any spiritual gift as you wait for the revealing of our Lord Jesus Christ. [8]He will also strengthen you to the end, so that you may be blameless on the day of our Lord Jesus Christ. [9]God is faithful; by him you were called into the fellowship of his Son, Jesus Christ our Lord.

## Theological Perspective

This text points to one of the unique characteristics of the Christian religion: the intimate relationship between God and the Christian community that God bestows in and through Jesus Christ. Among the world religions, Christianity gives witness to an intimate relationship among God, creation, and, in particular, the Christian community. This relationship is contextual: in other words, it takes its life and its shape from the particular terms of people's cultures. Hence, Jesus is our brother, our Lord, our ancestor, our beloved one, our enlightened spirit. While modern and postmodern arguments focused on historical evidence and/or propositional statements continue to frame most theological discussions about the uniqueness of Christ, Christianity's uniqueness springs from an intimate relationship between God and God's followers *in and through* Jesus Christ.

Paul celebrates the grace of God given to the community through Jesus Christ (v. 4). *In* Jesus Christ, the Christian community "has been enriched" in all ways of being—"in speech and knowledge *of every kind*." *In* Jesus Christ the Christian community in Corinth lives the way of Jesus, living out the faith *en lo cotidiano* (in daily life) and, reciprocally, strengthening the testimony of Christ among the church. Paul provides us with a

## Pastoral Perspective

In this lection Paul offers words of blessing and thanksgiving as part of his initial greeting to the church in Corinth. First words and last words often are vested with particular significance, because the hearer tends to them with unusual care. So Paul chooses his words carefully.

After brief words of greeting (not included in this lection), Paul proceeds to bless the Corinthian congregation. He has some urgent matters to take up with them, but those can wait for a time. Instead, Paul begins by offering a gift of blessing. It is an offering that, in itself, reminds his readers of the bonds they share as pastor and people. A pastor, after all—or, in this case, before all—is one who offers blessings. Marilynne Robinson's novel *Gilead* portrays the act of blessing as central to the pastoral vocation. At one point the narrator, Pastor John Ames, writes to his young son:

> I don't wish to be urging the ministry on you, but there are some advantages to it you might not know to take account of if I did not point them out. Not that you have to be a minister to confer blessing. You are simply much more likely to find yourself in that position. It's a thing people expect of you.[1]

[1]Marilynne Robinson, *Gilead* (New York: Farrar, Straus & Giroux, 2004), 23.

## Exegetical Perspective

Our canonical 1 Corinthians is not Paul's first communication with the Corinthian churches, nor is it even his first letter to them. The interpreter does well to bear in mind that contemporary readers of 1 Corinthians eavesdrop not only on someone else's conversation but on a rather small part of it.

The greeting, "grace to you and peace" (1:3a), which occurs in virtually every Pauline epistle, comes not from the letter writers Paul and Sosthenes (1:1) but from "God our Father and the Lord Jesus Christ" (1:3b). The apostles write not on their own but on behalf of the one who has commissioned them. The letter also ends with a reminder of the grace of the Lord Jesus (16:23) as well as the apostle's own love for his addressees (16:24).

The letter's thanksgiving (1:4–9) telegraphs to readers at the outset the basic concerns of the writer. In this case, Paul's concerns are several related issues pertaining to the welfare of the house churches in Corinth: their charismatic giftedness (vv. 4, 7), their wealth—particularly but not only in terms of speech and knowledge (v. 5), the revelation of Christ in glory on the Day of the Lord (vv. 7, 8), and the faithfulness of the God who has called them (v. 9). Each of these subjects recurs throughout 1 Corinthians.

Paul thanks God first for the grace that has been given the Corinthians in Christ Jesus (1:4). This

## Homiletical Perspective

In his letter to the Corinthians, Paul confronts a number of divisions and controversies in the church in Corinth. Here at the beginning of the letter, however, Paul does not even mention these conflicts. Instead, he gives thanks for the church. Even in speaking to a divided church for which he will later have some strong words, Paul is able to discern the gifts and the promise of the people.

In these opening words, Paul offers a helpful reminder for preachers who may be tempted to dwell on the challenges facing congregations and ignore the gifts that are already present and active in the church. Giving thanks for a congregation's gifts and promise provides one way to begin building up the community of faith, even in the midst of situations of conflict and division. Such words of thanksgiving may provide encouragement and vision for a congregation and possibly inspire them to begin living more fully into the realities for which the preacher gives thanks. Prophetic, challenging, critical preaching need not be thoroughly negative, but can take place in the context of thanksgiving and appreciation. Indeed, such words of thanksgiving may open congregations to hear more fully the words of challenge that also need to be spoken.

Paul's approach to thanksgiving, however, is carefully chosen. He does not simply celebrate the

# 1 Corinthians 1:3-9

## Theological Perspective

beautiful two-way movement. *In and through* Jesus we live like Jesus, so that our testimony is strengthened and our community's faithful are edified. *In and through* the grace of God in Jesus, we become partners in God's testimony in and for the world.

This gift of grace *in and through* Jesus Christ nurtures and prepares the community for its journey of faith. *In and through* Jesus Christ the intimate relationship between God and the Christian community generates life and perseverance, steadiness and testimony, so that we can wait for the complete revelation of our Lord Jesus Christ (v. 7). *In and through* Jesus Christ the faithful are equipped, "not lacking in any spiritual gift" (v. 7), to remain faithful until Jesus Christ is fully revealed. Living *in and through* Jesus Christ, the Christian community discovers and rediscovers the grace of God, over and over, fresh every time. *In and through* Jesus Christ, we are faithful witnesses of God's grace; and in our witness, which is Christ Jesus' witness, we rediscover an intimate and intentional relationship with God. Surprisingly, this is how we truly know who Jesus Christ is!

This two-way movement is part of a spiritual continuum. Unlike a tangent to a circle, the grace of God *in and through* Jesus Christ flows not only between God and the Christian community, but also in the Christian community's daily experience and history. The spiritual continuum constantly embodies "the testimony of Christ" that strengthens the community. It is this testimony of God's grace *in and through* Jesus Christ that "will also strengthen you to the end" (v. 8). The spiritual continuum is an eschatological vision and journey of the Christian community sustained throughout history by God's gift of grace. Again, "the testimony of Christ has been strengthened among you" (v. 6); consequently, we also give testimony of Jesus Christ's grace and "may be blameless on the day of our Lord Jesus Christ."

Paul reasserts that the Christian community will be sustained in this spiritual continuum for one crucial reason: "God is faithful" (v. 9). Briefly shifting his emphasis from Jesus Christ to God, Paul reminds the faithful that by God "you were called *into the fellowship* of his Son, Jesus Christ our Lord" (v. 9). This fellowship is what makes Christianity interestingly different from other world religions. As indicated above, it is an intimate relationship between God and the Christian community that God bestows in and through Jesus Christ. The character of the fellowship is God's embodied and

## Pastoral Perspective

Offering a blessing may not be a uniquely pastoral act, but it is so associated with the pastoral vocation that it warrants keen attention, in worship and elsewhere. When we tend to the task of blessing, to first words and last words, a benediction becomes so much more than familiar words intoned by rote. Such a moment is laden with possibility. God's presence can become palpably present. Indeed, in that hope, worshipers often listen to such words with expectant attentiveness.

Although Paul begins most of his letters with a blessing that includes the words "grace and peace," in the context of the Corinthian community, this greeting is anything but generic, because "grace and peace" are just the qualities that this particular congregation most needs and most lacks. In this one short sentence of blessing, Paul reveals that he knows them well. Blessings gain in power as they gain in specificity.

Paul then goes on to offer thanks for the ways God has graced the congregation with every spiritual gift. Those familiar with the rest of the letter know that shortly Paul will take them to task for the ways they have misrepresented the gospel in their teachings, in the ways they have ordered their lives, and, most particularly, in the ways they have created a fractious community. So are Paul's words of thanksgiving mere flattery? Is he trying to get the Corinthians to let their guard down, so that he can really let them have it? Or could he be indulging in a bit of sarcasm, as some commentators have suggested?

On the contrary, this is an instance when Paul shows his pastoral wisdom. He knows that he has difficult issues to take up with the Corinthians, so he chooses to begin by reminding them of the basis of their being together in the first place—because they are called by Jesus Christ and enlivened by the presence of Holy Spirit. He sets their sights on higher places so that they might begin to stop wallowing in the petty particulars of their present circumstances. Paul is reminding them of the very height and depth and breadth of their call, as a wise and experienced pastor finds frequent occasion to do.

When Paul says elsewhere, "Give thanks in all circumstances" (1 Thess. 5:18), he is commending thanksgiving as a spiritual practice. Practices help us to live out truths that we may have a hard time affirming at the moment: we are told to pray because sometimes God seems distant; we are told to forgive because our usual impulse is toward revenge; we are

grace is what creates the church and marks it as God's own, the grace that empowers Paul's ministry (3:10; 15:10), with which he thankfully eats whatever food God provides without being hampered by religious scruples (10:30), that marks God's victory over sin and death (15:57), and that evokes the Gentile churches' gift to the Jewish Christians in need (16:3). This grace is most particularly the source of the "grace gifts," the charismata (wisdom, ecstatic speech, prophecy, healing, and so on), that both enliven and threaten to divide the Corinthian fellowship (12:4, 9, 28, 30, 31).

Paul's gratitude for the church's spiritual wealth (1:5) sounds a bit ironic, if not disingenuous, when we read the rest of the letter. Although the Corinthian Christians may not lack any spiritual gift, they act as though they were themselves responsible, as if spirituality were a human endowment rather than a divine empowerment. "What do you have that you did not receive?" he asks at 4:7. The church's wisdom and knowledge, although great, are clearly insufficient when believers choose to settle their differences before non-Christian judges rather than among themselves (6:1–9). The Corinthians' conflict at the Lord's Table stems from conventional cultural attitudes toward unequal wealth: Paul says their practice of eating and drinking without regard for each other "show[s] contempt for the church of God and humiliate[s] those who have nothing" (11:22). Most significantly, he laments their poverty in regard to the greatest spiritual gift, love (chap. 13). Paul sees the church's giftedness not only in the proliferation of its charismatic gifts, but also in its knowledge (1:5), a subject to which he returns when he discusses the conflict over idol meat. Although "all of us possess knowledge" about the reality of God and the unreality of idols (8:1), that knowledge does not prevent members of the church from injuring one another, something only love can prevent (8:1–13).

Twice in the same sentence Paul points to the return of the risen Lord in glory: "you wait for the revealing of our Lord Jesus Christ . . . on the day of our Lord Jesus Christ" (1:7–8). This too sounds ironic in view of the fact that a good number of the Corinthians appear not to be waiting for much of anything. Their spiritual giftedness suggests to some of them that they already reside with Christ in glory. Paul says they are "puffed up" with pride or "arrogant" about their religious status and independence from one another (4:6, 18, 19; 5:2; 8:1; 13:4). They think that in their baptisms they have already been raised with Christ and no longer face

human efforts of the community. In fact, he does just the opposite. Everything for which Paul gives thanks is a gift of God's grace in Jesus Christ. His opening word of greeting in this text sets the tone: "grace" (v. 3). And his opening words of thanksgiving flesh out this greeting: "I give thanks to my God always for you because of the grace of God that has been given to you in Christ Jesus" (v. 4). Paul's thanksgiving leaves no room for human boasting, which, in fact, is part of the problem in the Corinthian community. His very thanksgiving begins to shift the focus of the church away from human standards and accomplishments that can create divisions to the grace of God that is the source of the community's "peace"—the second key word in Paul's greeting (v. 3).

Paul's understanding of grace in these few verses is worth careful consideration by preachers. Preachers often speak of grace primarily, if not exclusively, in terms of forgiveness. And, of course, that is an important dimension of grace. Here, however, grace is a dynamic power or energy within the people that bears fruit among them; grace moves with a power and activity similar to that of the Spirit. The grace of Jesus Christ enriches the community in speech and knowledge; it strengthens the testimony of Christ among them; it overflows in spiritual gifts; it enables the people to wait for the coming of Christ and to be strengthened to stand blameless on the day Christ comes. The grace of Jesus Christ encompasses the entirety of the community's life—past, present, and future—not simply as the forgiveness of sins, but as the power for faithful living.

Paul proclaims grace as an empowering force for discipleship. Grace and works are not somehow opposed to each other, but are integrally related. There is no "cheap grace" here; grace, by its very nature, bears fruit in faithful works. Rather than setting grace and works over against each other, Paul's words invite preachers to explore the deep relationship between the grace of Jesus Christ and the faithful discipleship of the church. Such an approach to grace might be exciting to congregations today, who ache not simply to be forgiven, but to be empowered for the adventure of discipleship.

Paul's emphasis on grace also serves a deep, social purpose in the context of the letter. Paul not only greets and gives thanks for the church, but he sets forth the theological grounds that will shape his response to the divisions and controversies in Corinth. Because grace is the source of the

# 1 Corinthians 1:3-9

## Theological Perspective

active faithfulness *and* our own struggle to live and give witness to God's grace *in and through* Jesus Christ. This fellowship is, hence, an incarnational experience of God's grace *in and through* Jesus Christ and the Christian community's spiritual continuum.

The Christian religion is experiencing one of the most dramatic demographic transformations in its history. As the old centers of the faith shift from the Euro/Atlantic context to the Southern Hemisphere—Africa, Asia, and Latin America—one crucial question is, "Who is Jesus Christ?" While many see Jesus Christ as a static mediator between God and human beings, Paul's description of God calling us "into the fellowship of his Son" opens possibilities for a fully embodied and culturally relevant intimate relationship between God and the Christian community that God bestows *in and through* Jesus Christ.

Fellowships are always shaped by culture. Ways of relating to the Divine, to other human beings, and to the natural world change with time and geography. For example, among many African Christians, Jesus Christ, as a protoancestor, honors God's calling to Africans into the fellowship of his Son. Ancestors nurture daily life and bring fullness to the community. Ancestors and community are in a reciprocal relationship. Therefore, when referring to Jesus Christ as a protoancestor, many African Christians discover a *new orientation* in their spiritual continuum: *in and through* Jesus Christ their faith is enriched, their testimony is strengthened, spiritual gifts are given for true testimony, and they live in fellowship with the Son of God—our protoancestor. Moreover, as they give testimony—*in and through* Jesus Christ—they rediscover their protoancestor. As a result, their African worldview is renewed by the discovery of Jesus Christ as an ancestor, and their Christian faith is renewed. They rediscover a new way of understanding what it means to be *in* Jesus Christ and to be, by God's faithfulness, pulled into the fellowship of his Son.

The two-way movement of God's grace *in and through* Jesus Christ for the community and the community's witness *in and through* Jesus Christ need not be seen as a menace to our monotheistic faith. In the fellowship of the Son, given to us by our faithful God, we continuously rediscover an intimate relationship that is contextual and dynamic.

CARLOS F. CARDOZA-ORLANDI

## Pastoral Perspective

told to confess our sins because we are practiced at seeing ourselves as innocent. And we are told to give thanks because sometimes it is hard to see reasons for thankfulness. When Paul received word about what was going on in the Corinthian congregation, his first impulse would not likely be thankfulness. Nevertheless, in such a circumstance the practice of thanksgiving is no less important; it is just more difficult.

When Paul speaks of the giftedness of the congregation, he is not attempting to induce guilt in them for having squandered what has been given to them. Rather, he is referring them back to the basis of their hope. Paul offers thanks for the Corinthians because the promises of God have not been abandoned. Even in the midst of the fickle Corinthians, God's faithfulness abides. So Paul's tone here is one of confidence.

The placement of this lection at the beginning of Advent is a reminder of the real setting of the anticipated birth—not in some pure and glittering place, but in the grit of Bethlehem. A liturgy in keeping with this lection will remind the congregation that that is just the sort of unlikely place where God is always showing up—in Bethlehem, of all places, and in other messy and unpromising places, such as the church.

This passage also affirms the eschatological hope, which reminds us that we are living between advents. At such a time, it is most appropriate that the liturgy be a celebration of God's steadfast promises.

The first Sunday of Advent often corresponds with the weekend when Americans celebrate the national holiday of Thanksgiving. This passage invites us to offer thanks to God, not for material gifts, but for spiritual gifts found in the church. A litany of thanksgiving appropriate to this passage will shift a congregation's focus to the kind of giftedness Paul celebrates. It might also serve as a reminder that the gathered body, the body of Christ, is itself intended to be a feast of abundance laid out for the sake of the world.

MARTIN B. COPENHAVER

death or judgment (chap. 15). They presume that their redemptions are complete and that they live in the private safety zone of the spiritually perfect. In response, Paul repeatedly reminds them of the unfinished character of redemption and the imminence of God's judgment (2:9; 3:13; 4:5; 5:5). Paul's discussion of resurrection in chapter 15 underscores the church's present life in the shadow of Jesus' cross as prelude to its resurrection on the Day of the Lord. The futurity of resurrection and the reality of death make right ethical relations essential in the church. The body is not irrelevant to spirituality, nor is it to be suppressed, so neither libertinism nor asceticism (both present among the Corinthians) is the proper response to the gospel.

The faithfulness—or trustworthiness—of God's call (1:9) surfaces repeatedly in 1 Corinthians. Rather than opposing "faith" to "works of the law," Paul uses the concept to talk about loyalty, both God's loyalty to the church and the church's loyalty to God in Christ. The character of Christian life as initiated and preserved by God, rather than by human beings, is a persistent theme in this letter. Even the believer's confession of faith is God's doing: "No one can say 'Jesus is Lord' except by the Holy Spirit" (12:3). By the same token, the Christian's loyalty to Christ in an idolatrous and seductive world is unavoidably part of the Christian's loyalty to the brothers and sisters for whom Christ died (8:11).

The contrast between Paul's thanksgiving to God and the realities of the Corinthians' life together is thus more than ironic. There is a theological conviction at the heart of the apostle's gratitude: Paul trusts God to complete in the church what God has initiated in the death and resurrection of Jesus. The church is not what it will be. The concrete reality of the Spirit's presence and the electricity of the church's experience of the grace of the Lord Jesus and the love of God provide assurance that they are indeed the body of Christ. The factionalism, competition, and privatism that mark the church disobey, but cannot destroy what God will accomplish in them.

E. ELIZABETH JOHNSON

Corinthians' gifts, boasting is prohibited. The grace of Jesus Christ, which is the source of the community's faith and life, undercuts all divisions in the community based on human accomplishments or status. Grace here has radical social implications; it is not simply a word spoken to individuals or a power at work in individuals. Grace creates a new kind of community—one in which the divisions and hierarchies of the world no longer function because the grace of Jesus Christ, not human accomplishment or status, is the source of the community's life. There is no room here for superior and inferior, because all gifts have the same source and are consequently equally valued. Even in his opening thanksgiving, Paul invites the Corinthian church—and the contemporary church—to become an odd, new people in the context of a culture divided between superior and inferior, honored and shamed, insider and outsider. The grace of Jesus Christ is the source of that new kind of community.

In his opening words, then, Paul not only greets and gives thanks for the church in Corinth, but he prepares to address the conflicts and divisions in the community. Most importantly, he does all of this at the *theological* level. His thanksgiving is thoroughly theological, emphasizing the grace of Jesus Christ. Similarly, in the rest of the letter he will address the divisions in the church at the theological level—also focusing on the grace of Jesus Christ.

Paul's approach is critical for preachers. The conflicts and divisions in the church will not fundamentally be addressed by conflict management classes or outside consultants or therapeutic interventions, as valuable as these may be. Rather, these divisions and conflicts will be addressed most significantly when preachers proclaim the deep, underlying *theological* affirmations that empower the church for life together as an odd people in the midst of a divided world.

CHARLES L. CAMPBELL

# Mark 13:24-37

24"But in those days, after that suffering,
   the sun will be darkened,
      and the moon will not give its light,
25and the stars will be falling from heaven,
   and the powers in the heavens will be shaken.
26Then they will see 'the Son of Man coming in clouds' with great power and glory. 27Then he will send out the angels, and gather his elect from the four winds, from the ends of the earth to the ends of heaven.
28"From the fig tree learn its lesson: as soon as its branch becomes tender and puts forth its leaves, you know that summer is near. 29So also, when you see these things taking place, you know that he is near, at the very gates. 30Truly I tell you, this generation will not pass away until all these things have taken place. 31Heaven and earth will pass away, but my words will not pass away.

## Theological Perspective

Does this text predict the future? If so, whose future? When? I shall argue, first, that Mark 13 anticipates multiple futures. Second, it reflects a common apocalyptic scenario about how God works. Third, the apocalyptic visions that present this scenario are recycled for new contexts; as such, they are comments on present circumstances more than predictions of future events. All this means that, fourth, we must understand how our context today may be similar to ancient contexts, so we may discern how to be faithful people of God in our time.

From the standpoint of the historical Jesus, "the Son of Man coming in clouds" (v. 26) sounds like the resurrection. Indeed, Christian theology sees the resurrection as a definitive, eschatological event. And this makes sense of 14:62, where Jesus offers the same saying to the high priest, who is looking for an excuse to have him put to death.

From the standpoint of Mark's original readers around 70 CE, much of this speech sounds like commentary on the Jewish revolt against Rome and the destruction of Jerusalem. After Jesus' prediction that the temple would be destroyed (13:2), the speech responds to the question, "When?" (13:4). The Jewish revolt is the most plausible historical context for Jesus' warning to flee (13:14) and his woes to women who are pregnant or nursing "in

## Pastoral Perspective

Most congregations do not need to be told to "keep awake" during Advent. They are already operating in a state of sleep deprivation. At a church in the western suburbs of Chicago, nobody could accuse us of being asleep at the wheel. Rather, we might be accused of scurrying and overscheduling, running but getting nowhere, like bourgeois bunnies on the rabbit wheel. As Advent begins, the fall season has swept us through the "back to school season" of taking children to sports practices, choir rehearsals, and dance lessons. The church has aped the rhythm of the world, with programs now in full gear, from youth groups to adult studies and festive events. And now, suddenly, the rush of Advent.

With all there is to get ready for the holidays, secularly and sacredly, nobody needs to tell us to "keep awake." As a pastor, it strikes me this may instead be the season to pass out the sleeping pills or the chamomile tea, to a revved-up, overcaffeinated culture of busy-ness.

But let us be clear that while the world's busy-ness may seem to be pointed toward Christmas, it is seldom pointed toward the coming Christ child. As Advent progresses, the number of shopping days left before the big day offers a countdown that stresses us out and keeps us up late. These days we are startled into extra hours of wakefulness in a

[32]"But about that day or hour no one knows, neither the angels in heaven, nor the Son, but only the Father. [33]Beware, keep alert; for you do not know when the time will come. [34]It is like a man going on a journey, when he leaves home and puts his slaves in charge, each with his work, and commands the doorkeeper to be on the watch. [35]Therefore, keep awake—for you do not know when the master of the house will come, in the evening, or at midnight, or at cockcrow, or at dawn, [36]or else he may find you asleep when he comes suddenly. [37]And what I say to you I say to all: Keep awake."

## Exegetical Perspective

*Watching and Waiting.* "It is the end of the world as we know it" is not simply the stuff of twentieth-century rock song lyrics or twenty-first-century televangelist sermons. Ideas inherent in both apocalypticism and eschatology can be found in today's gospel lesson.[1] The phenomenon of apocalypticism grows out of difficult political and social crises; thus, it is no surprise that an apocalyptic mind-set is reflected in the writings of the postexilic era of Israel. As the Judeans grapple first with Babylonian, then Persian, Greek, and Roman oppressors, the covenant theology of the prophetic era gives way to an apocalyptic worldview, as writings such as 4 Ezra, *2 Baruch,* and Daniel attest.

Scholars debate the origins of the worldview or mind-set known as apocalypticism; they also debate the constitutive elements of the literary genre known as an apocalypse; however, it is generally agreed that both include elements of dualism (good versus evil); pessimism (times are extremely tough); and imminence (so tough, in fact, that the world as we know it is about to end).[2] This final tenet,

[1] Eschatology as a technical term was not coined until the nineteenth century, but apocalyptic thinking is often filled with talk of the end times.
[2] For an excellent analysis of apocalypticism in antiquity, see David Hellholm, ed., *Apocalypticism in the Mediterranean World and the Near East: Proceedings of the International Colloquium on Apocalypticism, Uppsala, August 12–17, 1979* (Tübingen: J. C. B. Mohr [Paul Siebeck], 1983).

## Homiletical Perspective

On the first Sunday of Advent, as the church begins its telling of the Christian story once again, this lection turns our attention to last things. The passage, which is a portion of what is often called "the little apocalypse," puts us in the presence of the adult Jesus offering both prophetic judgment and prophetic comfort. He anticipates the end times when heaven will literally quake and stars will begin to fall out of the sky. What sounds like a disaster, however, actually prepares the way for the "Son of Man" and his gathering of the elect. Advent eventually takes us to a babe in a manger, but it begins by traversing the cosmos. Those who assigned the lectionary texts for Advent seem to have been following the advice of epic movie director Cecil B. De Mille: "Start with an earthquake, then build to a climax." Certainly, from the very first word, there can be no doubt that there is much at stake in this season, and in the very beginning of the story we are given a glimpse of its ending.

It can seem strange, at first, to begin our anticipation of the birth of Jesus by being exhorted to wait for his coming again. After all, this talk of Jesus' return seems out of sequence because, in the context of the liturgical year, we are still awaiting his birth. In one important respect, however, it is entirely fitting, because it places us squarely with

# Mark 13:24-37

## Theological Perspective

those days" (13:17). And the calamitous events of 70 CE account for Jesus' statement that "this generation will not pass away until all these things have taken place" (30).

From our standpoint today, however, 70 CE hardly qualifies as the end, no matter how traumatic that year was at the time. We might notice, therefore, that Jesus predicts not one but multiple wars and calamities (13:7–8). Also, the Son of Man "will gather his elect . . . from the ends of the earth" (13:27). This sounds like preparation for the judgment. Further, verse 32 ("about that day or hour no one knows") seems to rule out a date in 70 CE. And again, Jesus urges, "What I say to you I say to all" (13:37), indicating that his words apply beyond his immediate circle of disciples to Mark's readers, even to us.

So the predictions in this speech seem ambiguous, applicable to multiple circumstances. How, then, do we make sense of them? We must notice that the "Son of Man coming in clouds" (13:26) is from Daniel 7:13, and the "desolating sacrilege" (13:14) is from Daniel 9:27; 11:31; 12:11 (cf. 1 Macc. 1:54; 2 Macc. 6:1–6). Mark instructs us to pay attention to Daniel ("let the reader understand," v. 14). What we have in Mark 13 is a basic apocalyptic scenario lifted from Daniel and applied to new situations. The basic message of apocalyptic visions is this: The rebellion against the reign of God is strong, as the wicked oppress the righteous. Things will get worse before they get better. But hang on just a little longer, because just when you are sure you cannot endure, God will intervene to turn the world right side up.

In Mark 13, things are bad, and they will get worse. The "end is still to come" (v. 7); this is "the beginning of the birth pangs" (v. 8); "suffering, such as has not been from the beginning of the creation" (v. 19). It will feel like the cosmos is falling apart (vv. 24–25). But before things become unbearable God will "cut short those days" (v. 20).

In 167 BCE, the Seleucid emperor Antiochus IV Epiphanes banned all foreign religions. For Jews, that meant no circumcision and no sacrifices. It was illegal even to own a copy of Torah. In the context of the Maccabean revolt against Antiochus, the author of Daniel reached back into Jewish lore and recovered stories of the slave Daniel, who kept his faith in a pagan land even under threat of death. The book of Daniel exploits an analogy between the Babylonian oppression of Jews in the sixth century BCE and the Seleucid oppression of Jews in the

## Pastoral Perspective

liturgical season that annoyingly presumes we might be asleep. No wonder we tune it out, like teenagers hearing a parent's repetitive lecture and knowing that mom simply does not understand.

But of course, God does understand. In this way, the Scripture from long ago reads us, not the other way around. In Advent, we are indeed asleep to much of what matters.

Like people who have lived by the train tracks for years, we no longer hear the sound of the train. After years in church, we get used to the noise of Advent, to the coming of Christ, so much so that we no longer notice it. Or if we do, it has ceased to jolt us awake and has become instead a low, dull rumble.

As children, when we first learned of Advent, we anxiously awaited the Christmas pageant, and even the God it pointed to. But now tired parents might see that pageant as one more activity to drive the kids to, in a busy week. New members who have been away from sacramental life return to the season of Advent with delight and wonder as the purple banners and Advent wreath appear. But after a few years, these signs of the season become mere decoration.

Like the house hunter who noticed the train tracks on moving day, but later sleeps through the whistles and the engines that rush by, we can miss the thing in the season of Advent that might have been most obvious and important at one time—the coming of Christ.

We may not be physically asleep; quite the opposite. But in our wakefulness to worldly ways, we fall asleep to the spiritual season, and so we need a wake-up call from the Gospel of Mark.

It is a strange wake-up call for people who no longer hold fig trees as key metaphors in our cultural life. When we do encounter figs, they tend to be mashed inside that moist little comfort food cookie, or we might have a fig alongside a piece of fine cheese.

But as for the fig trees themselves, I do not see any on the carefully mowed lawns outside Chicago. If we do mow our lawns, rake our leaves, it is as a chore, often for appearance's sake. We do not normally find ourselves considering the branches of the fig tree and how they produce or do not produce fruit. Fruit production happens at the grocery store, when we take the food from shelf, to bag, to car trunk, to pantry; and then suddenly, on our granite countertops, fruit has been "produced."

Yet most of us long for a richer sense of how fruit comes into the world, with its rhythms of leaves and

imminence, is related to the concept of eschatology, the doctrine of the end times. Apocalyptic reflections often address the imminence of judgment and the hope of better times ahead.

Today's Gospel lesson is from a chapter often referred to as "the little apocalypse." The material in Mark 13 is a narrative break in the Gospel, set between Mark's recounting of Jesus' teaching on the temple mount (Mark 12) and the passion narrative (Mark 14–16). In the opening verses of chapter 13, Jesus predicts the destruction of the temple and then, crossing over to the Mount of Olives, he begins to talk with Peter, James, John, and Andrew about the end of the age. Mark 13:5b–23 comprises a series of warnings regarding false indicators of the end. Jesus admonishes his disciples to watch and wait, for the end will come and they must be alert. The Gospel reading for this first Sunday in Advent is the second half of this chapter, and easily divides into three sections: Mark 13:24–27; Mark 13:28–31; and Mark 13:32–36.

*Cosmic Signs.* In the first section, the author shifts the readers' attention from false prophets and deceptive omens to the actual signs of the times. With apocalyptic imagery borrowed from Isaiah (13:10; 34:4); Joel (2:10; 3:4; 4:15); Ezekiel (32:7, 8); and Daniel (7:13), the evangelist employs a common trope of disturbances in the cosmic order to herald a significant event. It is not unusual in apocalyptic writing to call on cosmic imagery to describe the indescribable; in this instance it is the coming of the Son of Man that is spotlighted. Just as Isaiah, Joel, and Ezekiel use cosmic imagery to predict divine judgment, and just as Daniel writes of the coming Son of Man, here the evangelist creates a synthesis of images and allusions from the biblical tradition for the readers/hearers of the first century.

*Lesson from the Fig Tree.* An earlier story of the fig tree (Mark 11:20–22) focused on the destruction of the temple; Mark 13:28–31 is a short parable about a fig tree with the focus not on an end but on a beginning, offering hope in the imminence of the coming of the Son of Man. Just as the fig tree is the harbinger of summer, so will the signs Jesus is describing portend the coming of the Son of Man. One difficulty in this section lies in the statement in Mark 13:30, "this generation will not pass away until all these things have taken place" (reminiscent of Jesus' words in Mark 9:1). Although some of the events were realized by the first century, not all were. It is not unlikely that the qualifications offered in

those who awaited the birth of the Messiah. Neither those who awaited the first coming of the Messiah, nor those who now await his return, know when he will appear.

In other respects, our contemporary anticipation of the coming of God's Promised One at Christmas is quite different from the experience of those who awaited the Messiah. After all, we know whom we are waiting for. We know the day he will arrive. It is circled in red on our calendars. We have Advent calendars and Advent candles to help us count down to the promised day.

By contrast, of course, those who lived before the birth of Jesus did not know the day or the hour of his arrival, so they needed to live in a continual state of watchfulness. The birth of the Messiah could only be celebrated as a surprise party that could take place on any day, at any moment. By anticipating the return of the Son of Man here, at the beginning of Advent, we wait in the same way those who lived before Jesus was born waited, not knowing the day or the hour when the Messiah would appear. We also join them in hearing—and needing—the same exhortation to be watchful and to keep awake.

A preacher might approach this text by considering the differences between waiting for Christmas and waiting for Christ. Obviously, we know when Christmas will arrive and what it will be like when it does. We know the script, and all we need do is follow it. But waiting for Christ to come—or to come again—requires something more, an expectant watchfulness, because we never know when he will appear.

This requires from us a different kind of waiting. Some waiting is passive. But there is also active waiting. A girl who stands on a street corner waiting for the bus to arrive will experience one kind of waiting, a passive waiting. That same girl on the same corner hearing the sound of a parade that is just out of sight will also wait, but it will be a different kind of waiting, full of expectation, a waiting on tiptoe, an active waiting.

A fisherman finds it burdensome to wait for spring to arrive because it is a passive waiting. Once he is fishing, however, he does not find it a burden to wait for the trout to rise to his fly because it is an active kind of waiting, full of expectation. At the pool of his favorite trout stream his waiting is filled with accomplishing all the many things he must do, all injected with an active sense of anticipation because he never knows when the trout may appear. That is the kind of active waiting Jesus had in mind

# Mark 13:24-37

## Theological Perspective

second century BCE. So also Mark exploits analogies between the Seleucid oppression and the Roman oppression of God's people in the first century.

Apocalyptic visions are always available to be recycled and applied to new situations. The point is not to predict specific events in the future. Rather, apocalyptic theologians look to understand God's mighty acts in the past as a framework for understanding how the people of God should respond to the present. It turns out that the enemy is not any one empire; but all political and economic powers are liable to be co-opted by Satan.[1] They seek their own, worldly agendas at the expense of ordinary people.

The theologian must find analogies between the present and past circumstances in which God acted decisively, as recorded in Scripture. From an apocalyptic perspective, we might ask, How does Satan try to influence every situation? How does God remain faithful in the midst of a crisis that is spiraling out of control? How can people of God tell the difference between following Satan and following God in any situation?

Amid the smoke of battle, the fog of politics, the confusion of economic distress, the babble of would-be leaders wearing God masks and claiming divine authority, how shall we know which way to turn? God's people should not be surprised or confused, because Jesus warned us ahead of time that such things would happen.

The powers that be will lull us to sleep by reassuring us that they have our best interests at heart as they pursue their worldly agendas. They play to our fears, our prejudices, our self-interests, so we do not notice their demonic behaviors. Beware. Keep alert. Keep awake (vv. 33, 35). The one who endures to the end will be saved (v. 13).

CHRISTOPHER R. HUTSON

## Pastoral Perspective

seasons. So whether we walk in orchards or drive around the suburbs, the image of the fig tree transports us to another world. There we imagine people who tend branches, not for the fun of it or to decorate a garden that decorates a house. We imagine a place where fruit trees are tended to because they make a difference in our survival. We imagine a time when figs were a regular part of the diet and helped fill stomachs that might have been left empty, if someone had not faithfully tended those branches.

In a season that is gearing us up to shop, we consider what it would mean to stay away and engage the natural world, rather than the world of neon malls and sales. This life is precious and unpredictable. Its seasons are short. Let us not have it slip away, only to realize that we spent it shopping.

On the first Sunday of Advent, there is still time to wake up from that bad dream. There is still time to encounter instead the presence of Christ in our waking hours.

An agricultural, natural image pulls no punches. The seasons pass, and the fig tree's growth follows an order, but that fig tree is fragile itself. Some figs will not make it; they simply will not flourish. Staying awake matters, not so much to protect ourselves, but also to notice the beauty in the moment. By staying awake, we may catch the second when the branch is tender, and learn that summer is near. By staying awake, we may be there to see the master who arrives when we are least expecting it, at midnight, at cockcrow, or at dawn.

Amidst the holiday parties and late-night shopping trips, the gospel reminds us to be awake to God in the world. This is a way of being awake that might actually be restful, and give us peace.

LILLIAN DANIEL

---

[1] "Satan" is a metaphor for the negative (fallen) form of what Walter Wink calls "the inner aspect of material or tangible manifestations of power" (*Naming the Powers* [Philadelphia: Fortress Press, 1984], 104). For thoughtful analysis of how to confront fallen powers, see Wink, *Engaging the Powers* (Minneapolis: Fortress Press, 1992).

verse 31 come from the Markan era as the community grappled with the delay of the coming.

*Parabolic Warning.* The closing parable of chapter 13, the story of a man on a journey, seems to serve several purposes in the narrative. Just as Mark 13:31 seems to reflect the evangelist's attempt to deal with the delay of the Parousia, so too does Mark 13:32 call the hearer to think beyond the moment because "about that day or hour no one knows." The lessons here admonish the hearer to be more concerned with being prepared and alert than with knowing the day or hour.

In addition to offering a window onto the audience of Mark's Gospel and their concern over the delay of the second coming, the parable in this final section of chapter 13 also serves a proleptic function in the narrative. Note, for example, how in verse 35 Jesus warns his listeners to "keep awake," because the time of the return of the master is unknown; it could be "in the evening, or at midnight, or at cockcrow, or at dawn." Here in the close of this narrative break is a foreshadowing of significant elements in the passion narrative to follow.

*A Word for Today.* The Gospel reading for today fits well with the other readings (Isa. 64:1–9; Ps. 80:1–7, 17–19; and 1 Cor. 1:3–9) for this first Sunday of Advent. They all carry the theme of waiting. In this Advent season we must watch and wait! As we move through the season, as we move closer to the coming of the Christ child, the admonition to be alert once again cries out across time and space. With the people of the texts we cry out this Advent season, "Where are you, God? When are you coming? Come now." Jesus reminds us now, as he reminded them then, that he will come again. We need not get lost in the details. Better to concentrate on being ready.

JUDY YATES SIKER

when he enjoined his followers, "Beware, keep alert; for you do not know when the time will come" (Mark 13:33).

It is clear that Jesus does not intend for us to predict when he will return. Rather, he is urging us to live as if his return were just around the corner. So there is no time to nod off in a waiting room. Rather, we are to be more like a waiter who is continually busy in serving others and so has no time to sit down and count the tips.

At the same time, we are to be attuned to the signs of his rule around us, because, indeed, he has already arrived. It would be a mistake to preach so persuasively about awaiting Christ's return that listeners might forget, for a moment at least, that he came in the first place.

This text forces the preacher to wade into one of the most important paradoxes of the gospel: the "already/not yet" quality to the portion of the divine drama in which we live. *Already* Jesus has established the means through which we are drawn into relationship with God, but *not yet* do we live in complete communion with God. *Already* the realm of God is evident, but *not yet* is that realm fully established.

In this portion of Mark's Gospel Jesus addresses those who have to live in the meantime, the challenging meantime between the "already" and the "not yet." By keeping alert and awake, by living our lives in accord with the One who has already come, died, and been raised, not only will we be prepared to live in the promised realm of God when it comes, but we may experience even now some of what life in the realm will be like.

MARTIN B. COPENHAVER

# SECOND SUNDAY OF ADVENT

## *Isaiah 40:1-11*

<sup>1</sup>Comfort, O comfort my people,
    says your God.
<sup>2</sup>Speak tenderly to Jerusalem,
    and cry to her
that she has served her term,
    that her penalty is paid,
that she has received from the Lord's hand
    double for all her sins.

<sup>3</sup>A voice cries out:
  "In the wilderness prepare the way of the Lord,
    make straight in the desert a highway for our God.
<sup>4</sup>Every valley shall be lifted up,
    and every mountain and hill be made low;
the uneven ground shall become level,
    and the rough places a plain.
<sup>5</sup>Then the glory of the Lord shall be revealed,
    and all people shall see it together,
    for the mouth of the Lord has spoken."

## Theological Perspective

The opening words of Second Isaiah announce good news or "gospel" about God (v. 9). Hence three of the significant theological themes in this text concern God: the relation between God's judgment on human sin and God's grace and forgiveness; the relation between God's "almightiness" or omnipotence and God's love; and what it means to hope in God in the midst of disaster and uncertainty.

First, the initial verses of Second Isaiah give rise to an important theological principle. First Isaiah differs significantly from Second Isaiah, not only in terms of historical location (late eighth century for First Isaiah, and the last half of the sixth century for Second Isaiah) and context (Assyria's attack on Israel in First Isaiah, and Judah's experience of exile and homecoming in Second Isaiah), but also in terms of theological content. What is announced in First Isaiah is God's judgment by means of Assyria on Israel's sin. Hence the news in First Isaiah is not good; "cities lie waste without inhabitant, and houses without people, and the land is utterly desolate," and "the Lord sends everyone far away, and vast is the emptiness in the midst of the land" (6:11–12).

The news in Second Isaiah is altogether different: not bad news but good. The message of Second Isaiah is good news about God's comfort and God's promise of redemption for a people who have lived

## Pastoral Perspective

The first pastoral word at the beginning of Second Isaiah is given in the prophet's turn from past tense to future tense. The turn brings to mind Cambridge don George Steiner's contention that whenever human speech dares the future tense of the verb "to be," the power of death has been negated. He says that when we begin a sentence with "if," we refuse the brute inevitability, the despotism of the fact.[1] God commands the heavenly council tenderly to comfort God's people with news that their punishment—their life at a chosen and then imposed remove from God's presence in Babylon—is past tense. God further commands that a way to the future (which seemed foreclosed by "brute inevitability and the despotism of the fact") is now to be made in the desert.

The way commanded is already a way known by God's people: it is a way through the wilderness. The comfort promised, therefore, does not preclude a waiting and a wandering in desert places. In the past tense, of course, even God's people grew impatient in the wilderness and threatened to turn back to the comfort of slavery. In the future tense promised by Second Isaiah, the fleshpots of Babylon receive no mention. Rather, with joy the exiles will be led

[1] George Steiner, *Grammars of Creation* (London: Faber & Faber, 2002), 5.

<sup>6</sup>A voice says, "Cry out!"
   And I said, "What shall I cry?"
   All people are grass,
      their constancy is like the flower of the field.
<sup>7</sup>The grass withers, the flower fades,
      when the breath of the LORD blows upon it;
      surely the people are grass.
<sup>8</sup>The grass withers, the flower fades;
      but the word of our God will stand forever.
<sup>9</sup>Get you up to a high mountain,
      O Zion, herald of good tidings;
   lift up your voice with strength,
      O Jerusalem, herald of good tidings,
      lift it up, do not fear;
   say to the cities of Judah,
      "Here is your God!"
<sup>10</sup>See, the Lord GOD comes with might,
      and his arm rules for him;
   his reward is with him,
      and his recompense before him.
<sup>11</sup>He will feed his flock like a shepherd;
      he will gather the lambs in his arms,
   and carry them in his bosom,
      and gently lead the mother sheep.

## Exegetical Perspective

*Ecstatic Words for the Fearful and Despairing.*
Disasters make people numb, afraid, and hopeless.
They undermine faith in God and in traditions that
once presented the world as orderly and secure. In the
beginning of the sixth century BCE, Babylon invaded
Judah, destroyed much of Jerusalem, interrupted the
economy, and deported leading citizens to Babylon; it
occupied the land for fifty years. The exquisite poetry
of the anonymous prophet known as Second Isaiah
(Isa. 40–55) emerges in the decades after the invasion
like a healing, life-creating song. It seeks to bring back
to life a people crushed under a shroud of death.
Second Isaiah probably writes among the deportees
and is concerned with their interests, but he imagines
a nation restored, a city rebuilt, and a people reunited
in Zion.

Today's reading (Isa. 40:1–11) introduces major
themes of the book and stands in sharp contrast to
the interpretation of the Babylonian disaster
presented by other biblical books. Jeremiah and
Ezekiel generally accuse the people of causing the
catastrophe by rampant sinfulness, but Second Isaiah
shifts the conversation in a radically different
direction. He puts aside blaming and accusing
speech, bursting out, instead, in lyric poetry of
comfort, hope, and joy. This passage creates a
theological terra firma for a fearful people, not in the

## Homiletical Perspective

One of the challenges of preaching during this
season is to find something fresh from texts made
familiar by frequent use. Who can think of this text
without hearing "Comfort ye, comfort ye, my
people" from Handel's *Messiah* rendered in a crystal
clear tenor's voice? It may seem at first that this text
has been worn so thin that it sounds "quaint," just
another decoration for the holiday season. Closer
study will show that it is a bold declaration about
the character of God offered to a demoralized
people.

Picture the scene. YHWH the God of Israel has
assembled a heavenly host. This is no council of
bickering gods but servants of the sovereign of the
universe, whose compassion and regard for justice
distinguish this God from other gods. At issue is the
situation of God's children, the people of Israel. We
can hardly imagine their misery, unless we think of
peoples of the earth in our own time who share their
agony. Stripped of the institutional structures that
shaped their lives, their temple destroyed, their
homeland laid waste, the people of Israel languish
under the thumb of Marduk, the Babylonian god. To
get some sense of their dire predicament, think, for
example, of the ways in which Native American
peoples have been treated in our own history. They
have been victims of a calculated attempt to destroy

# Isaiah 40:1-11

## Theological Perspective

in exile for some 150 years. Hermeneutically we must not read the first thirty-nine chapters apart from Second Isaiah. Theologically, that means God's judgment always serves the more encompassing purpose of God's forgiveness and redemption of the sinful community. So too in reading this text we must not forget the message of the first thirty-nine chapters. Theologically, we must not separate God's grace and forgiveness from God's judgment on human sin. To do so renders God's grace and forgiveness cheap and capricious and renders God's judgment on sin sheer retribution.

Can human sin be known apart from God's grace? If an essential feature of sin is its capacity to deceive, and if self-deception is a vicious cycle from which sinners cannot extricate themselves, then are not self-deceived sinners dependent on intervention from without—that is, dependent on God's grace—in order to escape the captivity of self-deception?[1] Put somewhat differently, how should one understand the relation between sin and grace, God's judgment and God's forgiveness, between law and gospel? Is it God's law that exposes the enormity of human sin and prepares the way for the gospel of God's grace and forgiveness, or is the gospel, the good news about God's grace, the necessary presupposition for the law's indictment and exposure of human sin?

Second, the good tidings in the opening verses of Second Isaiah are words of comfort for Israel. There is finally an end to God's judgment and wrath because they are for the sake of God's redemption of sinners. The God who rebukes and sends into exile is also the God whose mighty arm can mend what is broken and make right what has been distorted. This mighty God, however, is also like a shepherd who gathers, carries, and gently leads her flock (40:11) down the highway through the desert that leads home to Jerusalem.

The text gives us two quite different, even conflicting, images for God. On the one hand God has a mighty arm and can do what no human being can, namely, lift up, make low, level the uneven, make plain the rough places (v. 4). On the other hand, God is the gentle, nurturing shepherd whose love knows no limit or bounds (Matt. 18:12–14). Texts such as this one have compelled theologians through the centuries to describe God dialectically. In scholastic theology a distinction is made between God's incommunicable, metaphysical attributes

[1] On sin as self-deception, see Reinhold Niebuhr, *The Nature and Destiny of Man*, 2 vols. (New York: Charles Scribner's, 1964), 1:203–7.

## Pastoral Perspective

straightaway home by the God whose glory all people will see together. No doubt the culture of our captivity would keep us from these places, especially in this season; but God's people have come to hear the preacher counter the culture. With Isaiah we may offer a word of comfort that only exiles who know they are exiles can hear.

These commands of God, spoken to the heavenly council, were first overheard by a people for whom the future tense had been eclipsed. So too do we listen from out of a cultural captivity that has left us unconscious concerning our exile from God's always hidden presence. In what sense do we hear Second Isaiah's promise of comfort as a people that has ceased to pine for home? Lest the preacher cry "comfort, comfort" when there is no discomfort among the happy inhabitants of Babylon (readying themselves for a holiday), we would do well to begin by speaking of God's judgment, of God's absence, of God's silence. Our text presumes that our dwelling place is in a far country. Honoring the repentant imperative of Advent, we might begin by naming those corporate and personal places of exile that find us dwelling at an inconceivable remove from the God whose promises we once believed. Without the context of exile and punishment, we may confuse this costly word of comfort with the sentiment of the season.

But what if our people are those who live well aware of the brute inevitability, the despotism of the fact; and what if, along with the disputed "I" of verse 6, the preacher asks God in the study, "What shall I cry?" Cry, "All people are grass," says the Lord. How easy it is to miss the pastoral comfort of this cry in congregations of power and privilege! Those who live with the illusion of control over their circumstances will feel only dread when such a cry enters speech. But those who suffer under the brutal might of the oppressor will hear the gospel. For these, the passwords of hope, according to Steiner, are "shall" and "will" and "if."

These passwords are given to those who suffer under political oppression for sure, but they are given as well to those who bend "beneath life's crushing load," be that load disease, domestic violence, discrimination, or economic deprivation. To hear (the angels sing) "*All* people is grass" is to be assured that the despot, no less than the displaced and the disappeared, will wither and fade when God comes to reign. Lives secured by position and privilege will hear and tremble, but those who long have suffered under another's death-dealing rule will rejoice. In the end, one distinction alone remains:

destroyed temple, the collapsed monarchy, or the broken covenant of the past, but in God's never-failing word. At a time when other tangible and intangible ways of relating to God have collapsed, the prophetic word is their anchor. This may be why vocabulary of speaking and calling, voice and word, calling and commanding dominates the text. Though everything else fails, God's word endures forever, and that God comes to lead them home.

The passage divides into four movements: words of comfort (vv. 1–2); words of preparation (vv. 3–5); words about the word (vv. 6–8); and words of the herald (vv. 9–11).

*Words of Comfort (vv. 1–2).* For a grieving, futureless people, few words could be more surprising than Second Isaiah's first line, "Comfort, comfort my people." The divine command to comfort responds directly to the unmet yearnings of personified Jerusalem depicted in the book of Lamentations. There the destroyed city, known as daughter Zion, cries out for comfort and for God to notice her suffering (Lam. 1:2, 9, 16, 21). There God remains silent, but Second Isaiah opens with the longed-for consoling speech. Jerusalem has suffered "double for all her sins." Zion's suffering is massively disproportionate to anything she may have done. For Second Isaiah, the people's sin does not adequately explain the historical disaster. He reinterprets the past, argues with other interpreters, and with imaginative daring challenges the theological status quo of blame and despair.

*Words of Preparation (vv. 3–5).* Unidentified voices obey the divine command to comfort Zion in the next two movements (vv. 3–5 and 6–8). The first voice calls out urgent instructions; be at the ready; prepare now, for the king is coming. Smooth out the highway, flatten the mountains, raise up the valleys, make the way clear for a speedy arrival: the "glory of the LORD (YHWH) shall appear" (v. 5, my translation). The Jewish Publication Society translates this traditional Hebrew phrase with the richly resonant "Presence of the Lord." To this abandoned, battered community who supposed God had left them or had been defeated by stronger Babylonian gods, Second Isaiah announces that God approaches on the highway they are preparing. And this urgent announcement is utterly reliable because "the mouth of the LORD has spoken" (v. 5).

*Words about the Word (vv. 6–8).* The second comforting voice hammers home the utter reliability

their own respective cultures and religion for the purpose of "assimilation." So it was for Israel.

God responds to such conditions by bringing together the council. He is prepared to announce a message that God intends for the people of Israel. In it, one can see into the very depths of the character of the one the church calls "Sovereign." God wills comfort and consolation to those in the very depths of despair and depends upon human as well as divine agency to bring that message from God's royal realm. One question to ask as one shapes a sermon: whom is the message of this text for? Is it just for Israel in a particular time or place? Is it just for the church as it formulates its understanding of Jesus' life and ministry? Or is the text saying something about God's compassion for *all*? Another question one might ask is this: who is to *bear* this message? Is it a task only for angels, priests, or prophets? Would the text allow a preacher to commission the church to become bearers of the divine message of comfort and consolation?

Indeed, at this time of year we tend to think of the church only as the recipients of these words from on high. We like to cast ourselves as the shepherds who hear the choirs of angels broadcast the startling announcement of God's coming as warrior and shepherd. Surely the church does need to hear these ancient words again and again, to be reassured that the God in whom we trust does indeed honor promises and covenants. As the church wonders about its future—the shape of its life together, what its worship practices will be, and the nature of its witness—it experiences a high degree of confusion and *dis*comfort about itself. The church takes solace in its traditions particularly during this time of year when we speak to one another in the timeless language of divine consolation.

The uneasiness we feel about our own situation as the church in rapid transition cannot compare with the degree of suffering that God's word of comfort intends to address. These words are not just for us to savor like food at a holiday feast. We are in the situation of the celestial ones and the prophets in the text, trying to find a way to speak them to others that God loves. One of the questions that leaps up from the text is "What shall I cry?" Presumably it is the prophet's voice, as the prophet tries to understand how to formulate the message that God intends. The prophet uses the imagery and idioms of the time to proclaim that God's glory has been, is being, and will be revealed in the natural order and in the unfolding of human history, a dramatic

# Isaiah 40:1-11

## Theological Perspective

(God as God is in God's self) and God's communicable, relational attributes (God as God is known in relation to the world). Modern theologians, however, have worried that these two descriptions of God's attributes have not always been related to one other. Karl Barth, preferring the term "perfections" to attributes, described God in terms of God's freedom and God's love, but insisted that the two must be understood dialectically; that is, the one entails the other. God's freedom is always loving, and God's love is always uncoerced and free.[2] In the language of Second Isaiah, God's mighty arm is not that of an arbitrary tyrant but that of a gentle shepherd who carries her flock in her bosom. Her gentle nurture is indeed mighty, and her might is her gentle nurture. This is no ordinary shepherd.

Finally, for those who live in the midst of exile, cultural collapse, and communal disaster, there can be no true hope except in God. It is futile to hope in individuals or even in the strength of the community, for human beings are inconstant, are fickle, and break their promises. Eventually they wither and fade, not simply because they are mortal, but because they are untrustworthy. The only one who can be trusted to make right what is so badly wrong, who can lead Judah out of exile and into the promised land, is the one whose Word will alone "stand forever" (v. 8). The implication in this text is that Judah can hope because God is present, but Judah is not yet at home in Zion. Hope, therefore, must live in the tension between the Word that is present and the promise which is not yet, but is coming.[3]

And what is Judah to do in response to this shepherd with a mighty arm? To what kind of hope is Judah called? A hope that works hard in the wilderness to prepare the way.

GEORGE W. STROUP

## Pastoral Perspective

the distinction between those who rejoice at the word of God's coming and those who see God's rule as a threat to their own power and position. With echoes of Mary's Magnificat, therefore, a second pastoral word is at once a word of discomfort for the proud who *will be* scattered or for the powerful who *will be* toppled from their thrones (these will be past tense in God's coming reign); it is also, in the same breath, a tender word to the lowly, the meek, to them that mourn and the persecuted, for they "shall" and "will" see God.

Finally, the God we shall see, says Second Isaiah in this pericope, looks like this: on one hand, God will come with might and God's arm will rule; on the other hand, God will feed this flock like a shepherd. Both are pastoral words to a people whose long exile has found them questioning both God's power and God's love. Steiner identifies the same doubt in this age and calls it "the eclipse of the messianic." He says, in so many words, that we have quit hope in favor of actuarial tables. In contrast, the "'Word' that was in the 'beginning' . . . comprised a generative, dynamic eternity out of which time could spring forward, a present indicative of 'to be' pregnant with 'shall' and 'will'. Future tenses are an idiom of the messianic."[2]

Future tenses are also an idiom of the preacher who would, with present indicatives, take the words of Second Isaiah *to be* word from the same God become flesh in Jesus Christ. "Here is your God!" we say and so turn those who dwell in unforgiven past tenses to a Word made flesh, pregnant with God's "shall' and "will." "Here is your God!" we shout to those whose impending death has made them demand a miracle and so insinuate the mighty Word that alone negates our mortality against its every rival. "Here is your God!" we sing, and with Handel lift up our voice with strength, heralds one and all of good tidings.

CYNTHIA A. JARVIS

---

[2]Karl Barth, *Church Dogmatics*, II/1 (Edinburgh: T. & T. Clark, 1956), 257–677.
[3]Jürgen Moltmann, *The Coming of God: Christian Eschatology*, trans. Margaret Kohl (Minneapolis: Fortress Press, 1996).

[2]Ibid.

of the divine word by drawing attention to speech itself (vv. 6–8). "Call out!" a voice says. "What shall I call out?" someone replies. This miniconversation draws attention to the content of the speech. Flesh, grass, and flowers fade and wither; everything perishes, but "the word of our God will stand forever" (v. 8). Survivors of disaster know with profound certainty the ephemeral nature of life. Now, in bracing contrast, the prophet assures them of the steady, durable, and reliable foreverness of the divine word.

*Words of the Herald (vv. 9–11).* The passage climaxes when a commanding voice commissions a herald to climb to a high mountain. She must go up high to project her voice far and wide as she proclaims the good news, the message of joy. The unnamed speaker urges her to cry out fearlessly. But what is fearful about her task? Are her words too improbable to be believed by the cities of Judah to whom she is to proclaim it? Are they too hard to speak fearlessly about Judah's new life during Babylonian occupation? Is her joyful news too world-reversing even to be imagined?

The prophet-poet draws emphatic attention to the content of the herald's message. Three times he repeats the attention-grabbing word "Behold," more colloquially translated "Look" ("See" in NRSV). The three calls to look build upon one another: "Look, your God! Look, your God comes with strength . . . ! Look, your God's [his, in Heb.] reward is with him, his recompense before him!" Like any self-respecting king in the ancient world, the herald's God comes with gifts for the people. But the shock is that this God comes at all and that this God is not weak, powerless, or ineffectual. The God proclaimed by Second Isaiah comes in strength with arms stretched out in triumph. But this strength itself is paradoxical, because it is not the strength of a bloody avenger, a violent brute, or a demanding judge. No, this God's strength appears in the barely thinkable power of gentleness, in tender and caring presence, in intimacy such as a shepherd expresses when gathering the wounded, scattered flock. This God draws together the scattered lambs of Judah and rebuilds Zion. This God speaks with them in this fertile, life-producing word that, once spoken, accomplishes that for which it is sent (Isa 55:11).

KATHLEEN M. O'CONNOR

display of God's certain compassion and care for those who receive it.

To those whose ears are not tuned to this divine doxology, the message is preposterous. It seems clear to some that this God being touted has been defeated by the stronger god of the reigning empire. How is one to take seriously the claim that this God will appear in glory?

Take a look at our own world, and see how preposterous the message we carry will sound. It does indeed seem that the God of Israel and of Jesus Christ has very little power in relation to the other "gods" that seem to reign in our "empire." Consumerism demands more of our resources, and lust for oil and mobility threatens our environment. The conduct of war robs us of precious lives and international respect. Religious zealotry pits one image of God against another, leaving the human community fractured and cynical. How dare we speak of this God who promises to become present in a way that "all people shall see it together" (v. 5)?

That is precisely what the faithful people of God are being commissioned to do. In the face of derision and indifference, we are to speak of this God whose fierce compassion and care for humankind trumps the power of the other "gods" who seem to enjoy sovereignty in human relationships.

Advent is a time to hear the promises spoken or sung to the community of faith once again and then sit with them through the season. It is also a time for that community to find its own voice, overcome its objections, and speak words of comfort and assurance to anyone who feels separated or abandoned by God that God *will* arrive and *will* come in gentle power.

RICHARD F. WARD

# Psalm 85:1-2, 8-13

¹Lᴏʀᴅ, you were favorable to your land;
    you restored the fortunes of Jacob.
²You forgave the iniquity of your people;
    you pardoned all their sin.

*Selah*

. . . . . . . . . . . . . . . . . . . . . . . . . . . . . . . . . . .

⁸Let me hear what God the Lᴏʀᴅ will speak,
    for he will speak peace to his people,
    to his faithful, to those who turn to him in their hearts.
⁹Surely his salvation is at hand for those who fear him,
    that his glory may dwell in our land.
¹⁰Steadfast love and faithfulness will meet;
    righteousness and peace will kiss each other.
¹¹Faithfulness will spring up from the ground,
    and righteousness will look down from the sky.
¹²The Lᴏʀᴅ will give what is good,
    and our land will yield its increase.
¹³Righteousness will go before him,
    and will make a path for his steps.

## Theological Perspective

In this Psalter lection our attention is drawn to the depiction of the character of shalom in the vision that occupies the latter half of Psalm 85. It is a depiction worth lingering over, particularly when "the things that make for peace" (Luke 19:42) seem increasingly remote from our experience, nationally and internationally.

According to the seer or prophet who is listening to the Lord in these verses, the peace that the Lord will speak, or the salvation that is at hand, is nothing less than the glory of God dwelling with the people in the land. What this means is that land and people together will be permeated by the divine character, so to speak. They will be animated by those features of God's own manifest reality that were so central to the prophetic tradition: steadfast love (*hesed*) and faithfulness (or truth, *emet*), righteousness (*tsedeq*) and peace (*shalom*), all dynamically interrelating or "co-inhering" in a way that brings to mind the concept of the divine *perichoresis*, the lively mutual indwelling of the members of the Trinity.

Earth and sky and all in between will be caught up into and enlivened by these divine "perfections" (to borrow Karl Barth's term for what are conventionally called the divine attributes); each of these entails or includes the others, so that in a way they are only different ways of speaking of the same

## Pastoral Perspective

What does salvation look like? Is it the man on the corner with his sign "The End Is Near"? A cosmic final battle between good and evil? Is salvation to be found, as our culture claims, in how much we possess or how many weapons we have?

Psalm 85 offers a different vision. It starts with the reminder of how God has saved the people in the past—blessing the land, restoring the people, forgiving their sins and iniquity. Then beginning in verse 8, the psalm puts forth a vision of God's intentions for the future.

One might expect that vision to come through a prophetic oracle, offered in some mystical or mountaintop setting. It doesn't. Instead the vision comes in a typical act of worship, where an everyday priest does what any priest, preacher, rabbi, or pastor does every week—listens to sacred texts and asks, "Let me hear what God the Lord will speak."

No smoke or seraphim here. No "thus saith the Lord." Just an ordinary person trying to discern God's word and what to say in a sermon. First the psalmist hears and offers an echo of Isaiah. God will "speak peace to his people. . . . Surely his salvation is at hand . . . that his glory may dwell in our land." (Cf. Isa. 40:5; 52:7–9; 56:1.)

But then as all preachers must do—be they temple associates, big-steeple pastors, or lay

## Exegetical Perspective

Psalm 85 resists strict analysis of genre.[1] It displays a mix of genres, one of which, the lament (vv. 4–7), has been excised by the lectionary. The superscription, not included above, attributes the psalm to the Korahites, who first appear as a Levitical family group in Exodus 6:24. The books of Chronicles list them among the warriors and gatekeepers of King David, but their appointment for singing God's praises does not appear until 2 Chronicles 20:19–23, when King Jehoshaphat of Judah calls upon them to sing, "Give thanks to the LORD, for his steadfast love endures forever." Upon their singing, God initiates a rout of Judah's enemies. Although the line above does not appear in Psalm 85, the important term "steadfast love" (*hesed*) appears in verses 7 and 11, and a cognate term, his "faithful" (*hasid*), appears in v. 8. Other Korahite psalms are 42–49, 84, 87–88.

The first two verses recall God's saving acts in the past. Notably the parallel lines of verse 1 link God's favor to the land with the restoration of the people, a theme that returns in verse 12. Verse 2 explicitly recalls God's forgiveness of sin in the past. This pardon is comprehensive: it covers all the sin of all

[1] For a discussion of the various proposals, see Frank-Lothar Hossfeld and Erich Zenger, *Psalms 2: A Commentary on Psalms 51–60*, trans. Linda Maloney (Minneapolis: Fortress Press, 2005), 362–64.

## Homiletical Perspective

It is characteristic of the lectionary system to select only certain verses from a passage for a given Sunday. Sometimes such selection is a necessity. Who could possibly preach from all of Psalm 119 and do it justice? At other times the selection of particular verses makes for interesting possibilities. Is it not true, however, that most of the psalms are a unit, and that carving them up leaves behind a deformed piece? The tradition of using only part of Psalm 85 as an Advent reading raises just this question. If we read only the part assigned by the lectionary, we have before us a wonderful affirmation of God's forgiveness and transcendent goodness. What is the effect of leaving behind the darker, questioning, even agonizing part of the poem? What challenges and risks does that present to the preacher? What opportunities arise from those challenges and risks?

The lectionary leaves the preacher with a detached oracle of salvation. Oracles of salvation announce God's favor, grace, compassion, and power. Usually they are a response to either a lament or a confession. By excising the poignant lament portion of this psalm, the lectionary reading presents an oracle of salvation that has no corresponding situation from which anyone needs salvation. Salvation never happens in a vacuum; it is always salvation *from* something. The preacher must decide how to fill in

# Psalm 85:1-2, 8-13

## Theological Perspective

reality, calling attention to different implications. Other English translations of the Bible, both old and new, use other renderings for the key terms in Psalm 85:11–12: for example, mercy and truth, righteousness and peace in the King James Version; and kindness and truth, justice and peace in the New American Version. Because these English terms bring out different features of the underlying concepts, and have different and sometimes complementary resonances in our time, it may be well to keep more than one set in play in one's reflection upon and interpretation of this passage.

A reference to the Trinity may not be at all out of place, in the context of Christian reflection on this text. Our preeminent, if sometimes problematic, American theologian Jonathan Edwards (1703–58) provides some useful guidance in this general direction, and might lead us to a still more fruitful engagement with the vision presented in these verses. Being taught from childhood, through the Westminster Shorter Catechism, that our "chief end" is "to glorify God, and to enjoy him forever," Edwards turned in one of his theological writings to consider, on the basis of both reason and Scripture, just what the glory of God, and our creaturely glorification of God, might amount to.

His work on this topic—the results of which were published posthumously in 1765 as *A Dissertation concerning the End for which God Created the World*—included a close examination and exegesis of the concept of God's glory throughout the biblical canon. Edwards concluded that God's glory consists in an internal and an external glory, the first a glory proper to God's own being, and the second the communication of this glory—a glory flowing outward or shining forth in creation.

In each of these aspects, God's glory consists in three things: internally, in "his infinite *knowledge;* his infinite virtue or *holiness,* and his infinite joy and *happiness*";[1] and externally, in the knowledge, holiness, and happiness of God's creatures, mirroring God's internal glory; that is, the creatures' knowledge of God, love of God, and joy in God. God "delights in the knowledge and love and joy of the creature."[2] The creature glorifies God and attains its own proper end when, to the extent of its capacity, it knows, loves, and rejoices in God in all things, and

---

[1] *The Works of Jonathan Edwards,* vol. 8, *Ethical Writings,* ed. Paul Ramsey (New Haven, CT: Yale University Press, 1989), 528. The work is widely available in nineteenth-century editions and reprints, but this critical edition (pp. 403–536 of the volume cited) combines a reliable text with a very illuminating editorial introduction and notes.

[2] Ibid., 533.

## Pastoral Perspective

preachers for country churches—the psalmist offers *his* vision of that word.

And what a vision it is. The psalmist promises that in God's salvation,

> "Steadfast love and faithfulness will meet;
> righteousness and peace will kiss each other." (v. 10)

There is no more beautiful image in all Scripture, nor a richer pastoral word. The psalmist offers a vision of salvation and God's intention for this world that stretches from earth to heaven and back again. It is also a vision of salvation that runs counter to many current understandings.

For the psalmist, salvation is not the experience of the solitary individual, but includes all "who turn to [God] in their hearts" (v. 8). Faith and trust in God, not ethnicity, skin color, or nationality, are the criteria. In fact, even the land itself is included in God's salvation.

The basis for salvation is blessing, not terror of divine judgment. Even "those who fear God" in verse 9 are more accurately understood as being "in awe of God" than being terrorized by God. The vision that follows is not a hellfire-and-brimstone sermon, but God's fourfold promise of steadfast love, faithfulness, peace, and righteousness.

That vision affirms also that salvation is more than deliverance from one's enemies or release from captivity. It is the *presence* of God, as known in those four characteristics. It is an *active* presence, one that defines salvation as a dynamic process, not a one-shot "I've-been-saved" experience. Steadfast love and faithfulness don't just coexist; they meet. Righteousness and peace aren't static states; they kiss. Faithfulness springs up. Righteousness looks down. The Lord gives. The land yields. Righteousness goes before God.

In their meeting, the four characteristics interpret and expand the meaning of one another to give a fuller vision of God's salvation. "Steadfast love" (*hesed*) is not a mere emotion or passing passion, but a conscious decision that needs the truth and strength of faithfulness. In turn, faithfulness (*emet*) is not simply a dogged determination to remain loyal, but a commitment that must be nurtured and fed by love.

Similarly, to be true *shalom*—meaning not just the absence of conflict but the fullness of life—peace needs righteousness (*tsedeq*). Not the puffed-up morality the word has come to connote, but righteousness in its original meaning, that is, right relations, be they with God, with others, in our families or among nations. Sometimes we call it

God's people. Not only does this serve as a reminder to Christians that God's forgiveness of sin predates Christ's work on the cross; it also supports a broad application of the pardon granted at the cross.

Verse 3 (omitted in the lectionary) relates God's forgiveness and pardon to the withdrawal of God's anger. The communal lament (vv. 4–7) calls upon God to repeat his acts of salvation, asks whether God's anger must continue forever, seeks a revival of God's people, asks that God once again display steadfast love toward God's people, and reiterates the request for salvation.

Whereas the psalmist uses first person plural pronouns in the lament, verse 8 switches to first person singular: "Let me hear . . ." The "peace" that the psalmist expects God to proclaim is shalom, a comprehensive well-being that encompasses the fulfillment of every individual and corporate need, as well as the health and fecundity of the natural order, in addition to the absence of violence and conflict. Throughout the ancient Near East, *shalom* or a term similar to it appears in treaty texts as the promised consequence of a vassal state's fidelity to a great or conquering king. These treaty texts provide the backdrop for the divine covenant in the Hebrew Bible, which casts God as the great king, with Israel, as well as any other people who will consent, as the vassal. Thus verse 8 goes on to describe the recipients of shalom as God's "faithful." This presents a paradox that threads throughout the Bible: the covenant bringing shalom is God's gift, yet the people must also play their part in remaining faithful.

In the last line of verse 8, "to those who turn to him in their hearts," the NRSV depends on the Septuagint, the ancient Greek translation of the Hebrew Bible. Part of the difficulty is that the NRSV has condensed four lines of Hebrew into three. A closer approximation of the poetry, using the NRSV words but incorporating the translated Hebrew in the NRSV footnote in place of the Greek in the final line, would read:

> Let me hear what God will speak,
> the LORD, for he will speak peace
> to his people, to his faithful,
> but let them not turn back to folly.

Both the Greek and Hebrew versions thus amplify the meaning of "his faithful," though in different ways. Both readings also perpetuate the paradox that God's gift of shalom requires continuing faithfulness by God's people. Verse 9 similarly juxtaposes salvation with the fear of God. Where God's salvific

the gap. If the preacher does not fill the gap, the sermon could end up a mushy pep talk about the goodness of God. Such a sermon runs the risk of feeding what some observers call the "theology lite" tendency in modern "spirituality." Modern church-goers are increasingly reluctant to face such turnoffs as sin, God's anger, or judgment. This tendency is the flip side to another pitfall in our faith: the inability to see God as anything but angry. The preacher must decide how this oracle of salvation offers salvation. From what does God save us?

One possibility, of course, is for the preacher to explore fully the verses the lectionary lops off. In verses 4–6, the psalmist portrays an angry God. At least the people perceive God as angry. The preacher can explore how the congregation might understand such talk. Are the people too frightened of a wrathful God? Do the people imagine God as a kindly old soul who could never muster even mild indignation? What are the dangers for a particular congregation of either distortion of God's character? If God becomes angry at the church, what prompts such anger? What lies behind such anger? Do we perceive God as angry when such an assumption is unwarranted? These questions can guide the preacher who decides to reflect on the excised portion of this psalm.

Another option for the preacher is to ask what situation in the congregation needs an oracle of salvation. Because the lectionary recommends these verses as a complete thought, the preacher can proclaim them to a variety of situations. The congregation may be downcast, but may not assume that God is angry with them. The congregation may perceive God as distant, but not angry. The congregation may simply question why God does not act in some manifestation of suffering. The careful pastor can diagnose the needs of the congregation, to prepare them to hear the magnificent words of salvation this psalm offers.

Having determined the needs of the congregation, the preacher has a beautiful answer to them. These images and metaphors for God's salvation are among the most evocative and sublime in Scripture. The poet presents the components of God's peace in delightful tropes. Steadfast love and faithfulness meet each other. In whatever ways these qualities have been estranged—from each other or the world—they are now reconciled. Righteousness and peace kiss each other. If this translation is correct, whatever has kept them apart has been removed. If the creation has experienced a drought of faithfulness, it now

# Psalm 85:1-2, 8-13

## Theological Perspective

when it knows, loves, and rejoices in all things in God. And, for Edwards, it is in the *human* creature that creation thus truly comes into its own. Our calling, on behalf of creation, is to reflect the glory of God overflowing.

In other places,[3] Edwards was to explore the correspondence between this triadic structure in the articulation of God's glory and the triune reality of God (Spirit with holiness, Son with knowledge, Father with happiness) in ways that indicate how deeply in Christian language and experience this Trinitarian "grammar" is embedded, and how far its illuminating power can extend. The Spirit of holiness works holiness in us: "God's love has been poured into our hearts through the Holy Spirit that has been given to us" (Rom. 5:5). The eternal Word enables the knowledge of God and of God's creation to which we are called. And our joy in God and in creation is a mirroring of the joy and delight of the Father in the Word and the Spirit and in their shared life. It is, finally, a proper creaturely participation in the triune life of God that is our "chief end," and this is not to be understood—indeed, cannot be under-stood—only in terms of individual human beings. It is our common, corporate vocation. Moreover, it is one through which our cocreaturehood with all creation, as well as our distinctive role within that creation, is to be realized.

Edwards was not going out on a limb or engaging in fanciful speculation in his understanding of what human beings are meant for. Although he may have brought unusual insight and unusual gifts for expression to the task, the essential principles of this account would have been recognized and affirmed by Christians of many different times and places. One who approaches Psalm 85 with this sort of preparation might well place the dynamic harmony of steadfast love and faithfulness, righteousness and peace that is envisioned there into the more comprehensive context of our calling to be "participants of the divine nature" (2 Pet. 1:4). And one who lacks this preparation might be helped toward it through this psalm's eloquent depiction of the salvation that is to come.

CHARLES M. WOOD

## Pastoral Perspective

justice. But for that righteousness or justice to be more than legalistic fairness, it needs the breadth of vision found in God's shalom.

The psalmist's signs of salvation—peace, justice, faithfulness, and steadfast love—stand in stark contrast to the violent vision of Armageddon so popular in our time. The psalmist's proclamation means that we will know God's salvation is near, not when there are war and conflict in the Middle East (or anywhere else), but when God's peace—and love, faithfulness, and right relationships—prevail.

In addition, contrary to the view of salvation in which this world and most of its people get "left behind," the psalmist promises that "the LORD will give what is good, and our land will yield its increase." From beginning to end, the psalm affirms God's blessing of this earth, where we will not only see God's glory revealed, as Isaiah foretold, but where that glory will actually make its home.

As Christians, that glory dwelt among us in the person of Jesus Christ, the one whose name means salvation (from the Heb. *yeshua*) and in whose life the four gifts of salvation met. Both Bethlehem's manger and Calvary's cross are signs of salvation for us. But so is the life lived in between, in all the ways Jesus made flesh those words of love, faithfulness, righteousness, and peace. Moreover, for Christians, salvation is not just believing in Jesus Christ, but embodying what he embodied in this world. When steadfast love and faithfulness meet in our lives, when righteousness and peace embrace in our business practices, our family relations, or our nation's policies, God's salvation is near at hand. When we work for justice, we make way for God in our world.

Psalm 85 can open our eyes to signs of God's saving work even beyond the Christian church. In the 2006 war between Israel, Lebanon, and Hezbollah, when two of Motti Tamam's brothers were killed by a Hezbollah rocket, the Israeli man asked that their eyes be available for transplant. One of the recipients was Nikolas Elias, an Arab man who was blind. The two men, one Israeli and the other Arab, later met, shook hands, and exchanged phone numbers.[1]

"Salvation is at hand," says the psalmist, "when steadfast love and faithfulness shall meet, righteous-ness and peace shall kiss." May we see such salvation through Mr. Tamam's vision and Mr. Elias's eyes.

TALITHA ARNOLD

---

[3]The editorial note on p. 432 of the critical edition indicates some of these places, and some of the lines of correspondence that Edwards explores in them.

[1]"Eyes to See," *Christian Century*, September 5, 2006, 6.

initiative encounters faithful response, God's glory permeates the land.

This interrelationship between shalom and faithfulness continues into verse 10, though here "faithfulness" translates a different word, 'emet, which also means "truth." Each line juxtaposes an attribute of God with a corresponding consequence for God's people. The "steadfast love" (hesed) is God's obligation under the covenant, and it meets that faithfulness grounded in truth. The intimacy of encounter intensifies as righteousness and shalom kiss. "Righteousness" (tsedeq) refers not only to moral purity, but also to justice. The shalom that humans desire depends upon their truthful faithfulness to the steadfast love and righteous justice of God.

The psalmist now opens up his lens to macro, as the earth brings forth truthful faithfulness, and justice peers down from the heavens. The NRSV's "ground" and "sky" unnecessarily demythologize the richness of the Hebrew terms "earth" ('eretz) and "heavens" (shamayim). The juxtaposition of heaven and earth hearkens back to the creation stories of Genesis, as does the "good" of verse 12. The NRSV's choice of "increase" curiously diminishes the Hebrew yabul, which signifies all the richness of flora and fauna that becomes sustenance for God's people, indeed for all the people of the earth. The ancient Israelites did not view the earth's fecundity as in opposition to the human use of it per se. Rather, to the extent that humanity remained truthfully faithful to God, the earth would yield its produce, and humanity could benefit from it with clear conscience. By the same token, the image of truthful faithfulness springing forth from the earth would indicate that humanity's obligation toward God demands faithful and righteous stewardship of the earth, as well as truth and justice in all our affairs.

The final verse spans the entire Bible. It hearkens back to God walking in the garden of Eden in Genesis, and it points toward the footsteps of Jesus Christ, identified as the Son of God in the opening of Mark's Gospel. Throughout the Bible the divine footsteps define justice and blaze a path for God's creatures to follow.

PAUL D. BRASSEY

springs up from the ground. If anyone has perceived that righteousness has been looking the other way, it now points its gaze right at creation. The poet has taken seemingly abstract qualities and created brief scenes that invite mental pictures. One might even say that this psalm's portrayal of God's ultimate purposes for creation outdoes the eschatological promises of the New Testament. Surely this psalm's images are as elegant as anything in early Christian literature. With no expectation of an end time with new heavens and a new earth, the psalmist points to the possibilities in this life of the incursion of God's goodness and power.

One of the obstacles for the contemporary preacher may well be finding a way adequately to express the wonder of this psalm for contemporary listeners. We do not want to shortchange the rich promises of this poem, but we do not want our sermons to be so otherworldly that the psalm seems to be pure fantasy. With all of the hostility, mistrust, and alienation in our world, how can we hear this wonderful vision of the psalmist? In the midst of concentrations of wealth and deprivation, how can we hear this psalm's proclamation of abundance? Often, what we hope for is that things will become a little better. This psalm dreams of a world where everything works the way God intends for creation to work.

Advent is a time of waiting and expectation. This psalm reminds us what we are waiting for. This psalm presents many tasks for the preacher. It calls us to affirm that the future is in God's hands, but to motivate the congregation to live into these promises. It calls us to interpret abstract qualities such as steadfast love, faithfulness, righteousness, and peace, but to render them in the same animated, even sensuous way that the poet does. It calls us to announce God's activity to fulfill these promises in a way that creates hope, but to acknowledge that the full fruition of these promises will be in God's time and place.

CHARLES L. AARON JR.

# 2 Peter 3:8-15a

[8]But do not ignore this one fact, beloved, that with the Lord one day is like a thousand years, and a thousand years are like one day. [9]The Lord is not slow about his promise, as some think of slowness, but is patient with you, not wanting any to perish, but all to come to repentance. [10]But the day of the Lord will come like a thief, and then the heavens will pass away with a loud noise, and the elements will be dissolved with fire, and the earth and everything that is done on it will be disclosed.

[11]Since all these things are to be dissolved in this way, what sort of persons ought you to be in leading lives of holiness and godliness, [12]waiting for and hastening the coming of the day of God, because of which the heavens will be set ablaze and dissolved, and the elements will melt with fire? [13]But, in accordance with his promise, we wait for new heavens and a new earth, where righteousness is at home.

[14]Therefore, beloved, while you are waiting for these things, strive to be found by him at peace, without spot or blemish; [15]and regard the patience of our Lord as salvation.

## Theological Perspective

Nowhere does 2 Peter more thoroughly betray the theological significance of the late date of its composition than in this passage. These are not the eschatological concerns of Jesus ("But about that day or hour no one knows," Mark 13:32) or Paul ("we do not want you to be uninformed, brothers and sisters, about those who have died," 1 Thess. 4:13). These are the concerns of a community so removed from shared belief in the imminent return of Christ that they instead ask, "Is he *ever* going to get here?" Waiting will do that to you. What the author provides us, then, is a theology of waiting, first addressing time, then reiterating an eschatological outlook developed earlier in the letter, and concluding with the outlines of an ethical response appropriate to the eschatology, all the while dropping hints of a view of salvation that may be surprising.

*Time.* Any theology of waiting is built on two concerns: expectation ("Will it be worth the wait?") and response ("What should I do in the meantime?"). Second Peter 3:8–15a artfully addresses the former and forcefully deals with the latter, but first steps back and invites the reader to ponder the very nature of time and delay themselves. Second Peter 1:1–3:7 has all, more or less and always

## Pastoral Perspective

Fuller Seminary president Richard J. Mouw has observed that questions about what God is doing in the world and the role that human beings have in that equation are among the most urgent with which Christians deal. Mouw cites the work of missionary anthropologist Paul Hiebert, who discovered during his work in rural villages in India that when Christian converts wrestled with their personal experience of troubling questions about " 'the uncertainty of the future, the crises of the present life and the unknowns of the past'—concerns they had about sick family members, worries about finances, fears about the destructive forces of nature—they would typically not turn to the church for answers. Instead, they would return, Hiebert observed, to the local diviner, an authority whom they saw as capable of giving them specific answers" for how they should live their lives. The experience convinced the missionary of the need for Christians to develop "a holistic theology" that would deal with the ways of "God in human history."[1]

One can imagine the early church of 2 Peter following a similar pattern as they endured scoffers who taunted this Christian community with the failure of the second coming (v. 3). Why did they

[1]William C. Placher, ed., *Essentials of Christian Theology* (Louisville, KY: Westminster John Knox Press, 2003), 337ff.

## Exegetical Perspective

The issue that puzzles twenty-first-century preachers already puzzled the first-century author of 2 Peter: how do we understand the promises of Christ's second coming? For 2 Peter as for us, it seems clear that the initial promise, that Christ would return soon, was not fulfilled—at least not in the way that many Christians from that day until now have expected it to be fulfilled.

This letter was probably written in Peter's name a generation or two after his death. Like 2 Timothy, this letter was written by a theological follower of a great apostle, using the apostle's name to give authority to ideas that needed appropriate weight. In the case of both 2 Timothy and 2 Peter, that weightiness is further enhanced by the fact that each of these letters is shaped as the farewell discourse of · a great leader.

Our passage epistle starts by providing an expository answer to the query, why has Christ taken so long to return? Like early rabbis and like the early church fathers, the writer interprets Scripture by turning to Scripture. He alludes to Psalm 90:4: "For a thousand years in your sight are like yesterday when it is past." The psalmist is not trying to provide revisionary, theocentric arithmetic: for God one day equals one thousand years. Neither is the author of our epistle. Both know that God's time is not our

## Homiletical Perspective

The coming of the Lord is put squarely in the face of the worshiper in this passage. There is no way to soften the confrontation of the eschatology that lies at the heart of this text. It forces the modern Christian to the crisis mode that was ever present for the early church. One might say the hazard exposed here is that of "counting behind God."

*The Tension.* There is a tension in this passage: time as a measure of duration for the human creature, set in contrast with the life of God. Actually, it can be a great deal of fun to play with the numbers generated out of the ratio between one day and a thousand years. One year would equal approximately six seconds, and forty years would be slightly less than one hour.

The point is not to slip into some crass literalism; rather it is to explore the tension that comes to the fore when the perspective is changed and we look at matters from a vantage that begins to approach the way God knows the world. A stanza of a well-known hymn says, "A thousand ages in thy sight are like an evening gone, short as the watch that ends the night before the rising sun."

The flawed move being challenged is the equivalent of collapsing the promises of God onto the grid of modern epistemologies—that is, science

# 2 Peter 3:8-15a

## Theological Perspective

pointedly, been intended to "refresh your memory" (1:13). In 3:8 the author steps out of the morass built on the rhetorical excesses of the letter of Jude, extends a more welcoming hand to the reader, and asks, echoing the psalmist ("a thousand years in your sight are like yesterday when it is past," Ps. 90:4), "Does anybody really know what time it is?"

The answer, of course, is that only God knows what time it is, and unless one's sense of time is as finally attuned to God's as faith allows, one's timing will always be off. What surprises and excites is that not only is God's timing different from ours, but so perhaps is God's eschatology. First things first, however, and following the troubles and traumas of most of 2 Peter, that is a good thing. God's timing is different from ours. We know that, having missed the creation of the cosmos (3:5) and like the author being fully aware of our mortality (1:14), but what difference does it make? "The Lord is not slow about his promise, as some think of slowness, but is patient with you" (3:9). Or rather, what looks to us like *delay* looks to God like *patience*. And God has all the time in the world.

*Eschatology.* Biblical scholars have often enjoyed passionate debate about Jesus' eschatological self-consciousness, or lack thereof. Since Jesus, or most frequently "the Lord (and Savior) Jesus Christ," seems more like an idealization in 2 Peter than anywhere else in Scripture, here we would better ask about God's eschatological self-consciousness. What does the Creator have in mind for the creation? Given 2 Peter's dependence on Jude, it does not surprise to find that most of the figures and features come directly from central casting—false prophets, deepest darkness, scoffers, fire, day of judgment, and so forth. But 2 Peter does not convey a conviction that all this is either already happening or about to begin. God's primary eschatological disposition seems, oddly if not uniquely in 2 Peter, to best be described as patience, *makrothymia*; and the eschaton, while not cancelled, seems to be held in suspense. In 2 Peter we meet a combination of full-blown apocalyptic and halfhearted eschatology, because, while well aware of the central images for the end times, the author has come to understand the "delay" as central to the divine soteriology. God has not delayed the end in order to gather more sinners for the lake of fire; God is waiting with patience for another reason. "The Lord is not slow about his promise, as some think of slowness, but is patient with you, not wanting any to perish, but *all*

## Pastoral Perspective

continue foolishly to await Jesus' imminent return? Why not instead indulge themselves and live for the day? The critique was not just about the failed doctrine of the Parousia, but also about the larger question of how God relates to humankind. Rather than an enduring pastoral relationship between creator and creation, the scoffers charged there is no evidence that God intervenes in the life of the world and its inhabitants. Rather, life is a continuum—from creation until now—with no expectation of heavenly intervention. Not only is Jesus' return in glory not a legitimate expectation, but such a return would interrupt their worldly lifestyle.

The writer objects by pointing out that the scoffers' analysis has failed to take into account three things: the power of God's word both to create and to destroy (vv. 5–7), the difference between the reckoning of God's time and human time (v. 8), and the character of God (v. 9).[2] In other words, there is at once a power, a patience, and a graciousness that characterize this God, and the question remains, then as now, what disposition will our waiting take?

The writer indicates that a life turned toward repentance *(metanoia)* is the proper response to God's gracious patience (v. 9), and that life is characterized by holy conduct and godliness *(eusebeia)*. Rather than thinking that the Parousia has been delayed and that therefore licentious behavior is inconsequential, believers are exhorted to adopt an early postmillennialist view that holy conduct and godliness not only exhibit faithful waiting but can actually hasten the coming of the day of the Lord.

The writer's use of *eusebeia* exhibits echoes of its Platonic roots connoting right conduct in relation to the gods and of its Stoic heritage as knowledge of how God should be worshiped. But the Christian appropriation of *eusebeia* goes deeper than intellectual assent. *Eusebeia* bespeaks one's relationship with God, as well as the way that relationship influences one's association with fellow human beings. This godly living should never be confused with material prosperity—a salient point during a time in the twenty-first-century church's history when the gospel of prosperity is enjoying an unfortunate resurgence. As a mark of the Christian life, *eusebeia* points the believer to saintly living—life characterized by such communion with God that it become a witness, enabling others to believe as well.[3] The placement of

---

[2]Fred B. Craddock, *First and Second Peter* (Louisville, KY: Westminster John Knox Press, 1995), 119–20.
[3]William Barclay, *More New Testament Words* (New York: Harper & Brothers, 1958), 67ff.

time, not even multiplied by a factor of one thousand. The psalmist says "a thousand years are *like* yesterday." The author of the epistle says: "with the Lord one day is *like* a thousand years." If our authors were simply doing math, eager Christians might try to figure out how many "days" the Gospels anticipated before Christ's return and multiply that by a thousand. The poetic nature of God language is made clear in verse 9. "The Lord is not slow about his promise, as some think of slowness." Both the writer of Psalm 90 and the writer of 2 Peter know that faithful talk about God's time is always both metaphorical and real.

Indeed, as in the Synoptic apocalypses (Mark 13, Matt. 24, Luke 21), the epistle writer can talk about the unimaginable only through the use of imagination. The Day of the Lord will come like a thief, that is, precisely when we are not expecting it. (See Matt. 24:43; Luke 12:39; 1 Thess. 5:2.)

If we look at the first part of 2 Peter 3 (vv. 1–7) we will notice that what matters is not the way God counts but the way God speaks. God's word created the cosmos; God's word speaking through the prophets pointed ahead to the present messy days when scoffers refuse to believe in God's promises. God's word preserves the earth until its consummation in grace and judgment—grace and judgment that will also come by God's word.

There is a reason that God has delayed the final act of the cosmic drama. The reason is to allow time for repentance. What looks like tardiness is really mercy. Second Peter does not raise the vexed question of how many get saved from the wrath to come, but it makes clear how many God wants to save from the wrath to come: everyone, God "not wanting any to perish, but all to come to repentance" (v. 9).

As with other apocalyptic material in the New Testament—Mark 13, Matthew 23, Luke 21, 1 Thessalonians 4–5, 1 Corinthians 15, Romans 8—the function of prophecies about the end of time is not to encourage speculation but to encourage faithfulness.

What we are waiting for is not simply a new revised edition of our present world, or that all earth should be caught up into heaven. We are thinking poetically; what we want is neither an earth made like heaven nor heaven swallowing up earth. Again the writer draws on the Old Testament, Isaiah 65:17. What we await is new heaven and new earth—a godly scenario. We cannot say much about what new heaven and new earth will look like. We can say what will be at home there: righteousness.

and history. Then what we have is gross misunderstanding of the sayings of the Lord, or failed prophecy.

*Challenges to the Hearer.* An exciting challenge for preaching this passage is how to release the power of this tension into the life of a worshiping community. How does this passage "talk back" to scoffers? Where is the recipe (antidote) for arrogance?

Another exciting challenge that comes from this text is how to reiterate eschatological implications in a manner that is relevant and penetrating. Strong efforts need to be made to avoid the trap the scoffers have already set within the text itself. Obviously, the claims of this text are not to be taken literally—that is, within the epistemological boundaries the scoffers set. Within the scheme of human history, half a century can be said to be a long time. Clearly, this text is about more than numbers and arithmetic. Otherwise, the scoffers are right.

"Talking back" to the scoffers is a prophetic skill that does not assume that the despisers of the faith have all the questions or that their frame of reality is the only one. In this we follow the Anointed One, who refused to be the "answering machine" for those who sought to trap him or depreciate his ministry. Indeed, he had questions for them that put their questions for him into a perspective that challenged their view of reality.

There is no better time than Advent for believers to practice this skill. Unless we practice this skill, the culture becomes the tutor of the church, telling us what time it is. Our time is then dominated by the market forces and pressures that have nothing to do with the way of God and the coming of the Lord. Advent is swallowed up completely by the malls and their vendors, who no longer wait for Thanksgiving to display the trappings of the pagan rites that have replaced the celebration of Christ's coming into the world.

*Relevant Questions.* How can an "other world" be articulated as the very heart of the gospel? See, the theme of the cosmos—as human arrangement of life—is not a new theme at all within the framework of Scripture. Claims regarding its temporal endurance can be found with frequency.

As the lection comes to an end, the theme that emerges as prominent is purgation of the heaven, the earth, and all creation by fire. This is reminiscent of the "refining fire" of Malachi and the "baptism by fire" promised by John in his preaching of

# 2 Peter 3:8-15a

## Theological Perspective

to come to repentance" (3:9, emphasis added). All (*pantas*)? Whew. Universal salvation in 2 Peter? Who knew?

*Response.* How does the reader understand the patience of God in 2 Peter's theology of waiting? "[R]egard the patience of our Lord as salvation" (3:15a). Not, "Regard the patience of the Lord as *our* salvation" but a reiteration of the apparently universal soteriology of the epistle. The response called for is not what one has come to expect from the letters found earlier in the NT. Second Peter includes some Jude and Jude-like exhortation, yet the emphasis is not on behavior, but on understanding. The response is theological, not ethical, and the theologial burden of 2 Peter is nothing less than to share the mind of God, to see the cosmos, from creation to climax, as God sees it. "Since all these things are to be dissolved in this way, what sort of persons ought you to be in leading lives of holiness and godliness, waiting for and hastening the coming of the day of God, because of which the heavens will be set ablaze and dissolved, and the elements will melt with fire? But, in accordance with his promise, we wait for new heavens and a new earth, where righteousness is at home" (3:11–13).

If you stop and think about it, which we rarely do, the mix of patient waiting for a fiery ordeal is an odd juxtaposition. Eschatology yields not an ethics of the end times but a theology of patience, our patient waiting, imitating God's own. There is a hint that we are to be up to something in 3:12, "hastening [*speudontas*] the coming of the day of God," but the phrase itself is more rhetorical parallel and alliteration than theological statement about the faithful's capacity to accelerate the divine chronology.

So we wait. Just as we are to accept the vast difference between God's sense of timing and our own, if we apply God's patience in expectation of the salvation of all for our hurried desire for denouement, we may find the waiting more to our liking.

WILLIAM BROSEND

## Pastoral Perspective

this passage in the lectionary cycle between All Saints' Day and the season that celebrates the incarnation of Christ is a demonstration of its exhortation—it shows what it tells.

And it has a significant message to tell. The letter of 2 Peter was written presumably toward the end of the first century CE (perhaps as late as mid-second century)—in other words, in a time of transition to a church in transition. The church was moving out of its Jewish heritage into a Gentile world. It was moving from apostolic to postapostolic leadership. These are significant credentials to speak to churches in successive ages that have evolved from the patristic to the medieval era, from the modern to the postmodern era, and that have seen a movement away from the dominance of Roman Catholic and mainline Protestant denominations toward nondenominational megachurches, the emergent church, and subsequent iterations.

Will God be at the end of this tortuous road? If our traditional churches crumble, will God still be there? The church of 2 Peter says a resounding yes to churches that have been burned to the ground and are trying to find where God is in their future; to mainline denominations who once thought their dominance on the religious landscape was about *their* power and uniqueness; to the poor who are overlooked in the midst of political posturing and bickering; to faithful believers who cannot make sense of the rising tide of acrimony that infects fundamentalist strains of all religions.

Then, as now, this word to Christian believers in the church of 2 Peter echoes the wisdom that the doxological ending of Christ's prayer teaches us— that the kingdom and the power and the glory belong to God, not to us. Our right response to God's providential care is faithful living evidenced by the practice of *eusebeia,* pointing others to be in communion with the one who has formed and redeemed creation. That kind of waiting echoes Charles Wesley's poetic confession in his hymn "Love Divine, All Loves Excelling":

> Finish then thy new creation; pure and spotless
>   let us be;
> Let us see thy great salvation perfectly restored in thee;
> Changed from glory into glory, till in heaven we take
>   our place,
> Till we cast our crowns before thee, lost in wonder,
>   love and praise.

LEE W. BOWMAN

**Exegetical Perspective**

In the meantime we live in this unrighteous realm as if we were already citizens of that righteous one. "Holiness" and "godliness" in verse 11 do not correspond precisely to the theological gifts of "sanctification" and "justification," but they point in the same direction. Another way of saying that we seek holiness is that we seek to live "without spot or blemish." Another way of saying that we hope for justification is that we "strive to be found by him at peace."

In the meantime, we have to rename the meantime. This is not the time of despair, but the time of waiting (v. 14). This is not the time of our frustration, but of God's patience (v. 15). This is, thank God, not yet the fire next time. Because this is the time of God's patience, this is—still—the time of our salvation.

This epistle text fits well with the texts and themes for the second Sunday of Advent. Isaiah 40:1–11 is itself an oracle that calls for courage in the confidence that God reigns. Perhaps Isaiah 40:8 is echoed most directly in the larger context of our assigned epistle passage. In 2 Peter 3:1–8 it is the word of God that creates, pronounces, judges, and redeems, even in a world of fragile flesh. In Isaiah 40:8 "The grass withers, the flower fades; but the word of our God will stand forever."

Mark 1:1–8 reminds us that the coming of the Messiah is always a time of repentance. Second Peter reminds us that the invitation to repentance is always a grace-filled invitation. What seems to be a long delay in Christ's return is really God's gracious way of saying to us, from generation to generation, it is not too late. Wait in penitence and hope.

DAVID L. BARTLETT

**Homiletical Perspective**

preparation for the Messiah. The winnowing fork is in the hand of the Holy One who shall purge his threshing floor. Indeed, cleansing precedes the restoration. This time the cleansing that prepares for the new heaven and new earth is not with water, but with fire.

*Options for Sermon Structure.* One can do a straightforward exposition, which would be much like a repetition of what is found in the commentaries. The question is whether it will be so "demythologized" that it no longer has any power. One can "move" with the text; or one can set forth a series of "points" to give motion to the design.

*The Proclamation.* Good news needs to be proclaimed during Advent. It is more than some hindrance or slowdown before the real season begins. The temptation among some is to rush to Christmas. Then the incarnation is reduced to the showing of a doll in a basket. Commercialism runs amuck, leading to every crass form of celebration that can be imagined. No preparation exceeds that of restoration through the baptism of fire. In this restoration, hearts are turned back to one another, and the curse is lifted. Here we have come to the very "hinge" of the gospel. It is the call of God's people to live in defiance of history as human story.

The "strangers" suffering persecution are thereby reminded that there is indeed another world that is given by God and fashioned on God's terms. They could not hope to fathom or hasten their blessing through their methods of counting. Or, counting behind God leads to more despair that could pass over into joy. This critical mistake, to be eliminated at all costs, was "counting behind God."

I heard a Maronite priest from Palestine make reference to the "rabbi in our village a few days ago." The context was an experiment in harmony, where Christian Arabs, Muslim Arabs, and Jews come together in unity. More wonderful stories are yet to be told.

W. C. TURNER

# Mark 1:1-8

¹The beginning of the good news of Jesus Christ, the Son of God.
²As it is written in the prophet Isaiah,
"See, I am sending my messenger ahead of you,
    who will prepare your way;
³the voice of one crying out in the wilderness:
    'Prepare the way of the Lord,
    make his paths straight,'"
⁴John the baptizer appeared in the wilderness, proclaiming a baptism of repentance for the forgiveness of sins. ⁵And people from the whole Judean countryside and all the people of Jerusalem were going out to him, and were baptized by him in the river Jordan, confessing their sins. ⁶Now John was clothed with camel's hair, with a leather belt around his waist, and he ate locusts and wild honey. ⁷He proclaimed, "The one who is more powerful than I is coming after me; I am not worthy to stoop down and untie the thong of his sandals. ⁸I have baptized you with water; but he will baptize you with the Holy Spirit."

## Theological Perspective

Imagine you live in Galilee around 70 CE. There's a war on. Some radical Jews have revolted against Rome, and Jerusalem is under siege. Reports are that conditions in the city are bad. People are divided. Some see God raising up leaders to push the infidels from the Holy Land. Others urge submission to Rome as the path to peace and security. Everyone is anxious, caught between resentment of heavy-handed soldiers and fear of extremist guerrillas. Furthermore, Emperor Nero died last year, and there is unrest in Rome. Four men have been acclaimed emperor, only to be assassinated. Now Vespasian, the very general besieging Jerusalem, has been crowned. What does this mean for the war? Things are uncertain. The price of oil is skyrocketing—olive oil, that is. The world is in turmoil. Where do you look for the future?

Your village population is mixed, Jews and Gentiles, and tensions are high. Neighbors fear one another. Families fracture along ethnic lines. One small sect refuses to fight on either side, followers of a Galilean rabbi named Jesus, who was crucified for insurrection about forty years ago. Roman loyalists suspect them of continuing the alleged insurrection of their founder. The rabbis call them heretics, and the Zealot rebels dismiss their founder as ineffective against Roman oppression. But you are intrigued by

## Pastoral Perspective

Most of us want to get the credit. We want to be known as the one who got the job done.

Business leaders do not make it onto the front page of the newspaper for saying, "Well, it wasn't all about me. You see, there was a messenger who came before me, and in fact prepared the way." No, that would never fly.

No politician would ever stop to thank the person she replaced from her rival party. Newly elected senators and representatives seldom acknowledge the work that happened before they arrived on Capitol Hill. Rather, they behave as though their appearance on the scene marks the beginning of time itself.

Our culture loves everything new and easily forgets our debt to history. So our leaders portray themselves as masters of the turnaround. To hear today's stories of leadership, you would think nothing good happened until they got there to turn around the general incompetence of the organization. Often such leaders are called "saviors."

So it is interesting that when it comes to Jesus, the real savior, modesty makes an appearance. The Bible makes it clear that before he arrived on the scene, even Jesus had some help with the prep work.

The Gospel of Mark starts the Jesus story by looking back to Isaiah, who said, "See, I am sending my messenger ahead of you, who will prepare your

## Exegetical Perspective

*Prophetic Beginnings.* The good news of Mark's Gospel begins not with a birth story of Jesus (as in Matthew), not with the birth story of John the Baptist (as in Luke), and not with the beginning of time (as in John). Rather, the good news of the Gospel of Mark begins with a hearkening back to the words of the prophets. The Gospel reading for today is the opening of the prologue of Mark's Gospel and, although it is argued whether the prologue ends at verse 8, 11, 13, or 15, Mark 1:1–8 comprises a discrete section about John the Baptist that parallels the section on Jesus in Mark 1:9–15. Dense with references to the Old Testament, this section of Mark's Gospel proclaims the coming of Jesus the Christ. The passage is easily divided into three sections: verses 1–3, verses 4–6, and verses 7–8.

*Hearkening Back (1:1–3).* What the audience is about to hear/read is good news! It is the good news of God through Jesus, Jesus who is God's anointed, the Christ. One must be careful not to underestimate the impact of the opening phrase; one must not confuse the brevity of verse 1 with simplicity. This first-century audience of Jesus followers could use good news as they struggled to survive in the years during or just after the Jewish War with Rome (ca. 66–70 CE). Thought by some to be the title for the book

## Homiletical Perspective

Mark begins his Gospel like a breathless messenger who is eager to make an unexpected announcement. Mark does not begin his story by letting us linger with the baby Jesus for a time, as Matthew and Luke do in their nativity narratives; and Mark does not begin at rarified heights, as John does in the prologue to his Gospel. Instead, Mark begins with a brief fanfare: "The beginning of the good news of Jesus Christ, the Son of God" (1:1) and then launches into his story about another messenger, John the baptizer, who also bursts on the scene with good news to tell.

The preacher will need to consider, what is "the beginning of the good news" to which Mark refers? Where does this story begin? In a sense, of course, the beginning is the story of Israel, and particularly Israel's prophets. Mark situates his narrative in the sweep of salvation history by quoting Isaiah and by making sure that we see the ways in which John is identified with Elijah, the one who would prepare the way for the Messiah. In another sense, the beginning is with John himself, this larger-than-life character who, at every turn, wants his listeners to understand that he is only a transitional figure. So, if we listen to John, "the beginning" is not with him, or with the prophets before him, but with Jesus Christ, the Son of God. This prologue to Mark's Gospel,

# Mark 1:1-8

## Theological Perspective

their claim that Jesus' crucifixion is a symbol of God's "good news" for Israel and Rome. You ask, if this Jesus really was God's prophet, how is his execution good news for us? Someone hands you a scroll with a title scribbled on it, "The Beginning of the Good News about Jesus, the Messiah, the Son of God."

The title is provocative. The "good news" is foremost a story about Jesus. The word "messiah" reflects Jewish apocalyptic traditions about the eschatological inbreaking of God, who shakes the world, turning it right side up to restore the proper order under God's reign. The designation "Son of God" challenges the claim of *divi filius* found on many Roman coins next to portraits of emperors. So we might expect this story to challenge the established political order and side with Israel against pagan oppressors. But the story opens with John the Baptist preaching repentance. How does this make sense of the present political turmoil?

To help his readers understand their troubled situation, Mark proclaims Jesus. But to understand Jesus, he looks back to the Scriptures of Israel. Indeed, we cannot understand Christian faith adequately without understanding the Jewish roots of that faith. Whatever we think God is doing in our world today, and whatever we think God did in Jesus Christ, should be consistent with what God was doing all along in Israel.

Mark says the beginning of the gospel is "just as" Isaiah said. It is not that Isaiah was predicting John the Baptist, but Mark sees an analogy between Isaiah 40:3 and the preaching of John "in the wilderness" (v. 4). Isaiah provides a frame of reference for understanding the Baptist. In its own context, Isaiah 40:3 looks for God's intervention to restore Israel from Babylonian exile. For Mark, John is like the voice that announces "comfort" (Isaiah 40:1) to the exiles in Babylon. Although first-century Jews were not in exile, they were under foreign occupation. It was as if the Babylonian exile had followed them home,[1] and Isaiah 40 offered a fitting analogy for those who looked for restoration.

But lest his readers get the wrong idea of a triumphalist stance toward Rome, Mark prefaces his quotation of Isaiah 40:3 with one from Malachi 3:1. That oracle also looks forward to God's intervention, but not for restoration. In Malachi 3–4, God's messenger clears the way (3:2) by calling God's people to repentance. Mark sees an analogy between "Elijah" (Mal. 4:5) and John (Mark 1:6, cf. 2 Kgs.

[1] N. T. Wright, *The New Testament and the People of God* (Minneapolis: Fortress Press, 1992), 268–71.

## Pastoral Perspective

way; the voice of one crying out in the wilderness: 'Prepare the way of the Lord, make his paths straight.'" Even the Lord needs people to prepare the way.

But ironically, in congregations, the pastors may be the least likely to admit that others prepared the way for their ministry. Churches, wrapped up in the culture of the turnaround savior, can lead the pastor to believe that nothing happened until she got there. But pastors should know better.

The second Sunday of Advent is a time for all of us, clergy and laity, to remember the humility that comes with honoring our antecedents. If Jesus can admit it, so can we. We all have ancestors in our callings, people who prepared the way.

After Isaiah's prophecy, John the Baptist, locust stuffed and honey dripping, makes a big entrance. Now John could have decided that he was the end of the story, the alpha and the omega himself. There were probably people around him, captivated, who told him he was exactly that. But instead he looked out to the future with a humble heart and imagined the one who would really get the job done.

Imagine the reaction among his followers when John said, "The one who is more powerful than I is coming after me; I am not worthy to stoop down and untie the thong of his sandals." People who are willing to follow someone at least want the reassurance that they are following the right person, and not wasting their time. Who wants to follow the one who is preparing the way for someone else? From a management perspective, John probably should have kept his thoughts about better and future saviors to himself, at least until they had all agreed on a smooth transition plan.

But John is not operating from a management perspective; he is a servant of God. Therefore, as a servant, he has no leadership technique—just the call to tell the truth. That is a messy truth that God has stuck to his heart like the wild honey he eats. He cannot fling it aside; he wears it like a freak who does not fit in with the powers around him.

Thank God for freaks like that. Thank God for freaks who refuse to buy the publicity the world throws their way and trust instead in God's proclamation. Had John not prepared the way, and then admitted it, Advent would be a season not of waiting but of mistakenly believing it has all been accomplished by the latest guru. And that would have been a short season, I suspect, not one we would remember two thousand years later. For charismatic godly figures come and go, from Isaiah

itself and by others to be the title for the story of today's lesson, verse 1 reflects the historical setting of the Gospel, as it cries of "joyful tidings," good news (the same term used in the inscription from 9 BCE announcing the birth of the emperor Augustus), as well as the theological setting of the Gospel in its proclamation of Jesus as "Christ, Son of God."[1]

With echoes of language and imagery from the Jewish Scriptures, verses 2 and 3 hearken back to the prophets. Although many manuscripts read "in the prophet Isaiah," other manuscripts read "in the prophets," recognizing that what the author of Mark has done is to blend the prophecies of Isaiah (40:3) and Malachi (3:1) with a reference to Exodus (23:20) in order to set the stage for the first character, John.

*Presenting John the Baptizer (1:4–6).* The author moves from prophecy to fulfillment in the presentation of John the Baptizer as the one crying in the wilderness. In this section John is described as a preacher and baptizer, calling those who listen to confess their sins and be baptized. Some scholars argue that, because baptism is not a fixed initiation rite at this time, this baptism may be original to John. It does not appear to be the same as that of proselytism, nor what is known of the Qumran baptism rites. Whatever the origin, John's preaching and baptism for repentance of sins is successful. His success as a preacher is validated in the proclamation that "people from the whole Judean countryside and all the people of Jerusalem" came out. The endorsement is followed by a description of John's clothing and eating habits, and the image of Elijah (2 Kgs. 1:8) comes quickly to the minds of readers/hearers, then and now. The portrayal of John as an Elijah presence heightens awareness of the apocalyptic overtones of the presentation, recalling not only the saving activity of God in the past, but also the understanding that with Elijah all prophecy ceased—until the coming of the Messiah.

*Looking to the Future (1:7–8).* In verses 7 and 8 the focus shifts to the future as John calls attention not to himself, but to the one who is coming after him. While the preaching of John the Baptist is present in all three Synoptic Gospels, it is important to recognize that in Mark the preaching of John includes no threats. Unlike the polemical role of John in Matthew (see Matt. 3:7–10) and Luke (see Luke 3:7–9), the major role of John in Mark's Gospel

[1] The phrase "Son of God" appears in some ancient manuscripts and not in others.

then, offers a proclamation that is similar to the one with which the prologue to John's Gospel begins: "In the beginning was the Word" (John 1:1a).

The narrative style of this text suggests that a preacher should seek ways to offer a proclamation in the manner of both Mark and John the baptizer, with a sense of joyous urgency. A way to test that sense of urgency would be to ask, "Can I imagine gathering a group of people together for the sole purpose of hearing this word?" A sermon that does not meet that test is not in keeping with the mood of this passage.

The text is replete with the Advent themes of anticipation and preparation. In this passage, John draws people from the countryside and from the city, and from whatever occupies them, to consider for a time what it might mean to prepare for the one who is to come. In essence, this is the preacher's task as well. In the sermon the preacher can draw aside listeners for a time and invite them to consider what it might mean to prepare for the coming of the promised one.

John the baptizer proclaimed that preparation involved repentance and confession. The preacher will want to be frank that this does not at first sound like the promised "good news." Repentance and confession entail facing the truth about ourselves and changing the direction of our lives. And who wants to do either of those things? So the good news can often sound like bad news, at least at first. Repentance and confession both require a searching and honest look back. There are no shortcuts. It is worth noting that John, the one who insists on keeping the focus on the future and the one who is to come, also hearkens back to the past in his call for repentance. He represents a visual reminder of the past in his manner of dress. John's camel's hair outfit was several centuries out of fashion, just the kind of clothing worn by the prophet Elijah. The retro clothing and the prophet it recalls are themselves reminder that any movement forward first will require a retrospective look back, both to our own personal histories and to the salvation history of God's people. This bracing look back that John insists upon is so very different from the kind of nostalgia that always threatens to take center stage during the Advent season in the culture—and sometimes in our churches as well.

The preacher may want to spend some time naming, and perhaps describing at some length, our reluctance to embrace John's call to repentance and confession. A sermon that does not take seriously

# Mark 1:1-8

## Theological Perspective

1:8). Just as Malachi warned of God's judgment against the sins of Israel, so John preached repentance for the forgiveness of sins (Mark 1:4). Mark's juxtaposition with Malachi 3:1 causes us to notice that there is also a reprimand in the comforting oracle of Isaiah (40:27). We who look to God to deliver us from our enemies must first examine ourselves to see whether we are fit to stand before a righteous God.

Scripture proclaims hope for troubled souls and judgment for the self-assured. Against our human tendency to read the Bible in self-justifying ways, confirming our prejudices and excusing our resentments, we must learn to read self-critically, allowing Scripture to correct us. As the Swiss Reformed theologian Karl Barth says, "only when the Bible grasps at us," does it become for us the word of God.[2]

Mark teaches us to see God by looking to Jesus. But to understand Jesus correctly, Mark looks way back to the prophets of Israel. He sees them looking forward in anticipation of God's intervention. When he stands with them and looks as they look, he sees John the Baptist in line with them and looking in the same direction. As Mark looks at John looking at Jesus, he sees himself in perspective (vv. 7–8). And so, with eyes trained by the prophets to look repentantly and trustingly for God, Mark too looks to Jesus. Mark's story invites his readers to see Israel, Rome, and themselves in a different light.

We are like the crowds listening to the prophet John, seeking direction for our future. We look for God's definitive intervention to set things right. John points us to Jesus, who came so long ago and who for us is yet coming. As in the past, Jesus may shock us when he comes and shows us who we really are before God. Our only hope is to join with John in confessing our sins and looking to the coming of the Mightier One. Come, Lord Jesus.

CHRISTOPHER R. HUTSON

## Pastoral Perspective

to John. In fact, preparers of the way are still around. We may be preparers ourselves.

But there is only one savior of the world. And in Advent, we are still waiting.

Waiting for the savior is humbling. It forces us to admit that the world does not operate on our schedule. And by waiting for the savior, we have to admit the obvious: that he is not here yet. If he is not here yet, that pretty much rules out the possibility that the savior is one of us. It guarantees that it is not me.

"I have baptized you with water," John says, "but he will baptize you with the Holy Spirit." Thank God, is our Advent prayer. Thank God we get to prepare, but Christ gets to do the rest. Thank God we can wait, and trust that he will get here in the end.

On television, the latest contestants line up to compete in the national singing talent show. They get voted off one by one, by a fickle audience. The winner, the last performer left standing, seldom admits, and perhaps does not realize, that she is not the last at all.

At the moment when she triumphantly sings the winner's song, which is often about reaching the high point of one's life, she is actually already slipping down from the mountaintop. The last contestant standing is a temporary place holder, merely preparing the way for the next season's winner. Her moment of being the idol will pass very quickly. That is why she is only an idol. No one gets the last word but the living God. And so we wait.

LILLIAN DANIEL

---

[2]Karl Barth, *Church Dogmatics* I/1, trans. G. W. Bromiley, 2nd ed. (Edinburgh: T. & T. Clark, 1975), 109–10.

## Exegetical Perspective

is as herald of Jesus.[2] Verse 8 serves as a transition statement between the section on John (1:2–8) and the section on Jesus (1:9–15), as the author presents some of the strongest parallels between Jesus and John. John diverts attention from himself and casts it onto Jesus. Jesus is the stronger one; John is the servant character. John fades into the background quickly in this Gospel and does not appear again in Mark (after 1:10) except in 1:14; 9:13; 11:30; and 6:14–29.

*A Word for Today.* This Gospel lesson works well with the other lectionary passages for today. Isaiah 40:1–11 contains the portion of Isaiah from which the Gospel writer framed the opening verses, declaring "prepare the way of the Lord." Just as Isaiah declared God's coming in deliverance, comforting those who sought salvation, so too Mark speaks to those in the first century who are concerned about the delay. The reading from 2 Peter (3:8–15a) also speaks to the concern about the delay of the coming of the Lord. As the lectionary passages are read, so too must we bring a word of good news to the hearers in the twenty-first century. It is a good time to seek prophetic voices of our day. As Mark ties the words of Isaiah to his own setting, so too God's word speaks today. Mark's John is intent on heralding the coming of Jesus. Who are the heralds of today?

Clearly, this is not the birth story of Matthew or Luke. No manger scenes derive from this Gospel. Yet, here in the opening lines of Mark we have a "birth story" of sorts. On this second Sunday in Advent, it is good to tell of new beginnings, to tell about a God who breaks into our time with good news. In this Advent season he comes. Perhaps not as might be expected; perhaps not in the time frame desired— but he comes.

JUDY YATES SIKER

## Homiletical Perspective

such reluctance will not win the same hearing for the good news that follows.

John's words seem to pour hot into the ears of his listeners. Nevertheless, they also meet us in a familiar place, because they are traced with an unmistakable longing for what is just out of sight. That must have been a large part of why people traveled a considerable distance to hear John, and people will still travel to hear a preacher who is able to articulate the largely indefinable and yet inescapable yearning for God that resides in the human heart, leaning toward fulfillment. Beginning the liturgical year on the first Sunday in Advent is a way of saying that the Christian story begins with longing.

This passage helps us lean forward into the future in two other ways that are particular to Mark's Gospel. First, by starting with an adult John awaiting an adult Jesus, Mark reminds us that Jesus grew up. It is an important reminder for such a time, when it is a temptation to linger too long at the manger. A baby can be demanding, but in the case of this baby, the adult he will become is infinitely more so. Second, the final words of this passage point even beyond Jesus, to the continuing presence of the Holy Spirit. The Holy Spirit is a gift to anticipate even at the beginning of the liturgical year, because it is the culmination of the whole story. In his own life and ministry, Jesus also pointed beyond himself to one who is to come—in this instance, to the Spirit who will follow and be a continuing presence in the world and among the people of God. So this passage, which begins by gathering up ancient echoes of Israel's history, concludes by reaching into the present moment.

MARTIN B. COPENHAVER

---

[2] The role of John as herald is emphasized in next week's lectionary reading, John 1:6–8.

## Isaiah 61:1-4, 8-11

¹The spirit of the Lord God is upon me,
because the Lord has anointed me;
he has sent me to bring good news to the oppressed,
to bind up the brokenhearted,
to proclaim liberty to the captives,
and release to the prisoners;
²to proclaim the year of the Lord's favor,
and the day of vengeance of our God;
to comfort all who mourn;
³to provide for those who mourn in Zion—
to give them a garland instead of ashes,
the oil of gladness instead of mourning,
the mantle of praise instead of a faint spirit.
They will be called oaks of righteousness,
the planting of the Lord, to display his glory.
⁴They shall build up the ancient ruins,
they shall raise up the former devastations;
they shall repair the ruined cities,
the devastations of many generations. . . .

## Theological Perspective

Theologically, these verses from Isaiah center around the themes of salvation and mission. Whenever we speak of salvation (which is from the same root as the word "save"), we need to ask the question, what are we being saved from? from God's punishment? from the devil? from our own sins? from death? In some ways each of these answers has been a part of the Christian theological tradition, but in different times and places certain ones have been emphasized. For many Christians today salvation means "getting into heaven," which is a way of saying that human beings are saved from God's punishment (by being in heaven and not hell), from death (by being alive and not dead), and from sin and the devil (neither of which has power in heaven). This way of thinking about salvation leads to an understanding of "mission" as the work of getting as many people as possible into heaven. Even in liberal Christian traditions that tend to think more broadly about who will be saved, there is still a tendency to describe salvation in otherworldly terms (that is, "who will be saved" equates with "who will be in heaven"). In contrast to this, Isaiah challenges readers to name salvation as a quality of life here and now that reflects God's desires for human community.

What is salvation in Isaiah 61? It is good news, healing, liberty, release, and comfort (61:1–2). It is

## Pastoral Perspective

"Do not despise the words of prophets," the epistle for the day commands (1 Thess. 5:20). To be specific on this third Sunday of Advent, "Do not despise the words of the prophet Isaiah." And on the surface, what is to despise? The litany of the prophet's preferential care for the least of these can be made to serve the sentiment of the season as seamlessly as the manger. I think of Jesus' hometown congregation who spoke well of him even after he claimed that the prophet's words had been fulfilled in their hearing. It was Jesus: Joseph's son. What was to despise?

But when Jesus' exegesis quit the general categories of the oppressed, the brokenhearted, the captives, and the criminals, in favor of naming the religiously outcast—when he became specific about the wideness of God's mercy—the congregation heard and therefore despised Isaiah's words as well as the one who dared to speak them. Given the season wherein we also must stand and open the scroll of Isaiah in the assembly of the faithful, our pastoral instincts recoil from following the lead of this teacher of Israel! What would be gained pastorally by proclaiming the "in your face" grace of God when people have come in hopes of finally being allowed to sing a Christmas carol or two? The scandalous particularity of Isaiah's words-become-flesh in people

> [Dotted line at top]
>
> 8For I the LORD love justice,
>     I hate robbery and wrongdoing;
>     I will faithfully give them their recompense,
>     and I will make an everlasting covenant with them.
> 9Their descendants shall be known among the nations,
>     and their offspring among the peoples;
>     all who see them shall acknowledge
>     that they are a people whom the LORD has blessed.
> 10I will greatly rejoice in the LORD,
>     my whole being shall exult in my God;
>     for he has clothed me with the garments of salvation,
>     he has covered me with the robe of righteousness,
>     as a bridegroom decks himself with a garland,
>     and as a bride adorns herself with her jewels.
> 11For as the earth brings forth its shoots,
>     and as a garden causes what is sown in it to spring up,
>     so the Lord GOD will cause righteousness and praise
>     to spring up before all the nations.

## Exegetical Perspective

Shrouded in historical anonymity, a prophet asserts a mission, and good news is proclaimed to the oppressed. The initial section of the text (vv. 1–2a) is well known from Jesus' public reading of Isaiah in the synagogue at Nazareth, where he was nearly killed (Luke 4:17–19). The originating context of the lection, however, comes from the aftermath of exile (586–538 BCE) and the historically modest beginning of Israel's restoration in the land, particularly Zion, "the City of the LORD" (60:14). A central text from so-called Third Isaiah (chaps. 56–66), the lection recalls the exilic songs or poems ascribed to the Suffering Servant, especially the first one in Isaiah 42:1–4 (cf. 49:1–6; 50:4–11; 52:13–53:12).

The passage is part of a larger section that spans chapters 60–62, anticipating Zion's glorious destiny (e.g., 60:1–7; 62:1–12). Zion is depicted as a bride eagerly awaiting restoration (62:4–5; cf. 54:4–8; Hos. 1–3). Earlier she is personified as a desolate mother and widow (49:14; 51:17–20; 52:1–2), whose husband is God (54:4–8). Zion figures prominently in the lection, for her voice resounds in 61:10–11.

As with many texts from Isaiah 40–66, our passage contains a mixture of voices engaged in dialogue. The first four verses are voiced by the anonymous prophet proclaiming good news. The

## Homiletical Perspective

The Old Testament reading for the third Sunday of Advent provides a job description and a mission statement about God's intention. The words spoken are full of promise and reassurance. The themes of justice, hope, anticipation, and deliverance are spoken to the people as a reminder that God has not forgotten them. The prophet Isaiah tells us that God's presence before all the nations is viable and real.

Preachers will need to struggle with the tension between the reality of today's world and the world of Isaiah. Is God responding to our situation, or only to the situation of the people in antiquity? A simple approach to the sermon is to share biblical pictures depicting how it was then and news stories about how it is now. Our ears may not hear the biblical imagery of yesterday, but we cannot deny the condition of our world today. Specifically, we cannot overlook the fact that many people are feeling "oppressed," "brokenhearted," "captive," or "imprisoned" in some way and wondering when God's transformation will take place. The preacher's job description includes reminding people that Advent is a time of waiting and preparation for God to transform the world through Jesus Christ. Isaiah's words tell us that this transformation is not to be an empty hope but a sure promise.

# Isaiah 61:1-4, 8-11

## Theological Perspective

"the year of the Lord's favor," a reference to the jubilee year, in which debts are wiped away, slaves are freed, fields are allowed to rest, and land is returned to its original owners (Lev. 25:1–23; Deut. 15:1–15). Salvation is imaged both as a restored city (61:4) and as an abundant garden (61:11). The nations of the world will see what God has done for Israel and will know "that they are a people whom the LORD has blessed" (61:9). This recognition by the other nations reaffirms that Isaiah's vision is not a promise of pie in the sky. God's deliverance is real, tangible, and this-worldly. It can be seen by others. Though Christians have come to think of the promises of the New Jerusalem as having an eschatological fulfillment at the end of time, we must not lose sight of the ways in which God's salvation is meant to transform the world here and now. Jews and Christians are invited to participate in this salvific living, even in the midst of a world not yet fully redeemed.

If salvation is not another place and time but the reality of this world as it should be (what Christians have come to call the "reign of God"), then Isaiah asks us to think about how we might participate in ushering in what is, theologically speaking, the "real world." Being missional, in light of this passage, means profoundly challenging all forms of cultural Christianity that would make "church" an end in itself, a community of the saved devoted to maintaining a building, a set of programs, and a fellowship of the like-minded.

If Isaiah reveals what salvation looks like, then what is the proper form of mission that corresponds to God's salvific intentions? First, mission happens when Christians and Jews turn their attention to those who are named as the recipients of the good news: the oppressed, the brokenhearted, the captives, the prisoners, the mournful, the faint of spirit. The text reveals God's special concern for the lowest and the weakest. In order to participate in God's mission of restoration, the people of God are sent first to those who most need to hear that God will provide for them and will redeem their losses. Mission is not primarily something that *goes out from* God's people—by sending money or sending missionaries—but something that *defines* God's people, as existing for the sake of the oppressed, brokenhearted, imprisoned, and mournful.

Second, mission happens when the nations of the world notice that the people of God live differently, that "they are a people whom the LORD has blessed" (61:9). Twice we are told that the nations will notice the blessing of Israel (61:9, 11), and while there may

## Pastoral Perspective

categorically despised by a congregation does not bode well for the Sunday in Advent set aside for joy.

What must we say and how can we proclaim the word of the prophet when we are more inclined to speak in the tender cadences of Second Isaiah than we are to dare the darker tones of Third Isaiah? In the first place, we would do well to consider the coincidence between the social context of Third Isaiah and our own. Though the words of the prophet come close in this text to the same words that had given Israel hope in exile, they must have been received as salt poured onto an open wound. The prophet had been anointed and sent to a nation divided, where leaders played to privilege, justice was for sale, and iniquity persisted. He bore good news to a religious community where acrimony rather than accord won the day, where a rigid sectarianism rather than an expansive embrace of the other prevailed.[1]

So also some of our people have returned to the family and the pews as those first exiles must have returned to a homeland and a temple in ruins. The home they had expected often turns out to be a place filled with disappointment, disillusionment, and division. Furthermore the word of the prophet concerning the invisible "other" simply intensifies the dissonance between the national ruins we apparently do not care to rebuild and the reign of God. Alongside the backdrop of war, injustice, poverty, and greed, the word of the prophet taunts a nation that has grown rich in things but poor in soul. What is *not* to despise?

Therefore again I say, would it not be more pastoral to speak in generalities, play along with the culture's merrier *kitsch-mas* and, by definition, keep all of these unpleasant realities offstage? The congregation might even marvel at our nice message as they take our hand at the door!

But what if, instead, we dared to be specific? What if, to begin locally, we named those conditions closeted in the human heart and made acute by the culture's merriment: the relationships severed, the addictions hidden, the violence barely domesticated, the depression denied, the affair raging, the self-loathing cut deep into the flesh, the greed, the hatred, the fear? What if, to think globally, we named those peoples refused a room at the inns of privilege: the elderly poor, children without health care, refugees of Darfur, the homeless schizophrenic? Have we not been anointed to bring good news to

[1]Paul D. Hanson, *Isaiah 40–66*, Interpretation Series (Louisville, KY: John Knox Press, 1995), 186.

## Exegetical Perspective

lectionary leaves out verses 5–7, which ascribe to Israel a collective priestly function for the Gentile world (v. 6a; cf. Exod. 19:6) and promise inordinate wealth from the nations (vv. 6b–7). Zion will receive a "double portion" in correspondence to the double "penalty" Zion paid in exile (40:2). The lection resumes in verses 8–11, which opens with divine discourse (vv. 8–9) and shifts to Zion's voice (vv. 10–11), finalizing the passage. The passage, in short, begins with a pronouncement of good news and concludes with a response of joy.

A closer analysis reveals more profound discoveries. The discourse, like all of Third Isaiah, recalls older traditions and molds them in new ways. The prophet is a recycler! He proclaims, as it were, an "apostolic" mission: he is "sent" by God to proclaim "good news" for the victimized, the imprisoned, and the despairing (literally, "brokenhearted"; cf. Pss. 34:18; 147:3). The message is one of "release" and "liberty" (61:1). The latter term (*deror* in Hebrew) is used elsewhere to designate the release of slaves during the sabbatical year (Lev. 25:10; Jer. 34:8, 15, 17); its cognate (in Akkadian) refers to tax exemption. The subject of the proclamation is the "year of the Lord's favor," that is, the jubilee year (fiftieth year) of release, a holy year that marks the return of property to its original owners and the return of indentured Israelites to their familial households and land (Lev. 25:8–17). "Liberty" thus means more than freedom; it involves a socioeconomic reconfiguration of community (see Lev. 25:18–55).

The prophet proclaims this "year of favor" as a "day of vengeance" or, better, "vindication" (v. 2b). In God's timing, Israel's fortunes will be reversed and the nations will in turn acknowledge Israel's legitimacy. The phrase admits that Israel's captivity was a travesty of justice; release will be both Israel's vindication and God's! The expressed aim is to "comfort," a prominent theme in Isaiah (40:2; 49:13; 51:3, 19; 52:9), but more than wiping tears is involved. God's comfort of Zion is inextricably tied to Zion's restoration. It is the comfort of new creation. And the result is so extraordinary that it must be described in lush botanical terms. Zion's restoration is the miraculous work of the divine gardener. The poets and prophets of ancient Israel frequently employed agricultural imagery to describe Israel's settlement of the land and restoration (e.g., Exod. 15:17; Amos 9:15; Pss. 44:2; 80:8). A strong parallel is found in Isa. 51:3: "the LORD will comfort Zion; he will comfort all her waste places, and will

## Homiletical Perspective

The good news of Isaiah addressed to our world today could possibly be found in what is not said versus what is said. Isaiah's call "to proclaim the year of the LORD's favor" (v. 2) hearkens back to the "jubilee year" of Leviticus 25, when the restoration of past wrongs becomes the new order of the day. The analogy could be made that both Leviticus 25 and Isaiah 61 offer hope and restoration while concluding that God is the Lord of all times and places. Isaiah guarantees that God will cause "righteousness and praise to spring up before all the nations" (v. 11).

Moreover, no preacher can fail to note God's guarantee fulfilled as Jesus repeats Isaiah's words in the Gospel of Luke. In Luke 4:18–19, Jesus states his job description and mission statement when he echoes the words of Isaiah (v. 1–2) and the law of the jubilee year. Subsequently, Jesus proclaims that he is the one who will bring God's transformation to a broken world.

Still, the preacher may need to ask, "Where is God's transformation revealed today? What is God doing today in the lives of the people that offers hope and restoration to our broken world?" It is far easier to see the transformation of the secular world during this season of the year. Many of us get caught up in giving gifts, indulging in food and sharing the holiday traditions with our family and friends. Our homes, workplaces, and communities are transformed with bright lights, Christmas music, and Christmas pageantry galore. Our schedules are suddenly transformed into tireless activities leading to near-exhaustion and fatigue.

Even amid the greenery, candles, and mangers in our sanctuaries, it is often difficult to see God's transformation "spring[ing] up before all the nations" (v. 11). The real definition of Advent is something that Isaiah challenges us to ponder on this second Sunday of Advent. We do not need to look too far to see the injustice of poverty, abuse, hunger, oppression, and war. Yet our Christmas distractions often speak louder than Isaiah's call for God's transformation. Our eyes tend to drift away from the biblical text, and Isaiah's words fall on deaf ears. Jesus speaks the words of Isaiah again as a reminder that God's advent is a transformation that will alter our personal lives and the world in which we live.

The two questions of Advent always seem to be the same; "How is the advent of God trying to come into my life/our world?" and "What do I need to do to prepare for God's advent?" Another way of asking the same questions is, "What do I need to change in

# Isaiah 61:1-4, 8-11

## Theological Perspective

be a bit of payback in this (let those who have oppressed us see how well off we are now!), this is not all that is going on. The concern that the nations *see* God's salvation of Israel makes sense if we look back to Second Isaiah's prophecy in which God says, "I will give you as a light to the nations, that my salvation may reach to the end of the earth" (49:6), and ahead to the last chapter of Isaiah, "I am coming to gather all nations and tongues" (Isa. 66:18).

A restored Israel, living as a jubilee community, will stand as a sign of God's blessing to the nations around it, a kind of sacramental enacting of the salvation toward which it points. To be missional is to live as a people of good news, liberation, justice, and comfort in such a way that the world may take notice and be drawn to the ways of God (just as First Isaiah imagines "all the nations" streaming to a glorified Jerusalem, Isa. 2:2). So long as Christians live as divided people, known to the world as those who judge, fight, and exclude, the church will fail to be missional, no matter how much money it gives and how many missionaries it sends.

Though we must be careful not to read Isaiah through the lens of the New Testament, a Christian reader cannot help but note the significance of Isaiah 61:1–2 as a description of Jesus' mission in Luke's Gospel (Luke 4:14–21). Jesus declares himself to be the fulfillment of Isaiah's prophecy, the one to bring good news, healing, and release. As we walk through the last days of Advent, we remember not just *that* Jesus came but *why* Jesus came—to usher in a jubilee celebration that would have no end.

SCOTT BADER-SAYE

## Pastoral Perspective

these? No doubt the prophet's word will not sound like good news initially. As Flannery O'Connor once wrote to a friend, "All human nature vigorously resists grace because grace changes us and the change is painful."[2] Yet the God who can build up ancient ruins is also the God who can redeem the ruin a prodigal son believes he has made of his life; the God who shall raise up the former devastations is also the God who means to pick up a daughter's broken parts; the God who shall repair the ruined cities and the devastations of many generations is also the God who can repair even the ruined nation that has forgotten its way in the world.

Moreover, what if (more in keeping with Jesus' exegesis) we went on to name those who are oppressed, brokenhearted, captive, and imprisoned not only by the world but particularly by the church's narrow take on God's wide mercy: the gay uncle, the unwed mother, the woman who has chosen to abort her pregnancy, the non-Christian, tortured enemy combatants, the illegal immigrant, the hapless in a hospital waiting room. Have we not been anointed to bring good news to these as well? Curiously left out of the lection (vv. 5–7) are the strangers who stand and serve in silence, the foreigners who till the land in fear of being found out; they are those whose shame is double and whose lot among the chosen has been dishonor. Shall we dare to be called their priests? One begins to see the cliffs of fall waiting for us after the benediction is pronounced! No matter, for the One whose sandals we are unworthy to untie has gone before us, and we are here merely to prepare the way, to shout in so many words, "Repent!"

The carol that comes to mind (albeit on the Sunday when *Joy to the World* is on tap) is *O Little Town of Bethlehem*. Fortunately it is listed among the Christmas carols, a point to make with those huffing out the door. Our congregation is that little town: the crossroads where the hopes and fears of all the years meet and where souls made meek by the word of the prophet may receive the grace they have, heretofore, so vigorously resisted.

CYNTHIA A. JARVIS

---

[2]Flannery O'Connor, *Letters of Flannery O'Connor: The Habit of Being* (New York: Vintage Books, 1980), 307.

*Third Sunday of Advent*

make her wilderness like Eden, her desert like the garden of the LORD." Zion shall become the new garden of Eden, populated with "oaks of righteousness," cultivated by God's salvific work, like the tree planted beside streams of water in Psalm 1:3. The garden is nothing short of miraculous; it is the garden of God's glory (cf. Isa. 41:17–20) as well as the nursery of a nation. And how does God's garden grow? Genuine restoration, the servant claims, is cultivation in righteousness.

The latter half of the lection drives home the fundamental importance of Israel's reconstitution: God proclaims a passion for justice (v. 8), the kind of justice that sustains and shapes community. And out of such justice Zion will be restored and receive "an everlasting covenant," one founded upon God's unconditional covenant to David, but now extended to include a whole people (55:3). But the promise behind the covenant sounds more Abrahamic in scope: "descendants" and "offspring" are guaranteed. Yet the covenant ensures more than simply Zion's survival. It guarantees international renown: Zion will be acknowledged by the nations as preeminently blessed by God (61:9). The restoration of Israel, the recipient of divinely ordained shalom, bears testimony to God's grace unleashed in the world.

Zion's response to this pronouncement is total, unabashed joy, with whole heart, mind, and being (vv. 10–11; cf. Deut. 6:5). Her restoration as tantamount to being clothed by God in fine array: garments and jewelry become emblematic of God's saving work (cf. 52:1). Zion thus obtains a new identity as one uniquely blessed by God. The clothes make the city.

And as Zion is clothed with new garments, so the earth is clothed with new life. The conclusion of the lection returns to the garden. The earth's fructification is a sign of righteousness resurrected (see also 45:8). God has plotted this restoration with care, wielding not the sword but a garden spade. The proclamation of freedom sounded at the outset breaks and waters the fallow ground of exile, from which sprouts forth the beloved community.

WILLIAM P. BROWN

order to allow God's transformation to take place in me and ultimately the world?"

Yet that is not enough, for too often the words spoken from our pulpits focus on what one individual can do. Isaiah speaks of a systemic change and transformation. According to the prophet, God will bring about systemic transformations as an "everlasting covenant." Is it possible that the promises of God could produce a major transformation in the local faith community?

Another approach to the text might focus not on how it was then and how it is now, but on the future that Isaiah describes. Given the promises that God makes to the world in Isaiah 61, do these same promises make us feel uncomfortable today? If so, how do God's promises make us uncomfortable? What can we do to help bring about God's transformation? Do we even want to ask the questions? Is the spirit of the Lord God upon us, or simply upon Isaiah and Jesus?

Again there will be several listeners to the sermon who may feel "oppressed," "brokenhearted," "captive," or "imprisoned" in some way. Sometimes we do not see such conditions when they reside so close to where we live, work, and worship. Isaiah would want us to face into the future while recognizing that God brings about transformation in our life together.

A third viable sermon approach is to zoom out to a more global concern for God's transformation. What is the faith community doing in the world to bring God's good news of transformation? What activities beside the hanging of the greens and singing of Christmas carols follow from the prophet's words? Is the church adding to the confusion while seeking to promote its own calendar of events and activities? The preacher may seek to project a picture of God's transformation that is life-changing instead of simply one more season of Advent, just like the season of Advent last year and all the years before.

DONALD BOOZ

# Psalm 126

<sup>1</sup>When the LORD restored the fortunes of Zion,
    we were like those who dream.
<sup>2</sup>Then our mouth was filled with laughter,
    and our tongue with shouts of joy;
then it was said among the nations,
    "The LORD has done great things for them."
<sup>3</sup>The LORD has done great things for us,
    and we rejoiced.

<sup>4</sup>Restore our fortunes, O LORD,
    like the watercourses in the Negeb.
<sup>5</sup>May those who sow in tears
    reap with shouts of joy.
<sup>6</sup>Those who go out weeping,
    bearing the seed for sowing,
shall come home with shouts of joy,
    carrying their sheaves.

## Theological Perspective

In its two parts, this psalm appears first to recollect a past event of salvation (a homecoming, or a being brought back) and then to look forward in hope, from a present anxious situation, to another gracious act of restoration. Actually, it may all be anticipation, if verses 1–3 are construed as a depiction of the envisioned future—a kind of dream narration. In any case, the contrast between the present situation of restlessness and uncertainty and the time of singing and laughter is clear.

"Restore our fortunes, O LORD, like the watercourses in the Negeb. May those who sow in tears reap with shouts of joy" (126:4–5). The psalm moves from recollection to anticipation through this central petition. Amid the images of dramatic transformation in these verses, the theological issue that may linger in the reader's or hearer's mind has to do with the relation between tears and joy. How are we to construe their connection? Any of several possibilities might come to mind—and several of them have been attributed to the psalmist, in older and more recent commentary literature on this psalm.

One possibility is to associate the tears with repentance and contrition. On this reading, those who repent will be saved; or, to use the language common in news reports on the sentencing phases

## Pastoral Perspective

For ten years, the American Southwest experienced a devastating drought. Centuries-old pinyon trees that covered the hills throughout northern New Mexico became susceptible to bark beetles and died by the thousands. Once green landscapes turned grey with dead trees. For longtime residents, it felt like a death in the family.

Then one summer, it rained. Within days, fields of wildflowers sprang up. People could not believe their eyes. Every patch of ground was covered with yellow cow-pen daises, purple asters, and other flowers not seen in a century. But the rain alone was not the reason for the riot of color. The needles of the dead pinyons provided mulch and nutrients needed by long-dormant seeds. The trees would never be restored, but their death gave birth to new beauty as far as the eye could see.

"Those who go out weeping . . . shall come home with shouts of joy." Psalm 126 seems out of place for the third Sunday of Advent (the "Joyous" or "Rose" Sunday, for Mary, the rose in winter). Granted, the psalm speaks of joy, even "shouts of joy." But with images of seeds, sowing, and sheaves of harvest, it seems better suited for Thanksgiving than Advent. A "Song of Ascents," used by pilgrims going up to Jerusalem for a festival, it has more in common with

## Exegetical Perspective

The superscription of Psalm 126, omitted above, identifies it as "a song of ascents." The psalms so designated (120–34) take up the middle portion of Book V of the Psalter (107–50). Many explanations have been offered about the designation "of ascents." Proposals generally share some sort of processional either into Jerusalem or up the steps into the temple. The cultic occasion for such a procession, however, is much in dispute. Earlier scholarship associated the psalm with the return from Babylonian exile, ca. 520 BCE, based upon the term "fortunes" (*shibat*), which had been thought to mean "captivity." Discovery of Semitic cognates during the twentieth century CE led scholars to understand the term more broadly, which also unhooked this psalm from its identification with the event of the exile, if not with that period.

One of those scholars of comparative Semitic literatures was Mitchell Dahood, a Jesuit priest who specialized in the analysis of biblical texts in the light of Ugaritic, a language closely related to biblical Hebrew that was discovered in the archaeological excavation of Ras Shamra on the Lebanese coast. In light of his linguistic studies, Dahood thought that the verb tenses in this psalm had been misunderstood. Specifically he argued that "Restore" in verse 4 was not

## Homiletical Perspective

The structure of this rich psalm suggests a flow for the contemporary sermon. The psalm moves from one powerful emotion to another in distinct segments. Beginning with deep joy, moving to petition, and ending with an affirmation of faith, the psalm lends itself to almost effortless sermon design. The contemporary sermon could mirror this visceral journey. It would begin with reminders of joy at God's presence and activity among the community in the past, name the present problems that create a crisis of faith, and then finish strongly with a resounding proclamation of God's trustworthiness. The passage contains both outline and emotional content. The preacher breathes a sigh of relief that half of the sermon-producing task is already accomplished.

Despite appearances, however, the sermon from this psalm will not write itself. The problems in taking a congregation on this psalm's path are at least twofold. The first obstacle is the sense of community presupposed in the psalm. The second problem, the flip side of the psalm's potential, is the emotional tone of the poem.

The psalm pinpoints an emotion shared by the whole community. Although some translations render verses 1–3 in the future tense—as though the whole piece is anticipatory—the consensus among

# Psalm 126

## Theological Perspective

of criminal proceedings, one who "shows remorse" may be shown mercy in return. To construe the connection between tears and joy in this way is to see *sin* as the key problem to be addressed: the sorrow of contrition for our offenses leads to divine mercy, reconciliation, a restoration to favor with God. Read this way, in the "penitential" season of Advent or Lent, this psalm "teaches that only those who move toward God with the 'tears' of repentance and need may enter into the joy of 'the great thing God does for us.'"[1]

Another possibility is to interpret the tears as symbolic not of repentance, but rather of the ordinary trials and sorrows of life. Our existence entails suffering. Life is hard. But if we bear this suffering patiently, there will be compensation. The more sorrow, it may be, the richer the harvest. A still more intrinsic relation might be seen here, in which the experience of suffering *fits* us for the joy to come, renders us capable of sharing in it. There is "a hidden divine law: sowing in tears and reaping in joy are inseparable. To the eye of faith temporal suffering is a necessary stage on the way to joy in God's glory."[2] On this construal, our situation is not so much one of sin and consequent alienation from God as it is one of immaturity or unreadiness and a need for growth. The approach to human suffering in John Hick's classic work *Evil and the God of Love*[3] might favor this reading of the relation of tears to joy: the "vale of tears" of this world is in reality a "vale of soul-making"—a phrase of John Keats that Hick cites approvingly. Like the first construal of the tears-to-joy path, this one has an ancient lineage and is well represented in Christian literature and hymnody.

A variety of ways of thinking of what it means to share in Christ's sufferings (cf. Rom. 8:17–18; Phil. 3:10; 1 Pet. 4:13) leads to a third possibility, or family of possibilities, at least relatively distinct from the first and second. Here, the tears symbolize neither repentance nor the ordinary cares of human life, but rather the sufferings of Christ on behalf of humankind, in which we are called to share. Just what this sharing involves, how we are called to it, and what it is meant to accomplish, are subjects deserving some more extended reflection. Perhaps, in the wake of the *Joint Declaration on the Doctrine of Justification*, Catholics and Protestants of various

[1] James Luther Mays, *Psalms* (Louisville, KY: John Knox Press, 1994), 400.
[2] Artur Weiser, *The Psalms: A Commentary* (Philadelphia: Westminster Press, 1962), 763.
[3] John Hick, *Evil and the God of Love*, rev. ed. (New York: Harper & Row, 1978).

## Pastoral Perspective

"Come, You Thankful People" than "Come, O Long-Expected Jesus."

But a closer reading reveals its Advent message. Like "Watcher, Tell Us of the Night," the psalm looks for signs of God's promise in dark and difficult times. It first finds them in the remembrance of things past, in the joy and the laughter the people knew when God brought them home from exile and even their neighbors acknowledged God's mighty deeds on their behalf (vv. 1–3).

Their remembrances can resonate with us in Advent, when we often look back at Christmas pasts to recall long-ago joys and perhaps better times. Like the psalmist, we can "remember when"—when *our* mouths were filled with laughter, our family was all together, our church was full, our nation was at peace, and the world seemed, if not joyous, at least a safer place.

But Psalm 126 is not an exercise in nostalgia. The remembrance of things past has a present purpose. Recalling God's deliverance long ago leads directly to the call for God to use that same transforming power *now*. Verse 4 even asks God to demonstrate *greater* power than before. Not content with Isaiah's vision of "streams in the desert," Psalm 126 wants "watercourses [*aphiq*, "rivers, torrents"] in the Negeb," a desert whose very name means "dry," "parched," the hottest place around.

Isaiah predicted that "sorrow and sighing shall flee away" (35:10; 51:11). Psalm 126 proclaims such sadness will be transformed into "shouts of joy." Like "watercourses" (not just "springs"), the psalmist's word for joy incorporates abundance and power. This joy is not just *masos* ("rejoicing") or *simchah* ("gladness," "mirth") but *rinnah*—a loud cry, a proclamation of joy, a shout of victory. Moreover, the *rinnah* echoes three times (vv. 2, 5, 6) through the short psalm, a grammatical technique in Hebrew underscoring this ultimate joy.

In promising such joy, the psalm offers an important pastoral insight into its nature. This is no jingle-bells joy bought with a swipe of a credit card. The seeds of this joy have been planted in sadness and watered with tears. This is the honest joy that often comes only after weeping has tarried the night.

Such an understanding of joy is vital in the life of faith, particularly in Advent. For all their celebrations, the weeks leading to Christmas can be a time of sorrow. Sometimes we experience Advent's tears as a personal sadness, remembering a loved one who has died or a relationship that has ended. It can also be a sorrow we share as a nation or as churches,

an imperative but an archaic form of the past tense. Thus he translated the verse "Yahweh restored our fortunes like torrents in the Negev."[1] If he is correct about this, then the psalm is not a lament that calls upon God to restore Israel's fortunes once again, but simply a psalm of thanksgiving, celebrating God's past saving acts throughout. Certainly the temporal aspect of biblical Hebrew verbs, especially in poetry, is very complicated.

A structural feature of the psalms of ascents is that many, though not all, of the verses repeat a word or phrase from the preceding verse. We find the following repetitions in Psalm 126: verses 1 and 2 "the LORD" (*yhwh*); verses 2 and 3 "The LORD has done great things for"; verses 3 and 4 "LORD"; verses 5 and 6 "sow/sowing" and "shouts of joy" (*rinnah*), which also appears in verse 2. Another significant repetition is "When the LORD restored the fortunes of Zion" (v. 1) and "Restore our fortunes, O LORD" (v. 4; or, with Dahood, "Yahweh restored our fortunes").[2]

The first three verses celebrate the beneficent consequences of the Lord's restoration of Zion, a term which often stands for all of God's people as well as their political and religious institutions. The first effects are upon the people themselves. Their elation approaches an ecstatic state. They become "like those who dream"; laughter explodes within them and morphs into shouts of joy. All this is involuntary: the verb is passive; mouth and tongue are filled. This is a visceral, spontaneous response to God's acts that restore the community to its proper relationship with God and the world.

The people's internal response with its joyous external expression has its own consequence: the "nations" (*goyim*), that is, those who are not followers of the Lord, notice and start talking about it. They see God's people rejoicing, and they properly identify the cause: their God has done great things for them. The psalmist goes on (v. 3) to affirm that the "nations" were not wrong; God's great deeds among God's people indeed caused their rejoicing. In our contemporary milieu, this is jarring. It is rare today for anyone to attribute the happiness or well-being of a person or group of another religion to the actual deeds of their deity. Indeed, we rarely attribute our own well-being to God.

As already mentioned, the reading of verse 4 depends on a grammatical technicality. The NRSV

scholars is that the first stanza of the poem looks back to God's deliverance at the end of the exile. Enabling our congregations to identify with the experience of the exile is a difficult task for North American pastors. Although the terrorist attacks of 9/11 and the aftermath of Hurricane Katrina gave us some insight into massive devastation, they were not the utter defeat of Judah at the hands of the Babylonians. The sense of abandonment that was Israel's theological interpretation of their political humiliation lasted half a century. If we cannot understand the pain of exile, how can we grasp the joy of return and restoration? One might ask, to what shared community experience might a preacher point to create the sense of solidarity the first stanza of the psalm is based on? We find most of our deep joys on an individual or family level. A wise pastor can name those kinds of joy: a negative medical test, a new job, the birth of a baby, a new employer moving to town. Each of those experiences, however, would identify joy for some, but remind others of regrets. Do we discover our joys and experiences of God's presence based so much on individual or family events that we have great difficulty saying in the same way as the psalmist, "The Lord has done great things for *us*, and *we* rejoiced"? Do we not lose something of the psalm's emotional power if we cannot name shared joys?

Once we turn to verses 4–5, the tone of the psalm changes, but the burden of the preacher does not lighten. Again, the psalmist speaks to some situation that affects the entire community. We cannot be certain of the situation. Does the psalm lament the continuing problems of the returned exiles? Does the community face a literal drought? Has some new crisis of which historians are unaware confronted the community? We know only that some new event has threatened the faith of the people. The trust of the people, renewed by God's gracious action in retrospect, is once more at stake. The contemporary preacher again faces the challenge of identifying a crisis that affects the faith of the entire community. Once again, the preacher can readily think of individual or family situations that might serve as analogies to the crisis of the psalm. After intense prayers, the cancer went into remission. Now it is back. The family has healed after a near divorce. All seemed well. Now the husband has stormed out again. The breadwinner has settled into a promising new job preceded by prayers after a long layoff. Now the new company feels forced to downsize. Any of these scenarios could name the faith crisis of some in the community. Some communities might face

[1] Mitchell Dahood, SJ, *Psalms III: 101–150*, Anchor Bible, vol. 17a (Garden City, NY: Doubleday, 1970), 217–21.
[2] Ibid., 217.

# Psalm 126

## Theological Perspective

sorts may find themselves talking together in new ways about this important set of issues. For the present, this may simply serve as a reminder that Christian understanding of sorrow and joy must be somehow centered here, in what is going on with Jesus Christ.

A fourth (and, for these comments, a final) possible construal of the relation of tears to joy may be closer to the psalmist's own intent—impossible as that may be, finally, to discern. This construal is also quite consistent, to say the least, with the heart of more specifically Christian commitment on these matters. The connection between the two in this case is simply the steadfast love of God. It is a sense of human vulnerability that is evoked by the image of the sowers' weeping (and if there is anything behind the hints of ancient rituals of seedtime associated with these verses in some commentaries, it may be just the reality of human vulnerability before the uncertainties and mysteries of our existence); and it is that same vulnerability, that mere need, which is addressed here by the psalmist's final confident avowal, which might also be taken as God's promise. "Those who go out weeping, bearing the seed for sowing, shall come home with shouts of joy, carrying their sheaves" (126:6). The weeping sowers weep, let us suppose, because they are afraid. They are putting the seed into the ground under quite unpromising circumstances, not knowing what to expect. God will turn their tears to laughter, we might then imagine, not because they have been properly penitent or properly diligent (this is not a fable about ants), nor because they have grown spiritually through adversity, but because they are needy creatures and because God is God.

All the motifs mentioned here, and not just the last one, have a rightful role in the Advent season of preparation. This brief psalm may serve as a catalyst for reflection on a number of important issues in Christian life, personal and corporate. It may also bear the promise of more good news than we know how to handle. That, too, makes it an apt text for this time.

CHARLES M. WOOD

## Pastoral Perspective

when our preparations for the Prince of Peace make us realize how far we have strayed from that path.

Such sorrow can separate us from God, particularly if we confuse Advent's true joy with our culture's teachings about happiness and prosperity. In contrast, Psalm 126 acknowledges the reality of sorrow. It also remembers and points to God's power to transform sorrow into joy.

The joy the psalm both remembers and anticipates is a particular kind, namely, the joy of the harvest. That could reinforce the argument that the psalm is better for bringing in the sheaves than preparing for the birth of the Messiah—were it not for the fact that, for the Hebrews, harvest joy celebrated far more than good crops. When the people of Israel brought their firstfruits to the temple, they not only thanked God for the abundance of that particular year. They also gave thanks for God's deliverance in the past. In a ritual commanded in Deuteronomy (26:1–11), they remembered God's faithfulness and transforming power that went all the way back to Abraham, that wandering—and childless—Aramean of whom God had made a great nation. Their harvest prayer also recalled how God's power had transformed them from Pharaoh's slaves to sowers of their own seed, a free people in a promised land.

The natural power of God to turn seeds into grain would be miracle enough. But Psalm 126 makes an even greater statement. The seeds are not ordinary seeds, but *seeds of sorrow*. The fruit they bear is not grain or wheat, but *shouts of joy*.

This is not the conventional wisdom of "you reap what you sow" that Paul affirmed in Galatians (6:7). Instead the image—sow in sorrow, reap in joy—incorporated an ancient Near East belief that weeping or keening while you planted made the crops more productive.[1] By linking that understanding to the celebration of God's deliverance, the psalm changes an agricultural practice into a powerful theological statement. It affirms both God's power and the people's faith. They "*shall* come home with shouts of joy" (emphasis added).

Thus the psalm not only calls upon God to use that transforming power, but also calls *us* to be open to its possibilities. It challenges us to trust God's joy, wherever we encounter it—in a stable in Bethlehem, at an empty tomb, or in acres of cow-pen daisies and purple asters.

TALITHA ARNOLD

[1] William R. Taylor, *The Interpreter's Bible* (Nashville: Abingdon Press, 1955), 9:666.

renders it as an imperative, imploring God once again to restore the people. If Dahood is correct, the psalmist simply continues his hymn of thanksgiving, glorying in God's great deeds. In either case, the psalmist likens the past or coming restoration to "watercourses in the Negeb." The Negeb is a desert region in the south of Israel lacking any year-round streams. Thus the "watercourses" are streambeds or wadis that remain dry most of the year, but occasionally flow with the runoff from infrequent rains. Shortly after the Babylonian invasion of the early sixth century BCE, the Nabateans moved into the area and built a civilization based in large measure on their expert utilization of these "watercourses." They diverted runoff toward crops and stored the remainder in cisterns.[3] Thus the "watercourses in the Negeb" truly became the lifeblood of the region.

The complexities of Hebrew tenses return in verses 5 and 6. The NRSV renders verse 5 as a jussive, an expression of the speaker's will or desire. The verb "reap," however, is in a simple imperfective form, which has many temporal nuances. Dahood translates, "Those who sowed in tears, amid shouts of joy did reap." It might also read, "Those who sow . . . shall reap." In light of verse 4, one can imagine desert farmers scattering their seed with trepidation, knowing that it is time, though the rains have not yet come. When the rains finally come, germinating their seeds and providing them with abundant crops, the farmers would surely rejoice.

The final verse builds on this image of agricultural blessing. The verbs "go out" (*halok yelek*) and "shall come" (*bo' yabo'*) are doubled with their corresponding infinitive absolutes, which adds a layer of certainty to the enterprise. The NRSV captures this with the word "shall." The metaphor offered here is that in times of crisis or suffering, God's people can count on God's restoration, just as the desert farmers know that the life-giving rains will come eventually, though they know not when.

PAUL D. BRASSEY

situations that affect nearly everyone in the congregation. A drought could affect a farming community. The closing of the town's main factory might put half of the people out of work.

The emotional movement of the psalm holds much value for the contemporary preacher, but may not resonate fully with the congregation. How many of us really have experienced joy that seems like a dream come true (v. 1c)? When has laughter filled our mouths (v. 2)? Often our experiences of God's presence are quieter than what the poet expresses. In reflecting on the joy of our congregations, we must be careful not to overstate the case. A wise pastor knows the joys of the congregation. Some may have experienced delirious rapture, but many more may have found God's presence to be an abiding strength or a reassuring peace. To find one's joy in these quieter ways is not a lack of faith. Such experiences can sustain us.

A preacher can tap into the emotional power of this psalm by careful insight into the faith experiences of the congregation or community. The preacher may identify smaller sources of joy on an individual or family level, if that is what is needed. Perhaps larger, community-wide experiences may present themselves. Deep engagement with this psalm and the congregation will most fruitfully evoke preaching that creates community. The joys of some can become the joy of all. The threats of faith to some can become the faith question of all. An effective sermon from this psalm will use language to create the sense of trust that closes out the psalm. Sowing in the face of a threat is an act of faith.

God has acted in the first advent. The whole community draws joy from that event. Despite the birth of the Savior, threats to faith still erupt. Whether in the eschaton or in the life of the community now, God will act again. Psalm 126 enables the preacher to proclaim God's trustworthiness, so that faith can grow and flourish.

CHARLES L. AARON JR.

[3]Daniel Hillel, "Negev: Land, Water, and Civilization in a Desert Environment," in *Freshwater Resources in Arid Lands*, ed. Juha I. Uitto and Jutta Schneider (New York: United Nations University Press, 1997).

# 1 Thessalonians 5:16-24

16Rejoice always, 17pray without ceasing, 18give thanks in all circumstances; for this is the will of God in Christ Jesus for you. 19Do not quench the Spirit. 20Do not despise the words of prophets, 21but test everything; hold fast to what is good; 22abstain from every form of evil.

23May the God of peace himself sanctify you entirely; and may your spirit and soul and body be kept sound and blameless at the coming of our Lord Jesus Christ. 24The one who calls you is faithful, and he will do this.

## Theological Perspective

Last Sunday's epistle, 2 Peter, is arguably the last document written in our NT. First Thessalonians is inarguably the oldest. Between them is a span of fifty years, a difference fully evidenced in the eschatology and admonitions preceding these, the final verses of the body of the letter. It is common to describe the exhortation offered here as an example of eschatological or interim ethics—how should one live in light of the imminent expectation of Christ's return? While not entirely discounting that tradition, it seems Paul offers something more, something reflecting his own rhetorical and perhaps philosophical training. What he offers is a discourse on the good life, a discourse that will be repeated in one form or another in almost of all of his letters, and in those letters attributed to him.

First Thessalonians is as affirming, positive, and hope-filled as any of the letters to follow. The Thessalonians are "beloved" (five times) "brothers and sisters" (NRSV thirteen times), and Paul "a nurse tenderly caring for her own children" (2:7), "a father with his children" (2:11) filled with eager longing to see them again (2:17, 3:1–6). What he wants for them is salvation, of course, and for them to lead lives that please God, and in fact "to do so more and more" (4:1). In later letters Paul will come to describe that life primarily from a balanced

## Pastoral Perspective

As British theologian N. T. Wright reminisced about his ordination to the ministry of word and sacrament some thirty years ago, he recalled receiving a number of cards and letters expressing heartfelt sentiments on that momentous occasion. The one that made the deepest impression on him—and the only one he remembers specifically to this day—was one that quoted three Greek words: *Pistos ho kalon.* "The One who calls [you] is faithful."[1]

So writes the apostle Paul to the church at Thessalonica in what is thought to be one of his earliest letters, written about 50 or 51 BCE. This is Paul's letter to a newly formed church addressing their calling in Christ Jesus (1:4); as such, it is an early, nonsystematic expression of his theology of election, a topic Paul would delineate with notable sophistication in the book of Romans.

Paul speaks to the church of 1 Thessalonians with the heart of a pastor—comforting the afflicted and afflicting the comfortable, as Reinhold Niebuhr has described that role. Using the triad of faith, hope, and love (later expanded in 1 Corinthians) to bracket the letter (1:3 and 5:8), Paul addresses the new *ekklēsia* of the Thessalonians, literally "assembly" or "community" but later called "church"

[1]Tom Wright, *Paul for Everyone: Galatians and Thessalonians* (London: SPCK, 2002), 133.

## Exegetical Perspective

First Thessalonians is almost certainly the earliest Christian writing that we have. It was written early in Paul's apostolic career and not many years after Jesus' death and resurrection. Yet already the Thessalonians are concerned with an issue that has perplexed the church ever since: how do we understand the fact that Jesus has not returned in glory as soon as we had been led to expect? This is also an appropriate question for our preaching during Advent—how do we continue to hold out hope for a consummation devoutly wished but now so long delayed?

In 1 Thessalonians 4:13–18 Paul comforts the Thessalonians with the assurance that Christians who have already died will nonetheless be included in Christ's final victory. In 1 Thessalonians 5:1–11 Paul encourages the Christians to live wakefully, alert for the salvation that may be completed any time.

In 1 Thessalonians 5:16–24, however, Paul shows the Thessalonians how they are to live in the meantime—the time between Christ's first and second advents. The time between is the time in which we still live. Paul's exhortation really begins with 1 Thessalonians 5:12. First Thessalonians 5:12–13 tells the Thessalonians how to treat their leaders. First Thessalonians 5:14–22 talks about how all the Thessalonians are to treat one another and

## Homiletical Perspective

The early Christians believed that Jesus was soon to return. The expectation was taken at face value, and the assumption was that God's sensibilities in the matter matched human expectations. The Spirit, whose manifestation was the sign of the risen Christ's presence, kept the church stirred and filled with vitality. Yet, as the Lord's return was awaited, there were matters of daily, mundane concern that demanded attention.

*The Tension.* There is an interesting axis that lies at the heart of this passage—namely, pneumatology is put in tension with eschatology and ecclesiology, prophecy with order. The Holy Spirit, of which prophecy is a sign, seems to have unsettled the order preferred by some. Passages like these give great insight into ancient practices of the church. A question that can be drawn is whether the charisms of the first believers continue throughout the duration of the church, or whether "ordinary gifts" have supplanted "extraordinary ones," following the baptizing of the nations. On the one hand, this question was responsible in large measure for the rise of Pentecostalism in the twentieth century. On the other hand, it forced all churches to revisit their pneumatology and recover the teaching and experience of the continuing presence and activity of

# 1 Thessalonians 5:16-24

## Theological Perspective

combination of the negative and positive, offering lists of vices and virtues, or fruits of flesh and spirit. In 1 Thessalonians, however, there is little mention of what not to do in terms of vices; a cursory "abstain from every form of evil" in 5:22 sufficient for that task. Instead, great positive emphasis is given to the shape of life in Christian community.

The verses before us for Third Advent, *Gaudete* (Rejoice) Sunday, begin, appropriately, with joy. What gives coherence, however, is not joy but completeness and wholeness, in which the good is expressed as the *telos*, a word that occurs in an adverbial compound in 5:23 but is the presupposition of the entire passage. "Rejoice *always*, pray *without ceasing*, give thanks in *all circumstances*" (5:16–18 emphasis added). Be sanctified *entirely* (*holoteleis*) (5:23). The whole (*holoklēron*) of spirit, soul, and body is to be spotless (5:23). This is an ethic not of moderation, but of thoroughgoing devotion.

Wholeness is at the foundation of Paul's understanding of the good life. This reflects all sides of his education, the purity code of Hebrew Scriptures and popular Hellenistic thought, both emphasizing completeness as perfection. It is in this sense that we better understand the call for unceasing joy, prayer, and thanksgiving—not as hyperbole or temporal impossibility, but as unrestrained action. We are to rejoice, pray, and give thanks (*eucharisteite*) (5:18) unreservedly and absolutely, just as the whole of our being, spirit and soul and body, are to be unblemished. The shape of the Christian life is not contoured in measured apportionment—one part work to one part prayer, or some other recipe for spiritual fulfillment—but in unreserved and all-consuming self-giving. As Paul will later write, "I appeal to you therefore, brothers and sisters, by the mercies of God, to present your bodies as a living sacrifice, holy and acceptable to God, which is your spiritual worship. Do not be conformed to this world, but be transformed by the renewing of your minds, so that you may discern what is the will of God—what is good and acceptable and perfect [*teleion*]" (Rom. 12:1–2).

The exuberance of expression is to be matched by an exuberant life. While all should be tested, the Spirit must not be quenched, a little-used verb generally applied to extinguishing a lamp (Matt. 25:8). The parallel between not quenching the Spirit and not despising prophecy suggest an embrace of charismatic ministry that will later fade in Paul (1 Cor. 14), but well fits the emphasis on an unrestrained expression of faith at the heart of this passage.

## Pastoral Perspective

in a nuance of the original meaning. The significance of this *ekklēsia* is not derived from its location in a particular place but from its "location" in a particular god, namely the one God of Jews and Christians—known to both traditions as the Creator and Father of all.

Paul addresses this new extension of God's family, giving thanks that the church has remained faithful amid persecutions. He is well aware that the worship of a pantheon of gods is ubiquitous in the culture of Thessalonica—much like the endless offerings in the self-help sections of our local bookstores. The forswearing of those gods puts this newly formed Christian church at risk of being targeted by neighbors and colleagues with whom they had earlier dealings.[2]

As the church of 1 Thessalonians intentionally develops their faith in the one God, Paul encourages them to exhibit *agapē*. As he would describe in more detail in his letter to the Corinthians, this love is not characterized by the emotion of the moment but is more nearly an act of will. For that reason the conduct of the new church is critical as a witness to the community around them. Paul delineates the difference between *agapē* and the sexually licentious behavior that marked temple cult rituals. Unlike those who primarily sought self-gratification, persons of the Christian church should display a self-giving love as they care for and nurture one another. Though Paul does not use our popular term "dysfunctional," he certainly knows the danger of family members abusing or ignoring their responsibilities toward one another (4:9–12); hence his use of agape, a love that models the self-giving of God in Jesus Christ.

In addition to addressing the Thessalonians' struggle with both persecutions and temptations, Paul acknowledges their anxiety about the delayed Parousia. As he maneuvers between the *already* (what God has accomplished in the resurrection of Jesus Christ) and the *not yet* (the culmination of God's salvation in the second coming of Christ), he encourages the Thessalonians to engage the tension between living in the present and looking toward their apocalyptic hope. As we step into that tension, the church of 1 Thessalonians gives us a model for ways we can acknowledge God's future plan for the world at the same time we recognize and accept God's judgment upon this world's values and mores—our complicity in laying waste God's

[2]Ibid., 89, 91.

those outside the church. Then verses 23–24 represent a kind of closing benediction, both to the list of instructions and to the entire letter.

Verses 12–13 suggest to the congregation members that they can have peace with one another because they respect their leaders—leaders presumably appointed by Paul.

Verse 14 is a brief compendium of instructions for the good church leader. Note that though all the verbs suggest strong leadership, every verb is positive in its connotations: "admonish," "encourage," "help." There is no explicit word about nagging or punishing (though a good "admonition" might carry a note of severe urgency). The heart of the matter and the key to good leadership is the final line: "Be patient with all of them" (the verb is the imperative form of *makrothymeō*). We remember Paul's other word about what it takes to build peace in the church: "Love is patient (*makrothymeō*) and kind." Looking back from 1 Corinthians, we can see that Paul in his early writings is already moving toward a picture of leadership that unifies through love.

Some have thought that Paul's instruction to leaders to "admonish the idlers" may have something to do with the fact that some Thessalonians, thinking Christ would soon return, saw no need to worry about such niceties as daily work. This is an enticing speculation, but there is not much further evidence for it in the letter.

Beginning with verse 15, we have two sets of instructions for the entire congregation. Verse 15 echoes a theme that is central to early Christian tradition—the demand for nonretaliation. See, for instance, Romans 12:17 and Matthew 5:39–42 and 1 Peter 3:9. Paul indeed pushes the Thessalonians beyond nonretaliation to positive "doing good." Perhaps most strikingly, he insists that believers not only refuse evil and choose good toward one another, but refuse to do evil to anyone and choose to do good toward all. This is a contrast to other writings in the New Testament that sometimes suggest the only concern of Christian ethics is behavior toward fellow Christians.

The passage now moves to concern with the worship life of Christians and of the Christian congregation—beginning generally and then focusing on the particular issue of prophetic speech. The first three admonitions of verses 16–18 present a kind of synonymous parallelism. The way that Christians rejoice and the way that Christians give thanks is by praying. Put the other way around,

the Spirit. This tension, to which Advent points, is crucial to the church's vitality and power.

*Challenges.* The setting here seems to parallel 1 Corinthians 12–14. From the few clues we get from the canon, it seems abundantly clear that one of the elements in the liturgy was for the prophet to be allowed to speak. Prophetic utterance came by direct inspiration. It was unplanned, unrehearsed, not particularly the byproduct of study. It could give guidance, reveal secrets, or deepen the faith of those undergoing trials and persecution. Like miracles and other charisms, this was a sign that the Spirit was alive and present within the body. By the Spirit the risen Christ breathed life into the church. More, quite often the content of prophecy was a word regarding the return of the Lord as promised.

While prophecy was to be welcomed and not despised, any claim to speak in the prophetic voice was to be tested. So with one voice the instruction for believers was not to quench the Spirit. Still, it was demanded of them that they prove all things. Specifically, whenever there was a claim for the prophetic voice, a corresponding gift of discernment was in order. This critical line and delicate balance are not removed from one generation to another. Without manifestations of the Spirit, the life of the church becomes dull and fades. Yet, without the accompanying charism of discernment (*diakrisis*), some of everything can be credited to the Spirit.

*The Plot.* On the one hand, the church is called to live in full expectancy of the Lord's return. This is what keeps us ready, busy, on the post of duty. The expectation has the world and all to do with the urgency in ministry and mission, or lack thereof. When the church no longer expects the Lord's return, it is like the wicked stewards who spoil the lord's assets. They grumble and complain about what has been given.

On the other hand, the church must live as if the Lord is depending on it indefinitely. For its ongoing life it must care for matters that are mundane, like seeing to it that the servants receive their care, that the altar is tended to, that property is kept up, that schedules are made and observed. No one fit of piety, emotion, or sincerity takes the place of such vigilance.

*Relevant Issues.* What are some consequences for quenching the Spirit? For worship, a consequence is that all is done as a matter of mere ritual—a rote

# 1 Thessalonians 5:16-24

## Theological Perspective

Paul addresses and implicitly raises again for the reader the question of what life lived out in response to the gospel, "a life worthy of God" (2:12), looks like. For Paul such life is joyous, prayerful, eucharistic (in the multiple meanings of that word), Spirit-filled, prophetic, and tested. How that looks for each brother and sister will differ. Asking the question is the important thing, and it is a question too rarely asked. Contemporary Christians are profoundly moved by, for example, Dietrich Bonhoeffer's *Life Together* because, with the notable exception of David Ford's *Shape of Living*,[1] there is little literature to help the believer reflect for herself or himself on the nature and contours of a well-lived Christian life. There is, to be sure, an overabundance of literature to *tell* the reader how to live, and Paul is of course more than capable of doing that himself. What is needed is something different, an invitation to a profound reflection on the Christian life. Paul implicitly offers the invitation here.

Paul also gives an important, and suitably Pauline, explanation of how the brother and sister in Thessalonica and ever after are to manage to live such a life, spirit, soul, and body. She isn't. "Faithful is the one calling you, who will do even this" (v. 24, my translation). It is God's faithfulness, not the effort of the believer, that makes such life possible.

The tradition, perhaps beginning with Paul himself later in life, has struggled with the exuberant abundance that characterizes 1 Thessalonians 5:16–24. It is telling that verse 18b, "this is the will of God in Christ Jesus for you," is without fail applied only to negative and disheartening life events— illness, death, and so on—so that the exhortation in verse 18a, "Give thanks [*eucharisteite*] in all circumstances," is seen as a challenging demand rather than a gracious invitation. Paul, a masterful rhetorical craftsman, knew exactly what he was doing by beginning, "Rejoice always!" Sometimes, believe it or not, the good things in life are God's will too.

WILLIAM BROSEND

## Pastoral Perspective

creation and failing to honor the mantle of Christ's reconciling Spirit that we have inherited.[3]

In his closing paraenetic section of the letter, which comprises the epistle for the third Sunday of Advent (5:16–24), Paul fires off eight imperatives in seven verses. Taken together, they are Paul's admonitions about the way life in Christ should be lived—not for its own pleasure or even in the glory of its own accomplishment, but solely in the *hope* of a future secured through *faith* in the *love* of God in Christ Jesus.

Paul's exhortations—though tailored to the church of 1 Thessalonians and the specifics of its historical and cultural milieu—have much to say to twenty-first-century lives that are damaged or fearful. Our inclination in a post-9/11 world is to distrust those who have wronged us and to build security walls higher and stronger, in order to separate and protect ourselves from any perceived threat. Imagine using Paul's vision of openness based on the triad of faith, hope, and love to speak to a fearful member of the congregation. Imagine painting a scene of the Christian life balanced like a three-legged stool. First, we might say to those we are called to serve that if we can express thankfulness in all things, then we can say yes to whatever is, and we can embrace the reality of our lives rather than live in conflict with it. Second, if we can accept the notion that God uses everything, then we can enter into the now. Third, we discover in this process that God makes all things new. Rather than have all our no's about life quench the Spirit of God, we are able to pray, "Give me your eyes, God, for how my spouse is treating our children. Give me your eyes, God, for what life looks like in the wake of abuse or infidelity or betrayal."

To be sure, as Paul admonished, we should test everything. This reality testing is one of the primary ways the community of faith discerns that the power in us has emanated from the Spirit of God revealed in Jesus Christ. But with this kind of openness toward life, we can have curiosity, rather than dread, about the future of God's unfolding. And most important, we are able to risk this day, and the one after, in the sure and certain hope that the three-legged stool rests on a firm foundation—*Pistos ho kalon*—the one who calls [you] is faithful.

LEE W. BOWMAN

---

[1] David Ford, *The Shape of Living* (London: Fount, 1997; republished Grand Rapids: Baker, 2004).

[3] Abraham Smith, *The New Interpreter's Bible, The First Letter to the Thessalonians* (Nashville: Abingdon Press, 2000), 11:680–81.

constant rejoicing and regular thanksgiving are themselves perpetual prayer.

"For this is the will of God in Christ Jesus for you" might point forward to the discussion of prophecy that follows or might point back to the exhortation to give thanks. Abraham Malherbe suggests that more likely this is the conclusion of the sentences on prayer and the "for you" may suggest that the Thessalonians have a particular need to give thanks, that, for whatever reason, thanksgiving has not come easily to them.[1]

The last admonitions have to do with the role of prophecy in worship (see also 1 Corinthians 14). Prophets were Christian leaders who declared aloud in worship words that they claimed to have received from God's own spirit. The role of the congregation is twofold: (1) Listen attentively and generously. ("Do not quench the Spirit.") (2) Listen thoughtfully. ("Test everything.") The "good" and the "evil" in this context surely refer to the good and evil that are found in or result from true or false prophecy.[2]

The last two verses of our passage are both a prayer and a promise. The prayer is for wholeness: that the believers may be wholly sanctified, that spirit, soul, and body may be knit wholly to one another. The promise is that it is not up to the Thessalonians to make themselves whole: God will do this.

The reason for the prayer and the promise is the claim that has driven this epistle from the first verse to the last. Christ will come again. God calls the faithful to be ready for that coming—and enables their readiness.

It is not clear how this text might be read with the Gospel text on John the Baptist, except that the passage from John 1 is also about the right discernment of prophets. John the evangelist tries to help the priests and Levites, and through them the readers of John's Gospel, discern who John the Baptist really is. He is not the Messiah and not Elijah and not that prophet that Moses prophesied would be greater than himself (Deut. 18:15). However, John is *a* prophet, because his voice cries the truth. That truth points straight to Jesus. Jesus is more than John, and therefore more than a prophet and more than Elijah and more even than the Messiah. As the other verses of John's chapter make clear, Jesus is the Word made flesh.

DAVID L. BARTLETT

exercise. The church is not energized or invigorated. Worship is a chore that takes but does not return vitality. Churches in this condition experience difficulty keeping their children from one generation to the next. The decline seen in many churches attests to this dilemma. Another consequence of quenching the Spirit is the loss of prophetic consciousness. In this state the church can become a despiser of the poor and a hater of the weak.

The challenge of Advent, forced by a lection like this, is the discernment (*diakrisis*) to know the voice and the motions of the Spirit. Many churches struggle in this tension over the form worship should take and over how contemporary strands might be blended with traditional ones. All that may be well and good, but how do the prophetic impulses of the Spirit press the case in matters of justice? What is quenching the Spirit when issues of poverty, care for the destitute and the wretched, are at stake?

John the Baptist, who stood in the shadow of Elijah, prepared the way for the Messiah's coming. His work was that of turning the hearts of the fathers to the children and the children to the fathers, that the curse might be lifted from the land. Again, there was the prayerful wish of Moses that all the people of God would be prophets, and that God would pour out the Spirit upon them all. Are there prophetic voices speaking to the church in this day? What is the prophetic role of the church in the face of the domestic and global scenes? Does the order of the church, so closely aligned with the state, so much as register the frequencies in which prophetic tones come?

*Proclamation.* The dynamics of this lection can be seen with clarity in a figure like Zecharias, a priest of God, who was the father of John. When he was told that his aged wife would bear a son, he was stricken with dumbness for not believing. But when the child was born and he wrote the name given by the angel, his tongue was loosed, and he blessed the Lord God of Israel.

The church that quenches the Spirit similarly suffers a sentence of dumbness as it faces a world that needs blessing from the horn of salvation. Advent is a time for the tongue to be loosed and the mercies of God proclaimed.

W. C. TURNER

---

[1] Abraham J. Malherbe, *The Letters to the Thessalonians*, Anchor Bible, vol. 32B (New York: Doubleday, 2000), 330.
[2] Ibid., 333–34.

# John 1:6-8, 19-28

⁶There was a man sent from God, whose name was John. ⁷He came as a witness to testify to the light, so that all might believe through him. ⁸He himself was not the light, but he came to testify to the light. . . .

. . . . . . . . . . . . . . . . . . . . . . . . . . . . . . . . . . . . . . . . . . . . .

¹⁹This is the testimony given by John when the Jews sent priests and Levites from Jerusalem to ask him, "Who are you?" ²⁰He confessed and did not deny it, but confessed, "I am not the Messiah." ²¹And they asked him, "What then? Are you Elijah?" He said, "I am not." "Are you the prophet?" He answered, "No." ²²Then they said to him, "Who are you? Let us have an answer for those who sent us. What do you say about yourself?" ²³He said,

## Theological Perspective

This text focuses on the role of John the Baptist, the witness sent by God to testify to Jesus as the light of the world. These verses provide a bridge between the eternal preexistence of Jesus as the Word (*Logos*) (present with God at creation, vv. 1–5) and the historical manifestation of the Word (who became human and walked the earth, v. 14). The testimony of John is about who Jesus is, and this testimony is consistent with two important foci of this Gospel: incarnation (Jesus as the human embodiment of God) and Christology (Jesus as the Christ).

In verses 6–8, the relationship between John and Jesus is clarified. Set within the prologue (vv. 1–18) of this Gospel, these verses become a lens for interpreting the identity of Jesus with reference to a temporal and cosmic perspective. John is a man sent by God to witness in history to Jesus who was present with God at creation and who will be the eternal presence of God within history. The juxtaposition of the temporal and cosmic (eternal) accentuates the significance of John's place within the drama of creation and redemption for the world. John did not simply announce the coming of another prophet, but he proclaimed the coming of the Word who would embody God's presence within the world. The presence of this embodied God is described in a translation from the Aramaic: "And the word took

## Pastoral Perspective

"John the Baptist is no independent figure. He belongs entirely to Christ . . . he is only there to collect and give back the light that falls upon him from the figure of the one and only Christ. Thus standing there, being totally dependent, being totally man and sinner, totally serving."[1]

From a pastoral perspective we want to ask who is present on this second Sunday of Advent and what hopes and fears we bring to this service.

In the light of this text, all of us who come to Advent worship are witnesses. Our witnessing turns us from the excessive preoccupation with ourselves. Witness turns us to the Christ who is the focus of our worship and to the brothers and sisters who are the object of our witnessing.

The pastoral temptation of Advent is to turn from attention to our waiting for *Christ* and to focus instead on *our* waiting for Christ. Are we sufficiently prepared for the events of the days ahead? Are we sufficiently content to enjoy them? Faithful anticipation can turn quickly into frenzied activity and anxious self-examination. Advent turns from waiting to scurrying. Just when we should be looking forward to the manger, we are looking inward, taking our own spiritual temperature.

[1]Karl Barth, *The Great Promise*, trans. Hans Freund (New York: Philosophical Library, 1963), 1.

"I am the voice of one crying out in the wilderness,
'Make straight the way of the Lord,'"
as the prophet Isaiah said.

[24]Now they had been sent from the Pharisees. [25]They asked him, "Why then are you baptizing if you are neither the Messiah, nor Elijah, nor the prophet?" [26]John answered them, "I baptize with water. Among you stands one whom you do not know, [27]the one who is coming after me; I am not worthy to untie the thong of his sandal." [28]This took place in Bethany across the Jordan where John was baptizing.

## Exegetical Perspective

The Gospel of John begins in the land of time before time. It echoes the earliest cadences of Genesis, the Wisdom myth of ancient Judaism, and anticipates much of the *logos* poetry of second-century CE gnostic literature. There is little consensus on the origin and nature of the first eighteen verses of John's Gospel, but scholars such as Gail O'Day, Lamar Williamson, and C. K. Barrett concur with Raymond Brown's assessment of "the prologue" as "an early Christian hymn, probably stemming from Johannine circles, which has been adapted to serve as an overture to the Gospel narrative of the career of the incarnate Word."[1]

The text for the third Sunday of Advent begins at the precise point where the prologue moves from cosmic and mystical to incarnational and concrete. In Brown's translation, verses 6–8 are a parenthetical thought. Other scholars argue that they are misplaced prose in this poetic prologue. I suggest they are neither. Both R. A. Culpepper and Charles Talbert (Talbert, 66) see verses 6–8 as the B movement in a chiastic construction that is later complemented with a B' movement in verse 15. In verse 6, the Gospel writer begins his lengthy,

[1]Brown, *The Gospel According to John I–XII*, Anchor Bible, vol. 29 (Garden City, NY: Doubleday, 1966), 1. Charles Talbert makes almost the exact argument on p. 72 of his book *Reading John* (New York: Crossroad, 1992).

## Homiletical Perspective

The first chapter of John's Gospel upsets familiar tellings of the Jesus story in several notable ways. There is no birth story, for one thing. A Christmas pageant based on the Fourth Gospel would feature one child, speaking one line, in front of a curtain of black velvet: "And the Word became flesh and lived among us, and we have seen his glory, the glory as of a father's only son, full of grace and truth." While this might constitute great savings in the costume and props department, it would no doubt leave the audience feeling seasonally shortchanged.

What we have today is an Advent pageant—still starring one character saying much the same thing, still short on costume and props—only in this case the minimalism is both intentional and revelatory. The one character is a man sent from God whose name is John. He is not John the Baptist (as in Matthew), John the baptizer (as in Mark), or John the son of Zechariah (as in Luke). He is just plain John, who will not even say that much when the religious authorities come to question him.

They want to know who this noisy man is, this man who will not shut up about the light he saw fall to earth, who is baptizing people to help them see the same light, although he has no license to do this, from them or anyone else. They want him to say who he is, but all John will say is who he is not. He is

# John 1:6-8, 19-28

## Theological Perspective

human form and dwelt [tented] among us; and we saw his preciousness [glory], a preciousness like that of an only beloved son of the Father, who is filled with loving kindness and justice." (1:14)[1]

Likewise, verses 19–28 set forth the importance of John for understanding the identity of Jesus with reference to the history of the Jewish religious community to which Jesus belonged. In these verses the religious authorities question John about his identity as they seek to ascertain the identity of the one about whom his message speaks. The questions of the authorities provide markers for understanding both the identities and the roles of John and Jesus. Interestingly, before the questions begin, John declares that he is not the Messiah. This declaration thus leads the authorities to ask if he is one of these figures foretold in Scripture—Elijah or the prophet—who is to announce the coming of the Messiah. Although John says that he is neither of these figures, his words do signify that he has a prophetic role as "the voice of one crying out in the wilderness" (v. 23).

The authorities turn next to challenge John because he is baptizing without the authority to do so. John's response to this challenge (as in the case of vv. 6–8) establishes his distinction from and relationship to Jesus. John is a forerunner to Jesus, and this establishes his authority to baptize with water. He understands, and he wants the authorities to understand, that his actions are only preparatory in relation to the one whose identity they actually seek, but will not acknowledge.

These two sets of verses (1:6–8, 19–28) thus point us toward theological reflection upon the subjects of incarnation and Christology. First, holding these verses together, we are reminded that the humanity and divinity of Jesus are not competing aspects of the One we confess to be the Christ. The challenge of under-standing Jesus' identity is not therefore about how he is fully human and fully divine; the task is to accept the gift of the incarnation as we confess its fulfillment in Jesus the Christ. According to feminist theologians, the gift of the incarnation is that it helps us to rethink our understanding of embodiment and relationship. As the divine became human in the body of Jesus, we can reclaim healthy connections between the body and the spirit, the goodness of our embodiment. Likewise, Jesus' incarnation makes possible the human ability to live in relationship with one another in ways that we incarnate God's love for humanity.

## Pastoral Perspective

At Advent, our worship, always in danger of being self-contained, slouches toward self-satisfaction. How beautiful the decorations, soothing the sermon, uplift-ing the music, cute the children lighting the candles!

The questions we ask of every Sunday's worship are especially questions for Advent. Is God worshiped? Is Christ proclaimed? Do we bear witness to those who wander into this family celebration puzzled and lonely?

It is a little odd that the lectionary banishes John the Baptist to his own Advent week, bracketed out from the great prologue to John's Gospel and therefore strikingly absent from the great Christmas prologue where the evangelist put him. Maybe John becomes a symbol of those of us who stand slightly at the margins every Advent and Christmastide, knowing that something big is about to happen but not quite knowing how to be part of the party. Certainly an appropriate pastoral concern for this season is always for the many folk who find Advent and Christmas more as occasions for loneliness and sorrow than for community and joy.

Part of the theological and pastoral wisdom that John the Baptist exemplifies here is his confession of who he is not. There is an honorable tradition among the prophets of the self-knowledge of reticence. Amos: "I am no prophet or a prophet's son." Isaiah: "Depart from me, for I am a man of unclean lips." Jeremiah: "I am but a lad." The traditional Greek admonition "Know yourself" surely means "Know who you are and who you are not."

The Stoic or common-sense reminder that a healthy self-knowledge includes a healthy knowledge of one's limitations only touches the surface here. The limitation the Baptist confesses is the gap between the person he announces and the person he is. To say that as Christians we bear witness to Christ is a far cry from saying that we are somehow "little Christs." To say that the church is Christ's body does not simply conflate his lordship with our service. We point to him; we serve him, and we stand entirely under his judgment.

In this way pastoral health and theological fidelity come together. The soul freed from pretension is free to exemplify God's mercy, and the church freed from anxiety about its own fading authority has a better chance of bearing witness to the authority of Christ. My Protestant bias, indeed, is that we are invited to follow Jesus—at a distance—more than to imitate him.[2] "What would Jesus do?" the button asks. He

---

[1] Holy Bible from the Ancient Eastern Text: George M. Lamsa's Translation from the Aramaic of the Peshitta (New York: HarperCollins Publishers, 1968).

[2] I am indebted to Gene Outka's apt phrase, as Christians we are always following Christ "at a distance."

sometimes labyrinthine, theological commentary on how *ho logos* (the Word) and *to phōs* (the Light) survive even the greatest forces of darkness (see v. 5).

The first *anthrōpos* (human) introduced in this grand prologue is a man named John. This is the same John whom Mark defines as *baptizōn* (the baptizer, Mark 1:4) and Matthew names by the noun, *ho baptistēs* (the Baptist, Matt. 3:1), the one who preaches a fiery form of repentance. Luke describes John by his family name and the geographic locus of his ministry, *Iōannēn ton Zachariou huion en tē erēmō* (John, the son of Zechariah, in the wilderness, Luke 3:2), one with deep and apparent roots in the Jewish prophetic tradition.

While it is tempting to refer to the first human in the Fourth Gospel as "John the Baptist," to do so obscures the author's understanding of John's unique vocation as a holy human, "sent by God" to bear witness to "the Word" and to point to "the Light." In this Gospel, John is not introduced by family name or place of origin. He is not principally a baptizer, a prophet, an exhorter, or even a messenger from God. John is a *martyria*, a witness, sent by God to testify to "the Word made flesh," "the Light" that no darkness has or will ever extinguish. The principal vocation of John in this Gospel then is to bear witness, a verb that occurs thirty-three times in the Fourth Gospel and only twice in the entirety of the Synoptic Gospels.

"Can I get a witness?" is a cry heard from many an African American pulpit. If John "the First Witness" whom we meet in the Fourth Gospel were in the congregation, he would surely respond, "I'll be a witness."

"Witnesses say what they have seen and heard or attest to the truth of another's testimony," writes Lamar Williamson. "John's role is to recognize the true light when it appears, and to call attention to it so that others may recognize it and believe—that is, recognize, trust in, and commit themselves to the light." Indeed, some read John's Gospel as a prolonged trial about the person and nature of Jesus, with John the Baptist being summoned as the lead witness on Jesus' behalf.

In this Gospel of contrasts—light and darkness, the world made by God and the world that does not recognize God—John is a human example of the possibilities and limitations of a witness. While John is *apestalmenos para theou* "sent by God," just as the *logos* is "sent by God," John is sent not to be the *logos*

not the Messiah (never mind that no one asked him that). He is not Elijah. He is not the prophet-like-Moses awaited by Israel since Moses' death.

When the authorities press John to say something about himself, he will not even choose his own words. Instead, he paraphrases the prophet Isaiah. "I am the voice," he says. He is neither the light nor the Word. He exists to testify to the one who is those things. His being is for the sole purpose of bearing witness to the one whom he is not.

By the time John tells the authorities that they do not know this one, though he stands among them, and that John himself is not worthy to untie the thong of this one's sandals, the negatives in these thirteen verses reach a grand total of ten "nots," "neithers," and "noes." Here, then, is a stunning refusal to place the coming one into any of the theological boxes prepared for him, along with an equally emphatic rejection of the religious authorities sent to vet John the Voice.

It is as if the author has asked his readers to watch while John performs the old trick of yanking the tablecloth off the table that has been set for the Messiah. Everything is in place—the best china, the six-piece silverware settings, the Waterford wine glasses. The whole point of the trick is to yank the cloth so quickly that all these treasures are left trembling where they stand, but that is not how it happens this time. When John yanks the tablecloth, he takes everything with it: not, not, no, neither, not. The expected crash never comes. All the tableware simply vanishes as if it never were. Only then can John, standing all by himself in front of the black velvet curtain, do what God has sent him to do: testify to the light, and to the light alone.

Depending on local conditions, preachers will want to spend some time thinking about the ways in which faith and hope can cancel each other out this time of year. Faith, by definition, is radical trust in what God is doing, even when the divine mode of operation is far from clear. Even in the wilderness, even without a proper title for himself or a proper name for the coming One, John the Voice goes on testifying to the light. Without costume, props, supporting cast, or a production budget, he survives on the bare minimum of certainty about what God has sent him to do. In the words of Meister Eckhart, God is found in the soul not by adding anything but by subtracting.

Hope, on the other hand, can easily assume the dimensions of individual and corporate wants. I hope for a white Christmas, a less contentious

---

[2] Lamar Williamson Jr., *Preaching the Gospel of John* (Louisville, KY: Westminster John Knox Press, 2004), 4.

## Theological Perspective

Second, in the context of the Advent season, these verses remind us of our identity and our role as witnesses who must testify to Jesus' birth in the midst of the ever-encroaching consumerist claims regarding the meaning of Christmas. Like John we are to witness to the light of Christ as a voice in the wilderness of twenty-first-century consumerism. As voices in the wilderness, we must make a counter-cultural claim that dislocates the consumption of things, even when we offer these things as Christmas gifts. An example of such a counterclaim might focus on the buying and wearing of brand-name items that have become markers of our identities. The countercultural claim is that being fully human means the quest for our identity must be grounded upon the relationship we have to Jesus. Just as John knew who he was in relation to who Christ was, we must claim our identity, especially remembering that we are not the Christ but witnesses to him. Our role in our time is, like John's role in his time, to confess who we are not and proclaim the One to whom we testify.

Third, like John we live as witnesses to the light of Christ, for the light of Christ is life (v. 4, "in him was life, and the life was the light of all people"). Thus, as we testify to the light, we also embody that light as believers who reveal the life of Christ anew in the world this Advent season. To embody the light and reveal the life of Christ anew means that we are to live so as to nurture our humanity—especially the capacity to love our enemies—and to act humanely, offering compassionate and restorative justice.

Finally, the faithful response to and moral imperative of this text may be succinctly found in the words of an African American spiritual, "This little light of mine, I'm going to let it shine." Believers have a responsibility both *to be* persons who reflect the light of Christ and *to live* in such a way that our lives proclaim the light of Christ in the world.

MARCIA Y. RIGGS

## Pastoral Perspective

would walk on water, give sight to the blind, and raise the dead. Our text suggests the better question: "What would Jesus have us do?"

We cannot read the story about John the Baptist without remembering that the world regularly offers resistance to our witness. Though the Fourth Gospel never directly alludes to John's fate, we know from our reading of the Synoptics that he was beheaded for his faithfulness. In polite North American society, resistance is far more subtle. The danger is not that we will be executed but that we will be ignored. The Word made flesh turns into the word made papier-mâché, displayed on the lawn with all the charm and all the power of Santas, elves, and red-nosed reindeer.

We remember the call to bear witness means attending to resistances in our own congregations too. In one fairly typical mainline church, the governing board got a mailing asking them to support a Billy Graham Crusade. The chair started to toss the letter toward the circular file: "We don't believe in evangelism," he said. But we do believe in evangelism. Given the gift that Advent celebrates, it is simply selfish to keep our good news to ourselves.

The separation between "evangelical" and "mainline" or "old-line" Christians is entirely artificial. All of us are Christians because we have been evangelized—have heard and believed the gospel. All of us are under orders to bear witness to others.

The truly evangelical Christian is not ashamed to talk about faith. The claim that religion is an entirely private matter, never proclaimed and seldom mentioned, is very far from the convictions of John's Gospel. But the truly evangelical Christian does not seek to manipulate, coerce, con, or charm another into faith. Truly evangelical Christians and evangelical churches keep pointing to Jesus, saying, "Here he is." Evangelism borrows other language from John's Gospel. We proclaim not "Believe or perish," but "Come and see" (John 1:46).

From 1921 until his death Karl Barth kept over his desk a copy of a painting by Matthias Grünewald. The crucified Christ hangs in the center of the picture, and to one side stands John the Baptist—Barth's model for himself, and for all Christian believers—"with his hand pointing (to Jesus) in an almost impossible way."[3]

In an almost impossible way, we keep pointing to Jesus too.

DAVID L. BARTLETT

[3]Barth, cited in Eberhard Busch, *Karl Barth: His Life from Letters and Autobiographical Texts*, trans. John Bowden (London and Philadelphia: SCM and Fortress Press, 1976), 116. The painting is the frontispiece for the book.

of God. Neither is John *to phōs* (the Light) of God. The prologue of John's Gospel makes a clear narrative emphasis on John as "the witness" who was sent by God to bear witness to the light.

Two things are clear about the first human that is introduced in the Fourth Gospel—he is sent by God not to compete with the Word of God coming into the world, but to bear witness to him; not to be the light of God to the world, but to testify to the light of God that has transcended the realm of Hebrew myth and gnostic philosophy in the person of Jesus. In this Gospel of signs, John "the First Witness" is the signpost and the standard for any subsequent signposts to God's *phōs* and *logos*. No sign is from God in this Gospel unless it bears witness to the *logos* and the *phōs* and leads all to come to believe in God through him.

Deep into Advent, this Gospel text does not offer images of a young family on a holy trek to Bethlehem. Readers will see no shepherds and hear no cantatas in the fields. There are no villainous innkeepers and no sage magi in John's prologue. In fact, there is little in today's text or the entire prologue that supports a tendency in the church to obscure Advent and romanticize Christmas.

On the contrary, John 1:6–8 is a signature Advent text, as it reminds careful readers that the first witness to Jesus arrived on the earthly scene before Jesus did. He arrived not to get everything decorated and everyone ready for Christmas, but to "prepare the way of the LORD" (Isa. 40:3). He came to "bear witness" to the coming Light of God, reminding all who would listen that the darkest forces in the world are not finally as powerful as they appear. He came to bear witness that the most enchanting words spoken by forces of darkness lose their charm when measured against the "Word [who] became flesh and lived among us . . . full of grace and truth" (John 1:14).

GARY W. CHARLES

church, a closer relationship with Jesus, a God who makes sense. While there is nothing wrong with any of these hopes, they still carry considerable cargo, suggesting that I know not only what my community and I need from God, but also how God might best come to us. The only hope that belongs on this Messiah table is the bare hope of God's arrival, sweeping all clutter away.

Preachers who wish to explore historical themes may benefit from learning more about the messianic expectations of the late first century, especially as they relate to the Dead Sea Scrolls. Since the prologue to John's Gospel echoes the first chapter of Genesis, it is also important to note that the light revealed in Jesus is not the sun, moon, or starlight created by God on the fourth day, but the divine light created on day one.

Practical concerns for preaching this passage include helping listeners understand what the Fourth Gospel means by "the Jews," especially since this phrase will come up again in chapter 8 with far nastier overtones. The NIV translates "the Jews of Jerusalem" here, which is some help. While the author of John's Gospel employs the phrase more than sixty times in telling the Jesus story, "the Jews" most commonly refers to the religious establishment in the nation's capital, not to every person of Jewish descent.

Finally, there are plenty of devout Christians who think that the John who wrote this Gospel was the same John who baptized Jesus. Today's passage offers the preacher a clear opportunity to distinguish between the two, highlighting at the same time some of the differences between the Fourth Gospel's portrait of John and that of the Synoptic Gospels.

BARBARA BROWN TAYLOR

# 2 Samuel 7:1-11, 16

¹Now when the king was settled in his house, and the LORD had given him rest from all his enemies around him, ²the king said to the prophet Nathan, "See now, I am living in a house of cedar, but the ark of God stays in a tent." ³Nathan said to the king, "Go, do all that you have in mind; for the LORD is with you."

⁴But that same night the word of the LORD came to Nathan: ⁵Go and tell my servant David: Thus says the LORD: Are you the one to build me a house to live in? ⁶I have not lived in a house since the day I brought up the people of Israel from Egypt to this day, but I have been moving about in a tent and a tabernacle. ⁷Wherever I have moved about among all the people of Israel, did I ever speak a word with any of the tribal leaders of Israel, whom I commanded to shepherd my people Israel, saying, "Why have you not built me a house of

## Theological Perspective

Sitting at the very center of Deuteronomistic history, 2 Samuel 7 brings together the threads that hold that history together: David's conquests and ascension to kingship, the saga of the roving ark, and God's covenant to be with David and his descendants forever. The passage is both rhetorically clever and theologically profound. Having won peace and stability, David determines to do something for God, only to be reminded that in their relationship God is principally the provider rather than the recipient: God has brought David to this place, and rather than David building a "house" for God, God will build a "house" of him. At first blush, this passage joins many of the great theological themes of triumphant Christianity:

— God's presence cannot be contained by temple, tent, or tabernacle;

— God's peculiar election of a people is the basis for (re)establishing an eternal covenant;

— God's prevenient grace is, itself, a corrective for untoward human ambition.

All these themes warrant sustained attention. As Advent draws ever closer to its Christmas culmination, they are especially worth our attention, for each of them becomes literally embodied in the infant Jesus.

But there is more theology to this passage than meets the eye, and that "more" can both enrich those

## Pastoral Perspective

An apt and succinct commentary on this lesson may be found in Isaiah 55: "For my thoughts are not your thoughts, nor are your ways my ways, says the LORD" (v. 8). In 2 Samuel 7 the thoughts of both king and prophet are contradicted by "the word of the LORD" (v. 4), and human ways of honoring God are not only rejected but reversed (v. 16).

While not the main thrust of the text, one pastoral consideration is the interplay of king and prophet, the motivations of each, and the matter of speaking truth to power. On the surface, David's motivation appears honorable. Yet enough is known about the mixture of motives from which we all act, along with the knowledge of how the politically powerful sometimes use religion for their own purposes, to cause one to wonder. The expressed motivation is the honor of God.

Might David also wish to honor himself as the one who will forever be known as having honored God? Is the house meant to confine God? The "word of the LORD" that comes to Nathan infers as much. Why does David consult Nathan? Is it because the king values the prophet's wisdom? Or is it in order to secure a religious blessing on a political project? Does Nathan speak his genuine conviction in giving his initial blessing? Or is he simply playing the part of a court chaplain (see Amos 5:10–17)? To his

cedar?" 8Now therefore thus you shall say to my servant David: Thus says the Lord of hosts: I took you from the pasture, from following the sheep to be prince over my people Israel; 9and I have been with you wherever you went, and have cut off all your enemies from before you; and I will make for you a great name, like the name of the great ones of the earth. 10And I will appoint a place for my people Israel and will plant them, so that they may live in their own place, and be disturbed no more; and evildoers shall afflict them no more, as formerly, 11from the time that I appointed judges over my people Israel; and I will give you rest from all your enemies. Moreover the Lord declares to you that the Lord will make you a house. . . . 16Your house and your kingdom shall be made sure forever before me; your throne shall be established forever.

## Exegetical Perspective

This text is the culmination of God's promise made to Abram in Genesis 12. Finally, the people can claim the land as their own and live in peace. Yet, even as the promise is fulfilled, the tension between God and humanity, part of the story since Genesis 3, is also evident. This text represents God's grace and promise freely given to a humanity that still desires to use this grace as personal power.

*The Tension (vv. 1–3).* The narrator sets the stage from God's perspective. The king was "settled in his house" because "the Lord had given him rest." The promise given in Genesis 12 has now been fulfilled in God's good time. God has delivered on God's promise of a land for the people.

Against this backdrop, verses 2–3 are a shock. A reader of the Bible might expect this pronouncement to be followed by the thanksgiving and praise that are so closely associated with David in the Psalms. But instead, King David makes a pronouncement to the prophet Nathan; now that David has a house, he will a build a house for God. Several things seem amiss in the king's statement. First, David has decided for God instead of following God. Second, prophets usually advise kings of God's will, not the other way around. Here David has made the pronouncement alone. The David of Jerusalem

## Homiletical Perspective

What did the earliest Christians—and Jesus' own contemporaries—think they meant when they called Jesus "Son of David"? Today's Gospel mentions David twice: Joseph is "of the house of David" (Luke 1:27), and Mary's son will be "called the Son of the Most High, and the Lord God will give to him the throne of his ancestor David" (Luke 1:32). David's importance to the story of our faith is indisputable, but many Christians are familiar with only the barest outlines of the dramatic narrative of his rise and reign. This reading from 2 Samuel, then, offers the preacher an opportunity to expand on the meaning of those titles and references to enrich our understanding of how the earliest Christians identified the Christ.

David has only recently solidified his control over all Israel and Judah, and with his own personal troops has captured Jerusalem, which lies outside the established boundaries of Israel and Judah. Thus his capital is truly the "city of David," a new addition to the united kingdom. To this capital, with great fanfare and dancing, he has now brought the ark of God. The importance of this move of David's cannot be overestimated: the king is paying honor to the ancient stories of the tribes, while establishing a monarchy that departs significantly from the old models of tribal leadership; and he is identifying the

# 2 Samuel 7:1-11, 16

## Theological Perspective

themes and help us make sense of why 2 Samuel 7 is particularly appropriate in the days leading up to Christ's arrival.

Begin by noticing that this passage did not actually come together at a time when "the king was settled in his house, and the LORD had given him rest from all his enemies around him." Instead, it came together during the Babylonian captivity. There was no rest, no house, and no king. The lament of Psalm 137 would seem more fitting for such a context than claims about God's presence, election, and grace. Questions abound: Can this passage make sense to the defeated? Is this good theology? Can the God described in 2 Samuel 7 be the same God that is worshiped in exile? Ought we focus on God's presence, election, and grace in such a context?

Those questions could be answered negatively: perhaps the God of exile is absent, impotent, or cruel, and to worship the God of 2 Samuel 7 while in exile is an act of delusion or masochism. There is scriptural warrant for that approach in, for example, Job's and Jeremiah's accusations, Lamentations, and elsewhere. Indeed, many of these other Scriptures challenge the Deuteronomistic historian's tendency toward too-simple claims that obedience is rewarded and disobedience punished. But before writing off 2 Samuel 7, three points are worth noting.

The first point has to do with a tendency to oversimplify the theology of the Deuteronomistic historian. This passage, which sits at the very heart of Deuteronomistic history, doesn't conform to the Deuteronomist's "reward obedience and punish disobedience" pattern. There are neither "if-then" statements nor moral caveats here. Unlike the covenant at Sinai, the covenant established here is unconditional. Unlike 1 Kings 5:3, in which David is not allowed to build the temple because he is a warrior, God's word to David that he should not build the temple has to do with God's freedom, not the blood on David's hands. If Advent teaches us to expect the unexpected, then we might carry that Advent learning even into the way we read texts: coming to Scripture with fresh eyes is, itself, an Advent practice.

This leans into a second point: claims about God's uncontainable presence, peculiar election, and prevenient grace may have a place in settings of hardship and exile. Where exile forces us to face the existential threat that God is absent, the claim that God's presence cannot be contained opens the possibility of considering that God is here, too. Where exile calls God's power into question, the

## Pastoral Perspective

credit, when Nathan hears "the word of the LORD," he has the courage to deliver the same to David (v. 17), even though it contradicts the king's wishes.

According to the text, both king and prophet have misjudged the mind of the Lord. Despite their experiences as people of faith, and despite their being in possession of the story of divine activity "since the day I brought up the people of Israel from Egypt to this day" (v. 6), David and Nathan misconceive the character and purpose of the One they worship. In our own day there are examples aplenty, from both the political and religious realms, of those who have no doubt as to God's purposes and plans. This text serves as a warning against such a confident reading of the will of God and serves to underscore Lincoln's assertion that "the Almighty has his own purposes."[1]

The king and the prophet discover that they are in the presence of One who confounds human expectations and surprises even the faithful—or especially the faithful, who presume to know how God is acting because it is the way God *must* act. No small part of the challenge of preaching on the fourth Sunday of Advent is opening the eyes, ears, hearts, and minds of parishioners to the God who is not captive to human expectations and who—not only once upon a time, but time and again—scatters "the proud in the thoughts of their hearts," brings "down the powerful from their thrones," lifts "up the lowly," fills "the hungry with good things," and sends "the rich away empty" (Luke 1:51–53).

"If faith responds to the living God," writes Luke Timothy Johnson, "then faith is an open-ended enterprise, for the living God always moves ahead of us. If theology articulates faith, then theology also is a matter of constant catching up with the work of the God who acts before we do and most often catches us by surprise."[2] It may be easy for Christians, worshiping on this Sunday, to see how the promise of a house for David and a kingdom that will be forever has been fulfilled in a surprising way by the gift of God in Christ. Far more challenging—and perhaps of more benefit to those as familiar with the Christmas story as were David and Nathan with the story of Israel—would be to wonder where today God is moving ahead of us and acting in ways that will catch us by surprise.

The challenge presented to the preacher by 2 Samuel 7:1–11, 16 is to assist the congregation to take its place alongside David and Nathan as people

---

[1] Second inaugural address.
[2] Luke Timothy Johnson, *The Living Gospel* (New York: Continuum, 2004), 43.

seems to need neither God nor human advisors. Yet despite the king's lapse of protocol, Nathan answers that he should go ahead with his plans (v. 3).

*God's Answer (vv. 4–11).* Nathan leaves, and God speaks to him later that night. Nathan is told to speak two oracles to David. The first (vv. 3–7) addresses the nonissue of God's desire for a permanent home. The second is a warning to the human David (vv. 8–11) of his place in God's kingdom and the lessons he needs to remember.

Verse 5 is God's command to Nathan to go and speak for God, using the standard prophetic formula, "Thus says the LORD." Yet notice that Nathan is not told to go to the king, the title used in verses 1–3, but "to my servant David." This is a much more intimate address, yet at one and the same time should remind the king of his place as God's servant.

The oracle is the answer to the question that the king failed to ask God, and is couched as two questions itself. It is also a history lesson that stresses the relationship of God to humanity. "Are *you* to build me a house?" God asks, "I have not lived in a house since *I brought* Israel from Egypt and *I myself moved* in tent and sanctuary" (emphases added). The verb "moved" or "walked" is especially important, since it is a verb form that implies self-determination and also appears in Genesis 3:8, where God "walks about" the garden looking for those first humans. God is God and will walk where God wishes to walk.

The second question (v. 7) is an additional reminder for the king that God was with Israel long before David appeared; "Did I ever ask the leaders of Israel who shepherded my people to build me a house?" God did just fine without David and his offer of a home. The message God sends is clear: God will not be domesticated or controlled by David or anyone else. If God wishes to cease walking about and settle down, then God and only God will make the decision.

The second oracle (vv. 8–11) begins with the words of verse 5, except now Nathan is to say, "Thus say the LORD of hosts," a name that is not intimate; indeed, it indicates God's power over God's enemies. God tells David what God has done both for David and for Israel. Verses 8–9 remind David not to be too power hungry. "I took you from the pasture, from following the sheep to be prince over my people Israel." David should never forget that it is God that put him where he is and it is God who has given him victory over his enemies (v. 1). It is God who has

religious cult of his people with the political and military dynasty he intends to found.

We need to keep this background in mind as we hear David's question about building a house for the Lord, and the prophet Nathan's response. While Nathan assures David that the Lord is not in need of a permanent place to live, he confirms David's decision to establish a capital and a dynastic monarchy. Although the Lord God himself still resides in a tent, David's "house" will be permanent. Eventually, David's son Solomon will erect for the Lord the splendid permanent structure that will physically symbolize the identity between David's dynastic "house" and the presence of God.

The promise to David that "your house and your kingdom shall be made sure forever" (2 Sam. 7:16) proves to be a false assurance, for David's dynasty falls about 400 years later. Nevertheless, the identification between the Davidic monarchy and the cult of YHWH gives birth, in times of oppression, to a messianic hope that is firmly attached to the notion of the continuity of David's line. The longed-for Messiah must be of David's "house" or lineage, and is expected to mimic David's military and political success: he should lead a rebellion against the domination of the Roman foreigners and restore the monarchy—the monarchy that has been symbolized and remembered by the presence of the temple (the Lord's "house") connected with the physical palace (David's house) in Jerusalem. The Messiah should usher in a kingdom of God.

These are the associations that the title "Son of David" would have conjured to the minds of Jesus' contemporaries, and they are a significant factor in the misunderstandings and disillusionment that marked the thinking of those who opposed his prophetic teaching and precipitated his arrest and execution. And although contemporary Christians may understand the connection with David more metaphorically or spiritually, the association between David's name and the imagery of political and military success is emphatically current in many of the hymns and prayers associated with the risen Christ as Messiah. A Sunday focused on the unlikely birth of a holy child to an unmarried peasant girl might offer an opportunity to explore the dangers and possibilities inherent in familiar expressions such as "Son of David," and "kingdom of God."

Nathan's prophecy to David offers another, more imaginative direction to take the connections between this story and the birth of Jesus. Nathan

# 2 Samuel 7:1-11, 16

## Theological Perspective

claim that the covenant is forever raises the possibility that God's promises will continue after exile ends. Where exile raises questions about whether God has turned cruelly against us, the claim that God's grace is, itself, an answer to human arrogance hints at the possibility that the God who brought the people out of Egypt and established David's kingship may do something that looks more like unmerited redemption than undeserved punishment.

So understood, these are not *answers* to exile—as if believing them relieves pain, loneliness, and heartbreak—so much as *challenges* to a different and too-simple set of claims about unmitigated and endless horrors. They are alternatives to answers that proclaim that giving up on God is better than hoping against hope. They create openings for us to think differently about the world around us. They turn us away from attempts to force the world (or the gospel) to conform to our answers, and toward treating our claims as opportunities to learn anew about the world and how God acts in it. If Advent anticipates a new thing happening, we should be wary of thinking only in the same old ways.

Which leads to a third point. When those of us who preach and teach from the comparative comforts of the First World read Advent texts into our relatively luxurious lives—when we speak of an uncontained God from well-contained places, an electing God from seats of power, a graceful God from positions of plenty—we don't miss the point of the gospel that inheres in these things so much as we miss some of its power. As the First-World church watches itself become ever less tethered to that setting, no small amount of hand-wringing has ensued. Even the increasingly common church metaphors of "exiles," "resident aliens," and "strangers in the world" can carry within themselves wistfulness about the way things were. Yet if the Babylonian exiles could turn to 2 Samuel 7 as a way of hoping for a future based on what God has done in the past, then perhaps we might do so as well. Indeed, we might even watch the gospel be born anew.

MARK DOUGLAS

## Pastoral Perspective

of faith who nevertheless have considerable catching up to do with the One whose thoughts are not our thoughts and whose ways are not our ways. The preacher may serve best in this regard, not by offering answers, but by posing questions. What are *our* assumptions about what will be pleasing in God's sight? What are the ways by which *we* seek to enshrine and confine God? Should *we* not exercise more reticence before linking God's purposes with our political (David) or religious (Nathan) agendas? Where in the world, where in our life as a congregation, where in one's personal life, may God be wanting to do something that is being blocked by human aspirations and agendas, however seemingly noble? How receptive are we to the God who will not be confined or enshrined but retains and cherishes the freedom to surprise us—as in the coming of Christ down the back stairs of Bethlehem, to be born of Mary, grow up in the hick town of Nazareth, spend his time with the least, the lowly, and the lost, and, most surprising of all, become "obedient to the point of death—even death on a cross"? Could that same God be leading the church in new and unthought-of directions?

A sermon on this text could and should shape the liturgy to reflect "the God who acts before we do and most often catches us by surprise." The prayer of confession might acknowledge that we confuse our aspirations and ambitions with God's purposes. The congregation might confess how little it expects of anything new or surprising. The song "Sweet Little Jesus Boy," with its haunting refrain, "We didn't know who you were," could serve to underline the surprising way the kingdom promised to David has come to be. The hymn "O How Shall We Receive You?" could serve to highlight a Christ who continues to come among us in surprising ways.

EUGENE C. BAY

given David a great name. Verses 10–11 further make the point that it was not just David whom the Lord favors, but all of Israel. The final part of verse 11 pulls together what David had forgotten, "The LORD will make you [David] a house." David's house, of course, is a dynasty. Verse 16 reminds the king that humans can build houses of wood and stone, but God will build a "house" that only God can build, one of children, one of a dynasty.

David is as human as the rest of us. The promises of God in Genesis stand in deep contrast to the actions of the people in those formative stories. The God that walked around in the garden is the same one that has walked with Israel throughout its early history. Here, when David seems to forget his place in God's kingdom, he receives a warning, just like Cain in Genesis 4. Unfortunately, both ultimately disregard the warning given by God and take things into their own hands; murder of another is the result (2 Sam. 11).

This text is a powerful one to preach as the frenzy toward Christmas is peaking. Like David, we can use some warning. We may not be kings, but we too are tempted to make our plans without God, even on a holiday that celebrates God taking flesh. We need the history lesson as much as David. We too need to be reminded where God found us and what we would be without God's grace. We too need to be reminded that God saved more than just us, but is reconciling the world to God's self. David's lesson is a lesson that fits well as the culmination of our preparation for the coming of God incarnate.

BETH LANEEL TANNER

quotes the Lord as saying he is comfortable living in the tent of a nomadic people, as he has done since "the day I brought up the people of Israel from Egypt" (2 Sam. 7:6). This notion prepares the way for the prologue of John's Gospel, "And the Word became flesh and lived among us" (John 1:14). A more literal translation would be, "And the Word became flesh and *tented* among us." John is consciously choosing vocabulary that recalls the most ancient description of God in the company of his nomadic people.

Human beings—perhaps, especially, powerful ones—seem to have the need to build temples and monuments to proclaim the stability or permanence of their power. Certainly, it was David's strategy, brought to fruition later by Solomon, to build the temple as a monumental proclamation of God's support of and identification with the monarchy. What might it mean, in a day when the symbolism of the temple was compromised by the presence of a foreign occupying force, to say that God was "tenting" with God's people in the form of a human being—even a child?

Think about the vulnerability of a tent. The tents of David's day would have been made of animal skins and woven materials or rugs. They would have been patched probably and torn by the winds. Even the tent of the Lord would have been threatened by the forces of nature and would have had to be rebuilt periodically.

And is it too fanciful to compare contemporary tents? A ripstop nylon construction with spring-loaded poles that can bend flat in a strong wind? Or a bivouac on the face of a cliff, with only a few grams of fabric between a climber and hundreds of feet of free fall?

The tent's fragility is the price paid for its mobility. As we take the last steps toward our celebration of the incarnation, it seems appropriate to linger for a moment over the idea of a God who is constantly ready to pull up stakes and move where we go, sleep where we sleep, and be buffeted by the same winds that blow sand in our eyes and tear the roofs off the shelters we erect: Emmanuel!

LINDA LEE CLADER

# Luke 1:47-55

"My soul magnifies the Lord,
   [47]and my spirit rejoices in God my Savior,
   [48]for he has looked with favor on the lowliness of his servant.
      Surely, from now on all generations will call me blessed;
   [49]for the Mighty One has done great things for me,
      and holy is his name.
   [50]His mercy is for those who fear him
      from generation to generation.
   [51]He has shown strength with his arm;
      he has scattered the proud in the thoughts of their hearts.
   [52]He has brought down the powerful from their thrones,
      and lifted up the lowly;
   [53]he has filled the hungry with good things,
      and sent the rich away empty.
   [54]He has helped his servant Israel,
      in remembrance of his mercy,
   [55]according to the promise he made to our ancestors,
      to Abraham and to his descendants forever."

## Theological Perspective

The status quo does not obtain in God's economy. When God moves into the life of the world, everything changes. The old ordering of life is displaced in no uncertain terms, and a new ordering of life is put in its place. The old has gone, the new has come, and nothing will ever be the same again. Theologically, Advent means this: when God announces the divine intention to act decisively in the incarnation of the Word, everything gets turned on its head.

Mary's song of praise in response to her pregnancy and her awareness, at least in part, of its theological significance are an expression of hope in the God of Israel now acting in eschatological power. The kingdom that has been promised in Israel's past is coming to pass. Advent announces its inauguration. The content of the new work of God is not given in lofty theological images but as the ethic of a changed world order. In concrete and specific terms, Mary sings in the language of revolution (a turning around) to record her understanding of the great reversals that have unfolded, albeit, we must add, in a hidden way. The effect of the "prophetic perfects," suggests Geoffrey Wainwright, may incite the reader, in political terms, to a "revolution of the left," as one aligns oneself with the revolutionary action of God.[1]

[1]Geoffrey Wainwright, *Doxology: The Praise of God in Worship, Doctrine, and Life* (New York: Oxford University Press, 1980), 426–27.

## Pastoral Perspective

The fourth Advent candle will be lit this Sunday. Some people in the congregation will have been waiting anxiously, others waiting expectantly, some waiting in deep grief, and others waiting with a threatening diagnosis received during Advent. All are waiting with memories of Christmases past, including memories of as many sermons on the Magnificat as they have experienced years in worship. The waiting is almost over. So as Mary sings her song of praise and liberation, let us listen afresh as pastoral caregivers.

In the first stanza, as we enter this expectant time with Mary and Elizabeth, we know that they both have said yes to the plan of God, which leads us to wonder what will be asked of us. Mary quickly clarifies that question as she sings that God is doing a new thing. God's Son is coming into the world and she is the bearer of God. This young Jewish girl not only accepts her calling but also sings praise to God for this amazing grace.

Then she continues her song in the second stanza, announcing how the wrongs of history will be made right. Actually, she sings as if they have *already* been made right, since she uses the past tense. Through her song of justice, Mary calls us to be change agents for a better world for all. God's call to Mary was for a specific purpose, which her cousin Elizabeth

## Exegetical Perspective

The Magnificat is one of the most famous passages in the New Testament. Mary's song, which most believe to be based on the song of Hannah in 1 Samuel 2:1–10, is one of four poems in the Bible placed in the mouths of women who play key roles in the lives of ancient Israel and Judah, those women being Miriam (Exod. 15), Deborah (Judg. 5), Hannah, and now Mary. All of these songs are placed in the narrative at key points in the history of the nation: the exodus from Egypt, formation of the nation during the period of the judges and Philistine oppression, and now Roman occupation, colonization, and oppression. All of these women are either noted in the narratives or called mother or function as substitute mothers, as in the case of Miriam and Moses at the bathing scene with Pharaoh's daughter. The men children associated with these women serve key roles in the history of the nation.

All of these songs have some relation to the liberation of the nation from oppression.[1] On the one hand, these stories and these songs are really odes to the men and the male God who empowers the men to rule. On the other hand, these songs function to reinforce the primary social role of

[1]Jane Schaberg, "Luke," in *The Women's Bible Commentary*, ed. Carol A. Newsom and Sharon H. Ringe (Louisville, KY: Westminster John Knox, 1998), 371–73.

## Homiletical Perspective

Just when the pre-Christmas frenzy has reached its height, we are treated to the voice of the Poor One with this hymn of praise. Young Mary sings a song rooted in the legacy of her people Israel, the spiritual lineage of Miriam, and the sisterhood of Hannah, Judith, and Leah. All of them before her sang of God's reversals; but although reversal of power is one overarching scriptural mark of the Spirit's work, the Magnificat fine-tunes its paean of praise to focus upon God's handiwork in the socioeconomic arena. Here, the playing field is *more* than leveled: her stanzas envision the powerful stripped of their entitlements and the humble given preeminence. Mary speaks in two voices: for herself, initially (vv. 46b–50), although her song is anything but self-referential; and then in the third person (vv. 51–55), associating herself with all *anawim*, "handmaids" of "low estate" whom God has helped, whether by filling their barrenness or delivering Israel from its oppression.[1]

Experience indicates that the casting of Mary in the annual Christmas pageant (a nonspeaking role traditionally cast as placid and passive) can be tricky. While some little girls prefer to be angels because

[1]See Raymond E. Brown, *The Birth of the Messiah* (Garden City, NY: Image Books, 1979), 361. Note that exodus imagery predominates here as Mary describes God's acts.

# Luke 1:47-55

## Theological Perspective

Before we look at the reversals, however, let us pause for a moment to reflect on the effect that God's acts have on Mary: her soul magnifies the Lord; her spirit rejoices in God her savior. Her inner knowledge of what God has done calls her to worship. The repetitive affirmation is a declaration of worship of the God in whom she delights. The act of Mary's worship reminds us that the hope for the reign of God is in the God who acts, who alone is worthy of praise. This immediately places the statements of the reversals in a context that is far more that the outline of a political manifesto. The reign of God no doubt has profound political implications, but political action, no matter how noble, does not inaugurate the reign of God. Nevertheless, there is content to the acts of God, and Mary's song is not bashful in announcing what may be summed up as good news for the poor and downtrodden, and as very bad news indeed for those who hitherto have wielded economic, political, and military power.

There are five reversals. The first is the reversal that Mary experiences herself. She is of low estate, a peasant girl, unmarried, living in an economically poor and militarily occupied country. Yet she is *theotokos*, God-bearer. Protestants can surely find a place in their piety for the celebration of Mary as a blessed woman, for the Mighty One did great things for her, and through her, for us. In no sense, of course, should we depict Mary as mediatrix, as having soteriological status. Yet as a woman who was singular in her vocation from God to carry the Son of God in utero, she is one for whom we thank God that God found such a one as her worthy. God's mercy is for those who fear God.

Second, God has acted with a strong arm to scatter the prideful. Pride has conventionally been seen as the core sin, from which arise all other aspects and expressions of a broken relationship with God and, consequently, with one another. Self-satisfied and gratuitous self-referencing is not what God wants from us. God's response to our pride has a military overtone, for God has scattered the proud by the wielding of a strong arm. With the same arm, God, third, has brought down the powerful from their thrones and lifted up those who are without status and rights. The images are violent and thrustful. Similarly, fourth, God has filled the hungry and sent the rich away with nothing. The reversals are dramatic, purposeful, and final. There is no ambiguity concerning what God has done.

The final reversal is more hidden. Israel, the servant of God, has throughout her history been the

## Pastoral Perspective

affirmed. God's call to us on this fourth Sunday of Advent is coming to us through Mary's song. We need one another's affirmation, just as Mary needed Elizabeth's, to live into God's plan for the world. When a child is baptized, the parents vow to raise the child in the nurture and admonition of the Lord; the congregation affirms this commitment with its collective blessing and promise to support the family in this endeavor. This affirmation enables the child and the church to live into God's plan, just as Elizabeth's affirmation enabled Mary to do the same.

Looking at the poetic structure of Mary's song, we see in the second stanza seven strong verbs showing parallels or reversals: "has shown strength," "has scattered the proud," "has brought down the powerful," "[has] lifted up the lowly," "has filled the hungry," "[has] sent the rich away empty," and "has helped . . . Israel." It is important to note that God's mercy in Mary's song is described in the context of God's original covenant. "I will be your God and you will be my people." Mary's song maintains inclusion of all people in God's plan, even as her words echo both Hannah's song in 1 Samuel and the words of the prophets, preaching a strong reminder that God's purpose will always turn the status quo upside down. We can be better friends, spouses, mothers, daughters, grandmothers, and neighbors as we say yes to the new thing that God is doing with and within us.

Mary sings of the yes of God that she has learned through her Jewish faith. She knows God can be trusted, and she is therefore willing to say yes to God, even when she does not understand how a virgin like herself could bear God's Son. All of us, men and women, are included in Mary's and Elizabeth's times of expectancy, calling us together in partnership with God in God's plan for this world. This song addresses all the ways we set ourselves apart from one another, which is the excuse we need to set us over and against one another. We are all uniquely made in the image of God, meaning that we are to see God in one another and are called to say yes to justice for all.

For years Mary has been portrayed as submissive because of her yes to God at the annunciation. Today it is time to recognize that this prophetic woman also says no to all that negates God's purposes in human history. First, Mary celebrates the greatness of God, and then she proclaims God's liberating compassion for the poor. Mary sings the joy that she is feeling and sings blessing for the oppressed, whether that oppression comes from being

women as mother and as comforter within the patriarchal order in which they live. As Exum argues, they serve the patriarchy.[2] In terms of structure, the song has two parts, one relating to the individual (vv. 46–49) and one to the nation (vv. 50–55).

In both the vow of Hannah (1 Sam. 1:11) and the song of Mary, these women self-identify as servants, or more appropriately slaves, since verse 48 uses *doulēs*, as does LXX for 1 Samuel 1:11. This is most interesting, since both of these women come from upper-class families, as noted in the lineage of Elkanah in 1 Samuel 1:1 and Mary's priestly relatives as well as Joseph's royal background. It is as though their social class, which is prominent in the larger narratives,[3] has to be diminished by their designation as slaves of the deity. While the rich women listed in 8:2—who are reported to fund Jesus' movement—can literally maintain their social class standing, the songs and vows of these two women must deny or misrepresent their own. While this use of *doulos* may be likened to the terminology used to describe Moses' relationship to YHWH and Paul's to God, these women are in no way equal to these men in leadership of the nation; rather they are bearers of the children who will lead/save the nation.

Scholars have long struggled against the implications of *tapeinōsin* in v. 48. As the NRSV translates this, it is "lowliness," suggesting lower social class. The word is used four times in this form in the NT. While some suggest "humiliation" as a translation, the other usages of the term in Acts 8:33, Philippians 3:21, and James 1:10 speak to the lynching of the revolutionary by the state. *Tapeinōsin* is, however, used in LXX to speak to the oppression, exploitation, and misery of individuals, such as Hagar (Gen. 16:9), Leah (Gen. 29:32), and Hannah (1 Sam. 1:11), and of the nation by external oppressors (Deut. 26:7; 1 Sam. 9:16; and 2 Kgs. 14:26). In regard to the three women who experienced individual oppression, the reference is to the exploitation of their bodies, all with divine complicity. Some current scholarship suggests that this is the case with Mary in this passage from Luke.

In regard to the references to the national calamities, the one who comes forth is the one to lead the people in defeating these colonizers. Thus, were one to go along with "lowliness," this could not be a social-class designation as argued above. It

they *do* something, those who *want* to be Mary aspire to be the queen with royal prerogatives—an unfortunate commentary on the church's traditional interpretation of Mary's part. At the same time, we also see her as a "bit player" compared to the more energetic shepherds. But what if we restored the Magnificat to the Christmas pageant and understood Mary as a primary role model for serious disciples, bearer not only of the Savior but also of the news that God's reign has broken through our status quo?

It is a bracing focus (if also an ironic one) at the crux of a long commercial season, where all in the secular realm is focused upon acquisition and dancing to a Muzak of images angelic and snowy. At this juncture, most of us bear more resemblance to the self-satisfied than to the *anawim*. And yet those with listening ears may discern the clarion melody of a new realm in which economies are just and social injustice is undone. Preachers can help by applying Mary's template to their own communities, inviting hearers to measure their social realities by its dimensions. How do things look in "our town" today, and how *would* they look if the lowly were lifted up?

The aorist verbs of Mary's canticle suggest one intriguing trajectory for preaching on the cusp of Advent, the full weight of Christmas yet to come. Scholars have long puzzled over the past tense on the lips of this pregnant young woman, who *before* giving birth speaks of her offspring's approaching mission as already accomplished—finished and done. Merely agreeing with the proposition that in her prenatal announcement Luke expresses the community's postresurrection proclamation does not fully plumb its profound depth; for this intriguing use of the past to announce a consummated future has life-changing ramifications. We might hear Mary's aorist, ultimately untranslatable in English, as a combination of anamnesis and prophecy. The first makes past history a present reality, so that we ourselves are experiencing it; the second pulls a future vision into the present. The resulting synergy reveals a vibrant *now* in which God's realm is complete and dwelling among us.

"The end is where we start from," wrote the poet. "Or say that the end precedes the beginning."[2] If so, then the saving justice of God's reign is as good as accomplished among those who can articulate its outlines. We are not used to seeing the realities

[2]J. Cheryl Exum, *Fragmented Women* (Valley Forge, PA: Trinity Press International, 1993), 135–39.
[3]Itumeleng J. Mosala, *Biblical Hermeneutics and Black Theology in South Africa* (Grand Rapids: Eerdmans, 1989), 186–89.

[2]T. S. Eliot, *Four Quartets* (New York: Harcourt, Brace & World, 1943). The quotations are taken from "Little Gidding," stanza V, and "Burnt Norton," stanza V.

# Luke 1:47-55

## Theological Perspective

subject of God's judgment. Now, Israel is the recipient of God's mercy, as God remains faithful to promises made long ago. The people who angered God—they offended God's holiness and compassion; they violated God's love and justice—to them God shows mercy. God has helped Israel.

The issue now is to establish what the reversals mean. Certainly they are moral warnings. There are two conclusions: (1) God does not approve of prideful people, or of powerful rulers who disregard the lowly in their charge, or of rich people who get fat while the hungry starve; (2) God uses in special ways and looks with favor upon those of low estate. Further, the reversals are goads to lifestyle decisions and ethical action. Against any easy reduction implying that we are dealing with less than matters of eternity, recall, for example, the similar eschato-logical message of reversal found in the teaching of Jesus at Luke 16:19–31, a story that Helmut Gollwitzer used rather famously as the basis for a provocative book, *Rich Christians and Poor Lazarus.* That title surely causes us to take notice. The ethics of the kingdom of God lead to a certain ordering of action and values: to raise up and bless the poor, the weak, and the hungry persons among us, and to denounce and bring down those who perpetuate such hurt and disadvantage. That is work with a meaning for eternity.

There is one final point: we are reminded that God acts as God acts, according to God's covenant mercy, in history. Mary's song is a prophylactic against inappropriately spiritualizing the gospel. The Lord's work means the coming of a new heaven and a new earth. To live on earth, in history, in anticipa-tion of its fulfillment, is the great challenge of faith.

ANDREW PURVES

## Pastoral Perspective

underprivileged or overprivileged. So for the people in our pews, whatever their circumstances, Mary's new song announces the reality of "both/and." Just as she embodies the polarity of being virgin and mother, she shows us how we can be people both of the heart and of the head, both mystical and resistant, both contemplative and justice oriented, both spiritually alive and socially active.

On my first trip to the Monastery of the Holy Spirit in Conyers, Georgia, I met *Theotokos,* the God-bearer, depicted in a magnificent rose window above the altar. I was shocked by the size of Mary's womb. Mary sits in this glorious stained-glass circle with outstretched arms and a womb so large it contains Jesus standing as a grown man, with his arms open wide and enough room left over for God's rebirthing of all creation.

Every time I sit in that dark sacred womblike monastery sanctuary, being rocked back and forth by the sound of the monks chanting the Magnificat as evening falls, I am in awe of the *Theotokos* in the pregnant circle over the altar. The circle reminds me that Christ will come into the broken places in us and into the world where healing is needed. The circle reminds me that we are all pregnant with the possibility of new life, becoming more than we are, for God is with us and God is in us. Because our memories can be very short, we need Mary's song to remind us of God's twofold promise to deliver God's people and to lift up the poor. Mary sings because she has new life in her. Are we ready to join in singing with her? O come, let us adore him and follow him into new life.

TRISHA LYONS SENTERFITT

would instead have to be a gender designation that presumes women to be worth less than men. On the one hand, this is not an unusual argument in the biblical literature, namely, that the unity of the nation or church is primary to the liberation of women from patriarchal oppression and slaves from economic exploitation. On the other hand, the term could be multivalent, speaking both to the oppression of women and slaves in the society and the Roman colonization.

In both the song of Hannah and the song of Mary, the second part of the song revolves around the theme of reversal of fortunes, namely, that the high are going to be made low and the poor are going to be raised up. The hungry will be fed, and the rich will be hungry. It is these sentiments that make these songs so powerful for those who press liberation as a major theological scheme to be found in the text. Schaberg even notes the song as paradigmatic of God's special option for those on the margins. It is this song, along with the so-called Lucan inaugural in 4:18f., that gives this Gospel its claim to being "poor friendly." Part of the difficulty with this line of argument is that nowhere in the Gospel, or in Samuel, do we find evidence of this programmatic reversal being incarnate. While these songs raise structural problems relative to social inequalities, the subsequent narratives speak more to the amelioration of the problems of individuals (as in the miracle stories) but the confrontation with the Roman Empire and its acts of colonization seems to be pushed to the background.

Finally one has to explore whether liberation of one group has to be predicated on the oppression of another group. Would not a theology of relinquishment, where those who benefit from the oppression relinquish the privileges that come from sinful social orders, serve better as a model? Or do we use such passages that have women sing in ways that support patriarchal order to model how other oppressed groups should sing about reversals that still keep them oppressed?

RANDALL C. BAILEY

around us that way. "Realists," we call ourselves—ignoring the deep implications of incarnation no less than resurrection, the new thing God has already done that sleeps below the surface of our perceptions. Our challenge is to cultivate the ability to see God's promises as already having come to pass.

Mary's words foreshadow Fred Craddock's principle that the perceptive preacher gives voice to not only what people need to *hear* but, at least occasionally, what they want to *say*. "Yes, that is it," comes the response; "that is our message; that is our faith."[3] What is it regarding divine promises fulfilled that wants articulation (and then a thankful song of praise) in your congregation or community of faith? For the preacher, the question requires seeing into the deep heart of things, to all the metaphors for liberation that even now surround us.

Can preaching offer a new set of eyes—the eyes of those perhaps *not* represented in most of our sanctuaries? How does the world look to the *anawim* of our communities? Making that vision concrete for our hearers offers them opportunity not only to look beyond the commercialism of the season but to enter a stance of *solidarity* with all whose condition was shared by Mary's child. Seeing the present world with the eyes of the poor may give us for the first time true eyes of faith to perceive the mighty acts of God now operative in the world.

The preacher should be aware that this central word of the Magnificat—that wealth and power have no ultimate influence but are brought into subservience to the lowly—will be no more a popular Christmas message in our time than it was in the culture to which Jesus' witness first came. Prepare for the possibility of ruffling some shop-weary feathers, but persist in framing the message the way Mary did: as a song of praise and the celebratory news for which all generations have been waiting!

GAIL A. RICCIUTI

[3]Fred B. Craddock, *Preaching* (Nashville: Abingdon Press, 1985), 26, 44.

# Romans 16:25-27

<sup>25</sup>Now to God who is able to strengthen you according to my gospel and the proclamation of Jesus Christ, according to the revelation of the mystery that was kept secret for long ages <sup>26</sup>but is now disclosed, and through the prophetic writings is made known to all the Gentiles, according to the command of the eternal God, to bring about the obedience of faith—<sup>27</sup>to the only wise God, through Jesus Christ, to whom be the glory forever! Amen.

## Theological Perspective

As Romans begins, so it ends. Starting with God and ending with God, forcefully, clearly, and consistently. The themes of the benediction, echoing those from the opening salutation (1:2–5), are both central to the epistle and to this Advent Sunday, especially with regard to "the revelation of the mystery" (v. 25) that proclaims the coming of Jesus the Christ. The text is about God's very being, what God has done (the *kerygma* or good news), and the implications of God's action for human beings (*paraenesis*).

*Who Is God?* Speaking about God and for God is what Christian preachers do! Biblical resources are inexhaustible with images, titles, and characteristics of the Divine Reality. Here, most notably, the claims that God is "able" (v. 25) and "wise" (v. 27) draw the theologian's attention.

God's "ability" is reference to the distinctive biblical emphasis on God's actions or "doings." Almost every theological symbol includes God's activities; for example, as creator, redeemer, sustainer, and completer. The idea that "God is a verb" derives from this emphasis on divine doing. The prayer that Jesus taught his disciples emphasized this in the words "Thy will be done." This Advent Sunday marks particularly the end of the anticipation that God is about to act decisively and prepares for God's redemptive action.

## Pastoral Perspective

The mood of our annual Advent journey has shifted as we move closer to the celebration of Christ's birth. Advent is a season of hopeful anticipation, but it begins with the acknowledgment of human despair. We are all sinners in need of a Savior. Left to our own devices, we find life unbearable. Yet gradually, Advent prepares us for the gift of Emmanuel—God-with-us. Because of all God did, and continues to do, in and through Jesus Christ, life today can yield abundance and assure our future. Our epistle lesson is a joy-filled doxology (from the Greek word *doxologia*, meaning "word of glory") praising God for the greatest of all gifts.

On the Sunday before Christmas, many worshipers yearn to move beyond worldly worries and constraints into the joyful praise that God's goodness and generosity evoke. Procrastinators in our culture of consumerism are beginning to panic. Fatigue and financial concerns weigh heavily on others. Grief overwhelms those facing their first Christmas without a loved one. We prepare again to welcome the Prince of Peace amid a world filled with war, terrorism, poverty, disease, and natural disasters. The juxtaposition of our hope and our reality make today's epistle reading especially poignant as we guide worshipers toward the celebration of Christ's birth.

## Exegetical Perspective

In a concluding, magnificent doxology, Paul epitomizes the message of his great epistle to the Romans. The passage is appropriate for Advent because it incorporates themes pertinent to the season. One such theme is Jesus' key role in fulfilling the divine plan that a descendant of David should be enthroned to lead God's people (cf. Psalm 89; Rom. 1:3–4; also the day's lections from 2 Samuel 7 and Luke 1). Another such theme was that the messiah would bring the Gentiles to worship God (cf. Luke 1:78–79; 2:32; Matt. 2:7–11).

Grammatically the passage is one long sentence. With regard to verse 26, modern translations of the Greek move the phrase "to bring about the obedience of faith" from the middle to the end of that verse. With regard to verse 27, a word in the last clause is awkwardly translated "to whom" in the NRSV; some ancient manuscripts have "to him" instead, and most modern translations simply omit the word in question.

One of several text-critical difficulties with the passage has to do with the placement of the doxology (vv. 25–27): some manuscripts include the verses at the end of chapter 14 or chapter 15, or eliminate them altogether. Because of this variance, some scholars have doubted whether the passage is by Paul. But its vocabulary and phrasing reiterate those in the

## Homiletical Perspective

Many a preacher has passed over these closing verses of Romans year on year, turning gratefully to a less awkward text for this last Sunday of Advent. Doubtful authorship (more likely from the hand of an eager compiler of the Pauline corpus than from the apostle himself), broken syntax, and heavily theological language in a season that begs for stories can put the preacher off. In addition, there is awkwardness in preaching on a text that is essentially an expression of praise. Who in their right mind stands up after a breathtaking performance of *Messiah* to say, "Now, let me explain that"? Doxology seems to resist commentary.

Yet these verses deserve attention in a sermon. Regardless of who penned the closing lines of the received text of Romans, they are an authentic expression of the church's glad response to news of God's outreach to humanity, Gentile and Jew, in Jesus Christ. A sermon that takes its point of departure in these verses, however, will not explain or analyze doxology but seek to usher listeners into a place where they can experience the impulse toward praise—specifically, praise of God through Jesus Christ.

The doxology proper in the text is a brief summons to praise that could be imagined in the mouth of a worship leader, joined to a liturgical response from the congregation: (Leader) "Now to

# Romans 16:25-27

## Theological Perspective

The reference to God's "wisdom" draws theological attention to God's most inner being or essence, from which God acts in the drama of redemption, and also to the OT wisdom traditions. This combined emphasis of doing and knowing is accentuated here at the closing of Paul's most extended theological writing, highlighting that God's purposes, as fulfilled in the birth of Jesus, "make sense." Paul's letters and the Gospel birth narratives include reasoned attempts to understand "the revelation of the mystery" (v. 25). Christmas, the climax of God's intentions from the creation to the eschaton, contains specific theological content pertinent to this central drama of the cosmos and human history.

*What God Does.* Theology is all about God. At the same time, it is also about humanity, because theology speaks of what God does for people! This text highlights two intentions of God: that the able God intends (1) to "strengthen" us (v. 25) and (2) to enable obedient living (v. 26). Central to being empowered for the journey of one's days are the experiences of forgiveness and grace. As Paul earlier enunciates, by being renewed and recreated, the believer in Christ is accepted (though unacceptable) and forgiven (though guilty) and, in Christ, is transformed into "a new person." For Paul, typically, it is the Holy Spirit who enables living by grace. Imbued with "gifts," one "walks in the Spirit," strengthened by the power of God. The wonder of Christmas includes the humbling recognition that God came to humanity (and continues to come) in weakness as a vulnerable child. Nothing is more amazing than the gift of unmerited grace. Therefore, whatever gifts are brought to the manger in thankful obedience, whatever sacrifices are made for the Lord, whatever praise is uttered, no human responses to God can compare to the gift of God's grace that redeems human beings, adopts us into God's family, reconciles us to God and one another, and atones for our sin, enabling and empowering us to faithful obedience.

*The Implications of God-Happening.* Standing in grace, kneeling as forgiven, and walking by faith result in believers doing two things. First, they glory in God (v. 27). Like Isaiah in the temple (Isa. 6) and Job in the whirlwind (Job 40–41), they are overcome by the experience of grace and forgiveness. To glory in God is to be reduced to silence, driven to fall prostrate on the ground, awed by God's appearance, as at Christmas, when "silently, silently, the

## Pastoral Perspective

Romans 16:25–27 grounds us in God's plan of salvation. Foreshadowed over the centuries by the prophets and fulfilled in and through Jesus Christ, salvation is now offered to all people. From a pastoral perspective, all debates over authorship and placement of this passage within Romans are inconsequential. What is important is the benediction's liturgical summarization of the epistle's great theological themes. If "all good theology ultimately must come to expression in worship,"[1] this passage is key in drawing worshipers closer to holy moments of transcendence. We are challenged to create a worship environment in which they can more fully open themselves to the presence of God in the midst of everyday life. Only then can they more fully appreciate the transformative power within God's arrival in human form in Bethlehem more than 2,000 years ago, the spiritual rebirth of the risen Christ in the present, and our pregnant waiting for Christ's future return, at which time all creation will be redeemed.

Romans 16:25 begins with God's present desire to strengthen us with the good news and proclamation of Jesus Christ. Yet the mystery of the incarnation through which we are justified, sanctified, and strengthened is squarely rooted in human history. The great cloud of witnesses, and especially the prophets, heralded God's promise and plan. In and through Jesus Christ, God bridged the chasm that human sin created, so that we can live in relationship together. This incredible gift is not offered to a select few, but to all who accept Christ as Lord.

What does God want from us in return? Our epistle reading simply says "the obedience of faith." As we guide worshipers to the crescendo of Christmas, the obedience that is faith must be understood as the way in which we live out the gospel. Rather than adding legalistic requirements for people who often feel overwhelmed by the challenges of daily living, the obedience that is faith calls us to trust in God's promises, anchor our hope in God's goodness, and glorify God with hearts filled with joy. Our attitudes and actions spring not from an insatiable desire to earn God's favor, but from gratitude for God's grace, redemption, and love that we have already been given.

Christians can find authentic meaning and goodness in our lives only to the degree we trust in God's promises. As we prepare to celebrate the incarnation—the birth of God in human flesh—we are reminded how completely trustworthy God is.

[1] Walter Brueggemann, Charles Cousar, Beverly Gaventa, James Newsome, *Texts for Preaching—Year B*, (Louisville, KY: Westminster/John Knox Press, 1993), 37.

rest of the letter, and the placement problem likely resulted from scribes' effort to reconcile multiple manuscripts, some of which omitted chapter 16 (or chaps. 15 and 16). Moreover, important ancient manuscripts support the inclusion of the verses at their present location. The passage may therefore be regarded as genuinely Pauline.

It is appropriate that Paul should conclude the epistle with a declaration of glory to God, since God's glory—and humans' sharing in it—is an important theme throughout the letter. "Glory" is an attribute of God (Rom. 3:7, 23; 9:23) and virtually the power or force by which God accomplishes God's aims, including the raising of Jesus from the dead (6:4). Righteous humans such as Abraham give glory to God (4:20; 11:36 [another doxology]; 15:6, 7, 9), but the unrighteous fail to do so (1:23). The faithful hope and expect one day fully to share in the glory of God (2:7, 10; 5:2; 8:18, 21; 9:23).

Especially noteworthy for our passage is Paul's repeated use of "glory" and "glorify" in 15:5–9: here Paul prays that God will enable the Roman Christians to unite in giving glory to God, for "Christ has become a servant of the circumcised on behalf of the truth of God in order that he might confirm the promises given to the patriarchs, and in order that the Gentiles might glorify God for his mercy" (15:8–9a). Four scriptural quotations in verses 9b–12 then demonstrate that *the glorifying of God among and by the Gentiles has always been part of God's plan.*

When Paul refers to "my gospel" in verse 25 (cf. 2:16), he is not suggesting that he preaches a message different from all other Christian preachers' message, for there is only one authentic "gospel of God" (1:1–2; cf. Gal. 1:6–12; 2 Cor. 11:4). But certainly Paul has aimed throughout the letter to display the central content of that singular gospel *as he preaches it* to the Roman church, which he did not found and from whom he hoped to raise monetary support for future mission work (Rom. 15:24, 28). Paul's "proclamation of Jesus Christ" is the preaching of *Jesus crucified and risen* (10:8–9; 1 Cor. 1:23). This word of the cross had proven to be a stumbling block to faith among the Jews (Rom. 9:32–33; cf. 1 Cor. 1:23), who concluded from Torah that one who was crucified was cursed (Deut. 21:23) and so could not be the messiah.

Amazingly, Paul proclaims in Romans, God has been using the Jews' present (but temporary) period of unbelief as *an opportunity for the Gentiles to turn to God in faith.* Paul has explored this "mystery" of

God (v. 25a) . . . to the only wise God, through Jesus Christ" / (People) "[to God] be glory forever!" (v. 27). Bracketed between these opening and closing phrases, we find the acclamations that evoke this outburst of adoration. Either the practice of doxology itself or the specific acclamations of these verses can become the focal point for preaching.

The preacher may decide to dwell on the simple *fact* of this doxology, evidence of the church's long habit of glad acclamation in response to gospel news. Such a sermon might invite the gathered church to recognize and appreciate its own voice of praise. In addition to formal liturgical doxologies, some congregations erupt in spontaneous acclamation—"Amen!" "Tell it!" "Praise God!"—in response to the gospel heard in sermon, song, testimony, or anthem. Other congregations can be helped through this doxology to recognize how they have risen as one to sing, "Praise God, from whom all blessings flow," in response to astonishing news of God's interventions on their own behalf or on behalf of persons they love and causes they care about. Someone reports a life spared, a case for justice won, a mission launched—and the congregation erupts in praise to God.

Individual experiences abound of a palpable sense of divine presence, or the sense of being the recipient of a gift from an unseen, mighty hand. The birth of one's child, employment found after months of searching, financial disaster averted or overcome— such experiences can leave one "lost in wonder, love, and praise." But the preacher will do well to point beyond the strictly personal and individual to the communal experience of doxology. Weary demonstrators in Montgomery, Alabama, were strategizing their next move when someone burst into the room to declare, "God has spoken from Washington, D.C.!" and reported that the Supreme Court had ruled that segregated seating in public transportation systems was unlawful. The room erupted in tears, laughter, and spontaneous songs of praise to God.

Handling the theological warrants for praise embedded between the lines of the doxology proper is also worthy of preaching; but there are pitfalls to avoid here. For people of the ancient world, the gospel news of the God of the Jews offering salvation to all was boundary breaking, world shattering, and world renewing—more than enough to get the congregation on its feet and singing. This same news, however, may or may not evoke the same kind of spontaneous outburst from twenty-first-century listeners. Many a preacher has labored trying to

# Romans 16:25-27

## Theological Perspective

wondrous gift is given" to human hearts. "Glory," Frederick Buechner says, "is what God looks like when for the time being all you have to look at him with is a pair of eyes."[1]

Second, believers become infused with the wisdom of God as they become learners of Logos. Praising the glorious God is linked to living in a new situation. The wisdom of God provides the believer with perspective, a new way of being. We are recreated; reunited with God, ourselves, and others; and resurrected to a new life in Christ.[2] In Karl Barth's words, "We have found . . . a new world, God, God's sovereignty, God's glory, God's incomprehensible love. . . . Not the virtues of men but the virtues of him who hath called us out of darkness into his marvelous light!"[3]

This climactic passage provides the preacher with the dual themes of promise/anticipation ("according to the revelation of the mystery that was kept secret for long ages," v. 25b) and fulfillment/actuality ("but is now disclosed," v. 26a, and "is made known to all the Gentiles," v. 26b). Thus, with these words Paul enunciates both the good news of God's gift of the Christ and its salvific effects to receivers of that One.

Advent worshipers live in promise, hope, and expectation. Daily, the old is passing away. Daily, the new is coming to be. But, though this rhythm is undeniably at work in our lives, the Advent preacher often encounters a congregation that has little anticipation of the "new" inbreaking in Advent sermons. They have "heard it all before." This common attitude blunts their hearing.

I have sought to manifest the theological actuality of the coming of God in benedictions at some Advent services. Walking slowly up the aisle, I would pause at every pew and utter a personalized word of a hope for a better tomorrow to aisle-sitting congregants. Multiple benedictions, personal words of blessing, words of promise, hope, and expectation that speak to the fear, pain, dread, and hopelessness of real-life situations, the situations into which the Christ comes, fresh and new.

DONALD W. MUSSER

## Pastoral Perspective

Reaching out to humanity in spite of "the fall," our Creator loves us enough to have become like us so we can become more like God. Sin, born from and leading to our alienation of God, is overcome through Jesus Christ. The great German theologian Helmut Thielicke wisely said, "Faith can be described only as a movement of flight, flight away from myself and toward the great possibilities of God."[2]

As we open ourselves to God's power and goodness, the final doxology of Romans, as well as today's other lectionary passages, guides us to glorify God through our worship and praise. Presbyterian author Donald McCullough writes, "God's gracious self-giving in Jesus Christ calls for the response of faith, and faith's first expression will be the applause of praise. Worship—the word comes from middle English, meaning to ascribe worth—is both an instinctive response and an inexhaustible source of joy."[3]

The worship that invites God to strengthen our faith issues in doxology, in joy! Joy is a critical component of the Christian life because it functions as a thermostat; it sets the temperature or environment for our soul. The joy we know in the company of God is not dependent upon our immediate circumstances. Paul talks frequently about the joy he feels even when confined to a prison cell. Four walls could in no way diminish his love for God and his commitment to Christ, which were the source of his joy.

It is important not to confuse joy and happiness. The New Testament says a great deal about joy and very little about happiness. The root of the word *happiness* is "hap," which means "chance" (as in "happenstance"). Happiness is a mood, an emotion that changes as circumstances around us change. It is like a thermometer that goes up and down as it interprets the events around us, making us vulnerable to happiness one minute and despair the next. Joy, on the other hand, sets the temperature of our environment, rather than responding to it.

The final Sunday of Advent calls us to focus on what is most important. In a world that too often seems random and fraught with pain, it is not the presents we can touch that matter. Christ's birth reminds us of God's eternal gifts: radical hope, faith-filled trust, inner joy, and redemptive love. To God, through Jesus Christ, may all glory, praise, and honor be given.

CATHY F. YOUNG

[1]Frederick Brechner, *Wishful Thinking: A Theological ABC* (San Francisco: HarperSanFrancisco, 1973), 30.
[2]These Pauline concepts are helpfully explicated in "The New Being," a sermon that appears in Paul Tillich, *The New Being* (New York: Charles Scribner's Sons, 1955), 15–24.
[3]Karl Barth, *The Word of God and the Word of Man*, trans. Douglas Horton (New York: Harper & Row, 1957), 41.

[2]Helmut Thielicke, *Theological Ethics—Foundations*, ed. William H. Lazareth (Grand Rapids: Eerdmans, 1979), 283.
[3]Donald McCullough, *The Trivialization of God* (Colorado Springs, CO: Navpress, 1995), 104.

## Exegetical Perspective

Jewish unbelief/Gentile faithfulness already in Romans 9–11 (see esp. 11:25). The prophets, Paul has insisted, long ago foretold that the Gentiles would one day glorify God. But the means by which this would come about had been hidden until Jesus' expression of faithful obedience on the cross. Thereafter, for those with eyes to see, Scripture is read in a wholly new way. The one cursed by Torah turns out to be the very aim or goal toward which all Torah had been driving (10:4). It is this prophesied-yet-hidden "mystery" of God's working to bring about "the obedience of faith" among the Gentiles to which Paul makes reference in 16:26, and which he sees as the very heart of his gospel (cf. 1:5).

In Advent and in all seasons, the preacher must be careful in statements about present or past Jewish unbelief, lest he or she contribute to possible anti-Jewish sentiments in the congregation. It is good to remember that Jews who rejected Jesus' messiahship often did so precisely out of deep commitment to Torah; the proclamation of a crucified messiah seemed offensive and nonsensical to them (as it previously had to Paul himself). The correspondences between Jesus' earthly life and certain prophecies in the prophets and the psalms, which so many Christians find persuasive (for example, the prophecy of a virgin giving birth in the Septuagint version of Isa. 7:14) would not have seemed adequate to contradict the stumbling block of a crucified messiah. In the doxology (and throughout Romans) Paul does not focus on the *psychology* or *blameworthiness* of Jews for their unbelief. The preacher's attention rightly falls where Paul has placed his own: on *giving God glory* for working to bring about something that God has so long intended—the faithfulness of the nations. At Christmas and in all seasons, the God who through Jesus has brought us into covenant relationship and who strengthens us in faith deserves our highest honor and praise.

SUSAN R. GARRETT

## Homiletical Perspective

induce twenty-first-century worshipers to see the world through first-century lenses, experience consternation over first-century conundrums, and get excited about first-century solutions to first-century problems. On the whole, however, this is an exhausting homiletical effort. The crisis of Jewish-Gentile tension is not precisely our crisis. While it can be instructive to any Western congregation to be reminded that *we* are the ones grafted in to the beloved tree, on the whole, the announcement that God intended all along to include the Gentile may evoke appreciation but not exultation.

And yet we know plenty about division and exclusion. One way to approach this text, theologically, is to venture theologically sound, twenty-first-century analogies to the first-century scandal of the inclusion of the Gentiles. God continues to be astonishingly inclusive; and we have learned to read and reread our Bible in light of the evidence of God's Spirit breaking out in the lives we assumed were not qualified. God's goal is unchanging: that all should join in the "obedience of faith," that all should experience a being-redeemed way of life.

A third sermon focus, especially fitting in Advent, would be the praise-evoking wonder of the incarnation itself. The doxology is pointedly oriented to good news that cannot be told except by proclaiming Jesus Christ. The congregation is bidden to praise God "through Jesus Christ." To praise through Jesus Christ is to come to terms with the scandal of God incarnate. Perhaps no medieval theologian more fully understood the intimacy of incarnation than Dame Julian of Norwich. Jesus is the brother at our side; but, said Dame Julian, also the mother feeding us at her breast. If this shocks us, it should! But it may shock us for the wrong reasons: the noisy nuzzling of an infant at the naked breast seems too earthy for church. Maybe we need this shock, however, to come face to face with the staggering truth that God has willed to make our flesh-and-bone, our digestion-and-desire, our vulnerability his own. By grace, shock may give way to holy stillness, holy stillness to rising joy, until we leap to shout "Praise!" to the One who took flesh for our redemption.

SALLY A. BROWN

# Luke 1:26-38

26In the sixth month the angel Gabriel was sent by God to a town in Galilee called Nazareth, 27to a virgin engaged to a man whose name was Joseph, of the house of David. The virgin's name was Mary. 28And he came to her and said, "Greetings, favored one! The Lord is with you." 29But she was much perplexed by his words and pondered what sort of greeting this might be. 30The angel said to her, "Do not be afraid, Mary, for you have found favor with God. 31And now, you will conceive in your womb and bear a son, and you will name him Jesus. 32He will be great, and will be called the Son of the Most High, and the Lord God will give to him the throne of his ancestor David. 33He will reign over the house of Jacob forever, and of his kingdom there will be no end." 34Mary said to the angel, "How can this be, since I am a virgin?" 35The angel said to her, "The Holy Spirit will come upon you, and the power of the Most High will overshadow you; therefore the child to be born will be holy; he will be called Son of God. 36And now, your relative Elizabeth in her old age has also conceived a son; and this is the sixth month for her who was said to be barren. 37For nothing will be impossible with God." 38Then Mary said, "Here am I, the servant of the Lord; let it be with me according to your word." Then the angel departed from her.

## Theological Perspective

The fourth Sunday of Advent may be the only Sunday of the year that Protestants are comfortable focusing on Mary. Mary stands at the center of this lection, which tells the story of the annunciation—the *announcement* of the incarnation by the angel Gabriel. In twelve verses, Mary is described as favored, perplexed, thoughtful, and afraid. She questions, believes, and submits to her vocation. Given this array of images, it is not surprising that Mary is depicted in rich and varied ways. A cursory perusal of artwork titled "The Annunciation" reveals Marys who are afraid, who are demure, who are assertive. Some show Mary and Gabriel talking as two old friends sharing a secret. Others show Mary sitting at Gabriel's feet in submission, agitated by the news he is sharing.

Theologians have traditionally depicted Mary as the model Christian believer, the unblemished representative of the church. Mary has the reputation of being in perfect sync with God, responding to God's command in absolute obedience. She is the "blessed one" who is called by God to bear the Christ child, the "servant of the Lord" who desires that God's will come to fruition, even in and through her. All agree that Mary is elected to a particular purpose in which she wholeheartedly participates. But the character of

## Pastoral Perspective

On the Sunday before Christmas, people are in the mood for miracles. The annunciation contains all of the ingredients needed to satisfy this yearning. An angel appears as if out of nowhere, and a virgin learns that she will defy nature and bear a child. To add to the abundance of wonder, the angel alludes to another noteworthy occurrence: a woman well beyond childbearing years is in the sixth month of a pregnancy. Beyond their exquisite mystery, these marvelous prospective births offer multiple layers of meaning for holiday churchgoers seeking encouragement and affirmation amid life's quandaries and questions.

Mary's reaction to the angel Gabriel's visit is cautious at best. Living in a remote village far from the busy religious center of Jerusalem, she had no hint that she was destined for a singularly distinctive role. The tendency to think that leading unassuming lives in out-of-the-way places isolates us from the extraordinary is debunked by Mary's surprise visitor, just as it is dismantled by television broadcasts of school shootings and forest fires, or small towns that take pride in the accomplishments of members of their communities. Neither notoriety nor acclaim is confined to major metropolitan areas. The selection of Mary to be the mother of Jesus is an occasion to spur Christians to exit the realm of predictability

## Exegetical Perspective

In many ways, the angel Gabriel's announcement to Mary of the coming miraculous birth of Jesus reads almost exactly like the announcements of the wondrous births of Ishmael (Gen. 16:7–13), Isaac (Gen. 17:1–21; 18:1–15), Samson (Judges 13:3–20), and most obviously John the Baptist (Luke 1:8–20). This passage tells the Jesus version of this classic account of wondrous birth by using a wide variety of biblical images associated mostly with kingdom promises. In this way, Luke places the birth of Jesus into the context of a series of interventions by God into human history by way of wondrous births and into the context of the promises to Israel.

However, this story also deviates from the classic pattern. The unique character of Jesus strains both the classic form of a wondrous birth and the meaning of the promises to Israel. In Luke's account, the wonders of Jesus' birth will exceed those of any other birth. And the peculiar messianic destiny of Jesus will rewrite the meaning of all the ancient promises.

The biblical stories in which a special birth is announced follow a consistent pattern: the appearance of a divine figure; fear or confusion in the one to whom the figure appears; the announcement of the message; an objection by the one receiving the message; and finally a concluding promise or blessing from the divine figure. This

## Homiletical Perspective

It is daunting for most preachers to approach texts so familiar and beloved as those from the infancy narratives. Yet the Gospel for the day remains a source of rich possibilities for preaching. Three prominent themes present themselves: the inbreaking of the holy, the favor of God, and Mary's response to Gabriel's remarkable announcement of the coming birth of Christ.

*Holy Inbreaking.* In Henry Ossawa Tanner's painting *The Annunciation* (1898), there is no mistaking that this messenger whom Luke identifies as Gabriel is a holy being. The angel is represented as a bright column of light appearing before Mary as she sits on her pallet. This is no being that she—or we—have seen before, but a radiance beyond human experience or understanding. The holy being bursts into the earthly realm, into a particular time and place (v. 26), sent by God to a particular person in a particular community (v. 27). Already we see that we cannot anticipate the ways that God will break into human history—into our history! Even this announcement of the long-awaited birth of the Messiah makes it clear that we do not create our own salvation, nor do we have the capacity to imagine the ways of God. As Gabriel says about Elizabeth's own pregnancy, "nothing will be impossible with God"

# Luke 1:26-38

## Theological Perspective

Mary's election and her response have been energetically debated in the history of interpretation.

When Gabriel addresses Mary as "favored one" or "blessed one," what is being conveyed? Roman Catholic moral theologians understand Gabriel's greeting as highlighting Mary's extraordinary nature. Mary is *unlike* other Christian believers insofar as she is sinless and because she is both mother and perpetual virgin. In Protestant theology, by contrast, the extraordinary thing about Mary is precisely her ordinariness—Mary is a member of the "priesthood of all believers" who emulates for all of us sinful, embodied saints the mysterious reality that we are integrally included in the work of God. Reformer John Calvin rejects the idea that Gabriel's identification of Mary as "favored" suggests she is "worthy of praise." Rather, Gabriel recognizes Mary as the "*happy* one" who has received "the undeserved love of God," who alone is to be adored.[1]

Another matter for debate is how we are to understand the character of Mary's response. Was she doubting the words of Gabriel when she asked, "How can this be, since I am a virgin?" If so, why isn't she chastened by God, as Zechariah is punished for his disbelief in 1:18–20? Even more pressing for us, in an age and culture that values freedom and autonomy, is the matter of whether and how Mary participates as a free and active agent in relation to the incarnation. When she proclaims that she is "a servant of the Lord," is she resigning herself to functioning as a passive vessel in the work of God? If so, does Mary then model that human beings are called merely to be used by God, without making any contribution to the divine work?

Three Reformed doctrines that help us reflect on the character of Mary's response to Gabriel are total depravity, Christian vocation, and "double agency." Perhaps Mary's statement about her virginity does not reflect doubt as much as amazement at Gabriel's message in light of her own incapacity to conceive and give birth. Mary recognizes what all Christian believers must recognize—that we, creatures before the Creator God, are incapable, in and of ourselves, of accomplishing God's will. We are all depraved; we are all, in this sense, virgins.

However, Gabriel reminds Mary that to be incapable of conceiving in and of ourselves is not the end of the story, that "nothing [is] impossible with God." The best discussions of Mary's response recognize the pitfalls inherent in rendering Mary either

## Pastoral Perspective

and open themselves up to the unexpected and the unimaginable.

In the fourth century CE, Augustine of Hippo expressed in his *Confessions*, "For all I want to tell you, Lord, is that I do not know where I came from when I was born into this life which leads to death—or should I say, this death which leads to life? This much is hidden from me."[1] There is a natural inclination to wonder why we were born. An only child who knows how desperately his parents wanted to bear children may feel weighed down by the responsibility that accompanies being the fulfillment of someone else's dream. A youngest daughter may ruminate about whether or not her parents intended to raise a large brood, and rue the impact of her birth on the family finances.

God knew the prophet Jeremiah before he was formed in the womb (Jer. 1:5). Echoing Jeremiah's experience, the angel Gabriel's words provide a reminder that our lives are not initiated wholly by human effort and intention. God had specified the circumstances preceding Jesus' birth, and designed a plan that greatly affected Mary. Although the details rarely are readily apparent, God takes part in the unfolding of human existence from before the moment of conception. This realization may extend solace to parishioners who harbor guilt, regret, or disappointment.

The awareness that we are not fully in charge of our destiny ebbs and is revived repeatedly throughout our lives. Startling news—whether joyful or sorrowful—frequently evokes the question that Mary voiced when she was told that she was to bear a child who would be the "Son of the Most High," whom the Lord God would give both divine and royal authority: "How can this be?" A hospital patient may astonish his or her caregivers when a tumor shrinks or a precarious blood count is corrected, contrary to a bleak prognosis. Likewise, word that a friend has died suddenly may stir someone to exclaim, "How can this be? I just had lunch with him yesterday." A collective cry of anguish is raised when calamity or catastrophe befalls a neighborhood, community, or school. Mary's puzzlement grants permission to take time to adjust to astonishing news, to question whether or not trials and tragedies, or God's magnificent promises, are for real, and to contemplate potential repercussions. The query "How can this be?" is a reverberating refrain that shapes our faith by

---

[1] John Calvin, *Commentary on a Harmony of the Evangelists* (Grand Rapids: Baker Books, 1999), 33.

[1] Augustine, *Confessions*, trans. R. S. Pine Coffin (Harmondsworth, UK: Penguin Books, 1961), 25.

structure does more than provide a framework for the details of the story. It displays clearly the difficulty of divine intervention in human history. It arrives accompanied by human protest. It fulfills and does not fulfill promises. It leaves other promises in its wake. Jesus' own messianic history shares, to some extent, this structure.

This announcement is, of course, the second announcement of miraculous birth in the Gospel of Luke. Gabriel appears not only to Mary but, in 1:8–20, to Zechariah, the father of John the Baptist. Thus, this passage is part of Luke's careful interweaving of John the Baptist and Jesus, in which John serves largely in the role of Elijah preparing for the day of the Lord (Mal. 4:5). Consequently Luke emphasizes John's special calling and high status, while carefully elevating Jesus above John. As Jesus himself remarks in Luke 7:28: "Among those born of women no one is greater than John; yet the least in the kingdom of God is greater than he."

Although Gabriel becomes a key figure in Christian tradition, his biblical appearances are limited to these two birth announcements in Luke and an appearance to Daniel in which he announces details of the coming wrath (Dan. 8:15–27). Here Gabriel is sent by God to Nazareth to a virgin engaged to a descendant of David. The key christological claims of this passage are anticipated in the way Mary and Joseph are identified. Joseph is "of the house of David." This lineage is crucial to Jesus' messianic and kingly status. Mary is a virgin. Of the many terms used in Greek to refer to young women, Luke picks the one most associated with virginity. As Mary herself will insist, "I do not know a man" (literal trans. of Gk., 1:34). Mary's virginity enables Luke (and early Christianity) to transform the pervasive and general title "son of God" into a specific and unique claim about Jesus.

Gabriel's opening greeting signals the special character of both Mary herself and the coming announcement. Mary is "favored" and "the Lord is with [her]." Mary's perplexity is natural and follows the standard format of such angelic announcements, but the exact reasons for it are not given. In any case, Gabriel signals again the positive character of this announcement, when he says to Mary, "Do not be afraid, Mary, for you have found favor with God."

Then Gabriel gets to the heart of his message. Mary will conceive and bear a son. The series of messianic images in 1:32–33 concerning the destiny of this son forms the christological heart of the passage. Each image in these verses is fundamental to

(v. 37). It is tempting to imagine that the human predicament, whether we define that as the state of our warring world or the state of our broken lives, can never be healed or overturned. Yet Luke tells us that not only is redemption possible; it has already happened. Because of the birth, life, death, and resurrection of Christ, the holy continues to break into our lives, to bring us closer to the completion of creation and the already-and-not-yet reign of God.

*Being "Favored" by God.* Twice Gabriel lets Mary know that she is the recipient of God's favor. Contemporary Christians might do well to ask what it means to be favored by God. In popular piety it is often assumed that God's favor is earned by our good behavior, in either the moral or the political arena, or both. In other words, the theory goes that God's favor comes to those who give something to God; or, conversely, the ones blessed by God are those who have the power to bless God back. Yet, as Robert Tannehill suggests, God chooses Mary because she has nothing—she is a young girl in a society that values men and maturity; in her song of praise (1:47–55) she identifies herself as lowly and poor.[1] In other words, this is not one who is favored in the human realm, but God has shown favor with her. The divine choice of Mary anticipates the Magnificat and the great reversal that anthem proclaims. God's coming reign of justice and favor for all people is embodied in God's choosing to pour out the divine Spirit upon Mary, even within her, to bring about salvation for the whole world.

Ernesto Cardenal's *The Gospel in Solentiname* records the discussions of Gospel readings that were held among campesinos, farmers and fisherfolk who lived in the country around Lake Nicaragua. In this text they hear Gabriel's greeting of favor extending not only to Mary, but also to them; for according to the angel, this savior, this liberator, is going to be born among them, the people who were poor. "It's not the rich but the poor who need liberation," says one. "The rich and the poor will be liberated," answers another. "Us poor people are going to be liberated from the rich. The rich are going to be liberated from themselves, that is, from their wealth. Because they're more slaves than we are."[2]

That's the sort of good news that we can hardly conjure up on our own. Dare we proclaim that God breaks in, to restore, reveal, and redeem the mess we

---

[1]Robert C. Tannehill, *Luke* (Nashville: Abingdon Press), 48.
[2]Ernesto Cardenal, *The Gospel in Solentiname*, vol. 1, trans. Donald D. Walsh (Maryknoll, NY: Orbis Books, 1976), 14.

# Luke 1:26-38

## Theological Perspective

a passive participant, who has no choice but to submit to God's will, or an autonomous individual, who can choose differently than to bear God to the world. The doctrine of Christian vocation offers clarity. Mary's obedience is neither optional nor forced. Mary acts freely when she offers herself as a servant of the Lord. To embrace her identity as the Mother of God is the only choice that is true to her calling, because it is consistent with who she actually is.

As the story unfolds, Mary acts as creative partner and agent with God in the coming of the Christ child. One crucial place in which the "double agency" of Mary is affirmed is in the Chalcedonian Definition, adopted at the fourth ecumenical council in 451 CE. According to the Definition, still the standard of orthodoxy, "the very same one" who was, in relation to his deity, "born from the Father before the ages" was, in relation to his humanity, "born in the last days from the Virgin Mary, the Mother of God."

In addition to inviting us to think about who we are and what we do in relation to God and God's work, this passage challenges us to be reoriented by what the incarnation tells us about the character of God. Gabriel arrives at a particular time ("in the sixth month" of Elizabeth's pregnancy), in a particular place ("a town in Galilee called Nazareth") to a particular woman ("a virgin engaged to a man whose name was Joseph"). Theologians speak of the "scandal of particularity"; they recognize that it can offend our sensibilities to ponder how the omnipotent, omniscient Creator of the universe entered into the particularities of historical existence. The fifth-century debates about Mary as Theotokos ("God-bearer") reflect that the reality of God's entry into the womb of the virgin Mary changes forever understandings of God that dismiss the divine vulnerability as inconsistent with the divine omnipotence.

Related to this scandalous specificity is the revolutionary impact of the divine immanence. "God with us," known supremely in Jesus, barges in and meddles not only with our affairs, but with our very persons. Recent studies of this passage register concern that Mary is violated by the Holy Spirit. Instead of dismissing such risky interpretations, Christian believers might consider how God's call *does* violate the selves we imagined ourselves to be— transforming us from "virgins" who are unable to bear God to the world, to creative agents for whom, with God, "nothing is impossible."

CYNTHIA L. RIGBY

## Pastoral Perspective

reminding us, to paraphrase Augustine, how much is hidden from us. The exclamation of these four words may well signify the nearness of God.

The notion that anyone will receive a personal visit by a celestial being is improbable. Yet, in the manner of the angel Gabriel, persons whose authority or neediness seems too poignant to decline often recruit individuals for perplexing or onerous duties. When an employee is proffered a daunting promotion, he or she, like Mary, is the "favored one," having attained a privileged position laden with responsibility that may stir a sense of unworthiness or unreadiness. Congregants elected to leadership offices, although flattered by their fellow church members' trust in them, confide insecurity, whispering, "Why was I chosen for this office? How can I possibly live up to everyone's confidence? How can this be?" Sometimes opportunities are presented that convey seemingly unachievable expectations.

The angel Gabriel overturns Mary's dubiousness by explaining that the Holy Spirit will overshadow her. The angel then underscores God's incomprehensible capacity to accomplish wondrous aims by telling Mary that her relative Elizabeth had conceived a child at an advanced age, and explains, "For nothing will be impossible with God." This refrain conveys support, comfort, and courage for those confronting overwhelming expectations.

Mary's assignment from God is an honor yoked with struggle. In her day, an unmarried woman expecting a child was cause for disgrace. Nonetheless, her neighbors' prospective disdain does not hinder Mary's willingness to proceed according to God's entreaty. Her response to the annunciation is exemplary: "Here am I, the servant of the Lord; let it be with me according to your word." Mary compre-hends that her life, and not only hers, but the whole world's, is about to be rearranged. She ascribes more credence to God's vision for the human community than to naysayers whose words suppress courage. Perhaps Mary's words deliver God's Christmas wish, that followers of Christ will believe that nothing is impossible with God, and invite the Holy Spirit to work through them to attain miracles.

ASHLEY COOK CLEERE

Luke's story of Jesus. Jesus is portrayed as the Davidic messiah, who as the son of David sits on David's throne and whose rule, astonishingly, will never end. There is no hint here, as there is in Matthew, of the coming crucifixion and the historical irony of these promises. Jesus is also named here as "the Son of the Most High." In the context of these messianic announcements, the term "son of God" could have its usual meaning of "one endowed with divine powers and duties." But in the context of Mary's virginity, it comes to mean something else.

Mary's response points to this new meaning. She wonders how this can be, because, she points out, "I do not know a man." As readers have long noted, her response is a bit illogical. In the normal context of engagement Mary would expect to consummate her marriage with Joseph. In so doing, she could conceive and give birth, by way of Joseph of the house of David, to the Davidic messiah. Mary is not necessarily announcing in this protest her perpetual virginity or even a theological need for this new messiah to be born of a virgin. It is best to see her question as an articulation of a general puzzlement.

In any case, Gabriel removes the puzzle with his second announcement. He appeals to the Holy Spirit and "the power of the Most High." He points to the miraculous pregnancy of Elizabeth, which demonstrates that nothing is impossible with God. There is nothing sexual in his imagery of the Spirit coming upon her or the power overshadowing her. Luke does not attempt a biological explanation of this virgin birth. Luke evokes instead the presence and power of God. For all the boldness of this new Christian confession, Luke maintains the mystery of what it means to call Jesus "the Son of God."

Given the astonishing and mysterious character of this announcement, Mary's response is a model of Jewish (and Christian) righteousness. She abandons her questions and names herself "the servant of the Lord" and submits her destiny to "your word." In all of this, Mary's journey into her special place in Christian tradition begins.

LEWIS R. DONELSON

have made of the world? Dare we proclaim that God's gospel of justice and peace may turn our world upside down—and that this news is very, very good?

*Mary's Response.* Joseph gets all the attention in Matthew's infancy narrative, but Mary is the focus here. And a compelling figure she is. While it is rarely wise to psychologize a biblical character, we might consider what Scripture tells us about this young woman, and take note of her response to the remarkable surprise of an angelic announcement. In the aforementioned Tanner painting, Mary still has the skinny, knock-kneed look of a young teenage girl. Her face wears an expression that somehow communicates, all at once, wariness and curiosity, caution and boldness. Although she cannot comprehend the full meaning of Gabriel's message ("how can this be?"), she is not a passive recipient of the news. She responds actively, a willing partner in the holy disruption that befalls her.

Because of her response, Mary's womb brought forth the very Son of God and new life to the world. Bernard of Clairvaux saw Mary as a wellspring of living water, "an Aqueduct which, receiving the fullness of the Fountain from the Father's heart, has transmitted to us, if not as it is in itself, at least in so far as we could contain it."[3] Those congregations preparing candidates for baptism, or looking toward reaffirming baptismal vows on the Baptism of the Lord, might anticipate that event by contemplating the womb as the source of life. In the early centuries of the church, some baptisteries were circular, suggesting the shape of the womb, reminding believers that in baptism we receive new life. Because the living waters of Mary's womb served as a channel of grace from the fountain of the throne of God to humanity, we too are reborn from the womb of the font, made one with God in Christ and with one another, as grace is poured out upon us.

KIMBERLY BRACKEN LONG

[3]Bernard of Clairvaux, "Sermon for the Feast of the Nativity of the Blessed Virgin Mary," in *Sermons for the Seasons and Principal Festivals of the Year*, vol. 3 (Westminster, MD: Carroll Press, 1950), 284ff.

# Isaiah 9:2-7

2The people who walked in darkness
   have seen a great light;
those who lived in a land of deep darkness—
   on them light has shined.
3You have multiplied the nation,
   you have increased its joy;
they rejoice before you
   as with joy at the harvest,
   as people exult when dividing plunder.
4For the yoke of their burden,
   and the bar across their shoulders,
   the rod of their oppressor,
   you have broken as on the day of Midian.
5For all the boots of the tramping warriors
   and all the garments rolled in blood
   shall be burned as fuel for the fire.

## Theological Perspective

First Isaiah is a series of prophetic warnings about political maneuverings and their implications, broken up by staccatos of promise about a brighter political future, with Isaiah 9:2–7 being perhaps the best known of these staccatos. The passage describes a king to come who will lift the yoke of burden from his people's shoulders, because authority rests on his own, and who will end war, because his kingdom is defined by endless peace. Between the descriptions of the king in verses 6–7 and those of the kingdom in the surrounding verses, the church has long and fittingly associated this passage with the incarnation of Jesus the Messiah.

But partly because the Year B lectionary passages focus on the staccatos to the exclusion of the sweep of First Isaiah, and partly because the promises in those staccatos seem so extraordinary, it has been easy to depoliticize this text. Or, rather, it has become easy to see it as a text that portrays a divine politics but not a politics that is applicable to the vagaries of events on earth. If this text is about a king, it is only about a cosmic one.

There are good reasons to place this text at political remove—to treat it as a source of inspiration in dark times or to view it as a series of compliments about Jesus. After all, if we take this

## Pastoral Perspective

Whatever the original meaning of Isaiah's prophesy, and no matter whose birth prompted the prophet's lyrical expressions of rejoicing and hope, for Christmas Eve worshipers the "child . . . born for us" (v. 6) will be the baby in the manger, and the "son given to us" (v. 6) will be God's very own. The congregation can be expected to share Isaiah's joy and to join him in rejoicing (v. 3).

The congregation will readily identify with some portions of the lesson. Other parts of the text will seem to be mocked by current events. The sensitive pastor will acknowledge both aspects and the corresponding pastoral and prophetic dimensions of the text.

One approach to the pastoral dimension is by way of the theme of "darkness" and "light" (v. 2). Once worshipers grasp that "darkness" is a metaphor suggestive of evil, sin, suffering, distress, and death, they will recognize the world in which they live: a world of war, violence, torture and prisoner abuse, terrorist bombings, hubris or the wrongful use of power. Worshipers will know, not just the darkness of the world, but the darkness of their own lives: the darkness of family quarrels (perhaps even on Christmas Eve!), disease and death, enfeebled parents, rebellious children, fear and guilt, loneliness

> [6]For a child has been born for us,
>     a son given to us;
>   authority rests upon his shoulders;
>     and he is named
>   Wonderful Counselor, Mighty God,
>     Everlasting Father, Prince of Peace.
> [7]His authority shall grow continually,
>     and there shall be endless peace
>   for the throne of David and his kingdom.
>     He will establish and uphold it
>   with justice and with righteousness
>     from this time onward and forevermore.
>   The zeal of the LORD of hosts will do this.

## Exegetical Perspective

This text can generate a great deal of theological debate about the purpose of Old Testament prophecy and how it relates to the life of Jesus Christ. However, these debates are best saved for another time. For this night, debate has been put aside, and the church comes together to sing and praise God. The text the people have come to hear is from Luke 2, and only the bravest or most foolhardy of preachers would stray far from the manger this night. Yet the text from Isaiah, set in its historical context, provides additional insight into who God is and how we can more deeply understand the importance of this night.

The context of the Isaiah passage is one of fear. It is a dark and frightening time in the history of Judah and Israel. Assyria has become strong and is systematically taking over the whole region. Within a few years, Judah will become a resident captive, and the northern kingdom of Israel will be no more (722 BCE). Part of the oracles and narration leading up to Assyrian domination are found in chapters 7–11, which begins with saying that "the heart of Ahaz and the heart of his people shook as the trees of the forest shake before the wind" (7:2).

Ahaz and the people of Judah are caught between a rock and a hard place. The kings of Israel and

## Homiletical Perspective

Only three nights ago was the longest night of the year, the deep darkness of the winter solstice. Even if we did not know that the celebration of Christmas probably evolved from a pre-Christian solstice celebration, we could recognize that the theme of light triumphing over darkness resonates with our midwinter longings in a visceral, fundamentally human way. Our Christmas poetry and hymnody capitalize on the associations provided by elements of the natural world: the dark, cold, uncertainty, and fear of a long winter night being overcome by the light, warmth, and hope of new life and the promise of God's presence among us.

The imagery of Isaiah's oracle expands beyond light and dark, in circles eddying outward through metaphorical associations. With the shining of light comes a spirit of fecundity—the people rejoice as at the harvest. Or maybe the idea of military success is the point—and that joy over a rich harvest is replaced with the exultation of a people collecting the goods of a conquered enemy and dividing it among themselves, the victors. The imagery of warfare continues with the release experienced by captives or vassals shaking off the yoke of servitude. The idea of light overcoming darkness has been translated into liberation from slavery.

# Isaiah 9:2-7

## Theological Perspective

text to describe an earthly politics, then to judge from events around us, we are seemingly still people walking in darkness—a perambulation familiar to those who take seriously the taint of sin in all human actions, including (and perhaps especially) political ones. But beyond the mental acrobatics involved in taking a text about a king, placed in a book about the relation of divine action to human politics, and making it apolitical, there are at least three reasons to avoid depoliticizing it.

First, exegetes have highlighted the importance of understanding Isaiah 9:2–7 as a political text, suggesting that at one time it served as part of a coronation ritual or announcement of royal birth. Indeed, most rabbinic and modern Jewish scholars have argued that the text points to Hezekiah, who enacted a series of reforms after he succeeded his father, Ahaz, as king of Judah. Christians may quite properly interpret the text as referring to Jesus (the Hezekiah vs. Jesus debate being a matter pertaining to conflicting interpretations by two faiths that grow out of a common root tradition about an unnamed referent in a shared text); to depoliticize the text in the process, however, is a form of hermeneutical supersessionism. Debating about who the text refers to is one thing; abrogating its meaning is another thing entirely.

Second, when Christians depoliticize Isaiah 9:2–7, even as they make it about Jesus, they take a step down the road toward evacuating the political significance of Jesus' life, death, and resurrection. As writers as diverse as Augustine, John Calvin, John Howard Yoder, and Rosemary Radford Ruether have shown, what Jesus said and did has far-reaching implications, not only for the status of our souls, but for what happens to our bodies. Indeed, the great irony of spiritualizing this Christmas Eve text would be that it contradicts one of the very things that the incarnation most strongly affirms, namely, that Jesus' body and actions matter.

Finally, depoliticizing Isaiah 9:2–7 risks giving us an excuse to think of our own spiritual lives as apolitical. We go to Christmas Eve services to feel uplifted, refreshed, and hopeful in the face of all the various global, local, and personal problems that weigh us down, leaving us feeling dirty and depressed. What could be less political than a cooing baby and serene parents surrounded by well-wishers and barnyard animals? But treating Christmas Eve as a respite from politics does little to disconnect this particular night—silent and holy though it may be—from the other nights and days where such problems

## Pastoral Perspective

and bereavement. The preacher will take seriously the darkness for at least three reasons: because the text does, because darkness is no small part of the everyday life of the congregation, and because darkness is what the light of Christ makes its way into.

"The people who walked in darkness have seen a great light" (v. 2). The preacher can enable the congregation to know it is not only Isaiah who says so, but the Christian tradition. One could say that the meaning of Christmas, even of the gospel, is to be found in Isaiah 9:2—"The people who walked in darkness have seen a great light."

"Light" is a metaphor suggestive of the presence of God, the approach of God's grace, mercy, and peace. Isaiah refers to "a great light" (v. 2). The preacher may want to suggest that the light of Christ, while "great" indeed for those who have seen and welcomed it, was not "great" at its coming, in the sense of being a blazing or blinding light, and is not "great" in that sense now. It was and is now a gentle, modest light that Christ brings, so as not to overwhelm or coerce.

Neither Isaiah nor the NT suggests that the light does away with the darkness. (See John 1:5.) Yet the light of Christ has proved to be tough and tenacious. So, however great the darkness—and sometimes it is very great indeed—the Christmas Eve congregation can be encouraged to trust that the light of God's goodness and grace continues to shine, as well as to approach Christ with whatever darkness is within themselves.

There is, of course, more to the text than its opening verse, and it is this larger portion that seems to be mocked by the news of almost any day. "All the boots of the tramping warriors and all the garments rolled in blood" have not in fact been "burned as fuel for the fire" (v. 5). The child "born for us," the "son given to us" (v. 6), has not brought about "endless peace for the throne of David and his kingdom" (v. 7), or any other. "Justice" and "righteousness" have not been established (v. 7). All of which makes for a prophetic dimension to the text.

Any honest dealing with Isaiah 9:2–7 will have to acknowledge that the prophecy is as yet unfulfilled. With regard to the person of Jesus, the preacher may wish to acknowledge that the question of John the Baptist, "Are you the one who is to come, or are we to wait for another?" (Matt. 11:3), is unavoidable. Underlying the question is the messianic expectation that one will come to fix everything. It is that expectation that Jesus does not meet. So the preacher

## Exegetical Perspective

Aram form a coalition to fight Assyria. They ask, then demand, that Ahaz and Judah join with them. When Ahaz refuses, Israel and Aram declare war and move to attack Jerusalem. It is into this crisis that God sends Isaiah to speak to the king in Isaiah 7. Isaiah tells the king to stand firm and not join either the coalition or the Assyrians (7:4–9). Through Isaiah, God tells the king to ask for a sign of assurance. The king refuses. Isaiah declares God has sent a sign anyway. He points to a woman sitting in the room and says that before the baby she is carrying "knows good from evil" the threat of the coalition will have passed (7:14–17).[1] The message of assurance given in this great crisis is so ordinary that many miss its significance. And for those that missed the point of chapter 7, God sends the *very same sign* in chapter 8. A son is to be born to Isaiah, and before he can speak, Israel and Aram will not be a threat (8:4). God again sends the sign in the gift of a new life, in an innocent and vulnerable child.

In the face of two warring threats, the birth of babies and their growth seems like no sign at all. Great fear calls for a great and powerful sign. A sign of babies seem less than what one needs for reassurance in dark and fearful times. Indeed, at the end of chapter 8, Isaiah is content to wait on the Lord (8:17), but the people want to turn to other spirits and gods (vv. 18–22). Isaiah knows they will see only "distress and darkness." The king and the people are reacting from fear, and that fear drives them to do the unthinkable. Indeed, the king may have gone as far as to sacrifice his own son to try and appease the gods of Assyria and stop the coming invasion.

It is in this context that the oracle of 9:2–7 appears. Again the good news comes in the birth of a baby (v. 6). Assyrian rule will lead to death, but God's reign is seen in new life and birth. The shadow of slavery looms, and the regions named in verse 1 have already fallen into exile and death. God's world signals the end of war as joy returns (v. 3), the plunder is divided (v. 3), the garments of war are destroyed (v. 5), and the threat of shouldering the yoke of another is removed (v. 4). The Lord of hosts, literally "Lord of the armies," has risen up in zeal to bring the end of all war (v. 7). This great act is reflected in the names the king is to carry. John Goldingay has suggested instead of titles for the

[1] As with the text in chap. 9, this text is also heavily debated concerning how this relates as prophecy to Christ, who the woman is, who the baby is, etc. For an excellent discussion of these issues, see Christopher Seitz, *Isaiah 1–39*, Interpretation Series (Louisville, KY: John Knox Press, 1993).

## Homiletical Perspective

We are familiar with this series of associations, prevalent as they are in our biblical tradition and Christian poetry and hymnody. But no matter how familiar the notion of liberation from slavery may be, it is still a theme that moves even the most affluent or autonomous worshiper. There is no one, it seems, who does not feel in some sense trapped, enslaved, or limited by circumstance or personal history. This almost instinctive identification with the oppressed can sometimes be the door through which the powerful find their way to reach out to those who even now live on the margins of society. The appearance of the marginalized shepherds in the reading from Luke might offer a way to link a nativity story that is often associated with a spiritual liberation with the very literal kind of liberation celebrated by Isaiah.

Our tendency to dwell on the glory and the hope in this reading from Isaiah is encouraged by our familiarity with some of his language. It is likely that someone who has heard the reading will remember verse 6 ("For a child has been born for us . . . Wonderful Counselor, Mighty God, Everlasting Father, Prince of Peace") because the strains of Handel's *Messiah* make those words literally singable. And the words have been attached to the celebration of Christmas for so long that by now we even think of them as Christ-words rather than oracles from the Hebrew Bible. The language is familiar, hopeful, and—it would seem—Christian.

How many people, then, will remember or will even have noticed the verse immediately preceding, "For all the boots of the tramping warriors and all the garments rolled in blood shall be burned as fuel for the fire" (v. 5)? We may have been eager to associate the coming of the Messiah with liberation from oppression, or with the cosmic reversal of light out of darkness; but the imagery in this verse demands that we attend to the realities of war. The prediction of a fire fueled with warriors' boots and bloody shirts should evoke not only a vision, but the sting of oily smoke in one's eyes; rank smells of burning leather, fabric, and perhaps even flesh; heat scorching the hands and faces of those hurling wood onto the flames. It is a grisly vision.

The king celebrated in Isaiah's vision has not arrived as a savior from afar, swooping in and rescuing people from slavery. This messiah has been a leader of warriors, overcoming the strength of the oppressors with the sword. The king mounts his throne stepping over the bodies of those—from both sides—sacrificed for his victory.

# Isaiah 9:2-7

## Theological Perspective

engage us, and even less to connect us to a king who comes to establish justice and righteousness. The incarnation does not simply affirm Jesus' body; it helps us see that *our* bodies and actions matter.

But how? The passage says almost nothing about what human beings will (or ought to) do in the process of bringing about this kingdom. Perhaps, though, that is something to keep in mind: that the advent of the kingdom that comes with the incarnation of God turns not on our skills, talents, efforts, or luck. Instead, God brings about the kingdom. That, in itself, could feel uplifting, refreshing, and hopeful for those whose feelings of filthiness and hopelessness are the product of their fear that they have failed to establish a better world and gotten dirty in the process.

There is one thing that human beings do in the passage, however: they see a great light. They have a vision of the righteous reign of the coming king who is already at work in the world. They look out at a world that was no less corrupt, corrosive, cruel, or confusing than our world, and they see God at work in it. The power of God moves in and through it, shaping it according to God's will.

All of which suggests one final theological reason why it is important not to depoliticize this text: Any attempt to separate politics from the holy risks missing the chance to see God working in and through the political world. For the first political act in Isaiah's theology—and perhaps in a Christmas Eve theology as well—is to see the world and its politics differently: not as a field of heroic struggle against overwhelming force (though it may feel that way) or a prison in which humans are stoically trapped (though it sometimes seems so), but as a site of divine activity. There is hope because God is already working here, and there is renewal because the God who is already working is establishing a reign of justice and righteousness—even, and perhaps especially, on Christmas Eve.

MARK DOUGLAS

## Pastoral Perspective

can help the congregation think about the kind of Messiah Jesus *is* and is *not*. What he is not is someone who solves all problems and makes it unnecessary for us to do the hard work of peace-making or establishing "justice" and "righteousness" (v. 7). The preacher may link Good Friday with Christmas and speak about the Messiah who, instead of destroying evil, allowed himself to become its victim, and in that way to reveal the "Mighty God," the "Everlasting Father" (v. 6).

The text is subversive, contradicting what we imagine is the way the world has to work and inviting us to imagine the world as God intends it. Why is the world not the way God intends it? The prophetic dimension of the text will require the preacher to confess that we are a part of the reason "the boots of the tramping warriors" (v. 5) are still tramping. We have "seen a great light" (v. 2) in the person of Christ, but we choose to "walk in darkness" (v. 2).

The preacher will be wise *not* to use the Christmas Eve sermon to indict the congregation. Yet the preacher can remind the congregation that the child "born for us" (v. 6) became a man and asked certain things of his followers. If indeed we are those who believe that "authority" rests upon the shoulders (v. 6) of the One whose birth we are celebrating, then we are bound to listen to him. The preacher can relate the work the congregation is called to do to the Christian practices of peacemaking and the ministries of social outreach and justice (v. 7), and encourage Christmas Eve worshipers to celebrate the birth of the Christ child by walking in "the light" (John 8:12), doing what they can to honor Isaiah's vision of a world where justice and righteousness flourish. The preacher may acknowledge that by their doing of these things the people may not change the world, but they themselves will be changed, which is where it must all begin if God's intention for the world is ever to be realized.

EUGENE C. BAY

## Exegetical Perspective

human king, the names in v. 6 should be understood as a commemoration of God's act, reading, "One who plans a wonder is the warrior God; the father forever is a commander who brings shalom."[2] The king who is so named is to remember always that God provided all that he is and has.

The period of encroaching Assyrian domination and the fear in the hearts of the people have much in common with the time of Jesus' birth. Judah is a resident captive of Rome, and Herod, who is not in the line of David, sits on the throne in Jerusalem. The people long for freedom from oppression and look for a Messiah to arise and take the throne and make Israel a great power again. What they need is a big sign.

The people in both periods long for a powerful sign that God will redeem them from oppression, and the birth of a baby seems hardly the great sign they have awaited. But looked at in another way, this sign of new life is not ordinary at all. It is a sign that only the Creator God can give. It is the sign promised to Abraham and Sarah (Gen. 12–21). It was the sign that the midwives protected during the Egyptian captivity (Exod. 1). It was the sign of God's promise offered to Ahab. What more fitting sign of God's love than the creation of a new life, even in the midst of a broken world? It is no wonder this new baby will be named Jesus, meaning, "YHWH saves." God's sign of love for the world is now God's own Son, born so the world might be saved.

BETH LANEEL TANNER

## Homiletical Perspective

What if we stopped for just a moment to recall these grim details of Isaiah's messianic oracle, before embracing the happier prediction of the child to be born? What if we stopped for just a moment to take in the fact that the glorious throne of David was steeped in blood? Indeed, most of the rulers celebrated in biblical history secured their power through ruthless oppression of their enemies. And in that moment we recognize as "the fullness of time" (Gal. 4:4), the people of Israel were suffering under a succession of violent puppet kings who sold them to the domination of a foreign empire. How might an honest reflection on the violence and death that marked the stories of the kings color our understanding of the nativity we await, and the incarnation we celebrate?

This passage from Isaiah challenges us to push a few inches beyond the comfortable picture of the nativity tableau. The child whose birth we attend tonight was born into a world painted not in pastels but in dust and blood. This incarnation is not a spiritual, otherworldly concept, but the mystery of God present in a real human child, welcomed into a real world with all its agonies and ambiguities and challenges and joys.

Once we have reconnected with the earthiness of Isaiah's vision, we can step away again to the wider perspective of the prophet, who is fundamentally singing of the zeal and the steadfastness of YHWH. The people who have suffered persecution and been liberated are the people to whom the Lord has declared eternal faithfulness. The king who is announced in these verses is a king chosen and elevated by the God of Jacob. And the peace, justice, and righteousness with which the king will establish rule are gifts of the Lord of hosts. Our celebration tonight invites us to wonder at the mystery of this cosmic creative power, steadfast love, and irrepressible force for justice embodied in the fragile flesh of a newborn child.

LINDA LEE CLADER

---

[2]John Goldingay, "The Compound Name in Isaiah 9:5(6)," *Catholic Biblical Quarterly* 61 (2006): 243.

# Psalm 96

[1]O sing to the LORD a new song;
    sing to the LORD, all the earth.
[2]Sing to the LORD, bless his name;
    tell of his salvation from day to day.
[3]Declare his glory among the nations,
    his marvelous works among all the peoples.
[4]For great is the LORD, and greatly to be praised;
    he is to be revered above all gods.
[5]For all the gods of the peoples are idols,
    but the LORD made the heavens.
[6]Honor and majesty are before him;
    strength and beauty are in his sanctuary.

[7]Ascribe to the LORD, O families of the peoples,
    ascribe to the LORD glory and strength.

## Theological Perspective

A number of interconnected theological themes immediately jump off the page: the universal kingship of the Lord, the repeated summons to worship, and the anticipated advent or coming of this king. While only a forced exegesis will allow us to draw specific christological connections, nevertheless the psalm points forward to the fulfillment of God's intentions for creation.

The universal kingship of the Lord is stated explicitly at verse 10. This affirmation is set in the context of the creation of the world and God's providential rule over it. This king is also the universal ruler who will judge all the people of the earth with equity, whose righteous and truthful judgment is anticipated at verse 13.

Under this head we need to reflect, first, on what it means to speak of the kingship of the Lord. Increasingly today, at least in the West, constitutional monarchy is a diminishing form of government, while absolute monarchy is long gone. As a metaphor for the rule of God, monarchy seems now rather dated. Yet the intention remains clear: God created, rules, judges, and has future as a mode of divine being—note Revelation 1:4: "Peace [to you] from him who is and who was and who is to come."[1] There is a singularity

## Pastoral Perspective

Christmas Eve is one of those high liturgical moments when there is standing room only as all God's children gather for a sacred celebration of Jesus' birth. We know we will sing as many of our favorite Christmas carols as time will allow. Then we read Psalm 96, a hymn of praise that is perfect for Christmas Eve. As I read this psalm aloud, I am reminded of the live Christmas pageant that took place every Advent in the field behind the neighborhood church where I grew up. Christmas pageants have a way of indelibly imprinting our souls with the songs and stories of our dear Savior's birth.

No matter how many times we play the parts in the drama and sing the songs in the heavenly choir, when we declare the glory of God on Christmas Eve it is as if we sing to the Lord for the first time. Just as Christmas music reminds us of who we are, the powerful rhythm of Psalm 96 helps us remember that something important is about to happen.

The rhythms of the psalm flow back and forth, rocking the ear like a newborn baby. There is a sense of urgency not unlike that of a woman panting in labor: "Sing to the *Lord*, sing to the *Lord*, sing to the *Lord*—bless, tell, declare—ascribe, ascribe, ascribe—bring, come, worship, tremble. Say, 'The *Lord* is King!'"

What better way to enact the regime change announced and celebrated in Psalm 96 than to

---

[1]Jürgen Moltmann notes that in this verse, instead of the future of the verb "to be" we have the future of the verb "to come," in *The Coming of God: Christian Eschatology*, trans. Margaret Kohl (Minneapolis: Fortress Press, 1996), 23.

<sup>8</sup>Ascribe to the Lord the glory due his name;
 bring an offering, and come into his courts.
<sup>9</sup>Worship the Lord in holy splendor;
 tremble before him, all the earth.

<sup>10</sup>Say among the nations, "The Lord is king!
 The world is firmly established; it shall never be moved.
 He will judge the peoples with equity."
<sup>11</sup>Let the heavens be glad, and let the earth rejoice;
 let the sea roar, and all that fills it;
<sup>12</sup> let the field exult, and everything in it.
 Then shall all the trees of the forest sing for joy
<sup>13</sup> before the Lord; for he is coming,
 for he is coming to judge the earth.
 He will judge the world with righteousness,
 and the peoples with his truth.

## Exegetical Perspective

This psalm is a hymn of praise to YHWH, the God of Israel. It is most probably chosen for this day to supplement the idea of God/Jesus as "Lord of Lords and King of Kings." The psalm appears to be divided into two parts, with verses 1–6 speaking to the reason to praise YHWH and verses 7–13 making a claim of YHWH as potential universal deity.

The addressee of the psalm is not clearly stated. Verse 1 calls for "all the earth" to sing. Verse 7 opens by speaking to "families of the peoples," while verse 9 returns to addressing "all the earth." On the other hand, verses 11–12 address nature in the form of heavens, sea, field, trees, and forest, but it is not clear to whom the imperative in verse 10 ("Say!") is addressed.

Since the attributes ascribed to YHWH and the actions attributed to YHWH by the psalmist speak to YHWH's actions not just among Israel but also among the nations, one wonders whether such a hymn was used in a worship setting where foreign dignitaries were present in the temple in Jerusalem. On the other hand, the references to other nations could function in the expectation that they would influence Israel by getting Israel to see and acknowledge the wide-ranging power and influence of their deity.

Since verse 6 mentions YHWH's sanctuary, *miqdašô*, and verse 8 calls for bringing offerings or

## Homiletical Perspective

The joyful expectation that climaxes in our Christmas Eve liturgies finds its focal point in the twin psalms we will hear this night and on Christmas Day, here expressed as the joyous anticipation of God's judgment: "for he is coming, for he is coming to judge the earth" (v. 13). It is a judgment often conceived as evoking dread; but in the eyes of the psalmist, it is a promising juncture in which God's just and restorative purpose for all things animate and inanimate is being accomplished.

Right at the outset, the lectionary confronts preachers with a dilemma. On first encounter, the Psalter seems to be a minor stepsister to the "real" text of the occasion, the Gospel's birth announcement with its attendant shepherds and angels, the implied sounds of animals lowing and the rich aroma of straw. What preacher considers preaching the psalm text at *this* juncture? But because juxtaposition—the setting of one thing next to another, whether in liturgy, proclamation, or the arts—reveals "communal meaning,"[1] the invigorating juxtaposition of psalm superimposed on Gospel can lead us to the manger with new eyes.

[1] Gordon Lathrop, *Holy Things: A Liturgical Theology* (Minneapolis: Fortress Press, 1993), 11. See also p. 220, where Lathrop reminds us that Christian liturgy "always invites the many assembled people to participate in *juxtapositions* that ought never to allow one thing, one word, one action to be absolute."

# Psalm 96

## Theological Perspective

about the assertion made here for the authority of God. The Lord is greatly to be praised, to be revered above all other gods, which are really just idols, both weak and worthless (vv. 4 and 5). The Lord alone has majesty and is worthy of honor (v. 6). In fact, the presence of the Lord rightly induces trembling, a response similar perhaps to that identified by Rudolf Otto when one is confronted by what he called the "mysterium tremendum," meaning the awe, majesty, and energy of God, which shows itself as something uniquely attractive and fascinating, but which creates a feeling of creature-consciousness.[2]

The second point to notice is the inclusivity or universality of this kingship: everyone and everything is included. All the earth is summoned to sing (v. 1); God's glory is to be declared among the nations, and God's works announced to all the peoples (v. 3); God is to be affirmed by the families of the peoples (v. 7); all the earth is to tremble before God (v. 9). And definitively: "Say among the nations, 'The Lord is King'" (v. 10). Even the world of nature is included in the work of being required to respond to the kingship of God. The boundaries of an Israel-specific, localized divinity are here broken open, and a universal note is sounded as "the inevitable corollary of the character of the Lord. . . . The Lord is no petty, minor tribal deity."[3] There is a parallel with the patristic concept of Jesus Christ as *pantokrator*, Lord of the cosmos. Lordship is a concept without limits.

The contemporary theological problem is this: How do we speak of the singularity of the Old Testament's affirmation of lordship in the context of competing claims to divinity? Some people today urge us to think in terms of the Abrahamic faiths—Judaism, Islam, and Christianity—and to find a common ground in the shared ancestral heritage. The "God has many names" approach, however, flies in the face of the biblical testimony. If the Lord is king, whose name alone is to be blessed (v. 2), the blessing of God by another name amounts to blasphemy. The psalm states what the psalmist believed to be the case: The Lord, the God of Israel, is king. The New Testament equivalent is Acts 4:12, "There is salvation in no one else [Jesus Christ], for there is no other name under heaven given among mortals by which we must be saved." For the Christian, of course, Jesus is YHWH.

[2] Rudolf Otto, *The Idea of the Holy*, trans. John W. Harvey (London: Oxford University Press, 1958), 10.
[3] Robert Davidson, *The Vitality of Worship: A Commentary on the Psalms* (Grand Rapids: Eerdmans, 1998), 318.

## Pastoral Perspective

gather in worship on Christmas Eve? By this point in Advent we have tired of trying to find joy through decorating, baking, shopping, and wrapping. It is now time to sing a new song, ascribing "to the Lord the glory due his name" (v. 8). As we come to "worship the Lord in holy splendor" (v. 9), perhaps the sacrament of the Lord's Supper will be served, so that we celebrate the kingship of the Lord in our own particular way.

Each Advent, Emmanuel comes to us: God with us in the manger, God with us in the carols sung by the angel choir, God with us as the shepherds arrive and the wise ones ride in on their horses. As the promise of God is rehearsed and played out over and over through the years, can we hear often enough that divine love is real? For some present on Christmas Eve, life experience has shown that God can be trusted. For others who have not sensed God's love in their lives, perhaps this is the night, in the beauty of God's sanctuary, that the divine connection will be made. As the gathered community sings to the Lord and blesses God's name, those who have felt estranged from God and the family of faith sometimes reconnect as they "worship the Lord in holy splendor" (v. 9). The wonder and promise of this night is contagious. As the Spirit moves through God's people, both those experiencing it for the first time and those who have returned again and again, all those present are offered fresh experience as if for the first time.

For some the new song may involve figuring out how to celebrate Christmas without a spouse who has died or without a child away on military assignment. For others it may mean finding the voices they have lost to the horror of domestic violence or in the aftermath of a painful divorce. For some it may mean finding a way to celebrate the birth of baby Jesus, even though all their efforts to get pregnant have produced no baby to rock in their arms. This new song touches all those broken places where healing is needed, as well as those places of unrest where peace is demanded.

On Christmas Eve the new song that is about to break into the world is so mysterious, we need the memory of Christmases past to see what those wise ones saw, to hear what the shepherds heard, and to treasure the words that Mary pondered in her heart. Celebrating God's kingship can make us breathless. The people sitting in the pews on Christmas Eve may feel a little out of breath after all the hustle and bustle of the commercial world vying for attention and dollars during Advent. But finally, they can sit

## Exegetical Perspective

gifts, *minḥah,* into YHWH's courts, it is clear that this psalm was used in liturgy in the temple. Thus, most probably the psalm is addressed to the congregation of men assembled in the temple for worship.

There is much argument among scholars as to whether this psalm was written during the monarchic period, when Judah was an independent nation and the notion of king would have been most understandable, or in the Second Temple period, with language depicting YHWH as a universal deity who controls history and to whom all nations will turn, which has precedence in the theology of Second Isaiah.[1] Since there are no specific historical allusions in the psalm itself, dating it is more speculative, reflecting the ideological and theological interests of the interpreter.

The psalm begins with a series of imperatives to the congregation to sing. There is reference to a "new song." However, unlike Psalm 137, which gives the words to the songs to be sung "in a foreign land," this psalm does not give the words of the "new song." It does give the contours of the song, blessing YHWH's name and telling of YHWH's salvation and YHWH's works (vv. 2–3), but the words of the exact song are not recorded.

Following the imperatives to sing and declare, there are reasons for the singing, all introduced by *kî* clauses. Interestingly the reasons for singing about YHWH's salvation are not because of what YHWH has done for Israel. They are rather because of what YHWH has done "among all the peoples" (v. 3) and because of YHWH's importance and relationship to other deities (vv. 4–5). Again, there are no specific references in the psalm as to what deeds YHWH has done for other nations. One has to wonder if the other nations would agree that YHWH has done "marvelous works among" them (v. 3). As one reads through the Deuteronomistic History and the Chroniclers' work, first, other nations are used as pawns of YHWH to punish Israel and Judah for their apostasy by oppressing them; then, the nations are destroyed for these actions.

In referring to YHWH's relation to other deities in verse 4, the psalmist says YHWH is "to be revered above all gods." On the one hand, we again get acknowledgment in the Hebrew Bible of the existence of other deities and that YHWH interacts with them. The psalmist does not, however, tell us who is the one doing the revering. Is this Israel or the other deities? Or is this a claim of what *should* be

[1] Marvin E. Tate, *Word Biblical Commentary, Psalms 51–100* (Nashville: Thomas E. Nelson, 1990), 504–9.

## Homiletical Perspective

Here the psalmist clearly relishes the role of choral composer, playing the theme whose echoes will recur on Christmas Day as well: "the Lord reigns!" The primary act upon which this reign is founded is creation, so that on Christmas Eve, in an intriguing way, the lectionary is directing us back to *origins.* An unfamiliar carol of God's justice toward the earth is put forth as the central anthem for our candlelight service.

This psalm also fulfills a unifying function among the lectionary texts: the song to be sung is a *new* one, prefigured by Mary's Magnificat of freedom and justice. The Liberator of whom she sang *is* doing a new thing, the holy arm cloaked in infant form. Reading the psalm through the lens of nativity, it is plain that the truth with which the peoples will be judged is lying in a manger, the most meager of conditions. The "old" songs *lament* that we are bonded to material reality, sorely imprisoned in flawed flesh. Whether the lamentation is voiced in country western, blues, or rap, it bears the marks of regret, loss, incompleteness. Either here, or later on Christmas Day (when Ps. 98 will take up the refrain), the preacher might explore the dimensions of this "new song."

But be forewarned: the newness of the song reaches beyond the usual strains of Christmas Eve! It leads us from the quiet awe of Bethlehem, our captivation with the infant, even our astonished reverence before the mystery of Incarnation, to embrace the nations—"all the peoples" and indeed "all the earth." It tells of God's glory expressed in "marvelous works," not manifested only through Israel's history, but through the stories *we* bring to the manger as well. What new corporate song would the people of your parish sing on this night that so adeptly opens hearts and hallows memories? Would it be a ballad celebrating how God "brought us through" a critical, dangerous, or risky time? Or should it be the aria of an unexpected vision gestating among us?

For us who wait at a stable door, the psalmist's words are not a completed revelation but a fervent hope: we "read into" this holy night the affirmation of faith that God "will judge the peoples with equity" (v. 10). The cosmological intensity of the song, however, validates our hunch, as the sea and its inhabitants roar, the fields and their denizens exult, and all the trees "sing." In stanzas reminiscent of Romans 8:19–23, creation now joins in a celebration connecting incarnation with God's ultimate intention for the denouement of all things. Nature

# Psalm 96

## Theological Perspective

The response of faith to such a divine and universal kingship is not arrogance, or pride, or any kind of violence toward those of other religions. The response is worship, and it is worship of a sort that invites all others to participate. The Lord's glory is to be declared among the nations (v. 3), so all people can sing a new song to the Lord (v. 1).

The psalm begins with the threefold summons to song; this is followed with the summons to bless, tell, and declare. The psalm is one of celebration: it looks back at what God has done, and it looks forward, creating a horizon of expectation. As it builds up pace and intensity, as it were, the psalm seems to throb with anticipation and excitement. Faith here is expectant, for God's ultimate purposes will be fulfilled. This is the language of hope and, although the word is not used, also of joy. The faith of the psalmist, and the understanding of God contained within the psalm, lead to vibrant worship.

It is appropriate to suggest that worship is a criterion for the adequacy of theology. An understanding of God that does not cause us to shout out, to sing praises, to tell the story with enthusiasm, to be bonded into communities of hope and joy, is a poor theology indeed. Psalm 96 is a theology that sings and shouts its faith. This is a faith that cannot be contained in sensible propositions or ordered in calm ways of response. The metaphors are stretched to breaking point: "let the field exult . . . all the trees of the forest sing for joy" (v. 12); the exuberance can hardly be contained.

The psalm ends on a note of eschatological expectation that makes it an appropriate lection for Christmas Eve, the time when Christian anticipation is surely at its highest. As Robert Davidson notes in his remarks on this psalm, "In Christian vision, as contained in the book of Revelation, it climaxes in the words of the risen, exalted Jesus, 'Surely I am coming soon,' to which the response of faith can only be, 'Amen. Come, Lord Jesus!'" (Rev. 22:20).[4]

ANDREW PURVES

## Pastoral Perspective

and rest for a few minutes, trying to absorb what this new song is going to mean in their individual lives as well as the life of the church and the world.

We can dare to pray and work for justice in the world even in the midst of war and violence. "Say among the nations, 'The Lord is King! The world is firmly established; it shall never be moved. He will judge the peoples with equity'" (v. 10). We can dare to testify, along with the psalmist in verses 4 and 5: "For great is the Lord, and greatly to be praised; he is to be revered above all gods. For all the gods of the peoples are idols, but the Lord made the heavens." We can dare to sing a new song expecting a miracle, especially when life is not following the plan we expected.

God's response in verse 10 is to hold the world in God's hands and to judge the people with equity. The Messiah is coming tomorrow, no matter how ready we are. Just as we can never really be ready for the birth of a child, how can we be ready for the Messiah? Whether we are in a calm or anxious rhythm, whether we are afraid or prepared, in the natural rhythm of God's time Christ is born. But tonight we will await his birth as calmly as we can. "O holy night, the stars are brightly shining. This is the night of our dear Savior's birth." O sing a new song to the Lord!

TRISHA LYONS SENTERFITT

---

[4] Ibid., 319.

the case? In verse 5, YHWH is compared to other deities by referring to them as idols, in contrast to YHWH being the one who made the heavens. In this verse we see the translators of the NRSV softening the wording of the Hebrew text, which refers to these other deities not as idols but with the word *'elîlîm,* which is a negative epithet meaning "nothing." In essence the text claims that YHWH is a better deity than the others, who can do nothing. This wording can be problematic in relating to people from other religions who live in the same geographic area, and this change could explain the nuancing of the NRSV translators.

A key to interpreting the psalm is a determination of the phrase "families of the peoples" in v. 7. While *mišpahâh,* family, refers to one of the units of organization of Israel below the level of tribe,[2] the other references, to "all the earth" in verse 9 and "the peoples" in verse 10, lead most exegetes to see this as a claim for YHWH's being the ruler of all nations of the world. The call for them to worship YHWH in the temple and to bring gifts (v. 8) and the claim that YHWH will judge them (v. 10) is on the order of Isaiah 2:1–4a//Micah 4:1–3a and Psalm 68:28–31. Interestingly these notions of YHWH's judgment in verses 10–13 follow the upper-class concerns of order and omit both the hopes of the underclass for a transformative economic and world order (Isa. 2:4b and Mic. 2:4b) and the prophetic claim to *mišpat,* justice, referring to social redistribution.[3] Rather, the psalmist stresses the judgments will be in terms of righteousness and truth, which suggest more cultic than social radical forms.

Perhaps such omissions of prophetic and social concerns of the underclass make the choice of this psalm ironic, in terms of the radical transformation to which Jesus calls us.

RANDALL C. BAILEY

itself is a recipient of the redemptive event of this birth, and knows it—joining the blessing, participating in the ascription of praise to the Lord's glory and strength. The psalm reminds us that we are not sole beneficiaries of the divine hallowing of flesh and turns our eyes again toward our proper partnership with all creation.

The note sounded by 96:10 is "YHWH reigns" (in the NRSV's rendering, "the LORD is king!"). It is a decisive assertion not open to debate, a foregone accomplishment: YHWH has *already* begun to rule. Juxtaposed with the other texts for the occasion, it is quite a birth announcement. *This* is the hope for which we have come to the manger; for this reason, the whole creation—nations, seas, creatures, trees— is beckoned to sing a new song of praise to YHWH. Nothing is excluded as unworthy to join the praise.

Professor Jannie du Preez of the University of Stellenbosch responds to the enthronement psalms with a growing conviction that justice towards the earth forms an integral part of the mission of the church.[2] It may be inconvenient to speak on Christmas Eve of global warming, the destruction of rainforest and deep-sea habitats, and the over-consumption of earth's resources by the vast minority of earth's people; but nothing can be more appropriate than to allow Christ's birth to remind us of the great web of life in which we share, and for which God's entry into earthly flesh is accomplished. Toward that end, the psalmist's words illumine a renewed vision of our part in a world where indeed "all is calm, all is bright."

GAIL A. RICCIUTI

---

[2]Norman K. Gottwald, *The Tribes of Yahweh* (Sheffield: Sheffield Academic, 1999), 257–70.
[3]Itumeleng J. Mosala, *Biblical Hermeneutics and Black Theology in South Africa* (Grand Rapids: Eerdmans, 1989), 37–38.

[2]J. du Preez, "Reading Three 'Enthronement Psalms' from an Ecological Perspective," *Missionalia* 19, no. 2 (August 1991): 122.

# Titus 2:11-14

<sup>11</sup>For the grace of God has appeared, bringing salvation to all, <sup>12</sup>training us to renounce impiety and worldly passions, and in the present age to live lives that are self-controlled, upright, and godly, <sup>13</sup>while we wait for the blessed hope and the manifestation of the glory of our great God and Savior, Jesus Christ. <sup>14</sup>He it is who gave himself for us that he might redeem us from all iniquity and purify for himself a people of his own who are zealous for good deeds.

## Theological Perspective

The text provides a salient message for Christmas Eve. The drama of promise that occurs throughout Advent is made manifest in the appearance of Christ the Savior on Christmas. The eve of the Promised One's birth lies at the border between promise and fulfillment, darkness and light, despair and hope, all themes of the birth narratives. The theological loci of revelation, grace, salvation, and the disciplined life of faith, are present in the passage.

The location of the text in Titus is significant. Both before and after the passage, the author provides an ethical template for church leaders and laity on the isle of Crete. Moral imperatives dominate, as they do throughout the Pastoral Epistles. But, here, possibly recognizing how a legalism can twist the "laws" of Christ into a brittle code that drains the joy out of faith, the author reminds readers of the theological underpinnings of righteous living.

*The Appearance of Grace.* One core emphasis is the inseparability of gift and response, of a grace freely given and a faith that lives in disciplined gratitude. Christmas Eve worship typically bubbles with emotions of expectation and joy because of the underlying wonder that unto us a precious gift has been given. God's initiative and human response go hand in hand. First, the reception of grace; then, the life of

## Pastoral Perspective

The Advent journey has brought us to our destination. On this, the holiest of nights, pastors and worship leaders have two special challenges.

As on Easter Sunday, the congregation includes people who routinely worship only twice a year. For them, December marks the "Christmas season" rather than an Advent journey through the winter darkness that prepares us to receive God's ultimate gift of grace. How can we, in one hour, involve strangers in a service of worship that glorifies God and also touches their souls?

At the other end of the spectrum are those who have heard the Gospel infancy narratives dozens of times and have long since memorized cherished Christmas carols. How can we create a fresh worship experience without negating the rituals that are so meaningful?

Our epistle reading offers powerful insights about how God's incarnation affects our lives as contemporary Christians. The starting point for both this passage and our Christian faith is grace. Grace, God's unmerited favor, is a divine gift rather than an achievement. Grace is something we can never get but only be given. In the birth of the Christ child, we see grace in human form.

All world religions stress the importance of seeking to live in relationship with the divine.

*Christmas Eve*

## Exegetical Perspective

In a statement both beautiful and profound, the author of the epistle to Titus locates the Christian life squarely between the two advents of Christ: his first coming, which inaugurated the dawning of salvation, and the second, glorious appearing of Christ, yet to come.

There are no significant textual problems or translation issues. The passage (which properly continues through v. 15) both concludes and serves as the theological rationale for the preceding "household code" (vv. 2–10). As throughout the Pastoral Epistles, the author seeks to inculcate conventional moral norms for respectable people, as a way of commending the Christian movement to outsiders and deflecting critique (2:8; 1 Tim. 2:2). Though perhaps appropriate for the time, these instructions are problematic today. They approve hierarchical social arrangements that many see as incompatible with the gospel's call for freeing of the captives and resistance to the fallen principalities and powers. Yet there is a bedrock of truth in verses 11–14 upon which today's interpreter can build a strong and lovely dwelling for Christian families and for the church.

In verse 11 the author makes oblique reference to the (first) coming of Christ, described as the appearing of *grace*. (The Greek words for

## Homiletical Perspective

Several approaches to a Christmas Eve sermon are suggested by this text, with its strong emphasis on the bracketing of time by the two "appearings" of the Lord and on righteous living. Here the two advents that have claimed our attention for four weeks are brought into view in a single text, heightening our sense of "living between the times." This sense of time is joined to a communal and ecclesial vision of God's redemptive purpose, and the connection between Christ's coming and ethics is unmistakable.

A sermon might foreground the double vision, first-and-second-coming consciousness that, according to Titus, is the permanent time-consciousness of the believing community. The two "appearings"—the first a manifestation of grace, the second a glorious fulfillment—bracket and qualify Christian experience. Anticipating the reappearance of someone who has visited before is an idea that has found its way into North American Christmas celebrations by way of a familiar pre-Christmas jingle ("You'd better watch out, better not cry, better not pout . . . Santa Claus is coming . . . !"); yet, if this is mentioned, the *contrasts* should receive far more attention than the similarities. Jesus disclosed grace in all its challenging depth—he does not hand out goodies; and we are not occasionally bad-tempered children who should watch our manners, but a

# Titus 2:11-14

## Theological Perspective

faith. Only by receiving the light of grace that comes to us in and through God's visitation in the Son are we able to join the communities of worship and walk in the light that has shone.

Despite the centrality of this rhythm in Scripture, too often the imperatives of the Pastorals become "the rules" by which people of faith become legalists. As the faithful prepare to give and receive Christmas presents, they need to be reminded that salvation does not depend on whether they have been "naughty or nice." Perhaps the preacher can empha-size the mystery of the manifestation (epiphany) of grace, recalling possibly the Pauline theme that we love, praise, and serve God because God has first loved and graced us. Robert McAfee Brown, in concluding a discussion of grace, cites the closing of a sermon in which Augustine says, "I do not say to thee, seek the way. The way itself is come to thee; arise and walk."[1]

*The Purpose of Grace.* God's grace is the source of our salvation (v. 11). In grace we are rescued from sin, delivered from evil, and made whole. "By grace" one lives in the eternal grace and wisdom of God. One becomes a learner of God who purposes to train one in grace (v. 12a). To be a learner is to seek to live a wise life that renounces sin (v. 12a) and embraces righteousness (vv. 12b, 14b). Titus appears to follow patterns of OT wisdom here. Negatively, believers must renounce ungodliness and sensual lusts. Positively, they must be purified; that is, come under self-control, be upright, and be godly (v. 12b), learning to say no to attitudes and behaviors that are unacceptable to the renewed life, and yes to the marks of the redeemed. The celebrated birth of Christmas Eve is the beginning of our training for the journey we walk in Christ.

Graced moments and grateful living are two touchstones of the Christian life. They also may become separated and result in distorted attitudes and expectations. On the one hand, if the spiritual formation that renounces sin and evil and savors a godly life now, between the advents, is neglected, one may become caught up in a whirlwind of spiritual ecstasy at the wonder and joy of the manifestation of grace through the advent of God (v. 11) and the expected second advent of God in glory (v. 13). On the other hand, in doing for God in good works, ties to grace may be severed, which is the basis for

## Pastoral Perspective

Judaism, Christianity, and Islam identify God as the only object of our worship and adoration. Christianity proclaims the glorious assurance that it is God who first seeks us, loving us before we can even respond. Christianity values divine grace as few other religions in the world do.

Christianity becomes distorted whenever it is seen as a code of conduct apart from grace. The focus then shifts from God's gracious gift to human striving, sin, and guilt. In his book *Guilt and Grace*, the late Swiss physician Paul Tournier, a man of deep Christian faith, writes, "I cannot study this very serious problem of guilt without raising the very obvious and tragic fact that religion—my own as well as that of all believers—can crush instead of liberate."[1] Tournier valued the acknowledgment of sin because it leads to repentance. Yet many of his patients carried such immense guilt that they were unable to appreciate the present, remaining enslaved by the past. What people need most, Tournier concluded, is the *acceptance* of God's grace. Christmas Eve is the perfect time to be reminded that God has already given that gift to us in and through Jesus Christ. It is now our responsibility to acknowledge the gift, allow it gradually to transform us, and respond with gratitude.

Our response, this passage from Titus reminds us, must be ethical. A Gentile converted by Paul, Titus was sent on two urgent missions to Corinth and then to Crete, where he ministered to the fledgling congregations Paul planted. Gentile Christians had to make tremendous changes in their lives, turning away from the idols that had been the objects of their devotion and worshiping God alone.

Similar changes are needed within our own secular culture. A myriad of things vie for our atten-tion and devotion: good looks, social status, worldly success, money, intellect, politics, patriotism, and even morality. We fall into idolatry every time there is something more important in our lives than God. The insightful author Frederick Buechner writes, "Idolatry is the practice of ascribing absolute value to things of relative worth."[2]

Amid the close and holy darkness surrounding our celebration, Christians are called to turn away from all that separates us from God. This is precisely what we cannot do and so is what God graciously does for us in the birth of Christ. Christ's birth marks the inauguration of the kingdom of God here on earth. When Christ comes again, that kingdom

---

[1]Robert Brown, *The Spirit of Protestantism* (New York: Oxford University Press, 1965), 66. Brown notes that H. Richard Niebuhr ended his *The Meaning of Revelation* with this citation.

[1]Paul Tournier, *Guilt and Grace* (San Francisco: Harper & Row, 1962), 23.
[2]Frederick Buechner, *Wishful Thinking* (New York: Harper & Row, 1973), 40.

"appearing" in vv. 11 and 13 are related to the English word "epiphany.") This is a reference not to the birth of the earthly Jesus in Bethlehem but to the onset of a new season in the life of God's people, inaugurated by Christ's life, death, and resurrection. One may compare Paul's reference to the coming of *faith* in Galatians 3:23—an allusion to Jesus' own faith, which liberated us from bondage to the law and brought us into a changed relationship with God. According to the author of Titus, this epiphany of *grace* in the world has brought with it *salvation*. The author goes on to suggest in verses 13–14 that salvation has both a future and a present dimension. In the future, Christ will make a second appearance and claim us as his own (cf. 2 Tim. 4:8, and note the unusually high christological formulation in Titus 2:13). But in the present, we live changed lives, because Christ gave himself "to redeem us from all wickedness and to purify for himself a people that are his very own, eager to do what is good" (NIV).

Some Christians chafe at all the instructions for good behavior in the Pastoral Epistles, not only because they dislike the hierarchical social order assumed by the author, but simply because they view so many regulations as antithetical to the gospel. The author was not, however, prescribing a new law to replace the old, but envisioning a new sort of community that would glorify God and adequately reflect Christians' changed identity. *Because we are recipients of grace, we are empowered to live in a new way.* This same conviction is stated many times throughout the NT.

For example, Paul tells us that because we are no longer slaves to sin, we are free to "walk in newness of life" (Rom. 6:4). Elsewhere he contends that because we "are all children of light and children of the day" and are "not of the night or of darkness," we should "be sober, and put on the breastplate of faith and love, and for a helmet the hope of salvation" (1 Thess. 5:5, 8). The author of 1 Peter writes that we were "ransomed from the futile ways" of our ancestors and by obedience to the truth have purified our souls, in order that we might love one another "deeply from the heart" (1 Pet. 1:18, 22). Salvation through Christ carries with it both the potential and the imperative to live a changed life.

Titus 2:13 reminds us that as Christians we live in a time of waiting. God's promised redemption was achieved in Jesus' first coming, yet we have a joyful hope that there will come a day when the broken creation will be *wholly* restored (see, e.g., Rom. 8:19–23; Rev. 21:4). The NT statements about Jesus'

people claimed for costly testimony to the new-created world of God's grace and glory.

Better than explaining what it is like to live between the advents, and admonishing the congregation to live accordingly, will be a sermon evoking a qualified sense of time that results in changed behavior. The congregation already knows about living between decisive moments from ordinary human experience. Between engagement and marriage, between the moment of the positive pregnancy test and the longed-for moment of birth, between admission into degree candidacy and conferral of degree, between the diagnosis of incurable illness and—as used to be said in my childhood church, perhaps euphemistically but also faithfully—the "entering into glory," altered expectations come to bear, priorities shift, self-assessment changes, relationships take on heightened significance. Something has happened that makes this time like no other time; something is going to happen that will alter life again. Between-times living cannot be business as usual; and the Christian sense of what matters is uniquely defined by acts of God unrepeatable and decisive.

A second, quite different sermon could focus on a single verse, verse 14. We learn that the one who has appeared and will appear again came for us; but there is nothing here of individual salvation. While the popular reassurance that "Jesus would have come to earth if you were the only one who needed saving" contains a grain of truth, it suggests a horizon of salvation far smaller than Titus envisions. On Christmas Eve in particular, congregations are at risk of privatizing the incarnation. We watch *our* dear children play angels and shepherds around the manger that Mr. Green built with *his own hands*; and that is *Katie's* doll there in the manger—or in years when the timing comes out right, maybe even Katie's *little brother*. In other words, the whole candlelit scene is cozily *ours*, and we can imagine that Christian life means just this shoulder-to-shoulder closeness with God. While this makes the story accessible, especially to awestruck children, the socially radical significance of this entry of God into the world should not be lost. Jesus came to alter the deep structures of human life, not only on the individual level, but socially. God's purpose, states the writer of Titus, was the construction of nothing short of a new society, liberated from the clutches of all that is life denying ("all iniquity") and dedicated to what is life affirming ("good works"). The work of redemption includes us, and is not merely about *us*.

# Titus 2:11-14

## Theological Perspective

"giving cups of cold water," or regressing into legalism.

*The Experience of Grace.* Titus's theological excursus reminds us of the holy hush that constitutes so much of Christmas Eve worship. Amidst the rush of preparation and the fervor of expectations, the lights are dimmed and silence takes hold of us, our frantic fussing stilled. Weary and pensive we sit, eyes closed, dazzled by the glitter of holiday festivities. Our vision inexplicably clears, and things previously unseen are brought into focus. We are embraced by the overwhelming impossibility that the Center of Ultimacy has come, in love, to us. Out of that silence wells a joy that transcends our doubts, fears, and ambiguities.

While revelations always have consequences, such as the imperatives for godly living that Titus sets forth, the foundation of our "doing" is always in the indicative, in the event of the coming of God's grace. Friedrich Schleiermacher, writing from a heart of deep grief due to a broken relationship with his beloved Eleanore, captured the holy silence and exquisite joy of Christmas in his *Christmas Eve: Dialogue on the Incarnation*. To the question of what constitutes the joy of Christmas, one of the dialogue partners, Ernst, states: "And this inner ground cannot be other than the appearance of the Redeemer as the source of all other joy in the Christian world; and for this reason nothing else can deserve to be so celebrated as this event."[2] In the manifestation of grace on Christmas Eve, the Christ comes once more to us.

From the beginning of this text to the end, Titus writes from the perspective of one who has experienced the wondrous gift of God's coming to him, and to us, in grace. Being graced includes personal knowledge that reorders and reorients us, both in our thinking and our doing. Thus, in the congregation in which I commune, it seems so appropriate that folks whose lives were tattered, broken, and sick are being mended, repaired, and healed in a Sunday school class called "New Beginnings." As Dietrich Bonhoeffer suggested, our "life together" in Christian community is made possible only by the manifestation of grace in our imperfect lives.

DONALD W. MUSSER

## Pastoral Perspective

will be fulfilled and all God's creation restored to its original glory. All Christians live in the "now and not yet." Today's congregations, like the fledgling Christian community with whom Titus ministered, give humble thanks for the gift of God's Son and wait with expectation and hope for Christ's eventual return.

Waiting with expectation is different from passively watching time go by. Two very different Greek words, *chronos* and *kairos*, are translated into English as "time." In the original New Testament texts, *chronos* is used for human time that can be displayed on a clock or calendar. *Kairos* means the fullness of time. It is God's time. Our daily schedules revolve around *chronos* time; babies are born on *kairos* time. Christ will return when the time (*kairos*) is right.

Until that time, all Christians are called to live in response to God's grace as faithful disciples who act with integrity while we actively wait with hope and expectation. Rather than viewing waiting as a burden, we welcome it as a time of opportunity. Because God loves us enough to have become like us, our response is a desire to become more like Christ. The epistle to Titus calls Christians to be increasingly "self-controlled, upright and . . . zealous for good deeds." Rather than being the means by which we earn God's favor, good deeds should spring naturally from our gratitude for God's grace. How we live our daily lives puts our faith into action. We turn away from the things of relative worth fully to embrace God. We allow God to lift the burden of guilt we carry and replace it with grace. We open ourselves so that Christ can be reborn in us. Because Christ lives within us, all of life begins to take on a sacred quality. We become Christ's hands and feet in the world.

It is not enough to hear the glorious music of this holy day and retell the Christmas story. God calls us to be transformed by grace and wonder. The divine love that God pours out to us expands as it is shared with others. We seek to do what is good because of God's goodness. God's gift to us this Christmas is perhaps best summarized by Phillips Brooks, who wrote the lyrics for "O Little Town of Bethlehem" in 1868: "We hear the Christmas angels the great glad tidings tell; O come to us, abide with us, our Lord Emmanuel."

CATHY F. YOUNG

---

[2] Friedrich Schleiermacher, *Christmas Eve*, trans. Terrence Tice (Richmond: John Knox, 1967), 78.

## Exegetical Perspective

Parousia or second coming are understood in differing ways by Christians today. Some mainline Christians pay little attention to them and might prefer that they were not there at all. By contrast, some dispensationalist Christians focus almost exclusively on getting ready for "the rapture," with each new moment of unrest in the Middle East reinvigorating speculation that Christ is at the gates. But there are problems with any approach that either denies our hope that one day death will be "swallowed up in victory" (1 Cor. 15:54), or that claims to know too much about how God will bring about God's promised aims. The preacher may want to point out that the author of Titus puts no emphasis on prognostication and puts strong emphasis on how our lively hope for a *new* age affects the way we live *here and now.*

The bottom line for the author of this letter is that our families and our churches are to testify to the grace of God through Jesus Christ, who has freed us from the powers that rule the world and transformed us into his own people, who strive always to do what is good. Christ gave himself for us in order that we might resist the dominant yet ungodly passions or spirits of the age—spirits of anger, hatred, and divisiveness, for example, or spirits of acquisitiveness and idolatry—and bear *communal witness* to a better way.

We bear such witness most effectively not by trying to replicate first-century social arrangements, but by seeking to establish grace-filled relationships with members of our family, church, and wider community. Such relationships will manifest the same self-giving love for God and for one another as were exhibited by Jesus himself. Christmas—a season when many are filled with a sense of love and generosity—is an excellent time for us as God's people to consider how we will live our lives to bear witness the whole year through.

SUSAN R. GARRETT

## Homiletical Perspective

The preacher might capture Titus's social vision of redemption by reaching retrospectively into events of the past year, highlighting events in the local and world news that have caused the congregation to long and yearn with others for a redemption not yet fully realized, or in which the congregation has seen redemption being worked out, against all odds. Perhaps our Christmas pageants would ring more true if the familiar stable scene were set against a changing backdrop of photographs from every corner of the world depicting ways that God is at work through social and political action to confront and address all that diminishes human life.

A third approach to preaching from this text would make the connection between God's taking on flesh among us and ethics. The text of Titus is preoccupied nearly from beginning to end with behavior appropriate to believers. Exactly what behavior is required is a matter for each age to discern. The admonitions that seemed fitting when the text was written (see esp. 2:5–10) may seem either culturally irrelevant or downright appalling today. Yet, what should not be missed is that the behavioral imperatives do not come out of the blue; the imperatives are attached to theological indicatives laid out in the opening verses of the letter and here. In both places there is reference to the revelation of God in Jesus' coming among us, as well as the bracing hope of change still to come (see 1:2–3).

Jesus came to claim a people—not to lord it over them, but in order to turn them into a society that exists for the astonishing purpose of doing good works for the benefit of all. The preacher could expand on what it looks like today to be delivered from "iniquity"—for example, delivered from cycles of greed and the abuse of power for personal gain. The sermon can imagine vividly what a society looks like where every mental and physical skill is bent on doing good for others. Such a sermon throws the significance of Christmas forward into the coming year, enlarges vision beyond the domestic and personal to the radically social and global. Such a celebration of the incarnation would ring true for the writer of Titus.

SALLY A. BROWN

# Luke 2:1-14

¹In those days a decree went out from Emperor Augustus that all the world should be registered. ²This was the first registration and was taken while Quirinius was governor of Syria. ³All went to their own towns to be registered. ⁴Joseph also went from the town of Nazareth in Galilee to Judea, to the city of David called Bethlehem, because he was descended from the house and family of David. ⁵He went to be registered with Mary, to whom he was engaged and who was expecting a child. ⁶While they were there, the time came for her to deliver her child. ⁷And she gave birth to her firstborn son and wrapped him in bands of cloth, and laid him in a manger, because there was no place for them in the inn.

## Theological Perspective

A travel-weary couple gives birth to a baby and lays him in a manger. That which is ordinary fills the room: sweat; blood; makeshift blankets and diapers; the raw, immediate joy that comes with new life. There is neither expectation of, nor need for, visitors. It is one of those stop-still moments when not even an angel could add anything more. But visitors do intrude, reporting unfathomable things. And so the story of the manger becomes something even more than beautifully ordinary.

We forget the strangeness of this story because it is so familiar. What can be said that is new? One preacher, desperate to draw his listeners freshly into the text, preached his Christmas Eve sermon from the perspective of a curious dog curled up in the corner of the stable. The sermon did not go over well, probably because people who come to church on Christmas Eve do not want to stand, confused, on the sidelines. They want, instead, to be caught up with the starry-eyed shepherds, privy to a miracle. "*Gloria! In excelsis deo!*" They hope to hum, even as they exit the sanctuary, blow out their candles, and head toward their next Christmas festivity.

Maybe preachers should capitalize on the nostalgic sentiments of their listeners. Surely, those who are "home for the holidays" (or wish they could be) should readily sympathize with the dislocation of

## Pastoral Perspective

A couple that was planning to adopt a child of another race was told by their social worker that they would become what is known as a "conspicuous family." This term was coined to prepare prospective parents to be the object of others' attention in public places. Intended to be helpful, the description is sometimes met with resistance because it highlights difference as an obstacle, instead of coaxing the culture to be more accepting.

Luke's account of Jesus' birth suggests that Mary and Joseph were *not* conspicuous when they went to Jerusalem to register for the census. The passage makes no note of anyone going out of the way to accommodate this young couple that was a long way from home, wearied by travel, and probably visibly preoccupied with the impending birth of their baby. Christmas pageant scripts sometimes embellish the plot by assigning curt lines to an officious innkeeper whose hotel is full, but the text presents that aspect of the story almost as an afterthought, including it as a way of explaining why this young mother placed her newborn son in a manger instead of the more traditional and comfortable cradle.

Church school pageant directors are also inclined to incorporate farm animals into the story, but there is no reference to them in the actual text. While a stable is often presumed, the location of the manger

8In that region there were shepherds living in the fields, keeping watch over their flock by night. 9Then an angel of the Lord stood before them, and the glory of the Lord shone around them, and they were terrified. 10But the angel said to them, "Do not be afraid; for see—I am bringing you good news of great joy for all the people: 11to you is born this day in the city of David a Savior, who is the Messiah, the Lord. 12This will be a sign for you: you will find a child wrapped in bands of cloth and lying in a manger." 13And suddenly there was with the angel a multitude of the heavenly host, praising God and saying,
14"Glory to God in the highest heaven,
    and on earth peace among those whom he favors!"

## Exegetical Perspective

This passage is the third announcement by an angel in Luke of a miraculous birth. This announcement evidences no explicit knowledge of the other two. The story has moved from the inner workings of the families of Mary and Elizabeth into the public arena. Luke begins to name emperors and governors and to configure the social order. There are echoes of the Magnificat (1:46–55) with its condemnation of the rich and blessings on the poor. And there are anticipations of Luke's constant theme of social and economic justice. Governing it all, however, is the sense of promise and divine blessing that it offers to the earth in the birth of Jesus. Modern readers have no trouble identifying the Roman characters in this passage, but we do have trouble figuring out the precise timing of Luke's account. Luke 1:5 dates the appearance of the angel Gabriel to Zechariah during the reign of King Herod the Great. Herod died in 4 BCE. The Caesar Augustus named in the passage is, of course, Octavius, who was born in 63 BCE and began his official rule in 27 BCE. He died in 14 CE and was succeeded by Tiberius, who is referenced in Luke 3:1. Quirinius, who is named here as "governor of Syria," is mentioned in a variety of Roman sources and by all accounts became governor of Syria in 6 CE when Archelaus, the son of Herod, was deposed. Thus, normal Roman dating of these careers cannot

## Homiletical Perspective

On Christmas Eve, the fulfillment of a long wait is realized, as "Come, Thou Long-Expected Jesus" gives way to "Joy to the World." At the beginning of Advent, the world aches for a Messiah; now those who walked in darkness see a great light, for a child is born (see Isa. 9:2–7). Christmas is not merely an anniversary celebration of Jesus' birth—that is, it is not just the marking of an event in history—but the active remembering of what God has already accomplished in Jesus Christ and the promise of the coming completion of God's reign. At Christmas we proclaim not only the birth of Jesus, but the birth of the new creation (see Rev. 21). Despite what the newspapers seem to say every day, the way has been made clear; the chasm between God and humanity has been bridged because of the birth of Christ, and God's reign of justice and peace has already begun.

The vivid narratives of Christmas help us remember this actively, as is seen in the Gospel lesson recommended for Christmas Eve. What a story! The divine breaks in once again, this time in the form of a whole host of angels. And once again the natural response is fear. This should come as no surprise by now—Zechariah and Mary reacted this way, too. The angels' words are always the same: do not be afraid. But perhaps the preacher would do well to recapture that sense of fear of the divine—not a cowering

# Luke 2:1-14

## Theological Perspective

the figures in the story. Mary, Joseph, Jesus, and the shepherds do not travel with the anticipation that they will arrive to a familiar, homemade Christmas. They are headed to that which is uncomfortable and utterly new. Mary and Joseph are moving further and further *away* from their homes as they make the journey to register. The Son has left his place at the side of the Father and gone into the "far country" in order to be with us ("Emmanuel"). And the shepherds are minding the business of their own familiar domain when they are compelled, by the Good News of the angels, to travel and seek.

Theologically speaking, the juxtaposition between the warm sentiments of the average Christmas Eve listener and the unsettling responsibilities undertaken by the figures in the story presents unique opportunities for the hearing of the Word. What spiritual insight might be given in this space in which listeners attuned to *returning home* are confronted with the *leaving home* of Mary, Joseph, Jesus, and the shepherds? Those who assume that being away from home at Christmas would be unsettling might be surprised that the dislocation of the figures in the story does not appear to destabilize them. Mary and Joseph make a home where there is no home; Jesus nestles in the manger and is nurtured in his parents' arms; the shepherds tell the story of the angels, gathered in the dim candlelight of the stable, as if they are with old friends.

There is something theologically correct about our nostalgic portrayals of the nativity: the happy family and guests huddled 'round the manger made of straw, a warm brown cow looking on, softly chewing. What is right about this is that there is a home—a home whose hearth is Jesus Christ himself. He is the center of Mary and Joseph's life, the song of the angels, the mission of the shepherds. Where the Christ child lays, the story tells us, is home. This child is born for "all the people." He is our Savior, our Messiah, the one in whom our unsettledness gives way to great joy and peace.

The tension between the ordinary and the extraordinary is another theme of this text that Christmas Eve listeners, in particular, might be prepared to examine. How is it that Mom's pumpkin pie—made straight from the recipe off the label on the canned pumpkin—tastes better than any other? What is extraordinary, as told by the story, is entirely ordinary. The Messiah who is the good news for the people is an ordinary baby, born to an ordinary mother, wearing ordinary diapers, lying in a crib that is so ordinary we are apt to take pity, remembering

## Pastoral Perspective

is unspecified. In fact, nothing in verses 1–7 suggests that Jesus' birth was noteworthy. Quietly Mary and Joseph go about their business as good citizens and expectant parents. When Jesus is delivered, no midwife is mentioned, nor does the passage name anyone else who was present in the unspecified setting where the manger was located. Despite the secluded location where Jesus was born, word of his arrival quickly gets out! Before the orange of dawn pales the sky, the new parents find themselves greeting strangers: shepherds who show up in grimy work clothes, summoned from the fields by angels who serenaded them with news of the triply superlative birth of an infant who was Savior, Messiah, and Lord, born in the city of David. Although the angel Gabriel had informed Mary that her child would be the Son of God, it is doubtful that a social worker had primed her and Joseph for the unprecedented attention they received on the night Jesus was born. At that moment, Mary, Joseph, and Jesus must have felt as if they were a conspicuous family. Persons who prefer anonymity will relate to this experience by observing that Mary and Joseph may have desired privacy in their first hours of parenthood.

Many pastors have heard ironic regret expressed by active church members who indicate that they will not be in attendance on Christmas Eve because the timing conflicts with their family gatherings. Among those whose circumstances are conducive to worshiping on Christmas Eve are childless adults who are not granted sufficient time off from work to journey to see relatives, or others whose financial situations prevent them from doing so, as well as elderly individuals who do not feel up to traveling. In other words, those whose sparse schedules and geographic isolation from their families facilitates their availability to worship on Christmas Eve may be individuals who do not receive an excess of adoration or attention. Like the shepherds who lived outside the mainstream of society, these devoted churchgoers may feel overlooked by the world. For that very reason, they just may be the ones who are most deeply touched by the angels' announcement and the shepherds' contagious amazement. According to the angel's song, the Messiah's birth conveys goodwill. No one is inconspicuous in the eyes of the savior. Therefore, in this case, the special attention is positive. Jesus' birth carries peace to those whom he favors. This pastoral word can compel households that once echoed with emptiness to resound with incomparable joy!

be squared with Luke's account. Unless there is something we do not know, Luke seems to be incorrect about Quirinius or Herod or both. In fact, the traditional dating of the birth of Jesus would locate it during the reigns of neither Herod the Great nor Quirinius.

The worldwide enrollment creates a second problem. Romans were, of course, fond of various registrations for tax purposes. Historians know of several large-scale enrollments that Augustus conducted during his reign, although none of them fits the description we have here. According to Josephus, when the Romans took over direct Roman rule of the territory of Archelaus, Augustus sent Quirinius to conduct a census. But this would have been in 6–7 CE. Furthermore, we know of no Roman enrollment of any kind that required people to return to their ancestral cities. From the perspective of the modern historian, such a requirement seems implausible. We must remember, of course, that Luke knows the norms of Roman rule better than does any modern historian. Nevertheless, we are uncertain how to resolve the precise history of Luke's account.

On the other hand, as a theological and literary piece, this passage is remarkably successful. It is no accident that this story is a longtime favorite of Christians. The story is told with a simplicity and clarity that intensify the wonders of Jesus' birth.

The naming of Caesar Augustus and Quirinius does more than provide a date; it creates the proper political and social context for Jesus' ministry. Throughout the Gospel, Luke articulates a tension between the manifest Roman political powers and the hidden and almost ironic rule of Jesus. Wondrous births and the public announcements of the "good news" of those births had become a standard part of the public myth of Roman rulers. The birth of Jesus and his coming rule is contrasted here with those Roman political myths. The simplicity of the story heightens the contrast. Nothing striking is attributed to either Mary or Joseph in the birth itself. Mary simply gives birth to her "firstborn." Due to the requirements of the registration, Jesus is born in the city of David and thereby acquires messianic credentials. However, the famous lament that "there was no place for them in the inn" shows that Jesus is not part of the political elite. He is placed in a manger, which suggests humble social status. On the other hand, a manger is not a baby bed; it is a feeding trough for animals. Luke may be evoking an image of God feeding the world in the quiet birth of this unlikely Messiah.

before some malevolent spirit, but an awe before that which (or Whom) is far beyond our comprehension or knowledge, greater than our fragile, flawed, and mortal selves.

The main human actors in this narrative are the shepherds, of course. They seem unlikely messengers, until we take note of Luke's reminders that Joseph is a descendant of the house of David—David, the quintessential shepherd-king. This newborn son of David is born the ultimate shepherd-king, and an unlikely Messiah. These shepherds are hardly the ones we would expect to be entrusted with such earth-changing news, and yet they are the ones who are led to his birthing place, the ones who leave rejoicing and telling the good news to everyone they meet.

Shepherds were held in low esteem in those days; they lived outside the boundaries of polite society, were assumed to lead shiftless lives, and would hardly be considered trustworthy sources for any news of import. And yet they are the first to hear, the first to see, the first to tell of Jesus' birth. Paul indicates that this is God's way, as he writes to Christians in Corinth:

> Consider your own call, brothers and sisters: not many of you were wise by human standards, not many were powerful, not many were of noble birth. But God chose what is foolish in the world to shame the wise; God chose what is weak in the world to shame the strong; God chose what is low and despised in the world, things that are not, to reduce to nothing things that are. (1 Cor. 1:26–28)

This theme is reflected over and over in the Lukan Christmas narrative: in the annunciation to Mary, in her Magnificat, in the mean circumstances of Jesus' birth, in the calling of the shepherds to see and tell. Reflecting on these words of Paul's from 1 Corinthians, Nora Gallagher writes, "What if those words are about something real? What if they are a hint about the kingdom? A hint about God? What if this religion I've been practicing and this Gospel . . . I've heard from the priest every Sunday, is not a metaphor but a description of reality?"[1] To ask this question is to take a deep look into the meaning of the birth of Christ, the possibility that gospel truth is found today in the lives and witness of people we would not see as strong or powerful. Preachers might do well to remind listeners of this element of the Christmas story in the midst of a culture that puts

[1]Nora Gallagher, *Things Seen and Unseen: A Year Lived in Faith* (New York: Alfred A. Knopf, 1998), 73.

# Luke 2:1-14

## Theological Perspective

that "there was no place for them in the inn." It makes no sense to us that the immutable God of the universe would enter into the bowels of our world in order to be with us. With the shepherds, we are terrified at what this might mean. And so we avoid the scandalous character of the incarnation by romanticizing the bedraggledness of the holy family and the shepherds, thereby isolating the extraordinary spectacle and message of the angels from the realities of our creaturely existence. In doing this, we inadvertently render the good news meaningless.

Resisting such inclinations and facing, head on, the scandalous character of Jesus' ordinary birth is to be awestricken by the reality of God's presence with us which in turn exposes the wondrous, sacramental character of the most banal dimensions of our day-to-day lives. After all, it is to the shepherds engaged in the very ordinary work of "watching over their flocks by night" that the extraordinary message is given. It is to us—ordinary people—that a son is born. He is finally born, on this very evening, to we who have been waiting for the Messiah to come and change the world. Contrary to our expectations, however, he does not seem to have come with the purpose of being a revolutionary. He is, as it turns out, just a baby. Surrounding the stable at Bethlehem, the forces of empire have orchestrated a census, will soon make plans to murder newborn sons, and will systematically crucify those who challenge conventional understandings of divine and human power. They, like us, are not expecting a threat to come from something so ordinary. Who suspects that this baby born today in the city of David will save us? That this baby born to Mary will bring us peace? That this baby's consistent, persistent, habitual *ordinary* obedience to God will have an extraordinary, revolutionary impact?

With the shepherds, we should tell what we know about this child. With those who hear, we should stand amazed. With Mary, we should treasure the extraordinary, ordinary things of Christmas, pondering them in our hearts.

CYNTHIA L. RIGBY

## Pastoral Perspective

For centuries, the country from which one's ancestors emigrated was emphasized and often influenced one's social station in the United States. In many communities, lineage still extends security to some residents, and erects hurdles that others struggle to overcome. Prejudice toward persons of particular ethnicities continues. At the same time, many ache to be associated with a people or in tune with a culture. Joseph's lineage was a critical factor in the events that unfolded. Because the governmental decree mandated that he return to his native city, he and his betrothed were far from home when their firstborn son entered the world. Like Mary and Joseph, many new parents today are also separated from their families of origin and experience the momentous occasion of birth without relatives there to provide support in person. And the nomadic tendency rarely ends at that juncture. Few children graduate from high school in the town indicated on their birth certificate. Joseph's return to his home-town affirms the importance of feeling connected to a place, as well as the inconvenience of it. A word of empathy arises for those who feel adrift or displaced from their roots.

The woe attached to a mobile society that scatters close relatives across the continent exists in tandem with a blessing. Unlikely acquaintances become intimately involved in one another's lives. Local churches frequently find themselves innately adept at facilitating these essential relationships, as they pray for and with one another and share meals together. Amid a populace that exhibits tentative hospitality toward atypical families, congregations celebrate the Lord's Supper, a sacrament that models what it means to be welcoming. The inclusive communion table invites and accepts persons of disparate backgrounds, illustrating the value of a broadened sense of family and making the church a "conspicuous family" in a world that is inclined to judge the stranger and exclude the other.

When their son was born, Mary and Joseph were away from their immediate families, yet shepherds with whom they may have thought they had little in common were present to share their immeasurable gladness. On Christmas Eve, some people have the privilege of spending time with their blood relatives, and all are embraced by the glorious news of peace and goodwill.

ASHLEY COOK CLEERE

## Exegetical Perspective

The hidden and understated tone of the birth story itself gives way to the drama of an angel announcing the birth to shepherds and a heavenly choir singing a response. Of course, the low social status of shepherds reinforces the sense of political and social irony. The angel does not announce the birth of the Messiah to the elite, or even in normal public space, but to shepherds in the field with their sheep. In keeping with the usual course of such angelic announcements, the shepherds are "terrified." The announcement of the unnamed angel focuses entirely on the messianic identity of Jesus. He is born in the city of David; he is a savior; he is the Messiah. Ironically, they will find this savior, this Messiah, in an animal manger.

The song of praise by the heavenly host is filled with translation and textual issues. Of the many versions of this song, the most likely one is "Glory to God in the highest, and on earth peace for people whom he favors." Thus, the point is not an exchange of goodwill among people, nor that only people of goodwill have peace, but that God "favors" all people and is offering them all "peace" in the birth of the Messiah. It is to this gracious God that "glory" is sung.

While the lectionary permits ending the reading at 2:14, to do so is to cut off the responses to the angelic announcement. Each response is offered as proper model for how to react to the hearing of the gospel. The heavenly choir offers the first response in their song of glory. One response is simply to praise God. The shepherds obey the angel and announce what they heard to other people who, in turn, are amazed. Finally, at the end of the story, the shepherds glorify and praise God "for all they had heard and seen." They not only praise God but announce the good news to others.

Mary offers a much quieter and more personal option. She "treasured all these words and pondered them in her heart." The good news also provokes private wonder in human hearts.

LEWIS R. DONELSON

## Homiletical Perspective

great stock in following the ways of the influential, the good-looking, and the wealthy.

What does it mean to proclaim that Christ was born in a barn? The preacher dares not romanticize this birth story. Finding the Messiah in such impoverished circumstances was as amazing then as it would be now. Would we believe it if we were led to a newborn Savior in a homeless shelter or a truck stop? But here it is, in Luke's story: the Savior of the world, the Word incarnate, takes on human flesh in the most ordinary way.

Those preachers who seek to lead worshipers to the eucharistic table on Christmas Eve might look to the manger itself. Luke mentions the manger three times, pointing to its significance.[2] That the shepherds greet God incarnate not only in a barn but in the animals' trough points us to the table—Luke does not show Jesus resting on a pile of quilts in the corner, but in the feeding place. This baby, resting in a manger on the night of his birth, will be "the bread of God . . . which comes down from heaven and gives life to the world," the very "bread of life" (John 6:33, 35). Each time the community gathers around the table, it remembers this mystery: that though it is beyond our comprehension, God took on human form, lived among us, suffered for us, died and was raised, that we might know true life, in this world and the next. How fitting, then, that the church celebrates the Lord's Supper on Christmas, remembering how God became one of us, remembering how Christ still joins us at the Table, remembering how we are fed by him in order that we might live as his body in the world. It is a mystery indeed that we celebrate on Christmas Eve, one that reaches beyond even what Luke can tell us. The birth of Jesus is an incomprehensible inbreaking of the holy, as is his presence with us at the Table, and each and every day—a mystery for which we can respond only with our thanks and praise.

KIMBERLY BRACKEN LONG

[2]Robert C. Tannehill, *Luke* (Nashville: Abingdon Press, 1996), 65.

# Isaiah 52:7-10

⁷How beautiful upon the mountains
   are the feet of the messenger who announces peace,
 who brings good news,
   who announces salvation,
   who says to Zion, "Your God reigns."
⁸Listen! Your sentinels lift up their voices,
   together they sing for joy;
 for in plain sight they see
   the return of the LORD to Zion.
⁹Break forth together into singing,
   you ruins of Jerusalem;
 for the LORD has comforted his people,
   he has redeemed Jerusalem.
¹⁰The LORD has bared his holy arm
   before the eyes of all the nations;
 and all the ends of the earth shall see
   the salvation of our God.

## Theological Perspective

Coming at the end of another long passage from Second Isaiah's proclamation of good news for Zion in exile (51:1–52:12), Isaiah 52:7–10 both describes the reason for that good news and signals its magnitude.

The reason is that after a long exile, God's sleeves are rolled up and God is taking action in the world. By his bared holy arm he has redeemed Jerusalem and established justice. For Second Isaiah, then, the historic events leading up to the return from exile ought to be interpreted within the context of divine activity. (For this reason, incidentally, we need not settle the question of whether Second Isaiah's regular use of the image of God's "arm" should be interpreted as synecdoche for the divine being or as metaphor for a human agent: synecdoche and metaphor theologically collapse into each other when historic events—including human actions— are interpreted as driven by divine action.)

The claim that God is working in and shaping world events is fraught with implication for how we think about God. On the one hand, it is cause for rejoicing: We are not left exposed to the whims of history, because history neither tells nor shapes itself. Nor are we left to the caprice of the powerful, because they control neither our destinies nor their own. On the other hand, such a claim compels us to

## Pastoral Perspective

There are multiple ways for the preacher to help the Christian community find itself in the Isaiah text as it worships on Christmas Day. First and foremost, the preacher will want the congregation to see itself as the glad recipient of a message described by the text as one of "peace," "good news," a message of "salvation," an announcement of the reign of God (v. 7).

The message is directed to "Zion" (v. 7), the text says, to the people of God, the community of faith. The Christmas Day congregation will likely be composed of the faithful, which means there is opportunity for the preacher, not only to focus substantively on the "good news," but to assume that the congregation is ready, willing, and wanting to "break forth together into singing" (v. 9).

The text is ambiguous as to the identity of the "messenger" (v. 7). At the first and on one level, the Christian community may identify the beautiful feet of the messenger with the angel in Luke's Christmas narrative, who startles the shepherds with the news of the Savior's birth. Both the preacher and the congregation will want to go deeper, however, and recognize and celebrate the babe of Bethlehem, the man from Nazareth, the Christ of the cross, the risen Lord, as being both the messenger and the message.

The text provides an opportunity to explore and celebrate the content of the "good news" as reflected

## Exegetical Perspective

For years the feet of the messengers have brought bad news to God's people: Assyria's coming invasion (2 Kgs. 18), Babylon's first visit (2 Kgs. 20), the message to Ezekiel that Jerusalem had fallen (Ezek. 33). After all of this bad news, there is no more dreaded sound than the arrival of the one who brings news of dead loved ones and of losses against stronger powers. In a world of bad news, good news can be hard to hear and believe. Second Isaiah's promise of restoration and hope certainly is eschatological, but within its ancient context these words were harder to believe than the bad news that the people had come to expect. Standing in the ruins, it is hard to envision a rebuilt city. Standing in the midst of death, it is hard to believe there will be a time of salvation and shalom.

Hope dies hard, as both testaments testify in story after story. But there comes a time when the promises of God seem like fanciful tales of a God unable to deliver, as they did to Abram (Gen. 15). Against the death of hope, the oracles of Second Isaiah proclaim a bold faith and unbelievable promises from God. Isaiah 52:7–10 calls on Jerusalem to sing the praises of the good news that the messenger is yet to deliver. The oracle calls for a complete reversal of the former life of despair.

## Homiletical Perspective

Although the messages we send through the Internet today are delivered in nanoseconds, we may still send them off into cyberspace by pressing an icon of a human figure in full stride. In spite of our advanced technology, we still imagine our messages being delivered by runners on foot. On this day when we celebrate God's incarnation in Christ, some attention to Isaiah's very concrete metaphors for the arrival of good news may usefully balance the Gospel of John's more mystical reading.

Isaiah begins his vision marveling at the beauty of the runner's feet—beautiful because of the glorious news the runner brings—but it might be helpful to expand for just a moment on the length of the run, the weariness of such a runner, and the rough terrain he must penetrate to carry his joyful message through. Think of a marathon runner whose goal is not just to finish but to carry critical news. Now we can feel the excitement of one who has come as fast as he can from a great distance, bringing the astonishing good news of the return of the Lord to Zion. The parallels with our Christmas celebration are clear, but in our day how many of us are in touch with the intense excitement that this snippet of Isaiah evokes? Imagine the runner's beating heart. Imagine his being so out of breath that he can barely pant out the news he carries. Imagine challenging

# Isaiah 52:7-10

## Theological Perspective

ask questions about the mysterious and dangerous ways this God works: the same God who delivers the exiles participated in carrying them off. Following theologically on First Isaiah's heels, Second Isaiah offers no vision of a beneficent (if removed) God who occasionally steps in to do good things. Instead, this God is powerful and intimately connected to all that happens—one who follows exiling with restoring. In such a theology, the incarnation would not be about God stepping into human history from the outside so much as God becoming flesh as a new way of acting in that history.

The claim is also fraught with implication in how we think about salvation. For Second Isaiah, God's activity in the midst of historic events means that the good news of salvation is neither a rapturous spiritual escape from the world (as if body and soul could be divided) nor a stoic mental escape from it (as if body and mind could be divided). The nature of the good news of salvation is that it does not demand that the exiles excise part of themselves to benefit from it. As Christians celebrate the incarnation of a Messiah today, it is wise to remember this: salvation is integrative, not divisive. That, in itself, ought to be a source of comfort and celebration.

How extraordinary is this good news? It is so good that the exiles rejoice even before it is achieved. They praise the very feet of the messenger who is bringing news to Zion that its citizens are on their way home; they break into singing when the sentinels send out word that the exiles can be seen in the distance; they are comforted even before they celebrate their reunions. The salvation they celebrate is so good that they need not feel its full impact to begin offering praise. Even the verb tenses in the passage play up the relationship between what has already happened, what is happening, and what has yet to happen, moving constantly between perfect tense ("has comforted," "has redeemed," "has bared"), present tense ("reigns," "see,") and future tense ("shall see," "will go before you").

This temporal tension sits at the theological heart of this passage. It sits at the heart of the Christian faith as well. In Advent, we waited for the God who came to us in the form of a manger-born baby, and we wait for God to come again. At Easter, we celebrate Jesus' resurrection, and await the second resurrection. Daily, we rejoice in creation, and, as Paul writes, we groan in labor pains for the new creation (Rom. 8:18ff.). Picking up on this tension, John Calvin wrote of this passage, "The Lord hath changed the mourning of the people into joy, and

## Pastoral Perspective

in the ministry of Jesus. Perhaps the focus should be on the announcement of "salvation," since that appears to be the emphasis of the text itself (vv. 7, 9, 10). While the Christmas Day sermon is probably not the place for a scholarly incursion into theology, the preacher can help the Christian community appreciate something of both the personal and corporate dimensions of salvation, as reflected in the Bible and in the ministry of Jesus. In this regard the preacher could benefit by consulting the chapter entitled "How Does Christ Save Us?" in Luke Timothy Johnson's *The Living Gospel*.[1]

Another aspect of the "good news" of the text that easily connects with the "messenger" Jesus is the announcement, "Your God reigns." That is, after all, similar to the announcement with which Jesus began his ministry (see Mark 1:15). The preacher should be able to help the congregation identify itself as belonging to "Zion," a community which is distinguished, among other things, by its trust that indeed "God reigns." The preacher might also call attention to what is both a pastoral and prophetic dimension of the message "Your God reigns." If indeed the message of the reign of God is trustworthy, it is liberating. For, if God reigns, then all manner of other would-be gods do not—imperial political claimants, terrorists, cancer cells, capitalism, public opinion, Wall Street, death, to name a few.

Once Jesus Christ is viewed as both the messenger and the message of "good news," there is opportunity to explore the incarnation. The focus for such an exploration could be verse 10 of the text: "The LORD has bared his holy arm before the eyes of all the nations; and all the ends of the earth shall see the salvation of our God." Herein lies a pastoral dimension of the text that should not be ignored. There are all kinds of notions floating around—even within "Zion"!—as to the nature and activity of the God who "reigns." Any pastor with eyes and ears open, who has listened to "God talk," or to hospitalized or grieving parishioners, will be aware of notions of God that are anything but Christlike. The preacher can help the congregation to reflect on what it means to say that "the LORD has bared his holy arm" in the person of Jesus. This is the basic Christian conviction (see John 1:18 and Col. 1:15). Perhaps nothing is more important pastorally than for the preacher to help the Christian community to Christianize its image of God, to begin and not to end its thinking about the nature of God with what

[1] Luke Timothy Johnson, *The Living Gospel* (London and New York: Continuum, 2004), 191–99.

*A Reversal of the Bad News.* In the ancient world, there were no CNN trucks and satellites to send news instantly from one end of the world to another. News came from runners who ran from one place to another, carrying the latest news. These messengers were seen by the sentinels of the city approaching the city long before they arrived. This gap in time led to speculation of the news the messengers were bringing. It was a time of anticipation and waiting, a time of knowing that news was coming, without knowing what the tidings would be (2 Sam. 18).

This period of waiting offers a connection to the previous season of Advent, for we are, even on Christmas morning, still a people of the now and the not yet. Christmas morning is not a period in the story of Christianity, but a semicolon. Often, it seems that Christmas Eve or Christmas Day is the culmination of something, and the church then goes into a holding pattern until Ash Wednesday or even Easter. This text from Isaiah reminds us that the best is yet to come. This baby will not remain docile and quiet in that manger. He will rise and grow, then preach, teach, heal, and show us the way to live lives in the kingdom. For the people of Jerusalem, the exile was not the end of the story. Good news was coming.

Christmas is also not the end of the story. More good news is coming. Christmas morning, even with all of its pageantry, has much in common with the message of Second Isaiah, for it calls on the people to rejoice before the actual culmination of God's kingdom on earth. Christmas celebrations are not an end in themselves, but an anticipatory celebration of Easter morning.

*Celebration in Anticipation of God's Marvelous Works.* The sentinels are to cry out in joy instead of alarm (v. 8). The ruins of the city are to join in the exuberant cries (v. 9). The fear and dread at the sight of the messengers should now be replaced, not with joyful anticipation, but with the celebration of good news already received. Indeed, the passage is full of words of God's mercy and love. The messenger will bring "good news," will announce "shalom" and "salvation," and declare "Your God reigns" (v. 7). The sentinels are to shout for joy because the Lord has returned to Zion (v. 8). The ruins also shout for God has "comforted his people" (the same verb that begins the joyful announcement of Second Isaiah, 40:1) and "has redeemed Jerusalem" (v. 9). In these bold declarations of the kingdom, the Isaiah passage is a parallel to the psalm for the day. Psalm 98 is an

our Christian community to carry the good news of God's gift to us with that kind of intensity, and that kind of exultation!

The image of the messenger gives way to the sentinels on the high walls of the city, singing for joy. They have been straining their eyes to catch sight of the runner, or of some other evidence of victory. And now they witness "in plain sight," according to Isaiah, "the return of the LORD to Zion" (v. 8). What might it mean that they "see" the Lord return? Is it the sight of the dust raised by the victorious army at a distance? Is it the feeling of elation they experience at the knowledge of their people's success, a feeling they identify as signifying God's presence? Is it important that their response is to break into song? Today church people might start singing the Doxology, or Handel's "Hallelujah Chorus." What might the sentinels have sung back then? The songs of Miriam or Moses or Hannah come to mind (Exod. 15, 1 Sam. 1).

The prophet turns now from the songs of the sentinels to address the very walls themselves, commanding "you ruins of Jerusalem" to break into song. This is a bold metaphor, calling on streets and buildings to sing (cf. the psalmist calling on the gates to lift up their heads, Ps. 24:9). In a whimsical mood, we might ask our gathered community what song the walls of our city might sing, or the walls of our church? Or what would it take to cause the streets to sing? A less whimsical direction might be to consider the ruins we see and read about in the news: the devastation of floods, earthquakes, and bombings. What could make those ruins sing? What message could come to those people in those places that would prompt their cities to celebrate the return of the Lord to Zion?

The last image in the passage is of the Lord "baring his holy arm." This literalized picture of the God of Israel as a warrior may startle us, and we may find ourselves resisting its very physicality. Did the prophet himself think of God as so very much like a human fighter? Since this is the same prophet who moments ago called on the buildings of Jerusalem to sing, it must be clear that he is comfortable in the world of metaphor. The literal depiction of the Lord as a warrior, however, may challenge us to think about how comfortable we are in that world.

On the one hand, certainly some who hear this reading will be able to say that in their own lives they have experienced rescue or victory by the hand of God that was so immediate and so palpable they have no problem imagining God as a warrior

# Isaiah 52:7-10

## Theological Perspective

out of captivity hath made them free. Yet some person will say that this has not yet happened. But in the promises of God, as in a mirror, we ought to behold those things which are not yet visible to our eyes, even though they appear to us to be contrary to reason."[1]

Most of us are academically and existentially familiar with living between what God has done and what God will do. But how peculiar to highlight that tension on Christmas Day! Weeks of Advent waiting end with this day; some type of celebration at the culmination of the last four-plus weeks would seemingly make more sense than to be told that our waiting is not over. Today is about a newborn, not a pregnancy.

Perhaps, though, this is a particularly appropriate text for Christmas Day, for it serves to remind us of two things. First, Christmas (and for that matter, all of our holidays) are not points of temporal conclusion but proleptic participants in a time when all things reach their consummation: to use Calvin's metaphor, the joys we feel here are reflections as in a mirror of what will be when God's promises are ultimately fulfilled. As magnificent as it is, the incarnate presence of God with us only hints at that time when we are present with God. Second, our response to living between "the already" and "the not yet" is neither quietism nor anxiety; instead, it is gratitude and praise. As we learn to see even the feet of the messenger as praiseworthy, we gain practice in praise for that day when the ends of the earth do see the salvation of our God and praise is all that is left to do.

MARK DOUGLAS

## Pastoral Perspective

is revealed in Christ. If God "has bared his holy arm" in the person of Jesus, what "good news" that is.

As recipients of the message, the congregation may see itself in turn as the "messenger" who "announces peace," "brings good news," "announces salvation," and says, "Your God reigns" (v. 7.) In its own secondary way, the Christian community is both the messenger and the message. It has a story to tell to its children and youth: Christian education. It has "good news" to share: evangelism—not just spoken testimony, but the community's embodiment of the message in its life and work, its care for its own and for those in the greater community. If "all the ends of the earth" are to "see the salvation of our God" (v.10), then the Christian community itself will need both to speak and to embody the message. It will have to do so without making itself the center of attention or of people's affection.

On Christmas Day the Christian community will want to join in the "joy" of the "sentinels" who "see the return of the LORD to Zion" (v. 8). Worshipers will want to "break forth together into singing" (v. 9). They will be celebratory, grateful, joyful. A spirit of praise and thanksgiving will be present in both sermon and liturgy. Many carols may be sung, and the preacher might ponder how the words of the carols reflect the message of the text. The preacher may find that many of the carols join the text in announcing peace, bringing good news, announcing salvation, and proclaiming the reign of God.

EUGENE C. BAY

---

[1]John Calvin, *Commentary on the Book of Isaiah*, trans. William Pringle, in *Calvin's Commentaries*, 22 vols. (Grand Rapids: Baker Book House, 1974), 8:102.

## Exegetical Perspective

enthronement psalm, declaring, "YHWH reigns." Both call for the people and nature to make a joyful noise to the Lord.

*Celebration beyond the Covenant People.* The Isaiah lectionary text ends with another theme of Second Isaiah: God's deeds are seen not only by the people of Israel, but by the whole world. Both texts use the symbol of God's arm ("right and holy arm" in Ps. 98 and "holy arm" in Isaiah) to represent God's power and might. Each text declares that God's might has been shown to the nations and the ends of the earth. The salvation of God has gone global. In a world where might is often equated with imperialism, both Isaiah and Psalm 98 declare that God's military power will be used to free, not to enslave. God's holy arm is held up so that the world can see "the salvation of our God." God's victory as told by the arriving messenger is news of justice and equity (Ps. 98:9). God's judgment is not bad news but the best news; for justice and equity for all will be the hallmarks of this kingdom. God's gift to the world will not be a war, but a baby who grows to preach, teach, and show us the way to shalom and salvation.

Isaiah 52:7–10 can be the proclamation for Christmas morning, for it reminds us that this is simply another day of praising God. It is not the culmination of celebrating, but a stop along the way. We are a people who live in anticipation of the fulfillment of the kingdom. We are a people called to join with the whole world in seeing the wonders of our God. We are a people called to live in expectation of the good news of God's salvation for the world.

BETH LANEEL TANNER

## Homiletical Perspective

fighting personally for them. Some people in recovery from life-threatening illness or addiction, for example, often use this kind of language without embarrassment. For these people, it probably makes no difference how literally one takes Isaiah's imagery; they are secure in the reality of their experience.

There may be others, however, who view this image of triumph with suspicion. They may ask whether the God of the victors and the God of the vanquished are one and the same, or whether this image of the warrior God is at the root of some forms of Christian tradition they find repugnant. And they may go on to challenge the metaphorical language in which the Christmas celebration is cast: the Word becoming flesh, the light of the world, the literal truth of Jesus as God's Son.

The readings from Isaiah and John set for this occasion, filled as they are with rich metaphor, can provide a springboard for some exploration of the poetic nature of the language of the Christian tradition. John's prologue is virtually unintelligible to someone who stands outside the community of faith—he presents his "messenger," John the Baptist, for example, without any identification, as if we already know who he must be. Although Isaiah's description is less abstract and sketchy than John's, it also has to assume that an insider can hear the story of God the warrior and translate that into a vision of messianic hope. On Christmas Day it would not be inappropriate to reflect on how we celebrate the truth of our faith through metaphor, story, and poetry, and how our peculiarly Christian language both enlivens a vision for our community and challenges us to find common language to share our experience of God with others.

LINDA LEE CLADER

# Psalm 98

¹O sing to the LORD a new song,
    for he has done marvelous things.
His right hand and his holy arm
    have gotten him victory.
²The LORD has made known his victory;
    he has revealed his vindication in the sight of the nations.
³He has remembered his steadfast love and faithfulness
    to the house of Israel.
All the ends of the earth have seen
    the victory of our God.

⁴Make a joyful noise to the LORD, all the earth;
    break forth into joyous song and sing praises.

## Theological Perspective

*Cantate Domino.* The liturgical Latin title of this psalm emphasizes that with this psalm we are in the context of glorious and robust worship, the description of which stretches all the metaphors nearly to breaking point. Worship: always and everywhere the appropriate response to God. Sing to the Lord! Of course, because God has come to us in, through, and as the baby whose birth is celebrated. But the injunction is not just for believers to join in worship. There is joyous theological imagination at work here. Envision the chorus and the orchestra, if you will: all the lands shout to the Lord; with uplifted voice there is rejoicing and singing; the harp accompanies the singing; trumpets (the only time this word is used in the Psalter) and horns add to the praise; the sea and its creatures join the chorus; the clapping rivers add a backbeat; finally, the hills ring out with joy. This is not quite the full ensemble of Psalm 150, but nevertheless, it is a mighty acclamation of praise to the Lord. It is a worthy response of the created order to the redemption now begun.

The cause of all this praise is the victory of God, who has done marvelous things. Three times in verses 1, 2, and 3 reference is made to the victory of the Lord. While the language carries military connotations, there is also the sense of vindication. God's mercy and faithfulness to Israel has

## Pastoral Perspective

Joy to the world, the Lord has come. The long-expected Jesus has arrived, and how we love to express our joy through song. Few of us tire of singing Christmas carols, which in the retelling of our faith story remind us that the Messiah's birth brings a new song, a new day. The writer of Psalm 98 provides that song this morning, commanding us to sing a new song to the Creator and Savior of our lives. Remembering God's faithfulness and steadfast love in the spoken lines of the psalmist's song this Christmas Day, "How can we keep from singing?"

Having been reminded of what God has done in the past through the words of this psalm, we also remember all our Christmases. For some, those warm memories of family members celebrating Jesus' birth feel like being wrapped in yards of swaddling cloths, enfolded in the loving arms of God. For others, the painful memories feel like being left on a cold, dark night having to fend for ourselves, even though we know God is with us. Yet this text does not leave us in the past, but reminds us presently that our human singing of praise is joined by the whole of nature praising God.

So where does that lead us? The world situation is indeed troubling, with violence abroad, violence in our own cities and homes, exiles away from home after the devastation of natural disasters, and the

$^5$Sing praises to the LORD with the lyre,
   with the lyre and the sound of melody.
$^6$With trumpets and the sound of the horn
   make a joyful noise before the King, the LORD.

$^7$Let the sea roar, and all that fills it;
   the world and those who live in it.
$^8$Let the floods clap their hands;
   let the hills sing together for joy
$^9$at the presence of the LORD, for he is coming
   to judge the earth.
 He will judge the world with righteousness,
   and the peoples with equity.

## Exegetical Perspective

The use of this hymn of praise for YHWH as a triumphant war god is most ironic for a celebration of the birth of the Prince of Peace. Or is its choice for Christmas Day a caution to recognize there are battles to be fought for the liberation of the people? On the one hand, as with Psalm 96, there are no historical allusions in the text that could date the psalm, and both psalms refer to YHWH as a king. On the other hand, while many argue for this psalm being a parallel to Psalm 96,[1] which was used on Christmas Eve, the preponderance of war language and imagery that runs throughout this psalm speaks to a different dimension and a different message.

There is the similarity in some phrases, such as YHWH's *'emûnâh,* translated "truth" in 96:13b and "faithfulness" in 98:3a, but in the former this relates to the other nations, while in this psalm it relates to YHWH's relationship to Israel. Similarly, the opening call to "sing a new song," though present in both psalms, speaks to radically different songs. In Psalm 96 it is a song about YHWH's glory and mighty works. Here it is a song of YHWH's war exploits and victories. Thus, the similarities in language are muted by a dissonance of messages and may be a caution to the reader not to be too

[1] A. A. Anderson, *The Book of Psalms: Psalms 73–150,* in *The New Century Bible Commentary* (Grand Rapids: Eerdmans, 1980), 680.

## Homiletical Perspective

From the dark of Christmas Eve to the light of Christmas Day, the Psalter finds us singing again. But this psalm is "brighter" and more concise than Psalm 96 of the night before, now bearing within it the glorious metallica of trumpet and horn along with the mellower strings of lyre. An orchestra has been brought out to join in performance of the new song. Here, however, there is one significant differ-ence: the catalyst for the song shifts immediately to "victory." What an unlikely (even unsavory) earthly note that sounds, not only at Christmas but also in the context of today's post-9/11 world, where the eye is daily assaulted with images of human and environmental devastation as the global "war on terror" continues unrelieved. The "little town of Bethlehem" does not lie in "dreamless sleep," nor do we see the longed-for peace of the ages.

The startling juxtaposition of military-type victory with the liturgy of Christmas Day presents a challenge for preachers. It is important to recall, however, that today our congregations will be of a very different composition than those of Christmas Eve. To acknowledge the reality of the Western church, Christmas morning does not traditionally draw the crowd of twice-a-year worshipers whom we celebrate but doubtless will not see again until Easter. The storied "Christmas worshiper" is really

# Psalm 98

## Theological Perspective

triumphed. So much is the victory of the Lord in the foreground, those over whom the victory has been won have slipped into the background to the full extent. They are not even mentioned. The Lord is on center stage, in public view of all the nations, even to the ends of the earth, as the hosts of creation sing their praises with joy. This is a mighty "Amen," creation's response to God's marvelous work, and a reminder that redemption is a bigger reality than individual and personal salvation. It may not be stretching things too far to suggest that the vista opens out to a cosmic horizon.

This psalm is a lection for Christmas Day. One wonders if any preacher would use this text for the sermon. The pressure to preach again from the familiar nativity passages is compelling. Yet there is salutary benefit to pause a while with the psalm for a day such as this. Two reasons can be offered.

First, the psalm places the victory of God into a global and universal context. The God of Psalm 98, in a manner similar to Psalm 96, is no tribal or localized deity. This God is Lord of all the earth. The claim of this victory of God is universal. Nothing is outside the sweep and significance of what God has won this day. In familiar Christian language, this is the claim of the lordship of God. God is Lord of all and over all things. There is no special pleading only for religious life. The lordship of God extends to include economic and political life, personal and public life, private and communal life.

In the context of Christmas Day, one wonders what such a claim of universality means for Christians living out the lordship of Jesus Christ amidst the spirit-numbing merchandizing and sentimentalizing of Christmas. Our little protests about putting Christ back into Christmas are only as good as the efforts we make to live through the season with a converted awareness of Christ's total claim upon us.

The second point gives content to the first point, namely, that the heart of the Christmas season is joyous worship focused on the new and wonderful thing that God has brought to pass. The future for all things has now unalterably changed, for God has moved, unilaterally and unconditionally, to reconcile the created order into communion with God. The powers of evil and death are now to be defeated once and for all, and persons broken in relationship with God and one another will be brought back into communion with God as the body of Christ. Perhaps part of the problem with the modern Western celebration of Christmas is that we have lost the

## Pastoral Perspective

threat of war always rattling a saber. Psalm 98 reminds us that the pastoral response includes reminding all God's children that God is coming to "judge the world with righteousness, and the people with equity." When God comes to set things right, change will be ahead for all of us. Depending on where we are situated, the offering of new life could present a threat or could be received as a gift. If we are overprivileged, what might our song be this year? We may want to keep singing "Silent Night, Holy Night." If we are underprivileged, we may be more in tune with Mary's Magnificat, singing of redemption and reversal of power that brings equity to all and balances the ledgers.

So, as Psalm 98 pushes us into the future, considering what our new song will be, one thing we know for sure is that we cannot stay the same when God comes afresh into our lives. The new life that God brings at Christmas and all the days of our lives promises to transform us, and through our faithful actions as cocreators with God, to bring justice and hope for the weary world.

Families work so hard through Advent to keep the traditional rituals the same. When our children were growing up, they wanted nothing to change from year to year: same nativities on the same tables, same food, same decorations, same music, same size tree, same stories, same grandparents visiting, and same Christmas Eve candlelight service. For a few years my husband and I were able to repeat the Christmas celebrations without much change. Then death broke into the warm glow of those candlelit years, taking both grandfathers in one year, causing us to sing the familiar carols that year with huge lumps in our throats and many tears. Sometimes we are forced to sing a new song whether we are ready or not. But the comfort we need is already present in God's Son, our Savior, who continues to be with us.

God's greatest gift to us, Jesus Christ, is the source of our joyful noise at Christmas. "How can we keep from singing?" When we hear the night sounds of frogs and crickets, the morning sounds of birds' songs, and the evening sound of dogs barking, the whole of creation is "making a joyful noise." All of nature praises God as the moon waxes and wanes, as the sun rises and drops below the horizon, as the stars twinkle and frost silvers the earth. Psalm 98 reminds us that praise is given to God not only by humanity, but by all of nature and all the creatures! "How can we keep from singing?"

When I was a young mother about twenty years ago, a good friend was diagnosed with cancer. Like

## Exegetical Perspective

quick to see these two psalms as two sides of the same coin.

Psalm 98 is divided into three sections. The first section, verses 1–3, is directed most probably to the male congregants assembled in the temple. The second section, verses 4–6, is addressed to the earth. The third section, verses 7–9, is directed to nature in terms of the sea, the floods, and the hills. While it was the custom for women to lead the nation in singing at times of war (Exod. 15:20; Judg. 11:34; and 1 Sam. 18:7), this worship in the temple, with the masculine plural verbs, seems to exclude the women from the ceremony. This could be in line with the tendency in Chronicles to diminish the roles of women in the retelling of the history of Judah, while at the same time increasing the centrality of the temple and of temple worship to the life of the nation.[2]

The reason to sing the new song to YHWH is given through the use of anthropomorphic imagery citing YHWH's right hand and holy arm. These bring YHWH victory, which causes YHWH to get others (nations) to recognize this victory. The importance of this victory is symbolized by the claim that its fame has spread to the "ends of the earth" (v. 3), a term associated with military expansion and destruction (Ps. 2:8 and 59:13). In essence the psalmist proclaims that what YHWH has done for Israel will be impressive to all other nations. Unlike Psalm 96, with its expectation that the other nations will come to worship YHWH, the emphasis in this psalm is that the other nations become aware of the military might of YHWH, as exemplified in the military accomplishments of ancient Israel. This hyperbolic claim makes dating such a psalm most difficult, since there is no sense of the extreme and impressive military might of the nations of Israel and Judah, except for the Omride dynasty, and this seems not to be in the purview of the psalmist. What is clear, however, is the need on the part of YHWH to be given recognition by these foreign nations.

The next section of the psalm concentrates on what is generally taken to be cultic concerns with the mention of musical instruments.[3] The instruments noted—lyre (v. 5), trumpets and horn (v. 6)—are used both in cultic ceremonies and in war situations. The shofar was used by sentinels on the walls to

## Homiletical Perspective

the "Christmas Eve candlelight visitor"; but in the bright light of Christmas morning, a generally much smaller and heartier congregation will return to hear the meat of the Gospel with a different attentiveness. And so it is our task to hold in rigorous tension the psalm's nuances of both triumph and grace.

Victory over our enemies, even for a faith community that might hold war to be justifiable, is hardly the theme that first leaps to mind in the glow of Christmas. And yet, here is the psalm—amid its shouts of joy, nevertheless tempering and toughening the message of Christmas for those with ears to hear (and the stomach to preach a strong text at the height of a celebration so often co-opted by the culture). In light of such variants as congregation, context, and culture, then, the preacher's primary concern should be where the psalm might provide doorways into the deeper meanings of Christmas.

First, it must be noted that no enemies are named or acknowledged in Psalm 98. At the outset, the language of victory (v. 1) is for the marvelous things God has accomplished. Perhaps it is why this victory is so liberally described with images of "all the earth" breaking into joyous song, with lyre and horn broadcasting joyful noise. The jubilant cacophony is joined once more by the sounds of a redeemed natural world: the sea again roars along with all its denizens, floods are clapping, and hills are singing. This victory does not seem to be an adversarial one, born of war or violence, but one born of an assurance that, remembering the good or ill of times past, the Lord "will judge the [whole] world with righteousness" and its peoples with the same fairness. Psalm 98 juxtaposed with Christmas implies that what God has done for God's own people will be done for all people. Extend that line of thinking, and we understand that because of this divine righteousness, all people have become "God's people." Victory indeed!

But joyous news, even so wildly joyous as to make the hills sing, is often not easy news to apply to the dailiness of life when the party quiets down. The reference to "new song" may actually be problematic at the birth of the Prince of Peace, since every occurrence of the reference in Scripture is situated in the context of a holy war[1]—a precarious allusion at the outset of the twenty-first century. A triumphalist

[2]Alice L. Laffey, "1 and 2 Chronicles," in *The Women's Bible Commentary*, ed. Carol A. Newsom and Sharon H. Ringe (Louisville, KY: Westminster John Knox, 1998), 117ff.
[3]Marvin E. Tate, *Word Biblical Commentary, Psalms 51–100* (Nashville: Thomas E. Nelson, 1990).

[1]The case is made, and the references (Pss. 33:3; 40:3; 96:1; 98:1; 144:9; 149:1; Isa. 42:10; Rev. 5:9; 14:3) enumerated, by Tremper Longman III in his article "Psalm 98: Divine Warrior Victory Song," *Journal of the Evangelical Theological Society* 27, no. 3 (September 1984): 267–74.

# Psalm 98

## Theological Perspective

plot. For some of us it is just too familiar; others simply have no idea what all the fuss is about, but it is good for a party anyway. Whatever the case, the Christmas story is cause for extravagant joy, because God has decisively entered into the fray, fighting for the right. That story must be taught once more, both to those who are overly familiar with it, and to those who have never heard it. And the medium for its telling, surely, is compelling, robust, and wide-ranging worship.

Psalm 98, as a Christmas Day psalm, tells us about the kind of worship we will be engaged in when we hear the story of the birth of Jesus with open ears and believing hearts. On Christmas Day, amid the exhaustion of getting and spending, come to the quiet for a few moments and listen: perhaps far off you might hear the angels singing. And as you tune into the meaning of the day, into the events commemorated, perhaps too something even more amazing might begin to be heard: the lands have lifted up their voices, and harps and trumpets and horns blow a song of praise from every corner of God's creation, while the seas and its creatures make their strange noise of praise, to the clapping of the rivers and the ringing of the hills. All this, because the Lord comes—to judge the world, but as an act of love and redemption.

*Cantate Domino:* sing to the Lord a new song, because the Lord has done wonderful things! Let glorious worship be our Christmas theme.

ANDREW PURVES

## Pastoral Perspective

us, she and her husband had three young children, who were counting on her presence and loving guidance as they grew up. But after all the treatment possibilities were exhausted without bringing healing, she began to face her mortality. Being a very gifted soprano, she brought much joy to all who heard her. Every Advent she and her husband would sing "O Holy Night" as their gift to us at our neighborhood Christmas party. When she realized she had only a short time to live, she said to me, "None of us knows the length of our days, so please find the song that makes your heart sing, and sing it!" God kept giving her songs in the darkness of cancer through her husband, her children, her mother, and her friends. And then one holy night when the stars were brightly shining, she went out of this life full of hope, singing a new song.

The paradox of our faith is brought clearly into the light of celebration this day as we celebrate Jesus' birth even as redemption and present reality meet. We are called to live in this place of paradox where both joy and suffering are real. We are called to remember that the place where we are today is sacred, not only because it is Christmas Day, but because it is the present that God is giving us. And when we take time to pay attention, every ordinary day can be just as holy as this one. The coming of Christ means that no matter where we find ourselves on our journey of faith, God is with us, redeeming, loving, and enfolding us with blessings.

TRISHA LYONS SENTERFITT

warn the people of oncoming military invasions (Ezek. 33). While the NRSV translates *harî'û* as "make a joyful noise" in verses 4 and 6, the term also means to shout and to make the sound to signal a military or war march. Given the references to YHWH's victories in verses 2 and 3, the second meaning of this verb seems more in line with the intention of the psalmist. In other words, the setting of this psalm is a liturgy practiced in the temple in Jerusalem when the nation was successful in wartime. The glory was given to YHWH and YHWH's arm. The celebration was intended to embolden the people, for they must use these instruments to keep the people committed to the military agenda. Just as Psalm 24 is a liturgy for returning the ark to the temple after victory in battle and Psalm 118 is a liturgy for thanksgiving in the midst of wartime, Psalm 96 is a liturgy praising YHWH for victory and encouraging the nation to remain "on the battlefield."

The final section of Psalm 98 invites all nature to join in the celebrations of the first two sections of the psalm. The psalm then concludes with the claim of YHWH being the universal judge.

How do these lessons converge? While the epistle lesson focuses on Jesus as the sinless messenger and the Gospel lesson stresses the creation mythology of John and connects Jesus to precreation, the Hebrew Bible lesson and psalm speak to militaristic struggles for the nation in which YHWH will be victorious, with national integrity both established and acknowledged by other nations. In such a collection of readings, one sees the mixed and varied understanding of the promise of Christmas. What is most interesting is that the Jesus story takes place under Roman oppression, colonization, and imperialism, but the New Testament readings do not address resistance to Roman imperialism, while the Hebrew Bible passages for the day are the ones that hold forth resistance to these forces.

So how do *we* celebrate Christmas as we live in the midst of empire?

RANDALL C. BAILEY

identification with victors in holy war would not only violate the spirit of the season but would be misdirected, since the psalm celebrates not human victory but YHWH's triumph over death-dealing forces. We who preach should be careful to locate that triumph in the proper hands and to note that, even now, what we are seeing is God's first volley in the battle with death itself!

The bottom line is this extravagant jubilation and praise, whose grounds are the "marvelous things" God has done and whose motivation is God's surprising judgment, upending our expectations by its righteousness even in spite of Israel's (and our) recurrent unfaithfulness (v. 3). On the festival of Christmas, a simple translation of the psalmist's insight would be that we have received not what we deserved but a justice beyond our wildest imaginations! With this in mind, the preacher might reflect upon the gift we pined for as children at a time when we knew, deep down, that our behavior had not earned any gift at all. The joy of finding it under the tree hints at the psalmist's tone in responding to such longed-for gifts at a cosmic level.

Finally, as Old Testament scholar Ellen F. Davis points out, we are reminded once more of the great web in which we live. The psalm comes to us "not as a matter for local or private celebration by the righteous and, correspondingly, dread for the wicked, but rather as the occasion of cosmic jubilation."[2] It is a voice impatiently eager for the full revealing of God's will, not least for human life, but for all things. By way of the psalm's own eloquence, our hearts have been inescapably drawn again into the old, new song that proclaims on this day, "Joy to the world! The Lord is come. . . . Let heav'n and nature sing!"

GAIL A. RICCIUTI

[2]Ellen F. Davis, "Psalm 98: Rejoicing in Judgment," *Interpretation* 46, no. 2 (April 1992): 171.

# Hebrews 1:1-4 (5-12)

[1]Long ago God spoke to our ancestors in many and various ways by the prophets, [2]but in these last days he has spoken to us by a Son, whom he appointed heir of all things, through whom he also created the worlds. [3]He is the reflection of God's glory and the exact imprint of God's very being, and he sustains all things by his powerful word. When he had made purification for sins, he sat down at the right hand of the Majesty on high, [4]having become as much superior to angels as the name he has inherited is more excellent than theirs.

[5]For to which of the angels did God ever say,
"You are my Son;
today I have begotten you"?
[6]Or again,
"I will be his Father,
and he will be my Son"?
And again, when he brings the firstborn into the world, he says,
"Let all God's angels worship him."
[7]Of the angels he says,

## Theological Perspective

When I was a college student, I sensed a calling to ministry, specifically to teaching, and more focally, to teaching theology. A friend suggested that theology had already been done. He had a notion that orthodox believers all subscribed to a fixed, unchanging set of standards. Hebrews is a book of extensive theological reflection. But, contrary to my friend's perception, the author of Hebrews eloquently composes a poetic narrative that, as Thomas Long points out, displays "the cadence, the alliteration, and the keen awareness of the musical flow of beautifully spoken language that signal a carefully and poetically crafted oral event."[1] The passage is a theological word-event. It is a perfect text for Christmas when "story," not brittle affirmations, is pertinent, and song, not sermon, becomes the medium for the message.

At the same time Hebrews is not just acoustical. It contains profound and developed theological insights. One can dissect the text with respect to its attention to the author of the message and the messengers who deliver it.

*The Author of the Message.* God, according to Christian faith, is both creator and redeemer. In creation God brought all that is into being, and in

[1]Thomas G. Long, *Hebrews*, Interpretation Series (Louisville, KY: John Knox Press, 1997), 4.

## Pastoral Perspective

Day has dawned. The luminous brilliance of the angels and the "glory of the Lord" that overwhelmed the shepherds on that dark night two millennia ago have faded.

Just as the shepherds were undoubtedly groggy from their nocturnal sojourn, it is easy to feel a bit let down on Christmas Day. Family gatherings may not have gone as smoothly as expected. Heightened anticipation has given way to trash bags filled with wrapping paper and ribbons. Those who live in poverty, fear, or despair have not escaped their harsh reality.

How can pastors and worship leaders help Christians rise above the malaise of this holy day amidst an all-too-secular culture? Today's passage from Hebrews is helpful because it offers a rich perspective on God's interaction with human beings, plumbing the depths of the incarnation as that miracle intersects our daily lives.

It is not by coincidence that all four lectionary readings for the day are, or include, songs. Members of our congregations deserve to be engaged with their heads and their hearts each time they worship. Good sermons challenge listeners to think, but the arts are often more effective in evoking feelings. God is encountered in many ways, and the importance of beautiful liturgy, music, visual arts, and drama should never be underestimated.

"He makes his angels winds,
    and his servants flames of fire."
⁸But of the Son he says,
"Your throne, O God, is forever and ever,
    and the righteous scepter is the scepter of your kingdom.
⁹You have loved righteousness and hated wickedness;
    therefore God, your God, has anointed you
    with the oil of gladness beyond your companions."
¹⁰And,
"In the beginning, Lord, you founded the earth,
    and the heavens are the work of your hands;
¹¹they will perish, but you remain;
    they will all wear out like clothing;
¹²like a cloak you will roll them up,
    and like clothing they will be changed.
But you are the same,
    and your years will never end."

## Exegetical Perspective

The New Testament lections for Christmas Day focus not on the birth of the human baby Jesus but, rather, on the preexistent Christ through whom all things were birthed. The texts invite the preacher to reflect on the true identity of the Savior whose advent we celebrate—an identity so glorious that it defies the humble circumstances of his earthly origin.

The purpose of Hebrews 1:1–12 (along with vv. 13–14, which conclude the section) is to elicit a sense of awe at the exalted status of the Christ and to confirm his superiority over all contenders for human praise. The author achieves these aims through the use of two contrastive arguments, couched in elegant prose. First, the author contrasts God's speaking through the prophets with God's definitive self-revelation through the Son. The prophets served as instruments of divine speech, but the Son served as cocreator of God when the foundations of the world were laid and now upholds the creation "by his powerful word" (v. 3). Second, the author contrasts Christ's identity as perfect mediator with the lesser identity of the angels. Some Jews of the era viewed angels as heavenly priests and mediators between God and humanity; the author of Hebrews insists that it is *Christ* who has mediated, by making purification for sins. Angels are but *servants* of those for whom Christ has secured salvation (v. 14).

## Homiletical Perspective

This text, with its highly developed Christology expressed in a style both poetic and majestic, could not be more fitting for Christmas Day. Elegant language is put in service of the gospel in verses 1–4, while verses 5–13 skillfully weave a series of Old Testament citations, mainly from Psalms, to argue the superiority of Christ to the angels—those shimmering figures whose presence awes us at Christmas.

Yet the fine craft of the text can be a problem for preachers: how do they get their arms around a text like this? From its sweeping vision of revelation from ancient times to the present, to its sophisticated splicing of Wisdom philosophy with Royal Son theology from the Psalms, the text's sheer theological "size" is daunting. The danger, of course, is that a preacher can emerge after hours alone with this text in the study so dazed and dazzled that she cannot quite negotiate the journey from study to pulpit and make her experience accessible in any way to the congregation on Christmas Day.

One of several good ways to bring this text to proclamation is to focus on the announcement in the first two verses of God as the One who speaks. Crucially, God's speaking, culminating in incarnation, is thoroughly embodied and historical—and remains so today, as the living Christ continues to

# Hebrews 1:1-4 (5-12)

## Theological Perspective

redemption God has provided for human renewal. And how has God accomplished these twin acts? Both the OT and NT emphasize that although God is a potter who molds the clay, God is more than the fashioner or architect of the worlds. More centrally, God's actions are often "speech-events," his words causing events to occur and orbs to come into being. In creation "God said . . ." (Gen. 1). In redemption "the Word" (John 1) came in the flesh. God's doings result from the pronouncements of God's voice. Word/words become the media.

The eternal God often acts alone; but God also speaks through fine media. Hebrews begins with this affirmation. Both "long ago" (v. 1a) and "in these last days" (v. 2a), from creation to redemption, God has spoken through human voices: earlier, "in many and various ways by the prophets" (v. 1b); now, at Christmas, "by a Son" (v. 2).

*The Messengers.* Isaiah, Jeremiah, Amos, Micah, and others pointed to the coming of One who would embody and fulfill the hopes of the covenant people of God. At Christmas believers celebrate the coming of another prophetic voice and wisdom teacher. But the coming of the Son is not merely another speech-event of God. The Son's appearance is an embodiment of both God's message of redemption and the messenger. Not only by the Son's words, but in his very being, do Christians claim to "hear" God and also "see" God. They both listen to God and watch God in the "imprint" (v. 3) of God's being, the Son. In both his words and his acts God "speaks." The marvel of this miracle exacts an effusion of eight distinct claims about this messenger (vv. 2–4). Like a stunning display of fireworks, the author creates a collage of claims about the Son. He is heir, creator, reflection, exact imprint, sustainer, purifier, superior, and most excellent. Each of these images is a picture in itself and evocative of theological reflection.

First, Hebrews announces that the Son is both the creator ("through whom he also created the worlds," v. 2) and the heir of creation ("heir of all things," v. 2). These claims suggest a highly developed Christology and a nascent Trinitarian understanding of God. The Son is present at the beginning and at the end, as the Alpha and Omega. As incarnate Son, he splits history into "before" and "after." Christmas Day therefore takes on cosmic and redemptive significance.

Second, the Son is like God's own self as a "reflection" (as in a mirror, perhaps) and as an "exact

## Pastoral Perspective

The book of Hebrews is an eloquently crafted sermon rather than an epistle. We do not know the identity of the preacher, but we are given several clues about the congregation. Attendance is down at congregational gatherings (10:25), and many are desperately in need of being reenergized (12:12). They are struggling to hold on to their faith. Contemporary preacher and author Tom Long writes,

> Hebrews, like all good sermons, is a dialogical event in a monological format. The Preacher does not hurl information and arguments at the readers as if they were targets. Rather, Hebrews is written to create a conversation, to evoke participation, to prod the faithful memories of the readers. Beginning with the first sentence, "us" and "we" language abounds. Also, the Preacher employs rhetorical questions to awaken the voice of the listener . . . and keeps making explicit verbal contact with the listeners to remind them that they are not only supposed to be listening to this sermon, they are also expected, by their active hearing, to be a part of creating it.[1]

In the Greek, the first four verses of Hebrews are filled with rich alliteration, imagery, and poetic cadences. In trying to articulate the wonder of the incarnation, the preacher either incorporates an early christological hymn or takes prose to new lyrical heights. The ecstasy of the Christmas message explodes beyond the intellect as it touches the center of the soul.

From the Bible's earliest verses (Gen. 1:2), God speaks creation into existence. In that act of communication, God is revealed as involved, caring, and relational. The Creator remained engaged "in many and various ways" with people throughout Old Testament times. The transcendent God who is "wholly other" chose to come close to Abraham as a flaming pot, to Moses through a burning bush, to Elijah as a still, small voice. The God whose majesty exceeds all imagination chose to interact with humanity through the prophets, who spoke on God's behalf. God continued to speak, awaiting our response. And when the time was right, God spoke to us through a Son, born of Mary in a Bethlehem stable. The Word became flesh. While there is an emphasis in this passage on the continuity of the divine purpose in God's plan of salvation, there is also a great contrast. God's act of speaking through Christ is superior to all previous speaking. God's Son is preexistent; through Jesus, God created the

---

[1]Thomas G. Long, *Hebrews*, Interpretation Series (Louisville, KY: John Knox Press, 1997), 6.

## Exegetical Perspective

The claims made for Christ in verses 2–4 are remarkable. In naming Christ as "heir of all things," the author continues the tradition of reading God's promises that the Hebrews will inherit the land (Deut. 12:9 and 19:10) as metaphorical for inheritance of still greater realities: the kingdom of God, for example (James 2:5), or eternal life (Matt. 19:29; Mark 10:17; Titus 3:7). Christ is the ultimate heir of all such promises, and the faithful will share in his inheritance (Heb. 1:2, 14). In naming Christ as the agent through whom God created and sustains the world (vv. 2–3), the author claims for Christ the roles assigned to divine wisdom by other Jews of that era (all tracing back to Prov. 8:30). The language in verse 3 about Christ as "the reflection of God's glory and the exact imprint of God's very being" likewise recalls contemporary assertions about wisdom (see esp. Wis. 7:26–27). Finally, in asserting that Christ "made purification for sins" and then sat down "at the right hand of the Majesty on high" (v. 3), the author anticipates the epistle's later argument that Christ as high priest has offered the definitive sacrifice of himself at the *heavenly* altar (7:26–27; 9:11–14).

The author's vocabulary and phrasing in verses 1–4 would have been highly resonant for many first-century Jews, because the language evoked contemporary discourse about wisdom and other divine attributes, including God's glory, power, word, and name (all mentioned in vv. 3–4). These attributes were sometimes described in personified terms, almost as if the attributes were themselves angelic beings. Philo of Alexandria, for example, sometimes wrote about the *logos,* or word of God in ways that sound nearly as though he conceived of it as a second deity or an angel. Against this backdrop, the author of Hebrews insists that it is Christ who encompasses all such divine attributes or realities. The preacher might draw an analogy to how some great hymn writers have taken popular folk songs and transformed them by making Christ their subject: so also the author of this epistle has taken language conventionally used to describe quasi-angelic beings and refashioned it to describe and honor Christ (cf. John 1:1–14; Col. 1:15–20).

As one who comprehends all divine wisdom, glory, and so on, Christ is *superior to the angels* (Heb. 1:4). Here the author likely had in view Jewish tales from the era that describe the jealousy of some angels because of God's high regard for humans. According to rabbinic legend, angels were envious because God gave Torah to Israel instead of to them.

## Homiletical Perspective

speak through those who in flesh and blood continue to testify to God's purposes. Many possibilities suggest themselves: the bond of reciprocity established between one who speaks and one who hears; the will to be known that speech implies; the specific nature of what God has spoken.

A second sermon, challenging but important, could address the challenge of religious diversity. The text by implication brings up the subject of the relationship between Jews and Christians with its handling of themes of continuity and discontinuity in the mode of God's self-disclosure in ancient times and in "these last days." Many Christians, especially those living in diverse communities, with children in class side by side with children of other faiths, experience tension at this time of year. The text does not hint in the least that the God who spoke in the prophets is different from or inferior to the God we have heard in Jesus; so the preacher will want to avoid opposing the portraits of God in Old Testament and New, or acting as if God never spoke until Jesus appeared. God has made Godself known in many times, in many ways—and yet we indeed celebrate as Christians the distinctive and full self-disclosure of God that we have experienced through Jesus Christ.

Another sermon might amplify the text's description of Christ as creator, sustainer, and heir of creation. It can be refreshing for faith on Christmas Day to step back from our close focus on the details of adoring mother and babe in the manger to appreciate that the Incarnate One becomes one with what is his own. The risk in such a sermon will be that its language will remain so loftily theological and conceptual that it never touches ground. In keeping with the text's lyricism, poetics rather than the language of deduction may be more suited to the preacher's purpose in such a sermon.

In C. S. Lewis's children's book *The Last Battle,* the stable at Bethlehem strangely proves to be larger on the inside than the outside. At the last, a whole parade of beings, all creation in fact, flows to the one in the manger. One can imagine Christ intimately involved with the stuff of creation, exerting the energies that hold its conflicting forces together, and embracing every created thing with joy when all has been made whole.

Christmas is a season populated with angels. The subject of angels may seem to intrude oddly into the text halfway through verse 4, but it is helpful to remember that angels play a vital role in Old Testament revelation. They herald unusual births

# Hebrews 1:1-4 (5-12)

## Theological Perspective

imprint" (v. 3). Theologians have taken these assertions in two ways. The Son, a template of God's essence, is also a reflection of the purposes and actions of God. Perhaps the most "Christian" claim of theology is that believers see, know, and seek to do God's will by seeing, knowing, and following the Son. "Whoever has seen me has seen the Father" (John 14:9).

Third, the Son "made purification for our sins" (v. 3). Hebrews is replete with understanding the death of the Son as an atoning sacrifice for sins. Thus the Son becomes savior. The birth of the Son marks the beginning of our rebirth. The image of baptism may magnify the point: "We have been buried with him by baptism into death, so that, just as Christ was raised from the dead by the glory of the Father, so we too might walk in newness of life" (Rom. 6:4).

The fourth claim of Hebrews is of the Son's superior excellence to the angels (v. 4). Philo and other first-century Jewish writers emphasized the role of angels as "special agents" of God. That the Son is not an angel and is, in fact, exalted and more excellent than angels, may be the writer's critique of a low Christology among the recipients. The Son is the central Word of God, the climax of redemption, and the One-Above-All-Others; but unlike Marcion, Hebrews does not sever Christianity from Judaism or the Son from the prophets. While discontinuities and differences develop, connections with the OT are not obliterated. "Jesus does not void the previous promises of God; it fuses, clarifies, and fulfills them; it brings them 'to perfection.'"[2]

Hebrews puts the Son, the Christ, centrally into Christmas Day with these lyrical affirmations. Yet, the Exalted One comes on this day as one of us, affirming the abiding value of the created order and human life. By our births and rebirths we are grateful creatures of God and God's "reflection."

DONALD W. MUSSER

## Pastoral Perspective

universe. The incarnation is God's ultimate self-revelation; in Christ we see the "exact imprint of God's very being."

Because God's self-revelation came through a person, Christmas worshipers know that God is personal. In Christ, we have living proof of how far God will go to create an intimate, fulfilling relationship with each one of us. God loves us unconditionally, cares for and about us, and wants what is best for us. Through Jesus Christ, the faithful, regardless of the situation in which they find themselves, are sustained.

Yet Christ is also Lord, seated on God's right hand. Verses 5–12 contain six scriptural affirmations (most are from royal psalms) of Christ's exalted status. We live in a culture that tends to reduce the God of glory to a deity we can manage. Instead of worrying whether they are on the side of God, too many contemporary leaders imply that God is on their side. Instead of revering Jesus Christ, the Word made flesh is reduced to the level of a casual friend. Popular television series reduce angels—God's messengers—to personal helpers. But here we are reminded of the uniqueness and superiority of Christ. Jesus Christ is majestic and everlasting, the still point in our turning world.

Our only valid response must be reverence, awe, and worship. God is more powerful than any other force in the universe. In the person of Jesus Christ, the magnitude of that power is revealed. The miracle stories of Jesus demonstrate his power over the forces of nature, illness, sin, and death. The miracle of Christ's birth heralds a power greater than all God's angels combined. No matter how great our challenges, Christ has the power to redeem them. As our worship takes us beyond the physical manifestations of Christmas, we are apprehended by the mystery and wonder of the incarnation.

Albert Einstein once said, "The most beautiful emotion we can experience is the mysterious. . . . (S)he to whom this emotion is a stranger, who can no longer wonder and stand rapt in awe, is as good as dead."[2]

Worship leaders have a rich opportunity to build a Christmas service that witnesses to the glory of Christ through sermon, liturgy, and the arts. Hearts can be touched and souls can soar as the mystery of the incarnation is experienced and voices are raised in praise.

CATHY F. YOUNG

[2]Albert Einstein, "The Merging of Spirit and Science" (www.spaceandmotion.com/Albert-Einstein-Quotes) {Albert Einstein Quotes on Religion}.

[2]Ibid., 14.

## Exegetical Perspective

Another Jewish legend (transmitted by Christians) tells that Satan rebelled at the dawn of creation, when God commanded all the angels to worship Adam. Part of Satan's complaint in this account is that he should not have to worship one created *after* him.[1] By naming Jesus as *firstborn* and exalted to *God's right hand* (a place that Satan occupies in Zech. 3:1), the author of Hebrews preempts all arguments that any such figure can possibly compete with Christ for glory and honor. No angel can contend with Christ for praise, for there is no one like him in heaven or on earth. To reinforce the point, in verses 5–14 the author adduces a string of supporting OT quotations (from Ps. 2:7; 2 Sam. 7:14; Deut. 32:43; Ps. 104:4; Ps. 45:6–7; Ps. 102:25–27; Ps. 110:1). These argue for the Son's superiority to the angels (who are commanded to worship the "firstborn," v. 6), and address the Son directly as Lord and creator (vv. 10–12).

On Christmas Day we celebrate the astonishing news that, in the person of Jesus Christ, we come to know this exalted being as one who lives among us—who becomes, indeed, *one of us*. The Son through whom God created the world was born as a human baby, thus entering into the fragile fellowship of creatures who suffer and die. Indeed, because he shared our lot and suffered as all humans suffer, Jesus is able to sympathize with us in our weakness (Heb. 4:15). The birth narratives of Matthew and Luke help us to see Jesus' humanity and humility: he was born under the most modest of circumstances, a babe wrapped in swaddling clothes. The author of Hebrews helps us to see the Christ also in his breathtaking majesty: he is the one who is above all, and through whom all things exist.

SUSAN R. GARRETT

## Homiletical Perspective

(notably the births of Isaac and Samson) and issue messages. A heavenly being wakens Elijah not once but twice, as he lies exhausted in the wilderness on the way to Mt. Horeb, in flight from the wrathful Jezebel (1 Kgs. 19:5, 7). Yet angels in the Bible are not portrayed as the romantics, personal bodyguards, or playful tricksters of the popular media, but are obedient messengers of God.

Given our culture's fascination with the notion of angels, it would not be amiss to take up this text's comparison of Jesus to the angels. A successful sermon that takes this tack would steer carefully between killjoy lecturing on everything angels are not, on the one hand, and a romp into speculative angelology, on the other. A few scholars conjecture that, in fact, ancient philosophical speculation about heavenly beings is precisely one of the matters that concerns the Hebrews writer. The point, ultimately, is that these divine servants have work to do that concerns us; yet, although they may be able to warn or occasionally protect us, they cannot make whole the human-divine relationship. Christ's finished work of redemption and reconciliation is the help we finally need that no angel can ever grant us. Jesus comes to us in flesh and blood, "to share our human nature, to live and die as one of us," as the liturgy says.

The lyricism of the text should influence the sermon, whatever its content. In English, only the old King James Version, which declares its subject, "God," and then chants its claims in a series of rhythmic phrases, and the New Jerusalem translation, less robust and yet attentive to strophe and parallelism in its phrasing, capture any of the lyricism of the original. The preacher can reclaim the lyricism of this text by being attentive to parallel sentence structures and well-shaped language, making certain that a sense of majestic song infuses the worship that surrounds the Christmas proclamation.

SALLY A. BROWN

---

[1] See the discussion of ancient Jewish and Christian traditions about the angels' envy (including discussion on Heb. 1–2) in Gary A. Anderson, *The Genesis of Perfection: Adam and Eve in Jewish and Christian Imagination* (Louisville, KY: Westminster John Knox Press, 2001), 21–41.

# John 1:1-14

¹In the beginning was the Word, and the Word was with God, and the Word was God. ²He was in the beginning with God. ³All things came into being through him, and without him not one thing came into being. What has come into being ⁴in him was life, and the life was the light of all people. ⁵The light shines in the darkness, and the darkness did not overcome it.

⁶There was a man sent from God, whose name was John. ⁷He came as a witness to testify to the light, so that all might believe through him. ⁸He himself was not the light, but he came to testify to the light. ⁹The true light, which enlightens everyone, was coming into the world.

¹⁰He was in the world, and the world came into being through him; yet the world did not know him. ¹¹He came to what was his own, and his own people did not accept him. ¹²But to all who received him, who believed in his name, he gave power to become children of God, ¹³who were born, not of blood or of the will of the flesh or of the will of man, but of God.

¹⁴And the Word became flesh and lived among us, and we have seen his glory, the glory as of a father's only son, full of grace and truth.

## Theological Perspective

Our waiting is over. The Messiah has come. The one who has been prophesied, this long-expected child of Mary, is born. He is our life; he is our light. From this point forward, we expect, everything will be different.

John understands the event celebrated on this day to be about beginnings. This particular figure, Jesus of Nazareth, has been related from the start to the life of all things and all people. John the Baptist's testimony and Jesus' radical claims are historical occurrences that need be reported and processed. But knowing the facts as they are evident in time and space is not enough. John's concern is that the world does not know Jesus for who he actually is, that we have not yet received him as the Creator who made us and claims us as his own. Working to convey how radically related Jesus is to life itself, John dramatically identifies him with the organizing principle of the cosmos—the divine Logos. From "in the beginning *God*" to "in the beginning was the *Word*" to "And the Word became *flesh* and lived among us" in the person of Jesus of Nazareth.

The association of "Word" with "God" is, conceptually, not too much of a stretch. We are hooked by the elegant joining of a respectable philosophical idea with our deepest-held spiritual convictions. The linking of "Word" to the flesh of

## Pastoral Perspective

The service on Christmas Day holds the potential to be anticlimactic. The big event was the previous night, when four weeks of Advent waiting culminated for many with lessons and carols in a candlelit sanctuary made cozy by the presence of grandchildren and other guests. Those who worship on Christmas morning are likely to be wrapped in happy thoughts of gifts given and received, musing about touching stories of elaborate steps taken to keep secrets while planning surprises. It may seem as if the high point of the holiday has already been reached and the congregation has entered a period of denouement.

Compounding these obstacles to preparing a stirring sermon, the lectionary delivers a pericope devoid of the images and illustrations that are fondly associated with this jubilant occasion. Incarnation occurs in the elusive, almost intangible form of light rather than a baby boy who can be cradled in human arms and heard to coo and cry. Jesus is never mentioned by name, and John's opening verses, unlike Matthew's and Luke's, comment on the tragedy that is yet to come: "He came to what was his own, and his own people did not accept him" (v. 11). This foreshadowing of the crucifixion, albeit faint, gently imposes a touch of gloom on the cheeriness of the day.

## Exegetical Perspective

Readers of John have long noted that the opening verses emerge from a different perspective than the rest of the Gospel. The mysteriousness that characterizes the portrait of Jesus in the Gospel of John, along with the sense of limitation and modesty in the voice of the author, is lacking here. In a tone of theological confidence, these verses offer a summary of the cosmic and historical dimensions of the story of Jesus. It is as though the author of these verses is surveying the story not only from a distance but also from a place of great assurance. Thus, the prologue reads to many as a confident poetic meditation on the finished Gospel.

These verses also beautifully inaugurate the language world of John, with its famous combination of metaphor and dualism. Like the rest of John, the metaphorical character of these verses creates a spiritual reading experience that resists the rigors of exegesis. But, also like the rest of John, embedded in this poetic syntax is a series of stunning and powerful theological claims that invite further thought.

Of the many proposals for an outline of these verses, the most obvious one is still the most persuasive. These verses create a narrative of the Word that divides into four sections: the Word and creation (1:1–5), the Word and the witness of

## Homiletical Perspective

The Gospel reading from John for Christmas Day, the passage often referred to as the prologue, is more poem than narrative. And poetic language is exactly what is called for, because John is doing something different from the writers of the Synoptics. Mark begins his Gospel with an account of John the baptizer, whose baptism of Jesus is the occasion at which Jesus is identified as God's beloved child. Matthew's Gospel begins with the details of Jesus' genealogy and Joseph's doubt, and Luke's account begins with vivid descriptions of angelic appearances, first to Mary and then to the shepherds. Both Matthew and Luke make it clear that Jesus is known as the Son of God, even at his birth. In the Fourth Gospel, however, divine identity is clear from the inauguration of time. Long before taking on human flesh, Jesus, the Word, was with God "in the beginning"—even more, Jesus *was* God.[1] So perhaps only poetry will do to describe John's Jesus.

*Incarnation and Redemption.* As incomprehensible as it seems, the cosmic eternal Christ, the preexisting Logos, is also a flesh-and-blood person, who was born to a particular woman in a particular town at a

[1]See Alan Culpepper, *The Gospel and Letters of John* (Nashville: Abingdon Press, 1998), 110–11, for a fuller explication of the differences between the opening chapters of each Gospel.

# John 1:1-14

## Theological Perspective

this particular person named Jesus is another matter. It is, by comparison, crass, embarrassing, and nonsensical, leaving us a bit puzzled, perhaps, at John's liberal use of positive terms such as "light," "life," "glory," "grace," and "truth." How can the Word share at the same time both the life of the Creator God and the life of the enfleshed creature? It is no wonder that the world did not know him—why would we accept a fellow human being as the source of all life? Who would expect the divine wisdom to hide under such a thick veil of historical conditioning? How can it possibly be that through a creature darkness is overcome, all are enlightened, and we are given power to become children of God?

"And the Word became flesh" is not only an astonishing pronouncement; it is also, arguably, the most significant claim of the Christian faith. According to John, it is the very basis upon which we become the children of God. Gregory Nazianzus, a fourth-century theologian, testified powerfully to why it matters that God entered fully into creaturely existence. "That which is not assumed is not redeemed," he proclaimed. His words have shaped our understanding of Christ and salvation ever since. The humanity of Jesus Christ is no mere costume. It is not a temporary condition or thirty-three-year experiment on the part of God. The real Word really became real flesh. This is the content of the gospel. This is the miracle of Christmas. It is through entering into our flesh that Jesus reveals to us who God actually is, has been, and will be. It is through plunging deeply into the sinful, ignorant realities of our existence in this world that Jesus restores us to that for which he created us. It is in this unlikely way that he is our true light. Understandings of the doctrine of the incarnation that are docetic (i.e., that compromise on the full humanity of Jesus Christ) leave us stranded. Apart from God's assumption of our flesh, God is not really *with* us.

Correspondingly, understandings of the incarnation that compromise on the full divinity of Jesus Christ fail to convey that it is *God* we know, truly, in him. No theological insight has exercised more influence in shaping Christian doctrine than that the Word—known to us in Jesus Christ—was God. At the Council of Nicaea in 325 CE, the church affirmed that Jesus Christ is not simply *like* God the Father (*homooisios*), but is of the very same substance as the Father (*homoousios*). With John, the church concurred that this particular human being is not only godlike, but actually God. All other Christian doctrines are premised on this crucial

## Pastoral Perspective

For the more cerebral congregants, those who crave concepts to contemplate, as opposed to human action and dialogue, this passage is refreshing and satisfying. However, a Christmas sermon, more than most any other homily, must strive to touch the hearts of all who are present: right- and left-brain thinkers, children and adults, weekly worshipers and once-or-twice-a-year guests. The preacher may be tempted to dismiss the lectionary and choose a reading with more accessible imagery, but to do so would be to neglect the good news that seeps throughout these verses. In contrast to the recognizable tableau of shepherds and angels of the evening before, the prologue to John's Gospel invites the provocative pursuit of considering the world as both the earth that God created and the global community with whom God converses.

God has been working on behalf of humankind since the very beginning, when the earth was the formless void depicted in Genesis 1:1, before Adam named the animals of the field and the birds of the air. This allusion to the dawn of creation affords a welcome reprieve to the commercialism that has drenched the culture since before Halloween. The ears of those who adore the environment will find contentment, and others may be moved to cherish the earth. The God who said, "Let there be light," and who confirmed that the light was good transcends time. The light that shines in the December darkness year after year is the light of all generations! "The Word became flesh and lived among us" (v. 14). These words remind the Christmas congregation that the Creator dwells among the created. The artistic author of life is also an avid reader of all that transpires around the globe.

Yet we do not know how God participates in the script that dramatically represents the history of the world. Natural disasters such as the deadly tsunami of Christmas 2004 (described as having attained biblical proportions) cry out for a pastoral word of explanation. How can a loving God allow such devastation and seemingly wrathful destruction? Although the preacher will be hard pressed to answer this question directly, comfort is couched in the recognition that "the light shines in the darkness, and the darkness did not overcome it" (v. 5). Despite immeasurable catastrophe, hope persists. The text provides an opportunity to celebrate moments when the world, the congregation, or an individual glimpsed or was warmed by God's abiding light.

This annunciation of light is delivered by John (the Baptist), who functions as a lamp reflecting the

John (1:6–8), the Word in the world and the reaction of the world to it (1:9–13), the Word becoming flesh and the confession of the children of God (1:14–18). Thus, the theological structure is not that of descent and ascent, with its cosmology of above and below, coming and going, that animates much of the rest of the Gospel. The structure is that of classic Logos (Word) theology, wherein the divine Word is embedded in creation and is manifested in the appearance of Jesus.

The famous and unsuccessful debates about the origin of Logos theology have given way to a recognition of the multiple evocations of the term Logos. The Word in John evokes the creative word of Genesis 1, the cosmic and rational word of Greek philosophy, the word of Wisdom and Torah from Hellenistic Judaism, and the person and story of Jesus. The power of the image in the prologue lies to great extent in its capacity to unite these four theological narratives. The Word is the creative word of God that is embedded in creation. The Word is the ordering force of reason that resides in the cosmos and the human mind. The Word is manifestation of divine will that is revealed in the Torah and the orders of reality. The Word is Jesus himself and the gospel about him. Thus, Jesus is Wisdom, Torah, reason, and the ordering force of reality. The story of Jesus and the story of the cosmos is the same story.

While every verse in the prologue deserves comment and has occasioned exegetical discussion, there are several moments that are key to the course of the Gospel and to subsequent Christian thought. First, the relationship between the Father and Son in John is not articulated by later Trinitarian categories but by a sequence of affirmations that first affirm the unity of Jesus and the Father and then affirm their distinction. Here the imagery is "the Word was with God, and the Word was God." Later in the Gospel, Jesus will affirm that "The Father and I are one" (10:30) and "the Father is greater than I" (14:28). Second, the affirmation that "all things came into being through him" maintains a high status for creation itself. The world is not something alien to Jesus, to which Jesus comes as outsider or invader. As 1:10–11 will assert, "the world came into being through him. . . . He came to what was his own." Third, the claim that both light and life are in him unites old creation with the new. The new life in Christ is not something contrary to the nature of creation. Always, this new life was present. Fourth, the image of the light shining in the darkness inserts

particular time, and died a painful physical death. This incomprehensible mystery is, of course, what we mean when we talk about the central theme of Christmas, the incarnation. Sylvia Dunstan is one modern-day poet who has tried to get at the inscrutability of it all, in her poem "Christus Paradox."

She writes of the apparent polarities that Christ himself embodies: lamb and shepherd, prince and slave, one who brings peace and one who brings the sword. Then she turns the paradox toward praise:

> Worthy your defeat and vict'ry.
> Worthy still your peace and strife.
> You, the everlasting instant;
> You, who are our death and life.[2]

The incarnation—that is, the whole life, death, and resurrection of Jesus—is at the very heart of the paschal mystery. This means, then, that we cannot celebrate Christmas without having Easter in view. One who preaches on Christmas cannot proclaim the birth of the baby Jesus without also proclaiming the purpose of that birth. For the wonder of the incarnation is that when Word becomes flesh, human history is irrevocably changed; the relationship between God and humanity is forever altered. Athanasius (fourth cent. CE), bishop of Alexandria and perhaps the church's greatest teacher on the incarnation, asserted that Jesus "became human that we might become God. He manifested Himself by means of a body in order that we might perceive the Mind of the unseen Father . . . [and] endured shame from men that we might inherit immortality."[3]

*Incarnation and Revelation.* It is not only that the Jesus who lived and died for us achieved our atonement through his suffering and sacrifice, overcoming our alienation to God and drawing us into God's own eternal life. That would be enough—but there is still more! In his living, dying, and rising, Christ reveals to us the God we could not otherwise know. Through the story of how Jesus came to be born, the narratives of his life and ministry, the account of his suffering and death, and the proclamation of his rising—not just as an ethereal spirit being but as a body who eats breakfast with his friends on the beach after overcoming death—through it all, the words and deeds of the incarnate Word, we somehow know more of who

[2] Sylvia Dunstan, "Christus Paradox," in *In Search of Hope and Grace* (Chicago: GIA Publications, 1991).
[3] Athanasius, *De incarnatione Verbi Dei* (New York: St. Vladimir's Seminary Press, 1975), §54.

# John 1:1-14

insight. The doctrine of the Trinity holds that God is not a monad, but an actual fellowship of persons, including Jesus. The doctrine of humanity argues that, because God has entered into relationship with us in the person of Jesus Christ, we are exalted to participation in the very life of God. And the doctrine of eschatology reminds the church that, insofar as we await the return of this particular, embodied one who is God, all of our efforts are provisional.

The implications of the joining of the Word to the historical figure of Jesus have been pondered by theologians through the ages. Calvin explains that Abraham was redeemed through the very same Word by which Christian believers are redeemed, even though he never knew Jesus' name. Barth insists that, because God's acts are always consistent with God's being, the incarnation of the Word in the figure of Jesus Christ reveals not only what God has done for us, but also that God is with us and for us. E. A. Johnson argues, similarly, that God enters into solidarity with us when the Word becomes flesh, holding nothing back from us, even to the point of death on the cross.

In Jesus Christ we experience the glory, grace, and truth of God. His glory is known through that which is lowly, restoring those whom he joins in flesh to the life for which he created us. Calvin imagines God speaking "baby-talk" to us in the event of the incarnation, accommodating to our creaturely limitations so we might know the unknowable One. But we will still not, necessarily, accept him. While his presence with us is the objective reality, while the light that enlightens everyone has come into the world, some of us have rejected the glory of the enfleshed Word who lies right here, in the manger, in the center of our world.

Do we recognize this One who has entered into our midst? Have we received him, really, for who he is? Will we be born, on this day, with this One who is born? Will we become, with him, the children of God?

CYNTHIA L. RIGBY

true light that radiates grace and truth. The boundless quality of God's light is evident in Isaiah's anticipation of the event ages earlier when he prophesied the eventual arrival of a messianic king, and the day when "a little child shall lead them" (Isa. 11:6). This Gospel prologue proclaims that all who believe in the true light will become children of God. Together as leaders and followers, parents and progeny, brothers and sisters, we experience the world as we know it, collaborating with God and one another to dismantle injustice until that climactic moment when "the wolf shall live with the lamb." On Christmas morning, the praise lifted up to the Creator on Christmas Eve may be showered back upon a community of faith by applauding efforts to counter inequity and nurture neighbors in need. The sermon affords an opportunity to advocate extending the distinctive spirit of generosity that often characterizes Advent but has the tendency to subside as soon as the Christmas ornaments are tucked away for another eleven or so months.

As children of God led by God's beloved Son, we are summoned to express our concerns without inhibition and to exhibit unrestrained delight. This purposeful playfulness replicates the personification of creation in Third Isaiah when "the mountains and hills . . . shall burst into song, and all the trees of the field shall clap their hands" (Isa. 55:12), a spectacle at least as incredible as magi following a star to a stable! It is little wonder that the words that English Congregationalist Isaac Watts penned in 1719 are widely known and sung with gusto in both sacred and secular settings: "Joy to the world, the Lord is come! Let earth receive her king." The light that will come into the world full of grace and truth will not be the privileged gift of a select segment of the population, or even reserved for humankind alone. All of creation—fields, floods, rocks, hills, and plains—are overcome with glee! Awed by the Word of God, voices are raised in unison across the globe. Angels join the chorus and "repeat the sounding joy" as "heaven and nature sing"!

ASHLEY COOK CLEERE

a dualism into the picture of a unified created world; yet it does so not by separating light and dark into two realities, but by creating an intimacy and interrelatedness in which "the light shines in the darkness."

The accounts of John the Baptist (1:6–8) and of the light coming into the world (1:9–13) also offer a series of powerful images. For instance, John as a witness to the light models how all children of God must witness. The great puzzle in John as to why some people believe and some do not is not addressed here as it is in the rest of the Gospel. Here, everyone is "his own." Some receive him, and some do not. That is all that is asserted. The affirmation that these new "children of God" (v. 13) are "born not of blood . . . but of God" anticipates the complex images of faith and new life that frequent the Gospel.

However, apart from the geography of creation given in 1:1–5, the most influential affirmation of the prologue is that "the Word became flesh." The significance of this image in the Gospel and in Christian thought is almost impossible to overestimate. The Word becoming flesh undermines and even undoes the dualisms in John. The contrasts between light and dark, above and below, and so on, in the context of the Word becoming flesh, must be seen as rhetorical strategies rather than assertions of cosmic realities. The Word becoming flesh also tightens the focus on the person of Jesus. The story of Jesus in the flesh becomes the story of reality. The Gospel narratives are manifesting the internal structures of the cosmos. Finally, for all the manifestations, the seeing of his glory, the Logos remains hidden in the mystery and otherness of Jesus, in the opaqueness of his flesh. The puzzlement of the world and of the disciples over who Jesus is and what he is talking about is evoked in this astonishing claim that the Word became flesh.

LEWIS R. DONELSON

our God is. Of course we will never know it all, for what God has done for us in Christ reaches far beyond our most profound imaginings. As Athanasius put it, "to try to number [all that Christ has done] is like gazing at the open sea and trying to count the waves." We cannot begin to take in all that Christ has accomplished, he says, "for the things that transcend one's thought are always more than those one thinks that one has grasped." All there is to do is gaze in awe at the amazing mystery and gift of Christmas and to sing our praise.

*Incarnational Faith.* All of this means that celebrating the birthday of Jesus goes much deeper than "keeping the Christ in Christmas." Preaching the doctrine of the incarnation does not mean explaining some dry theory or reciting some old, long-ago history. Nor does it mean caving in to the sentimentality of the season to which it is all too easy to succumb. Preachers must proclaim nothing less than Jesus Christ the living Word, the one who brought the cosmos into being, the one who will bring creation to completion, and the one who lives today—"who was and is and is to be, and still the same." We encounter him in the reading and preaching of the Word; he invites us to the Table and meets us there; he is present in his body, the church. This is why we live an incarnational faith—why we seek Jesus not only in the words we say but in the sacramental life we share. If we are paying attention, we recognize too that God is in the ordinary moments of our life—in the making of lunches and the folding of laundry, in daily kisses good-bye, in the moment when we look into the eyes of one whom the world considers unlovely at best and unworthy of notice at worst. It is why we aim to live the Christian life by not only talking about it or thinking about it, but by doing it—why our prayers are not only those of the heart, but those of the hands and the feet.

KIMBERLY BRACKEN LONG

# Isaiah 61:10-62:3

<sup>10</sup>I will greatly rejoice in the Lord,
  my whole being shall exult in my God;
 for he has clothed me with the garments of salvation,
  he has covered me with the robe of righteousness,
 as a bridegroom decks himself with a garland,
  and as a bride adorns herself with her jewels.
<sup>11</sup>For as the earth brings forth its shoots,
  and as a garden causes what is sown in it to spring up,
 so the Lord God will cause righteousness and praise
  to spring up before all the nations.

## Theological Perspective

To a Christian theologian, the end of Isaiah 61 is a passage that looks both backward, to Israel's history with God, and forward, to salvation in Christ.

To begin with the former, no one familiar with Isaiah will read 61:11 without remembering the Song of the Vineyard in Isaiah 5, which includes the Lord's bitter accusation that he has not reaped in Israel what he sowed: "He dug it up and cleared it of stones and planted it with the choicest vines. He built a watchtower in it and cut out a winepress as well. Then he looked for a crop of good grapes, but it yielded only bad fruit" (5:2 NIV). What do the good and bad grapes symbolize? Verse 7 (NIV) explains: "he looked for justice, but saw bloodshed; for righteousness, but heard cries of distress." The harvest of justice and righteousness that God expected from God's people was perverted by human wrongdoing. In this later stratum of the book, a disciple of Isaiah looks for the restoration of the right relationship between Judah and its God: "For as the earth brings forth its shoots, and as a garden causes what is sown in it to spring up, so the Lord God will cause righteousness and praise to spring up before all the nations" (61:11 NRSV). The repetition of the word "righteousness" makes the echo of the earlier text unmistakable. YHWH's expectations for Israel are at last fulfilled.

## Pastoral Perspective

The couple bounces across the threshold of my office. They move their chairs together—a makeshift loveseat—and hold hands. Ginny and John, as we will call them, are old enough to be my parents; this will be their second marriage. After many years of matrimony John's first wife left home one Monday morning and did not return. Ginny married young and the relationship spiraled into a destructive cycle of emotional abuse. "It was bad," she whispers.

The mathematics of marriage looms above wedding canopies. In our time, half of the marriages in North America end in divorce. The dissolution of so many sacred unions seems incongruous with the delight and promise of a wedding day. Before God and witnesses, the pastor pronounces the beginning of a shared commitment, introduces the couple, and invites them to express their love with a kiss. Guests applaud. The buoyancy of that moment floats with hope.

In his reflection on Jürgen Moltmann's *Theology of Hope*, Miroslav Volf reminds us of the difference between optimism and hope. Volf writes, "Optimism is based on the possibilities of things as they have come to be; hope is based on the possibilities of God irrespective of how things are. . . . Hope is grounded in the faithfulness of God and therefore on the

¹For Zion's sake I will not keep silent,
　　and for Jerusalem's sake I will not rest,
　until her vindication shines out like the dawn,
　　and her salvation like a burning torch.
²The nations shall see your vindication,
　　and all the kings your glory;
　and you shall be called by a new name
　　that the mouth of the Lord will give.
³You shall be a crown of beauty in the hand of the Lord,
　　and a royal diadem in the hand of your God.

## Exegetical Perspective

Before the writings of Third Isaiah (Isa. 56–66), many of the best and brightest of Israel, most of them young men and women and children, were taken as captives, or exiles, into Babylon. Scripture tells us how they wept for their homeland and pined to be part of their own people again (Pss. 126, 137). For decades they lived, worked, married, and bore children. Many of them did their best to make a home in a land not of their choosing, but all the while, many of them struggled to keep the vision of their true home bright in their memories and imaginations, and to keep that vision alive for their children and grandchildren. They were the ones who welcomed with relief the prophecies that assured them that freedom would come. Freedom eventually did come, and the exiles—or, rather, their descendants—were allowed to return to the homeland they had longed for. Today's pericope is part of a song of praise for that long-awaited deliverance.

The first-person narrator switches from the Lord's voice, in verses 8–9 ("For I the Lord love justice, I hate robbery and wrongdoing") to the prophet's voice in verse 10: "I will greatly praise the Lord with my whole being" (my translation). The prophet speaks with the representative "I," that is, with the voice of the whole community. The

## Homiletical Perspective

This first Sunday after Christmas opens with a text of ferment. Here is the social radical, the visionary, the street warrior arming himself for the sake of the city. While the departments and committee rooms are closed for the holiday, this warrior seizes the moment to press for a broader vision.

This action stems from zeal, not rage. This revolution arises out of love for the gift of a city and from determination to have it known by its deepest name. It takes great courage to want this and to brave it. Resistance and entrenchment wait around the next corner. It takes great wisdom to consider the vision over time and to include it in the sacred text of a people. Ferment for the highest goals arising from the deepest wells is an essential ingredient in the recipe for a great society.

*"Your land shall no more be termed Desolate . . . for the Lord delights in you" (62:4).* Beneath such a clarion call, does anyone care about the "righteousness of the nation"? Our culture is concerned with other matters: the stability of the nation, its entrepreneurial skills, and with the nuances of international politics, how we fit and how we win. At first glance, talk of righteousness appears to put a damper on a free spirit.

# Isaiah 61:10-62:3

## Theological Perspective

Chapter 62 focuses on the theme of Zion's vindication and restoration, but the old idea of Zion's inviolability can never be quite the same again; instead Zion "shall be called by a new name that the mouth of the LORD will give" (62:2). This is only one of many new things that are promised in the later portions of Isaiah—the Lord is going to do a new thing (43:19) and declare new things (42:9; 48:6), in response to which the people are to sing a new song (42:10); and all this will culminate in new heavens and a new earth (65:17; 66:22). Despite the destruction of Jerusalem that brought to an end the old dispensation, newness flourishes everywhere by the grace of God. Indeed, the promise of new beginnings is integral to God's word of comfort (Isa. 40:1).

On the one hand, there is a strongly nationalistic bent to these prophecies of restoration; on the other, the very idea of a new earth suggests that the old geopolitical order may be irrelevant. The theologian should remember that in any case the nationalism of such prophecies is radically reevaluated in the New Testament in texts such as John 4:21–24 and that such texts presently stand in tension, awaiting divine rather than human resolution.

Who is the speaker, the one who will rejoice in the Lord ? The limits of the lectionary passage invite the hearer or reader to take on this role himself or herself by removing the larger context of the utterance, but it is still informative to consider that context. At the start of chapter 61, this same speaker says that the Lord has anointed him. It is probably not safe to connect this with the reference to Cyrus of Persia as the anointed one in Isaiah 45:1, since these chapters probably derive from a different historical situation. Nor does the author of these chapters appear to envision a restoration of the Davidic monarchy. There is little more to say from a historical perspective, but Luke 4:18–19 identifies the speaker of Isaiah 61 squarely with Jesus Christ by having him announce his ministry in a Nazareth synagogue with a modified reading of 61:1–2. In light of a Trinitarian and monotheistic understanding of God, the comparison in 61:10 is interesting: "[The LORD] has clothed me with the garments of salvation, he has covered me with the robe of righteousness, as a bridegroom decks himself with a garland, and as a bride adorns herself with her jewels." The Lord clothes the speaker as a human being clothes (or adorns) *himself* or *herself*. This shift from transitive action to reflexive action is odd in the context of the Old Testament alone, but considered from the standpoint of a God who is both unitary and

## Pastoral Perspective

effectiveness of God's promise."[1] Given their experiences, it would not be surprising if Ginny and John felt a mix of optimism and hope. As people of faith, they know well the sharp edges of a forsaken marriage, and they trust in God to bring light from the darkness. With hope, they write new vows, plan a ceremony, and move toward their wedding day in the shared pursuit of happily ever after.

The theology of hope and the metaphor of marriage surface throughout Second and Third Isaiah. Reading around this week's text (Isa. 61:10–62:3), we find both evidence of a painful separation and reason to hope.

Has Israel left God, or has God left Israel? The prophet asserts that the sins of Israel have brought about the exile. God speaks through the prophet: "Yet you did not call upon me, O Jacob; but you have been weary of me, O Israel! . . . You have burdened me with your sins; you have wearied me with your iniquities" (43:22, 24). Thus, Jerusalem— the feminine personification of Israel—has remained desolate during the years of exile, and she laments, "The LORD has forsaken me, my Lord has forgotten me" (49:14).

And yet God responds to Jerusalem's despondency with a pronouncement of reconciliation. God's capacity to save Israel transcends their capacity—and ours—to turn away. Not only will the exiles be reunited with God in Jerusalem, but they will adorn the city like the jewels of a bride; again, God speaks: "As I live, says the LORD, you shall put all of them on like an ornament, and like a bride you shall bind them on" (49:18).

In Isaiah 61:10–62:3 that future day arrives. Jerusalem beams like a bride. The city breaks into song: "I will greatly rejoice in the LORD, my whole being shall exult in my God" (v. 10). Joy returns to Jerusalem with all the hope and promise of a second marriage. In the wake of our pericope, God offers Israel a reason to hope; God says, "You shall no more be termed Forsaken, and your land shall no more be termed Desolate; but you shall be called My Delight Is in Her, and your land Married; for the LORD delights in you, and your land shall be married" (62:4). The ceremony of remarriage has begun.

As God adorns the bride Jerusalem, we might reflect on what "marriage" means to Isaiah's contemporaries. Marriage between God and Jerusalem signifies newfound fertility for Israel. Like her ancestor Sarah, Jerusalem's reunion with God promises

---

[1]Miroslav Volf, "Not Optimistic," *Christian Century*, December 28, 2004, 31.

## Exegetical Perspective

community rejoices to be returned home very much as it would rejoice at a wedding. Indeed, the nuptial imagery so common in Scripture is used here, as well, to connote the fulfillment of promise and to portray the renewed beauty of Israel. No longer a slave, she greets the Lord "as a bridegroom decks himself with a garland, and as a bride adorns herself with her jewels" (61:10 NRSV). This is not only a joyful reunion, but since the marital love between God and God's people is always creative, there is an expectation that the homecoming will be fruitful as well. The nuptial imagery is less about the separation of the past than it is about the promise of the future.

The narrative voice returns to the Lord in verse 62:1, and in its urgency the reader gets a hint of the trouble lurking below the surface of this reunion. The exiles are thrilled to be home, certainly, but Judah has not been a perfectly preserved paradise while they were away. Poverty, destruction, and corruption in the wake of the Babylonian raids have made the longed-for homeland an unwelcoming place, and it seems that the exiles' suffering is not over. Years of hard work lie before them, and though they are grateful to God for his deliverance, they are bitter that it is not as they dreamed it would be. But the history of God's people is full of stories that are much more complicated than they should be; between the Lord and his people, "the course of true love never did run smooth."[1]

It is in the midst of this profound discouragement that the Lord speaks a prophetic word, and makes it clear that this word is on the side of God's people: "For Zion's sake I will not keep silent, and for Jerusalem's sake I will not rest" (62:1). By God's act and word, a now-desolate land will not only prosper, but will become "a crown of beauty in the hand of the LORD, and a royal diadem in the hand of your God" (62:3). This is a promise of glory built on the promises of Isaiah 60:1–9, in which God's light shines in the darkness for God's reunited people, and all people are drawn to the spiritual health and prosperity given by God. Indeed, directly before this passage begins, God reiterates the promise that his people will not be taken away to live with strangers, but strangers will come to live with them: "Strangers shall stand and feed your flocks, foreigners shall till your land and dress your vines" (61:5).

It is also possible, in a slightly different reading, that verse 62:1 is not the Lord's voice but offers a personal comment by the prophet, speaking not with

[1]William Shakespeare, *A Midsummer Night's Dream*, act 1, scene 1, line 134.

## Homiletical Perspective

Of course there are people who do long for the righteousness of the nation: vulnerable people, citizens who know injustice or discrimination, and people with a sense of one world. The public text may expect a bland acceptance of the norm, but inside every heart visions speak.

In this Isaiah text, a servant of the Holy One longs for such righteousness. In this case, such awakening leads to a longing for a blessed and resilient society. Blessing is not simply about my life, my prospects, my family, or my values. It is about becoming an agent, moving us from where we are to where we need best to be.

*"[The LORD] has clothed me with the garments of salvation" (61:10).* Consider the meaning of "being clothed" for this significant work. "The whole armor of God" might jump to mind, but hold off. It seems too ferocious for this subtler, gentler work. Consider instead what you wear to do specific things: gardening, playing sports, supporting a cause. Imagine how it feels to turn up at an event inappropriately dressed. Think through the symbolic power found in costumes and the garb of public function. Then ask what outfit a righteous one might wear.

*"The Lord GOD will cause righteousness and praise to spring up before all the nations" (61:11).* It requires change for a nation to reach its true righteousness. Sometimes the battles last for generations before some heartfelt acceptance of a new ethic takes hold. Some folk will rise to the delights of promise. Others will resist bitterly to the end. So when nations "see your vindication, and all the kings your glory" (62:2), they will be looking beneath any surface display to what we have been through to arrive at this blessed state. Each institution would be expected to deliver its honest best. That would mean revealing the reworking of the hearts of the people.

How can this be done? We seem so small and so preoccupied with our lives as they are. Here the vision hurts more than it helps. It just points out the distance between us and such greatness.

Yet imagine a society that greets all comers with genuine welcome. This would be us at our best. One who discerns this quality of vision, painful as such discernment is, is truly blessed.

Clearly we are not there yet. Neither are we this writer. It is still too easy to preach these texts in ways that simply uphold the status quo. The image of a people "married" to the Holy One is compelling in that it reaches an audience beyond the church walls.

# Isaiah 61:10-62:3

## Theological Perspective

inherently relational, it takes on new meaning: in clothing Christ, God the Father in a sense adorns himself. As Augustine wrote of this passage: "Christ is preaching himself."[1] This passage could thus serve as a way into the mysteries of the Trinity.

The metaphor of clothing has been a rich one for Christian interpreters seeking to understand justification and sanctification. Paul more than once uses the same verb as the Septuagint translation of Isaiah 61:10's "clothed me with the garments of salvation" (*endyō*) in this way. For example, in Ephesians 4:24 he reminds the Ephesians, "clothe yourselves with the new self, created according to the likeness of God in true righteousness and holiness." In Romans 13:14, he adds a christological twist, exhorting his readers to "put on the Lord Jesus Christ (*endysasthe ton kyrion Iesoun Christon)*, and make no provision for the flesh, to gratify its desires." To "put on Christ" means to be sanctified, and the idea of cleansing and clothing has long been acted out in the sacrament of baptism; in the early church the one baptized wore a white robe for a certain length of time afterward.[2]

This vein of interpretation has been especially fruitful in Reformed theology, where the contrast between the sinfulness of humanity and the holiness of God is so starkly drawn. The image of sinful humanity being clothed in the salvation and righteousness of Christ is an attractive one, because it preserves both poles of the traditional anthropology/theology: Righteousness, however freely given, is not something inherent to humanity, but something granted by the grace of God in Christ. Calvin remarks that we as believers in Christ are like Jacob impersonating his brother Esau, hiding "under the precious purity of our first-born brother" although we do not deserve the blessing thereby won.[3] For those who struggle with feeling unworthy of God's grace, this can be an eminently important image.

CHRISTOPHER B. HAYS

## Pastoral Perspective

progeny. Like the ancient decree of Genesis, Jerusalem will again "be fruitful and multiply, and fill the earth" (Gen. 1:28). The rebirth of postexilic Jerusalem includes the promise of new life.

The prophet underscores this hope by planting his listeners in a springtime garden. Here we leave the image of wedding festivities to imagine God growing Israel from the ground. The wasteland of a broken relationship will now burst forth with green shoots. Past taunts from neighboring nations—*God has surely left you, Israel!*—will now give way to the world's newfound praise of Israel and her God. To imagine Israel turning green and to dream of foreign jeers turning to cheers is no small thing. It is the work of hope that is grounded in the faithfulness of God.

In 1945, in the wake of a world-rattling war, Ruth Krauss wrote a children's book called *The Carrot Seed*. The book is as profound as it is brief. A young boy plants a carrot seed. He tends to the weeds and waters the ground, but his parents and older brother are not optimistic. Still, the boy tends the plot and waters the ground. His family remains dubious. Then one day, "a carrot came up, just as the boy had known it would."[2] The carrot is larger than life, larger than the boy.

This image of that carrot underscores the promise of bounty and growth for Israel in this week's passage. It calls us to cross the threshold of hope, where old wounds are healed, where impossibility yields to God's ability to bring something green from the cold ground. And it calls us to consider the new life that God has brought forth in Bethlehem.

Like the carols that linger on this first Sunday of Christmas, this passage from Isaiah celebrates God's desire to be with God's people in a new way. The promise of reconciliation gives Israel hope. The promise of God's steadfast love gives Israel reason to sing again. From age to age, our congregations repeat the sounding joy: "I will greatly rejoice in the LORD, my whole being shall exult in my God" (v.10).

ANDREW NAGY-BENSON

[1]Augustine, *On the Psalms*, 75:4.
[2]Ambrose, *De mysteriis*, c. 7.
[3]John Calvin, *The Institutes of the Christian Religion*, 2 vols., ed. John T. McNeill, trans. Ford Lewis Battles, LCC (Philadelphia: Westminster Press, 1960), 3.11.23; cf. 3.11.10.

[2]Ruth Krauss, *The Carrot Seed* (New York: Harper & Row, 1945).

## Exegetical Perspective

the communal or divine "I," but as a man with a vision and a passion for his people—the "I" who will not keep silent or still for their sake. Since the author or authors of Third Isaiah are unknown, this would be a tantalizing glimpse at a person whose work has moved us for long ages. Who is this fierce prophet with such hope for his homeland? This individual voice may also be heard in the well-known passage that leads into this pericope, Isaiah 61:1 ("The spirit of the Lord GOD is upon me, because the LORD has anointed me; he has sent me to bring good news to the oppressed, to bind up the brokenhearted, to proclaim liberty to the captives, and release to the prisoners").

Such a reading certainly makes the mysterious figure of Third Isaiah seem more real to his readers; this prophet is a man of zeal, devotion, and fierce love for his people and their life, and the passion of his words is contagious. The original listeners were inspired to return home and claim the promises of God for this new life of freedom, and the contemporary reader may well be inspired to ask what his or her own part may be in bringing about this glorious restoration.

It is true that some of Judah's former glory was restored after this point in history. Though the promised land would never again be entirely free of foreign occupation or influence, under the patronage of King Cyrus, the Jews were able to rebuild the temple and repair the destruction to many of their cities. The passage foreshadows its Christmas proclamation when one considers that even before the birth of Christ, God's word was made flesh in those laborers who rebuilt temple and city, in those worshipers who sang and prayed, in those prophets who proclaimed a living Word, and in those families who lived and loved in trust that the word of God already dwelt among them.

KATHERINE C. CALORE

## Homiletical Perspective

How preachers handle this promise will release or restrict its power.

What are our people feeling just now? What is the preacher feeling? On the first Sunday after Christmas, expectations are dropping. The festive mood so doggedly maintained against deadly, daily news is replaced by the "post-Christmas exhale." People wonder what the season has to do with the days ahead.

Jesus cares about the righteousness of the nation. Touched by Isaiah's vision, he becomes the Righteous One alive in flesh, word, and spirit. The story of this Christmas child sows the seeds of cultural transformation. Such grace rises and walks among us—an endless stream of grace. Here is the preacher's chance to open the windows of the church to let this warm and radiant message do its work.

*"For Zion's sake I will not keep silent" (62:1).* We know we carry high explosives in our gospel. Christendom removed the fuses in the long years of its reign, but now at Christendom's demise the true nature of our message comes clear. We speak of a threatening freedom. People may not want to hear of it.

Preach it quietly, tentatively, as curious children touching and exploring a new thing. The rough and rowdy change agent, the newborn visionary, and the slasher of worlds will likely all fare poorly in this work.

This Isaiah text concerns news of one transforming everything for its good. It takes courage to risk dislocating our perspective in order to allow a strange light to enter. It takes imagination to ask where our ancient faith is leading us now.

One idea for a sermon on this text is to tell of a wedding scheduled for right after Christmas. Imagine the abrupt change of gears, the stresses and strains involved, and yet the joy of such a life-altering event. It is the stuff of family stories for generations to come. Not everyone is happy at a wedding. Indeed, it is deemed one of the most stressful times in a life. People must be kept happy and involved. Traditions must be satisfied or explained away. Old rivalries and unfinished business give way to the ceremony. And out of it all, the history of the world is changed as lives embrace, for the first time, some deep and timeless thing.

G. MALCOLM SINCLAIR

# Psalm 148

¹Praise the LORD!
  Praise the LORD from the heavens;
    praise him in the heights!
²Praise him, all his angels;
    praise him, all his host!

³Praise him, sun and moon;
    praise him, all you shining stars!
⁴Praise him, you highest heavens,
    and you waters above the heavens!

⁵Let them praise the name of the LORD,
    for he commanded and they were created.
⁶He established them forever and ever;
    he fixed their bounds, which cannot be passed.

⁷Praise the LORD from the earth,
    you sea monsters and all deeps,

## Theological Perspective

As the Psalter draws to a conclusion, Psalm 148 teaches that the praise it calls for is an expression of radical monotheism. It not only calls upon the reader to praise God for the creation, its stability, order, and benefits. It calls upon the creation, seen and unseen, to join in that praise. It envisions the creation as a community of praise, a choir, as it were, that finds its true interconnectedness in its vocation of praise. One thinks of the passages in the book of Revelation (chaps. 4 and 5) that envision the sovereignty and security of God's presence in terms of a comprehensive worshiping community. The encompassing vocation and obligation of praise that unites the composite elements of the creation are precisely what manifest the primary concern of the whole Psalter: "his name alone is exalted; his glory is above earth and heaven" (v.13).

There are two theological issues that are immediately suggested. First, even though the creation, seen and unseen, can not be worshiped as sacred or partaking of the divine, doesn't the vocation of praise assume a capacity to give back to God, to be eucharistically oriented? Secondly, is there an eschatological dimension to this psalm? Does it assume or invoke an eschatological horizon and anticipation? Psalm 96, among others, in anticipating the Lord's "coming to judge the earth"

## Pastoral Perspective

Psalm 148 whirls with exclamation marks. The expansive, exuberant praise uttered in this psalm begins in the heights of heaven, plummets into the depths of the sea, and then emerges to wend its way over the contours of the earth and through all sorts of animals, birds, and humans. Coming the Sunday after Christmas, it is as if the whole nativity cast of characters has gathered onto one page to join the heavenly host in praising God. In this psalm we can find angels, stars, sheep, cows and camels, heavens and fields, shepherds, mother, magi-become-kings offering praise to God at the birth of Jesus. Reading Psalm 148 aloud is akin to singing "Joy to the World!" It is the appropriately effusive liturgical response to God's great gift of the Messiah: "Praise the Lord!"

For many in the pews, this is a joyful season filled with visual and social exclamation marks. Special lights, candles, greenery, ornaments, gatherings with family and friends, gifts, and holiday foods give ample evidence that this a happy, busy season. In the best of our intentions, these decorative symbols are in service of our praise to God. Because of the faith we share, holiday gatherings and meals, even exchanges of gifts, can underscore the relatedness we have with one another spiritually as well as socially.

For others, however, this season is a difficult one. Seasonal depression, loneliness, strained finances or

<sup>8</sup>fire and hail, snow and frost,
    stormy wind fulfilling his command!

<sup>9</sup>Mountains and all hills,
    fruit trees and all cedars!
<sup>10</sup>Wild animals and all cattle,
    creeping things and flying birds!

<sup>11</sup>Kings of the earth and all peoples,
    princes and all rulers of the earth!
<sup>12</sup>Young men and women alike,
    old and young together!

<sup>13</sup>Let them praise the name of the LORD,
    for his name alone is exalted;
    his glory is above earth and heaven.
<sup>14</sup>He has raised up a horn for his people,
    praise for all his faithful,
    for the people of Israel who are close to him.
Praise the LORD!

## Exegetical Perspective

Hallelujah! So begins and ends this psalm for the first Sunday of Christmastide, in an expression of exuberant praise that echoes the angelic chorus addressed to shepherds on Christmas Eve, and evokes memories of Handel's *Messiah*. Praise the LORD!

Psalm 148 is the third of five hymns of praise that conclude the Psalter. Each is bracketed with the imperative summons to praise, and each offers a different set of reasons for obeying the command. The twofold basis for praising God known elsewhere in the Psalter—God's creative action in the cosmos and God's deliverance of Israel—is visible in these psalms. Other hymns in the Psalter elaborate the reasons for praise; these final five psalms focus almost exclusively on the simple act of summoning both creation and community to praise. So dominant does this summons become that in the final psalm of the series, Psalm 150, the command *hallelu*— "praise!"—initiates every line.

*Calling the Cosmos to Praise, verses 1–6.* Psalm 148 commands the praise of God to ring from every corner of creation. The skies are to render their adoration, and all their inhabitants are summoned to reply. Cosmic spaces and high places, angels and heavenly hosts; sun, moon, stars; even the watery

## Homiletical Perspective

This is challenging text to preach. In the first place, contemporary homiletical theory urges the preacher to observe not only the content but also the form of the text, that is, what it *does*. The sermon, it is said, should do in its new setting what the text did in its original setting. The psalm is a series of summons, one after another, to all people and all creation to praise the Lord. Can the sermon also be series of calls to praise? "Let the board of deacons praise the Lord! Let the young peoples' group praise the Lord, and the retired women in the Martha group also!" Of course, they *ought* to do so . . . but a whole sermon on the subject? The sermon would quickly become tedious. That little word "ought" leads to the second and more severe problem. A preacher can make a congregation feel they *ought* to praise God, but is praise that is duty, not delight, really what we want to inculcate?

Two words seem to sum up the psalm. One is *comprehensive*; from angels to creeping things, from shining stars to the frost under our feet, all are to praise the Lord! But the second word is *exuberance*. The psalm is one great shout of gratitude for the goodness of God and the wonder of creation. Here is the problem: preachers can easily make people feel guilty, but can they make them grateful? This is not just a preacher's problem, of course. It is a

# Psalm 148

## Theological Perspective

(v.13), speaks of the satisfaction and witness of the natural world: "Then shall all the trees of the forest sing for joy" (v.12b). Obviously this is poetic language, but it anticipates a sacramental witness to and participation in a divine act of righteousness that is yet to be but most certainly will occur. Because it is an act of this sovereign, merciful, and faithful God, one can speak of it as if it has already taken place. When the psalmist says: "Let them praise the name of the LORD" (148:13), it is an invocation of and confession of that moment. Does this suggest that Israel's miraculous existence makes it an eschatological community?

What is praise? Since the psalmist expects the whole creation to join in praise beyond the vocal expression and worship of people of faith, and even the whole human community, it is something like an orientation of existence. It is not only owed to God; it is essential to one's existence. It is not only an acknowledgment that existence and living is dependent upon God: "And God said . . ." (Gen. 1); it is also an agreement with and submission to the fundamental divine approbation: "God saw everything that he had made, and indeed, it was very good" (Gen. 1:31). Praise as the fundamental expression of worship is not solely an acknowledgment of dependent creatureliness. It is an expression of astonished gratitude. It is a confession that existence is a mysterious, miraculous gift. Rabbi Abraham Joshua Heschel has written: "It is so embarrassing to live! How strange we are in the world, and how presumptuous our doings! Only one response can maintain us: gratefulness for witnessing the wonder, for the unearned right to serve, to adore, and to fulfill."[1] The very practice of praise as an expression of gratitude is, therefore, also the recognition of the dignity of one's life and the acceptance of a calling within the panoply of the creation. Praise and gratitude as confession and testimony lead to invitation and encouragement of others. "I will bless the LORD. . . . My soul makes its boast in the LORD. . . . O magnify the LORD with me" (Ps. 34:1–3).

We have suggested above that the fundamental interconnectedness among the dimensions and elements of the creation is in the vocation of praise. The stewardship of this vocation is the particular calling of the community of faith. The mutuality of life within that community, ordained as the practice of justice and mercy, is the image of a mutuality that undergirds the whole creation. It is what the English

[1] Abraham Joshua Heschel, *I Asked for Wonder*, ed. Samuel H. Dresner (New York: Crossroad, 1983), 22.

## Pastoral Perspective

strained relationships, bittersweet memories bring emotional and spiritual darkness, in contrast to the commercial glare and liturgical glow all around. Even those who enjoy Christmas may find in the week that follows a kind of postholiday letdown, however mild. This is where the persistent presence of Psalm 148 for the first Sunday after Christmas might offer pastoral instruction along with the liturgical opportunity to praise.

Psalm 148 is the assigned reading in all three years of the lectionary for this Sunday. The Gospel readings change, but the psalm does not. One year, the Gospel confronts us with the massacre of the infants and the holy family's desperate flight into Egypt (Matt. 2:13–23). Another year, the Gospel presents us with Simeon and Anna, whose faces surely showed the years and the strain of waiting and hoping for God's promised salvation. As they look into the face of baby Jesus, they see the salvation they had hoped for but, like Moses gazing into the promised land from Mount Nebo, might not live to enter into fully in this life (Luke 2:22–40). Another year, this Sunday reveals a telling snapshot of Jesus as a child. Already slipping away from his parents' protection, Jesus is found in the temple where, early on, he is asking probing questions of teachers and authorities. It was not the first occasion, nor would it be the last, for his parents to be astonished or in "great anxiety" (Luke 2:41–52).

These three very different Gospel stories are accompanied by the same psalm . . . a psalm of praise. The persistent presence of this psalm, no matter what the Gospel readings are, no matter what the current headlines are, recalls us to what truly binds us together, the authentic source of our interrelatedness: offering praise to God. This is the purpose of creation, and the purpose of every creaturely being: to offer praise and glory to God. The reasons for offering such lavish and continual praise are stated. God commanded creation into being and fixed the bounds of heaven and earth (vv. 5–6). God, whose name we know (vv. 5, 13), alone is exalted in heaven and on earth. God called a people into community and "raised up a horn" for them; that is, God restores people to strength and dignity (v. 14). Praise of God, then, is not determined by how well things are going at the moment in our own lives or in the world, as though praise has to do with us or our circumstances. The praise we offer to God is wholly determined by, dependent on, who God is and what God has done and is doing in the universe. Praising God is what we—along with the sun and

chaos that surrounds the firmament—all are required to praise the Creator.

The reader who knows the common hymnic structure of summons to and reason for praise cannot but notice that Psalm 148 spends four and a half verses calling various aspects of creation to praise and only one half verse providing the reason for the celebration. The reason is clear enough: creation praises its Creator because the Creator is its lord, having established its boundaries and fixed the order of the universe. But the repeated pattern of the summons—praise imperative + object—in verses 1–4 is so overpowering as to force the reason for praise into the background. Adding to the effect is the repetition of the adjective *kol*, "all," in verses 2–3. The effect is not unlike a virtual tour of the cosmos, where at every stop there is a new voice to raise the song of adulation until the praise is universal.

The psalmist's choice of language evokes the creation narrative in Genesis 1:1–2:4a, where God crafts sun, moon, and stars, and where the firmament separates the waters above and beneath the earth. But a subtle shift takes place in the move between narrative and hymn. What was mute evidence of God's work in Genesis is now summoned to bear active witness to the Creator's greatness. There they were the objects of God's activity; here they are the subjects that themselves act in adoration. It is as though the works of creation have taken on life and now live to praise.

*Earth Echoes the Adoration, verses 7–14.* What begins in the heavens continues on earth. Once again, the psalmist shows the reader around the world, from the depths of the sea with its monstrous whales to the heights of storm clouds filled with snow and hail, and once again the reader hears each object called to praise its creator. Again, the language evokes the Genesis 1 creation account: sea monsters and deeps, fruit trees, wild animals, creeping things and birds in flight—all are the direct result of the Creator's handiwork in Genesis 1, and all are now summoned to bear witness to God's power. With verses 11–12 a new group joins the chorus: human beings. Kings, princes, rulers, and even nations are called to praise. No one is omitted: young, old, male, female—all human life is expected to praise.

Verse 14 advances the reason for the praise: God has delivered Israel. The expression "raised up a horn for his people" should most likely be taken to imply an act of God to strengthen or empower Israel (cf. its usage in Pss. 75:10; 89:17, 24; 92:10; 112:9). For the

widespread human problem. Children receive Christmas gifts from the grandparents or the uncles and aunts. You can make the child get on the phone and say, "Thank you," but a good parent instinctively knows that the words alone are not enough. The thanks are incomplete without gratitude. This may be where the sermon can begin, with a problem that is both theological and existential, a problem not unique to the preacher but also shared by the congregation.

A very senior and very wise psychiatrist once told me that she had begun to write an academic paper on the origin of gratitude in the human person. She found to her surprise that in all the literature in her field, she had found *nothing* on the origin of gratitude. Every conceivable condition or disease or syndrome had its own library shelf of studies, but not gratitude. How does a child become truly grateful? How does a church? With a child, it begins with love received. The little child can learn gratitude only if in her early years she is surrounded by love and made to know she is wonderful. In Christian terms, the child is told she is special because she is a gift from God. Whether a boy or girl, the child is Nathaniel, a name that in Hebrew means "gift from God." And for this gift the parents are grateful. Perhaps we learn gratitude by being loved by others who are themselves grateful. Gratitude grows in a matrix of love and concern and in the midst of examples of gratitude. The praise of the church, and more specifically Psalm 148, is just such a matrix.

Perhaps a third key word for the psalm is *wonder*. The psychiatrist at the conclusion of her paper wrote of her young grandson, filled with wonder, turning the gift over and over in his hands, noting with amazement all that the gift could do. The psalmist includes in our praise realities that fill us with wonder: sun, moon and shining stars, the heavens and the waters above the heavens, the sea monsters in the deep. Perhaps we have grown so used to our surroundings that we have forgotten wonder. Amid the city lights we cannot see the stars. But there is wonder aplenty for those with eyes to see and ears to hear. Some years ago, the Hubble space telescope was trained on an apparently empty patch of space. That patch of space, when viewed with the great telescope, teemed with the light of stars and galaxies. Then the scope was turned to what appeared to be a barren patch in that area and set for a long exposure. In that long exposure even what had been thought to be empty was still filled with distant galaxies. Light everywhere! It is wonderful, and let it all praise the Lord!

# Psalm 148

## Theological Perspective

author Charles Williams, following several patristic writers, refers to as "co-inherence." Life is a web of interdependencies. The psalmist begins Psalm 148 with a confessional: "Praise the LORD!" The following expression of praise (v.1bff.) is in the imperative voice, addressed to every dimension of the creation as well as the social order. It is a challenge. The third expression: "Let them praise . . ." (v. 13) is an invitation and expectation. The three different forms taken together constitute a rhetorical expression of that co-inherence out of which the praise of the whole creation proceeds. That vocation of grateful praise is what gives equal standing before God of all people, "kings of the earth . . . all peoples . . . princes . . . rulers . . . young men and women alike, old and young together" (vv. 11, 12). The "horn" (v. 14) that God has raised for the people of faith is not only the history of events by which Israel was created and has been sustained by God; it is also the word of the Law and its ordinances by which the community of mutuality is called forth. The life of that community constitutes being the people who are "close to him" (v. 14). It is the practiced expression of what the act of praise is for and about. In its worship and in its way of life, Israel, as the community of praise, is to be a confessional challenge and encouragement to the world. In the midst of the mystery, the richness and the diversity of the created world, it advocates for the vocation of praise that unites all there is before its compassionate Creator. The life of the community is to be a witness to what that compassion looks like and what it promises.

The eschatology of the Christian community, what it hopes for, expects, and serves, should include reflections on this psalm as well as others. The earnest that is inherent in the comprehensive and vibrant attention to God's glory can nurture and clarify the depth of what the community yearns for as it prays: "Our Lord, come!" (1 Cor. 16:21).

DWIGHT M. LUNDGREN

## Pastoral Perspective

moon, snow and wind, mountains and trees, creeping things and flying birds—are called to do.

There are seasons, Christmas included, in which it may not be easy to find a voice for praise. Sometimes the word or song of praise gets silenced by a lump in our throat, as though we have swallowed too much grief or sorrow or loneliness to utter a sound. Sometimes praise is no more than a whisper, because we are exhausted or afraid or ill. What happens when we ourselves are too sad or too weak to offer praise of God? This psalm exclaims the hopeful, comforting message that we are not isolated or alone in our vocation of praise. From start to finish, Psalm 148 places us within a vast, diverse universe where continual praise is being offered to God: Angels and stars, fire and frost, wild and domesticated animals, men and women, young and old, wealthy and poor . . . join in a terrestrial/celestial symphony of praise. So, when our own song or spirit is silenced, praise still fills the space all around us. In a time of personal darkness, we may stand in the midst of the congregation or with one other person, we may sit in a field or float on the water, we may listen to the birds of the air or sit with the family pet and let this creation, these creatures, these companions praise God for us until we find our voice again.

This common vocation of praise is the source of our true interrelatedness to God, to one another, to the universe. Praise, then, is a gift that brings us out of isolation and into communion. Communion is what Christmas is most truly about: God's desire to be at one with us, Immanuel, and the fact that in Christ God is reconciling all things. Psalm 148 will give voice for many to the joy experienced in this season. For others struggling through these days, Psalm 148 can offer assurance that they are not left in isolation and silence in creation or in the community of faith.

KIMBERLY L. CLAYTON

psalmist, God's deliverance of Israel—the people "who are close to him"—becomes the reason for the whole creation and all the peoples within it to offer praise.

James L. Mays raises the question that lurks in the back of most readers' minds: how does a sea monster or a fire, a mountain or a cedar tree praise God? Mays suggests that the answer lies in the phrase at the end of verse 8: the aspects of the natural order praise God by "fulfilling his command," by being what they were created to be.[1] If so, is it not also the case that the proper praise of human beings is also being what God created us to be? To the extent that human life is characterized by faithfulness and humility before the sovereignty of God, life is itself an act of praise, whether or not we use words to express it.

*Reading the Psalm at Christmastide.* The lectionary locates this psalm on the first Sunday after Christmas. At this time of year, the summons in verse 2 to the angels and heavenly host cannot but recall the angelic chorus that filled the skies in Luke 2, read on Christmas Eve. The "horn" God has raised for God's people becomes the Christ born in a manger, and the chorus of praise of all creation prescribed by the psalm seems to fit perfectly the mood of the season.

In another passage for Christmastide, Matthew sounds a discordant note against this chorus of praise. Herod's false promise of praise for the child (Matt. 2:8) and his evil plan to destroy him (Matt. 2:16) betray his failure to live in faithfulness. They are thus the precise opposite of the psalmist's call to praise, and they stand as a stark warning that not all creation lives out the Creator's intent. The contrast between the vision of an adoring creation and the scheming of its human inhabitants anticipates the struggle of the gospel in the world, a struggle that will lead inevitably to the cross.

PAUL K. HOOKER

Of course, it always helps if the child actually gets to know the grandparents. It is hard to be grateful to a name on a card or a voice heard on the phone at Christmas and birthdays and a few other times. "Let them praise the name of the LORD. . . . He has raised up a horn for his people . . . for the people of Israel who are close to him." The horn is a symbol of strength and we will hear that language in another psalm. In this case it is one of the lovely psalms in Luke's Christmas story, in which Zechariah praises God: "Blessed be the Lord the God of Israel, for he has visited and redeemed his people, and has raised up a horn of salvation for us in the house of his servant David" (Luke 1:68–69 RSV). In this context it is clear that Luke wants us to understand that "horn of salvation" is Jesus. God has drawn close to us in Jesus and we are indeed close to the divine heart.

And in the meantime, you teach children to say, "Thank you." Even if their heart is not truly in it, is not full of gratitude, you teach them to say the words because the words are still important. If they say the words, the words will become a habit, and in the soil of the habit, the seed of gratitude may grow. So yes, "Let the board of deacons praise the Lord! Let the young peoples' group praise the Lord, and the retired women in the Martha group also! Let them *all* praise the Lord!"

STEPHEN FARRIS

---

[1] James L. Mays, *Psalms*, Interpretation Series (Louisville, KY: John Knox Press, 1994), 444–45.

# Galatians 4:4-7

> [4]But when the fullness of time had come, God sent his Son, born of a woman, born under the law, [5]in order to redeem those who were under the law, so that we might receive adoption as children. [6]And because you are children, God has sent the Spirit of his Son into our hearts, crying, "Abba! Father!" [7]So you are no longer a slave but a child, and if a child then also an heir, through God.

## Theological Perspective

Today's passage was addressed to uncircumcised Gentile Christians who accepted, but now were reconsidering, the message that Paul has proclaimed about God's grace in redeeming and justifying Jews and Gentiles through faith in Jesus Christ without the works of the law. They received the "good news" that Gentiles could become heirs of God's promises and equal members of the people of God by abandoning their idols and trusting God's redemptive action in Jesus Christ, without observing the law. The acceptance of this message made possible the emergence of Christian Jewish groups in synagogues and churches that proclaimed and practiced full and equal membership of uncircumcised Christian Gentiles among God's people.

Paul claims in this epistle that the new (eschatological) reality of God's redemption of Gentiles without the works of the law (4:4–5) and their incorporation as uncircumcised believers into God's people was several things: something God intended from the beginning (3:6–9); a teaching in the law (4:21–30); a reality accepted by key leaders in Jerusalem (2:1–6); and a missional agreement between these leaders and Paul (2:7–10). Therefore, uncircumcised Gentile believers in Christ were encouraged to claim their new status as equal children of God and descendants of Abraham

## Pastoral Perspective

On the First Sunday *after* Christmas, commonly called a "low Sunday," Paul calls us to be lifted impossibly high. On a day when worship attendance is normally at its annual low, a day when church choirs often take a "vacation" after the vocal workout of Advent, and when the euphoria of Christ's birth has turned to postpartum exhaustion, Paul—ever the counterculturalist—calls the church and its culture to vivid, pentecostal transformation. *Our hearts*—our overindebted, oversweetened, very over-Christmas hearts—are directly injected with the Spirit of God's Son. If we listen closely, we hear a new, extra heartbeat within us, faintly echoing the cry of a baby's first words: "Abba! Abba! Abba!" Our blood is mingled with that of Jesus himself. We are no longer slaves—to the law, to others, or to ourselves. We are no longer second-class strangers to our salvation. We are now children and heirs of God, just as Jesus himself is God's child and heir. And so, on one of our "lowest" days, Paul would have the full impact of the heights of Christmas take hold of us and lift us above ourselves and beyond our culture. Paul calls us—the church—to be born again on the first Sunday *after* Christmas.

Paul composed his letter to the Galatians without the benefit of the written Gospels, so it is impossible to know exactly what nativity story Paul had in

## Exegetical Perspective

In three sentences that have been aptly called "the theological center" of this letter,[1] Paul offers his Galatian faithful the good news that God has sent the Son to rescue them from spiritual slavery and adopt them as God's children. Just as God has redeemed the Jews through faith (4:4–5), so now God has redeemed Gentiles (4:6), and all have become God's adopted children (Gk. *huioi*, sons) and therefore heirs. God has made all this evident by sending the Son's Spirit to cry out from faithful hearts, "Abba! Father!" On this first Sunday after Christmas, then, we consider *why* God sent the Bethlehem child: to redeem captives and welcome them, open-armed, into God's family.

Not all of Paul's news to the Galatians is quite so cheery as this, of course. The sentence that precedes our passage portrays Judaism as a kind of slavery from which one must be rescued (4:3), and the sentence that follows it will chastise the Galatians for what Paul counts as apostasy (4:9). It seems that after Paul's visit, a group of Jewish-Christian teachers arrived in Galatia offering a (friendly or unfriendly) amendment to his gospel—the additional demand that the Gentile-Christians complete their devotion to God by being

[1]J. Louis Martyn, *Galatians*, Anchor Bible, vol. 33A (New York: Doubleday, 1997), 406.

## Homiletical Perspective

Now we can catch our breath, pause, and reflect. If on this first Sunday after Christmas Day a homiletical letdown is to be expected (or at least widely experienced, the pastoral equivalent of postpartum depression), the opportunity for substantial, theological preaching is ripe.

Mary's last month of pregnancy has been frantic and uncomfortable—for her and for us who relive it with her year by year. The labor and delivery have proven, yet again, to be both endless and instantaneous. But now we are home, the first wave of visitors has gone (though more are on the way), the baby is asleep in the crib, and in the afterglow and wonder we begin to consider all this birth might mean.

The Gospel for today tells of Mary and Joseph's going up to the temple according to the law, for purification and presentation. It is left to Simeon and Anna prophetically to discern and declare the meaning and purpose of the holy birth. Paul takes his turn in our lesson from Galatians, and we are encouraged to do so as well.

Tucked into the middle of this small lection from Paul's most contentious epistle, and itself only a part of a much larger, multifaceted discussion about the "rights and privileges" of Gentile Christians, there are two concrete pieces of tradition related to or drawn from the life and teaching of Jesus. As Paul so

# Galatians 4:4-7

## Theological Perspective

(3:6–9), but free from the obligation to observe the law (3:10–29).

This message and its practical communal implications were opposed by some Christian Jewish groups who affirmed and practiced something different. In their view, in order for Gentiles to be redeemed by God and enjoy equal membership among God's people, they needed to become proselytes—that is, circumcised and law-observant converts. Like Abraham, they needed to be circumcised in order to become children and heirs of Abraham (Gen. 17). God's covenant and true faith in Jesus Christ required the observance of the law. Their faith was incomplete and their membership unequal until they were circumcised. Most likely, confused about their spiritual identity and threatened on their group status, uncircumcised Gentile Christians began to accept this gospel, complied with the new requisite, and submitted to the authority of these leaders. Paul's letter was an attempt to reprimand this turn away from the gospel. He tried to convince them not to believe this "different" gospel, not to comply with this assimilation policy, and not to consent to the threats of exclusion and expectations of subordination of those leaders.

Today's reading is part of Paul's arguments to justify the lawfree "gospel of Christ" and the policy of incorporation and equality (3:28) for uncircumcised Gentiles believers in Jewish Christian groups. Paul focuses on what God has done in Jesus Christ and the Spirit in order for Jews and Gentiles to acquire the new status of free children of God. There are three theological convictions in this passage that are part of Paul's understanding of the "gospel of Christ" (1:7) that grounds spiritual freedom and equality among God's people.

First, God is the redeemer of all people, Jews and Gentiles alike, who always makes real the divine promises of redemption. God is the universal and inclusive redeemer seeking to bless all of the children of God. God is enacting the promise made to Abraham: "All the Gentiles shall be blessed in you" (3:8). By God's grace and freedom and through the death and unity with Christ (3:28), uncircumcised Gentiles are now included as free and equal members in God's people.

Second, God's gracious and inclusive redemption is the work of God the Father, the Lord Jesus Christ, and the Spirit. Through the death and resurrection of the Son, God has: "set us free from the present evil age" (1:4); justified those who believe in Christ Jesus (2:16); "redeemed us from the curse of the law

## Pastoral Perspective

mind. Perhaps, "When the fullness of time had come, God sent his Son, born of a woman, born under the law" is all the birth narrative Paul had, or at least all he needed. What a refreshing alternative this is to the market-saturation of Christmas narratives—biblical and secular—spoken, aired, and wired throughout Western culture from Halloween until Christmas Eve. By the first Sunday after Christmas, we have heard so much about Christmas. Perhaps this is the day to hear so little. Perhaps this is the day we can be at rest and listen to the still, small cries of the Spirit of God's newborn Son within us.

Although Paul had no written Gospel texts to guide him, and although he most assuredly wrote long before the Gospel of John and in a different subculture of the nascent church, Galatians 4:4–7 sounds remarkably Johannine. In the third chapter of that Gospel, in Jesus' exchange with Nicodemus, a leader of the Pharisees, we hear echoes of Paul. "How can anyone be born after having grown old? Can one enter a second time into the mother's womb and be born?" Jesus answered, "Very truly, I tell you, no one can enter the kingdom of God without being born of water and Spirit" (John 3:4–5). What John would call "water and Spirit," Paul foresees as "adoption." Regardless of the mode of birth, whether by nature or by law, the end is the same. In both Paul's writing and John's, at the intersection of law and gospel, God does something miraculous. John called Nicodemus, Paul calls the Galatians, and God calls us—to a spiritual second birth.

Does a child know she is being born? Does an infant know he is being adopted? Perhaps there is some vague recognition of a change of environment, but the immediate consequences of a new baby rest on the parents. From the perspective of Reformed theology, the genesis of any spiritual birth is the providence of God. While our churches sing and rejoice in the days leading up to Christmas, is it possible that, like a new parent, God's rejoicing begins the first days *after* Christmas? Is Christmas a signal of renewed commitment on God's behalf to watch over us, to nurture our potential? Does God listen with a parent's anxious anticipation for our first, babbling attempts to say, "Abba"? Over time a newborn child will learn to recognize and respond to a parent's voice. Over time, a person emerging on the other side of Christmas may awaken to the change of spiritual environment both inside and out. This awakening to the voice of the Spirit takes time. God's love overflows, but we must learn to navigate

circumcised and observing the dictates of the Mosaic law (1:6–9; 3:1–5; 4:12–15, 17; 5:2–4, 7; 6:12–15). Even the prospect that his spiritual children will embrace this condition has Paul veritably apoplectic and produces some of his most derogatory characterizations of Jewish religious practice. Paul, the ex-Pharisee, shockingly claims that for the Galatians submitting to these Mosaic demands would be tantamount to resuming pagan religious practice. "Now, however, that you have come to know God, or rather to be known by God, how can you turn back again to the weak and beggarly elemental spirits? How can you want to be enslaved to them again? You are observing special days, and months, and seasons, and years" (4:9–10). Paul believes the Galatians are dabbling with law observance. For him the stakes are high and the consequences dire.

Against this embattled backdrop, Galatians 4:4–7 shines brilliantly forth. In it, Paul draws together the experience of Jews like himself and Gentiles like the Galatians as corecipients of God's gift. To do this, he calls upon the customs of familial inheritance. In this loose metaphor, the heir's minority is analogous to the period of Jewish and Gentile slavery under the elements of the universe. All were formerly minors/slaves—Jews through the observance of law, Gentiles through the worship of pagan gods; but just as at the time of the father's choosing, the heir receives the inheritance, so at the time of God's choosing, the Son appears to liberate them from the power of these elemental spirits of the universe.[2] Whether Jews or Gentiles, then, all have been redeemed through the Son, all have received the Spirit, all are adopted children and heirs.

Paul's hope of connecting the cosmic history of Jews and Gentiles may explain the most confusing grammatical element of this passage, namely, the strange alternation of first- and second-person pronouns in 4:4–7. Paul writes that God redeemed those under law so that "we" might receive adoption (v. 5); then, because "you" (pl.) are children (v. 6), God has sent the Spirit of the Son into "our" hearts (v. 6), so "you" (sg.) are no longer a slave but a child (v. 7). The confusion of both ancient copyists and modern commentators attests to the oddness of the language. Perhaps Paul here risks a moment of illogic in order to forge a close bond between the

rarely references the actual ministry or words of Jesus, their very presence here is enough to perk the ears.

The first is Paul's "birth narrative." He writes that in the "fullness of time"—which is to say, at the end of one age and the beginning of another—when a new time had arrived and a new day had dawned, "God sent his Son, born of a woman, born under the law." In context, of course, this latter description means the Jewish law, but readers of Matthew's birth narratives might find ample evidence to suggest that Jesus was born under Roman law, as well, as indeed he will in all the Gospels die by that law. If "God sent his Son" is Paul's affirmation of the divinity of Christ, "born of a woman, born under the law" is both Paul's characterization of Jesus' full humanity and a narrative bridge back to the particularities of today's Gospel lection. Paul's description of the true humanity of Jesus in no way trivializes the doxological confessions, but begins to indicate what that "true humanity" might comprise. In sum, verse 4 is first-order testimony to which Nicaea serves as creedal explication.

In the second, Paul quotes Jesus' prayer, preserving the Aramaic logion: "Abba, Father." If "born of woman" is confession of Jesus' humanity, "Abba" reveals the content and purpose of that humanity. The "full stature" of Christ's humanity (Eph. 4:13) is evidenced in his filial relationship with God and his determination to do the will of God. Quite unlike the prodigal who takes the inheritance of his father and wastes it on himself—Augustine said that "doing what I want to do" is but little freedom—Christ divested himself of his inheritance to make others wealthy, joint heirs with him, in obedience to God's will. This filial devotion, an act of radical freedom, exalts strangers and orphans and slaves to the status of family members.

One of the most important words in this passage, indeed in the entire New Testament, is also one of the smallest: three letters in Greek, transliterated *hina* and translated "in order to/that." The word is used twice in the parallel purpose clauses of verse 5: "in order to redeem those who were under the law, in order that [my translation] we might receive adoption as children." There is concrete purpose in God's sending of Jesus, reminiscent of motifs found in the exodus and Sinai: Christ is God's means both of liberating us from slaveries and of constituting us as a new and unified people.

Interesting is Paul's use of "we might receive" (v. 5): Paul intentionally self-identifies with the Gentile Christians to whom the letter is addressed,

---

[2] So NEB and NRSV. The NIV's "basic principles" indicates another line of interpretation, which views these elements of the cosmos (*stoicheia tou kosmou*) as ideas rather than powers. For a recent reading of *stoicheia* as principles, see Frank J. Matera, *Galatians*, Sacra Pagina, vol. 9 (Collegeville, MN: Liturgical Press, 1992), 155.

# Galatians 4:4-7

## Theological Perspective

by becoming a curse for us" (3:13); passed on the blessing of Abraham to Gentiles (3:14); made believers in Christ "children of God through faith" (3:26), Abraham's offspring (3:29), and adopted and free children of God (4:5; 5:1); and finally, made believers one and equal in Christ Jesus in spite of human differences in identity and status (3:28). God has given the (eschatological) promise of the Spirit (3:2–5, 14) in order for believers to be free children in communion with God and heirs of God's promises (4:6); "eagerly wait for the hope of righteousness" (5:5); overcome the desires and works of the flesh (5:16–21); bear the fruit of the Spirit (5:22); experience "the only thing that counts . . . faith working through love" (5:6); and become agents of love and care for the common good in the life of the community (6:1–10). Finally, God is committed to redeem and transform the life and destiny of Jews and Gentiles alike, especially those who are excluded and marginalized by human hierarchies and divisions (3:28).

The Christian gospel invites people to become aware of and respond to God's grace and mercy, which seek, among other things, to make humans free in order to live reconciled and reconciling lives with God and others. The church has the continuous task of discerning and enacting new ways by which God extends a gracious invitation of acceptance and freedom to those who are considered and treated as "others, outsiders, subordinates, strangers, and impure" by church and society. God's love and righteousness defy all attempts by religious people to establish policies of separation, exclusion, subordination, and assimilation on human terms that run counter to the gracious terms of God's policy and praxis of redemption, adoption, and hospitality. Old and new forms of all sorts of "slaveries" appear in different times and contexts. For this reason, churches are always challenged to live and proclaim their understanding and practice of the Christian gospel of peace, freedom, and justice in response to particular contexts where these "kin-dom" values and relationships are resisted and denied in society and church. The task of discerning the truth of the Christian gospel and the freedom of Christian life is not under our control and achieved once and for all, but it is sustained by the hope that the liberating work of God through the sending of the Son (4:4) and the sending of the Spirit (4:6) is still with us.

LUIS R. RIVERA

## Pastoral Perspective

its waters. Whether a person is conscious of a dramatic conversion or new birth in Christ takes a lifetime, our awareness is secondary to God's primary act of love. We are being made new because God has declared us heirs. Our status has changed, *after* Christmas.

In the days after Christmas, guided by the opening words of Paul's letter to the Galatians, we are directly led to hope. We are told anew of God's hope for all the world, and reminded that our hope rests in God. Wherever we stand, we have standing because God is willing to adopt us. Wherever God is, God stands hopeful that we can develop beyond societal limits, casting off whatever chains of situation tie us down, to become conscious of our position as children and then also heirs of God. Not merely students, nor even friends, we are brothers and sisters of Jesus Christ. Especially at our "low" times, this message of hope, this word of new birth must be proclaimed, whether heard by many or only a few. Slack attendance is no excuse for weak hope.

Lest the boundaries of hope become too narrow, we should remind ourselves that Paul proclaims the word of God's hope not to individuals, but to a church. In a culture driven by personal wants, public hope is easily privatized. Our status can quickly become another souvenir of Christmases past. Yet hope is a gift, not an entitlement. Hope cannot exist on its own. A church can fall on "low" times, just as its members do. Paul calls all the church to continual rebirth. On the first Sunday after Christmas, as the church looks in equal ways at the year behind it and the year ahead, we are reminded that we are surrounded by a Parent's love that will not let us go. Any willing congregation can find new life in the proclamation of Jesus Christ for the world.

JAMES W. MCTYRE

*First Sunday after Christmas Day*

Jewish Christian and Gentile Christian experience of redemption.

This good news of Galatians 4:4–7 should not have been new to the Galatians. They have heard about adoption and redemption before. In Paul's initial time among them, he spoke vividly to them about the cross of Christ (3:1), they were baptized into a new life as God's children in Christ (3:27), and they received the Spirit (3:2). To remind them of this shared history, Paul here retrieves a central image from their experience of adoption, when, fresh out of the baptismal waters in which they left their past life, with the first Spirit-aided words of their new life, they spoke their initial "Abba!" to God. Also, his presentation of redemption here summons Galatians 3:13–14.[3] There Paul writes, "Christ redeemed us from the curse of the law by becoming a curse for us—for it is written, 'Cursed is everyone who hangs on a tree [Deut. 21:23]'—in order that in Christ Jesus the blessing of Abraham might come to the Gentiles, so that we might receive the promise of the Spirit through faith." Here the history lesson Paul supplies the Galatians in 4:4–7, recollections of baptism and Spirit, begins to make sense. In 3:1–5, Paul has recalled the Galatians to their beginnings in faith—the crucifixion proclaimed vividly by Paul, the Spirit received powerfully in their lives. The cross of 3:1 becomes the tree of 3:13 and then the unspoken vehicle of redemption in 4:4. The Spirit appears in each setting. Thus, the Son has taken the curse of the law and the powers upon himself through the cross, and Jews and Gentiles alike are set free and inspired in him.

The circumstances in Galatia paradoxically evoke the best and worst in the apostle Paul, as crises are wont to do. While the polemical setting drives him viciously to castigate his opponents' (and his own former) pattern of religion, it also produces one of his purest communications of divine love. God is the parent who leaves a rich inheritance to all of the children. God is the liberator who sees human captivity and sends a Son to free slaves and give them a share in the Spirit's freedom. God has created in that Son's cross a way to widen the divine reach and welcome all peoples, Jew and Gentile alike, into the company of God's family.

ALLEN R. HILTON

as if to say that all who are children of God are so by virtue of adoption. Only Jesus is by nature the Son of God; all others—whether born under the law or strangers to the law—come into the relationship by the grace of adoption. All who are thus redeemed and adopted enjoy the same "rights and privileges" (and obligations!) of being in God's family.

In verse 7 there is a grammatical switch worth nothing: "you" is singular. If there has been and remains a strong urge among many Christians to critique and even lay aside the "individual piety" of some evangelical preaching (in favor of a social or political vision of the kingdom of God), here is an example of the particular consequence of Paul's universalizing faith. "You [sg.] are no longer a slave but a child, and if a child then also an heir, through God." Social renderings of the gospel are incomplete unless founded on or accompanied by personal transformation. And so a word of caution is offered on the other side of what might be called the "conversion wars": Paul's unequivocal affirmation that the implications of grace are, at least in part, individual.

A needful emphasis: all of this is God's gift, God's work, God's initiative. God sends the Son into the world, and God sends the Spirit into our hearts and prayers. The evidence of that Spirit in and among us is our use of "Abba," the prayer language of Jesus. Paul anticipates the teaching of the elders of the church: *lex orandi, lex credendi*; the rule of prayer is the rule of faith. In this case, as the prayers of Jesus are formed in us they form us, shape our faith and faithfulness. When we pray the prayer of Jesus and profess the faith of Jesus, we begin to do the works of Jesus. And should we die the death of Jesus, or any faithful death, we will be raised to the life of Jesus, and all of this as God's once and abiding Christmas present to the world.

THOMAS R. STEAGALD

---

[3]Richard B. Hays has called Gal. 3:13–14 and 4:4–7 "two tellings . . . of the same story" in *The Faith of Jesus Christ: An Investigation of the Narrative Substructure of Galatians 3.1–4.11* (Chico, CA: Scholars Press, 1983), 116.

# Luke 2:22-40

22When the time came for their purification according to the law of Moses, they brought him up to Jerusalem to present him to the Lord 23(as it is written in the law of the Lord, "Every firstborn male shall be designated as holy to the Lord"), 24and they offered a sacrifice according to what is stated in the law of the Lord, "a pair of turtledoves or two young pigeons."

25Now there was a man in Jerusalem whose name was Simeon; this man was righteous and devout, looking forward to the consolation of Israel, and the Holy Spirit rested on him. 26It had been revealed to him by the Holy Spirit that he would not see death before he had seen the Lord's Messiah. 27Guided by the Spirit, Simeon came into the temple; and when the parents brought in the child Jesus, to do for him what was customary under the law, 28Simeon took him in his arms and praised God, saying,

29"Master, now you are dismissing your servant in peace,
     according to your word;
30for my eyes have seen your salvation,
     which you have prepared in the presence of all peoples,

## Theological Perspective

Mary and Joseph dutifully take Jesus to fulfill the letter of Jewish law, and their diligence raises questions for Christians who feel no obligation to the Old Testament's laws. More personally, we see a family bringing their newborn child to the temple to make—a sacrifice? In our comfortable world, parents and newborn usually *receive* gifts instead of making them. What if we sacrificed something of immense value to mark a birth, to consecrate a child to God?

This purpose of the sacrifice in Luke 2? "For their purification." But there was no need for this child to be purified. No need for Mary to be purified either. Karl Barth rather wonderfully wrote that, when Jesus was baptized, he needed to be washed of sin—not *his* sin, but *our* sin: "No one who came to the Jordan was as laden and afflicted as He."[1] No one ever came to the temple for purification as laden with sin—not his, or his mother's, but ours—as Jesus. Notice the gender limitation in the text: "every male." Jesus bears even that narrow-minded injustice on behalf of all males and for all females.

Because of his purifying mission, Jesus is, as Oscar Hijuelos phrased it, "the most wanted child in the history of the world."[2] How lovely, how tender, the way aged Simeon, the frailties of his years draped

[1]Karl Barth, *Church Dogmatics* IV/4 (Edinburgh: T. & T. Clark, 1969), 59.
[2]Oscar Hijuelos, *Mr. Ives's Christmas* (New York: HarperCollins, 1995), 4.

## Pastoral Perspective

Anyone who has studied and practiced pastoral care knows the importance of case studies. A case, of course, is a situation that is located in a particular context with particular features, and exploration of this content yields perspective helpful in moving to deeper levels of understanding. Reflection on a case often is instructive and may accomplish several things. We may be reminded of realities and resources that have faded into the background of our experience and memory. In so reminding us, a case study can resensitize us to issues with which others are struggling and, at the same time, bring to mind other resources that may be helpful in understanding more deeply what is going on. A case provides an opportunity to gain new angles of vision on a particular human experience. It thereby enables us to generalize and add to our repertoire of knowledge as to resources, dangers, and opportunities to offer to others. And, of course, it widens our own capacities as we proceed along our way of caring for ourselves and others.

Though relatively brief, this lectionary text for the first Sunday after Christmas provides us with several "cases" for pastoral and homiletical reflection. The first case in the text is contained in verses 22–24. Mary and Joseph bring Jesus to the temple for the required Mosaic ritual of purification. Brief though it is, the scenario reminds reader and listener of at

³²a light for revelation to the Gentiles
  and for glory to your people Israel."
  ³³And the child's father and mother were amazed at what was being said about him. ³⁴Then Simeon blessed them and said to his mother Mary, "This child is destined for the falling and the rising of many in Israel, and to be a sign that will be opposed ³⁵so that the inner thoughts of many will be revealed— and a sword will pierce your own soul too."
  ³⁶There was also a prophet, Anna the daughter of Phanuel, of the tribe of Asher. She was of a great age, having lived with her husband seven years after her marriage, ³⁷then as a widow to the age of eighty-four. She never left the temple but worshiped there with fasting and prayer night and day. ³⁸At that moment she came, and began to praise God and to speak about the child to all who were looking for the redemption of Jerusalem.
  ³⁹When they had finished everything required by the law of the Lord, they returned to Galilee, to their own town of Nazareth. ⁴⁰The child grew and became strong, filled with wisdom; and the favor of God was upon him.

## Exegetical Perspective

The story of the presentation of Jesus in the temple concludes a larger narrative segment that introduces the reader to John the Baptist and Jesus. Luke parallels the material, presenting it in alternating segments.

| | |
|---|---|
| 1:3–25 | annunciation of John's birth |
| 1:26–38 | annunciation of Jesus' birth |
| 1:39–56 | Mary visits Elizabeth, two strands come together |
| 1:57–58 | John's birth |
| 1:59–66 | John's circumcision |
| 1:67–79 | Zechariah interprets the meaning of John's birth |
| 1:80 | summary of John's role |
| 2:1–20 | Jesus' remarkable birth |
| 2:21 | Jesus' circumcision |
| 2:22–39 | Simeon and Anna (=Hannah) interpret the meaning of Jesus' birth |
| 2:40 | Jesus' surpassing value over John (cf. 1:80) |

Beginning his Gospel in this fashion, Luke relates Jesus' birth to the history of Israel and his historical context, and he provides a glimpse of the greater divine purpose that Jesus will fulfill.

  The passage for this morning can be outlined as follows:

| | |
|---|---|
| 2:22–24 | the occasion and the mandate |
| 2:25–38 | the messengers and the message |
| 2:25–35 | Simeon |

## Homiletical Perspective

*The Reality of Congregational Time.* It is the first Sunday after Christmas Day. The cost of gift giving has been more than some members can bear. Some families entered the sacred season with great expectations, only to discover it was not what they thought it was. This is the time beyond means and expectations.

*The Context of Biblical Time.* Imagine the spiritual and emotional toll on Mary and Joseph during this past year. They are given a divine mission to complete in their human flesh, before they appear to be ready. These two new parents are within the first forty days of their baby's life. They have journeyed from Nazareth to Jerusalem, to Bethlehem, back to Jerusalem during a time of emotional and physical exhaustion. The text opens with the young and weary Mary and Joseph at the temple with their new baby boy. After many sleepless, uncomfortable nights, they meet two elders who also know something about time. These elders have been waiting for a lifetime to see the Messiah. It appears that Mary and Joseph have brought him to the temple in their arms.

  Simeon and Anna have waited a lifetime for this moment to find perfect peace. For Joseph and Mary it is only the beginning of their stewardship of a favored life. This is the beginning of a journey of

# Luke 2:22-40

## Theological Perspective

over him, cradles the infant Jesus in his arms. Imagine holding in your arms this most wanted child, the hope of the ages, the yearning of your entire life.

But Jesus was just a baby—and this is God's shrewdest device. As Luther put it, God became small for us in Christ; he showed us his heart, so our hearts might be won. Infants wield a kind of power. Muscular men with calloused hands become gentle as pillows when handed a baby; potent people with gruff voices adopt a falsetto and coo to an infant. God came down, not to thrash evildoers or crush the Romans, but as an infant, to elicit love, to nurture tenderness.

Simeon has waited all his life for this child. Now he can die in peace. This waiting and the dying in peace are theologically poignant for us who glance away from death anxiously, who die in considerable consternation. "Those who wait for the LORD shall renew their strength" (Isa. 40:31). "For God alone my soul waits in silence" (Ps. 62:1). We do not like to wait. We want to move, fill the time, stay in control, rush to the next titillation— and in our inability to be still and know that God is God, we miss God.

God is not a possession you nab and cling to now. God is like a lover at some distance. You are filled with longing—and the longing is sweet, delightful in anticipation, rippling with eagerness. Simeon waited, not for minutes or months but decades. Gregory of Nyssa understood this peculiar yearning and satisfaction: "constantly going on in the quest and never ceasing in ascent, seeing that every fulfillment . . . continually generates a further desire." This discovery, "far from making the soul despair, is actually an experience of God's fuller presence."[3]

Because of this child, Simeon can die calmly, confidently. He can be as hospitable to his impending death as he has been to the child Mary brought to the temple, embracing it, blessing God for it.

Then we see Anna, an octogenarian, having led a relatively uneventful life. Her gaze was focused on only one vista, God's salvation. God's blessing was not a continual smorgasbord of titanic experiences and shiny baubles. God's blessing was just one thing, and it was eighty years coming. "Purity of heart is to will one thing" (Søren Kierkegaard); "There is need of only one thing" (Luke 10:42), to be near Jesus, to see salvation dawn.[4]

[3] Jean Daniélou, *From Glory to Glory* (Crestwood: St. Vladimir's, 2001), 45f.
[4] Sören Kierkegaard, *Purity of Heart Is to Will One Thing*, trans. Douglas Steere (New York: Harper, 1938).

## Pastoral Perspective

least two things. Birth is both an ending and a beginning. In Jesus' case, of course, that is especially true. The realization of his special nature and mission is becoming more and more clear. But, even more to the pastoral point, this brief depiction reminds us of the importance of keeping faith. The Mosaic law required this ritual of coming to the temple and offering a sacrifice. Different sacrificial offerings were acceptable, depending on the parents' economic ability. In this case, given the modest, if not poor, circumstances of Mary and Joseph, the acceptable sacrifice was a pair of turtledoves. The birth of a child, regardless of family resources, brings with it responsibility. Jesus' parents are acknowledging and honoring their faith commitments and their recognition of the special quality of their child.

So these verses may serve a pastoral purpose in reminding all parents of the responsibilities that come with the birth of their own "special child." Further, this case reminds us that there are particular rituals available both to remind and to encourage mothers and fathers in their new tasks of parenting. And the resources extend beyond just the parents themselves. The temple represents the presence of a much wider array of persons, a community, and resources to undergird them. That was important in the life of Jesus, and it is important for all of us in our continuing care of children.

The second case is that of Simeon. Of course, as in every situation, his story is woven into a larger story, in this case the story of Jesus. Simeon is an old man carrying a vast hope. He has been waiting for this day, and by the providence of God his hope is fulfilled in the temple. While this aging saint rejoices in this particular moment, he represents a wider reality. At the birth of every child, there is a wider company of persons who have hopes and fears for the future. Some will remain silent and watch from afar. Others, like Simeon, will step forward and be devoted enough and courageous enough to tell parents what lies deep in their hearts. The parents of Jesus "were amazed" at what was being said to them. They heard the good news! But, Simeon was also honest and caring enough to tell them the painful news as well. No parent wants to hear a painful prospect for his or her child. But every parent, in order to fulfill the responsibilities of parenthood, needs to have someone prepare them for the difficulties that are likely to lie ahead. It was the good fortune of Mary and Joseph to have such a person come to them early in their parental life.

2:36–38   Hannah
2:39–40   you can go home again (cf. 2:4)
Luke 2:39 and 2:4 form an inclusio. It is time to look more closely at each narrative unit.

Luke 2:[21]–25. Luke's purpose in narrating these events seems clear. He wants to portray Mary and Joseph as obedient to God's revelation. Following Torah, they circumcise the baby Jesus on the eighth day, and according to Gabriel's instructions, they give the child his name (1:31). Both parents are attuned to divine revelation, whether it comes through an angel or the Torah. Notice that the Torah is first called "the law of Moses" (2:22) but is subsequently identified as "the law of the Lord" (2:23, 24). Their obedience to Torah is no less divine than their obedience to the angel. Both actions show their fidelity to God's purposes (Lev. 12:1–8; Exod. 13:2, 12, 15). Luke 2:23 is a free-flowing paraphrase of these texts, not a precise citation. Still, his point is clear. Jesus's parents bring him for circumcision (Lev. 12:3) and for the redeeming of their firstborn child (Exod. 13:2, 12, 15) in accordance with the "law of the Lord." Owing to their poverty, Mary and Joseph offer two turtledoves because they cannot afford a lamb (Lev. 12:8).

At first glance, the temple might seem to be an odd place for meeting prophets. It is customary to think of prophets and the temple at odds with each other. Yet throughout their histories Israel and Judah had prophets operating in the centers of power, including the likes of Nathan, Elijah, Elisha, and Jeremiah. In similar fashion, Simeon and Anna see in the birth of the child the beginning of a new order that will shake the foundations of the powers that be.

At the start, Luke provides a character description of Simeon to emphasize his trustworthiness as bearer of God's prophetic word. The messenger is congruent with the message. The Holy Spirit is mentioned three times in the introduction of Simeon (2:25, 26, 27); he is a Spirit-filled prophet on a mission for God. While it might seem to some that it is a chance encounter in the temple, Luke makes it clear that the Spirit made the appointment (2:27).

Simeon begins his inspired utterance with the emphatic "now," emphasizing the presence and nearness of salvation in the child. The request to "release" ("dismiss," NRSV) carries two meanings. First, release can mean, "let me die" (in fulfillment of the promise in 2:26), or, "release me from this vigil." Simeon has been, like Habakkuk before him, standing at his post, keeping watch and waiting for the Lord. The narrative provides a dramatic picture

unanswered questions for first-time parents. They know they have a long way to go in their responsibility as parents to fulfill the divine promise of parenthood they have made to God.

***The Dichotomy of Blessings in Poverty.*** Joseph and Mary were young people of limited means, who struggled to get to Bethlehem for the census. While there was no room at the inn, one might wonder if the new dad possessed the resources for a hotel stay. He stood by helpless, and poor, watching the mother of his child give birth next to beasts of burden. After his divine child's arrival in the world, he witnessed shepherds and others worship him. Then he was faced with his human role as a provider in the time beyond birth. All he had to offer his son was a life tied to the limitations of a father's social location.

The text tells us that Mary and Joseph, who Matthew says were later blessed with gifts from kings, could not afford to offer a lamb. They presented the gift assigned to the poor, a pair of turtledoves. Over and again, people told them of the blessing they had in their arms. Every day they struggled to make ends meet.

We live in a society where it is hard to understand the blessings in poverty. Mary and Joseph, like many poor parents in our midst today, were trying to be faithful, but the journey was not easy. In the context of the capitalism of our generation, it is hard to accept the idea of being blessed but not prosperous. The challenge for us to wrestle with is the injustice that many poor people of faith face. They are blessed. They hold new life and future possibilities in their arms. They possess faith, and yet they must find a way to afford the social expectations of church life. For many of the poor but faithful in our time, this is still a painful reality.

***The Call of Community to Bless beyond Words.*** The text tells us that Simeon was "guided by the Spirit" to come into the temple at the appointed time. When he arrived, he saw two young parents who had come a long way, to follow the law of the Lord and offer a sacrifice for their child. These young parents, like many others of that time, could have made the decision to give up on the faith, because it cost too much. Mary and Joseph remained committed to the rituals of the faith, even though religion cost them the daily resources they needed for survival.

Simeon was a seasoned man of faith. As one who had deep relationship with God, he had surely taken note of numerous young families coming and going

# Luke 2:22-40

## Theological Perspective

Just a child—but hardly safe and harmless. "This child is destined for the falling and the rising of many." This child provokes a crisis, a decision, for Simeon, for Anna, for all people of every generation. How we respond to this one person decides everything. The stakes are not trivial. It is not that, if we go with Jesus, our lives are 17 percent better, our happiness 14 percent higher, our marriages 16 percent healthier. It's all or nothing. You fall. Or you rise.

Notice the order. In the world, it's rise and fall. The rise and fall of the Third Reich, the rise and fall of the business tycoon, the rise and fall of a movie star. But with Jesus it's *fall and rise*. "Unless a grain of wheat falls into the earth and dies, it remains just a single grain; but if it dies, it bears much fruit" (John 12:24). Anna fasts "night and day," not "day and night." Jesus did not fly directly up into heaven once danger flared. He suffered and died, and *then* was raised to glory. We suffer and die—and not just at the end of life. "I have been crucified with Christ" (Gal. 2:19); I bear the death of Christ now. I deny myself. I am persecuted because I am in sync with Christ and out of sync with the world. We fall, and from that lowest point, we rise. We may just fall, but if we rise, we fall and then rise.

Perhaps Mary shuddered at Simeon's words. Mysteriously he spoke of a sword piercing her soul. It is moving to think of Mary, feeling Jesus kick in her womb, hearing his first cry, nursing him, watching his first steps. She witnessed the thirty years telescoped into a single verse: "The child grew and became strong." He left home and marshaled a following. But wicked men turned against her son, who was pure, good, all love. Mary had to watch as Simeon's prophecy was fulfilled. Her heart broke as she saw the lifeblood she had given him drain out of his beautiful body. The fall. But then the rise. Who, among all who witnessed Jesus risen from the dead, was more joyful to see him alive than his own mother?

JAMES C. HOWELL

## Pastoral Perspective

The story of Simeon and his interaction with the holy family reminds us of what we now know, that Jesus faces a life of glory and pain. But, this case reminds all of us as well of at least two things: more people than we know have an investment in those we love; and the most dedicated and courageous of those people will tell us of their hopes and of those things for which we should be prepared.

The third case is that of Anna, also in the temple. She, like Simeon, was a prophet. And, she, like Simeon, was a person with the wisdom of age, the inspiration of the Holy Spirit, and a lifetime spent in the temple. Her coming forward added to the power of what Simeon had already said, and she testifies again to the emotional and spiritual investment in the child Jesus and offers praise to God for his birth and life to come. Again, like Simeon she reminds us of the surrounding cloud of witnesses to whom we can turn with our hopes and our fears—and those who will approach us, whether we seek them out or not!

Those two saints, in combination with the faithfulness of Joseph and Mary, lead to the fourth, and final, case in this passage—the case of Jesus himself. With the grace of God and the commitment of his parents, and surrounded by the hopes and dreams of so many, he was launched toward becoming the person God intended him to be. And so should be the case with every child—created in the image of God, surrounded by God's grace, cared for by faithful parents, and encouraged by supporters, both known and unknown, within the community of faith and others in God's wider good creation.

WILLIAM V. ARNOLD

of Simeon sweeping down on Mary and Joseph, taking the child in his arms; before they can present him to the Lord, Simeon does the honors (2:27–28). In this way, Simeon's prophetic presentation trumps the usual temple ceremony. His declaration is composed of three simple couplets in 2:29, 2:30–31, and 2:32. What is remarkable is that the prophecy joins together the revelation to the Gentiles with the glory of Israel. The redemption of the nations is tied to the fulfillment of Israel.

Simeon's message comes in two parts. First, he speaks to the Master (*despota*). His prophecy has opened a door onto the future fulfillment of God's promises (2:29–32). Second, he blesses Mary and Joseph (2:33–35). They are understandably "amazed," a verb that suggests confusion. Joseph and Mary are present as "the child's father and mother." When Simeon addresses them, however, he speaks only to Mary (2:34). The "falling and rising" theme anticipates an important Lukan theme, the eschatological reversal that will become a hallmark of Jesus' ministry. Even Mary will feel the consequences of her son's work; "a sword will pierce" her heart as well. The phrase has been taken to refer to Mary's pain at seeing her son's rejection, or it has been taken as a symbol of judgment that will affect even Jesus' own family.

Anna's name in the Greek is Hannah. It is important to emphasize this in light of Luke's allusive use of 1 Samuel 1–2, the story of the birth of Samuel to Hannah and Elkanah. What the two events share is the sense that God is doing something new to facilitate the fulfillment of God's purposes in history. Both are transitional events. If Simeon spoke to God and then to Mary and Joseph, Hannah speaks "to all who were looking for the redemption of Jerusalem." The Word becomes public in a way it has not been. This means that Anna is more than a distant echo of Simeon, but has her own distinctive role to play.

Finally, the passage ends on a surprising note. The family returns home. The prophets have given us an anticipation and a faint glimpse of the future, but for the moment, people will return to the ordinary circumstances of their lives but living with a new expectancy and confidence in the fulfillment of God's purposes.[1]

WILLIAM R. HERZOG II

from the temple. Simeon was expecting a miracle and waiting for the Messiah. When he saw that this young family brought only turtledoves, he knew they did not have the funds to offer a lamb. In other words, Simeon in a moment knew the long-awaited Savior of the world was being raised by parents in poverty.

Imagine being this seasoned person of faith, who had the chance to witness a poor teen mom and a dad with the Anointed One in their care. Imagine knowing they had a child with tremendous promise and possibility for an entire people. If you were in such a position, would you do something more for this family than offer a blessing?

As people of faith in a privileged nation, we have an obligation to care for poor families in tangible ways, so they can raise their children with limited burdens. We miss out, as a community, when we do not acknowledge that all children in our midst are a gift to the world. Perhaps we are called to create a society with a positive regard for struggling, faithful parents, because we believe we are costewards of the future. Perhaps this text is pleading with those of us in this generation to create a more just society for the children who come into the world through parents of limited means.

We have questions with which to grapple. If Jesus were born today, to teen parents in American urban poverty, would he be better off now than he was 2,000 years ago? Will we answer the call to create a global community that makes sure all mothers and fathers have adequate health care, food, education, clothing, and shelter? When we consider the abundance of our nation, do faithful people of means have an obligation to the poor beyond offering them verbal blessings?

SHELLEY D. B. COPELAND

---

[1] Some works consulted in preparing this study: Joseph Fitzmyer, *The Gospel according to Luke I–IX* (Garden City, NY: Doubleday, 1979); Joel Green, *The Gospel of Luke* (Grand Rapids: Eerdmans, 1997); Herman Hendrickx, *The Third Gospel for the Third World* (Collegeville, MN: Liturgical Press, 1996).

# Jeremiah 31:7-14

⁷For thus says the LORD:
　　Sing aloud with gladness for Jacob,
　　　and raise shouts for the chief of the nations;
　　proclaim, give praise, and say,
　　　"Save, O LORD, your people,
　　　the remnant of Israel."
⁸See, I am going to bring them from the land of the north,
　　and gather them from the farthest parts of the earth,
　　among them the blind and the lame,
　　　those with child and those in labor, together;
　　　a great company, they shall return here.
⁹With weeping they shall come,
　　and with consolations I will lead them back,
　　I will let them walk by brooks of water,
　　　in a straight path in which they shall not stumble;
　　for I have become a father to Israel,
　　　and Ephraim is my firstborn.

## Theological Perspective

In this passage, the shepherd God (v. 10) leads his people home from exile in the north, in Babylon. The image of the Lord as shepherd is certainly an ancient one in Israel's thought (Ps. 23:1, Gen. 49:24). The text comprises a series of remarkable reversals, beginning with Judah as the "chief of the nations" in verse 7, which in the sixth century would have been a remarkable statement, most at odds with the apparent geopolitics of the day. Indeed the passage itself acknowledges this in crediting the Lord with redeeming Jacob (Israel) from the grasp of "hands too strong for him" (v. 11). Compared with the Babylonians who overwhelmed them and the Persians who continued to rule over them, the Judeans were a small nation. But in this instance, as at other moments in history, "God chose what is weak in the world to shame the strong" (1 Cor. 1:27).

One sees not only the reversal of the expected international power relationships and of the physical direction of exile, but also of some of the deeper ills inflicted by exile. For example, one of the most horrific yet common images of the destroyed Jerusalem is that of a violated woman (e.g., Lam. 1–2). Here the safe return of childbearing women affirms the possibility of new life for the restored community. The land that was scourged by the assaults of the Mesopotamians is to be rich and

## Pastoral Perspective

A young child is crouching over the sand, shovel in hand. Below her sustained yogalike posture—knees bent, head hung low—is a sandcastle.

Hours later, after high tide reaches its height and recedes, the child returns to the beach. Her castle has been reduced to an inexact mound. After a slight sigh, the child strikes her pose again and starts digging, dumping, and packing the wet sand.

We build something beautiful in our minds or with our hands, and we hope our work endures. Then the tide comes in and rolls over us. And yet, hurricane season after hurricane season, trial after trial, setback after setback, we rebuild. It is what we do. It is also what God does.

The prophet Jeremiah writes eloquently of such a God. Jeremiah 31 is part of a well-known collection of restoration oracles called the Little Book of Consolation (chaps. 30–33). This week's passage in particular reveals God's promise to refashion and rebuild the fractured covenant with the people of Israel. Upon that promise rests Israel's hope for homecoming.

On the surface, the language of exodus (literally, "departure") is replaced with the vernacular of return. Israel's memory of wandering in the wilderness gives way to the promise of a "straight path" (v. 9). The once murmuring congregation of Israel

<sup>10</sup>Hear the word of the Lord, O nations,
   and declare it in the coastlands far away;
   say, "He who scattered Israel will gather him,
   and will keep him as a shepherd a flock."
<sup>11</sup>For the Lord has ransomed Jacob,
   and has redeemed him from hands too strong for him.
<sup>12</sup>They shall come and sing aloud on the height of Zion,
   and they shall be radiant over the goodness of the Lord,
   over the grain, the wine, and the oil,
   and over the young of the flock and the herd;
   their life shall become like a watered garden,
   and they shall never languish again.
<sup>13</sup>Then shall the young women rejoice in the dance,
   and the young men and the old shall be merry.
I will turn their mourning into joy,
I will comfort them, and give them gladness for sorrow.
<sup>14</sup>I will give the priests their fill of fatness,
   and my people shall be satisfied with my bounty,
            says the Lord.

## Exegetical Perspective

The record of the prophet Jeremiah's work and words comes to us from a dramatic and intense time in Israel's history. The figure of Jeremiah himself was so intense and extraordinary, his words so threatening and frightening, that he was vilified in his own day as a traitor and heretic. Only much later, with several generations' worth of hindsight, could the Judean and Israelite communities see that Jeremiah's harsh words had indeed been both prophetic and accurate—indeed, had been words of love from God himself.

Jeremiah preached and prophesied from about 627 BCE (the thirteenth year of King Josiah's reign) to the fall of Jerusalem to the Babylonians in 587 BCE. In the reign of Josiah, the mighty Assyrian empire fell. Finally free of this ever-present threat, Judea's national mood took a turn (perhaps understandably) toward a strong religious nationalism. Most of the era's prophets saw this as a good thing, as a return to the faith and practice required by the Lord.

Jeremiah, however, was a lone (if loud) voice to the contrary. In his view, the new religious nationalism was not righteousness, but self-righteousness. It was not faith, but a self-satisfied arrogance that would eventually lead to worse trouble than before. Those who trusted in themselves and their own righteousness were

## Homiletical Perspective

Christmas has bloomed. The blossoms found in Jeremiah are lush and scented. Here is the gracious promise we've all been waiting for. God is among us in love and power. What a gift!

Yet, on second look, this passage brings before us the people we rarely see in church. There is a troubled quality to the crowd. There is a messiness about its business. Reverence is replaced by simple presence. What you see is what you get. People are gathering just as they are, warts and all.

Of course, in truth, we see such people all the time. We are those people. Our business is unfinished, and the rooms in our houses are cluttered with things too messy to show visitors. We have been scattered from deep things, from ourselves, from our kin. We wonder if anyone can see or hear us, if anyone will bring us home. This text presents what is going on behind the Christmas tableau. It shows what happens before the shepherds arrive and after the magi depart. This text may well speak to us more readily than the famous Christmas stories we have just heard. It offers a clean and undecorated tale of a caring God who does not forget who or where we are. This God accepts us in our disarray and gathers up every aspect of our lives. Gifts deepen to a sense of a gift of belonging. Greetings take the form of a personal touch and a

# Jeremiah 31:7-14

## Theological Perspective

fruitful again. Exile and return continue to be powerful metaphors for theology; many believers and communities experience real exile from home and family, like those from New Orleans who lost their homes to Hurricane Katrina. Furthermore, Christians have long pictured themselves as sojourners in this life, separated from their true homeland with God (see Heb. 11:13–16). Augustine's famous line reflects on this condition: "Our hearts are restless until they find their rest in you."[1]

The procession homeward depicted by Jeremiah is also a remarkable scene of healing and inclusion. The blind and lame, excluded from coming before God in Leviticus 21:18, are here welcomed back to Jerusalem. This fits with a broader theme of inclusion in postexilic prophetic texts; elsewhere, foreigners are also said to be welcomed to serve God in new and closer ways (Isa. 56:6). The return from exile might be envisioned as a new exodus, with a new "mixed multitude" seeking to reclaim the land of Judah in hard times (in the exilic and early postexilic periods, Judah was less wealthy and much less populous than before). If God is a Father (v. 9) then this passage describes God as exceedingly generous in love. One thinks of Psalm 68:5–6, where the Lord is called a "father of orphans," who gives a home to the solitary and abandoned. Churches today that are ministering in challenging contexts might take Jeremiah's inclusive word as a model; God has often chosen to use those whom humans do not expect. So it was even with Moses (with his speech impediment), David (the youngest son), and Jesus (of lowly birth).

From another angle, one might conceptualize this text as one in a sequence of passages incorporating water imagery: Psalm 23's "He leads me beside still waters"; Psalm 137's "By the rivers of Babylon—there we sat down and there we wept"; and now this journey home "by brooks of water, in a straight path in which they shall not stumble" (31:9). Walter Brueggemann has suggested that the Psalms can be thought of as leading the reader through three psychological stages: *orientation* (to the worship of God), *disorientation* (a loss of direction, or a sense of the failure of the promises), and *reorientation*.[2] One sees just such a progression in these three texts. God does not punish forever, nor has Israel abandoned its faith in its God because of its awful historical experiences. Indeed the proclamation of Israel here

[1] *Confessions* 1.1.
[2] See Walter Brueggemann, *The Psalms and the Life of Faith*, ed. Patrick D. Miller (Minneapolis: Fortress Press, 1995), 3–32.

## Pastoral Perspective

"shall not stumble" (v. 9) on the stones of complaint but will return with songs of praise. Thirst in the desert will be assuaged during this journey by "brooks of water" (v. 9). Indeed, the sojourn Jeremiah foresees moves not to a promised land but to land Israel knows well enough to call home.

Interestingly, the prophet preaches of such a homecoming before the people of Israel leave their land. As this book is structured, Babylon's dispersal of Israel looms ominously on the horizon (chap. 39). Even before the people of Israel fall to the deluge of that foreign foe, the prophet speaks God's word of reconciliation. God's promise will weather the gathering storm.

For our congregations, this welcoming embrace of Israel might call to mind the father's forgiveness in Christ's parable of the prodigal son (Luke 15). God's capacity to restore Israel might echo David's Good Shepherd God who "restores my soul" (Ps. 23). In essence, these familiar images of Scripture complement an important aspect of the God Jeremiah reveals. The God we encounter in this passage claims Israel as a child, "my firstborn" (v. 9) and "will gather him, and will keep him as shepherd a flock" (v. 10). In this passage God is depicted as both father and shepherd.

However, God's leadership and restoration of Israel will not be merely for the individual—for a wayward son or a shepherd-king. The prophet speaks of *communal* redemption. Not only will young women dance and men of every age rejoice, but the most vulnerable members of the Diaspora flock will return to Israel too. Through the prophet, God offers assurance to the "blind and the lame" (v. 8) and to "those with child and those in labor" (v. 8). God says, "I am going to bring them . . . and gather them" (v. 8). This redemption song is intended for a mighty chorus.

Thus the promise of communal salvation raises questions for both church and state: Who in our communities is not yet singing with joy? Who has been left behind? According to the prophet's vision of Israel's redemption, the "least" among us are as important as the "greatest" in the economy of God's salvation.

"Redeem" (v. 11) is a word not often spoken by the prophet. As John Bright reminds us, "redeem" appears only once more in the unquestioned poetic sayings of Jeremiah (Jer. 50:34).[1] Jeremiah paints this promise of redemption with colorful images, none

[1] John Bright, *Jeremiah*, Anchor Bible, vol. 21 (Garden City, NY: Doubleday, 1965), 281.

doomed to follow the same path as the Assyrians, as he makes clear in chapter 17: "Cursed are those who trust in mere mortals and make mere flesh their strength, whose hearts turn away from the LORD. . . . Blessed are those who trust in the LORD, whose trust is the LORD" (vv. 5, 7).

In the midst of Jeremiah's warnings and judgments, we come across a short, three-chapter section (chaps. 30, 31, and 33, interrupted by a short chapter of prose narrative). This section is so unique and such a unit unto itself that it has come to be known as the Book of Consolations. Jeremiah is not a happy or particularly encouraging prophet; he spends forty years trying to warn his people that disaster is coming, and for forty years the only attention he is paid is punishment and hatred. Jeremiah's frustration and anger are understandably clear in many passages. Nevertheless Jeremiah is a true prophet, and a true prophet's function is to speak the words of God. The words of God are ultimately words of love.

This Book of Consolations includes some of the Bible's most beloved passages and verses. "I have loved you with an everlasting love" (31:3) and "I will turn their mourning into joy, I will comfort them, and give them gladness for their sorrow" (31:13) are two examples. This is also a section in which Christians will recognize prophetic words that have come to be associated with the life of Jesus: "A voice is heard in Ramah, lamentation and bitter weeping. Rachel is weeping for her children, and she refuses to be comforted for her children, because they are no more" (31:15). "In those days and at that time I will cause a righteous Branch to spring up for David; and he shall execute justice and righteousness in the land" (33:15).

These echoes, though not specifically included in today's pericope, help the Christian interpreter tie Jeremiah's words to the Christmas season in which they are read. Jeremiah is offering God's people a promise of love, redemption, and renewal. He sees what is going to happen—defeat and exile—but he also sees that God will not abandon his people. Their punishment will not go on forever, and God will save them both from their enemies and from themselves. It is a pattern that is repeated in every aspect of the life of faith, from Jesus' crucifixion leading to the new life of resurrection, to the periods of decline and apathy that precede a people's vibrant renewal, to the dark and dry periods that precede spiritual consolations for individual believers. Nobody wants to hear that pain comes before

guided walk toward something deeply homelike. This text carries the promise uncluttered by the cultural Christmas we have just known. It speaks to the unguarded part of us and gathers up the longings that the Christmas season cannot fulfill. Grief, regret, anger, neglect, and chances come and gone are somehow reclaimed and dealt with in this generous and all-inclusive vision. Beneath our church smiles and Christmas glee, we long to know such richness of soul.

In the text, the recipient of the news seems to alone. He is suddenly overrun by relatives from near and far. The church can produce such hermits busying ourselves with our own things while outside the rest of the world goes about its business.

Christmas may display the hermit more than usual. It is our season, our gifts, and our expectations. Yet in the text the hermit is being pushed toward a broader welcome. The first thing to go is our penchant for control. The world is much bigger than what we see through the slit in our door. The Holy One is keeping covenant in ways broader than we imagine. God speaks through diversity. We might approve or disapprove, but the speaking continues. Tension rises. Suddenly we have strangers in our backyard. This is the small town facing the steady influx of urban sprawl, the seaside hamlet bracing for summer tourists, the church and its neighbors squaring off over social issues. It is the secular world climbing all over us.

Consider too the range of the holy call. It includes the blind and the lame, often found wanting in a culture that holds the notion of purity as sacred. We may pity, ignore, or build satisfying lives of service among the disenfranchised, but to imagine that God calls them may be a stretch. God calls them. What must change to hear and honor such a call?

We are outnumbered too. Those coming are the rest of us, the ones we never see, the ones with whom we have no dealings. Things will change. Our pew, our place, our policies, our posterity shall be put at risk.

Something in me is tempted to bar the door. However, this text proclaims that there is a broader purpose at work. Our conversations, intersections, and quiet moments, our sermons, prayers, affections, and convictions, shall then be tools in the hands of the Great Shepherd.

"I will give the priests their fill of fatness, and my people shall be satisfied with my bounty" (v. 14). Here is good news. This transforming parade may well freshen the religious systems meant to honor

# Jeremiah 31:7–14

## Theological Perspective

in Jeremiah 31 is very much like that of a psalmist who tells of his suffering at God's hand, only to follow with an account of his healing, and close with praise: "Declare it in the coastlands far away; say: 'He who scattered Israel will gather him'" (v. 10). Also like a psalm, this passage invites the reader to sing with joy.

In Christian theology the historical deliverance of Israel has been likened to God's spiritual deliverance of believers from sin. So wrote Calvin: "Hence the prophet . . . describing the spiritual redemption of the believing folk, speaks of them as 'redeemed from the hand of one stronger than they.' By this he surely means the tight fetters with which the sinner is bound so long as, forsaken by the Lord, he lives under the devil's yoke."[3] One could expand this comparison in new directions by considering the rich promises of verses 12–14. Deliverance from sin may seem to be an austere sort of blessing; that is, it may seem to indicate merely the absence of wrongdoing. These verses in Jeremiah, however, depict a restored life of wholeness (shalom) in which the entire creation, from fields to flocks to humankind, rejoices in right relationships and therefore flourishes. If sin is wrong relationship to God and to God's creation, then its absence is not a void but a joyful and harmonious dance.

Extending the idea of Babylon's power as a metaphor for sin's power, the book of Revelation might provide a fruitful set of texts to put in conversation with this one. Revelation recounts God's overthrow of a wicked city referred to as Babylon, although historically probably it was Rome. Just as God's overthrow of the historical Babylon was considered the prerequisite for the fruitful restoration of Judah, so God's overthrow of this metaphorical Babylon (sin) through Christ might be considered the prerequisite for the final restoration of right order on earth, symbolized in Revelation by the descent of the new heavens and new earth. Both cases call for the believer's faith in God's ultimate control of history, despite the sufferings and imperfections of our own times.

CHRISTOPHER B. HAYS

## Pastoral Perspective

more pregnant with possibility than that of "a watered garden" (v. 12).

The mere mention of a watered garden on the second Sunday after Christmas may pose a challenge to those who feel the cold clutch of winter's gusts. But as Israel looks forward to the softer soil of salvation, so may we remember and look forward to the summer garden bursting with flower and fruit. As Israel's homecoming resonates with the story of the exodus, the garden in this passage reaches deeply into the recesses of Israel's collective memory and points to a day when the people of Israel will come alive like a new and improved creation.

This image of the watered garden reveals something of God's nature and of Israel's new life. The "watered garden" suggests God's intention to tend Israel; the Creator's rains will fall gently upon their fields. And if the German root of "garden" (an enclosed, protected space) reflects the spirit of the prophet's message, perhaps we can imagine Israel enjoying the protective care of God. The watered garden of Israel's future foretells both God's nurture and fortification of the people.

Moreover, if the people of Israel—and the people of our congregations—are to live like a "watered garden," then the people share some responsibility too. Adam and Eve were cast from Eden, but the people of Israel are called upon to bear the good fruit of obedience. The bounty that awaits Israel pronounces both God's ability to raise a garden from the formerly hard soil of Israel's heart and Israel's renewed disposition to grow heavenward toward their God.

As the new year dawns, words of renewal fill the air. God speaks a forgiving word and promises the return of God's children. God plans to rebuild and refashion individual lives and communities of faith. Looking through the dim glass, we are witnesses to the power of God's reconciling love in the world. We are witnesses to redemption's "straight path" back to God. We are members of a mighty chorus that fills the air with a song of hope and homecoming.

ANDREW NAGY-BENSON

---

[3]John Calvin, *The Institutes of the Christian Religion*, 2 vols., ed. John T. McNeill, trans. Ford Lewis Battles, LCC (Philadelphia: Westminster Press, 1960), 2.3.5.

## Exegetical Perspective

healing, or darkness before light, or dishonor before glory, but Jeremiah could see that Israel itself was about to begin that cycle again. The grace present in the cycle, as Jeremiah offers in the passage, is the comfort God always gives in the hard times, the promise that when the hard times end, we will be closer to God than we were before.

The pericope for the second Sunday of Christmas, Jeremiah 31:7–14, evokes the same theme that the Isaiah readings evoke for the Christmas season. That theme is homecoming. The first Christmas reading talks of Israel's vindication, her exiles returning, and the homeland prospering. The Epiphany reading speaks of sons and daughters returning to their rightful home. Somehow, the birth of Jesus is seen as the fulfillment of these promises of homecoming and restoration. Jeremiah proclaims that the Lord will "bring them from the land of the north, and gather them from the farthest parts of the earth" (v. 8), and that "with weeping they shall come, and with consolations I will lead them back" (v. 9). Demonstrating God's own compassion, Jeremiah makes a point of proclaiming that even those who could not otherwise be expected to make the journey will be included, "among them the blind and the lame, those with child and those in labor [or according to some translations, the newborn], together" (v. 8). Jeremiah, perhaps counterintuitively, understood that if things are hard for most people, things are even harder for those whose lives present particular struggles, such as pregnancy or handicaps. Again Jeremiah speaks the hope of God to those who need it most.

In some ways (that Jeremiah doubtless never intended) these words evoke Jesus' own ministry, in which neither women, children, nor the handicapped were left behind. For now, though, it is still Christmas, and the emphasis remains upon the fulfillment of God's promises. Jeremiah tells us that God is faithful and will return the exiles to their homes. At Christmas we know that God did not stop there; he made his home with us, as well, in the presence of Jesus.

KATHERINE C. CALORE

## Homiletical Perspective

the holy. We know the soul's thinness these days, and a dearth of spiritual intimacy. Church life rides on a ceremonial surface, rarely touching the places most hungry in our lives. When God moves among us in the variety and freshness found everywhere, we may well then taste and see that the Lord is good.

As this rich passage settles over me, I am amazed at how much I need to hear its good news. I do not want to be alone with my people, and theology, and tradition, with my little hopes and dreams. It is not enough. I need to hear that the whole people is coming, that God is weaving the world through everyone.

"For the Lord has ransomed Jacob, and has redeemed him from hands too strong for him" (v. 11). Here is the saga of "resurrection" in a phrase. Is this experience not played out before us in the tales of the empty tomb? God's spirit will lift to safety all who wrestle for truth in turbulent times. The world is overwhelming. Changes are swift and drastic. Meaning is uncertain. Yet we are not alone. God is greater. God is here.

Please note that this human parade does not end up within denominational corrals. It picks us up as it sweeps along. Its destination is hidden in the God who calls. Still, there is a strange security in this. So much so that we may even choose to open our doors and risk the richness of the rabble.

One sermon sparker may be our remembrance of one time in a group in which we were not the leader. Someone else had the vision. Others took up the tasks. We helped and observed, and felt the enthusiasm rising. It was the spirit of group participation. We did it together. It was worthy, and we liked it.

G. MALCOLM SINCLAIR

# Psalm 147:12-20

<sup>12</sup>Praise the Lord, O Jerusalem!
    Praise your God, O Zion!
<sup>13</sup>For he strengthens the bars of your gates;
    he blesses your children within you.
<sup>14</sup>He grants peace within your borders;
    he fills you with the finest of wheat.
<sup>15</sup>He sends out his command to the earth;
    his word runs swiftly.
<sup>16</sup>He gives snow like wool;
    he scatters frost like ashes.
<sup>17</sup>He hurls down hail like crumbs—
    who can stand before his cold?
<sup>18</sup>He sends out his word, and melts them;
    he makes his wind blow, and the waters flow.
<sup>19</sup>He declares his word to Jacob,
    his statutes and ordinances to Israel.
<sup>20</sup>He has not dealt thus with any other nation;
    they do not know his ordinances.
    Praise the Lord!

## Theological Perspective

Woven throughout the Psalms is the theme of the special place of the city of Jerusalem as an expression of God's providence for and God's presence with the people of Israel. It is perhaps all summed up in Psalm 48:1–2, where Jerusalem is referred to as both "the city of our God" and "the city of the great King." Psalm 87:3 goes on to assert: "Glorious things are spoken of you, O city of God."

As the Psalter draws to a conclusion, Psalm 147 revisits this subject, revisits the city, as it were. In very concrete, human, even poignant terms it describes the blessings of life within the precincts of the city—manifestations of God's care for Israel and a testimony to God's essential, sovereign, and steadfast love. In doing this the psalmist provides a vivid portrait of what is at the heart of every effort to create a communal life with promise and integrity and lifts this concern to the level of a legitimate theological and ethical consideration.

Recognition and enjoyment of the blessings that are provided by God's sovereign actions point beyond themselves to a particular life of faith, in this psalm characterized, on the one hand, by hopeful confidence and, on the other, by a particular vocation from God to live daily in a manner that is itself a reflection of God's character. Simply stated, it is a life of hope and loyalty.

## Pastoral Perspective

Christmas, we say, is a time for giving. In this season, we have had many opportunities to give to others: Gifts to family and friends; or perhaps we "adopted" a family in need during the holidays—supplying food for a Christmas feast or toys and clothing for children; or at the least, we have dropped an extra few coins into the red donation bucket at the local mall. Spending money on ourselves, we feel better if we extend a portion of that generosity to others. But is Christmas primarily the season of giving? William Willimon, United Methodist bishop and provocative preacher, says the nativity stories in Luke and Matthew offer an alternative point that has the power to reframe our perspective and reshape us as a people.

Willimon writes that the Christmas of the Gospels puts us in the position of receivers, not givers—a position he suspects we find uncomfortable. We are better givers than "getters," he ventures,

not because we are generous people but because we are proud, arrogant people. . . . We prefer to think of ourselves as givers—powerful, competent, self-sufficient, capable people whose goodness motivates us to employ some of our power, competence and gifts to benefit the less fortunate [but which still leaves us the powerful ones]. Which is a direct contradiction of the biblical account of the first Christmas. There we are portrayed not as the

## Exegetical Perspective

"*Hallelu-yah!* How good it is to sing praises to our God, for he is gracious, and a song of praise is ever fitting." So begins the psalmist. However good it may be, it is not immediately apparent that this song is "fitting." In a world gone increasingly haywire, where hurricanes release their annual destructive fury against the coast and those who dwell thereon, and where nations and people regularly beat plowshares and pruning hooks into weapons of mass destruction, one is almost forced to ask, Why should we praise God? Psalm 147 begs to offer an answer. It is, to paraphrase the words of common liturgy, because God is good . . . all the time.

Psalm 147 begins and ends with the imperative, *hallelu-yah,* "Praise the Lord!" Within the bracket created by these first and final words, the psalmist offers a complex of reasons why the faithful should obey that imperative. In typical hymnic fashion, the reasons fall into two categories: God's providential act in creating and ordering the universe, and God's saving action in delivering and sustaining the faith community.

The psalm is easily structured in three parts, verses 1–6, verses 7–11, and verses 12–20. Each section begins with imperatives of praise, and each dwells on both God's creative providence and God's saving grace as justification for the praise. Many

## Homiletical Perspective

Our reading is the third section of a classic psalm of praise. The temptation when preaching such psalms is to turn delight into duty: "Israel praises God in this magnificent psalm. We Christians ought to praise God also. "The general homiletical strategy in such psalms might be to turn from the imperative demanding praise to the recitation of the blessings that call forth the praise. The naming or "counting" of the blessings takes up much of the psalm, and it can do likewise in a sermon.

An initial difficulty for "counting the blessings" in this psalm is its contrast between universality and specificity. There is from the beginning of the psalm a contrast, perhaps a tension, between praise for those mercies that God extends to all nations and those that God grants specifically to Israel. Although the psalm initially praises God for the restoration of Jerusalem, much of the early part of the psalm is about blessings that God has granted to all nations and indeed to the world as a whole. God's rule over nature—numbering the stars, providing rain for the earth and food for the ravens—is hardly manifest only in the neighborhood of Jerusalem. Moreover, one hopes that God "heals the brokenhearted" (v. 3) in other nations as well. As our reading begins, there is a return to thanksgiving for that which pertains directly to the covenant relationship with Israel. We

# Psalm 147:12-20

## Theological Perspective

Psalm 147:12–20 is clearly the second half of the psalm. As a parallel expression, it revisits what has been said in the first half of the psalm, but it intensifies that expression and in doing so it identifies the themes mentioned above. In the first half, Jerusalem is referred to as a subject of God's blessing. In this second half, the city is personified as if its corporate existence were more than the sum of its constituent lives. Its well-being is marked by security and safety. Thus the "gates" are watched and strong. Everyone's well-being is measured by the well-being of all the children. It is a place of prosperity, that is, "the finest of wheat" (v. 14). But the prosperity that is envisioned is more than wealth, for the word first used in the verse is translated "peace." Again, the corporate identity of the community suggests blessings that are experienced by everyone.

This is a theological vision, hope, and goal. As such it is also a plumb line. If this vision ever existed at a given moment, it certainly was not every moment. Psalm 55 speaks of "violence and strife in the city" (v. 9) as well as "oppression and fraud" in the "marketplace" (v. 11). No matter how preliminary and momentary are the experiences of that civic safety and peace, they are blessings that are real and exist as a compass heading for what is promised and intended by God.

Both halves of the psalm identify God's blessing for Jerusalem with the same sovereign power that orders the natural world. In the reference to the experience of the hardship of winter and then its timely passing, there is the affirmation that this is not a matter of some mechanical or even some semisacred cycle of nature. It is, rather, a manifestation of a timely divine forbearance that speaks of God's mercy and care.

The whole operation of the natural world in its diversity and richness is to the psalmist effected by the will and word of God. God "sends out his command" (v. 15) and "sends out his word" (v. 18). However, when it comes to Israel, God "declares his word" (v. 19) in the form of statutes and ordinances. As much as the events of exodus and the promised security of the covenant through David, these statutes and ordinances are a continuation of God's creation of Israel as a community that expresses in and to the world this God's character. Faithfulness to them is Israel's part in the establishment of that security and peace that is so appreciated and desired. The stakes are quite high! Safety and prosperity that do not include everyone or are at the expense of others are not going to endure.

## Pastoral Perspective

givers we wish we were but as the receivers we are. Luke and Matthew go to great lengths to demonstrate that we—with our power, generosity, competence and capabilities—had little to do with God's work in Jesus.

Willimon quotes Rabbi Michael Goldberg, who in his book *Jews and Christians* says that

> as a Jew he is impressed reading Matthew's account of the nativity by how utterly passive the actors are. As a Jew, he answers to the story of the Exodus, a story of how God liberated the chosen people through the enlistment and prodding of people like Moses, Aaron and Miriam. But the Christmas story implies that what God wants to do for us is so strange, so beyond the bounds of human effort and striving, that God must resort to utterly unnatural, supernatural means.

What God wanted to do for us was so far beyond our own imagining that God resorted to "angels, pregnant virgins, and stars in the sky to get it done." Says Willimon: "We didn't think of it, understand it, or approve it. All we could do, at Bethlehem, was receive it. A gift from a God we hardly knew."[1]

Psalm 147:12–20 helps us to see this alternative view of ourselves not as givers but as "getters," and to see that this "season of giving" is instead the season of receiving. Psalm 147:12–20 brings us empty-handed into Jerusalem, into God's presence, to receive all that God has done and gives. The action in this psalm, the power at work in the world, belongs to God, not to us. God is both subject and verb throughout these verses. God strengthens the bars of Zion's gates. God blesses the children within. God grants peace within Israel's borders and fills people with finest wheat. God sends out commands; God's word runs swiftly. God sends snow and hail—and melts them, too. God makes the winds blow and the waters flow. In the presence of this divine power, recounted verse after verse, God's people become keenly aware of their own powerlessness. In this recounting of God's bounty toward us, we see our empty-handedness and inability to meet our own needs.

Perhaps the congregation that first heard these words was especially aware of their need to receive from God. Perhaps they knew quite plainly of their powerlessness to supply their own future. While a precise date cannot be ascertained for Psalm 147, some scholars believe this psalm comes from the

[1]William Willimon, "The God We Hardly Knew," in *Watch for the Light: Readings for Advent and Christmas* (Farmington, PA: Plough Publishing House, 2001), 141–49.

scholars have argued that the three sections compose two, or even three, separate psalms. In fact, both Greek and Latin traditions of the Psalter preserve verses 12–20 as a freestanding psalm. However, each of the final five psalms in the Psalter begins and ends with the imperative, *hallelu-yah*, "Praise the LORD!" Separating Psalm 147 into two or three psalms breaks this pattern. This suggests that the arrangement of the Masoretic Text (the standard text of the Hebrew Bible) reflects the intent of the collectors of the book of Psalms.

Verses 12–20 exhibit within themselves the same hymnic structure visible in the psalm as a whole. Verse 12 begins with a double imperative of praise (*šebhi* and *haleli*). The first imperative translated "praise" is a form of the verb *šabah*, which occurs also in Psalms 63:4 and 106:47; Ecclesiastes 4:2 and 8:15. In these latter contexts, the verb carries the sense of "to commend," although it is likely intended here merely as a synonym for *halel*. The following verses convey the reasons for praise: God's benevolence to Israel and God's majesty and power visible in the forces of nature. Both God's deliverance of Israel and God's rule over creation are classical justifications for the praise of God.

Verses 13–14 detail the providence of God to Jerusalem: God provides strong defenses (v. 13a), blesses the progeny of the city (v. 13b), grants peace within the surrounding territory governed by Jerusalem (v. 14a), and fills the communal granaries with wheat (v. 14b).

Verses 15–17 focus on God's command of natural forces, especially those of winter: snow (v. 16a), frost (v. 16b), hail (v. 17a), and cold (v. 17b). God sends forth his "command" (*'imrah*), and the divine "word" (*dabar*) runs swiftly, covering the earth with snow and frost. In its ancient context, the readers of the psalm would have understood this language as polemical. The forces of nature, particularly storm and wind, were understood as the province of the Canaanite deity Ba'al. Yet the psalmist depicts God staking a claim over these very forces, in direct defiance of the divine division of labor. The psalm's polemic would have been clear: God commands, and even the realms of other deities must obey. The psalmist has an active image of God's word: it is a force released into the world to bring about change in accord with God's will.

Verses 18–19 continue the theme of the work of God's "word" (*dabar*), but now the psalmist directly compares the power of the word in the natural world ("he sends out his word, and melts them," v. 18a)

have just read that "the LORD takes pleasure in those who fear him, in those who hope in his steadfast love" (v. 11). It is no surprise, therefore, that the introductory summons in this section is then directed to "Jerusalem" and to "Zion," God's blessed partner in covenant. In our section of the psalm also, however, there is general praise, in the verses on winter and rough weather. Israel is not alone in experiencing winter blasts and spring thaws. (Some nations are in fact considerably more "blessed" than Israel in this respect, if blessed is the right word!) The psalm, however, declares at its climax that God "has not dealt thus with other nations." Though the difficulty ought to be named, it is more apparent than real. The blessings of nature, on the one hand, and of the covenant, on the other, are two sides of the same divine coin. Moreover, they are both operations of the "word," as we see in verses 15 and 19 respectively. Christians, perhaps particularly Protestant Christians with their orientation towards the "word," will not be surprised by this.

As Christians we must exercise particular care in interpreting the final and climactic blessing to Israel. In such a psalm the last blessing named is of special importance. If mere position were not enough to draw our attention, the words of the psalm do so quite specifically. There is one supreme blessing that has not been granted to "any other nation." That blessing is the "ordinances" of God. If it were simply the "word" of God as in verse 19a, there would be no difficulty. But the psalm is very specific; the "word" of 19a is expanded and explained by the "statutes and ordinances" of 19b. To many Christians, statutes and ordinances seem chiefly burdens, burdens that we may not rightly be able to carry. These two words appear elsewhere as synonyms for the "law" of God. In some Christian traditions the law is understood not only as a matter of duty, but as a theological category that points to our own vain attempts to please God by good works. Law is in this understanding the very antithesis of the gospel. Whether or not that is the case for us, "statutes and ordinances" do not sound like a great blessing in most Christian ears. They speak more of duty than of delight.

It may help to remember that the word "law" renders the Hebrew word *torah*. That word might be better translated as "instruction." We have all been frustrated by original equipment manufacturers who provide no "torah," no instructions at all or, even more frustrating, instructions that appear to have been prepared by someone with a only a very slight

# Psalm 147:12-20

## Theological Perspective

These statutes and ordinances, the law, are to be obeyed, but as a response of loyalty and hope. They are words of grace. At the end of the first half of the psalm, there is an affirmation that elucidates this dynamic. It says in part, "the LORD takes pleasure in those who fear him, in those who hope in his steadfast love" (v. 11). To fear God is not about fearing judgment or avoiding punishment. It is about appreciating the blessings and dreading the violation of God's pleasure in the community that reflects the character of this creating, sustaining, and redeeming love. It is to rely on a care and mercy, to live hopefully from it and toward it.

It is close to the logic of Paul's appeal to the believers in Rome when he begins his exhortation and instruction of them: "I appeal to you, therefore, brothers and sisters, by the mercies of God, to present your bodies as a living sacrifice, holy and acceptable to God" (Rom. 12:1). That sacrifice, that proper worship gets expressed through the creation of neighborhoods of grace that extend out as far as possible from the immediate relations within the church itself.

Those "neighborhoods of grace" signal the presence of a new city within the old city. It is the ancient tale of two cities, eloquently articulated by Augustine in *The City of God*, but previously announced by the author of the Revelation (21:2). While it celebrates and awaits the consummate reality, the Christian community is called to witness to it by the manner in which it graciously attends to the quality of the safety and peace of the earthly city in which it dwells for this moment.

DWIGHT M. LUNDGREN

## Pastoral Perspective

period of restoration after the exile. If that is accurate, these verses have special poignancy. The people of God were empty-handed indeed in those postexilic years. Defeated people whom God had yet preserved and returned home with joy, they faced many challenges: rebuilding Jerusalem; reestablishing worship patterns; restructuring daily life; and remembering God's laws to faithfully reorder their community. Yet even these good efforts would not secure what they most needed and desired: a covenantal life and future with God. That life and future could only be received as a gift from the God who had chosen them. On this and any other Sunday, there are people filled with such poignant longing and powerlessness.

Does such a realization of our own empty-handedness leave us mute, incapable of response or action? Not at all! The psalmist calls on God's people to respond to God's power and bounty with praise! To sing songs, make music, worship the Lord with thanksgiving. Why? Because God works not only in the vastness of creation, but also in the specific life of a people. God gives snow and is the force behind the wind and the source of precious water in creation (vv. 16, 18). Yet God is also the One who strengthens *Jerusalem's* gates and blesses *Israel's* children. God's word melts creation's cold, but God's word is also declared to Jacob, God's ordinances are given to Israel. God's power, then, is far reaching in the world *and* God's power and care are bestowed upon the life of a chosen people who are known by name, Jacob and Israel.

As William Willimon puts it: "This is often the way God loves us: with gifts we thought we didn't need, which transform us into people we don't necessarily want to be."[2] That is something to ponder on the second Sunday after Christmas Day. Now that our own gift giving is spent, perhaps we can reconsider this season, this story, and see ourselves not as givers but as "getters" from the true Giver of the truest Gift ever given, Jesus Christ. Then, faithfully empty-handed, we can reconsider ways to praise God that are responsive to this "strange," unimaginable gift we thought we didn't need. And living in those ways, we may be transformed into people we do not necessarily want to be, for God's sake and for God's purposes.

KIMBERLY L. CLAYTON

[2] Ibid., 149.

## Exegetical Perspective

with the power of the word in the faith of Israel ("he declares his word to Jacob, his statutes and ordinances to Israel," v. 19). The language makes clear that the God who has power over the forces of nature also claims authority to command the faith of Israel. And though the polemic is implied, it is no less present: just as God has made clear that no other deity commands the forces of nature, so also God makes clear that no other deity commands the worship of humanity.

Verse 20 makes the claim of Israel's uniqueness: God has not dealt this way with any other nation, and no other nation knows or understands God's intent as expressed in the commandments. This is a crucially important claim, given the historical context in which Israel sang this hymn. By the time of the hymn's collection into the Psalter, Israel was one province among many in the vast Persian Empire, confined to borders defined by a distant ruler and subject to the jockeying for position that characterizes the life of minor powers under the rule of an overlord. Without any military or political claim to greatness, Israel came at last to understand that its true greatness came not from itself but from its God. The God who has shaped the pathways of the wind and formed the storehouses of snow and rain is the very God who speaks the word of instruction and wisdom to Israel. Israel's position in the world came not from the size of its armies or its treasury, but from its place as the people of God: "God has not dealt thus with any other nation."

It is precisely this claim that makes this psalm a significant part of the Christmas liturgy. At Christmas, Christians claim that God has spoken the divine word anew. This time, however, the word is not indistinctly heard in the blowing of wind, nor is it to be found only in the cadences of the law. Rather, it comes to us as the Word, enfleshed and in a manger, and now at work in the world in a powerful new way. The Christmas gospel thus calls the followers of Christ to join their voices with those of ancient Israel in the awestruck acknowledgment that "God has not dealt thus with any other nation." Hallelujah, indeed.

PAUL K. HOOKER

## Homiletical Perspective

acquaintance with the English language. For the word "instructions" in such cases we might substitute synonyms such as "directions." In just the same way the psalmists use "ordinances" or "statutes" as synonyms for law. (See esp. Ps. 119.) Whichever word is used, we are speaking of the same reality. When putting together something complicated, a child's toy at Christmas, for example, we all want clear and ample instructions or directions. A good "maker" provides such instruction and directions. That is exactly what the Maker has provided for Israel, and so God's people are rightly grateful. Preachers will be able to image this notion vigorously and probably even humorously.

One can say even more. We fear that law limits our freedom and are impatient of any restraint except, perhaps, the whims of fashion. Law can become for us "regulation" and "red tape." In a very real sense, however, good instruction enhances our freedom. It makes it possible to do new and exciting things we could not otherwise experience. Many listeners will have paid large sums of money for instruction in leisure activities. We pay cheerfully for golf lessons, dancing lessons, music lessons. Such lessons make a richer and more vivid life possible for us and for our children. The principle extends to our work life also. Think of the frustration of trying to install and use new computer software or hardware. How grateful we are when a friend or a consultant explains clearly and shows us by example how to use the product. What a blessing it is! In fact, that is one blessing that comes not only from the word as instruction, but most clearly through the Word made flesh: Jesus explains clearly and shows by example how to carry out this complex task of living faithfully before God and with one another. So of course we too can offer praise!

STEPHEN FARRIS

# Ephesians 1:3-14

<sup>3</sup>Blessed be the God and Father of our Lord Jesus Christ, who has blessed us in Christ with every spiritual blessing in the heavenly places, <sup>4</sup>just as he chose us in Christ before the foundation of the world to be holy and blameless before him in love. <sup>5</sup>He destined us for adoption as his children through Jesus Christ, according to the good pleasure of his will, <sup>6</sup>to the praise of his glorious grace that he freely bestowed on us in the Beloved. <sup>7</sup>In him we have redemption through his blood, the forgiveness of our trespasses, according to the riches of his grace <sup>8</sup>that he lavished on us. With all wisdom and insight <sup>9</sup>he has made known to us the mystery of his will, according to his good pleasure that he set forth in Christ, <sup>10</sup>as a plan for the fullness of time, to gather up all things in him, things in heaven and things on earth. <sup>11</sup>In Christ we have also obtained an inheritance, having been destined according to the purpose of him who accomplishes all things according to his counsel and will, <sup>12</sup>so that we, who were the first to set our hope on Christ, might live for the praise of his glory. <sup>13</sup>In him you also, when you had heard the word of truth, the gospel of your salvation, and had believed in him, were marked with the seal of the promised Holy Spirit; <sup>14</sup>this is the pledge of our inheritance toward redemption as God's own people, to the praise of his glory.

## Theological Perspective

The proclamation and praxis of the kingdom by Jesus and the proclamation and praxis of the gospel by early Christians led them to challenge different structures and relationships of separation and subordination. In different contexts and ways, they announced a vision and enacted practices for alternative inclusive communities where social and religious boundaries of exclusion and hierarchical orders were challenged in the name of the redemptive and inclusive grace of God. All of them took the risk of living out a faith that announced the present reality and the future fulfillment of God's liberating and recreating eschatological realm.

The admission of Gentile Christians as Gentiles, that is, without the need of becoming Jewish proselytes, in Christian Jewish circles was a trans-forming and difficult process in early Christianity. Some Christian Jews saw the conversion of Gentiles to the faith in Jesus the Messiah (Christ) as one of the signals of the eschatological times: the recognition and worship of God by Gentiles together with Israel (1:9–10; 3:5–6). These Christian Jews embarked in a radical social and religious project convinced that God had called and accepted Gentile believers without the requirement of observing circumcision and the Law (1:4; 2:4–9, 14–16). They attempted to build an inclusive community of worship where the

## Pastoral Perspective

Is it ever too late to send a thank-you note? In this age when handwritten thank-you notes are becoming passé, the second Sunday after Christmas presents us with an overflowing page of thanks. Paul begins his letter to the Ephesians not by thanking them, but by raising a sweeping note of thanksgiving to God. "Blessed be the God and Father of our Lord Jesus Christ." Twice again in the same sentence, Paul uses a form of *eulogeo*, as if to say, "The Blessed One blesses us with blessings." Wherever Paul might go in this letter, he begins with doxology; he begins by saying, "Thank you."

By the second Sunday after Christmas, we should all be pastorally advised to complete thank-you notes for the gifts we received, returned, or recycled. Whether the Christmas gifts are treasured or even appreciated by us matters not. Whether the gift was painstakingly selected with love or merely tossed in a shopping cart out of obligation makes no difference. Without some kind of return of intentional thanks, the transaction remains incomplete, commercial, stripped of holier meaning. Only to receive is an empty and selfish end.

If this is true for earthly Christmas presents, then all the more pressing is the need to complete the cycle for heavenly gifts. God has provided every spiritual blessing. The riches of grace have been

## Exegetical Perspective

We have all experienced events that seemed small but were actually large. He registered for a science class in grade school and was assigned the seat next to his eventual life partner. She started a chatty conversation with the stranger on the train and ended up with a job offer and a career. That little gesture of kindness rescued the woman from abject cynicism, freed her for her own act of hope, which rubbed off on her children, who became . . . By means of an extended blessing, Ephesians 1:3–14 places the simple faith walk of first-century Christians in the larger world of God's plan for the cosmos.

Blessings abound in our passage. After a brief greeting, Paul (the author in the letter's narrative world, whether or not he was in the first-century world) launches his letter with a traditional Jewish *berakah*. In one long sentence that has been called "monstrous" by some and "liturgically majestic" by others,[1] the epistle to the Ephesians begins by blessing God for God's many blessings to the church. The *berakah* tradition seems to have begun with a simple response to divine benefaction, as when Melchizedek says to Abraham in Genesis 14:20,

[1] Eduard Norden called it "the most monstrous sentence conglomeration . . . that I have encountered in Greek" (*Agnostos Theos* [Berlin: Teubner, 1913], 253). Ch Masson marveled at the "fullness . . . , liturgical majesty, [and] perceptible rhythm" of the language (*L'Epitre de Paul aux Ephesiens* [Neuchatel: Delachaux et Niestle, 1953], 149).

## Homiletical Perspective

In 2 Corinthians 5:13, Paul makes the observation that if he is "beside" himself, it is for God, and if he is in his "right mind," it is for his readers. The ecstasy he experiences is restrained by his pastoral agenda, and both of them are bound together by the rule of love and the goal of evangelism.

We might well apply those same characteristics to the text before us—whether it is from the hand of the apostle, the pen of his secretary, or even the heart of a later disciple. We might also suggest that the best preaching of this text is rendered in two voices at once: the authentically joyful and doxological, the measured and precise. The latter voice is for many preachers far easier, despiritualized and rational as we in the West tend to be and have been trained to be. But out there on the edges of the mainline, our brothers and sisters are fluent in the language of joy and doxology; from them we might learn how to approach this kind of text without fear, how to echo and sustain and prolong this kind of text in our preaching.

The epistolary shape of the lesson is familiar, borrowing from the conventions of the day. Still, there is also something different here. Perhaps Ephesians is a circular letter with, as it were, a blank spot where any church's name might go. Or perhaps the lack of the usual geographic particularities make

# Ephesians 1:3-14

## Theological Perspective

ethnic distinctions between Jews and Gentiles were recognized but at the same time surpassed by their common faith in Jesus Christ and their unity in the body of Christ (2:17–22).

The recognition by Christian Jews of the equal status of Gentile Christians as members of the people of God remained a controversial issue. Many Christian Jews thought that the only way to belong to the people of God was through the practice of the Law and circumcision. Therefore, Gentile Christians felt the pressure either to assimilate by becoming proselytes (Galatians) or to suffer the stigma of being considered unequal members or even outsiders (Ephesians). The letter to the Ephesians is a manifesto that proclaims full membership, equal status, and honorable place for Gentile Christians in the people of God (2:12–14), the household of God (2:19), the temple in the Lord (2:21), and in the heavenly places with Christ (2:4–7). One of its purposes is to defend Gentile Christians and give them reassurance in the midst of discriminatory attitudes and practices by some Christian Jews, and to call and inspire both Jews and Gentile believers to live their unity and equality in love (4:1–3; 2:15–16; 5:1–2).

The incorporation of Gentile believers as members of the people of God became part of the gospel (1:13–14; 2:4–9; 3:1–6; 6:15, 19–20a) but posed a challenge to Christian Jews. How do we explain theologically this historical event and recent development in the life of Israel and the world? The answer required two theological insights. The first was a reaffirmation of God's sovereign and inclusive grace for Jews and Gentiles (1:3–14), and the second was a redefinition of Israel in light of God's revelation in Jesus Christ (2:1–22).

Ephesians 1:3–14 is a one-sentence eulogy that invites the community to do three things: (a) to praise God for God's grace and blessings in Christ for Jews and Gentiles; (b) to praise God's gracious, sovereign, and free decision to incorporate and honor Gentile believers in Christ; and (c) to praise God's inclusive grace and redemption for Jews and Gentiles, planned and accomplished in and through Jesus Christ (1:9–10) for Jews and Gentiles, as the theological foundation of the gospel of peace (6:15; 1:13–14; 3:5–6). This pericope is a doxological and theological answer to the question, why do we defend and promote the admission, membership, and equality of Gentile believers in the people of God? We do it because of God's revelation to us in the Spirit (1:5; 3:1–12) about what God has willed and done in and through Christ for us and all.

## Pastoral Perspective

*lavished* upon us. Therefore, our return of thanks ought to be equally lavish, or at least as lavish in scope as words will allow. Paul's doxology to God nearly spills off the page as he praises God from whom *all* blessings flow. Paul lifts up thanks for all blessings—not only personal blessings, not only blessings to the church. Paul's thanks reach to embrace God's overarching plan for all creation.

Measured against this scale of magnitude, our Christmas gifts and our thank-you notes seem miniscule, even trivial. The idea that we can begin adequately to thank God for this lavishness of grace is vanity and a striving after the wind. How could the art thank the artist? How could a book thank the author? How could the creature possibly thank the creator? Yet, any act of giving becomes a gift only when it is appreciated in return. Any person becomes fully human, becomes as God intended, only when he or she becomes appreciative. Paul is calling us not merely to fling up some obligatory, rote three-line card to God; Paul is calling us to live, wholly live, as appreciative persons of hope and trust. In order to be true to this calling, we must know who we are. Paul tells the Ephesians and tells us: We are those upon whom blessing has overflowed through Jesus Christ. Therefore, to live in blessing, to breathe in thanksgiving, continually to complete the cycle of gift and doxology is our highest calling and deepest meaning. We say, "Thank you," to God, not because we can do it well, but because we can do it at all. We are created—destined—to be people of thanksgiving. As begins Paul's letter to the Ephesians, a full life begins by saying "Thank you" to God.

Being "destined," though, also bears a weight of responsibility beyond the bubbling joy of thanksgiving. Being destined to be adopted into God's inheritance is also to be destined to be holy and blameless in love. Before we become overly impressed by God's good taste in choosing each of us before the foundation of the world, let us remember the cycle of gift and thanksgiving. Holy and blameless love like that of the Creator requires a perpetual (not merely annual) sharing of gifts, thanksgiving, and more gifts. Just as Paul taught the holy and blameless love of God to the Ephesians, thus must the Ephesians teach this love to their neighbors, and on and on. Saying "Thank you" completes the cycle of gift giving but doesn't finish it. God has set in motion an irresistible cycle of gift and thanks, of which we are destined to be a part, but certainly not the end. Rather than being entitled by God's spirit of adoption, we are obligated by its

"Blessed be God Most High, who has delivered your enemies into your hand" (see also Gen. 24:27). Later the blessing becomes a more formal practice of Israelite religion, as when Solomon begins and ends his dedication of the temple by blessing God (1 Kgs. 8:15, 56). The tradition is developed further when psalmists begin to use a *berakah* to close psalms (e.g., Pss. 41:13; 72:18, 19; 89:52; 106:48).[2]

Along with involving the audience in praise for God, and parallel to the customary function of Pauline thanksgiving sections, this introductory blessing provides a loose table of contents for the entire letter. Cosmic scope, mystery's disclosure, the location of blessing in Christ, God's grace, the seal of the Holy Spirit, the will of God. Notably these initial offerings also guide the audience both toward the theological vision of chapters 2 and 3, and toward the moral vision of chapters 4 through 6. In this *berakah*, God is blessed for blessing God's children.

The echoes of a profound story of God's blessing may lie in the background as well. The language recalls the baptism of Jesus (Mark 1:11; Matt. 3:17), with its use of a cognate to the term "son" (1:5), its mention of God's "good pleasure" (1:5), and its reference to Jesus Christ as "the Beloved" (1:6). This placement of the Ephesian folk in the river alongside the beloved Son with whom God is well pleased serves to unify the list of divine benefactions.

The blessing runs both ways. Woven through the listed benefactions for which God is praised in 1:3–14 is a unifying theme of praise: some version of "to the praise of [God's] glory" appears three times in these eleven verses (1:6, 12, 14)—first in the destiny of all the saints (1:5–6), then in the specific ordination of the Jews (1:11–12) and of the Gentiles (1:13–14). This repetition reminds the reader that all of these graces have a cyclical dimension: benefaction moves from God through the bliss of the faithful and back to God in the form of praise.

In their experience, Paul's Christians in Ephesus may have understood their decision to join the new community as a mere shift in religious focus—no big deal, just a changed habit of worship. But then the apostle's letter arrived, someone read it out after a meal, and they discovered that their small steps into this new community had been planned by God before the beginning of time, that the steps amounted to God's adoption of them through Christ, that they were now a part of a cosmic plan to bring all the separated fragments of creation

[2] See Claus Westermann, *The Praise of God in the Psalms*, trans. K. R. Crim (London: Epworth Press, 1966), 87–89.

this epistle at once more general and therefore more universal in its tone and scope. In any case, the thanksgiving here is unleashed, and the blessings of God cascade.

The text itself is breathless, a stream of doxological consciousness, as if the writer got started and could not stop. It is all one sentence, these verses before us, as is the next paragraph (vv. 15–23). The second long sentence is uninterrupted thanks regarding the Ephesians' prayers, but that benediction follows the author's praise to God and for God. The author blesses God for God's blessings, which is to say that God is the source and recipient of the author's praise.

Like Jewish *berakah*, the formal blessings of God customary in Jewish worship and prayer, this ecstatic utterance is liturgical in structure. It is a hymn, a doxology, a benediction: the once-for-all exaltation of God and the enthronement of Christ on the praises of the church—and the consequent blessing of those in every time and place who join the never-ending song.

Indeed, the passage is *musical* and *lyrical*, a kind of overture to the theme of salvation that will occupy the first half of Ephesians. For Paul (and his followers), "salvation" means nothing more or less than being a part of God's chosen people. To be a part of God's people—and we are!—is also to be a part of God's plan for the fullness of time and in fact to be a part of the agency for bringing that plan to pass.

This agency is not to be misconstrued: the vision is God's, the initiative is God's, the power by which it will come to pass is God's. God creates, God destines and blesses, God wills, reveals, and accomplishes according to his own purposes. Similarly, Christ is the locus of the choosing, the means of salvation, the sacrament of God's lavish grace, the instrument of God's will. Christ is the source and fulfillment of the divine purpose, which is salvation to all people.

Acknowledging who God is, proclaiming what God has done in Christ and is doing, allows us to know who we are, what we are made for now, and what we will be doing at the end: our purpose is praise, and God is the one to whom, for whom, and before whom our praise is uttered. The emphasis on God's initiative and our thanksgiving may make it a hard lesson to hear in our "if not us, who?" society, shot through as it is with presuppositions that we are self-determinative, self-interpretive, and make our own meaning. But for those who know themselves to be lavishly blessed, the only true and lasting exaltation is the praise of God in Christ.

# Ephesians 1:3-14

## Theological Perspective

Blessed be God! Jews and Gentiles have been chosen in Christ (1:3–4) to become the people of God in one reconciled body (2:14–16). Glory to God! God has changed the spiritual condition, identity, and destiny of Gentiles who have believed in Jesus Christ. They are equal to Jewish believers in the blessings (1:3) of election (1:4), call to holiness (1:4), adoption (1:5), forgiveness (1:7), the reception of the Spirit (1:13), and present and future redemption (1:7, 14; 2:7). Praise God! By God's grace, wisdom, and power, Gentiles are now members of God's people, household, and spiritual temple, and coinheritors of the covenantal blessings and promises to Israel in the new body and humanity (2:14–16) that God has created in Christ. For these reasons, discrimination should stop, and unity is sought in love in the church (4:1–3).

The church will always be challenged by God's revelation in Jesus Christ to love and serve God and humanity and to reinvent herself in worship, life, and mission in their sociocultural and religious contexts. Churches around the world and in human history have a mixed record of complicity with and resistance to exclusive boundaries, excluding walls, and discriminatory hierarchies that religious and social communities build and legitimate. Churches have been both victims and victimizers of the power systems and spiritual captivities that racism, sexism, classism, heterosexism, religious prejudice, and other forms of systemic domination and exclusion have generated in societies and their institutions. The presence and praxis of God's Spirit empowers and leads sectors in the churches to keep the memory and work faithfully for "kin-dom" communities that God envisions and the gospel promises. The encompassing grace of God stands as a judgment and a promise that help Christians to explore the inclusive love and ways of Jesus Christ in new contextual forms. The prophetic impulse that, on the one hand, resists relationships of separation and structures of subordination and, on the other, works for alternatives communities of inclusion and equality, in the name of a gracious, righteous, loving, merciful, and hospitable God, has led past and present Christians to ministries and worship that witness reconciliation, hospitality, and peace with justice in words and deeds.

LUIS R. RIVERA

## Pastoral Perspective

purposes. The mark of "the seal of the promised Holy Spirit" (v. 13) is not that we believe and then stop, satisfied of our own salvation. The mark of the Holy Spirit is seen when we continue to place this imprint of love upon our neighbors, our friends, and even our enemies. By the mystery of God's will, they too will continue the cycle of gift and thanksgiving.

That there is a "second" Sunday after Christmas is not a notation of later or lesser worth. The day's liturgical title reminds us there is always a second day, always a continuation of what God began through Jesus Christ before the foundation of the world. Completing thank-you notes and putting ornaments in their attic boxes is not the signal for the Christ child to go into hibernation until next year. A second Sunday is an admonition that, just as the liturgical calendar won't let Christmas end, neither should we. Like the echoes of bells pealing, what we have learned of God must ring forth throughout all the earth— from the first to set their hope on Christ to the last, until all from the very greatest to the very least have heard and experienced the good news of God's great plan. What plans do we have, what plans do our churches have in the coming year to live into the mystery of God's will? How do we propose to continue to write, say, and give thanks? How will we continue to share our spiritual, physical, and financial gifts? Will we live another year as people with possessions, or will we live as people with gifts? Will we cautiously parcel out our gifts, or will we heap them lavishly, as God has given them to us? Mercifully, even if we missed the opportunities of Christmas, there are always second Sundays, second chances to begin anew. Our lives can be grateful, again.

JAMES W. MCTYRE

## Exegetical Perspective

together in unity through Christ, and that this would all end in a glorious inheritance.

But does the letter go too far? Some critics have condemned the triumphalism of Paul's grand and cosmic language in Ephesians. Through the window of twenty-first-century Western culture, with steeples dotting the landscape and Christian televangelists filling the airwaves, seeing Paul as triumphalist seems appropriate. The charge of triumphalism may even be at home in fourth-century Rome, after Constantine has made Christianity the state religion. But in the scattered little communities of first-century Christianity, the words must be heard differently. Small conventicles of Christians met in houses. The newspapers did not notice them, and officials who did notice them most often opposed them. Even the survival of the movement was a long-shot bet. In that setting, Paul might seem to have delusions of grandeur, but a charge of triumphalism certainly does not fit. Paul is bolstering members of a fledgling community. In that context, "Paul's great prayer . . . is a celebration of the larger story within which every single Christian story . . . is set."[3]

This bolstering, story-lending quality of Ephesians 1:3–14 may offer a means of entry for a twenty-first-century Western culture for whom Christianity lives out a false and hollow bravado. The same culture that features those plentiful steeples and twenty-four-hour Christian cable channels— that culture also features a temptation to respond by trivializing Christian involvement. The laxity of old Christendom and the militant face of new fundamentalism can prompt a disinterested skepticism to which Christianity seems small and vulnerable to exploitation. Into that sociopolitical context comes the God of Ephesians 1. This God's plan for the cosmos involves not cultural or military hegemony, but the redemption of a beloved people who can become a community of lavish grace and forgiveness. A Christianity formed by this story may hope to be significant in a post-Christian age.

ALLEN R. HILTON

## Homiletical Perspective

In sum, the author proclaims that out of the love, power, and initiative of God we (meaning those who hope in Christ) have been *chosen for relationship with God.* This relationship is not bound by temporal, ethnic, or linguistic concerns. Indeed, it was forged in eternity and intended for all people everywhere, giving us the manifold blessing of being at once friends with God and friends with each other. This same grace enables us to befriend our enemies, for we know that they will not be our enemies forever.

The mystery of God's purposes—that Christ will be all in all—has been revealed to us. We are therefore not only *chosen for revelation from God* but also entrusted to convey that glad gospel. We are the storytellers, the harbingers, and messengers of the world to come. If no one could see it but God, and no one could accomplish it but Christ, no one but we can witness to it. We witness by means of our praise.

We are those *chosen for praise to God,* destined for worship, and appointed unto doxology. If we cannot yet see all that will be, we can already sing it. We sing of what will surely come by the grace of God. In so doing, we prove that we are marked by the seal of the Holy Spirit. The Spirit serves as a kind of retainer, or sustainer, until the fullness of time. In the day to come, all will sing and give thanks to God; until then, we who have received the lavish blessings and redemption sing on behalf of the rest.

If the origin of the message of Christmas is that the Word becomes flesh and dwells among us, the culmination of the season is that our flesh becomes the praise of God who makes us all one.

THOMAS R. STEAGALD

---

[3] Tom Wright, *Paul for Everyone: The Prison Letters, Ephesians, Philippians, Colossians, and Philemon* (Louisville, KY: Westminster John Knox Press, 2002/2004), 8.

# John 1:(1-9) 10-18

[1]In the beginning was the Word, and the Word was with God, and the Word was God. [2]He was in the beginning with God. [3]All things came into being through him, and without him not one thing came into being. What has come into being [4]in him was life, and the life was the light of all people. [5]The light shines in the darkness, and the darkness did not overcome it.

[6]There was a man sent from God, whose name was John. [7]He came as a witness to testify to the light, so that all might believe through him. [8]He himself was not the light, but he came to testify to the light. [9]The true light, which enlightens everyone, was coming into the world.

## Theological Perspective

The nature of Jesus was hotly debated at the Council of Nicaea. Was Jesus a creature made by God at some point in time? Or had he always been? John 1 provided the key to unlock the mystery. The Word—a theologically profound expression of Christ for John—always was God. Somehow, the fellowship that is God, the intimate relationships of love that are God's heart, have always been, and will always be.

The poetic genius of this overture to John's Gospel is astonishing, and moving. Even in our day, when words are cheap, John's words are eloquently beautiful, for they speak of the one true beauty. "Words take on meaning by the company they keep."[1] These words take on meaning because their company is God the Father, God the Son, and God the Holy Spirit.

This soaring symphony tries to express the inexpressible. God's inner self, God's loving heart, God's eternal fellowship, spilling over and making a world, knowing full well that world would miss the point, and be downright recalcitrant in reply. But Love loves anyhow.

Ask anyone: what was the most beautiful moment in your life? At first, most people recall some spectacular sight they once photographed. But if

[1]Nicholas Lash, *Believing Three Ways in One God* (Notre Dame, IN: University of Notre Dame, 1992), 14.

## Pastoral Perspective

In the first portion of John's prologue, verses 1–9, we are introduced to two "characters": the Word and John the Baptist. Each of them is presented briefly and purposefully. In the case of the Word, or Jesus, we learn of his origin, his place, and his power ("the darkness did not overcome it"). In the case of John the Baptist, we also learn his origin ("sent from God"), his name, and his purpose in the larger scheme of things. He is the "introducer" of the main character—who, of course, is Jesus—who is not even named until the end of the prologue. Reference most of the way through is simply (and significantly!) to "the true light."

The second half of the prologue provides the movements of the process of knowing. And in these movements we can begin to identify Jesus more practically and identify with him more clearly: "the world came into being through him; yet the world did not know him." In a very real sense, with these verses, John is already introducing us to the passion narrative; the horror and the injustice of being responsible for so much and yet being unknown.

First, there is the experience of not being known, not being recognized for who he was. We too know the pain of being unrecognized for who we are and what we have done and can do. That unknownness is something to be overcome. Jesus, the Word, was and

¹⁰He was in the world, and the world came into being through him; yet the world did not know him. ¹¹He came to what was his own, and his own people did not accept him. ¹²But to all who received him, who believed in his name, he gave power to become children of God, ¹³who were born, not of blood or of the will of the flesh or of the will of man, but of God.

¹⁴And the Word became flesh and lived among us, and we have seen his glory, the glory as of a father's only son, full of grace and truth. ¹⁵(John testified to him and cried out, "This was he of whom I said, 'He who comes after me ranks ahead of me because he was before me.'") ¹⁶From his fullness we have all received, grace upon grace. ¹⁷The law indeed was given through Moses; grace and truth came through Jesus Christ. ¹⁸No one has ever seen God. It is God the only Son, who is close to the Father's heart, who has made him known.

## Exegetical Perspective

The prologue to the Fourth Gospel presents a preview of coming attractions and frames the narrative of the Gospel. Wes Howard-Brook believes that the prologue has been shaped into a concentric structure.

> A 1:1–5, relationship of Logos to God, creation, and humanity
> > B 1:6–8, witness of John the Baptist (negative)
> > > C 1:9–11, journey of the light/Logos (negative)
> > > > D 1:12–13, gift of empowerment
> > > C' 1:14, journey of Logos (positive)
> > B' 1:15, witness of John the Baptist (positive)
> A' 1:16–18, relationship of Logos to God, creation and humanity[1]

In a concentric structure, the emphasis usually falls on the middle member (D). If so, the purpose of this reflection on the Logos is to explore how the Word becoming flesh empowered human beings.

The two references to John the Baptist were probably not part of the original hymn. For our purposes, it is important to leave the hymn as it is found in the Gospel narrative. The introduction of John the Baptist keeps the cosmic hymn rooted in the particularities of history. His appearance in the

[1]Wes Howard-Brook, *Becoming Children of God: John's Gospel and Radical Discipleship* (Maryknoll, NY: Orbis Books, 1994), 51.

## Homiletical Perspective

*Light Always Makes a Difference in Darkness.* Faith is not easy to come by for those living in this generation. We are living with a popular notion of no absolutes. This way of thinking has exploded in our culture because many people have been hurt by the scandals that have emerged from numerous religious organizations and leaders of our time. Many who do not "believe" in Jesus "believe" there is no black and white. Nothing is clear. The image of life is somehow gray and ambivalent. Right and wrong can be explained away by a culture of situational ethics. Some believe the right decision should be based on what makes one feel good rather than on what is good. Looking at life through the lens of feelings can be troubling at the least and devastating at the most.

John's description of Christ coming into the world is critical for the skeptics of this generation. It takes away the human drama of virgin birth, shepherds, and angels. It gives us another way to look at the gift of Jesus Christ to the world. In John's presentation of the Messiah, we are given a presentation of Jesus as *logos*. The Word of God is Jesus. Further, we can make sense of the Word of God through the eyes of spiritual reasoning. As we grow to understand Jesus in this light, we are brought to a place of faith through an understanding of the definitive power of the creative spirit.

# John 1:(1-9) 10-18

## Theological Perspective

they linger over the question, they arrive at some truly beautiful moment when words that matter are spoken. "I love you; will you marry me?" "I forgive you." "I am immensely proud of you." "I just learned that I am pregnant." Life is birthed through words.

God created everything by simply speaking. "Let there be light." Jesus is the primal utterance of God, the Word behind the words, framed in the triune heart of God before time, yet not content to be sequestered outside of time. David Bentley Hart has written elegantly of "the scandal of Christianity's origins, the great offense this new faith gave the gods of antiquity . . . a God who goes about in the dust of exodus for love of a race . . . who apparels himself in common human nature, in the form of a servant; who brings good news to those who suffer and victory to those who are as nothing; who dies like a slave and outcast without resistance; who penetrates to the very depths of hell in pursuit of those he loves; and who persists even after death not as a hero lifted up to Olympian glories, but in the company of peasants, breaking bread with them and offering them the solace of his wounds."[2]

John's Gospel sparks the fire that enflames theology, from the Nicene Creed's confession that God "came down for us and our salvation," through Anselm's "only God become man can save us," to Martin Luther's thundering ruminations on the hiddenness of God in the crucified flesh of Jesus, resounding through Barth, Moltmann, and a host of women and men among the rank and file of worshipers who delight in the Word made flesh.

We often think of the incarnation as an emptying: Christ, "though he was in the form of God . . . emptied himself, taking the form of a slave" (Phil. 2:6–7). But this Word made flesh isn't a hollow vessel, an empty shell. The humanity of Jesus is full, it is Fullness itself. The emptying is not an emptying of grace. The Word made flesh *is* grace. The flesh is God's glory. Jesus was not pretending to be human; he really did enter into our flesh of weakness, mortality, pain. There is no other God, no other secret truth about God. We do not apologize for the suffering as an aberration from the glorious nature of God. God's glorious nature *is* the suffering. The Word made flesh is very full of grace and truth.

We live in a culture that cares little for truth. Everything is about what works, what sells, what seems true. Yet truth matters. Truth is our best defense against evil. Truth is the ground of peace.

[2]David Bentley Hart, *The Beauty of the Infinite* (Grand Rapids: Eerdmans, 2003), 126.

## Pastoral Perspective

is in our midst, undergirds our life, and yet we did not and still do not know him. There is within this verse 10 an implication of the unfolding process. The first step in that process is awareness. We begin, as the world begins. We "did [do] not know him." We might well say that our coming to know Christ begins in ignorance. And in our ignorance we do not even know what we need to know! We are therefore helpless. If we were left there, there would be no process of knowing in which to participate. We would simply be in a "state" of unknowing. But here the process of knowing begins.

Second, we are told that "he came to what was his own." The initiative to bring us into a new state of knowing comes from outside of ourselves. This initiative, which comes from God, has implications for our own calling. Pastoral care often has had to take on the assertion by many that "you can't help people if you don't let them come to you first." Yet pastoral care in its best expression draws on the very essence of these first two stages described in John's prologue. People often, living in a state of ignorance, are not aware of the health that is possible for them. Someone must reach out to them (often in the name of God) to bring them into an awareness of what they need. We all begin by needing to know that we are needy. And here in this lectionary text lies the theological impetus for pastoral initiative. We reach out to others with compassionate understanding, knowing that others, like us, may not know what they need until it is offered to them. Jesus is the embodiment of God's grace. We can be the embodiment of Jesus' extension of himself to all humanity.

Third in this unfolding process: disbelief ("his own people did not accept him"). We certainly know human nature well enough to know that offering good news to someone is not a guarantee that it will be received happily. Disbelief grows out of any number of things: fear that daring to hope will result only in further disappointment; recognition that acceptance of good news brings responsibility; numbness that makes new reality difficult to comprehend. Our calling, reflective of Jesus' purpose in the world, is not to assure acceptance. Rather, we come to introduce good news, a new reality, into a previously uncomprehending context.

The fourth stage, if the third stage is overcome, is one of receiving new power, or energy. And it is more than that. It is recognition of who we are, and becoming who we were created to be ("to all who received . . . he gave power to become . . ."). And, it is

hymn anticipates the role he will play in 1:19–51, where John shows that he is not in competition with Jesus but accepts a willing subordination and a lesser role. It is John the Baptist who says of Jesus, "Here is the Lamb of God who takes away the sin of the world!" (1:29). In 1:6–8, John is characterized as "sent from God" with a mission and a purpose—to act as a witness (*martyria*) to testify (*martyreō*) to the light. John didn't need to occupy center stage because he too was focused on God's purposes, not his own reputation.

The beginning of the Logos hymn (1:1–5) explores some complex ground in deceptively simple language. The term *logos* had a long and storied history before it appeared in the Fourth Gospel. It was a term used by the Stoics to refer to the principle of reason that governs the universe, while Philo spoke of its creative power (named God) and its royal power (named Lord). The rabbis related *logos* to Torah, and *logos* also came to be associated with wisdom (*sophia* in Greek and *hokma* in Hebrew).

John uses *logos* to express a most astounding Christology, "and the Word became flesh and dwelled in our midst, full of grace and truth" (my translation). As Genesis 1 begins with creation, so John 1 begins with a new creation (1:3). Clearly, the hymn proclaims the activity of God in the coming of the *logos*.

John adopts two images to express this renewal of creation. The *logos* is life and light (1:3–4). Just as God created the heavens and the earth and all life therein, so the *logos* brings life to creation. The theme of life reverberates throughout the Fourth Gospel, especially "eternal life," the life made possible by the new creation. The *logos* is the agent of eternal life as surely as YHWH was the author of life in creation. In the world of this Gospel, eternal life is not reserved for the future but is already present, as Jesus's encounter with Nicodemus (3:1–21) or Mary, Martha, and Lazarus (11:1–44) indicates. In the same fashion, the theme of light reverberates through the Gospel (8:12–20).

The full drama of this renewal of creation has not yet been told. The protagonist, the *logos*, has been introduced, but the antagonists have not, though they soon will be characterized as forces of darkness (1:5). The conflict between the *logos* who is light and the forces of darkness defines the plot of the Gospel. The light of creation shines in the darkness, and although we are assured that the light will prevail, the implied struggle between darkness and light casts an ominous shadow over the story. The plot is clear:

In this presentation of the One who came to make a difference, we are given a metaphor of spiritual understanding we can wrap our minds around. In addition, the text presents us with the image of Jesus as the light of the world. Illumination always makes a difference in darkness. The world we live in is full of darkness. Wherever Jesus shows up, light enters the atmosphere. Without a doubt light always makes a difference in darkness and changes the atmosphere. That is an absolute truth to hold on to.

*It Is Hard to See When You Are in the Dark.* In our text we are told of Jesus' entry on the world stage. "He was in the world, and the world came into being through him; yet the world did not know him" (v. 10). As we ponder this pronouncement of our state, we can understand it. When light suddenly appears, it takes time for the eyes to adjust. In the initial moments of light, we may not really know what we are seeing, especially if we have been in the dark for a long time. As one comes out of the dark, there may be recognition of silhouettes in the light. The image may be familiar, but we do not quite know what it is. In many ways, this is how the world received Jesus. The text tells us that Jesus "came to what was his own, and his own people did not accept him" (v. 11). Perhaps it was hard for people to know and accept him because they had been living in darkness for so long.

*Believing Is Seeing.* To believe what one is seeing sometimes takes a leap of faith. It means trusting in something not quite understood. To believe in Jesus Christ as God in the flesh means relying on that something within that allows one to trust. It means opening up the heart to believe that God has so much love for humanity that God wants to walk in our shoes. We are compelled to accept the possibility that God chose to live as one of us—to be one with us.

*To Believe and See Means Making a Decision.* When the light comes, one must choose either to stay in the anonymity of darkness or to move forward in the familiarity of light. Darkness is somehow relaxed and distant. Light is intimate in the midst of visibility and understanding. The question we each must answer for ourselves is, would you rather live your life in the dark or in the light?

*Life Is More Stimulating in the Light.* Jesus came to the world to bring the spiritual gift of light. Light has a way of making things look better. We can see more

# *John 1:(1-9) 10-18*

## Theological Perspective

Truth is simpler than we might imagine. John the Baptist provides the clue: he simply pointed to Jesus, who is Truth.

Truth is more than mere facts. The historian David McCullough said, "You can have all the facts imaginable and miss the truth, just as you can have facts missing or some wrong, and reach the larger truth. 'I hear all the notes, but I hear no music,' is the old piano teacher's complaint. There has to be music. The work of history . . . calls for mind and heart."[3]

What is this music for mind and heart—this "fullness" of grace and truth? Don't we crave fulfillment? We stuff something into our gnawing emptiness to try to feel full: busy-ness, things, alcohol. Now the preacher is tempted to say, "Jesus is what fills that hollow place." Jesus does fill our emptiness, but we must be careful not to idolize our desires, our cravings. It is not the case that Jesus satisfies us with what we've always wanted. No one desired Jesus. His own people rejected him; he "dwelled" among us, but we did not even recognize him. "He had . . . no beauty that we should desire him" (Isa. 53:2 RSV).

The Word tutors our desires; they are converted into something truer. God has something far richer in store for us than merely what we thought would do. Consider this profound prayer from Hans Urs von Balthasar:

> We always wanted to measure your fulfillments by the standard of our desires. More than what our hollow space contains, so we thought, we cannot obtain from you. But when your Spirit began to blow in us, we experienced so much greater space that our own standard became meaningless to us. . . . And thus is fulfilled the promise which is the blowing Spirit itself in person: Because he blows the fulfillment toward us . . . if we are ready to allow ourselves to be surpassed in our desires. The religion and desire of all peoples means ultimately this: to get beyond one's own desires.[4]

JAMES C. HOWELL

## Pastoral Perspective

a gift to us, who began with not even knowing who we were or what we could become. The rest of this powerful passage is an expression of the joy that comes with such recognition.

The second half of John's prologue is a powerful and graphic theological description of the unfolding process of God's love revealed in Christ. The outcome of that process is new comprehension of who we are. In like manner, this theological description can serve as more than a theological statement. It also can be a pastoral word for us—bearing in mind that the word "pastoral" does not refer only to ordained clergy. We all are called to be pastors to one another. As pastors of the Word, we are called to recognize the helplessness of many who do not even know what is possible. Our recognition of their helplessness, combined with an awareness of God's recognition of our helplessness, can become an occasion—or perhaps a call—to offer them good news. That news, of course, is that they are more than they even know. Our bringing them that message may generate instant gratitude, but in more cases it will first generate disbelief. To believe would be to take a risk. So, we stay with them, still reflecting the sustaining love of Christ. We will hope to share with them the joy that comes with the recognition of who we are and whose we are. Then we, and they, become more of who God created all of us to be.

WILLIAM V. ARNOLD

---

[3]David McCullough, *The Course of Human Events* CD-ROM (New York: Simon & Schuster, 2005).
[4]Hans Urs von Balthasar, *Spiritus Creator* (Ft. Collins, CO: Ignatius, 1993), 479.

the conflicts between Jesus and his antagonists are historical skirmishes in the larger campaign of light against darkness (e.g., 9:1–41).

While it would be possible to focus solely on this conflict, it would not tell the full story. The coming of the true light into the world (1:9) inspires not only conflict and rejection (1:10–11) but acceptance and empowerment (1:12–13). The key phrase here is found in 1:12, "to those who received him, he gave to them authority [*exousia*] to become children of God, to those believing in his name" (my translation). This is the definition of discipleship for John and his community, whose members have received their commonly shared authority from the same source, unlike those who were born amid bloodshed (the plural of "blood" is used here, a Hebrew idiom for "bloodshed"[2]) or by human scheming ("the will of the flesh" as what opposes God) or by human status seeking (the will of human beings to propagate and perpetuate their bloodlines). The major forces that dominated the social world of empire and rule are dismissed. What counts is God's authority to enable all people to become children of God. This is the empowerment brought by the *logos*, and it is a direct challenge to the violence, privilege, power, and oppressive rule found in John's world.

The closing members of the concentric structure focus on the Word set against human systems of rule. "The Word became flesh." This is an astonishing statement, for "flesh" is often used (as in 1:13) to express what opposes God's rule and creation. Jesus came into just such a world (1:5, 10–11); he was not protected from the forces of the flesh. Yet even in his incarnate state he exhibited God's "glory, full of grace and truth" (1:14, 17). Grace (*charis*) implies that Jesus, as the Word and Son, mediates God's benefits for God's people; truth (*alētheia*) carries the sense of revealing what had not been known before, in this case, the identification of the *logos* with Jesus.

The hymn closes with a reflection on the consequences of this unveiling for the Torah. The revelation at Sinai must make way for what the coming of the *logos* has made possible—a more transparent understanding of God that can come only from the Son.

WILLIAM R. HERZOG II

detail and color. Light creates warmth and gives us a richer point of view. With this in mind, Jesus Christ came into the world as light, so those of us who have the desire to know God better can see God, through Jesus Christ. We can make the choice to accept the light and adjust to the light as people who choose to accept God and adjust to life in the midst of God's revelation to the world. In the light, we can better see things as they really are, and we can see truth placed before us.

*The Challenge of Community Life in the Light.* As a child, I recall my mother telling us to turn off the lights when it was hot outside. When I asked her the reason for this, she would reply, "Light draws heat." As an adult, I am not sure if this is a scientific reality, but I know it is a spiritual reality. To decide to live as people in the light often means stirring up controversy. It means calling attention to things that others may not want to see. This is why we need the support of other believers. We need people of like mind and faith who will stand together as people of the light. It is not easy to live in the light. It means standing out as one on the hot seat, when many of us prefer life in the coolness of noncommitment.

SHELLEY D.B. COPELAND

---

[2] Raymond E. Brown, *The Gospel according to John, I–XII* (Garden City, NY: Doubleday, 1966), 12.

# Isaiah 60:1-6

> [1]Arise, shine; for your light has come,
>    and the glory of the LORD has risen upon you.
> [2]For darkness shall cover the earth,
>    and thick darkness the peoples;
> but the LORD will arise upon you,
>    and his glory will appear over you.
> [3]Nations shall come to your light,
>    and kings to the brightness of your dawn.
>
> [4]Lift up your eyes and look around;
>    they all gather together, they come to you;

## Theological Perspective

Isaiah's vision of the glorious restoration of Jerusalem was probably originally intended to inspire returnees from exile, but it has also inspired theologians ever since, especially in their reflections on revelation, heaven, and Christ. The chapter is first and foremost a call to perceive and participate in the glorious work of God.

The image of the nations bringing their wealth to the capital of Judah, which has roots in earlier strata of the book (e.g., 18:7), was always idealistic. It is historically grounded in a political image from the ancient world: kings coming to an emperor to present their tribute and tax. Such political power was only rarely achieved, if ever, during the period of the kingdom of Judah, and it certainly was not evident during the postexilic period, when Isaiah 60 would have been written. Still, the idea of Zion's centrality to the earth, due to God's favor and the unique wisdom of the divine teaching (Isa. 2:3, etc.), was a profoundly powerful message—*especially* in times when God's rule of the earth and favor for the people were not immediately apparent. This was the case not only in the midst of the struggles of the Persian period, but also for John, the author of Revelation, who clearly drew on this passage in his vision of the heavenly Jerusalem. The new Jerusalem, like the one in Isaiah 60, was to be characterized by

## Pastoral Perspective

On May 9, 1961, the Dave Brubeck Quartet recorded a short piece at the Thirtieth Street Studio in New York. It is called "Charles Matthew Hallelujah," a tune that burst into being the day Dave and Iola Brubeck's sixth child was born.

That day Brubeck stopped by the hospital in Norwalk, Connecticut, on his way to a recording session in the city. When he arrived at the hospital, he learned that Iola had just given birth to their grand-finale son. When Brubeck finally arrived at the studio, he told the band the good news, went directly to the piano, and started playing.

Light notes announced the birth. The saxophone, bass, and drums responded with joy. The song was inspired and recorded on the spot, but listening to it today we might think every note was meticulously placed and well rehearsed.

When she first heard the piece, Iola Brubeck said it sounded as if each band member was presenting her newborn with a gift. Paul Desmond on saxophone. Eugene Wright on bass. Joe Morello on the drums.[1] These "three kings" of the 1960 jazz scene have something to teach us about the Sunday and season of Epiphany.

---

[1]Dave Brubeck, *Dave Brubeck Time Signatures: A Career Retrospective* (Sony Music Entertainment C4K 66047; compact disc, 1992).

your sons shall come from far away,
    and your daughters shall be carried on their nurses' arms.
⁵Then you shall see and be radiant;
    your heart shall thrill and rejoice,
because the abundance of the sea shall be brought to you,
    the wealth of the nations shall come to you.
⁶A multitude of camels shall cover you,
    the young camels of Midian and Ephah;
    all those from Sheba shall come.
They shall bring gold and frankincense,
    and shall proclaim the praise of the LORD.

## Exegetical Perspective

In a time of despair and discouragement, the prophet of Third Isaiah offers more than encouragement; he offers a vision so glorious and compelling that anyone who trusts the Lord will be inspired and motivated to work hard to rebuild and renew the land and the people. The exiles have returned from Babylon, but instead of the welcoming and peaceful homeland of their grandparents' stories, they find ruin, decay, and corruption.

One can almost picture the forlorn returnees in the midst of it all, their lifelong hopes cruelly dashed. When the best of the best were taken from their homeland seventy years ago, those who were left behind did not have the skills or qualities required to run the government, to educate the young, to see to the spiritual health of the community. Perhaps those left behind can hardly be blamed that Israel was not the place after the exile that it was before, but when the exiles returned home, they found a mess that they did not expect. Instead of glory and health, they found crumbling buildings, incompetent and corrupt authorities, and a terrible apathy in the nation's religious practice. The returnees were devastated. This was not at all what they had set their hopes on.

In the midst of this grief and desperation, the prophet speaks an incongruous invitation: "Arise,

## Homiletical Perspective

Only a tribe that has known total defeat and scattering can reach into such a deep, poetic place.

As a family mourns its lost children long after their deaths, so this ancient tribe recalls the richness of its faith being diminished by each reversal and period of oppression. No matter what happens, the shadow of what is lost, of what might have been, leaves the circle broken. The great hymn is sung without all its verses. The great proclamations are read without all their words.

We too know thick darkness. It comes with feeling small and helpless. It comes when our power to protect and champion is lost. It comes when there is nothing left to say beyond simply guttural phrases that get us from here to there. Then, if we are fortunate, a poet arises in our midst. She sees the distension in us and explores its strange shapes. He grasps the absences and crafts them into words. The poet comes as spring rain soaking our parched land with hope.

For Christians, this poet's artistry rings again through Matthew's story of the magi. Scenes of Christmas pageants come to mind. Yet, to replace the former with the latter is unfair to the Isaiah vision. The two texts are separate. The writer imagines the long-awaited glory of Jerusalem. Here is the feel of a surprise party. The recipient is stunned by the sudden change of circumstance.

# Isaiah 60:1-6

## Theological Perspective

the glory of God (Rev. 21:11), so that it "has no need of sun or moon to shine on it, for the glory of God is its light, and its lamp is the Lamb" (Rev. 21:23). Countless Christian interpreters since John have also seen in Isaiah 60 an eschatological dimension. Calvin wrote that the vast riches described here "cannot properly apply to the land of our pilgrimage, or to the earthly Jerusalem, but to the true homeland of believers, that heavenly city wherein 'the Lord has ordained blessing and life forever more' [Ps. 133:3]."[1]

Who exactly is to enjoy the divine light of this heavenly city? There is an evident tension running through the passage itself. On the one hand, the peoples are to be covered in a "thick darkness" (interestingly, a Hebrew term that is itself associated with divine *presence*, e.g., Exod. 20:21), but on the other hand, the nations and their kings are expected to come to the light. It seems that what is envisioned is not the permanent banishment of outsiders, but rather the revelation of divine favor for God's people, a grace to which others will ultimately be drawn. This image of the (conditional) inclusion of outsiders is consonant with the overall message of this portion of Isaiah (cf. 56:6–7)—and also, of course, with the evangelistic thrust of Christianity. It is to be hoped that Christian communities will manifest a gracious and blessed way of life that is attractive to outsiders.

The foregoing discussion already hints at the way this passage underlies aspects of later christological reflection. Isaiah 60's references to light and darkness evoke the whole book's extensive immersion in those images (2:5, 9:2, 29:18, 42:16, etc.). In Christian tradition, this text is linked with Epiphany—from the Greek *epiphaneia*, literally the "shining forth" of God's glory in human form at the birth of Christ. The phrase "your light has come" (60:1) is thus inextricably linked in the tradition with John 1: "The light shines in the darkness, and the darkness did not overcome it" (1:5). Thus the light has multiple layers of signification: the favor of the Lord shining on the people, the divine word that enlightens the hearer, and Christ who is the light of the world. Our passage suggests that the light of God's people in every age is a *reflected* light: like precious metals or stones flashing in the sun, God's people themselves do not generate light; they can only gather and disperse the light that shines on them.

## Pastoral Perspective

In this passage from Third Isaiah (Isa. 60:1–6), God speaks an oracle of magnanimous gift giving. The opening verses of the pericope rest on a foundation of cause and effect. Because God's glory shines upon a new Jerusalem, Israel will rejoice. Because God and Israel radiate joy, the neighboring nations will come bearing gifts.

Like the bright countenance of Israel, these gifts from foreign kings shine too. A train of camels from Midian, Ephah, and Sheba bear a heavy load of gold and frankincense. The weights and amounts of these treasures seem less important than the implication of abundance. The reference to Sheba recalls the queen of Sheba's extraordinary gift to Solomon (1 Kgs. 10:1–13) and suggests a similar display of generosity and submission to the God who resides in Israel.

The current of this passage marks a swift departure from the preceding chapters and, more significantly, from the political climate of the day. Biblical scholar Walter Brueggemann rightly asserts that Isaiah's vision is an "inversion of geopolitics." He states, "For as long as anyone can remember, Israel has paid imperial tribute to others—the Assyrians, the Babylonians, the Persians—all money going out. Now the process is reversed."[2] Indeed, rather than Israel remaining in the shadows of other nations, those nations are drawn to Israel's light; three of the six verses in this passage end with "you," accenting Israel's political and theological place in the region. As God promises, "they all gather together, they come to you" (v. 4). The image is striking: powerful leaders pour into Israel in a unified act of tribute to God and God's people.

This promised watershed event marks the reestablishment of Israel's *identity*. Isaiah's oracle makes it clear. The people of Israel are people of God. Who they are, as a nation, is indelibly bound to whose they are. They belong to God. They are no longer under the thumbs of foreign rule but rather in the care of God.

Similarly Epiphany invites our congregations to consider who we are and to ask, "Who is Jesus?" On the Epiphany of the Lord and throughout this season, our congregations will become reacquainted with John the Baptist, who proclaims, "'The one who is more powerful than I is coming'" (Mark 1:7). We will marvel at the power of Jesus to call fishermen into discipleship (John 1:43ff.). And we will hear the crescendo of good news build to the heights

---

[1]John Calvin, *The Institutes of the Christian Religion*, 2 vols., ed. John T. McNeill, trans. Ford Lewis Battles, LCC (Philadelphia: Westminster Press, 1960), 2.11.2.

[2]Walter Brueggemann, *Westminster Bible Companion: Isaiah 40–66*, (Louisville, KY: Westminster John Knox Press, 1998), 205.

shine, for your light has come, and the glory of the LORD has risen upon you" (60:1). It is perhaps hard to believe, but it does stir memories of Second Isaiah, the prophet of the exile, who also promised that the Lord's light would shine in their present darkness (e.g., chaps. 40 and 43). Darkness is an overarching metaphor for many ways in which life is difficult and human experience seems to shut out joy. This is especially true in Second and Third Isaiah, which are composed of long poetic passages mourning the darkness of the current circumstances and praying for God's light, which includes both spiritual faithfulness and material prosperity, to shine once again on God's people.

The next part of the prophecy offers this hope but, in the usual way of God, offers so much more than God's people could have asked for or imagined. Not only would God's glory shine upon this forsaken place—this *dark* place—but it would shine so brightly that Judah would be envied by the rest of the world. From far and near, God's own children would return home, and the days of homelessness, of wandering in the dark among strangers, would be over forever, because the light of God—again, spiritual faithfulness and material prosperity—would never be extinguished. There would be no wandering in the darkness among strangers, because strangers and foreigners would also come to Judah, bringing gifts and wealth and begging to be included in this glorious restoration. Not only would Israel be brought back to their proper glory, but the rest of the world would be drawn to the light that shone only there.

This fulfillment is no less than a reversal of history itself. A desperate and oppressed people are asked to stand tall and confront their own darkness—to shine with the light given by the glory of the Lord. For centuries, Israel had been abused and trampled on—literally—from all sides. From Egypt and Mesopotamia armies marched through on their way to more important wars, trapping Israel in the middle of all of it. But now Israel is to be not a place to be exploited on the way to somewhere else, but the ultimate destination for the nations. Instead of seeing war horses march across their land, the people will welcome camels, animals that represent domesticity and economic prosperity. Instead of helping themselves to the wealth of Israel, the nations will come bearing their own wealth as a gift to Israel and Israel's God. Most importantly, those children and young men and women who have been torn away from their families as spoils of war will

"For darkness shall cover the earth, and thick darkness the peoples" (v. 2). Root around in the concepts of "darkness and thick darkness." What darkens the earth and its peoples? Is there a difference between "darkness" and "thick darkness"? Is the one natural and the other of human origin?

"But the LORD will arise upon you, and his glory will appear over you" (v. 2). What does that look and feel like? Is it a slow dawning or a fresh realization? Does it involve strange visitors or key responses in a critical moment? Whatever it is, it begins to attract attention. To follow these questions is to stir the imagination. Images may come. Incidents and illustrations may arise to enrich the preaching. Our thoughts and remembrances are part of the weave. The texts are not complete for preaching until we add our own stitching.

"Lift up your eyes and look around; they all gather together, they come to you" (v. 4). Here is a family reunion. The scattered children have come home. How lovely it would be to push past our losses and fixations on our glory days, in order to hear what our work has in some way accomplished. Our children have come home. We have been instruments of grace for homecoming after all.

Next come the treasures. Nations bring their wealth to lay at the feet of God. To offer our wealth is the deepest sign that something has moved us greatly. Wealth is the goal. Wealth is that which defines, protects, secures. Some massive shift has occurred in this vision. We are spectators who marvel that the Holy One has influenced strangers so profoundly. Perhaps we then realize that our own city is not ours after all. We only live here. Our deeper dwelling place is in the God who owns and lives within this familiar metropolis too.

This text disturbs. What if we respond badly to this turn of events? Our churches may reject the broader crowds. Our returning relatives may not be accepted at our door. We may simply choose to live where we live and to don our "Sunday faces" to cover these sadder realities.

It eases this discomfort to tell the plain truth. This text is a "dream/vision." Jerusalem was never like that in real life. The glory of the Lord was never fully realized in any regime or perfect society. Jerusalem was a city of kings and courtiers, intrigues, violence, and petty tyranny. People lived as we live, to the level of their abilities and depth of character. They were chewed on by their times as we are. They made their way as they could. Nations did come to the city gates, sometimes to trade and sometimes to conquer.

# Isaiah 60:1-6

## Theological Perspective

The passage has thus been taken up in more specific ways by later Christian writers; for example, if Jesus Christ is the light, then he ought to receive the gifts promised by Isaiah. Indeed, gold and frankincense are specified by the author of Matthew as the gifts of the magi to the newborn Jesus (Matt. 2:11). To the reader whose ears are attuned to the Scriptures, such details as these point to the kingship of Christ, part of Calvin's threefold office of Christ—as prophet, priest, and king. The addition of myrrh among the magi's gifts perhaps reflects a christological reading of the Song of Solomon in which Christ is understood as the lover whose "lips are like lilies dripping with myrrh" (Song 5:13, my translation).

With so much else of interest in the passage, it would be easy to overlook the imperative of 60:4—"Lift up your eyes and look around!"—but it too has theological significance. The glorious state of affairs is not only eschatological. It is already present, the text hints, but it is obscured by the hearer's refusal to see. In that respect, the light of the glory of the Lord is akin to the kingdom of heaven: it is already breaking into reality around us, but we often fail to see it. Insofar as the light is also identified with Christ, one might also reflect on Matthew 25's description of Jesus as present all around us in the hungry, sick, and imprisoned, but recognized in none of these forms. During the holiday season, rather than being too downcast to lift our eyes, we may instead be too busy and distracted, and may thus miss the true light of the world.

CHRISTOPHER B. HAYS

## Pastoral Perspective

of the transfiguration, where a heavenly voice will make it plain: "'This is my Son, the Beloved; listen to him!'" (Mark 9:7).

Today, in advance of that holy—and perplexing—mountaintop experience, we sing of kings who bring bountiful gifts to the newborn in Bethlehem. Gold. Frankincense. Myrrh. The contrast between the magi's riches and the humble "cattle shed" echoes the "wealth of the nations" (v. 5) knocking at the door of a downtrodden Israel. So, too, the revelation of Christ's identity—"my Son, the Beloved"—begins today, like Israel's eyes adjusting to the bright light that shines anew in Jerusalem.

These revelations of increasing light, in Jerusalem and in the Christ, draw us closer to the nature of God and allow us to see ourselves more clearly. Indeed, we might ask ourselves: How do I respond to God's initiative of grace? What gift do I bring to the Christ and to this congregation gathered in his name? How is the global church drawn together in adoration of the Christ? What do the "outsiders" in the passages from Isaiah and Matthew's Gospel teach us about who we are and who Jesus is?

In 1907, in his parting address to the National Council of Congregational Churches, Washington Gladden urged his peers to see the church as a manifestation of Christ. For Gladden, one of the chief reasons for Christ's life and for the life of the church was "to make men and women feel that the great joy of life . . . is the joy of service; to populate this world with a race of people whose central purpose it shall be, not to get as much as they can, but to give as much as they can—this is what Jesus came into this world to do."[3]

In light of today's passage from Isaiah, "giving as much as they can" seems to be a most fitting response to the revelation of God in Jerusalem and in the life of Jesus Christ. The foreign rulers cross the threshold of Israel with riches. The magi cross the threshold of Bethlehem with riches. Likewise, when the light shines in our darkness and the darkness does not overcome us, we are invited to cross the threshold of joy.

ANDREW NAGY-BENSON

---

[3]Washington Gladden, "The Church and the Social Crisis," in *The Living Theological Heritage of the United Church of Christ*, vol. 5, *Outreach and Diversity*, ed. Barbara Brown Zikmund (Cleveland: Pilgrim Press, 2000), 418.

## Exegetical Perspective

return home, unharmed, safe, and happy. In fact, the homecoming will extend beyond just Israel and Judah, but all people will be drawn by this light into their true home.

The images of this ingathering hearken back to God's call to Abraham to be a blessing upon all the families of the earth. Abraham's homeland will be the gathering place for all God's children, who will come bringing their finest treasures as an offering to God and for the benefit of God's people. For the Christian, these images hearken forward to the redemption of all creation in Jesus Christ—the One who on the cross opens his arms wide to draw all people to himself. However, here in the between times, readers are shown a people willing to be inspired by and work hard for a vision that is, as yet, out of their reach. The proclamation of this passage is one of hope, of something that is promised, but for which we are still waiting in faith.

When this passage is proclaimed at Epiphany, the verses envisioning the arrival of foreign worshipers, camels, and strangers bearing gifts of gold and frankincense evoke images of Matthew's Gospel, with its visit of foreign wise men bearing these exact gifts (plus the significant addition of myrrh for burial). In Matthew's theology, the promises of both Second and Third Isaiah are fulfilled in Jesus. But as Matthew Henry says, for believers the promises of God are our starting point, not the end nor even the goal of our life of faith.[1] Knowing what God promises, that "the glory of the LORD has risen upon you," and "the LORD will arise upon you," we begin our journey toward him, bringing our finest gifts and bringing others along with us, until all are gathered to him in the light of his glory.

KATHERINE C. CALORE

## Homiletical Perspective

Poetic visions still go begging among lesser, blunter things.

If the city envisioned is not yet real, perhaps it is the visionary himself who is the gem. The gift of seeing this beautiful thing opens the door to untapped joy. Maybe we live best through such moments of vision. Though we do not have it—indeed though we have never seen it writ large—we sense its truth and the rightness of it. Then light comes and floods the ordinary with the glory of God. When we tire of the decline and brave the reversal of course necessary to prepare for the poet, larger dreams are born and that city appears at the horizon.

This very day the Holy One may arrive as an unassuming guest on the street, or a minstrel in the park, in a gentle touch, or a good word. The light shines. When it does, we begin to know who and where we are.

One way of fashioning a sermon on this text might be to consider the greatest gifts you have ever received. What are their nature and their impact at the time and over time? What would you rush to keep, and how would you share with others what they have come to mean? To whom would you bequeath your great gift? For me the gift itself is always a sign of something more, be it the giver, the relationship, or the quality of perception found in the gift, how it says it all. Gift giving is the beginning of an adventure. It involves a lowering of the guard to let the power of a relationship have its way.

G. MALCOLM SINCLAIR

---

[1] Matthew Henry, *Matthew Henry's Concise Commentary*, http://www.christnotes.org/commentary.php?com=mhc&b=23&c=60.

# Psalm 72:1-7, 10-14

¹Give the king your justice, O God,
   and your righteousness to a king's son.
²May he judge your people with righteousness,
   and your poor with justice.
³May the mountains yield prosperity for the people,
   and the hills, in righteousness.
⁴May he defend the cause of the poor of the people,
   give deliverance to the needy,
   and crush the oppressor.

⁵May he live while the sun endures,
   and as long as the moon, throughout all generations.
⁶May he be like rain that falls on the mown grass,
   like showers that water the earth.

## Theological Perspective

The choice and consideration of this passage from the Psalms is set within the context of Epiphany. And understandably so! Matthew's Gospel opens notably with the announcement of Jesus' place within the lineage of David and, of course, his identity as the Messiah, the culmination of both God's promise and Israel's hope for a king who will minister God's care and will with integrity and strength.

But the story that recounts the world's first public recognition of his presence, the journey of the magi and their exchanges with Herod's court, unfolds a challenge to the waywardness of the collective human situation and the individual heart that harbors that waywardness. When the magi recount to the court their mission and their message, we are told that "he [Herod] was frightened, and all Jerusalem with him" (Matt. 2:3).

Psalm 72 sums up everything Israel's history expected and needed in a king. As a petition of praise it also recognizes that for Israel's hopes to be fulfilled, the king would have to be endowed by God with God's own justice and righteousness. Those endowments are the source of the justice, prosperity, and vindication that promise that the blessings of life will be experienced by all. They are the only guarantee that vindication will find its way to the poor, the needy, and the oppressed (72:1–4). Each

## Pastoral Perspective

Psalm 72 is the concluding psalm of what is called the Davidic Psalter (Pss. 51–72), and its placement there is probably no accident. This psalm presents a compelling, culminating description of the kingship God and the people of Israel expected and hoped for from the person who occupied the throne. According to its inscription and placement, this psalm comes when David hands over his throne to his son Solomon, who prayed to rule and to judge the people with wisdom. Like all of Israel's kings, however, Solomon both succeeded *and* failed "royally" in that calling. Perhaps it was a setup for failure, because Israel's king had an impossible standard for any mortal to meet: he was to mirror the justice and mercy of the only true king, YHWH, as he ruled in the life of the people. At their best, the kings of Israel wanted to rule by God's definition of justice and mercy. At their most faithful, the kings of Israel desired and worked for peace, shalom, to fill the land. Still, the lure of power and honor was great—and corrupting.

The tension between best intentions and baser motivations is not a problem reserved for kings—or for ancient people. Every person, king or citizen, then and now, struggles between living according to God's standards of justice and mercy and living for our own interests and gains. We seem to feel a pull

> [7]In his days may righteousness flourish
>    and peace abound, until the moon is no more. . . .
> . . . . . . . . . . . . . . . . . . . . . . . . . . . . . . . . . . . . . . . . . . . . . .
> [10]May the kings of Tarshish and of the isles
>    render him tribute,
>    may the kings of Sheba and Seba bring gifts.
> [11]May all kings fall down before him,
>    all nations give him service.
> [12]For he delivers the needy when they call,
>    the poor and those who have no helper.
> [13]He has pity on the weak and the needy,
>    and saves the lives of the needy.
> [14]From oppression and violence he redeems their life;
>    and precious is their blood in his sight.

## Exegetical Perspective

Psalm 72 is a royal psalm, one of a group of psalms that celebrate various aspects of the reign of the Davidic king. Specifically, this psalm is a prayer for the reign of God to be realized through the reign of the human king. Structurally, the psalm has five sections: verses 1–7, verses 8–11, verses 12–14, verses 15–17, and a doxological conclusion in verses 18–20 that serves as the conclusion for both Psalm 72 and Book II of the Psalter as a whole.

The psalmic prayer begins with a call to God to give to the king God's "judgments" (the Hebrew word *mišpateka* is plural, despite the singular rendering, "justice," in both NIV and NRSV). The vocative + imperative pattern in verse 1—"O God, give"—is the only direct address in the psalm; most of the remaining verbs are jussive, expressing a wish or desire: "May he." The king is never addressed directly, but throughout is referred to in third person. Thus the psalm is a prayer to God on behalf of the king.

The opening call to God (v.1) to give the king the divine "judgments" serves as the foundation for all that follows. The judgments of God—the acts of God in creating the world and deciding the course of human welfare—are the very acts for which the psalms repeatedly praise God. For God to give these "judgments" to the king is to imply that the king shall rule the people as God rules the earth. As God

## Homiletical Perspective

The preaching problem in the psalm is obvious. It is the gap between what is and what we want, for our land or, for that matter, for our church. The preacher's task is to explore the gap. The first thing we will note is that this gap is nothing new. It was that way in Israel also. No king ever really made it by the standards of Psalm 72. Certainly, King David never did. Though he ruled from the Mediterranean to the Gulf of Aqaba and to the upper reaches of the Euphrates, his kingdom never reached "the ends of the earth" (v. 8.) Nor did he always judge with righteousness, even in his own family, and still less with Uriah and Bathsheba. Still less did Solomon, named in the superscription of the psalm (not shown above), live up to the psalm's contents. He did not always defend the cause of the poor of the people. Remember the forced labor, the high taxes, the foreign entanglements with the daughters of the great. He did not crush the oppressor; in some ways, he became one. Nor did any of the successors of David and Solomon live up to the dream of the psalm. Though the words are truly wonderful, the reality of kingship in Israel was not. If the psalm is mainly a dream, it is a failure.

Many readers of this commentary will be American. The United States began as a dream, as a "city set on a hill." Its founders went out on an

# Psalm 72:1-7, 10-14

## Theological Perspective

generation, disappointed by circumstances but more by the failures and limitations of the reigning powers, looks hopefully to the future. This looking toward the future becomes an eschatological horizon, the theme of the later prophets.

The blessings of that petitioned kingship are so manifold and secure that they draw the tribute of foreign sovereigns. But it is not the political or military power of this Davidic king that initiates this tribute; it is the effective commitment to the poor, the weak, and the needy that commends their attention (vv. 12–14). This kingship surpasses the wonders of Solomon's reign as mirrored in the story of the visit of the queen of Sheba (1 Kgs. 10:1–13; 2 Chr. 9:1–12). There it is the "wisdom and prosperity" of Solomon as well as the attendant splendor of his court that is noted (1 Kgs. 10:7). For the psalmist, it is the well-being of the marginalized that constitutes the splendor of the court. Just as importantly, this king does not decline to the liabilities of Solomon's reign. The reign of Solomon and David's successor will invoke the same renown as theirs for the secure establishment of a communal life that actually creates hope for the nations and peoples that surround it. "May the kings of Sheba and Seba bring gifts. . . . For he delivers the needy when they call" (Ps. 72:10, 12).

Matthew's Gospel has Jesus say that "the queen of the South will rise up at the judgment with this generation and condemn it, because she came from the ends of the earth to listen to the wisdom of Solomon, and see, something [God's action in Jesus] greater than Solomon is here" (Matt. 12:42). Being greater is not a matter of degree but rather of kind. It is a matter of the graced one who is also the vehicle of grace, the forgiveness of sins.

So the story of the magi begins the public story of Jesus, the Messiah, by referring to what for the psalmist and the prophets is the end of the story. It is taking place now. Here are the foreign visitors seeking the new king. They have come for a magnificent exchange. They have come to present their gifts; they hope to return with the gifts of the awaited reign of peace. Their search, the journey that is more than geographical in nature, becomes part of the evangel process. The inquiry at the court in Jerusalem, in one sense a straightforward request, becomes a judgment upon that court. Herod's reign by itself is not at stake. The whole system is being questioned. As magi they hearken back to both the kings of the psalm and the visitor to Solomon's court who was in search of wise judgment and

## Pastoral Perspective

toward power early on in life. In a church I once served, we held a late afternoon Christmas Eve service especially designed for younger children. As they arrived for the service, children could choose one of three tables filled with costumes so that they could take a part in the Christmas pageant as it unfolded in the sanctuary. Most of the girls chose the table piled high with glittery wings and halos. They would be the angels, the heavenly host. We expected the boys to favor the other two tables, one loaded with paper crowns and cloaks of bright fabrics, the other offering brown headdresses along with some wooden staffs: kings and shepherds. For two years in a row, however, as we made our way through the Christmas story in that worship service, there were no shepherds. Every boy, and a few girls, wanted to be kings! They wanted the tall crowns with the glued-on shiny plastic jewels and the bright cloaks. No one wanted to be a lowly shepherd dressed in drab brown—however tempting it might be to wield that staff.

Every pastor and every church nominating committee can testify that it is easier to fill the more prestigious church offices than the more humble ones. The Davidic kings simply represent the human condition writ large.

Psalm 72 contains within its verses this tension many of us feel between power and service if we are honest enough—or have the innocence of children enough—to admit it. Verses 1–4 focus on the matter of service and mercy for poor and oppressed people. Majesty and power then shape the prayers of verses 5–11 in grand ways before returning to mercy and compassion again in verses 12–14. In reading the psalm itself, we sense and read the competing pulls, the tension between God's calling and our own desires.

In writing of this psalm and its use in the liturgy of kingship, Walter Brueggemann notes that for kings "it is predictable that one's inclination would be toward the matter of majesty, because majesty generates authority, power, prestige and security. On the other hand, to be a creature, child, and heir who is to submit and be shaped by the liturgy is to be pulled toward the matter of mercy, to understand that the world now constructed is a world in which the marginal are cared for." He notes that liturgy does its proper work when majesty and mercy are kept in balance and tension.[1]

[1] Walter Brueggemann, *Israel's Praise: Doxology against Idolatry and Ideology* (Philadelphia: Fortress Press, 1988), 69.

has brought order out of chaos, so the king will impose the divine order on the nation. As God delivers the people and gives them land and identity, so the king will deliver the poor and oppressed, giving them hope.

Central to the theology that supported the Davidic monarchy was the belief that from Jerusalem God distributed to the world righteousness (Heb.: *tsedaqah*) and wholeness, peace (Heb.: *shalom*). In God's reign, even the mountains will yield *shalom* (NRSV and NIV both render the term "prosperity," but *shalom* means much more: "integrity," "wholeness," and "peace") and the hills will bring forth *tsedaqah* (v. 3). The agency through which the land yields up its produce of goodness is the just and righteous rule of the king. Bracketing the image of the hills and mountains bearing *shalom* is the expectation that the king will exercise his power and authority for the benefit and defense of the poor and needy, the vulnerable and oppressed. The psalmist understands that there is a direct connection between the just and right treatment of those most at risk in the society and the material and spiritual health of the realm as a whole.

The psalmist is confident that such a reign will attract the loyalty of the whole earth. In verses 8–11 the psalmist depicts the just and righteous king as having dominion from one end of the earth to the other. Kings from the known world—Tarshish (Spain), the "isles" (probably Cyprus and Sicily), Sheba (east Africa), and Seba (Arabia)—will offer tribute, obeisance, and obedience.

Verses 12–14 explain why the king is internationally influential. Verse 12 begins with the conjunction *kî*, "because," signaling the reason for the king's power. Significantly, it is not military prowess or economic power that makes the king important. Rather, the foes bow and kings obey because the righteous king "delivers the needy when they call" (v. 12) and "from oppression and violence . . . redeems their life" (v. 14). Once again, the psalmist emphasizes the connection between the success of the king's reign and his commitment to justice for the vulnerable.

Perhaps this language of wealth and international influence explains the dedication (omitted above) of the psalm in verse 1: *leshlomeh*, "To Solomon" (NRSV and NIV: "Of Solomon"). Of all the Davidic kings, Solomon is most remembered for his fabulous wealth and international prestige (see 1 Kgs. 10), and as the one who sought wisdom to rule the people justly. But even Solomon falls short of the vision of

"errand into the wilderness." From the Declaration of Independence, to the Constitution, to Lincoln's Second Inaugural, to Martin Luther King Jr., there have always been wonderful words and a dream. But there has also been, sadly but also obviously, a gap. Nor is this sad reality only true of the United States. My own nation, Canada, got its formal name, Dominion of Canada, and its Latin motto, "A mare ad mari" ("from sea to sea"), from the King James Version of verse 8 of this psalm. But the poor do not always find justice from their rulers in Canada either. And if we turn to the rulers of other nations, the picture stays the same. We speak high-sounding words at the inauguration of a new leader, the formal equivalent of the setting in life of this psalm, but do the rulers ever live up to the high-sounding phrases? The question remains, with all countries, to what degree does the nation live out the vision of justice contained in the psalm? And the answer is clear: not well enough. The words may be wonderful, but the reality falls sadly short of the words. If a nation is mainly a dream, it's also a failure.

For preaching purposes, the appropriate analog to the Israel of the psalm may be not a nation but a church. The equivalent setting today is not the inauguration of a president but the ordination of a minister or priest. No Western nation is a theocracy. But the church is supposed to be the place where God does rule. And indeed the church is present to the ends of the earth. Moreover, we have such wonderful words in our churches, including these noble words from Psalm 72. But our churches also fall sadly short of the reality envisioned in the psalm. The true church is where the word is rightly preached and the sacraments rightly administered, to quote one ancient formulation, but too often our sermons are dull and our sacraments perfunctory. Yet tedium or liturgical sloppiness is scarcely the worst charge one could bring against the church! Even if we are not in open conflict with one another, as is often the case, in far too many churches, the reality of our life together does not show forth the loving presence of the Prince of Peace. We instinctively understand the bumper sticker: "I love God; it's his followers I can't stand." If we turn from the church to the leaders of the church, the picture remains very much the same. There are some fine clergy, but none of us live up fully to the high words we proclaim. Even for the best of us, our performance does not live up to the words spoken at our ordinations. If a church is mainly a dream, it is probably a failure also.

# Psalm 72:1-7, 10-14

## Theological Perspective

understanding. Perhaps all our questions and pursuits of justice and peace as expressions of an "ultimate concern," to use Paul Tillich's term, are part of the evangel when they call into question the "current arrangements" as well as our acquiescence in them.

Herod's commendation of their search is an evasion. It is not just a political evasion; it is an evasion of the spirit of their search. "Go and search diligently for the child; and when you have found him, bring me word so that I may also go and pay him homage" (Matt. 2:8). There can be no second-hand search for this sovereign. The search for grace is prompted and sustained by grace. Psalm 72 prays for a king who is animated and guided by God's own goodness. But the vision and hope that gives birth to the prayer is the work of grace. The little drama that is played out between Herod and the magi is a drama that is replicated in every human. If we continue to desire to rule ourselves, we continue as oppressors of ourselves, and perhaps of others.

Matthew's Gospel, as well as the others, is a narrative of how Jesus' ministry fulfills the results of the reign of God's "anointed one" in this psalm, but not in any mechanical way. The discernment of faith is always required. Jesus' encounter with the woman who suffered from chronic bleeding can easily call one back to the psalmist's poignant acclaim: "he redeems their life; and precious is their blood in his sight" (v. 14). Jesus' life and ministry do not fulfill a script; they fulfill a promise. The miracles are always a challenge to hope, the same hope that animates the prayer that is Psalm 72. What is announced by a star rising in the east becomes Isaiah's "great light" (Matt. 4:16; cf. Isa. 9:1, 2) shining over a world, not just a nation, that dwells in the shadow of death.

DWIGHT M. LUNDGREN

## Pastoral Perspective

A pastoral sermon on Psalm 72, then, will bring together the competing visual and scriptural images of kings that are contained in Epiphany and help us to find our own practices of power and service, of majesty and mercy, restored to balance and tension. With the reading from Matthew that tells of the magi coming to pay homage to the infant Jesus, we encounter King Herod and all the power and terror that kingship afforded him. We are called to examine our own use of power collectively and individually and its effects on others. But we have also made these magi into kings themselves, and three in number. They bring evidence of their wealth as they offer gifts to Jesus and his parents. We are called to consider how we use our own wealth—sometimes as good gifts rightly given, at other times to insulate us from the dangers others face daily. Wealth enables us to live apart from those who are poor and vulnerable.

There is, of course, another king offered at Epiphany: king Jesus. Some scholars think that over time, as Israel watched its long procession of kings come and go and fail, Psalm 72 took on a plaintive longing. This psalm became liturgy about more than the next king; it became a prayer for the long-awaited Messiah.[2] Jesus is the king who will redefine power and majesty and security. He is the one who will finally mirror—no, embody—the divine blend of majesty and mercy for people, especially people who are poor, vulnerable, oppressed, and hurt. The ancient dream and longing voiced in Psalm 72 still is ours today as we await the coming of God's kingdom in its fullness. In this "meantime" there are tables set before us offering choices about who we want to be. Epiphany is a time to consider what it means that we have been called to be servants of this particular Sovereign and citizens of this kingdom of God.

KIMBERLY L. CLAYTON

---

[2] James L. Mays, *Psalms*, Interpretation Series (Louisville, KY: John Knox Press, 1994), 238.

## Exegetical Perspective

the faithful king contained herein, finally becoming more fascinated with his wealth and prestige than with his faithfulness to God (see 1 Kgs. 11). After Solomon, no other descendant of David does even so well. In the end, we are forced to admit that the king described in this psalm is ideal, not historical.

The idealized vision of the king whose power comes from his commitment to God's justice for the poor is an eschatological vision. No historical ruler has fulfilled it, and judging from the course of human events, none is likely to do so. How then is the faith community to understand it? To nurture this vision of the righteous ruler is to entertain simultaneously two apparently opposite inclinations: we must maintain a critical distance from human rulers, because they inevitably fail to live out the divine intent and become more enamored with power than with justice. At the same time, we must keep alive the hope and expectation that the righteous ruler will one day come, and the vision of God's judgments enacted in human life will at last be realized.

For Christians, who read this psalm on Epiphany (the feast of the revelation of the rule of God expressed in Jesus Christ), that day has come, at least proleptically. We read Psalm 72 alongside Matthew's narrative of the adoration of the magi and with the Isaianic call to Jerusalem still ringing in our ears to "Arise, shine; for your light has come, for the glory of the LORD has risen upon you" (Isa. 60:1). In this context, Psalm 72 reminds us that the only king whose life reflects the rising of divine glory and who merits our adoration and worship is the one king who eschewed the throne for the sake of the cross. For Christians, it is the reign of Jesus, revealed in time but still expected eschatologically, that realizes God's judgments and distributes to the world God's *shalom* and *tsedaqah*. To read this psalm on Epiphany is to capture a glimpse of God's new reality, born in a manger, enthroned on the cross, and coming to transform the earth, until even the mountains and hills glow with divine glory.

PAUL K. HOOKER

## Homiletical Perspective

But in our preaching we do more than explore gaps or name the ways in which all our institutions and leaders fall short of our best intentions. We note that the psalm is not just a dream; it is a prayer, "Give the king your justice. . . . May he judge your people with righteousness. . . . May he defend the cause of the poor." We pray the great words even if we know we will fail fully to live up to them. And we stick with the church, even as we recognize its failures. Perhaps we stick with the church precisely because it has those great words and occasionally, at its best moments, its people and its leaders actually approximate them. But above all we stick with the church because in it we meet another son of David, another King's Son. The language of Psalm 72 "fits" with him, as the church has always recognized. While recognizing that this is a Hebrew psalm, whose first referent is to some unknown king of David's line, when it is used in a Christian church, it also points beyond its original setting in life to this new King. The preacher has the marvelous privilege of pointing to the presence of that King in church and in world. When the sermon is over, it is time for the prayers of the people. In those prayers, we ask that the church and its leaders may live up to his presence.

STEPHEN FARRIS

# Ephesians 3:1-12

[1]This is the reason that I Paul am a prisoner for Christ Jesus for the sake of you Gentiles—[2]for surely you have already heard of the commission of God's grace that was given me for you, [3]and how the mystery was made known to me by revelation, as I wrote above in a few words, [4]a reading of which will enable you to perceive my understanding of the mystery of Christ. [5]In former generations this mystery was not made known to humankind, as it has now been revealed to his holy apostles and prophets by the Spirit: [6]that is, the Gentiles have become fellow heirs, members of the same body, and sharers in the promise in Christ Jesus through the gospel.

[7]Of this gospel I have become a servant according to the gift of God's grace that was given me by the working of his power. [8]Although I am the very least of all the saints, this grace was given to me to bring to the Gentiles the news of the boundless riches of Christ, [9]and to make everyone see what is the plan of the mystery hidden for ages in God who created all things; [10]so that through the church the wisdom of God in its rich variety might now be made known to the rulers and authorities in the heavenly places. [11]This was in accordance with the eternal purpose that he has carried out in Christ Jesus our Lord, [12]in whom we have access to God in boldness and confidence through faith in him.

## Theological Perspective

God is the God who wants to be known in order to reconcile and redeem humanity and the rest of creation. God's revelation takes place not to remain secret or within the control or for the benefit of an elite group. God's redemptive revelation in Jesus Christ is for all and is made known by the public and cosmic proclamation of the gospel (1:13; 3:8, 10). The revealing and redeeming God calls forth the ministry of apostles and prophets (3:5; 4:11) and demands the readiness of a church to proclaim the "gospel of peace" (6:15). The *apocalypsis* (revelation) of God (3:3) requires the apostolicity (sending) of an evangelizing church.

The author of Ephesians wrote this letter emulating the message of and advancing the agenda of his mentor, the apostle Paul. He wrote in Paul's name and for Paul's cause, the evangelization of the Gentiles (3:8). Like Paul, he was a defender among Christian Jews of the divine will and call for Gentiles to become part of the people of God through faith in Jesus Christ without circumcision and the works of the Law (God's affirmative action in Christ for the Gentiles!). He taught and fought for the recognition of the equal spiritual identity, status, honor, and blessings of Gentile believers, who previously had been outsiders and aliens from God's people, but now were cosharers with Jewish believers through

## Pastoral Perspective

Paul describes his personal epiphany of faith as a *mystery*. Yet a popular understanding of a mystery might mislead us. Most bookstores have an entire section devoted to mystery, but the kind of stories will be quite different from Paul's. A mystery television show or novel is usually tied to the apprehension of criminals. Within these artificial boundaries, the case is certain to be solved within an hour or by the last page. A mystery keeps our attention by providing enough plot twists to keep us guessing. Will the author surprise us? Are we skilled detectives, able to deduce an elementary solution in advance? In popular culture, a mystery is a contest of minds, pitting "us" against "them," sleuth against conspirator, reader against author. A mystery is a game.

Paul's mystery is vastly different. His mystery concerns not the apprehension of criminals, but the *comprehension* of Jesus Christ. And so, mystery writer Paul turns the tables on the reader with delicious irony. In Paul's plot, the reader is not the one who declares to the perpetrator, "I got you!" In the mystery of faith, Christ is the one who apprehends *us*. Paul writes in 3:1 that we are made Christ's prisoners, not vice versa. Our individual moments of epiphany come, as did Paul's, when we finally realize we are the hunted, not the hunters. We will not escape the loving justice of the long arm of

## Exegetical Perspective

More of us fail than succeed at the dicey business of telling our own stories in sermons; but we tell them anyway, because when it works, it really works. Personal epiphanies make powerful proclamation. In Ephesians 3:1–12 Paul (the author in the letter's narrative world, whether or not he was in the first-century world) reaches for some of that experiential clout. In Paul's epiphany, God tells long-kept secrets about the wide identity of God's people and the height of their purpose in the world.

The cosmic good news of this passage is that God's people hail from all corners of the human community. That is good news to Gentiles because in Christ God has made them heirs to Israel's promises. The Jewish Messiah will be also the Lord of all. This radical inclusion is not new to 3:1–12. Already in chapter 2, we heard how through Christ's cross God has embraced the Gentiles, who "once were far off," so that they are "no longer strangers and aliens, but . . . citizens with the saints and . . . members of the household of God" (2:13, 19). Together with their Jewish Christian brothers and sisters, they are called to be nothing less than "a dwelling place for God" (2:22). The glory of inclusion resounds.

To reiterate the dearness of that inclusion, Paul begins here with a brief reference to the punishment

## Homiletical Perspective

Epiphany as a season has been celebrated since at least the fourth century. The Scriptures that have come to be associated with the feast and the season, and especially Matthew's narrative concerning the visit of the wise men, call us to honor the One who is, by God's gracious initiative, both King of the Jews and Savior of the world.

While the presenting motif is the unveiling of God's will and ultimate purpose to the Gentiles—and their "discovery" of the light that is for all people—this "good news" is no less a revelation to the Jews: that God intends to unite divided humanity into one people. And so there is an interesting interplay between today's Gospel account and the epistle: in the former, the Gentiles bring gifts to the Christ child; in the latter, Paul (whether in person or by secondary witness) brings the gifts of Christ to the Gentiles.

The primacy of Christ in God's gracious initiative and the consequent unity of all God's children—and all people, now, beneficiaries of Christ's unsearchable riches (v. 8)—are the heart of this day's proclamation. While the full scope of God's plan, along with the identity of the One who will accomplish it, have been mostly hidden until now, Epiphany unveils, proclaims, celebrates God's gift to all people.

# Ephesians 3:1-12

## Theological Perspective

their faith in and unity with Christ (God's preferential option for the Gentiles in Christ!). He joined his voice to those Christian Jews who proclaimed and celebrated God's redemptive and inclusive grace for Gentiles (3:1–2, 6) and conceived the present people of God as the eschatological reunion of Jews and Gentiles in a reconciled body under the Lordship of Jesus (God's new humanity on earth! 2:15).

The author of Ephesians conceived Paul and himself as part of the apostolic and prophetic community (3:5; 4:11–13), that, guided by the Spirit (3:5) and enabled by God's grace (3:2, 7–8), received the revelation of the mystery of God's will (1:9) for the purpose of making it known (3:8) in the appropriate time of God (3:5). This mystery was the divine plan (3:9; 1:10) "to gather up all things" in Christ (1:10) and to make Gentiles "fellow heirs, members of the same body, and sharers in the promise in Christ Jesus through the gospel" (3:6). Paul and the author are represented in the epistle as apostles, servants, and ambassadors (1:1; 3:7; 6:20) of God's secret plan that has been revealed and now should be proclaimed. They were members of a church in apostolic mission serving the mission of God for which Christ himself was an example and foundation as one who "proclaimed peace" to Gentiles and to Jews (2:17).

In remembering Paul's commission, the author establishes the apostolic paradigm for the churches to follow. Inspired by Paul's example and authority, churches should be ready to continue the evangelizing mission to the Gentiles (6:15) and their witnessing to the "rulers and authorities in the heavenly places" (3:10). As a "new humanity" created in and through Christ (2:15), the church stands as an embodied witness to the "fullness of time" and is a present sign of the future "gather[ing] up" of "things in heaven and things on earth" (1:10). By its existence as a "new humanity" (2:15) and by its status of sharing with Christ "in the heavenly places" (2:6), the church makes known God's will and plan to the "rulers and authorities" that still keep humanity apart from God and one another (2:2; 6:12). The church is a beneficiary, creature, and agent of God's redemptive revelation. The existence of the church as a "new humanity" where Jews and Gentiles are reconciled to one another (3:6; 2:13–16) and where humanity is reconciled to God (3:11–12) is evidence that "the plan of the mystery hidden for ages in God" is underway (3:9). This ministry of the mystery is sustained in the church by the exercise of the gifts to build up the body of Christ (4:11–12).

## Pastoral Perspective

God. We have already been captured. Perhaps the greatest mystery of faith is why Christ would choose to make us his servants in the first place, we who would be in the last place when compared to greater saints, we who are sinners, we who consistently break the laws of God. The mystery of faith is not a case to be solved, nor a problem seeking solution, nor a contest of wills. Paul's mystery reaches its pinnacle at the precise moment we understand there is no game. The contest is already won. Epiphany.

So many church members struggle with their faith. They struggle to reach a perceived goal, some imagined level of sainthood at which they can declare, "I've got it!" Perhaps Paul, when he was Saul the arch-Pharisee, felt the same. Perhaps he felt like a detective, tracking down criminals, hoping for a final notch in his belt. Now as then, the quest to uphold the faith produces restlessness and anxiety. There will always be more infidels, no matter how effective our efforts to convert the masses. There will always be a part of ourselves that resists our best efforts. Sin will remain. The problem of sin will not be solved by our resourcefulness. Enter Jesus Christ.

The comprehension of Christ's entry into our lives is a moment of purest epiphany. We become wise men and women, not when we find the baby Jesus, but when we realize the crucified Jesus has found us. An epiphany is a relief, a release from the struggle with anxieties and interpersonal wars. Paradoxically, an epiphany is not a triumph, but a surrender. Surrender was a difficult concept for Pharisees and Ephesians. Surrender is difficult for modern-day Christians too. Surrender sounds like failure. We view defeat as shameful, a public demonstration of inadequacy, the triumph of evil. We are trained from early in life to compete—for status, for jobs, for wealth, even for love. If we must cheat, so be it; we will change our game from beating competitors to beating authorities. What a life-changing mystery it is to discover a God who is not playing games. God neither answers all our questions nor solves all our problems. But God loves. God loves with a love that stretches from creation to our next breath, to our final breath, and beyond. Instead of anxiety and restlessness, God through the Spirit of Christ brings us the boldness and confidence to confess our faith, to turn ourselves in, to be free at last.

Is it possible, then, that beyond individual epiphanies, the church might experience a corporate revelation of the Spirit? Surely this is the hope in which Paul writes to the Ephesians. When Paul

he incurred for announcing it. "Gentile freedom had cost [Paul] his liberty," wrote J. A. Robinson,[1] and mention of his imprisonment speaks subliminally the costliness of the gift. Later, Paul will pray for his audience to fathom "the breadth and length and height and depth" of *Christ's* love that made their belonging possible (3:18). Here he tells *his own* love and the chains he has endured so that they could hear about that belonging.

If Paul's experience of prison tells the *cost* of Gentile inclusion, he grounds its *trustworthiness* in the authority of direct revelation. About the mechanics of this revelation, Paul is customarily reticent.[2] We only know that, though God kept the secret from generations of men and women, God's Spirit has now told it to apostles and prophets. As one of that august company, Paul now passes it on to the Gentile audience of this letter. To any who doubt their belonging, he answers, "I've got it from God that you're in!"

After assuring the Gentiles of their inclusion, Paul turns quickly to their calling. Just as they celebrate being "fellow heirs, members of the same body and sharers in the promise in Christ Jesus" (3:6), Paul interrupts their reverie with the enormous responsibility of their new status. They will be messengers. After telling his own example of servanthood (3:7), he quickly passes the communication baton to the church. But if Paul's audience has been "the Gentiles" and "everyone," the church is called to publish the rich and various wisdom of God "to the rulers and authorities in the heavenly places" (3:10).

The cosmic specter of "rulers and authorities in the heavenly places" will appear again in the spiritual battle pictured in chapter 6, where war is waged "not against . . . blood and flesh, but against the rulers, against the authorities, against the cosmic powers of this present darkness, against the spiritual powers of evil in the heavenly places" (6:12). How will the church make cosmic mysteries known to such as these? This question gains force when we picture, not an idealized church, but the real and tiny and flawed one meeting in the chance living rooms of a few first-century Mediterranean cities. The sheer motleyness of this crew would make Paul's claim laughable, if not for its thematic fit with Israel's own motleyness, that lowly Bethlehem birth, and the unexpected turn of a few fishermen's and tax collectors' and prostitutes'

And so we think today first of the Gentile magi, a long way from where they might ever have imagined themselves to be, on a strange mission to bring gifts to a young stranger, a Hebrew male child: gold, frankincense, and myrrh, as signs of their fealty and faith in a reality beyond their conventional wisdom. The star is pure grace; their travel is sheer faith; their worship is the dawn of a new age whose fullness will see all peoples come to the mountain of God. The "wisdom" of the magi may seem so much foolishness, and not least in their visit to Herod, but their "foolishness," both the travel and sacrifice, anticipates Paul's own (see 1 Cor. 4:10).

And so at Epiphany one thinks also of the "other" wise man, Paul, whose "too much learning," Festus declared, had driven him (Paul) insane (Acts 26:24). Paul indeed refers to himself as a fool for Christ (1 Cor. 4:10), but his is a foolishness that he perceives as the very wisdom of God (after 1 Cor. 1:21). Educated at the feet of Gamaliel in the strictest and most conventional Jewish wisdom, Paul finds himself now a very long way from where he might ever have imagined himself to be. Imprisonment is the least of it, he says, for, though bound, he has been set indescribably free on a strange mission to bring gifts to the Gentiles. He brings words of grace and inclusion in the family and purposes of God, a truth that could only come by revelation: that the Gentiles are, and have been all along, in the ultimately inclusive plans of God.

These plans have not always been clear or self-obvious. To be sure, there have been, here and there, angelic hints and prophetic whispers, indications now and then, and evidence too in the Jewish traditions and texts. Jesus himself drew upon such stories as he preached in Nazareth. That he was almost killed for it demonstrates that the inclusive word is often the least welcome word. Still, the fullness of God's plans is now unveiled, born and raised in the world in a dramatic and unmistakable way.

A friend of mine's little girl asked her the perennial question: "Mommy, where was I before I was born?" In a moment of high inspiration my friend answered, "In the heart of God." Indeed. Likewise, the plan of full inclusion for Gentiles in the family of God was always in the heart of God, and now that plan has been revealed for all to see and for all to hear through the preaching and fellowship of the church.

We have changed seasons, from Christmas to Epiphany, but we are still in the birthing chamber. The story of Jesus' nativity is but one part of a

---

[1] J. Armitage Robinson, *St. Paul's Epistle to the Ephesians* (London: James Clarke & Co., 1922), 10.

[2] Cf. Gal. 1:16 to the account of Paul's conversion and call in Acts 9.

# Ephesians 3:1-12

## Theological Perspective

In light of this concern for the apostolic mission to the Gentiles, the petition for prayer that the author solicits in the name of the apostle in order to have the words and courage to speak the "mystery of the gospel" (6:19) is also a prayer extensive to all the saints (6:18). They also need the divine power (3:18–20) to accomplish their call to advance the gospel. God's manifestation is mediated by the apostolic annunciation of the "news of the boundless riches of Christ" (3:8).

Ephesians has inspired past and present theologians to discern the "marks" and the "missions" of the church. The church has a vocation to be one, holy, catholic, and apostolic. The church has a call to engage in worship, proclamation, communion, and service. By calling attention to the key role Paul played in the revelation of the mystery of God, and by recognizing the church as a place and instrument where revelation takes place, the pericope for today emphasizes the apostolic nature and the evangelizing task of the church.

The church of Jesus Christ finds its identity and mission in proclaiming to the world the gospel of peace. The vocation to share the good news in speech and life constitutes an essential part of its apostolic nature and mission. The church becomes church by God's epiphany in Christ, and it remains church by embodying and communicating for the whole world through words and deeds and in the power of the Spirit the mystery of the gospel of peace (6:15, 19). The vocation to confess the gospel of peace (*shalom*) takes many forms in a fragmented, convulsive, and conflicted world. The task of being witnesses and artisans for God's peace and a world of peace with justice requires ecumenical, interfaith, and public local and global initiatives and networks that address the conditions and negative consequences that deny and prevent the blessing of God's peace with justice for all. The church is renewed by the Spirit who leads it, as servant of God and humanity, to preach and live the gospel in places and borders where the dynamics of alienation, exclusion, and domination of the old age still resist the new time of the blessing and praxis of God's peace.

LUIS R. RIVERA

## Pastoral Perspective

speaks of the "wisdom of God in its rich variety" (3:10), he points to the church as the vessel by which this mystery will be poured out, that even the "rulers and authorities in the heavenly places" might hear and understand. Paul's ministry to the Gentiles will be joined into God's grand scheme for all creation, not through individual enlightenment, but through the church. Therefore, with the same boldness and confidence that allows us to confess our personal faith, so must the church publicly declare what it believes. In acts of servanthood, in responses of gratitude, in generous giving and in prophetic speech, the church is called to share its epiphany. In this age when so many churches wonder what, if anything, they have to offer, Paul writes a word of basic revival. Even churches trying to solve mysteries of disappearing membership and budgets based on smoke and mirrors are part of the eternal purpose of God. Yet, because faith is not a competition, a church should be mindful not to fall back into a spirit of "us against them," whether "they" be other churches, other religions, or any other perceived perpetrator of second-class saintliness. The church is called to proclaim Christ, not conquer sin. Some mysteries can be solved only by God.

But what if a church has no group epiphany to share? How does a congregation touch the untouchables? The church and Paul have always held conjoined the paradox of mystery *and* the gift of sacrament. Like an epiphany, a sacrament is the slightly open window through which we slide a finger toward relief. The Lord's Supper is a prime example of an activity in which we neither act nor accomplish, but through which we mysteriously draw closer to each other and find access to Christ. In the sacraments we stop solving mysteries and, for a marvelous epiphanic moment, allow the mysteries to solve us.

JAMES W. MCTYRE

careers. In this latter context, though, it seems par for the course: ragtag and inauspicious little ones are called again into the grand and significant movement of God in the cosmos.

And so it goes for us. As dazzlingly new as it is to Paul and the Ephesians, the cosmic good news of 3:1–12 is most assuredly not news to God. The inclusion and employment of Gentiles through Christ is an "eternal purpose" (3:11), planned by God before the beginning. But for reasons Paul does not explore with the Ephesians, God has kept humanity out of the know for centuries. This theme of mystery and disclosure is widespread in the New Testament: the God who keeps secrets becomes the tell-all God in Christ.

But was *all* truly told with Christ? Or are there divine secrets still longer kept? Looking back at church history through the lens of Ephesians 3, can we spy other such cosmically significant epiphanies? Christians through the centuries have probed this question with every passionate debate—about the Bible's endorsement of slavery, the place of women in ministry, and the moral status of gay and lesbian unions, to name a significant few.

The Puritan worthy John Robinson spoke his heart on the matter four centuries ago: "God has yet more light and truth to break forth out of his[3] holy Word." If he was right and God *is* still *speaking*, Paul assures us here that God is *not* still *growing*. Whatever kept humanity from hearing the expansive inclusiveness of God through those long generations before the Nazarene, it was not God's limitation. The plan preceded the people. In this blessed Epiphany lection, Paul tells his own epiphany of God's old-but-new inclusiveness. There were more such dramatic moments to come. In an ecclesial irony too splendid to be anything but divine, abolitionists and feminists and gay-rights activists alike become the apostles Paul of their day—prophets handing on their own dear-but-belated epiphanies from a misunderstood God who ever was so. And, lest we self-congratulate, many more will come after and expose our own smallnesses. Before the rulers and authorities in heavenly places, and to all of us who once were far off, Paul and all these latter-day prophets speak powerful words of inclusion and embrace: "I've got it from God that you're in!"

ALLEN R. HILTON

greater birth announcement: that light is born into darkness, that salvation (in the sense of inclusion in the people of God) is born among the Gentiles, that the fullness of God's will is delivered into the world for all with eyes to see. The church exists to reiterate that message in full hearing and view of the powers and principalities of this world.

However one understands the authorship of Ephesians or this somewhat "autobiographical" section, in the first movement of the text (vv. 1–4), the author grants his audience authority to plumb the validity of this rendering of the gospel. The text itself evidences an assumption as to the shared (pneumatic?) authority that exists in the church— itself a demonstration of Epiphany's message: the light has, in fact, come to all.

Similarly, in the last movement (vv. 10–12) the proclamation that begins with Paul's preaching to the Gentiles is extended and broadened: the church (including these Gentile Christians) now shares the authority and responsibility to continue the preaching of this unifying gospel. This word to the "principalities and powers in the heavenly places," and indeed to the world, is that God intends and is already at work to unite all humankind through Christ. That proclamation defines the church's "social mission," for it is indeed the will and wisdom of God. If, in many instances and in many ways, the church has waited for the world to "set the agenda" for justice and inclusion—leaving the church the embarrassing task of catching up to the world—the Epiphany announcement is that the reverse is the actual *ordo salutis*. As we preach this gospel, we have boldness before God and the world, because we have access to God's wisdom through the gift of Christ.

A caution seems in order, however: though we are recipients of this gospel, we have no hold on God or wisdom. Epiphany reminds us that our best wisdom is foolishness and that God's plans, though in the vanity of our thoughts we might deem them impossibly foolish, are wisdom and light indeed.

THOMAS R. STEAGALD

---

[3]In the early seventeenth century, the gender-transcendence of God had yet to break forth!

# Matthew 2:1-12

[1]In the time of King Herod, after Jesus was born in Bethlehem of Judea, wise men from the East came to Jerusalem, [2]asking, "Where is the child who has been born king of the Jews? For we observed his star at its rising, and have come to pay him homage." [3]When King Herod heard this, he was frightened, and all Jerusalem with him; [4]and calling together all the chief priests and scribes of the people, he inquired of them where the Messiah was to be born. [5]They told him, "In Bethlehem of Judea; for so it has been written by the prophet:
[6]'And you, Bethlehem, in the land of Judah,
    are by no means least among the rulers of Judah;
  for from you shall come a ruler
    who is to shepherd my people Israel.'"

## Theological Perspective

Having sat through enough Christmas pageants, it may be hard to banish the image of graying dads pressed into service, wearing bathrobes and Burger King crowns, trying to appear as wise and regal as possible. But the magi of Matthew's narrative would have been exotic novelties in a backwater like Bethlehem. Who were these travelers from faraway Persia, who studied star charts and discerned fates in the night sky? Who could be less likely to have discovered the Christ child? Their mystical craft, handed down from the ancient Sumerians, predated even Moses. Judaism and then Christianity regarded their arts as deceptive, even dangerous. Instead of waiting expectantly for some messiah, they were taking notes on comets and planetary movements. Yet they are the ones who have come to worship the Messiah.

What did they see? A supernova? Jupiter and Saturn in conjunction? A comet? How would a star point to a particular house anyhow? Medieval writers believed the magi saw a bright angel, which they mistook for a star—but that angel led them directly to the manger.[1]

Matthew isn't endorsing astrology. Instead, he cleverly testifies to the power of God, not merely to bring foreigners and those who have up until now

[1]Dale Allison, *Studies in Matthew* (Grand Rapids: Baker, 2005), 17–41.

## Pastoral Perspective

The word "epiphany," in a standard dictionary, has two meanings. When capitalized, of course, it refers to the manifestation of Christ to the Gentiles, as described in the lectionary text for this day. In lower case, the term applies to any manifestation of a deity. But the word increasingly has been used as a referent to any insightful or dramatic moment that instills new spiritual insight, vision, or perspective.

The Epiphany story offers rich opportunity for insight into a set of "stages" for these "wise men from the East." Their epiphany (*the* Epiphany in Christian history) was the recognition that the prophecies of the Messiah had become a reality. There are a number of observations to be made.

First, these wise people had been studying. They knew their history. They hadn't merely stumbled onto this momentous event. They had searched their own past and their sacred texts, and the result of their study was a readiness, or at least a willingness, to recognize the sign when it appeared.

Second, these scholarly folk did not keep their noses in the books all the time. They also were keen observers of the world around them. Without those two characteristics, knowing the prophecies and being observant of their contemporary world, the Epiphany might well have been missed by these

[7]Then Herod secretly called for the wise men and learned from them the exact time when the star had appeared. [8]Then he sent them to Bethlehem, saying, "Go and search diligently for the child; and when you have found him, bring me word so that I may also go and pay him homage." [9]When they had heard the king, they set out; and there, ahead of them, went the star that they had seen at its rising, until it stopped over the place where the child was. [10]When they saw that the star had stopped, they were overwhelmed with joy. [11]On entering the house, they saw the child with Mary his mother; and they knelt down and paid him homage. Then, opening their treasure chests, they offered him gifts of gold, frankincense, and myrrh. [12]And having been warned in a dream not to return to Herod, they left for their own country by another road.

## Exegetical Perspective

The story of the visit of the magi is a drama in five acts. Act 1 (1:18–25) describes Joseph's dream concerning the child, act 2 (2:1–12) the visit of the magi and the actions of Herod. Act 3 (2:13–15) describes Joseph's dream warning him to flee to Egypt for safety (an ironic reversal), act 4 (2:16–18) the slaughter of the innocents by Herod. Act 5 (2:19–23) describes Joseph's return to Nazareth (again, prompted by a dream). The alert reader will note that acts 1, 3, and 5 involve Joseph and his response to divine prompting through dreams. The magi are the next players in importance. Herod is, of course, the other primary character in the drama, along with his scribes.

Who were the magi? Why do they occupy so central a place in the story of Jesus' birth? Traditionally, one of three answers has been given to the question of their identity: (1) They were magicians and frauds who practiced the forbidden arts of divination. (2) They were a class of courtly priests serving the rulers of Persia. As such, they had access to power and wielded the kinds of power appropriate to court retainers. Richard Horsley argues that the magi also led a rebellion that attempted to end the rule of excessively cruel and arbitrary rulers. If so, their presence in the story may carry overtones of subversion and change.[1]

[1]Richard A. Horsley, *The Liberation of Christmas* (New York: Crossroad, 1989), 39–60.

## Homiletical Perspective

*The Revelation of King Herod.* To some, King Herod was a man at the top of "his game." He held a position of significance, but that was not enough for him. He hungered for more. His appetite for power left him vulnerable in his leadership, relationships, and life. Imagine what it was like for those who served in his administration. They knew the king was prone to disquiet. They also knew what could happen if his uneasiness was left unrestrained. So, on that fateful day when the intellectuals from the East appeared in Jerusalem, asking questions, it was a day of trepidation for the staff, the chief priests, and all the people of Jerusalem.

Imagine the expression on King Herod's face when his staff informed him of erudite philosophers of wealth and status entering the city. At first, he must have believed these individuals of brilliance and prestige had traveled for months to know more about the one who was great in his own mind. After all, from Herod's perspective, he was the most important person in Jerusalem. The king might have believed he had "arrived." Sadly, he learned, the magi were not inquiring about how to meet with him. They were asking the natives, "Where is the child who has been born king of the Jews? For we observed his star at its rising, and have come to pay *him* homage" (2:2).

# Matthew 2:1-12

## Theological Perspective

been clueless about God's plan into the fold, but even to manipulate nature itself. Augustine wrote, "Christ was not born because the star shone forth, but it shone forth because Christ was born; we should say not that the star was fate for Christ, but that Christ was fate for the star."[2] God is "the love that moves the stars" (as Dante[3] put it); we are not the star-crossed victims of fate. This newborn Jesus is our destiny.

The tragic comedy of this story is underlined by the way Matthew juxtaposes the magi over against King Herod's Bible scholars. The Scripture experts have scrolls; but they miss the Messiah's birth—and when they get a whiff that the Scripture might actually be taking on flesh, they recoil and lash out defensively.

Of course, when Matthew writes he is keenly aware of the sorrowful heartbreak of the early church: that although Gentiles were flocking into the body of Christ, so many Jews simply did not believe. Even today, we might ask: Do we ever hold the truth in our hands but miss the living Lord? God is determined to be found, and will use any and all measures, even tomfoolery (like astrology!), to reach out to people who are open.

Who is the king? Herod isn't, although he brandishes all the gaudy symbols of kingship. Herod was history's most hysterical megalomaniac. The magi were lucky to get away after saying to his face, "Where is the king of the Jews? We have come to worship him." The irony is as rich as when a grownup Jesus was asked by Pontius Pilate, "Are you a king?" (John 18:33). When the first Christians declared, "Jesus is Lord," the implication was "Caesar isn't." Jesus was not a military subversive trying to take over the empire. But he was king, and Herod, Pilate, and Caesar were exposed as mere pretenders.

If Jesus is king, there is something upside down and just plain unkingly about his royal bearing. Poor fishermen stood as his court, his standard was a cross, his boast was not iron-fisted dominance but tender love. Little wonder King Herod was "troubled." All who cling to power, all who lust for dominance, are in for a headlong tumble before this Christ child.

Theologically, we have good reason to shrink back from the manger scenes and children's pageants—or at least to use them as teaching moments. Surveying the scene, a child would quite naturally identify with Jesus. I am the child in that picture. There's Mary

[2] Benson Bobrick, *The Fated Sky: Astrology in History* (New York: Simon & Schuster, 2005), 79.
[3] Dante, *The Divine Comedy. Paradise* xxxiii, l. 145.

## Pastoral Perspective

figures around whom so much mystery, hymnody, and inventive detail have been created.

Third, they were willing to seek confirmation of what they had learned and seen. They moved, put their feet (or perhaps their camels' feet) in motion to follow this sign. They took a chance on being proven wrong—or right!

Fourth, they were willing to ask for directions along the way, even if they were wrong in their choice of resources (Herod).

Fifth, having found the confirmation of their convictions (the child with Mary his mother), they responded with all the gratitude they could muster.

Sixth, after seeing the child and having all their hopes realized, they still remained vigilant and attentive—open to further visions and insight—and thus they were responsive to their dream-delivered warning to go home by another road.

Popular literature too often treats spirituality as simply a matter of attitude. In many cases it even provides an excuse for avoiding the discipline demonstrated by the wise traveling scholars in Matthew. But the likelihood of a deeper encounter, if we are to use the model offered in this Gospel account, begins with motivated and devoted study. Scripture, of course, is at the heart of such discipline, but commentaries, devotional materials, study groups, prayer groups, worship, and meditative practices—all are ways of devoting oneself to a deeper understanding of the roots that make for readiness for epiphanies.

There is a danger, however, that burying ourselves in the study of revelation can become too detached. One must also be attentive to what is going on in the immediate world—local and national, cultural and familial, earthly and heavenly. At some point, what is happening now may just correlate with what we have found in our study. And when that apparent correlation is seen, it is time to investigate. It's time to move with anticipation, with cautious optimism, and with some skepticism, to probe the validity of what seems to be coming together, not unlike what the wise men did so long ago.

As we travel—by foot, by camel, by auto, or in our mind—it is very important to seek guidance along the way. No one of us, not even any small group of us, can know it all. There are others who are seeking, and there are others who have a stake in what we are seeking—for good or for ill. The wise ones, in their encounter with Herod, provide us with a twofold commentary on investigating: it's important to seek help, and it's possible that we will

## Exegetical Perspective

(3) They were astrologers who read the heavens and advised rulers on their plans. Of course, their occupation was precarious, and they could pay a heavy price if their message was not palatable to the rulers whom they served.

If the magi were astrologers, their presence places the so-called "star of Bethlehem" in a different light. The star has been thought to be the result of a supernova explosion, a conjunction of planets, or a comet. But it need not be any of these. The star of Bethlehem was not necessarily an extraordinary celestial event, but an ordinary star seen through the extraordinary eyes of the magi. They had "eyes to see," but Herod and his scribes did not.

Being acquainted with centers of power, the magi journeyed straight to Jerusalem and Herod's court. Perhaps the magi were not particularly wise in their decision to visit Herod's court. However, once they visited Herod, they knew that they had made a serious mistake and did not return. In Jerusalem, the magi experienced the fear induced by a despot. Historically, when Herod was frightened, people died. His paranoia led to more and more extreme actions as he tried to secure his throne from all threats. But Herod had to respond, so he called "together all the chief priests and scribes of the people." The chief priests are mentioned in the plural because the phrase includes the high-priestly houses who supplied the candidates for the high priesthood. The scribes were a retainer class of experts in the law and its interpretation.

It has been noted that the magi were able to get to Jerusalem by following a star but required some "special revelation" (the prophets) to augment the "general revelation" (the star) that led them to Jerusalem. Whatever the case, the scribes produced a reading of Micah 5:2 that pointed to Bethlehem of Judea, one of the smaller and less important clans. Now the magi had the prophetic word as well as the celestial event to guide them.

Perceiving an opportunity to eliminate another claimant to his throne, Herod tried to turn the magi into his emissaries by holding a secret meeting to enlist their help. If the magi were unaware of their mistake in coming to Herod, they were by now well aware of their blunder. No reigning monarch willingly travels to pay homage to a child born into a peasant family who is being proclaimed as his successor. The contrast between the magi and Jerusalem is captured by the contrast between the fear that pervaded Jerusalem (2:3) because the king was feeling threatened and the exceedingly great joy they experience at the reappearance of the star (2:10).

## Homiletical Perspective

In an instant, the king's lifted head of arrogance declined as the rage of humiliation rose. In a moment, Herod's ego-driven expression changed. He was afraid people might discover there was one born so significant that a star was placed in the heavens to announce his arrival. Fear of losing control took over. The limitations of his unrestrained ego affected his leadership.

*The Weak Witness of the Oppressed.* The birth of the Messiah was a time of celebration. In the national consciousness the people of Israel held an understanding of their place as God's chosen people. All their lives, they heard stories of God's promise to send "a ruler who would shepherd the people." When the star appeared in the sky, its meaning was clear. For generations, the job of the chief priests and scribes was to teach the people how to read the signs of God. The angels proclaimed the arrival. This was their moment. A time of liberation and new possibilities was upon the people. Tragically, the news preordained the inevitability that things would change for those who had finally reached the place of having something to lose. For a people who had suffered much, this was not the good news they were seeking.

More than fifty years ago, the Reverend Dr. Martin Luther King Jr., pastor of Dexter Avenue Baptist Church, helped to organize the Montgomery, Alabama, bus boycott. The protest was in response to the injustice of southern Jim Crow laws. For a year, people of conscience coordinated efforts to bring attention to a public wrong. With the Supreme Court ruling, the Montgomery city bus lines reluctantly changed their policy, and all people could sit on the bus where they pleased. This shift in public policy created a new dynamic in many relationships. Some people were ready to walk in this dimension of the unknown, and others were not.

The story of the civil rights movement has been homogenized. Today's version of the story makes some believe all black America marched on the side of Rev. King. Many African Americans of the establishment were not in support of the man and the movement, because they feared losing their status in the community. My father was a civil rights activist in the North. Many vivid memories of my grandmother's disgust with my father's participation in the movement prevail. Grandma believed my dad's activities risked her reputation as a dignified, exemplary "colored" woman. She was not alone. Many black Americans of that time believed going

# Matthew 2:1-12

## Theological Perspective

and Joseph, just like my mom and dad. And the magi have come, bearded travelers from afar, and they have brought gifts—to me! Just like Santa Claus. Christmas becomes for most of us a grand festival of gift giving, a frenzy of gift receiving. But the gifts of the magi aren't little child-appropriate presents for Jesus to enjoy. They are symbolic of the grandeur of all of creation being gathered at the feet of the Lord of it all. Isaiah 'twas foretold it: the enigmatic passage, Isaiah 60:1–6, speaks of nations and kings coming to the light and paying homage.

Yes, through this passage's exegetical history, commentators have devised all kinds of allegorical schemes about the three gifts. Gold reflects Jesus' royalty, frankincense his divinity, and myrrh his sorrowful death. Did God fire a synapse in their brains back in Persia so they would know what symbolic gifts to bring? They simply brought what was precious, what they wanted Jesus to have.

They did not build a mansion in Bethlehem to stay near this one they had worshiped. And you wouldn't need to be warned in a dream not to revisit nasty king Herod! Yet an angel—perhaps the same one who flew so brightly leading them there in the first place—warned them, so they departed "by another road" (v. 12). Quite simply, they took an evasive route to avoid Herod's clutches. But could it be Matthew is offering a tantalizing hint about life for those who have met Christ? Nothing is ever the same. You don't take the old road any longer. You unfold a new map, and discover an alternate path.

T. S. Eliot imagined the thoughts of the magi back home: "We returned to our places . . . but no longer at ease here, in the old dispensation, with an alien people clutching their gods."[4] Jesus does not make my life more comfortable; Jesus doesn't help me fit in and succeed. We are no longer at ease in a world not committed to Jesus; we notice false gods all over the place. We detect royal pretenders. Nothing is the same; nothing comes easy. A strange, unfamiliar road is now our path—but the road is going somewhere.

JAMES C. HOWELL

## Pastoral Perspective

be wrong in our choice of help. Nonetheless, mistakes in making our choices should not tempt us to withdraw and rely only on ourselves.

Excitement is not out of place along the way of spiritual awakening. Certainly it is appropriate (and, perhaps, not even avoidable!) in the process of study, awareness, further exploration, and the receipt of heartening counsel and direction. But when confirmation is found, the time is right for full expression of our joy and gratitude. An epiphany is not something to be hidden. It is something to be shared. In fact, if one is inclined to hide an epiphany, as if it were some private possession to be protected, then there is reason to question whether it is a genuine epiphany at all. Spiritual maturity inspires one to be generous, rather than fearful or stingy. It triggers eagerness to share, rather than protectiveness and hoarding. The wise men again are our model in their giving priceless gifts and adoration.

Of course, there is always the temptation to assume that once a discovery has been made, once a high spiritual moment has been experienced, we are then to remain focused on that achievement. There may even be the temptation to presume that there is no further need for consultation with others. But the wise men, still open, received another dream after the glory of their meeting the Christ child. And consistent with the way they had lived their journey of faith so far, they continued to listen and were obedient in respecting the warning they received. So they returned by another way. We too need to be careful about falling into arrogance, as if there were no more to learn.

In reading the story of the magi, we can rejoice in their discovery and their greeting of the Christ child. We can also learn from their discipline and do likewise in pursuing our own pilgrimages of faith.

WILLIAM V. ARNOLD

---

[4] T. S. Eliot, "Journey of the Magi," *Collected Poems, 1909–1962* (New York: Harcourt Brace Jovanovich, 1988), 100.

## Exegetical Perspective

When the magi arrived at the house where Jesus was born, they brought their gifts of gold, frankincense, and myrrh. Traditional Christian interpretation has read the gifts as foreshadowing the child's life. Gold is fitting for royalty and frankincense for priestly duties, and myrrh points to the prophet's death he would suffer. Even more important than the gifts was the magi's response to the child: "they knelt down and paid him homage" (2:11). In short, they were believers, even though they were Gentiles from the East who practiced astrology, an activity considered suspect by the Torah.

Ironically, one would expect "the king of the Jews," the religious leaders of the temple, and the scribes who devoted their lives to studying the law to have shown some interest in God's activities, yet they showed none. The scribes identified Micah 5:2, which points to a town just a few miles away, but showed no interest in checking things out. They seemed unable to translate what they read into action. Once they answered Herod's question, they were through and disappeared from the scene. They lived at the center of power. Who cared what was happening at the margins? Their behavior and attitudes contrasted sharply with the faith of the magi.

Clearly God was at work not at the center of power but on the margins, not in Jerusalem, paralyzed by fear, but in a small village that carried memories of a glorious past when David was anointed there by Saul (1 Sam. 16). The magi's visit seems to be a fulfillment of the vision in Psalm 72:8–11, the Gentiles streaming to Zion to learn the way of righteousness and justice. Yet what did they find but another petty tyrant who fancied himself "the great."

The opening scenes in Matthew anticipate how the Gospel will end. When Jesus is buried, the religious leaders urge Pilate to put a guard at the tomb lest the imposter's resurrection be proclaimed (27:62–66; 28:4, 11–15). Just as the powers that be try and fail to prevent the resurrection, so they try and fail to prevent the birth of God's child (1:18–2:23). God's purposes cannot be thwarted; God's purposes will prevail.[2]

WILLIAM R. HERZOG II

## Homiletical Perspective

against the white power structure was foolish. They could not consider the possibility of a better life for all people. Many of the black middle class preferred to hold on to the imperfect but better-than-some-other-people life they lived. The fight for justice came more easily for those who had nothing to lose.

*The Worship of the Wise.* The magi were learned people who lived a disciplined life of study. The text does not number or identify the gender of these travelers. What we know is they went a great distance and gave three thoughtful gifts. Traditionally, the gold represents Christ's majesty, the frankincense signifies worship of his divinity, and the myrrh gives a foreshadowing of his body's preparation for burial after his premature death. There may have been a multitude of diverse individuals in the traveling party. The arrival of these unusual researchers must have caused quite a stir. In our own experiences with small-town America, we know the excitement caused by uncommon out-of-towners coming to learn about one of our own.

The magi did not come to study Jesus. They came to worship a newborn king by following a special star. Sacrificing time and comfort, they brought gifts to a baby who demonstrated no outward signs of prophetic confirmation. They held no assurance of how the story would end. All they had was prophetic knowledge of a star and a coming messiah. Reflected in their eyes was an economically limited toddler, in modest surroundings, lying in a teen mother's arms. To the intellectually perceptive, this scene was not a scholar's formula for future success. Yet, by grace, the magi had the faith to experience unbridled joy. They beheld the substance of things hoped for and humbled themselves to worship the gift of God. Jesus was the promise of salvation for the world and the gift of joy that sent the wise home by another way.

SHELLEY D.B. COPELAND

---

[2]Some works consulted in preparing this study: Raymond Brown, *The Birth of the Messiah* (Garden City, NY: Doubleday, 1977); Warren Carter, *Matthew and the Margins* (Sheffield: Sheffield Academic Press, 2000); Craig Keener, *Matthew* (Downers Grove, IL: InterVarsity Press, 1997).

## Genesis 1:1-5

[1] In the beginning when God created the heavens and the earth, [2]the earth was a formless void and darkness covered the face of the deep, while a wind from God swept over the face of the waters. [3]Then God said, "Let there be light"; and there was light. [4]And God saw that the light was good; and God separated the light from the darkness. [5]God called the light Day, and the darkness he called Night. And there was evening and there was morning, the first day.

## Theological Perspective

The story of creation provides a fitting theological text for the first Sunday after the Epiphany. During this season of celebrating the manifestation of God in Christ, the creation story can be examined to learn about its testimony to the initial manifestation of God. The story of creation is a framing narrative that shows the dependence of all that exists upon God. It introduces ideas about the character of God and the purpose of creation. Because of its doctrinal density and relevance, this passage "cannot be easily overinterpreted theologically," as Gerhard von Rad insisted.[1]

In addition to its identification of attributes and actions of God and God's handiwork in the created order, the passage suggests several other distinct Christian beliefs. Among its embedded doctrines, the passage contains the roots for the classic doctrine of *creatio ex nihilo*—creation out of nothing—and it anticipates the climax of God's creative acts with the forming of humans in the divine image, thus establishing the foundation for the doctrine of the *imago dei*. It also introduces the concept of the congruity of God's voice with God's identity, specified when Moses at the burning bush hears the voice of God reveal God's name (Exod. 3). In Christian thought this dynamic idea is consummated in the proclamation of

[1]Gerhard von Rad, *Genesis: A Commentary*, rev. ed. (Philadelphia: Westminster Press, 1972), 48.

## Pastoral Perspective

There are two creation stories in Genesis, but here we consider only one. In the first chapter's account of creation, humanity is created last. There was a time, according to this passage, before humanity and human self-consciousness. We might call it the yeast of Eden. We might imagine a whole service renewing our baptismal vows, retouching our early water. Touching the water drives us back to the beginning of our beginning.

"In the beginning God." That is the whole story in a nutshell. Then comes the verb: "created." Then comes the object of the verb: "the heavens and the earth." The first thing that happened to the formless earth, which was void and darkness, but which had a "deep" face, is this: the Spirit of God moved upon the face of the waters.

When Jesus is later baptized, he has a significant connection back to the deep waters of creation. He goes from being without form to being someone with form. He goes back to the original. He has a heaven-opening event. He does what God did in the beginning: He reopens the world.

There is something almost pagan in this beginning creation time. "Pagan" originally meant "of the country," a kind of sensual simplicity. Surely that describes the time before us. It is just day and night.

## Exegetical Perspective

We all know the importance of context. The phrase "See you later" can mean one thing when tossed off as you leave the office on an ordinary day. Whispered by the bedside of a dying friend, it bears a deeper import indeed.

The opening words of Scripture, "In the beginning," are so familiar that we often do not pause to consider context before we begin our interpretation. For this text, such context is crucial, from at least three vantage points: literary, historical, and liturgical.

*Literary Context.* We begin with the literary context. Though these verses appear at the front end of the Scriptures, we must always remember they are not where the original story began. The story of this people, who now "remember" the story of the world's creation, began by the banks of some other waters, in a land that was also a "formless void": the land of Egypt, by the banks of the Nile, where these desert nomads found themselves crying out under hard labor as slaves. The kind of wondrous work they experienced in the birth waters of the Red Sea is thus the template within which they imagine the wondrous work of the Lord before the ordered world began. As they had experienced the spirit of God bringing order out of chaos in Egypt, so they now testified to the similar work of the spirit "in the

## Homiletical Perspective

As the house lights go down, a man in a hat with a pipe in his mouth carries a bench onto a bare stage. Only the barest of props indicate a house, gardens, a street; just a table and three chairs to stand for a kitchen. A blank wall serves as the horizon of this New Hampshire town. Before the action gets underway, the Stage Manager offers several homely words of introduction for Thornton Wilder's *Our Town.*

By contrast, the Hebrew Bible does not bother with preamble or prologue. These opening verses of Genesis are not mere stage setting. They are the story proper—a story of God's activity. The main actor is here. All the scenes to come will proceed from this actor. As many a preacher has placed the period, "In the beginning, God."

And yet something about this magisterial creation exalts humankind. Its movement is toward us. Creation moves from the cosmic to the mundane, becoming ever more beautiful and various. By the time God gets around to creating humankind "on the sixth day" (Gen. 1:26–31), we are presented as God's crowning work of art. The universe in its immensity, with its spiral galaxies and nebulae, finds a small but final fulfillment in us.

From ancient times until now, around campfires and through telescopes, humans have marveled at the vastness of creation. A typical example comes at

# Genesis 1:1-5

## Theological Perspective

the Gospel of John that the Word itself is none other than God, creative from the beginning (John 1:1) and ultimately incarnate in the life of Jesus as the Christ (John 1:14).

The idea of creation out of nothing is implied in the references to the "formless void" and the dark deep (v. 2) into which God introduced light, shape, and order. The concept of *creatio ex nihilo* was first inscribed in Hebrew texts during the second century BCE, when the writer of 2 Maccabees implored the faithful "to look at the heaven and earth and see everything that is in them, and recognize that God did not make them out of things that existed" (2 Macc. 7:28). The doctrine was introduced into Christian thought in the second century when theologians sought to counter developing ideas that, in creation, God worked with already existing matter. Then as now, the primary purpose for the explication of the doctrine of *creatio ex nihilo* is not to explain how creation occurred, but to affirm that all that exists depends upon the creative and sustaining power of God.

The deep darkness in which and over which God worked in creation provides a dramatic contrast for the initial creative act of God: illumination. Called forth by God's command, light bursts into being (v. 2) and enables the possible perception of all other elements of creation. In the dark void, even chaos could not be perceived. Light is the first step for order to be established and discerned. The separation of light from darkness begins a crescendo of creative action that is crowned with the creation of humans, who are formed in the image of God and who serve as God's companions. By separating light from darkness and by naming the light "Day" and the darkness "Night" (v. 5), God establishes the origin of time and divine dominion over history as well as nature.

Light is the palate for further creation. Yet light itself renders more than the possible perception of shapes and colors. Light is the basis of life and order, and light itself is judged by God as being good (v. 4), thus exhibiting its moral quality. Because of its sublime quality and ordering character, light subsequently serves as a profound symbol for the incarnation of God in Christ and for the fullness of life itself (John 8:12; 9:5).

By speaking, God commands creation into being. Each act or element of creation is generated by God's word. Consequently God is understood as an active God, as the source of history. God speaks, and actions occur. The uniqueness and supremacy of God is that God is best understood not as a noun but as a verb.

## Pastoral Perspective

What we can appreciate about the pagan approach to life is that it lives where it lives. It does not climb every mountain. It climbs one mountain. It does not ford every stream. It fishes one sea. My own definition of peace comes from the poet Billy Collins. He reminds me to know who I am: I live in Eastern Standard Time, as a white Western woman. I live locally. I live globally. I live "glocally." I live a far piece away from original creation but I am part of creation.

Billy Collins also has a great line that helps me move to my subject. He says, "People say that poetry speaks to everyone but here I would only like to address those in my own time zone." When I meet visitors from Tanzania or Guatemala, I say to them: "Forgive me for encouraging you to eat and sleep and drink and see. I plead ignorance. I am a white Western woman and resist taking sleeping pills, although I'll bet I could use one from time to time. Yes, I have forgotten how to sleep. I apologize. I used to know how to sleep; back in the beginning of time, humans slept with a night-and-day rhythm." How do we know? Because before humans were created, there was morning and there was evening.

The word "pagan" also comes from the Latin, *pangare*, "to fix or to fasten." I am fastened to my zip code, my latitude and longitude, my cultural latitude and longitude, and all the stuff that happened in it before I got to it.

A friend of mine just climbed Mt. Kilimanjaro with nine Western companions—and twenty-three schleppers. That is right: that is another definition of being a white Western woman. When you climb a mountain, you need other people to haul your self-definitions along with you. She said it was a great trip—and that most Westerners she knows should go to Tanzania and climb Mt. Kilimanjaro to get in touch with themselves. My friend took this trip because it was a form of personal renewal. She was trying to get back to her original. She no longer wanted to be a Xerox copy of herself. She wanted to get back to the garden.

How do we restore the reverence we have for creation and allow it be a part of our daily living? *Baptismatus sum*, said Luther. I am baptized and renewed in a creation that had my name in it from the very beginning. I am christened to creation. My DNA comes from the original light and lightness!

The biggest problem in my time zone is that we have lost reverence. Reverence is a deep understanding of human limitation. We got hoodwinked into thinking that there were no human limitations.

## Exegetical Perspective

beginning." This is a God who may occasionally create ex nihilo (out of nothing), but who usually prefers to rework tangible chaos into something "good."

*Historical Context.* Now we move to the historical context. The opening chapter of this "prequel" (Genesis) to the "main story" (Exodus) was so important to the later generations of this people that the final form of the Scriptures insists on telling it twice: once by the Priestly writers, here in Genesis 1, and once by the Yahwist, in Genesis 2. The key here is to recognize the distinction between these two historical contexts.

The Yahwist imagined this earlier creative work by God during the days of the united monarchy, the high point in Israel's collective history, then and now. It is therefore understandable why this creation would be remembered as God creating a creature out of dust in order tangibly to tend a garden under the guidance of the Lord. This is a story where we "dust creatures" are invited into the story of this ordering God, but quickly reminded that without due humility, we will fall. This is a story of creation for our *strong* days, when we may be tempted to overreach.

The Priestly writer, in contrast, most likely imagined this earlier creative work of God during the days of Babylonian exile, when all the earlier order of Israel's worship in Jerusalem had been brought to naught. Where does one look in order to trust the ongoing ordering of the Lord when the temple is destroyed, one's power has been shattered, and one's captors follow a different calendar and worship different gods? Shackled in a prison cell, with only a slender slice of sky visible from *tehom* (the "deep," v. 2), the ongoing division between day and night may be your only sign that the Lord is yet creating order out of chaos, the wind or spirit of the Lord yet moving over "the waters." This is a story of creation for our *weak* days, when we are tempted to despair.

This shift in context thus prevents this text from being used as it often is in the worship of the church—celebrating the order of creation that reflects the order resident in our lives ("and let our ordered lives confess the beauty of thy peace"[1]). No, this creation story is a way of holding onto hope when all signs of order in our lives have been destroyed and we must look out for signs of the

## Homiletical Perspective

the end of act 1 in *Our Town,* as Rebecca Gibbs mentions a letter that a friend got from her minister, addressed to "Jane Crofut; The Crofut Farm; Grover's Corners; Sutton County; New Hampshire; United States of America; Continent of North America; Western Hemisphere; the Earth; the Solar System; the Universe; the Mind of God."[1] Genesis offers a radically different perspective, one that looks in the opposite direction—essentially, from the Mind of God down to Grover's Corners.

Which brings us to baptism, the genesis of Christian life. Here too God assures us that we are not too small for notice; that in fact we matter immensely.

The beginning is all water: watery deeps, dark and formless, essentially a flood. God calls for light to illuminate this waste. According to Genesis, then, creation is not exactly ex nihilo, but is redemptive. The floods represent anything that threatens to upend, frustrate, and drown life. Waters have their own capricious ways of changing landscapes and can bring terror, for they are random and mindless; in other words, they represent an impersonal, naturalistic creation very different from God's. In the redemption story of Genesis, God installs a vault called the sky to keep such chaos at bay.

All the more impressive, then, that at baptism we are asked to submit to the primordial waters and a figurative death. And all the more important, the Creator calls us by our own names—in some Christian traditions, gives us new names. God's creative power is made powerfully personal in this second birth.

This first Sunday after Epiphany comes at the start of the new year, an evocative time to talk about beginnings. In my own church, we observe it by dipping our hands in the sacred waters and drawing wet crosses on our foreheads. The beginning of the year lends itself to this remembrance of baptism and the beginning of Christian life.

To read the first chapter of Genesis on such a day, however, does pose a dilemma. Inevitably it means that we are reading a Christian message into an ancient Hebrew tale—which is like painting blue flowers on a priceless plain urn. It could compromise the integrity of the original story.

A further dilemma is that at every turn the Old Testament suggests the New. Try as we might on this Epiphany Sunday, we cannot help having epiphanies. In Genesis, for example, God sees that the light on

---

[1]John Greenleaf Whittier, "Dear Lord and Father of Mankind," 1872.

[1]Thornton Wilder, *Three Plays* (New York: Harper & Bros., 1957), 45.

# Genesis 1:1-5

## Theological Perspective

God's word is dynamic because it expresses God's will (Ps. 33:6, 9). God creates, not out of coercion or obligation, but out of freedom. The creation is neither accidental nor random, nor is it self-generated (Gen. 1:2). It is intentional. Creation assumes significance not merely for being, but for order, for balance, for harmony between darkness and light, for unity within creation.

Created in the image of God (Gen. 1:26), humans also have the power to speak, to exercise dominion over the creation, initially by naming animals (Gen. 2:20). Unlike the words of God, however, human utterance does not generate action or materiality. Yet according to von Rad, "the idea of creation by the word preserves first of all the most radical essential distinction between Creator and creature. Creation cannot be even remotely considered an emanation from God; it is not somehow an overflow or reflection of [divine] being."[2] Nonetheless, human speech shapes ideas and images that define reality and order society.

The opening text in Genesis affirms the character of God, rather than providing a historical account or a scientific proposition about creation. The passage is one of revelation and testimony, rather than history, because no human observed the process and because no archaeological traces point to a reconstruction of this particular narrative. The text is not a scientific treatise, because science is concerned about the relation between finite causes and effects. In contrast, a question about the ultimate origin or first cause is essentially theological, because "it is the question of the [very] origin of the whole system of finite relations."[3] Consequently, when the creation story is heard as theological testimony, it permits consideration of all scientific theories about the process of creation, the relation between causes and effects.

The text is a theological affirmation that all of life, all aspects of order, and all possibilities within reality are dependent upon the primordial creative act of God. It grounds nature and history in the creative acts of God, and it establishes the bond between Creator and the creation.

JOSEPH L. PRICE

## Pastoral Perspective

Climb every mountain. Ford every stream. Follow every rainbow, till you find your dream. Trespass every time zone, till you steal their dream. Pagan people, those who know we belong to one country, are free of such trespass: we like where we are and who we are. We are better prepared for the place east of Eden, the new untarnished-by-civilization place. We see the yeast of Eden, east of Eden.

"Awful" and "awesome" come from the same root in "awe." They used to be two sides of the same coin. We have awe at awful things. We have awe at wonderful things. We have awe. Now awful is reserved for bad, and awesome is reserved for good—and you begin to see what the faithful have stolen from the heathen, which is Webster's idea of a synonym for "pagan." We have stolen integrity, unity, and oneness of experience. What we need is a return to reverence, an all-encompassing heathen appreciation of mystery and its root in human limitation.

One might have thought that reverence was just a religious value. It is not! Reverence is the virtue that keeps us from acting like gods.

How can we change? We can practice the great lightness of being that separates night and day. We can remember our baptismal waters. We can climb one mountain and carry only what we can carry. We can forget about needing schleppers. We can reclaim the moment before human, when God created. We can reclaim the time before time, when God's spirit moved upon the waters.

And then we can live in the awesome reality of whatever time and place our created selves live in today.

From our own country, we can open the heavens.

DONNA SCHAPER

---

[2]Ibid., 51.
[3]Langdon Gilkey, *Maker of Heaven and Earth: A Study of the Christian Doctrine of Creation* (New York: Doubleday & Co., 1959), 25.

creative work of God beyond our control. If God is still creating order out of chaos in the succession of day and night, maybe God will one day create order once more out of chaos in the lives of God's people. Hold on, and do not lose hope.

*Liturgical Context.* Finally, we turn to the liturgical context. Now we may be ready to rightly hear this familiar text within its lectionary-driven context on Baptism of the Lord Sunday. Now the story of Jesus' baptism in the waters of the Jordan becomes less a story about "sin" (and the conundrum of the one without sin submitting to such a rite) and more a story about solidarity (on the part of the Messiah and, through him, on the part of God). When Jesus steps down into the waters of the Jordan, with the Spirit now descending from above, he steps down into the chaos of the exiles and trusts the power of God to keep on creating order out of chaos, even through him. It is all a matter of context, for him and for us.

All this contextual work may help us resolve the most difficult exegetical problem in these opening verses of Scripture. Is verse 1 an opening sentence, declaring God's creative ordering of heaven and earth a task that is completed? "In the beginning, God created the heavens and the earth." Or is verse 1 a dependent clause, setting the stage for God's first creative act in verse 3? "In the beginning when God began to create—the earth being a formless void with the wind of God hovering over the waters—then God said, 'Let there be light.'" Set in context literarily, historically, and liturgically, this story can only be heard as the first in a long series of stories about God creating order out of chaos: at the beginning of ordered time, through the waters of the Red Sea, in the muddy waters of the river Jordan, and down to the chaotic situations of God's people today. Now we can hear these verses as a prequel to a story whose sequel is still being spoken and enacted today.

RICHARD BOYCE

the face of the waters is good; and declares that humankind is good; much as God declares at Jesus' baptism, "This is my beloved child, with whom I am well pleased."

There are essential differences between Genesis and the Gospels. No vault separates Christians from the waters of chaos; baptism insures no one against disaster. Of course, to die is to die in Christ, and that is life; for those who have been baptized, death and life have been re-created. And while God is plainly the main actor in both testaments, by the time Jesus comes to the Jordan, God seems more a stage manager, a voice from the wings.

Ultimately the cosmic drama recorded in Genesis challenges our modern assumption that the universe has no mind and that nothing hovers over the face of the deep. Genesis may seem just as removed from modern experience as the bucolic innocence of Grover's Corners.

Thornton Wilder and his brother Amos were raised by devout parents; their maternal grandfather had been a pastor. Baptized in such a family atmosphere, Amos Wilder quite naturally became a theologian. During the Second World War, he brought out a volume of poetry called *The Healing of the Waters,* taking the title from 2 Kings 2:21, in which Elisha heals waters in a bowl. Here is Wilder's "Homage" to those fighting the chaos of his day, fascism:

> These on the crumbling levees match themselves
>    with the infuriate flood.
> These beneath the waves toil at the primeval
>    sea-walls
> Whose courses were laid against chaos.
> These repair the moles erected of old against the
>    ravening deep.
> These descend where the nethermost piers of history
>    are building,
> And place their lives if need be at the foundation of
>    all the ages of glory to come.[2]

As we start Genesis, the house lights do not go down, but come up; struggles are all around us, and we share them as God's cocreators. It is God, however, who brings the healing of the waters. In the beginning, God.

LAWRENCE WOOD

[2]Amos N. Wilder, *The Healing of the Waters* (New York: Harper & Bros., 1943), 19.

# Psalm 29

¹Ascribe to the LORD, O heavenly beings,
  ascribe to the LORD glory and strength.
²Ascribe to the LORD the glory of his name;
  worship the LORD in holy splendor.

³The voice of the LORD is over the waters;
  the God of glory thunders,
  the LORD, over mighty waters.
⁴The voice of the LORD is powerful;
  the voice of the LORD is full of majesty.

⁵The voice of the LORD breaks the cedars;
  the LORD breaks the cedars of Lebanon.

## Theological Perspective

Psalm 29 is traditionally associated with the celebration of the baptism of the Lord. It stands as a reminder that the God revealed in the person of Jesus Christ is the cosmic ruler of the universe. The one who descended upon Jesus Christ and proclaimed him "my Son" is the Lord of all existence, the source, sustainer, and judge of all that is. In an age prone to characterize Jesus Christ as a supportive friend and God as an intimate, comforting presence, the fierce images of Psalm 29 shock our sensibilities like cold water splashed on drowsy eyes. Long dormant religious dispositions such as awe and fear emerge through these descriptions of the naked, threatening power of the natural world, challenging our safe, domesticated spirituality.

If contemporary Christians tend to emphasize God's grace expressed in the self-sacrificial love of Jesus Christ, this passage forcefully reasserts God's irresistible might and glorious power. If contemporary Protestant Christians tend to emphasize Scripture as the sole source of knowledge about God and God's way, this psalm reminds us that God also reveals Godself to all creatures through the general patterns and events of natural world.

A violent, destructive thunderstorm insists to pious and impious alike that our existence, for good

## Pastoral Perspective

The pastor calls the congregation to worship declaring, "The Lord reigns, let the earth rejoice!" In light of Psalm 29 it might be more appropriate to declare, "The Lord reigns, let the earth *tremble!*" The psalmist calls all creation—heavenly beings and human beings—to worship the Lord of glory at whose voice nature itself trembles.

The dominant image in the psalm is that of the mighty voice of God. Seven times the voice of the Lord thunders in the text. The psalmist declares that the sovereign Lord of creation speaks not only through the "still, small voice," but also "thunders . . . over mighty waters."

Yet too often worship in the mainline churches is not characterized by a sense of the awesome majesty of the God whose mighty voice "breaks the cedars . . . shakes the wilderness . . . causes the oaks to whirl, and strips the forest bare" (vv. 5–9) More often our worship is tame and thoroughly predictable. The writer Annie Dillard calls us to task. She warns, "The churches are like children playing on the floor with their chemistry sets, mixing up a batch of TNT to kill a Sunday morning. It is madness to wear ladies' straw hats and velvet hats to church; we should all be wearing crash helmets. Ushers should issue life preservers

<sup>6</sup>He makes Lebanon skip like a calf,
and Sirion like a young wild ox.

<sup>7</sup>The voice of the Lord flashes forth flames of fire.
<sup>8</sup>The voice of the Lord shakes the wilderness;
the Lord shakes the wilderness of Kadesh.

<sup>9</sup>The voice of the Lord causes the oaks to whirl,
and strips the forest bare;
and in his temple all say, "Glory!"

<sup>10</sup>The Lord sits enthroned over the flood;
the Lord sits enthroned as king forever.
<sup>11</sup>May the Lord give strength to his people!
May the Lord bless his people with peace!

## Exegetical Perspective

Psalm 29 is a hymn in praise of God as sovereign of the universe. It begins with a call to praise and worship (vv. 1–2). It continues in verses 3–9 with the reason for praise: the power of God made manifest on earth through a thunderstorm. The psalm concludes with an affirmation of God's eternal sovereignty (v. 10) and a prayer for God's blessing upon God's people (v. 11).

*Verses 1–2.* The call to praise is addressed to "heavenly beings" (v. 1; Heb. "sons of God"). In the Old Testament these divine beings are understood as subordinate to God, the servants and messengers who make up God's heavenly court (see, e.g., Pss. 89:5–7; 103:19–21; 148:1–2). Here they are summoned to fulfill their purpose by praising God's "glory." The term "glory" (vv. 1–2, 3, 9) is the organizing motif of this psalm. It serves as the summary term for God's attributes as king of the universe, incorporating God's strength (v. 1), holy splendor (v. 2), power and majesty (v. 3). "Glory" also refers to the manifestation of God's sovereignty in the world: in this psalm, the display of God's power in the thunderstorm.[1]

[1] James L. Mays, *Psalms*, Interpretation Series (Louisville, KY: John Knox Press, 1994), 136.

## Homiletical Perspective

The psalm describes a theophany as the psalmist poetically recreates the experience of a thunderstorm. God appears in glory and splendor in, through, and above the storm. The psalm tracks the storm moving inland from the Mediterranean Sea to the Lebanon mountains in the north, down through the Jordan Valley, and south out into the wilderness of Kadesh. The awesomeness of God is described by the loudest, most impressive noise that the ancient Israelites had ever heard, the clap of thunder.

As one develops the sermon, however, one must realize that the psalm is not about the storm, but about God. It is about "glory," God's glory (vv. 1–2, 3, 9). God is above the storm and enthroned over the flood (v. 10). A feeling of awe sweeps over the psalmist as he or she reflects on the mighty power of God and calls on everyone to break forth in praise (vv. 1–2, 9).

Through worship the psalm celebrates the reign and lordship of the almighty God. The psalm begins with a summons to the heavenly counsel to give praise to the Lord of the cosmos. It concludes with the temple worshipers joining in the chorus of praise (v. 9). The result of the awesome display of holy power is that God's people receive strength and peace (v. 11).

# Psalm 29

## Theological Perspective

or ill, is in the grip of a power we can neither fathom nor control. Whether one identifies such an event with God or the forces of nature, awe and fear are universal and appropriate dispositions. It is worth reflecting on the fact that this psalm was adopted into the Israelite cult almost without change from a Canaanite hymn to Baal, the storm god. Such blatant liturgical borrowing expresses a deep sense of legitimate religious commonality. Hebrew and Canaanite expressed shared religious sensibilities in response to the human condition—dependence on the uncontrollable power that is both the source of life and a threat to it. In his commentary on this psalm, John Calvin acknowledges that human beings are driven to religious awe and dread by the destructive power of the natural world. "With great propriety, therefore, does the prophet invite our attention to these instances which strike the rude and insensible with some sense of the existence of God."[1] Whether Christian or not, whether wise or otherwise, human beings experience fear, wonder, and reverence in response to the inscrutable and inescapable power in and behind existence.

The story of Jesus' baptism bears witness to the Christian confidence that the life, death, and resurrection of Jesus Christ correlate with the fundamental nature of this life-giving and life-taking, creating and destroying, awful and awesome power at the heart of things. On the Sunday of the Lord's baptism, this psalm forces the Christian community to acknowledge and integrate God's power and God's goodness as well as human experience and Christian revelation.

Human beings experience the power in and behind the universe and are driven to awe and reverence. But they cannot know whether faith, hope, and love are also appropriate religious responses. Can this power, which reigns over life and death, creation and destruction, be trusted? Ought it to be loved? Caught in its clutches, have we any grounds for hope? For Christians, such questions find their answer in the life, death, and resurrection of Jesus Christ. The voice from heaven that says, "You are my Son, the Beloved; with you I am well pleased," reveals the power of goodness and the goodness of power. In Christ's baptism Christians do not find the one who can save them from the threatening power that stands behind the universe. They find, rather, that the power in and through everything intends redemption. In the light of this

## Pastoral Perspective

and signal flares; they should lash us to our pews."[1]

The psalmist declares that "the voice of the LORD shakes the wilderness" (v. 8). When the Lord of hosts speaks, the foundations of life are shaken, for it is indeed "a fearful thing to fall into the hands of the living God" (Heb. 10:31).

The prophetic word we hear in the psalm warns against the ways by which we domesticate and trivialize the God of glory. God's voice, God's Word, has power to accomplish all that God intends, though not in the ways we might have imagined.

The lectionary appropriately links Psalm 29 with the baptism of Jesus on the first Sunday after the Epiphany. These readings represent quite different but inseparably related epiphanies: the manifestation of the Lord's thundering power in creation and the quiet manifestation of the glory of God in the face of Jesus Christ. The apostle Paul makes explicit the link between creation and redemption in writing to the church in Corinth: "The God who said, 'Let light shine out of darkness,' . . . has shone in our hearts to give the light of the knowledge of the glory of God in the face of Jesus Christ" (2 Cor. 4:6). The creator of all things visible and invisible, whose voice shakes the foundations of the earth, is uniquely revealed, not in fearsome displays of nature's fury, but personally in the face of Jesus of Nazareth.

The image of a thunderstorm, which provides the organizing metaphor for the psalm, was one of the most vivid images available to the psalmist of the powers that threaten human life. What image or images would play a similar role in our time? A category-five hurricane? A tsunami? An earthquake along the San Andreas fault?

The psalmist affirms that the "LORD sits enthroned over the flood" (v. 10). On this side of Hurricane Katrina and the tsunami that struck the day after Christmas in 2004, we hear those words with fresh ears and greater apprehension. Is the triune God indeed Lord over the raging waters of chaos in nature, in history, and in our personal lives?

At times the thunderstorms that batter our lives are terrifying events in nature. More often they are events in our own lives. A woman tells her husband she no longer wants to be married to him, or vice versa. Your doctor calls. "The pathology report came back. It doesn't look good. Can you come in Monday morning?" The phone rings after midnight. "Your child's been in an accident. You need to get to the ER

---

[1]John Calvin, *Commentary on the Book of Psalms*, 5 vols., trans. James Anderson (Edinburgh: Calvin Translation Society, 1845), 1:478.

[1]Annie Dillard, *Teaching a Stone to Talk* (New York: Harper Collins, 1982), 40–41.

*Verses 3–9.* The Bible often speaks of the revelation of God in the world through acts of history (e.g., Pss. 105 and 106). Here God is revealed through God's acts in nature. The "voice of God" causes and orchestrates the mighty storm—revealing God's presence and sovereign power in the world. The phrase "the voice of God" is repeated seven times in these verses, rolling through the psalm like thunderclaps over the landscape. The storm begins over the waters of the Mediterranean (vv. 3–4). It then moves across the mountain ranges of Lebanon with wind and lightning, tearing through trees and shaking the very foundations of the mountains themselves (vv. 5–7). Finally, it crosses into the wilderness region of Kadesh, causing still more devastation (vv. 8–9b).

For human beings in its path, such a storm would be terrifying and tragic—akin to a tsunami or hurricane. But this psalm is *not* the occasion to contemplate the storm as human tragedy or to question why God would allow such devastation to occur. Rather, this psalm views the storm at a distance, from the celestial court of God, and acknowledges the awe-inspiring divine power that created it. From that distance, from that perspective, the only possible response is "Glory!" (v. 9c).

*Verses 10–11.* The setting in life for the use of Psalm 29 was in Israel's worship. The human congregation, gathered for worship, was encouraged by the psalm to recognize God's sovereign power and to respond with praise as well. On earth as in heaven, all in God's temple say, "Glory!" in response to the revelation of God's power in nature.

Such praise of God's glory leads to other acts of worship. The congregation (on earth and in heaven) affirms their faith in God as "king forever"— sovereign over all of creation, including storms and floods (v. 10). And because this is so, because the Lord reigns eternally and universally, the people's prayer in verse 11 is also possible and hopeful. There is no clue in this psalm *why* God's people need "strength" and "peace." Their predicament could be a natural disaster (flood, famine, drought, etc.)—or it could just as easily be political oppression, war, or exile. The point is, it does not matter what the predicament might be. At any time, under any circumstances when "storm clouds" roll, God's sovereign power is available to bless and deliver God's people, to give them peace even in the midst of storms. The same God who rules over the universe, whose "voice" sends forth the thunderstorm, *is* the God of

Significantly, a parallel theophany occurs in the New Testament with the birth of Jesus (Luke 2:8–14). A heavenly being appears to announce the good news. The messenger is joined by "a multitude of the heavenly host" (2:13) who proclaim: "Glory to God in the highest heaven, and on earth peace among those whom he favors" (2:14). The heavenly host proclaims that God's power and reign bring strength and peace. Through the birth of Jesus, God is enthroned. In like manner, through the poetic re-creation of a thunderstorm, God is enthroned.

This psalm has much to teach a congregation about worship. It is on this theme one could focus the sermon. The praise and glory described in the psalm take place in the gathered assembly of worshipers. Significantly, the psalmist does not call the worshipers to go outside and wait for a thunderstorm to develop and then be overwhelmed with wonder and amazement. No, the storm is recreated in the worship assembly through the liturgy and through a hymn that the worshipers sing. While engaging in the liturgy that reenacts God's sovereign power, they shout, "Glory!" The worship experience brings blessing and peace and energy for daily living.

Humans long for experiences that energize, that generate zeal and passion in their lives. However, we so easily succumb to superficial experiences to fulfill that yearning. We rely on the cheap thrills provided by the entertainment world and the adrenalin rush that so often accompanies extreme sports. We look for passion in all the wrong places. These experiences provide only momentary exhilaration; ultimately like a drug they drain and weaken the soul. In contrast, through worship God imparts to us an energy, an "ecstatic experience," when we come into his presence.

The problem comes when believers do not expect anything to happen in worship. They approach worship casually, almost nonchalantly, hoping only to hear some practical piece of advice or to escape the problems of the world for an hour and lose themselves in an aesthetically satisfying experience. Worship is oriented horizontally toward the worshiper.

The worship the psalmist describes is directed toward the living God who sits enthroned in the heavens. The worship going on here expresses awe to a transcendent and sovereign God, a God who is shrouded in mystery and power. Annie Dillard is correct when she says that we don't come before the living God as "cheerful, brainless tourists on a

# Psalm 29

## Theological Perspective

revelation, awe is transformed into trusting reverence, fear into love, and resignation into hope.

This basic Christian proclamation about the relationship between the person of Jesus and the power at the center of everything is captured in Scripture passages like Colossians 1:15–16: "He is the image of the invisible God, the firstborn of all creation; for in him all things in heaven and on earth were created, things visible and invisible, whether thrones or dominions or rulers or powers—all things have been created through him and for him." This is also the focus of such essential Christian doctrines as the Trinity and Christology. The God who creates is also the God who redeems. The Father and Son are unified in power and goodness. Jesus Christ is both fully human and fully divine.

Psalm 29 read on the Baptism of the Lord Sunday points toward an essential aspect of the gospel: God is the unavoidable power at the center of everything, the source and end of all existence. The other essential aspect of the gospel is that through the life, death, and resurrection of Jesus Christ, Christians know that God is good—the faithful, loving source of our hope. The gospel does not exist without both of these aspects; neither goodness without power nor power without goodness constitutes good news. In an age that is infatuated with God's goodness, to the point of ignoring God's power, Psalm 29 is necessary to preserve the fulness of the gospel. In an age when the Christian imagination often limits God's activity to scriptural revelation and the life of the church, Psalm 29 reminds us that God's reign is cosmic in scope, revealed in and through everything that exists. It presents us with the real challenge of integrating human experience and Christian faith, the ruthless power expressed in nature with the self-sacrificial goodness of Jesus Christ. But this is also the source of our very real hope that, as Paul puts it in Romans 8:38–39, "neither death, nor life, nor angels, nor rulers, nor things present, nor things to come, nor powers, nor height, nor depth, nor anything else in all creation, will be able to separate us from the love of God in Christ Jesus our Lord."

TIMOTHY A. BEACH-VERHEY

## Pastoral Perspective

as soon as you can." In words like those you hear the roar of the thunder and the crack of the cedars breaking.

None of us is a stranger to the thunderstorms that shake the foundations of our lives and blow away our illusions of security. But over against all that shakes us to the core, all that threatens to wash away the very foundations of life, the psalmist ascribes glory to the God who has power to "bless his people with peace." It is the same Lord who declares, "I have called you by name; you are mine. When you pass through the waters, I will be with you; and through the rivers, they shall not overwhelm you. . . . Do not fear, for I am with you" (Isa. 43:1–2, 5). It is a mighty and precious promise that runs throughout Scripture.

The psalmist invites us to trust that the God of *shalom* is Lord alone over all the forces that threaten to "blow us away." Pastoral reflection on the psalm gives opportunity to affirm that in the midst of chaos we too may experience the presence and power of the One whom the voice of God would acknowledge in the waters of the Jordan, "This is my Son, the Beloved." Amid the storms of life, we too are invited to ask and exclaim with Jesus' storm-tossed disciples, "Who is this that even wind and sea obey him?" In these last days, we too have beheld his glory, not in nature's power, but in a cradle in Bethlehem, a cross on Golgotha, and an empty tomb at the dawn of the new creation.

Hymns that could be used effectively in a service in which Psalm 29 is the organizing center include "How Firm a Foundation," "Eternal Father, Strong to Save," "Out of Deep, Unordered Water," "O Splendor of God's Glory Bright," and the marvelous baptismal hymn, "We Know that Christ Is Raised."

A new creation comes to life and grows,
As Christ's new body takes on flesh and blood.
The universe, restored and whole, will sing,
  "Alleluia!"[2] and "Glory!" (Ps. 29:9).

ALLEN C. MCSWEEN JR.

---

[2]John B. Geyer, "We Know that Christ Is Raised," *The Presbyterian Hymnal* (Louisville, KY: Westminster/John Knox Press, 1990).

## Exegetical Perspective

Israel—the One in whom they can trust and to whom their prayers ascend.

*Relationship of Psalm 29 to Other Lectionary Texts.* The Old Testament reading, Genesis 1:1–5, affirms God as creator of heaven and earth. The brief reading includes only God's activity on the first day of creation. However, that activity sets the pattern for the entire creation story. As in Psalm 29, God's voice or word is the agent of creation. God speaks, and the world is created. Genesis 1:2 mentions the "waters" of chaos, before God's activity of creation begins. They are, in a way, reminiscent of the chaotic waters of the sea and flooding rains of Psalm 29 (see vv. 3 and 10). In the Genesis creation story, God separates and orders the chaotic waters (Gen. 1:6–9). In Psalm 29, God once again stirs up the ordered waters into a powerful and chaotic storm.

The Gospel reading, Mark 1:4–11, provides, in a sense, the ultimate answer to the prayer of Psalm 29:11. Here God's "glory" is revealed in the baptism of Jesus, particularly in the Holy Spirit descending upon Jesus (Mark 1:10). But God's "glory" (evident in the power and presence of the Holy Spirit) is not revealed only when Jesus is baptized. That "glory" will also reside in him and continue to be revealed in and through his earthly ministry. Note the words of John the baptizer concerning Jesus: "I have baptized you with water; but he will baptize you with the Holy Spirit" (Mark 1:8). The vocabulary of "water" and "voice" echoes that of Psalm 29. But here the "water" is the saving water of baptism, not the destructive water of thunderstorm and flood. And the "voice" of God, which created the world in Genesis 1 and the thunderstorm of Psalm 29, here acknowledges Jesus as beloved Son (Mark 1:11). While the "sons of God" (NRSV, "heavenly beings," Ps. 29:1) attend God in the heavenly court, Jesus is the only begotten and beloved Son of God—one with God and God incarnate in human flesh.

MARSHA M. WILFONG

## Homiletical Perspective

packaged tour of the Absolute." Rather as we enter the assembly we should all be wearing crash helmets![1] Playing off Dillard's image, the preacher might engage in some creative imagination envisioning a worship experience in which, rather than flight attendants, as we enter the sanctuary we encounter *worship attendants* who welcome us to worship, issue life preservers and signal flares, and announce, "Be sure that you are securely fastened into your body harness before takeoff. If we reach too high an altitude during this worship, oxygen masks will automatically drop from the ceiling." We are in the presence of the Holy God, creator of the universe! Energy is released.

However, the sermon should issue a strong word of caution. The worshiper must not misunderstand how public worship generates an ecstatic type of experience. Typically it is generated not by a lot of pomp and circumstance, but rather by openness to the presence of God. A fitting parallel to Psalm 29 is the worship scene described in Hebrews 12:18–28. The writer makes a contrast between these Christians in their little house church in Rome and the worship of YHWH at Mount Sinai by the Israelites (Exod. 19–20). As the Israelites approached Mount Sinai for worship, the Lord appeared in fire and smoke. A blast of the trumpet sounds; the clouds, the thunder, and thick darkness engulf the mountain. It was such a terrifying scene that Moses exclaims, "I tremble with fear." They stood in awe of God. Yet the Hebrews' writer tells this little group of Christians that they experience a worship even more amazing than their ancestors at Mount Sinai. Like this psalmist who invokes the whole heavenly counsel to praise, so this little house church gathered for worship is surrounded by a heavenly host of angels, a cloud of witnesses, by "God the judge," by "the spirits of the righteous made perfect" (those who've died in the faith), and by "Jesus, the mediator" (Heb. 12:22–24). These all gather to worship with the little group of Christians. Even though it may appear to them that nothing happens in worship, because this heavenly audience surrounds them, it becomes an electrifying energizing experience. So they worship with reverence and awe in the presence of a God who is "a consuming fire" (12:28–29)! And together all shout, "Glory."

DAVE BLAND

---

[1]Annie Dillard, *Teaching a Stone to Talk* (New York: Harper & Row, 1982), 40.

# Acts 19:1-7

¹While Apollos was in Corinth, Paul passed through the interior regions and came to Ephesus, where he found some disciples. ²He said to them, "Did you receive the Holy Spirit when you became believers?" They replied, "No, we have not even heard that there is a Holy Spirit." ³Then he said, "Into what then were you baptized?" They answered, "Into John's baptism." ⁴Paul said, "John baptized with the baptism of repentance, telling the people to believe in the one who was to come after him, that is, in Jesus." ⁵On hearing this, they were baptized in the name of the Lord Jesus. ⁶When Paul had laid his hands on them, the Holy Spirit came upon them, and they spoke in tongues and prophesied— ⁷altogether there were about twelve of them.

## Theological Perspective

The passage makes little sense apart from Acts 18:24–28. There we are told that Apollos, an Alexandrian Jew and eloquent evangelist whom Paul mentions in 1 Corinthians 1:10–17, came to Ephesus, spoke accurately concerning Jesus, but knew "only the baptism of John." Thus, when he spoke in the synagogue, Priscilla and Aquila "took him aside and explained the Way of God to him more accurately" (18:26). In 19:1–7, we are told that Paul passed through Ephesus while Apollos was away in Corinth. Paul asked some disciples there whether they had received the Holy Spirit when they became believers. Their reply, "No, we have not even heard that there is a Holy Spirit" (19:2), implies that Apollos's ministry continues to suffer significant deficiencies. Unfortunately, they had been baptized only into John's baptism. (Did the explanations of Priscilla and Aquila not take?) Paul explained that John's is a baptism of repentance that looks forward to Jesus. Hearing this, the Ephesians were baptized by Paul in the name of the Lord Jesus, and when Paul laid hands on them, "the Holy Spirit came upon them, and they spoke in tongues and prophesied" (19:6).

One point that stands out is historical. Our passage intimates some important tensions within the early Christian movement. Apollos is presented as being helpful at arguing with other Jews that the

## Pastoral Perspective

This passage raises important questions about what it means to be initiated into Christian community and what membership in these communities bestows on believers. In most churches, the process of initiation focuses on baptism by water. However, in the earliest Christian communities, as is evident in the Gospel of Luke and in the Acts of the Apostles, the reception of the Holy Spirit was at least as important as water baptism. Baptism by water was seen as being necessary for the forgiveness of sins, and was probably taken over from John the Baptist's baptism. This baptism by water was a precursor to baptism by the Holy Spirit, without which one could not be a full member of the Christian community. For this reason, the disciples whom Paul found in Ephesus, who had received John's baptism, but "[had] not even heard that there is a Holy Spirit," were missing out on one of the central aspects of Christian discipleship.

According to Luke, what these disciples were missing, and what they received from Paul when they received the Holy Spirit, was principally the power of prophecy. We tend to think that prophecy has to do with foretelling future events, but in Luke's Gospel and in Acts, to prophesy is to speak about the present; it is to speak in God's name on behalf of God's work in the world. This speaking is done with

## Exegetical Perspective

This pericope is part of a larger unit (19:1–41) that narrates the Ephesian period of Paul's ministry, which lasted for more than two years according to Acts 19:10 and 20:31. It came after his Corinthian stay and turned out to be the last residential ministry in his life. The entire chapter 19 can be divided into four sections: "Johannine" disciples in Ephesus (vv. 1–7), preaching to Jews and Gentiles (vv. 8–10), miracles by Paul (vv. 11–20), and riot by Demetrius (vv. 21–41). None of these events is mentioned anywhere in the letters of Paul. So, whatever their historical veracity, it will be exegetically sound to focus on the redactional tendencies of Luke reflected in this pericope.

In Luke 3:15–18, which is probably one of the few Synoptic passages where Q and Mark overlap, John declares to those who are asking him if he is the anointed one that he baptizes them with water, but the stronger one who is coming will baptize them with the Holy Sprit and with fire. This prophecy of John is not fulfilled anywhere in the Synoptic Gospels, but it is fulfilled at least in an indirect way in our pericope in Acts. Both the Synoptic tradition preserved in Luke 3:15–18 and the Lukan redactional work in Acts 19:1–7 seem to reflect the fact that the followers of John the Baptist continued to exist in parallel to and even in competition with the

## Homiletical Perspective

Every text has rabbit trails to lead the preacher off in false directions, and this text has more than most. It talks about baptism, but it is not about baptism; it mentions the laying on of hands and speaking in tongues, but it is not about tongues or laying on hands, or their order or importance. In the past, in some country towns, preachers debated these matters in courthouse squares. T. DeWitt Talmage, pastor of First Presbyterian Church in New York (1895–1902), criticized debates over baptism and compared such "ecclesiastical hydropathy" to his experience as a boy swimming with friends when they would splash water in one another's eyes. The only result, he said, was blurred vision. The Mandaeans of Iran and Iraq today still pursue their rites as disciples of John the Baptist, although he would be puzzled by many of their practices; yet our historic preoccupation with ecclesiastical differences may be just as foreign to the one who came to bring the good news.

What then, if anything, does this lesson have for us on this first Sunday after Epiphany? We do not "know only the baptism of John," and for many Christians, all denominational differences are off-putting. Epiphany may be behind us now in the church calendar, but it is not forgotten, as the lessons for today remind us. What is Epiphany? A season of

# Acts 19:1-7

## Theological Perspective

Messiah is Jesus, but at a loss when it comes to rightly understanding baptism and entry into the Christian movement. He misses something fundamental, namely, the relationship between baptism in the name of Jesus and empowerment in the Spirit. Indeed, it seems the reality of the Spirit does not accompany baptisms performed by Apollos at all. We may be unable to trace all of the parties and tensions that lie beneath the surface here (or for that matter beneath the surface of 1 Cor. 1:10–17), but Acts 19:1–7 makes it abundantly clear that the early Christian movement was more diverse and contentious than we often recognize.

Then there is the immediate theology of our passage. A prime conviction in Luke–Acts is that the true Christian movement or the Way is associated with the apostolic party of which Paul, who once famously persecuted it, is now a belated member (whereas Apollos is not). Another prime conviction is that the true Christian movement is both united and driven by God in the power of the Spirit. Thus, at his ascension Jesus tells the apostles they will receive power to witness to the ends of the earth when the Holy Spirit comes upon them (Acts 1). The Spirit gathers the church at Pentecost and inspires persons from many nations to speak about God's deeds of power (Acts 2:11), and the Spirit-empowered apostles perform awe-inspiring wonders and signs (Acts 2:43). In Acts 19:1–7, this same empowerment in the Spirit is repeated with Paul and "about twelve" (a number loaded with apostolic significance; v. 7) disciples at Ephesus. Unlike Apollos's ministry, then, Paul's apostolic ministry sets the Ephesians within the true Spirit-empowered movement.

This brings us to a theology of the Spirit. In Luke–Acts, the power of the Spirit expands the Christian movement in an ever-widening circle (according to God's plan). Indeed Acts chronicles the Spirit-empowered expansion of the Way from Jewish apostles to Parthians, Medes, Mesopotamians, Cappadocians, Egyptians, Cretans, and Arabs, to Rome, the center of the known world, where Acts will close with Paul himself preaching "without hindrance" (Acts 2:9–11; 28:31). The gift of the Spirit, which now is poured out even on the Gentiles (Acts 10:45), has an inherent evangelical and expansive dynamic, so that the Way comes to be universal, inclusive of all peoples and nations.

Somewhat similarly, classical discussions of baptism link it with entrance into the church but offer different accounts of baptism, gift, and

## Pastoral Perspective

the Spirit's power, and thus it is inspired utterance, and has the power to change the world. This powerful prophetic Spirit manifested itself at first in Jesus' life. The Spirit overshadowed Mary so that she conceived Jesus, and it was the Spirit of whom the angel Gabriel spoke when he said, "Nothing will be impossible with God"(Luke 1:37). The Spirit anointed Jesus with the mission to preach good news to the poor and liberation to captives (Luke 4:18–19). Jesus told his disciples that the Spirit would be with them when they were hauled before "rulers and authorities" (Luke 12:11 NIV) and were required to give an account of their faith: "do not worry about . . . what you are to say; for the Holy Spirit will teach you at that very hour what you ought to say" (Luke 12:11–12).

Jesus' promise to his disciples that they would receive this Spirit was fulfilled at Pentecost, when the Spirit was poured out on them. For Luke, this gift of the Spirit was an eschatological event, fulfilling Joel's prophecy that in the last day God's Spirit would be poured out on all flesh, so that "your sons and your daughters shall prophesy" (Acts 2:17). The gift of the Holy Spirit at Pentecost was this sign of the end times, and it meant that all of the followers of Jesus became prophets. Baptism by the Holy Spirit, in Luke's account of the early church in Acts, gave the followers of Jesus power to proclaim the gospel with boldness, and to do so in tongues that all could understand.

This prophetic calling was lived out in astonishing ways, as the book of Acts attests. The first followers of Jesus were able to proclaim the life-giving gospel of Jesus before "rulers and authorities," even at the cost of their own lives. The Spirit guided them to bring this gospel far beyond where they had initially thought it could go, leading them to open the church to Gentiles, like the Ephesians in today's text. With the Spirit's power, these early disciples discovered the truth of the angel Gabriel's words, that "nothing will be impossible with God." Through Jesus' first followers, the Spirit was a powerful wind that blew through the ancient world and transformed it.

There are many Christians today who, like the disciples Paul finds in Ephesus in today's passage, might say that they "have not even heard that there is a Holy Spirit." We may well underestimate the power bestowed on us at our baptism, thinking that the primary gift of this initiation into Christian community is the forgiveness of sins, and not realizing that this forgiveness and cleansing are only

## Exegetical Perspective

followers of Jesus for some time. If that is the case, the author of Luke–Acts is trying in both places to establish the superiority of Jesus to John by linking the coming of the Holy Spirit exclusively to Jesus. A very similar redactional motif is found in the immediately preceding passage (Acts 18:24–28).

Our pericope begins with a remark that Paul came to Ephesus and found some disciples there (v. 1). The exact identity of these people remains untold in the narrative. The word "disciples" (*mathētai*) and the expression "when you believed" (*pisteusantes*) in the following verse give us the impression that they are already followers of Jesus, just like Apollos in the previous passage. However, it is also possible that Luke intends to describe them only as followers of John. Scholarly opinions are divided on this issue. Whatever the case, one should not draw a conclusion from this passage that in Luke–Acts only those who have received the Holy Spirit are authentic followers of Jesus. In the combined history of Luke–Acts, even before the promise of receiving of the Holy Spirit (Acts 1:8) and its fulfillment on the Pentecost (Acts 2:1–4), the disciples of Jesus were authentic followers. However, it is the Holy Spirit that gives them power (*dynamis*) to become witnesses (*martyres*) of Jesus to the end of the earth (1:8), which is the very theme of the book of Acts.

Paul never mentions John the Baptist in any of his epistles. He also says in 1 Corinthians 1:14–17 that he baptized no one except Crispus and Gaius in Corinth and the household of Stephanas and that Christ did not send him to baptize but to proclaim the gospel. In contrast, here in Acts the Lukan Paul explains the purpose of John's baptism of repentance (*metanoia*) in terms of believing in Jesus (v. 4), and Paul himself performs the baptism into the name of Jesus (v. 5).[1] This indicates a highly redactional hand of Luke at work in our pericope. The rendering of *metanoia* as "repentance" in most English translations is not necessarily wrong, but it could be reductionistic. Its lexical meaning is "change of mind." Earlier, in Luke 3:8, John the Baptist talks about the "fruits (*karpous*) worthy of repentance," and in Luke 3:10–14 he addresses those who have means or are authorities and gives them concrete commands for what they should do for the change of mind. This should be regarded as part of the meaning of the same word *metanoia* in Acts 19:4. In

[1] Unless the baptism in v. 5 is a metaphorical expression, which is doubtful, it is the only instance in the New Testament where a double baptism is conducted (Ben Witherington, *The Acts of the Apostles* [Grand Rapids: Eerdmans, 1998], 572).

## Homiletical Perspective

appearings: of gifts, and gift givers, and a unique gift from God. All of these elements continue in the lesson from Acts. To find a suitable homiletical approach to this text, let us examine the unity in several apparently diverse themes.

First, notice that the *gift* of God's Spirit is central to the pericope. Those disciples whom Paul found in Ephesus did not know of the Spirit, or at least did not know that the Spirit of God had been given to all Christians. As those who had been baptized by John (or perhaps by disciples of John) and whose understanding was limited to John's baptism of repentance, this is not difficult to understand. Although God's Spirit is manifested repeatedly in the Hebrew Scriptures, the coming of that Spirit appears to have been limited to special persons, times, or places. The first disciples obviously did not understand the universal nature of that gift to Christians, either, as they remained puzzled, though obedient, until Pentecost. When Paul explained to these dozen disciples that John the Baptist pointed to the one who would come after him, they were baptized in the name of Jesus. Then Paul laid hands upon them, and they received the gift of the Holy Spirit. Like the central message of Epiphany, this text focuses on a gift.

Furthermore, this gift is *unique*. For some, the uniqueness of the gift of the Spirit may have been linked to the speaking in tongues that sometimes accompanied the experience of baptism. Yet the Greeks believed that it was necessary once a year to visit a shrine, such as the temple of Delphi, to be filled with a good spirit, in order to prevent the body from being possessed with an evil spirit. For them too, speaking in an "unknown tongue" was proof of the presence of the good spirit. But the gift of God's Holy Spirit was not merely prophylaxis against evil, as theirs was, but an empowering to accomplish the work of Christ. John A. Broadus, who wrote the classic treatise on homiletics *On the Preparation and Delivery of Sermons* (1870), said that baptism often is called the door to the church, but it also is the door into God's vineyard where there is work for all. The uniqueness of that work lies in the uniqueness of Christ himself.

The life of Jesus was an ongoing parable of the embracing arms of God. His life as a Galilean peasant under the tyranny of vast powers beyond reach, economic as well as political; his inclusion of the marginalized, women, children, tax collectors and lepers; his revelation of a God with such compassion that even the sparrow's trampled fluff of feathers in the gutter does not go unseen: these all

# Acts 19:1-7

## Theological Perspective

commitment. In the Augustinian traditions, baptism is a visible sign of an invisible grace. There is something divinely given, namely, the grace of adoption whereby we become God's daughters and sons, and so Augustinians baptize children as well as adults. Some Baptist churches regard the rite essentially as a marker of the faith commitment or decision of the person baptized, and so they baptize adults rather than infants. Reformed Protestants often try to acknowledge both points. They claim that, by the power of the Spirit, the baptized enter into God's covenant of grace, and so participate in the new reality of God's people. Even so, they insist that the order for infant baptism looks forward to the formation of baptized children in the community of faith; parents and congregation promise to nurture the child toward the end that she or he may make a good confession.

Acts 19:1–7 joins divine gift and personal commitment in a manner that may connect with a theme of major importance for theological ethics. The passage clearly insists that a chief difference between John's baptism of repentance and baptism in the name of Jesus is that the latter entails the gift of the Spirit. John's baptism of repentance points almost entirely to a personal turning away from evil and toward good. Baptism in the name of Jesus entails a divinely given reality, but this reality both empowers and disposes people to witness to God's deeds of power (Acts 2:11). The gift of the Spirit in baptism sweeps people up into the dynamic of the Spirit and its expansive Way. It drives believers to participate in the church's expansive mission. It empowers them to witness in word and in deed to a universally inclusive reality. And so by the Spirit they are empowered to witness to a truth that many in today's terrorized and war-torn world may need to hear. Now that the Way is come to all, we no longer need be Jews or Greeks or Egyptians or Romans or Arabs in order to be God's people.

DOUGLAS F. OTTATI

## Pastoral Perspective

the first step in embracing the Christian faith. The second, all-important step in this initiation is receiving the astonishing, world-transforming, dangerous power of the Holy Spirit. With the gift of the Holy Spirit at baptism, each new believer is drawn into the eschatological event of the pouring out of the Spirit, and thus becomes a prophet.

This gift of prophecy calls us to proclaim what God is doing even now in our world, and to do so with boldness. This Spirit moves us to proclaim God's good news to the poor and liberation to captives. This gift empowers us to "speak truth to power," confronting the "rulers and authorities" of this world with the revolutionary message of the gospel, and trusting that when we are called upon to offer this witness the Holy Spirit will give us the words to say. This Holy Spirit inspires us to risk our very lives for the sake of the good news of Jesus Christ, and to trust that with God nothing is impossible. This Spirit is a powerful wind that breathes through our speaking and our acting to accomplish more than we can ask or imagine, even to the point of transforming the world, as the Spirit did through the first disciples.

This is the day of the liturgical year when Christians celebrate the baptism of Jesus. This day is designated in many churches as a particularly appropriate one on which to baptize and welcome new members into the Christian church. Today's reading from Acts reminds us to claim the full power of that baptism, which includes baptism not only by water but by the Holy Spirit, and which gives us the ability and the inspiration to take up the prophetic calling of all Christians.

RUTHANNA B. HOOKE

that regard, it is important to recognize that the baptism into the name of Jesus in our pericope does not cancel out the baptism of John. Luke is not interested in denouncing the baptism of John the Baptist. Rather, the baptism into the name of Jesus and the coming of the Holy Spirit give them power to do what John's baptism originally intended to do.

The expression "they were baptized *into/toward/in regard to* [*eis*] the name of the Lord Jesus" in verse 5 indicates purpose or allegiance, rather than instrument, which would have been expressed either with a simple dative or with a preposition *en*. The precise meaning of this expression remains unexplained in the text. Earlier, in Acts 2:38, Luke had Peter speak of being baptized "upon [*epi*] the name of Jesus Christ for the forgiveness of sins" (my translation). Whether or not the same meaning is implied in Acts 19:5 cannot be determined exegetically.

The laying of hands in verse 6 does not seem to be part of the baptismal ritual per se. In the present context, it is closely linked with the baptism, but it could also be regarded as a separate ritual, as it was in Acts 13:3. In the narrative flow in our pericope, the Holy Spirit came upon them, not when they were baptized, but when Paul laid his hands upon them. In Acts 10:34–48, the Holy Spirit came down to the household of Cornelius while they were listening to Peter's speech. Only after witnessing this, Peter baptized them "in [*en*] the name of Jesus Christ" (Acts 10:48). In other words, baptism in Acts is not a magical ritual that automatically brings down the Holy Spirit whenever it is performed. The baptism provides an optimal environment for the coming of the Holy Spirit in the narrative world of Acts, but it is also true that in the book of Acts the Holy Spirit has absolute freedom to come and work in whatever way the Spirit sees fit.

EUGENE EUNG-CHUN PARK

preached a kingdom so gracious, so inclusive, that even our own contradictions of it over two thousand years have not destroyed its hope. If the unique power of God's Spirit in the Hebrew Scriptures seemed to have been limited to certain persons and places (or, more likely, if this was the perception of it), then baptism in the name of Christ promised grace to all.

So Paul became a *gift giver*, through his message, to these early disciples in Ephesus. Yet, the preceding chapter in Acts also needs to be recalled at this point. Apollos, the gifted preacher from Alexandria, Egypt, who preached Jesus with both ardor and accuracy, also knew only the baptism of John. Aquila and Priscilla therefore instructed him more fully in the Christian way (though nothing was said about baptism). In both of these passages, one concerning a gifted, accomplished preacher and the other concerning lay disciples, we are shown a willingness to receive further instruction in the way of Christ. The Ephesian disciples in our lesson were willing to receive the gift of instruction from Paul and to transfer their focus from John the Baptist to Jesus— never mind their previous history and loyalty. And Apollos? This much-admired orator was willing to be taught by two lay disciples, one of them a woman! There is not a hint of pride or objection in the accounts of either of these experiences. This too is a gift, a gift of grace, and one we might pray for, both for ourselves and for our congregations.

If we and those to whom we preach could know the humility of these earliest followers of Christ, what lessons might we learn, what changes might come over us? What transformations might we experience in our churches, our denominations, our communities?

CLYDE FANT

# Mark 1:4-11

⁴John the baptizer appeared in the wilderness, proclaiming a baptism of repentance for the forgiveness of sins. ⁵And people from the whole Judean countryside and all the people of Jerusalem were going out to him, and were baptized by him in the river Jordan, confessing their sins. ⁶Now John was clothed with camel's hair, with a leather belt around his waist, and he ate locusts and wild honey. ⁷He proclaimed, "The one who is more powerful than I is coming after me; I am not worthy to stoop down and untie the thong of his sandals. ⁸I have baptized you with water; but he will baptize you with the Holy Spirit."

⁹In those days Jesus came from Nazareth of Galilee and was baptized by John in the Jordan. ¹⁰And just as he was coming up out of the water, he saw the heavens torn apart and the Spirit descending like a dove on him. ¹¹And a voice came from heaven, "You are my Son, the Beloved; with you I am well pleased."

## Theological Perspective

Mark's story of Jesus' baptism provides the indispensable context for understanding everything subsequently recounted about Jesus' ministry and passion. God's dramatic acknowledgment of Jesus makes it clear that through the words and deeds of Jesus we humans are encountering the enacted intentions of God. Although the passage does not employ the later creedal terminology of divine and human natures, theologians have read it as a clue to the meaning of the doctrine of the incarnation.

Jesus is presented as the fulcrum of God's dealings with humanity. The figure of John the Baptist situates Jesus in the past, present, and future of God's activity. As the archetypal preacher/witness, John links Jesus to God's promises in Israel's past. The setting in the wilderness evokes memories of the preparation of the people of Israel for entrance into the promised land. John, the epitome of the prophets, also points forward to God's imminent intervention in human history to confer a new hope to humanity. Into the wilderness of our own broken lives and our own bleeding world erupts the promise of a baptism of new life. Poised like John's generation between a troubled past and an unprecedented future, our proper response in the present should be confession, repentance, and hopeful expectation.

## Pastoral Perspective

Here is a reminder that the gospel is down to earth, grounded in the real, tactile, sensual, fleshy world. In these few verses are references to river water, clothing from camels, diet from bugs, and tying shoes, a bird analogy, and an interesting weather phenomenon. Mark's earthiness gives us a hedge against faith and worship that are too ethereal, otherworldly, abstract.

We may ask, for example, how the dove descended. Gently, if classic pictures of this scene are to be believed. But birds sometimes dive-bomb (for example, to protect their young)! A dive-bombing Holy Spirit would fit with the accompanying "torn apart" sky. Many congregations love to sing "Sweet, Sweet Spirit," perhaps preferring the "sweet heavenly Dove"[1] to the wild-wind/fierce-flame Spirit. Are our baptism rituals sometimes so nice that we neglect to mention the uncomfortable implications of inviting God's Spirit to invade our lives?

The earthiness and the Spirit go together. I am informed that C. S. Lewis once told an audience that for Christians "spirit" is not lighter than matter, but heavier. Spirit is the real substance of God acting in creation and redemption and final reconciliation. And yet Spirit is always tied to material—real water, real bread, inexpensive wine,

[1] Words and music by Doris Akers (Manna Music, Inc., 1962).

## Exegetical Perspective

The setting for the beginning of Jesus' ministry is provided by the activity of John the Baptist. John was a prophet who preached and baptized in the Judean wilderness. He proved to be so popular that Herod Antipas found it necessary to arrest and execute him (Mark 1:14; 6:17–29). The discovery of the Dead Sea Scrolls has led to speculation that John was a member of the community that produced the scrolls. Certainly the eschatological nature of John's message resonates with the apocalyptic perspectives of Dead Sea community. Similarly, that community's concern for ritual purity with the elaborate water system in evidence at Qumran is similar to John's use of baptism as a sign of repentance. The Qumran community was composed largely of rural priests who believed that the aristocratic priests of Jerusalem had failed the Jewish community and were going to be replaced following a mighty manifestation of divine power. Luke asserts that John came from a priestly family (Luke 1:5), so the suggestion that John the Baptist was a member of the Qumran community or at least had some connections with it is plausible. Still, there is no direct evidence that John the Baptist had any connection with the Qumran community.

Another significant question is the nature of Jesus' relationship to John. Luke contends that John

## Homiletical Perspective

The baptism of Jesus invites a tangle of questions about Christology, Trinity, and baptism. If John offers "a baptism of repentance for the forgiveness of sins" (v. 4), why does Jesus come to be baptized by John? Was Jesus under the power of sin until this point? Or is he merely binding himself more closely to a sinful humanity? And does the voice that calls Jesus "Son" and "Beloved" simply announce what has always been true—or does it perform a kind of adoption? And what sort of self-consciousness does the event give to Jesus? What does he make of this voice from heaven? Does anyone else hear it? And if Mark describes the Spirit "descending like a dove" on Jesus (v. 10), how can Western Christians confess in our Nicene Creed that the Spirit "proceeds from the Father and the Son"? The questions multiply, and tugging at any one of them will pull a preacher and a congregation into the wondrous snarl of all the rest.

A sermon might start with any one of these questions. They lead very quickly to core Christian beliefs. And they arise not as imported impositions from ivory-tower theologians, but as urgent questions from a congregation's hearing of the text. The best sermons will sharpen and refine those questions and keep them in constant conversation with the living practices of congregations. For instance: if Jesus came to have his sins washed away—if Jesus

# Mark 1:4-11

## Theological Perspective

At the climax of the narrative Jesus is declared by God to be God's Son, the Beloved. To emphasize the importance of this appellation, the heavens are ripped open. Perhaps more than other traditions, Eastern Orthodoxy has stressed the significance of this celestial fissure. Through God's claiming of Jesus, the veiled mystery of God has now been made manifest and available. Karl Barth proposed that God's claiming of Jesus in this story summarizes the essence of the gospel: the astonishing claim that God does not will to remain hidden in the heights of heaven but descends to the depths of earthly life in order to be seen and heard by us finite creatures.[1]

The naming of Jesus as "Son" points to other crucial junctures in Mark's Gospel that help give content to this elusive term. At the transfiguration, "This is my Son, the Beloved" is repeated by a divine voice (Mark 9:7). The title is so dangerous that the unclean spirits who recognize Jesus' identity must keep it secret (Mark 3:11; 5:7). At the trial it is Jesus' acceptance of the title "Son of God" that fatally convicts him of blasphemy (Mark 14:61–62). The phrase is echoed in the human and public confession of the centurion at the cross (Mark 15:39). Here again a veil, this time that of the temple rather than the sky, is ripped and Jesus gives back to God the spirit that he had received. Golgotha confirms the title proclaimed at the Jordan. Putting all this together, theologians have concluded that God's hailing of Jesus as "Son" was Jesus' entrance onto the way that led to the cross, the inexorable journey that defines what "Son" means.

The cross reveals that the sonship declared at Jesus' baptism involves obedient suffering. This is evident in the baptism scene itself, for Jesus voluntarily joins the ranks of penitent sinners. This trajectory is continued throughout the Gospel as Jesus accepts multiple forms of suffering. In fact, Mark's notorious "messianic secret" is the scandal that the Messiah must suffer, even to death. The victory of resurrection and anticipated return is inseparable from the obedient suffering; the crown cannot be had without the cross.

Jesus' baptism does more than initiate the beloved Son's career of obedient suffering. A mysterious connection is implied between Jesus' identity as the suffering, obedient Son and Jesus' empowerment by the Spirit. This critical descent of the Spirit catalyzes Jesus' potent public ministry with its exercise of power over demons, sin, the law, and even nature.

[1] Karl Barth, *Church Dogmatics*, IV/2, ed. G. W. Bromiley and T. F. Torrance (Edinburgh: T. & T. Clark, 1958), 167.

## Pastoral Perspective

beautiful baptismal dresses for our children, or soaking robes for our adults. Spirit fills us in church and then drives us from church (as it will drive Jesus from the Jordan to the wilderness). There, outside the walls, we wrestle with the beasts and pray for ministering angels . . . angels heavier than air.

The text describes a ritual of confession, repentance, and forgiveness. The text would seem to suggest that everyone in that time (v. 5), whether they were sophisticates from the big city or bumpkins from the Judean countryside, knew that confession is good for the soul.

And here is a reminder of the value of communal ritual action: the laying on of hands and the feel of water make it all real. Baptism should be a powerful and memorable experience for participants and observers. There is a tangible sense of love and blessing when congregations lay hands on people who are moving away, who are going on a mission trip, who are facing major surgery, who are preparing to teach Sunday school, who are being confirmed and consecrated.

The text represents a striking interplay between Jesus' authority and his humility. In these verses it is John who declares that Jesus has the authority to baptize with the Holy Spirit. In the chapters that follow, we will see Jesus act out that authority—the authority to teach, the authority to heal and cast out demons, the authority to heal.

Jesus embodies his own humility. How odd, the early Christians must have thought, that their Lord should be baptized along with penitent sinners! Mark did not know of the doctrine of the Trinity, nor was he aware of Paul's claim that all the faithful people who are baptized are baptized into Christ's own baptism. What Mark knows and proclaims is the Suffering Servant, the crucified Messiah.

Jesus' authority and Jesus' humility are not two different things held together, even paradoxically. Jesus' authority is the authority of the humble one, and his humility is the (true) humility of the one to whom all authority belongs.

Of course our churches are not simply communal versions of Christ or hand-me-down remnants of his faithfulness. Yet we too want to balance the authority that can unashamedly claim that Jesus Christ is Lord and the humility that knows that he is Lord of all creation, and not just the church's Lord. Our Lord, but not our Lord alone.

When in the liturgy we claim to forgive one another's sins, we show forth the tension between authority and humility. The sins we forgive in

and Jesus were relatives (Luke 1:36). Both Matthew and Mark present the ministries of both John and Jesus as the fulfillment of prophecy (Matt. 3:3; 4:14–16; Mark 1:1–2). Mark claims that Jesus began his preaching ministry after Herod Antipas arrested John (Mark 1:14). Was Jesus himself a disciple of John who then struck out on his own when John was no longer able to continue his ministry? The Fourth Gospel asserts that at least some of Jesus' disciples were originally disciples of the Baptist (John 1:35). Was Jesus acquainted with them because he too was a disciple of John? The Gospels insist that John the baptizer's mission was to prepare for the coming of Jesus. Mark cites a portion of Isaiah 40 in 1:2–3 to present John's ministry as preparatory to that of Jesus in fulfillment of the prophetic word. Still, the exact contours of any personal relationship between John and Jesus are not precisely known.

What Mark tells us about John is minimal. He portrays John as a preacher who calls people to repentance and who baptizes those who respond to his call. Mark characterizes John's baptism as a rite of "repentance for the forgiveness of sins" (Mark 1:4). This likely means that the people who were baptized by John believed in his proclamation of a coming judgment. In view of that coming judgment, they repented of their sins and received forgiveness. Mark is really the only Gospel that explicitly states that John baptized Jesus. Matthew presents John as objecting to Jesus' intention to be baptized. Matthew, of course, says that Jesus was baptized but never actually says that John performed the ritual (Matt. 3:13–17). Luke follows suit (Luke 3:21–22). The evangelists, of course, considered such a ritual unnecessary in Jesus' case. The author of the Fourth Gospel, in particular, would never intimate that "the Word made flesh" needed to repent and receive forgiveness of sin, so that Gospel omits any reference to Jesus' baptism, though it is presupposed (John 1:32–34; 3:26).

Given the association with John's baptism and the repentance of sins, it is obvious that the evangelists faced a problem in presenting Jesus as having been baptized by John. In view of how circumspect the evangelists were in writing about Jesus' baptism, it is historically certain that Jesus was attracted by the Baptist's message and was baptized by him. For Mark, however, more important than the baptism were the vision and audition that Jesus has upon his emergence from the Jordan. Of course, these inform the reader of Jesus' true identity, clearing up any

didn't *really* become the Son of God until he was adopted at the Jordan River—then why did we just celebrate Christmas as the coming of Immanuel, God-with-us? But if Jesus did *not* come to have his sins washed away, what was his baptism for? And what, then, might *our* baptisms be for?

Such questions have dominated Christian reflection on the baptism of the Lord, and they remain full of promise. But it is worth noting that they are not Mark's first questions. Sermons that hugged Mark 1 more closely might focus instead on John the Baptist or on the tearing of the heavens.

Contemporary Christians trying to understand John the Baptist often have trouble getting beyond questions of style. Like a *Vanity Fair* report of a celebrity party, popular memories of John recall little beyond what he ate, what he wore, and some outrageous thing he said. Accessorized with camel's hair and a leather belt, dining on locusts and honey—and didn't he call someone a "brood of vipers"?—John has become an all-purpose container for any kind of radical content. And so everyone from John Brown to Mr. T has been called a "modern-day John the Baptist."

A sermon that engaged Mark's quick sketch of John would remember that radical style—but as a way of telling time. John's dress marks him as the new Elijah, whose coming some believed marked the arrival of the end times (cf. 2 Kgs. 1:8). His appearance in "the wilderness" recalls Israel's long wandering in between deliverance from slavery and entry into the promised land. In wilderness time the powers of sin and death have been broken, and the covenant has been kept, but the people of God still wait to receive the fullness of redemption. John baptizes people in the Jordan, the border between the wilderness and the land of milk and honey. He is not just any sort of radical, but the kind of witness who stands right at the edge of the reign of God and invites people to live into the now-and-not-yet reality of it. A sermon might describe this location and then take up this task.

John announces the time, and it comes quickly. Right after John promises that the coming one "will baptize you with the Holy Spirit," Jesus arrives on the scene (vv. 8–9). As Jesus arises from the waters of the Jordan, he sees "the heavens torn apart." The Spirit and a voice descend through this tear in time (vv. 10–11). In this moment of Jesus' baptism, heaven and earth are transparent to one another. Jesus looks to the heavens in love, and the voice calls out in love. The Spirit, the love between the first and

# Mark 1:4-11

## Theological Perspective

The bestowal of the Spirit upon Jesus is crucial for traditions that stress God's sanctifying grace. Jesus did not receive the Spirit in order to enjoy privately its spiritual benefits, but rather in order to pass it on. The church has claimed that Jesus underwent baptism so that we might commune with him in baptism and share his empowerment by the Spirit. If our baptism involves a participation in Jesus' baptism, and if Jesus' baptism initiates his ministry of suffering obedience, then our baptism must include a similar acceptance of self-denial. The path that baptism opens is a road typified by bearing one's own cross, and of saving one's life only by losing it (Mark 8:34–35).

These verses have generated two controversial questions in the history of theology. The most vexing one concerns the relationship of Jesus' obedience, God's approval, and Jesus' status as Son. At various times in Christian history groups known as adoptionists have argued that Jesus was "adopted" as God's Son at the baptism as a consequence of his obedience. For most believers, however, this suggestion ascribed far too much efficacy to the human agency of Jesus and undercut the conviction that Jesus' entire life was the enactment of God's eternal purposes. Consequently, interpreters from Athanasius in the fourth century to Karl Barth in the twentieth have argued that Jesus' baptism merely manifested his already-existing identity.

A second recurrent problem has concerned the relationship of John's baptism with water to Jesus' baptism of the Holy Spirit. Some Christians, including many Pentecostals, have argued that the church's baptism by water for the remission of sins must be supplemented by a subsequent spiritual baptism by the Holy Spirit. However, most Protestants have regarded the baptisms of John and Jesus as different dimensions of the church's ritual of initiation. According to Calvin, the church, like John, employs physical water, a visible sign, in a public ceremony, while the hidden work of the Holy Spirit upon the soul imbues that ritual with spiritual efficacy.[2]

LEE BARRETT

## Pastoral Perspective

Christ's name are really forgiven. But they are forgiven in Christ's name, and we are only servants of his own majesty.

Christian pastoral care listens humbly to the needs and wishes of the other. But Christian pastoral care is also given the authority to proclaim—to announce reconciliation, to require fidelity, to demand justice.

When John the baptizer testifies that Jesus will baptize with the Holy Spirit, he is declaring what all of Mark's Gospel declares: that the ministry of Jesus is the beginning of the eschatological reign of God. The Spirit that is the sign of the turning of the ages has now been poured forth on Jesus. From now on, he and those who follow him are blessed and stuck with an eschatological mission: to declare and embody God's reign.

We want to domesticate the gospel and hallow the present. Mark's Gospel calls us to unfamiliar territory and challenges us with the promise of the future. In this Gospel we are always moving forward, following our Lord.

*The New Oxford Annotated Bible* points out that "Jesus himself is baptized into the renewal movement that began before him."[2]

In part this reminds us that in Jesus Christ does a new thing, but not a brand-new thing. Israel, Torah, the prophets, John the baptizer all prepare the way. God did not wake up one morning and decide that all divine activity up until that moment had been in vain. Abraham, Sarah, Isaac, Jacob, Moses, Miriam, King David, Isaiah, Jeremiah, John the baptizer all "prepared the way." We who are clergy need to be wary of the temptation to march into our new congregational charge as if we were God's first thought for that people.

In part the *Annotated Bible* note reminds us that institutions, groups, movements tend to spin off new versions of themselves. Change and innovation—often good things—are to be expected.

Credit the hugely successful baptizer for recognizing that his innovative ministry was not the be-all and end-all of faith expressions. Credit Mark's Gospel for knowing that not even Jesus is contained by the movements established in his name: he is always "going ahead of [us]" (Mark 16:7).

ELTON W. BROWN

[2]John Calvin, *Commentary on a Harmony of the Evangelists, Matthew, Mark, and Luke*, vol. 1, trans. William Pringle (Edinburgh: Edinburgh Printing Co., 1845), 201–6.

[2]*The New Oxford Annotated Bible*, 3rd edition (New York: Oxford University Press, 2001), footnote on v. 9, NT 58.

misunderstanding about the significance of the baptism: Jesus is the divinely appointed Messiah. Matthew presents the baptism of Jesus as an act of humility and obedience by Jesus (Matt. 3:13–17). For Luke, the baptism is a prelude to Jesus' prayer during which the Spirit descends on him in the form of a dove and he hears God's voice identifying him as God's Son (Luke 3:21–22). Both Mark and Luke, then, use the tradition of Jesus' baptism to make a christological point. In particular, Mark wishes his readers to know who Jesus really is from the very beginning of his story of Jesus' ministry and death. The characters in Mark's story will come to such knowledge only gradually. The climax of Mark's Gospel comes with the confession of the centurion on Golgotha: "Truly, this man was God's Son" (Mark 15:39). Ironically, it was the death of Jesus that revealed his true identity.

A key element in the New Testament's portrayal of the Baptist's ministry was that his preaching and baptisms were preparatory (Mark 1:7–8). It is likely that the New Testament has this emphasis because the Baptist's movement continued after his death (see Acts 18:25; 19:3–4). John called people to repentance in view of the coming judgment. John's preaching had a definite eschatological flavor. He announced that "another" was coming after him. The "mightier" one would inaugurate the time of judgment announced by John. Mark 1:4–11 picks up on the theme of the coming judgment and like the Baptist exhorts believers to be prepared.

Though Christian baptism has a significance different from that of John's baptism, the preacher should use the opportunity presented by the Gospel lesson to lead the members of the congregation to reflect on the significance of their baptism. The words spoken by the voice from the heavens identify Jesus as God's "beloved Son" (Mark 1:11). The rest of the Gospel describes how this beloved Son fulfills the mission given to him by God—a mission that will result in his execution. Christian baptism has transformed us into God's beloved children. Will we commit ourselves to completing Christ's work on earth despite the cost?

LESLIE J. HOPPE

second persons of the Trinity, is manifest. And all creation is caught up in this great love. The prophet's prayer that God would "tear open the heavens and come down" (Isa 64:1) is answered, and the promise of "a way in the wilderness and rivers in the desert" (Isa. 43:19) is fulfilled.

The heavens will open again in Mark. There will again be talk of tearing, and of Elijah, and of the love between Father and Son. It happens at the hinge of Mark's story, in the transfiguration (9:2–8). And it happens again near the end, at the cross, when even the imperial powers get caught up in declarations of divine love (15:34–39). But for most of the Gospel this love lives out of sight, like a seed growing secretly (4:26–29). Only the demons know who Jesus is. The disciples stumble along, forever forgetting what they have seen and heard. The heavens seem not torn open, but sealed and silent—as they do so much of the time today.

Baptism of the Lord Sunday can be a great day for congregations to celebrate the tearing open of the heavens. The coming stretch of Ordinary Time will carry us into the hard work of discipleship, when the will of God can seem so elusive and the power of God so absent. But before Mark takes readers on that journey, the Gospel gives us a moment to taste and see and hear the goodness of the Lord. Preaching and worship on this Sunday might do the same, not just talking about the love of God, but making that love *manifest* in word, song, sacrament, and prayer. It is a day to wear white and shout hallelujah. The heavens have been torn open, and this is a day to bask in the love they reveal.

TED A. SMITH

# 1 Samuel 3:1-10 (11-20)

¹Now the boy Samuel was ministering to the Lord under Eli. The word of the Lord was rare in those days; visions were not widespread.

²At that time Eli, whose eyesight had begun to grow dim so that he could not see, was lying down in his room; ³the lamp of God had not yet gone out, and Samuel was lying down in the temple of the Lord, where the ark of God was. ⁴Then the Lord called, "Samuel! Samuel!" and he said, "Here I am!" ⁵and ran to Eli, and said, "Here I am, for you called me." But he said, "I did not call; lie down again." So he went and lay down. ⁶The Lord called again, "Samuel!" Samuel got up and went to Eli, and said, "Here I am, for you called me." But he said, "I did not call, my son; lie down again." ⁷Now Samuel did not yet know the Lord, and the word of the Lord had not yet been revealed to him. ⁸The Lord called Samuel again, a third time. And he got up and went to Eli, and said, "Here I am, for you called me." Then Eli perceived that the Lord was calling the boy. ⁹Therefore Eli said to Samuel, "Go, lie down; and if he calls you, you shall say, 'Speak, Lord, for your servant is listening.'" So Samuel went and lay down in his place.

¹⁰Now the Lord came and stood there, calling as before, "Samuel! Samuel!" And Samuel said, "Speak, for your servant is listening." ¹¹Then the Lord said to

## Theological Perspective

The season of the Epiphany celebrates the manifestation of God in the early life of Jesus, who, on the eighth day following his birth, was presented to the aged Simeon in the Temple (Luke 2:25–35). Centuries before the birth of Jesus, the story of God's revelation to Samuel established a model of divine selection of a boy to introduce a radical transition from a traditional priestly family to a new priestly lineage.

Luke probably drew upon the story of Samuel to establish parallels related to God's actions: between the story of God's call to Samuel to shift the priestly lineage from Eli to Saul and the transition from the temple priesthood to the priesthood of Christ. Parallels between the two narratives are seen in several instances. First, Luke echoes the recognition that the child Samuel "continued to grow both in stature and in favor with the Lord and with the people" (1 Sam. 2:26) when he relates that Jesus "grew and became strong, filled with wisdom; and the favor of God was upon him" (Luke 2:40). Second, like Luke's narrative about the aged Simeon's blessing the infant Jesus, the story of Samuel's call is also focused on the new beginning made possible by the divine call and willing human response. Third, Luke is the only Gospel writer who includes the adolescent story of Jesus instructing the rabbis in the

## Pastoral Perspective

God is going to do a new thing, so large that it will make us tingle. And God is going to do it through a young boy. God is going to give us pins and needles and use a child as the delivery system. This story from the First Testament sounds a lot like the Christmas story! It echoes the surprise of Mary at the movements in her womb, the amazement of Joseph as he flees to Egypt with a woman he barely knows.

The last time I felt tingle was when a two-year-old visited our house and played with our cat. In the middle of our living room is a large hassock. It is there to keep eyes turned toward each other in our "living" room and away from the TV, which is in the corner. Six chairs and a couch surround the hassock, on which many people put up their feet. On this particular evening the circle was comfortably made around the hassock, and only the child and I knew that the cat was hiding under it. The child kept confirming his wisdom, giggling and pointing out that the cat was under the hassock. The adults were amused for a while, then tired of the game, and went on in their own pursuits. The child kept pulling up the upholstered skirt of the hassock and giggling. Things moved on. We ate. We ate some more. The child built a few blocks and knocked them over. Then the child returned to the hassock, and the cat was not there. Disaster ensued. The child began

Samuel, "See, I am about to do something in Israel that will make both ears of anyone who hears of it tingle. ¹²On that day I will fulfill against Eli all that I have spoken concerning his house, from beginning to end. ¹³For I have told him that I am about to punish his house forever, for the iniquity that he knew, because his sons were blaspheming God, and he did not restrain them. ¹⁴Therefore I swear to the house of Eli that the iniquity of Eli's house shall not be expiated by sacrifice or offering forever."

¹⁵Samuel lay there until morning; then he opened the doors of the house of the LORD. Samuel was afraid to tell the vision to Eli. ¹⁶But Eli called Samuel and said, "Samuel, my son." He said, "Here I am." ¹⁷Eli said, "What was it that he told you? Do not hide it from me. May God do so to you and more also, if you hide anything from me of all that he told you." ¹⁸So Samuel told him everything and hid nothing from him. Then he said, "It is the LORD; let him do what seems good to him."

¹⁹As Samuel grew up, the LORD was with him and let none of his words fall to the ground. ²⁰And all Israel from Dan to Beer-sheba knew that Samuel was a trustworthy prophet of the LORD.

## Exegetical Perspective

A journalist reading declassified documents pays attention when she comes to text that has been blacked out. In a similar fashion, any disciple of the lectionary should be on guard when he encounters parentheses. Leave out the verses in the parentheses and you have a nice little story of an individual's call. Keep them in and you have a powerful story regarding the courage required to listen and to speak—especially if the one to whom you dedicate ears and lips is the Lord.

This passage stands at the beginning of the stories of kingship in Judah and Israel, a time when God's people grew weary with the occasional service of the judges who rescued them when their disobedience had made them prey to their enemies. Now Israel began to long for a king, like the nations round about them. From the beginning, this concentration of power in the hands of a human being, versus the strong arm of the Lord, was fraught with difficulty. How would such a fallible ruler stay attuned to the voice of God once he was seated on his own throne?

Thus the story begins on an ominous note. Not only is "the word of the LORD . . . rare in those days," but the leadership over Israel is corrupt. Eli's sons have been using their status as priests to satisfy their own desires: consuming the precious fat of the sacrifices and lying with the vulnerable women who,

## Homiletical Perspective

This passage begins with an arrestingly modern note: "The word of the LORD was rare in those days; visions were not widespread." So the story is placed in our time; with this verse, we have passed the age of miracles. After this there are no pillars of fire, no columns of smoke, no parting of seas or rivers; most of what follows is a worldly history of successes, defeats, and palace intrigue. In fact, Samuel's role in anointing human kings will be to further human independence from God. A shiver may come upon us at realizing that we are on our own.

And yet "the lamp of God had not yet gone out" (3:3). Although visions may be rare in the modern world, they can still happen; God only *seems* to be sleeping. Indeed, while Samuel sleeps, God turns out to be delightfully awake.

Modern Christians can identify with Samuel, who "did not yet know the LORD, and the word of the LORD had not yet been revealed to him" (3:7). Like him, we may be set apart for service, having had some years of religious instruction without really knowing the Lord in a direct way.

And like him, we are sleeping. We do not fully sense the divinity around us. Exhaustion has so dulled our hearts, minds, and souls that we can work all day in the temple but never hear God. "I never knew how tired I was until I retired," one colleague

# 1 Samuel 3:1-10 (11-20)

## Theological Perspective

temple (Luke 2:41–46), a vignette that reflects Samuel's assistance to Eli in sacred service.

Along with these clear literary parallels, three theological themes dominate this passage about the revelation of God to Samuel: the call of God, the response to God's call, and the justice of God.

*The Call of God.* God's call of Samuel provides the core of this story. Other prophetic call narratives include those of Isaiah, Jeremiah, and Ezekiel. Their reports of receiving a divine call are related as a confession or an immediate charge to prophesy. In contrast, the call of Samuel is told in the third person. It is a story of delayed recognition of God's voice and of Samuel's submission. In addition, at the time of his call, Samuel does not receive directions to deliver an oracle to wayward people or to proclaim the word of the Lord. Instead, the focus of his prophetic call is to prepare for the transition from Eli's household to a new priestly family.

To be called by God is an act of spiritual intimacy and divine urgency. To be called by God means that God knows one's name and, in knowing one's name, exercises a powerful influence on the person. To be called by God also indicates a need for immediate response because the Almighty has indeed summoned one to a specific vocation or course of action.

In the summons to Samuel, God instructs Samuel first to listen. God does not charge him to deliver the judgment to Eli. Instead, God confides in young Samuel, specifying the judgment that will be exacted upon Eli, without enjoining Samuel to pass the message along to the affected priest.

*The Response to God's Call.* Throughout the ages persons have perceived their call into ministry in a variety of ways—from the blinding experience of Paul on the road to Damascus, to the visionary perception by Ezekiel, to the intensifying sense of moral compulsion that Jeremiah increasingly discerned. Here we discern another distinct means of a call, so clear in its articulation that it is recognized as a call, a voice.

Initially Samuel does not understand God's call as a divine summons. Its accurate recognition requires an old priest suffering from encroaching blindness to interpret the repeated summons as being from God. Yet even when Samuel first hears the call, he responds to it immediately, submitting himself for service to the priest.

Once Samuel recognizes the voice as one from God—a means of revelation that even dim-sighted

## Pastoral Perspective

crying uncontrollably and had to be comforted, after which he went back to his blocks. Then I saw the cat slip under the hassock.

I told the cat's secret to the child. The boy lifted the skirt, began to giggle, run back and forth, yell, scream, carry on, and *tingle* with the joy he had in finding the cat. I found it contagious and added my pins and needles to his excitement. God is in the heavens, and all is possibly right with the world. That little feline experience carried me a long way toward understanding what happened with Eli and Samuel and God. I do not know much tingle—and just this little bit helped me understand the magnitude of the visitation of "tingle."

Eli and Samuel's encounter with God has a dramatic motion similar to my little hassock story. An old man and a young man collaborate to hear God's vision for a new Israel. They are unsure at first that something authentic is happening. The old man knows the ways of the Lord and guides Samuel to listen in. Eli senses the possibility of forgiveness—or at least an end to his mourning—and listens up. Samuel "did not yet know the LORD" (3:7) but finds his way by a superb guide. The news is said to "tingle" in the KJV. The NRSV reads, "I am about to do something . . . that will make both ears of anyone who hears it tingle" (3:11).

When was the last time you felt a "tingle" about the word of God to you? When was the last time you experienced hope kicking into high gear, forgiveness writ loud, pins and needles all over your body because you were so excited?

With its promise of "pins and needles," this passage is a kind of spiritual acupuncture. It brings us by way of thrilling news to a time of renewal and forgiveness.

Often we make decisions because we have experienced the tingle of fear. We heard the doctor say our cancer was back, or we heard the judge say the child would be convicted for using drugs or stealing computer data. We were put on full body alert at the possibility that our pension was going to be taken away. We were so scared at how close we came to hitting the other car that we had to stop and rest a minute in order to experience our body's adrenalin rush. When we heard that our father lost his job, after his heart bypass, fear got our full attention. When the fighting began in Lebanon, World War III crossed our lips. It swam into view. We tingled in fright.

What this passage recommends to us is that we begin to make decisions based on the tingle of hope.

like Samuel's mother Hannah, had come to worship the Lord at the tent of meeting (chap. 2). These are heinous sins in Israel's moral universe. Some judgment is on the way.

But who will speak truth to power? Who dares to stand and, by giving voice to the Lord's proclamation, unleash God's power into the affairs of rulers and nations? In this "nice little" story, a new office begins to emerge, preparatory to the later emergence of the king: the office of "trustworthy prophet of the LORD" (v. 20), an office that can place a later child "over nations and over kingdoms" (Jer. 1:10) and destine one still later "for the falling and the rising of many in Israel" (Luke 2:34). This is a little story with large implications.

Therefore note the following details:

First, the birth of this office is a cooperative affair. While Eli has failed to pass on faithfulness to his own flesh and blood, he now serves as a spiritual parent for his young charge, Samuel. Though Eli's eyes may be failing him, his knowledge of the Lord, and his experience of the revelation of God's word, are not. It takes both the attentiveness of the young Samuel's ears and the wisdom of the old priest's heart and mind to birth this new office in the service of the Lord. Likewise, it takes both the authority of this failing priest and the obedience of this youthful protégé to bring the Lord's judgment to fruition. Even though this prophecy will bring about the destruction of Eli and his two sons, this elderly priest receives Samuel's words as the trustworthy words of a prophet: "It is the LORD; let him do what seems good to him" (3:18). It takes a community to bear such a task.

Second, this is a "vision" of words and hearing alone. While the kings who will follow will build great palaces for others to see, and have at their disposal great armies with which to act, the prophet's tools remain twofold: the ears and the lips. This story is started rolling by something as ineffable as a voice in the night: "Samuel! Samuel!" This call leads to a response of audition: "Speak, Lord, for your servant is listening." This reception leads finally to a new act of speaking, this time courageously set loose by the lips of a human: "So Samuel told him everything and hid nothing from him" (3:18). As words of the Lord began this story back in Genesis ("Let there be light"), so words continue this story in 1 Samuel 3. Only this time they are given to a human being to open his mouth and speak in turn. This is no "nice, little story" after all.

Third, it is important to note on this second Sunday after the Epiphany that human speaking and

has told me. That is why our sleep is disturbed. The voice of God troubles us, even when we cannot identify it, and we cannot rest until we know who is calling us and why.

What a funny, biting commentary, that God's voice is so unexpected in the temple! We understand how the place could have become a museum instead of a home for the living God.

Characteristically, Scripture leavens this sorry situation with plenty of Jewish comedy. The Lord calls, "Sam-u-el, Sam-u-el," meaning "God has heard." The boy says, "Here I am!" and runs to the priest Eli (significantly named "my God"), who has not called for him. "God has heard!" God calls again, and again the boy goes to Eli, "my God," rather than his true God.

A third time the Lord says, "God has heard," and at last Eli (truly awake for the first time in many years) instructs the boy to answer, "Speak, LORD, for your servant is listening."

"See," the Lord tells Samuel, "I am about to do something in Israel that will make both ears of anyone who hears of it tingle" (3:11). Now the slapstick comedy crashes into God's seriousness. *Are you listening? Do you hear what I am saying now?*

The news will not be good for Eli, whose sons have disgraced the priestly line and illustrated the need for kings. Because the priests cannot rule, God must anoint a conventional king; and Samuel is to be kingmaker.

God help the boy—and God help us. In local and in national life, clergy and laity alike have long played the role of kingmakers. This has been true in progressive black churches, conservative white churches, Catholic as well as Protestant. The role has not often been to our credit.

At this point in his career, Samuel does not have all the answers, and unlike today's kingmakers, he is not looking for a man to front his own agenda. He is a frankly bewildered boy with questions rather than answers. "Samuel did not yet know the LORD, and the word of the LORD had not yet been revealed to him" (3:7). He needs Eli to help him makes sense of this voice calling in the night.

Eli—the one with the ironic name, the blind man, the disgraced priest who has failed to discipline his sons—is the man who introduces Samuel to God. Eli may be blind in more ways than one, but he has seen enough to be of help. Somewhat like the "whiskey priest" in Graham Greene's *The Power and the Glory,* he is a priest for life, and he does God's work in spite of himself.

# 1 Samuel 3:1-10 (11-20)

## Theological Perspective

Eli could apprehend and appreciate—he also perceives the message that the priesthood of Eli and his family will be destroyed. Yet the message is not directed to be delivered as judgment. Instead, it is announced by God as a means of legitimizing Samuel's authorization of new leadership that Eli's sons had been expected to fulfill.[1] At the time Samuel received the call of God as a revelatory word, vision was "rare" (v. 1), emphasizing the truly remarkable character of God's action and Samuel's reception.

Although there initially might seem to be a conceptual disjunction in the prophetic process, the shift from an oral summons (v. 11) to the report of visual perception of the message (v. 15) does not represent discontinuity. Both the voice and the vision are part of typical prophetic discourse. The point here is that God initiated contact and revealed a change of course in tradition.

*The Justice of God.* A third significant theological theme in this passage begins with Eli's earnest plea and words of warning: "Do not hide it from me. May God do so to you and more also, if you hide anything from me of all that he told you" (v. 17). The new beginning in leadership requires the faithful to face candidly the failures of Eli and his family. For Eli's sons had "treated the offerings of the LORD with contempt" (2:17). And so the new beginning requires an exercise of divine justice, not because of evil acts committed by Eli but because of Eli's aversion to act; Eli had failed to discipline his scoundrel sons for their corruption, which he had recognized and ignored.

The story of Samuel's call establishes his authority, empowering his transfer of priestly leadership from Eli to Saul, and reinforcing hope in God—that God will refresh and renew.

JOSEPH L. PRICE

## Pastoral Perspective

Oddly, the passage assures us that what God is going to do will make both ears tingle. Since I hate sermons that make us have to be more heroic than we really are, I say this. Let one ear tingle with fear. Fear is legitimate under most of the circumstances of most of our lives. Fear is spiritually legitimate. A lot has gone wrong. A lot of danger lurks. But listen now with the other ear. Hear what Samuel was reluctant to hear: God is going to do a new thing, which will make both of our ears tingle. Give the other ear a little exercise. Let it tingle too.

Imagine a world beyond gimmicks, with no gotchas, a world that restores the dash between "noblesse" and "oblige," a world where things are fair, where you are well, where those you love are well, where swords have become art schools and weapons have become warming centers for the elderly.

Imagine a world of enchantment, where you look outside at a child playing on a safe street, where good public transportation pulls up to take you to a good job, where economic obsession is gone and decent salaries replace it. Imagine a world where health is insured and life is insured and you have decent choices at the end to do what is right for you and your family. Imagine hospitals as good as homes and hospices as good as hospitals. Imagine good things and then believe that they are coming. God has plans, already executed in Jesus, to do good things. The way to tingle is to open both of your eyes and look around. Look under the hassock, look back to the Scripture, look forward in hope. Open both of your ears. Soon they will tingle.

DONNA SCHAPER

---

[1]See Walter Brueggemann, *First and Second Samuel*, Interpretation Series (Louisville, KY: John Knox Press, 1990), 25.

## Exegetical Perspective

hearing now become one of the main means by which the light of God's revelation breaks into the affairs of this world. We had seen this work at the individual level earlier in the stories of Moses: "The LORD summoned Moses and spoke to him from the tent of meeting, saying, Speak to the people of Israel" (Lev. 1:1). We will see this happen again at the individual level in the new Moses to come: "You have heard that it was said . . . but I say to you" (Matt. 5:21–22). But here, at this point in the story, when words from the Lord are rare, this listening and hearing becomes a communal affair, dependent on both the hearing and the speaking of the community together. As the stories of Saul and David spin on in 1 and 2 Samuel, there will be times when the Lord seems absent from the scene. All we will hear are words of human beings, on the one hand, counterpoised with actions of human beings, on the other. And yet even here we will learn that the Lord is at work. Indeed the Lord has drawn as near as the words and actions of our fellow human beings, attuned or not attuned to the voice of their God.

The inclusion of Samuel's words of judgment is thus a necessary precaution against the too easy domestication of this story by the church today. The light of God's revelation in Jesus Christ continues to strive to break forth with power into the lives of both Israel and the nations. These are indeed words meant to "pluck up and to pull down, to destroy and to overthrow, to build and to plant" (Jer. 1:10). But they are given birth and revealed in the conversations of older priests and younger disciples, who together are granted the courage both to hear and to speak. By God's grace, may it still be so today.

RICHARD BOYCE

## Homiletical Perspective

The drama deepens in the optional verses (11–20) as God tells Samuel the charges against his beloved teacher. These are the charges against us, the ineffectual priests who have watched our churches slip into trouble. (Or, just as uncomfortably, they are charges against our mentors.) Now Samuel is so troubled that he cannot sleep.

In the morning, Eli calls, "Sam-u-el," and the boy comes to him. Eli wants to hear God's message, however hard the news. And it is indeed hard. With deep affection for his flawed teacher, Samuel tells him everything: God plans to abandon this priestly line. Later, we will hear several different voices and meanings to the words, *Eli, Eli, lama sabachthani,* "My God, my God, why have you forsaken me?"

We would suppose that Samuel, the innocent, is the hero. When called, he readily answers, "Here I am," anticipating by several hundred years Isaiah's response to a heavenly vision. In Calvin's phrase, Samuel is "prompt and sincere in the work of the Lord."

And yet Samuel's own sons will be scoundrels no less than Eli's. In fact, the people will tell Samuel pretty much what they have told Eli: "You are old and your sons do not follow in your ways; appoint for us, then, a king to govern us, like other nations" (1 Sam. 8:5). He will become a kingmaker only after failing as a father.

This comic, tender, tragic story really does come from modern life. In an age of divine reticence and the all-too-human failings of religious leaders, it speaks to every servant weighed down with fatigue or regret. Are we Samuel? Are we Eli? Can we really be sure which? And what shall we do if the living God comes into our troubled temple? It is Eli, ironically enough, who tells us what to say: "Speak, LORD, for your servant is listening."

LAWRENCE WOOD

# Psalm 139:1-6, 13-18

¹O Lᴏʀᴅ, you have searched me and known me.
²You know when I sit down and when I rise up;
   you discern my thoughts from far away.
³You search out my path and my lying down,
   and are acquainted with all my ways.
⁴Even before a word is on my tongue,
   O Lᴏʀᴅ, you know it completely.
⁵You hem me in, behind and before,
   and lay your hand upon me.
⁶Such knowledge is too wonderful for me;
   it is so high that I cannot attain it. . . .
. . . . . . . . . . . . . . . . . . . . . . . . . . . . . . . . . . . .
¹³For it was you who formed my inward parts;
   you knit me together in my mother's womb.

## Theological Perspective

Speaking about God tends to tie theologians up in tense knots of contradiction. God is transcendent but also immanent, just but also gracious, omnipotent but also personal. The wonder of this cherished psalm is that it knits these complex threads of God's nature together into the single garment of divine providence. This essay explores the psalmist's interrelated vision of God and human selfhood.

Greek philosophical categories have done a disservice to Christian theology by conceiving God as superlative, unchanging perfection. They present an aloof, static God far removed from the cares and affairs of finite human beings. The psalmist, on the other hand, offers a Jewish vision of God as intimately involved and profoundly concerned as well as transcendent.

In fact, for the psalmist, intimacy with God is a function of God's ultimacy. Only because God is universally present, ultimately powerful, and all-knowing does the psalmist have such a profound sense of an immediate and personal relationship with God. Because God is at the farthest reaches of the universe and in the most secret depths of the human heart, God is the constant companion, who cannot be escaped, fooled, or ignored. "You hem me in, behind and before, and lay your hand upon me" (v. 5).

## Pastoral Perspective

According to the late Dr. John Leith, at the heart of the Reformed tradition is the conviction that "every human being has every moment to do with the *living* God."[1] That conviction is distinctly but not uniquely Reformed. In one form or another it is shared by virtually all Christian traditions. God is the encompassing reality in whom all that is "lives and moves and has its being." The psalmist insists that whether we are aware of God or not, we are known completely by the God to whom, as the Book of Common Prayer puts it, "all hearts are open, all desires known, and from whom no secrets are hid."[2]

The verses chosen for this lection (vv. 1–6, 13–18) focus on God's comprehensive knowledge of the human self. Other sections of the psalm (vv. 7–12) offer occasion for reflection on the inescapable presence of the living God, the "Hound of Heaven" (Francis Thompson), from whom we can flee but never escape. Here, however, the psalmist addresses in prayer the God who knows our every thought, word, and deed before they are uttered or performed.

The psalmist insists that before we know or name God, God knows and names us. It is a theme of great pastoral significance that echoes throughout

[1] John H. Leith, *Introduction to the Reformed Tradition* (Atlanta: John Knox Press, 1977), 67.
[2] *Book of Common Prayer* (New York: Seabury Press, 1979), 323.

<sup>14</sup>I praise you, for I am fearfully and wonderfully made.
   Wonderful are your works;
   that I know very well.
<sup>15</sup>My frame was not hidden from you,
   when I was being made in secret,
      intricately woven in the depths of the earth.
<sup>16</sup>Your eyes beheld my unformed substance.
   In your book were written
      all the days that were formed for me,
      when none of them as yet existed.
<sup>17</sup>How weighty to me are your thoughts, O God!
   How vast is the sum of them!
<sup>18</sup>I try to count them—they are more than the sand;
   I come to the end—I am still with you.

## Exegetical Perspective

Psalm 139 speaks of the relationship between the psalmist and God in terms of knowledge. God *knows* the psalmist through and through—his innermost thoughts, his every action, the meditations of his heart. Every aspect of the psalmist's existence is encompassed by God. The psalmist *knows* only that God's works are wonderful (v. 14). But God's ways remain incomprehensible to him (vv. 6, 17–18). Yet despite the mystery and the vast difference between them, the psalmist ultimately experiences God's presence and knowledge as pastoral (vv. 23–24).

The psalm is divided into two distinct parts. The first part, verses 1–18, is a hymn in praise of God's intimate knowledge and involvement in the psalmist's life. Almost every verse contains pronouns referring both to the psalmist (I/me/my) and to God (you/your). They are intertwined in such a way that God is the very context of the psalmist's life—indeed, of all human existence. The hymn has three stanzas. Verses 1–6 declare that God knows everything the psalmist thinks and does. Verses 7–12 acknowledge that God is present with him everywhere he might go. Verses 13–18 affirm that God has been present and actively involved with him from the very beginning, as his creator.

The second part of the psalm, verses 19–24, is a prayer for God to deal with wickedness. In verses

## Homiletical Perspective

As Americans we revere our privacy. We want our privacy protected at all costs. And when someone infringes on it, we are incensed. When we fall victim to identity theft, we feel our privacy deeply violated. We guard the information about ourselves we share with others. We take great care in revealing who we really are, sometimes even to our closest friends and family members. At the same time we possess a deep desire for another to truly know and understand us. A sermon on this psalm might explore this tension between protecting privacy and sharing ourselves with others. One of the themes this psalm develops is that, contrary to all our efforts to protect ourselves, God invades our privacy and knows us better than we know ourselves.

The psalm, however, contains ambiguity about God's knowledge of us. On the one hand, God's knowledge is a source of comfort for those who long for God's discipline in their lives (v. 23). On the other hand, God's knowledge is a source of discomfort for those who wish to keep their comfortable lives intact, who desire to be left alone (v. 3; the term "search out" carries with it a nuance of judgment). Thus the psalm comforts the afflicted and afflicts the comfortable. Human attitude toward God's knowledge remains ambivalent.

God knows us, however, better than we know ourselves. One key term in the psalm is the word

# Psalm 139:1-6, 13-18

## Theological Perspective

God's unyielding presence could be experienced as claustrophobic and threatening. The psalmist's opening line—"O LORD, you have searched me and known me" (v. 1)—concedes that judgment looms in God's intimate ultimacy. As Jonah found, to his dismay, it is easier to delude oneself than elude God. God's ultimate, transcendent power over us, God's immanent, intimate relationship with us, and God's absolute, accurate judgment of us are inescapably entwined.

Yet the general spirit of the psalm is not fear but trust, not guilt but praise, not judgment but grace. The psalmist reflects on his utter dependence upon God and finds it comforting as well as demanding. God "knit" and "wove" the psalmist together in "secret," in "the depths of the earth." God's intimate, loving attention (vv. 13–16) is reminiscent of Genesis 2:7, where God molds the human from dust with God's own hands and breathes God's own breath into the creature's nostrils. God's personal care makes even a mother's physical familiarity and loving nurture seem distant and reserved.

God's providence includes the psalmist's end as well as his origin. All the psalmist's days are recorded in God's book (v. 16). Nothing can befall him that is not included in God's loving providence. In a similar mind-set, the psalmist writes, "I come to the end"— whether the conclusion of endless reflection on God's goodness or of his own life—"I am still with you" (v. 18). The psalmist trusts that no extremity, whatever it is, can separate him from the loving presence of God. Wherever he goes, whatever becomes of him, God is there. This trust is echoed in Paul's comforting words to the beleaguered Christians in Rome: "For I am convinced that neither death, nor life, nor angels, nor rulers, nor things present, nor things to come, nor powers, nor height, nor depth, nor anything else in all creation, will be able to separate us from the love of God in Christ Jesus our Lord" (Rom. 8:38–39).

God is transcendent enough to overcome any earthly power, immanent enough to be present in the midst of whatever happens, and gracious enough to care about the destiny of each of God's creatures. In this beautiful and moving meditation on God's presence in his life, the psalmist captures the fundamental message of the gospel and unites the disparate features of the doctrine of God.

John Calvin opens his *Institutes of the Christian Religion* with these words: "Nearly all the wisdom we possess, that is to say, true and sound wisdom, consists of two parts: the knowledge of God and of

## Pastoral Perspective

Scripture. "Before I formed you in the womb I knew you, and before you were born I consecrated you" (Jer. 1:5a). Our knowledge of God is derivative of God's knowledge of us. The psalmist addresses and invites us to trust the God whose sovereign grace encompasses us in ways we can never fully comprehend. "Such knowledge is too wonderful for me; it is so high that I cannot attain it" (v. 6).

In a time when the worth of human life has been vastly cheapened, the psalmist affirms God's supreme valuing of the human. The psalm invites the preacher to reflect on the sanctity of life, not as a political slogan or wedge issue, but as an expression of the worth God gives to the work of God's hands. In reflecting on the psalm, the preacher can encourage a congregation to wrestle with what a consistent "ethic of life" would entail.

In Psalm 139 the work of God the creator is not only cosmic—it is inescapably personal. Six times in the first six verses the psalmist addresses God as "You." "It was you who formed my inward parts; you knit me together in my mother's womb" (v. 13). As the thoroughly known creation of God, humans have both an identity and a value that endure. The NRSV says, "I praise you, for I am fearfully and wonderfully made" (v. 14). The RSV takes a different tack. "I praise thee, for thou art fearful and wonderful." Both affirmations are true, and they need to be held together—the wonder of God, our creator, and the wonder of our creation as the "intricately woven" handiwork of God.

The question of identity, "Who am I?" is particularly urgent in our time. It is not only teenagers who struggle with a sense of identity. It is the parent whose children are all away from home for the first time. It is the retiree who has nowhere to go in the morning. It is the caregiver whose spouse has died after a long illness. It is the man or woman struggling with issues of sexual identity. One way or another, at one time or another, we all ask, "Who am I? Where do the meaning and value of my life come from?"

One who asked the question in a way that resonates clearly with the words of the psalmist was Dietrich Bonhoeffer. In his poem "Who Am I?" written in the Tegel prison shortly before his execution by the Nazis, Bonhoeffer contrasted what others said of him with what he knew of himself. He ends the poem by asking, "Who am I? They mock me, these lonely questions of mine. Whoever I am, thou knowest, O [God], I am thine."[3]

[3] Dietrich Bonhoeffer, *Letters and Papers from Prison: The Enlarged Edition*, ed. Eberhard Bethge (New York: Collier Books, 1977), 347–48.

19–22, the psalmist prays for God's ultimate judgment (death) against the wicked in the world, who are enemies of God. In verses 23–24, the psalmist asks God to search for any wicked ways in him and to guide him "in the way everlasting" (v. 24). This final prayer, "Search me, O God, and know my heart; test me and know my thoughts" (v. 23), echoes the opening affirmation of the psalm, "O LORD, you have searched me and known me," and ties the two parts of the psalm together.

The lectionary reading includes only the first and third stanzas of the psalm's hymn of praise (vv. 1–6 and 13–18). The two sections that are omitted from the reading (vv. 7–12 and 19–24) contain what might be viewed as the "difficult" parts of the psalm. In the middle stanza of the hymn (vv. 7–12), the psalmist affirms God's presence wherever he goes. However, he does so by raising the question, "How can I escape from you?" (see v. 7)—perhaps not the most faithful sentiment for God's people to express. The psalmist's prayer for God to kill the wicked (vv. 19–22) is even more fraught with difficulty for Christian sensibilities. We seem to feel that it is inappropriate to pray such a prayer. Nevertheless, the prayer for God to deal with wickedness—in other people as well as in the psalmist—is a reminder that God's divine knowing of human beings does not eliminate human responsibility for obedience to God's will. And it is not a passive knowledge on God's part, but rather a knowing that results in God's active intervention in human life—both to judge and to redirect our paths.

The two hymn stanzas remaining in the lectionary reading focus our attention on the contrast between God's all-encompassing knowledge of human beings and our very limited ability to know and comprehend God. In verses 1–4, God is the subject of the verb "know" and synonyms ("search," "discern," "be acquainted with") seven times. The object of God's knowing is the psalmist—his every action and thought. By contrast, the stanza ends with the psalmist stating that "such knowledge" is too wonderful and too high for him to comprehend (v. 6).

In the third stanza, the psalmist affirms God as his creator, the one who "formed" him and "knit" him together (v. 13). He was known by God even then—both his beginning and all the days of his life (vv. 15–16). Yet when the psalmist tries to meditate on God's thoughts, he is overwhelmed by the weight and number of them (vv. 17–18). The only things that the psalmist can know and comprehend about God are that God's works are wonderful (v. 14—cf. God's knowledge in v. 6), and that when his

"know" or "knowledge" (vv. 1, 2, 4, 6, 14, 23[2x]). A sermon on this psalm could investigate this theme. God knows the psalmist inside out because God knit the psalmist's innermost parts. God's knowledge penetrates time and space, light and dark (vv. 13–18). God knows the psalmist before birth (v. 13) and after death (v. 18).

To expand this theme, the sermon could explore what it means to know and be known by others. One might consider the genre of literature and movies devoted to individuals who attempt to trade places or spaces or bodies with another. For example, in a recent movie, a wife switches bodies with her husband; she becomes a professional football player, and he becomes a housewife. A mother and daughter switch bodies (*Freaky Friday*). A wealthy and a poor person exchange places of social status (*Trading Places*). One of our deepest desires is to get past the façade, to be understood, and to experience empathy with another person.

Because of human limitations and selfishness, however, we cannot fully understand another person, nor can they understand us. That is where this psalmist derives comfort. Knowing that God knows the psalmist better than she knows herself is the greatest of all comforts (vv. 4, 6).

As a preacher investigates this theme, it is important to understand the role the incarnation plays in God's knowledge of humans. God did not send Jesus in order to know what it was like to be human. Rather, because God *already knew* what it was like to be human, God sent Jesus. This psalmist declares that God knew every facet of our being, our frame, and our innermost parts (obviously long before the time of Christ). God has always known what it was like to be human. God's incarnation is primarily for our benefit, not God's.

This psalm serves as a tremendous source of comfort to all humans. The words of the psalm, however, provide special consolation to those suffering the loss of a loved one or experiencing pain or persecution or battling a terminal illness. Those, for example, combating a life-threatening illness often struggle with the feeling of aloneness, even in the midst of strong family support. No one can fully understand what she or he is going through.

Jesus struggled with the feeling of aloneness when he suffered on the cross. He cried out, "My God, my God, why have you forsaken me?" (Matt. 27:46; quoted from Ps. 22:1). It was Christ's honest expression of feeling abandoned by God. One explanation given for this cry is that Jesus carried the

# Psalm 139:1-6, 13-18

## Theological Perspective

ourselves. But, while joined by many bonds, which one precedes and brings forth the other is not easy to discern."[1] God and self are so intimately related that genuine knowledge of one entails the other.

The bonds that join God and self together are captured in the answer to the first question of the Heidelberg Catechism, "What is your only comfort in life and in death?"

> That I belong—body and soul, in life and in death—not to myself but to my faithful Savior, Jesus Christ, who at the cost of his blood has fully paid for all my sins and has completely freed me from the dominion of the devil; that he protects me so well that without the will of my Father in heaven not a hair can fall from my head; indeed, that everything must fit his purpose for my salvation. Therefore, by his Holy Spirit, he also assures me of eternal life, and makes me wholeheartedly willing and ready from now on to live for him.[2]

The conviction that human beings are autonomous, self-determining individuals is an illusion produced by pride. Human destiny is in the hands of a gracious God. Therefore genuine selfhood includes trusting dependence on God and grateful responsibility to God.

According to H. Richard Niebuhr, the prominent twentieth-century American theologian, the unity of the self depends upon an ultimate unity behind all things. "In religious language, the soul and God belong together; or otherwise stated, I am one within myself as I encounter the One in all actions upon me. . . . And my response to every particular action takes the form of a response to the One that is active in it."[3] A human being is a singular self in the midst of all her various roles and responsibilities only to the extent that she is responding through all of them to a unified power and presence in them. The unity of self and the universality of God go hand in hand. We are singular selves only as we live in trusting dependence upon the gracious One and as we respond in grateful joy to this One in all of our many actions and relationships.

TIMOTHY A. BEACH-VERHEY

## Pastoral Perspective

At the opposite extreme, among the saddest words in American literature are those spoken by Biff Loman at his father's grave. "He had all the wrong dreams, all, all wrong. He never knew who he was."[4] Yet even we, who do not know who we are, are nevertheless fully known and eternally loved by the Lord to whom alone we belong "body and soul, in life and death."[5]

Psalm 139 invites us to receive an identity rooted not in the things we say about ourselves or the labels others assign us, but in the One who knows us more deeply and more lovingly than we could ever know ourselves. Perhaps Paul had the words of Psalm 139 in mind when he wrote, "Now we see in a mirror, dimly, but then we will see face to face. Now I know only in part; then I will know fully, even as I have been fully known" (1 Cor. 13:12).

A second, equally important pastoral implication flows from our identity in God. Because the God who knows us thoroughly loves us fully, our lives have a worth that cannot be taken from us—by others or ourselves. The value of our lives does not come from what we achieve or possess or what others may think of us. It comes from the God who knows and names us, from whose steadfast love nothing in all creation can ever separate us.

The task of the preacher is to lift up the psalmist's affirmation of the worth of life in God in the face of the countless devaluations of human life all around us. The entertainment industry, which nurtures and shapes us in ways we barely perceive, often treats the human self in degrading ways. One of the challenges of the pastor is to lift up books, films, or dramas that affirm human identity and value in ways that are consistent with the witness of the psalmist and Scripture as a whole.

ALLEN C. MCSWEEN JR.

---

[1] John Calvin, *The Institutes of the Christian Religion*, 2 vols., ed. John T. McNeill, trans. Ford Lewis Battles, LCC (Philadelphia: Westminster Press, 1960), 1.1.1.

[2] *The Book of Confessions* (Louisville, KY: Office of the General Assembly, Presbyterian Church (U.S.A.), 1999), 29.

[3] H. Richard Niebuhr, *The Responsible Self: An Essay in Christian Moral Philosophy* (New York: HarperCollins Publishers, 1963), 122–23.

[4] Arthur Miller, *Death of a Salesman* (New York: Penguin Books, 1949), 110–11.

[5] Heidelberg Catechism, in *The Book of Confessions* (Louisville, KY: Office of the General Assembly, 1999), 29.

comprehension of God fails, God is still present with him (v. 18).

The difference between creator and creature, between God and human beings, is ultimately too great for us to fathom. Yet perhaps it is enough for us to know that God knows us—intimately and completely—and that we live our lives from beginning to end surrounded by God's discerning presence.

Psalm 139 finds echoes in each of the other lectionary texts. The Old Testament reading, 1 Sam. 3:1–10 (11–20), narrates the call of the young boy, Samuel, whose very conception and birth were the answer to his mother Hannah's prayer, and whom she dedicated from birth to serve God (see 1 Sam. 1). In chapter 3, God called Samuel to be God's prophet. Even beyond that night in the temple, God's active involvement and guidance in Samuel's life continued: "As Samuel grew up, the LORD was with him and let none of his words fall to the ground" (3:19).

In the epistle reading, 1 Cor. 6:12–20, Paul urges the Corinthian Christians to avoid fornication by reminding them that even their bodies are "members of Christ" (v. 15) and "temple[s] of the Holy Spirit within you" (v. 19). They belong not to themselves but to God, who in Christ has redeemed them ("you were bought with a price," v. 20). In sum, they have no existence apart from the purpose and presence of God.

In the Gospel reading, John 1:43–51, Nathanael is astounded by Jesus' knowledge of him before they have even met—so astounded that he declares, "Rabbi, you are the Son of God! You are the King of Israel!" (v. 49). Nathanael's response to Jesus' knowledge makes theological sense only in light of Psalm 139. Only God could have such knowledge. That Jesus possesses such knowledge leads to one conclusion: that Jesus is the Son of God.

MARSHA M. WILFONG

sins of the world on his shoulders and that God, who abhors sin, therefore had to turn away and leave Jesus to suffer alone for a time. Such an explanation is theologically absurd. Though Jesus experienced feeling abandoned, in reality God never abandoned Jesus during his darkest hour. Jesus, quoting Psalm 22, knew the whole psalm and also knew that midway in that prayer the psalmist announces with confidence, "For he did not despise or abhor the affliction of the afflicted; he did not hide his face from me, but heard when I cried to him" (22:24). God did not abandon Jesus on the cross, even for a moment! As Psalm 139 says, "even the darkness is not dark to you" (v. 12). William Brown fittingly observes, "There are no moments, distant and dark though they might be, in which God is absent. There are no traumas in which the psalmist does not own God's mercies."[1] Others may not understand the pain, the hurt, the abandonment, the rejection, and the loneliness, but God does.

The psalmist concludes by requesting that God invade his or her private life: "Search me . . . and know my heart; test me and know my thoughts" (139:23). The psalmist no longer remains ambiguous about God's involvement but invites God to intrude. The psalmist now understands God's intrusion not as a threat but as an act of grace. Again as Brown observes, despite all of our vigorous efforts to protect our privacy "there is someone who will always intrude, not like some unwanted guest, but as judge, advocate, friend, and savior, one who knows us better than we know ourselves and one who claims us in compassion."[2] The one who knows me intimately and knitted me together before I was born is the one who says, "I am still with you" (v. 18). And one day we can proclaim with Paul, "For now we see in a mirror, dimly, but then we will see face to face. Now I know only in part; then I will know fully, even as I have been fully known" (1 Cor. 13:12).

DAVE BLAND

---

[1] William Brown, "Psalm 139: The Pathos of Praise," *Interpretation* 50, no. 3 (1996): 283.
[2] Ibid., 284.

# 1 Corinthians 6:12-20

¹²"All things are lawful for me," but not all things are beneficial. "All things are lawful for me," but I will not be dominated by anything. ¹³"Food is meant for the stomach and the stomach for food," and God will destroy both one and the other. The body is meant not for fornication but for the Lord, and the Lord for the body. ¹⁴And God raised the Lord and will also raise us by his power. ¹⁵Do you not know that your bodies are members of Christ? Should I therefore take the members of Christ and make them members of a prostitute? Never! ¹⁶Do you not know that whoever is united to a prostitute becomes one body with her? For it is said, "The two shall be one flesh." ¹⁷But anyone united to the Lord becomes one spirit with him. ¹⁸Shun fornication! Every sin that a person commits is outside the body; but the fornicator sins against the body itself. ¹⁹Or do you not know that your body is a temple of the Holy Spirit within you, which you have from God, and that you are not your own? ²⁰For you were bought with a price; therefore glorify God in your body.

## Theological Perspective

The reading is set within the same instructions for faithful living that 1 Corinthians 7:29–31 (the epistle reading next Sunday) is, and comments on the two passages should be read together. The broader instructions address everything from a man "living with his father's wife" (5:1) and why Christians should settle disputes without recourse to Roman courts (6:1–8), to questions about marriages to nonbelievers (7:12–16) and eating food sacrificed to idols (8:1–13). There is a persistent concern with sexual morality, for example, conjugal rights in marriage and whether the unmarried should remain single (7:3–9). Our passage itself comments on visiting prostitutes and fornication, but largely as an occasion to present a thicket of more general arguments.

"All things are lawful for me" (6:12). Paul may not entirely disagree. In Christ we are put into right relationship with God by grace. This is the free gift (Rom. 5:15), the basis for Christian freedom—for the fact is that our standing before God does not depend on satisfying the law. Nevertheless, says Paul, "not all things are beneficial" (1 Cor. 6:12; cf. 10:23). What's more, if I am truly free, then I will not be dominated or enslaved by anything (6:12).

How shall we determine which things benefit and which dominate? We can try to determine what

## Pastoral Perspective

From a pastoral perspective, this text offers rich, complicated, and highly relevant material upon which to preach. The text addresses questions of sexual ethics within the Christian community in first-century Corinth, and also speaks to issues of sexual morality in our own churches today. The matters that Paul was addressing in this passage are closely analogous to those of our current cultural and ecclesial situation.

Our culture has an ambivalent relationship to the body. On one hand we glorify the body, and much energy goes into tending and beautifying it. This very energy, however, suggests that on a deeper level there is shame of the body, since it has to be constantly improved and worked on. Likewise the church, perhaps inheriting some of the body-spirit dualism held by the Corinthians, is at best squeamish or embarrassed about the body. Regarding sex, both culture and church are lacking in insight. Cultural forces tend to sexualize all aspects of our lives, while at the same time inculcating a certain prudishness regarding sex. The churches struggle to find a theologically and pastorally coherent way of addressing this cultural situation, and tend either to avoid altogether teaching about sexual morality, or to make rigid rules that are not beneficial to Christians. These

## Exegetical Perspective

First Corinthians is a letter Paul wrote to the Corinthian church while he was staying in Ephesus (1 Cor. 16:8). Unlike 2 Corinthians, which reflects a severe conflict between Paul and his opponents in the Corinthian church, 1 Corinthians presents Paul as someone who is quite confident about his pastoral authority in his former church. The present passage is located at the end of the first half of the epistle, which deals with the issues reported by Chloe's people (1:10–6:20). In the second half Paul addresses the questions raised in a letter sent him by the Corinthian church (7:1–15:58). In this first half Paul gives his pastoral admonition concerning what he regards as a troubled congregation on four specific problems: factionalism (1:11–4:21), incest (5:1–13), litigation at a civic court (6:1–11), and freedom and fornication (6:12–20).

The present passage registers Paul's disagreement with a philosophical position about human freedom that was apparently advocated by some members of the Corinthian church and served as a theoretical basis for going to prostitutes freely. The first clause of verse12, "All things are allowed for me" (my translation), is most probably a slogan used by the Corinthians. Paul cites it here and later in 10:23, in only partial agreement and in strong refutation of its application. The impersonal verb *exesti(n)* denotes a

## Homiletical Perspective

This text is a classic example of Scripture that poses two hazards for the sermon: moralistic preaching and, for lack of a better term, "deadly dull doctrinal preaching." Doctrinal preaching in its true form is much needed by the church today—but not if you ask the average church member. Doctrinal preaching has always been noted as difficult preaching. For listeners, and sometimes for the preacher also, there is the sense of, "Well, it's that certain Sunday, this certain doctrine has to be preached on, like it or not!" If doctrinal preaching is deadly dull, it is because it has been excised from its living situation, labeled, laid out on the examination table, and tediously lectured on by someone trying not to fall asleep before the audience does.

Moralistic preaching, since the time of the Puritans in this country, has single-handedly given preaching a bad name. Try to think of any positive idiom using the word "preach." ("Don't preach at me," "At that point the novelist began preaching at us," etc.) Furthermore, modern moralistic preaching has done exactly what its ancient counterpart among the Puritans did—turn the children against the church and produce generations of skeptics. The children of the Puritans turned against the faith of their parents, spurred on, in part, by the Puritan divines themselves who encouraged them to spy on

# 1 Corinthians 6:12-20

## Theological Perspective

things are meant for. Thus, food is meant for the stomach and the stomach for food. But food and stomach are material things that pass away; God will destroy them both. The body is different because "the body is meant . . . for the Lord, and the Lord for the body" (6:13b). In fact, our bodies (and indeed our selves) are members of Christ (v. 15a) that will not be destroyed but will be raised as Christ was. (Remember that, for Paul, our resurrected body is not flesh and blood, as the stomach and food are, but spiritual [1 Cor. 15:35–53].) Members of Christ should not be joined with a prostitute. Moreover, this does not correspond to what our bodies are meant for, namely imperishable life in God's kingdom.

Again, "anyone united to the Lord becomes one spirit with him" (v. 17). His body therefore becomes "a temple of the Holy Spirit" (v. 19) that is not to be defiled. Moreover, "you are not your own," but "were bought with a price," that is, Christ's cross. "Therefore glorify God in your body" (19–20). Now if glorifying God is what we are for, then it becomes a criterion. Activities that do not glorify God skew life. They indicate that we are not oriented toward what we are meant for, but are captivated by another object.

A definite eschatological current runs through 1 Corinthians. Paul thought Jesus would soon return, and that many of Paul's hearers would be living when he did (1 Thess. 4:13–18). But Paul was wrong about the Lord's return, and the world did not end on anything like the schedule Paul expected. How does this affect the continuing validity of his ethic?

Albert Schweitzer claimed Jesus' ethic—Sell all that you have and give it to the poor; Do not resist evil—was too radical for regular life in history and society, where we necessarily produce goods, build institutions, and plan ahead. It was appropriate only for an interim just before the end. Did Paul instruct people as he did only because he thought the time was short? Is his advice therefore now out of place?

Surely some of it is, for example, Paul's opinion that "in view of the impending crisis" (7:26) it is better for those who are married, single, and virgins simply to remain so. We generally don't dispense this kind of advice, although we might endorse some of Paul's other views, for example, about the mutual conjugal rights of husband and wife (7:1–6). Interestingly, however, the arguments presented in our particular passage, 1 Corinthians 6:12–20, do not depend especially on Paul's imminent eschatological expectation.

This is why the sixteenth-century Protestant John Calvin, who did *not* think the time especially short,

## Pastoral Perspective

rules oversimplify the complexity of human sexuality and thus do not help Christians discern how to exercise morality in this domain of their personhood. Rather than offering slogans, the church needs to provide rigorous theological reflection to Christians seeking to live faithfully as sexual beings.

Paul's teaching to the Corinthians offers this much-needed reflection, in that he places questions of sexual ethics within a larger theological framework. In this passage, as elsewhere in the First Letter to the Corinthians, Paul articulates the nature of Christian freedom. The Corinthians believed that their freedom as Christians, their possession of the Holy Spirit, meant that they were free of all rules governing their behavior. The phrase "all things are lawful for me" had become their slogan, used to justify all kinds of behavior, including sexual libertinism. Paul countered this position by teaching them that as Christians their freedom came from belonging to Christ, and thus "you are not your own."

The freedom that comes from this "slavery" is a freedom to follow God and to love one's fellow believers. The gift of the Holy Spirit, which makes people into believers and helps them to live as such, is to be used for building up the Christian community. Paul's ethical framework is foreign to our contemporary culture. Like the Corinthians, we tend to answer ethical questions in terms of "rights," according to what is "lawful." This language of "rights" presupposes individual autonomy, but belonging to Christ means we should orient our behavior toward glorifying God. What glorifies God, according to Paul, is what is "beneficial," not principally to ourselves, but to the Christian communities of which we are part.

Within this definition of Christian freedom, Paul insists that belonging to Christ includes the body as well as the spirit, and thus has implications for sexual behavior; sexual actions are among those that give glory or dishonor to God. The Corinthians' dualistic notion that God would destroy the body but save the spirit led them to believe that sexual behavior could not count as sin. Paul reminds the Corinthians that just as Christ was raised in the body, so too the body of the believer, as a "member of Christ," will be raised at the end time. This means that what people do with their bodies does matter in an eternal sense.

Moreover, Paul interprets being "members of Christ" in a radical way, arguing that this membership is a union with Christ that is analogous to sexual union. Our bodies are not our own but are

person's ability or an action/object not being prohibited. Since the subject of our sentence is *panta*, which is a substantive use of an indefinite pronominal adjective *pas* in the neuter plural nominative case, the latter meaning is more appropriate. Hence the connotation is, "I am free to do whatever I want."

Freedom (*eleutheria*) had long been valued highly throughout Greek antiquity. It is depicted in the funeral oration of Pericles as a characteristic of Athenian democracy that can be duly boasted of (Thucydides, *Hist.* 2.37). A saying of Socrates cited in Xenophon calls it a great asset both for an individual and for a state.[1] A more immediate background for the statement in 1 Corinthians 6:12 is found in the Stoic-Cynic ideal of a true philosopher as a free person (*eleutheros*) who lives as he wills.[2]

Paul himself cherishes the notion of the freedom (*eleutheria*) in Christ Jesus (Gal. 2:4; 5:1; 1 Cor. 9:1, 19). He might even have preached the same notion to the Corinthian church while he stayed there. Now he judges that they interpreted the meaning of freedom in a completely wrong way. By adding two exegetical remarks to the Corinthian slogan, Paul is trying to correct their libertine view. The first interpretive clause, "but not all things are beneficial" (v. 12), implies that for Paul the principle of behavioral ethics is not what is permitted but what is beneficial, especially for the community (cf. 12:7). The second interpretive clause, "but I will not be dominated by anything" (v. 12), intimates a Pauline notion that freedom, if misused, can lead into slavery to desire, which is also attested in Galatians 5:1, 13. Paul's logic here bears resemblance to the saying of Socrates cited by Xenophon: "As for the one who is ruled by bodily pleasures and is therefore not able to do what is best, do you suppose such a person to be free?" "Not at all!"[3]

Since there was no device for marking quotations in ancient manuscript, it is very difficult to distinguish between citations of the positions of the Corinthians and Paul's critique of them in verse 13, and there is no agreement among commentators. It seems most probable that the first half of verse 13 is the Corinthian position, while the second half of verse 13 and the entire verse 14 are Paul's own. That is, the Corinthians suppose they can do anything they want with their body, because they believed that God will eventually destroy both the body and what

[1] *Memorabilia* 4.5.2.
[2] Epictetus *Discourses* 4.1.1.
[3] *Memorabilia* 4.5.3.

their parents and uncover their hypocrisies. They were urged to "turn informer" and root out hidden sin. Of course, those children also turned against the hypocritical divines and the church. By the time of the founding of this country, the descendants of the Puritans were avoiding church in droves and fully embracing rationalism.

If people do not come to church to find out what really happened to the Jebusites, in Fosdick's famous phrase, or to the Corinthians, they do come for a living word for their living situation. Remember that all Scripture derives from some life situation. That is certainly the case here. Paul is once again forced to rehearse certain matters with his "problem child," the Corinthian church. First, he confronts the issue of Christian freedom versus responsibility. Second, he presents the reality of the believer's union with Christ and its implications for daily living. With regard to the local matters that prompted these remarks, Paul cites again issues pertaining to the body, food, and sexual relations. Archaeological evidence from the ancient city of Corinth gives us insight into the context of these matters for addressing this text to contemporary Christians.

Briefly, Corinth has been known in history as a licentious city. No doubt, as a seaport city it had its share of prostitutes. But most of its reputation derived from Athens, its bitter rival, which loved nothing better than to cast Corinth in the worst possible light (as if Athens had no prostitutes!). The temple on the Acrocorinth in which a thousand prostitutes supposedly plied their trade was so small as to make the claim ludicrous. Nevertheless, the temptations for licentiousness were certainly plentiful in the city. Corinth also had a healing center, a temple to Asclepius, which also functioned as the city's country club. With a swimming pool, dining facilities, and a garden setting just on the edge of town, this Asclepion was used by the gentry for elegant dinners at which meat offered to idols would often be served and to which, no doubt, some Christians would be invited. With the ferocious social climbing and status consciousness of the Corinthians, passing up such an invitation would be difficult even for the most dedicated Christian.

Now, having placed the parts of the text back into its living body, its context, we are ready to begin the sermon process.

Though our congregants do not live in Corinth, they do live in places not unlike it in many ways. Of course, they still struggle against the "tempta-tions of the flesh" perhaps at least as much as the

# 1 Corinthians 6:12-20

## Theological Perspective

was able to make famous use of a phrase from our passage in order to summarize his own understanding of faithful living. Calvin noted that, for Paul, we are "to present [our] bodies to God as a living sacrifice" (Rom. 12:1). We understand ourselves to be before God and responsible to God. This is why we should be transformed in our minds rather than simply conformed to the fashion and concerns of this world. This is why we ultimately should be oriented to God and God's glory rather than simply to the many mundane pleasures, rewards, and goods. Then Calvin wrote

> We are not our own: let not our reason nor our will therefore sway our plans and deeds. We are not our own: let us therefore not set it as our goal to seek what is expedient for us according to the flesh. We are not our own: in so far as we can let us therefore forget ourselves and all that is ours.
>
> Conversely, we are God's: let us therefore live for him and die for him. We are God's: let his wisdom and will therefore rule all our actions. We are God's: let all the parts of our life accordingly strive toward him as our only lawful goal.[1]

Let me update this. Our lives may be ordered by commitments to many different things: career, wealth, power, reputation, sex, nation, church, tribe, or ethnic group. But we are not meant only for these things. We are not fitted to live only for these things. These things, important as they are, need to be fitted into a broader context. They need to be put into their proper places. Indeed, when we are oriented toward these things alone, when our attitude and disposition is not adjusted by an appreciation for and loyalty to some greater and grander reality, we become skewed and enslaved. Then we do things that are neither beneficial nor helpful.

If Calvin was right, then our passage makes an enduring point. Our lives are appropriately ordered when they are oriented by devotion to a good that extends beyond our designs and indeed beyond both our control and our complete comprehension. Human life is well ordered when it is oriented toward the larger reality of God and God's glory.

DOUGLAS F. OTTATI

## Pastoral Perspective

a gift from God and a part of Christ's body; thus, to commit sexual immorality is essentially to defile Christ's own body. This argument not only radicalizes the depth of our connection to Christ, but insists that sexual acts are powerful, in that they create a lasting physical and spiritual union with other beings. Sex with a prostitute is wrong, not so much because it contaminates the believer, but because it is sex without spiritual union. Paul urges the Corinthians to remember that because their bodies are united to Christ, the Holy Spirit dwells in them, and their bodies are made sacred "temples" by this indwelling. What they do in their bodies should therefore be oriented toward giving glory to God.

Paul's teachings remind today's churches that the body and sex are good and that what we do with them matters. To be made as physical and sexual beings is to be given a powerful means of finding physical and spiritual union with other beings. However, this goodness and power also give us a profound responsibility to live in our bodies and express our sexuality in ways that glorify God and build up our communities. What might it mean for us to glorify God with our bodies, especially in the expression of our sexuality? What might it mean to think of our bodies as belonging to Christ and of sexual acts as done *with* Christ and *to* Christ?

Among other things, it might mean honoring the gift of our sexuality and recognizing it as integrally connected to our spiritual lives; sexuality is a dimension of our personhood that has the capacity to connect us not only to other human beings but also to God. It might also mean pondering the ways that sexual expression can either build up or undermine Christian community. Paul's touchstone for what benefits the Christian community is what is done in love. Christian love, *agape*, is described in 1 Corinthians 13 as patient, kind, generous, humble, truthful, self-giving. This is the kind of love that builds up the church and that can be the basis for Christian sexual morality in particular.

RUTHANNA B. HOOKE

---

[1] John Calvin, *The Institutes of the Christian Religion* 2 vols., ed. John T. McNeil, trans. Ford Lewis Battles, LCC (Louisville, KY: Westminster John Knox, 1960), 3.7.1.

## Exegetical Perspective

it desires. Paul retorts that God, who raised the Lord, will also raise our bodies; therefore fornication should not be practiced with the body (v. 14). There are three variant readings for the verb "raise" in this verse: *exegeiren* (aorist), *exegeirei* (present), and *exegerei* (future). Even though external evidence is almost equal among them, the future tense, which is adopted by the Nestle-Aland 27th, seems to be the best option according to the internal evidence.

The rest of the passage (vv. 15–20) consists of three rhetorical questions, each beginning with "Do you not know?" and followed by Paul's paraenetic statement. In verse 15 Paul uses the metaphor of the church as the body of Christ, which he will further develop later in chapter 12. This body metaphor lets him identify the bodies (*sōmata*) of the Corinthian Christians as limbs (*melē*) of Christ, which is therefore not to be made limbs (*melē*) of a prostitute. Verse 16 introduces a citation of Genesis 2:24, "The two shall be one flesh," as a basis for the idea that the one united with a prostitute becomes one body with her. Even though in Greek body (*sōma*) and flesh (*sarx*) are two different anthropological categories, Paul seems to use the two synonymously in this passage. In contrast, he uses a different noun, "spirit" (*pneuma*), for the union with Christ in verse 17. For the very reason that Paul is taking body as something that will ultimately be preserved, not destroyed, this choice of word almost anticipates the innovative parlance of Paul, "spiritual body" (*sōma pneumatikon*), in 1 Corinthians 15:44.

In verse 19a Paul reintroduces the idea that a Christian's body is a temple of God, in which the Holy Spirit resides (1 Cor. 3:16) and in verses 19b–20 he also touches on the redemption metaphor, "You are not your own, because you were bought with a price." Then comes the final paraenesis that goes beyond simply shunning fornication: "Therefore, glorify God in your body." For Paul, the body is not just an ephemeral entity inferior to the immortal soul. Rather, it is the locus of the union with Christ in the present life of a Christian. As such, it is what ultimately will be transformed into an eternal form of existence at the eschatological resurrection. Thus the anthropological dualism of the Corinthian church is overcome by a newly conceived Christian anthropological holism of Paul.

EUGENE EUNG-CHUN PARK

## Homiletical Perspective

Corinthians, and compromising one's beliefs to get ahead is certainly as prevalent as ever. A top salesman for a company is expected to provide entertainment for an important client coming to town; he would never sleep with a prostitute himself, but he is expected to "take care of whatever needs" the big customer has. A young teenager, self-conscious and lonely in a new school, desperate to be included, falls prey to any number of body- and life-destroying offers.

The importance of these issues cannot be minimized. But many who resist these particular temptations fall victim to other faith-damaging practices. Individualism in the Western world has created liberty and opportunity. But individualism has been raised to the level of divinity in this country, along with nationalism and the wallet. College students are deeply committed to a laissez-faire life: it may not be your way, but it is my way. Yet is that not also the mantra of the modern church? Are we willing to stand beneath the word of God, to bow down in humility at the feet of the Christ? Are we willing to obey anything beyond our own whims—particularly if something important is involved? Or do we not believe it has nothing to do with our faith and is nobody's business but ours—least of all, the church's?

These notions of individualism are equally deadly to the body of Christ, the church. Perhaps our sermon should focus on the unity of the individual body with Christ, but should it not also direct its attention to the corporate body, the church, the bride of Christ? And is that not, in truth, exactly what Paul is saying to the Corinthians? If the prophets could censure Israel for immorality on the basis of their worship of other gods, do we modern Christians not stand under the same judgment as those who have wedded ourselves to the autonomous, undeniable, all-powerful Self? Then is it not our duty as ministers of the gospel, as it was Paul's, to call our church members back to the true priorities of a Christian, back to their first love?

CLYDE FANT

# John 1:43-51

⁴³The next day Jesus decided to go to Galilee. He found Philip and said to him, "Follow me." ⁴⁴Now Philip was from Bethsaida, the city of Andrew and Peter. ⁴⁵Philip found Nathanael and said to him, "We have found him about whom Moses in the law and also the prophets wrote, Jesus son of Joseph from Nazareth." ⁴⁶Nathanael said to him, "Can anything good come out of Nazareth?" Philip said to him, "Come and see." ⁴⁷When Jesus saw Nathanael coming toward him, he said of him, "Here is truly an Israelite in whom there is no deceit!" ⁴⁸Nathanael asked him, "Where did you get to know me?" Jesus answered, "I saw you under the fig tree before Philip called you." ⁴⁹Nathanael replied, "Rabbi, you are the Son of God! You are the King of Israel!" ⁵⁰Jesus answered, "Do you believe because I told you that I saw you under the fig tree? You will see greater things than these." ⁵¹And he said to him, "Very truly, I tell you, you will see heaven opened and the angels of God ascending and descending upon the Son of Man."

## Theological Perspective

The call of the disciples in John's Gospel is the critical link between the prologue's description of the cosmic Word and the main text's narration of the signs and discourses of the flesh-and-blood Jesus of Nazareth. As such, theologians have perceived it to be a foundation of one of the church's most central affirmations, the doctrine of the incarnation. The passage helps introduce John's foundational theme, that, contrary to all human expectations, God's very own eternal Word is made available to us wayward creatures in the life of a human being from Nazareth, particularly in that life's mysterious coincidence of descent (crucifixion) and ascent (exaltation).

As soon as Jesus appears on the scene, his paradoxical identity is suggested by a striking tension in the text. The passage begins with no obvious indication that Jesus is anything other than an ordinary human. In this initial episode Jesus has performed no miracle, shown no sign, and engaged in no teaching. Jesus has presented no proclamation about the reign of God that could excite the imagination of Philip or anyone else. Philip has no evident reason to find Jesus to be remarkable. Ostensibly he is just Jesus from Nazareth, the son of Joseph. The fact of Jesus' humble and human origins initially causes Nathanael to scoff at Philip's

## Pastoral Perspective

This story begins with Jesus making a decision. "Where shall I go next? O, let's see . . . how about Galilee?" In this instance he was not driven (as in Mark 1:12), nor—apparently—was he led (as in Matt. 4:1), nor did he have to go (as in Matt. 16:21). It is comforting to remember that even Jesus, though utterly Spirit-filled and completely in tune with God's will, had to sort out his options and make his own decisions. God thus honors the gift of individual freedom.

Here the story of Jesus suggests the dilemma we all face in pastoral ministry. On the one hand, in John's Gospel Jesus is chosen by God—like every faithful person, only more so. On the other hand, in John's Gospel Jesus chooses God—like every faithful person, only more so. When we engage in leading worship or in the ministry of evangelism or even in particular acts of social service, we are always enacting both sides of this relationship: Of course we invite people to choose God and the new life that comes in Christ. Of course we know that God has already chosen humankind, through Christ, to be the heirs and recipients of that new life.

Jesus here is deciding not just where to go next but whom to take with him. He is selecting followers. John's Gospel and the Synoptics agree on this crucial point: it is not enough to believe in Jesus.

## Exegetical Perspective

"Can anything good come out of Nazareth?" (John 1:46) The rhetorical question that Nathanael posed to the enthusiastic Philip reflects an important literary and theological motif in the Fourth Gospel. That Gospel presents most of Jesus' contemporaries making the same mistake as did Nathanael in appraising Jesus and his message. They assumed that Jesus' origins could explain who he was. Nathanael's skepticism about the claims made for Jesus by his first followers allowed Jesus to suggest to Nathanael that his first impression was seriously flawed. A similar motif appears in the first lesson (1 Sam. 3:1–10). There the young Samuel at first mistook the voice of the Lord for that of Eli, who then helped Samuel realize who was calling him. Even when confronted by the Divine, it is possible for people to be oblivious to God's presence in their lives.

Nazareth was a village of 200–400 people. Like several other villages in the area, it was economically dependent on the city of Sepphoris, which was the capital of Galilee in the first years of Herod Antipas's reign as tetrarch. The Hebrew Scriptures never mention Nazareth, much less associate it with messianic expectations. Nazareth, then, lent no special status to its inhabitants, so when Philip told Nathanael that Jesus was the one of whom Moses and the prophets wrote, Nathanael concluded that Philip had to be

## Homiletical Perspective

On the second Sunday after Epiphany the church stands between Christology and discipleship, between the wonder of the Word made flesh and the gritty joy of our attempts to respond. The day comes after the feast of the incarnation, after the awe of Epiphany, after the tearing of the heavens in the baptism of the Lord—and before the long haul of discipleship leading up to Lent, when following Jesus will deepen through and toward the cross. John 1:43–51 stands at a similar place in the Fourth Gospel: between the great revelation of the prologue and the stories of signs and wonders (almost) seen by those who try to follow Jesus. The best sermons will grow out of just this spot where Christology and discipleship come together.

John's story of the call of the first disciples (1:35–51) is packed with christological language. The story is not just about John, Peter, Andrew, Philip, and Nathanael. It is first of all about Jesus. Readers catch glimpses of the fullness of Jesus' identity in the bold speech of John, the fumbling words of new disciples, and the mysterious responses of Jesus himself. The text is mostly talk, and the talk teems with christological titles and catchphrases. Jesus is called Lamb of God (v. 36), rabbi (v. 38), Messiah (v. 41), "him about whom Moses in the law and also the prophets wrote" (v. 45), son of Joseph from

# John 1:43-51

## Theological Perspective

invitation to come and see Jesus. The subsequent development of the Gospel of John will continue to reinforce the genuine humanness of Jesus, insisting that Jesus is a real person, who thirsts, gets hungry, sorrows, and dies. Nevertheless, in this passage Jesus the son of Joseph is also hailed as the Son of God and the King of Israel. A wild profusion of messianic titles like these, all suggesting Jesus' unique status and function, abound in John's Gospel. Here Jesus is described as the fulfillment of the hope of Israel, of both the Law and the Prophets, implicitly of the entire Hebrew Scriptures. Nathanael's confession indicates that these titles evocative of divine power apply to the human being from Nazareth. The overwhelming shock is that this person whose earthly origins can be identified, this Jesus, elicits a response appropriate to God.

The application of the titles Son of God and King of Israel to Jesus is justified by his exercise of divine power and royal authority. Such power and authority are evident in his ability to awaken in people a believing response not based on empirical evidence. Philip simply hears the imperative "Follow" and obediently does exactly that. Even more dramatically, Nathanael, with no verbal command from Jesus, comes, sees, hears, and spontaneously follows. Jesus is already exercising royal authority over Philip, Nathanael, and all like them who believe and obey. Theologians from John Calvin to Karl Barth have noted that in this passage the following of Jesus is not the fruit of any individual's deliberation and choice. Here confessing Jesus seems to follow with a certain necessity from merely seeing or hearing him. Calvin, and generations of Reformed theologians after him, would cite this as evidence of the election of certain individuals to fellowship with Christ.[1] Barth, changing the theological idiom, would describe it as the attractive power of a preexisting bond established by God's incarnation in Jesus.[2] In any case, the common theme is that the encounter with Christ is the potent force that propels Philip and Nathanael; it is the sheer presence of Christ that draws them.

Jesus' paradoxical identity is elaborated in these verses in terms of his critical role as the revealer of God. Jesus' call of Philip and Nathanael is not so much a call to mission as it is an invitation to an epiphany. The theme of the person of Jesus as the epiphany of God is suggested by Jesus' reference to

[1] John Calvin, *Commentary on the Gospel according to John*, trans. William Pringle (Edinburgh, 1847), 74–81.
[2] Karl Barth, *Church Dogmatics*, IV/3, trans. G. W. Bromiley (Edinburgh: T. & T. Clark, 1962), 584–86.

## Pastoral Perspective

Discipleship consists in following him (sometimes all the way to the cross: see John 21:18–22).

Jesus finds Philip, and Philip finds Nathanael—our best evangelists are often the most recent converts! Philip does not take the opportunity to subject Nathanael to a long homily full of messianic proofs. He makes the best possible invitation for evangelism both then and now: "Come and see" (John 1:39). (In Acts 8, Philip does practice the evangelism of exegesis, but only after the Ethiopian eunuch has shown considerable curiosity about the text; see Acts 8:26–40.) There may be the reminder for our own churches that one-size-fits-all evangelism or pastoral care is unduly rigid and insufficiently attentive to the winds of the Spirit. Philip deals with Nathanael quite differently from how he deals with the Ethiopian eunuch, but in each case Philip—with the Spirit—leads a new follower to the Master.

Nathanael is excellent disciple material because he is without guile. Nathanael would make a terrible poker player but a wonderful friend. God thus honors the qualities of honesty, genuineness, integrity, and open-mindedness. This is not one of those cases where God takes a miserable sinner and turns him into a saint. This is one of those equally remarkable cases where God takes a person who is humanly praiseworthy in every way and makes of him something even more—a disciple. The fact that Jesus, who has never met Nathanael, knows of his integrity suggests that here, as always in the Gospel of John, Jesus can read people's hearts. He is the light that illumines every person—he not only gives each person light; he sees each person in his or her true light (see John 1:9).

Nathanael is honest enough to express amazement that God's Messiah could come from an insignificant village. The story suggests two claims. First, God can accomplish great things in unlikely places. As is often the case, we are enabled to see the irony of Nathanael's question: "Can anything good come out of Nazareth?" (v. 46). The answer is, "Indeed." The second claim may be that God is perfectly capable of honoring ordinary people and apparently insignificant places. Scripture and our own experience bear witness to the fact that with God's help even dinky burgs like Aurora and Hoyt Lakes, the two-point charge I am serving, can nurture greatness.

Why does Nathanael decide to go with Jesus? Perhaps because of Philip's testimony, but the deal is sealed because Jesus apparently has gifts of perception that are more associated with divine life

mistaken, since Jesus was the "son of Joseph from Nazareth" (John 1:45). In Nathanael's view, Jesus could be nothing more than a simple Jew from an insignificant village in Galilee. The Messiah would certainly be of more prominent parentage and come from a more significant town.

Galilee had no association with any Jewish messianic expectations. In the period of the Israelite national states, it was part of the kingdom of Israel. Those who harbored royal messianic expectations believed that the Messiah would come from the territory of the former kingdom of Judah. The Fourth Gospel highlights these beliefs by having Jesus' enemies assert that the Messiah would belong to David's family and would come from Bethlehem (see John 7:42).

The reader of the Fourth Gospel knows that Jesus has another origin of which Nathanael was unaware. While Jesus was indeed "the son of Joseph from Nazareth," he was also the Word made flesh who was with God from the beginning and was God (John 1:1–14). The reader knows of Jesus' true identity from the very beginning of the Fourth Gospel. Jesus' opponents never accept Jesus, because they are unwilling to see beyond appearances. This is the great tragedy of the Fourth Gospel: "He came to what was his own, and his own people did not accept him" (John 1:11). The disciples were able to accept Jesus as the Messiah because Jesus chose them "out of the world" (John 15:19).

Though Nathanael at first maintained that Jesus could not be the Messiah, his first encounter with Jesus changed his mind. Jesus' foreknowledge was what convinced Nathanael that he was in the presence of an extraordinary individual whose origins, as far as Nathanael knew them, did not do him justice. Nathanael addresses Jesus as "rabbi" and confesses that he is the Son of God and the King of Israel. Jesus' response is that Nathanael will be a witness to greater things than a display of precognition.

The final verse of the pericope is an allusion to Jacob's dream near a town called Luz (John 1:51; see Gen. 28:10–19). Jacob dreamed that he saw angels ascending and descending on the ramp that stretched from heaven to the place where he was sleeping. Jacob recognized that he was in the very presence of God. Indeed, he renamed the place where he was resting Bethel, "the house of God." The allusion to this story identifies Jesus not merely as a messenger from God, but as the means by which human beings can have an authentic encounter with

Nazareth (v. 45), Son of God (v. 49), and King of Israel (v. 49). The talk about Jesus comes to a head when he seems to refer to himself as both the Son of Man promised in Daniel 7:13 and the ladder between heaven and earth dreamed of by Jacob in Genesis 28:12.[1]

The sheer multiplicity of words about Jesus is perhaps the most striking feature of this text. The multiplicity itself is a gift to church and world today, when the narrowness of talk about Jesus is so often paired with an insistence that the narrowness is all there is to say. Such narrowing happens in multiple ways. Jesus is made into no more and no less than Best Friend, Great Teacher, Radical Revolutionary, and Word of the Father. The many words about Jesus in John 1:35–51 resist any such reduction. They pile up past the testimony of any one person.

The first chapter of John also resists the breezy confidence in human perception that makes these narrow christologies possible. The disciples testify to Jesus, and sometimes they speak truly, but they don't know the half of it. Philip tells Nathanael that the one "about whom Moses in the law and also the prophets wrote" is this "Jesus son of Joseph from Nazareth." But readers of John's prologue know that the deepest truth about Jesus is not that he is the son of Joseph, but that he is the Word of God. And they know him not as the one who comes from Nazareth, but as the one through whom Nazareth and all things come into being (1:1–5). Even a beginning reader knows that Philip's testimony falls short of the reality of Jesus. And still, somehow Philip's testimony leads Nathanael to "come and see." The story gives preachers reason to take heart, even as it teaches us new humility.

Worship services engaged with this text might spend time with each of its christological confessions. Each snippet, title, and catchphrase deserves attention in itself. A sermon might reflect on the significance of the multiplicity of confessions and then do some teaching around the more complex passages—like the tangle of allusions in verse 51 or the irony in verses 46–47. Prayers, songs, and litanies could present other christological affirmations. The whole service might become not only a response to the text, but also a partner in its work. Like the text, the worship service might take up a whole array of fumbling, God-given words to speak of the love we meet in Jesus. Like the text, the service might let those christological words

[1]Gail R. O'Day and Susan E. Hylen, *John*, Westminster Bible Companion (Louisville, KY: Westminster John Knox Press, 2006), 32.

# John 1:43-51

## Theological Perspective

the "angels of God ascending and descending upon the Son of Man" (v. 51). Ever since Augustine, theologians have perceived a connection between this image and Jacob's vision of the ladder of angels at Bethel (Gen. 28:10–17). This scriptural parallel is reinforced by Jesus' description of Nathanael as an Israelite in whom there is no guile. Traditionally, Jacob's new divinely given name, Israel, was taken to imply that he was the personification of God's people rapturously beholding their God. Jacob, however, was regarded also as an inveterate man of guile. Jesus' address establishes Nathanael as the new Jacob, as the ideal Israelite. To further support the parallel, Jacob was also remembered as the one who saw God face to face and was utterly transformed by the encounter (Gen. 32:30). Consequently, concluded countless theologians, individuals like Nathanael who behold Jesus are seeing the very face of God, just as Jacob did. Jesus the Son of Man is the ultimate ladder stretching between heaven and earth. Jesus is the point of contact between the finite and the infinite, the conjunction of time and eternity. Jesus is the place where the heavens are opened and the divine glory can be contemplated. Similarly, Nathanael as the guileless Jacob, the true Israelite, is the prototype of a new humanity reborn in Christ.

Of course, theologians have not treated this manifestation of the divine to Philip and Nathanael as a self-contained, isolated episode in John's Gospel. Rather, it has been seen as the initiation of the disciples into an extended process that would eventuate, as they were promised, in the full beholding of God's glory. Belief, it was promised, would blossom into an unmediated vision of glory. Of course, such vision required the unfolding of the full narrative of Jesus' life, death, and resurrection. In the signs that follow in the Gospel, particularly the pivotal sign of cross, the heavens are indeed opened. The disciples will see the divine glory fully only when the work of crucifixion and resurrection is completed. The unveiling of the glory of God occurs in the history of Jesus, in the mysterious conjunction of crucifixion and exaltation.

LEE BARRETT

## Pastoral Perspective

than human life. Jesus seems to suggest that Nathanael is easily impressed. Wait until he sees how this story turns out. Is the text suggesting that the wonder of Jesus' special knowledge is of little import compared to the wonder of God's using Jesus as the one who comes from heaven and returns to heaven again? The great sign is Jesus himself and the way he reveals the Father. Or is the text honoring those who believe without seeing great wonders, as in John 20:29? God's greatness exceeds what we have already seen and what we can imagine.

The prediction of the last verse (angels ascending and descending) is reminiscent of Jacob's ladder, particularly the implication that intercourse between heaven and earth runs both ways (Gen. 28:12).

Of course Jesus himself represents a twofold journey between God and ourselves. He is the Logos who comes into the world from God. He is (esp. in John 17) the one like a high priest who intercedes with God on our behalf. When we are most faithful as pastors, we will try to imitate, however poorly, this twofold ministry of revelation and intercession. We bring God to our people, and we bring our people before God.

There is a word here too about the relationship believers have with God. Our relationship with God is a two-way street, both parties talking and listening and reaching out to each other. As in a verse from the spiritual "Every Time I Feel the Spirit": "There ain't but one train that's on this track, It runs to heaven and runs right back."[1] God wants to be in relationship with us, reaching out to us and inviting us to reach out to God. Thus again does God bestow honor and sacred worth upon humanity.

ELTON W. BROWN

---

[1] *African American Heritage Hymnal* (Chicago: GIA Publications, 2001), 325.

the divine. When Nathanael has this experience as promised by Jesus, he will know Jesus as he really is—not just the son of Joseph from Nazareth but the Word of God in the flesh. It is important to note that in Greek the second-person forms in verse 51 are not singular as they were in previous verses, but plural forms. The evangelist here is speaking to a wider audience. John wants his readers to see themselves as heirs of the promise Jesus gave to Nathanael.

Only the Gospel of John names Nathanael as one of Jesus' disciples. Popular tradition identified him with Bartholomew, who does not appear in the Fourth Gospel, though the Synoptic Gospels do include him among the Twelve (Matt. 10:2–4; Mark 3:16–19; Luke 6:14–16). The association is made because in the Synoptic lists Bartholomew always follows Philip, who introduced Nathanael to Jesus, according to John. This identification is somewhat plausible. Bartholomew is not a personal name, but simply identifies its bearer as "the son [Aramaic *bar*] of Tholomeus." While it is possible that this person had the personal name of Nathanael, there is no historical evidence supporting the identification of Nathanael and Bartholomew. The identification of Nathanael with Bartholomew reflects the tendency to harmonize the four Gospels.

Philip, the disciple who introduced Nathanael to Jesus, bears a Greek name and comes from Bethsaida, a predominantly Greek town in the territory ruled by Herod Philip along the northern shore of the Sea of Galilee. The same is true of Andrew, another of Jesus' early disciples, though Mark 1:29 identifies Capernaum as Andrew's home. Bethsaida, mentioned only seven times in the New Testament, was the site of Jesus' healing of a blind man (Mark 8:22–26), and the feeding of the five thousand took place in its vicinity (Luke 9:10). Apparently Jesus was very active in it, since Bethsaida along with Capernaum and Chorazin is condemned for its failure to respond positively to Jesus' ministry (Matt. 11:21; Luke 10:13).

The preacher may wish to focus on how our preconceptions of God and God's activity can prevent us from an authentic encounter with God. Such an encounter always broadens our horizons and helps us to see the divine in new ways.

LESLIE J. HOPPE

proliferate and pile up. And like the text, the worship on this day just might involve us in words that outrun even our best intentions.

The christological conversations of John 1:43–51 do not happen in a vacuum. They happen between Jesus and people learning how to follow him. And they happen as those followers try to tell the good news to other people. Christology unfolds in the course of discipleship. The best sermons on this text will therefore refuse to launch into Christology as an esoteric discourse. They will remember that the church learns to speak about Jesus in the process of giving thanks, singing praise, sharing good news, and speaking truth to power. A preacher might reflect on this dynamic in the life of the congregation she serves this Sunday. She might start from discipleship: How has this church tried to follow Jesus—in its programs, its prayers, and the life of its members in other spheres of life? How has it learned to speak along the way? Or she might start from Christology: What has this church said about Jesus—in its official documents, its favorite hymns, and its stained-glass windows? How has it tried to live into that testimony? Wherever the preacher begins, she might trace the complex relationship between Christology and discipleship in the life of her congregation. And she might connect that relationship to the one she finds in the first chapter of John.

Discipleship and Christology fit together so closely because discipleship is first of all a willingness to walk with Jesus. It is not obedience to an abstract set of codes, but consent to a costly, joyful relationship. In walking with Jesus, we learn who he is. As we learn who he is, we learn what it means to follow him. The best sermons for this day will lead us a little further along both of these braided journeys.

TED A. SMITH

# Jonah 3:1–5, 10

¹The word of the LORD came to Jonah a second time, saying, ²"Get up, go to Nineveh, that great city, and proclaim to it the message that I tell you." ³So Jonah set out and went to Nineveh, according to the word of the LORD. Now Nineveh was an exceedingly large city, a three days' walk across. ⁴Jonah began to go into the city, going a day's walk. And he cried out, "Forty days more, and Nineveh shall be overthrown!" ⁵And the people of Nineveh believed God; they proclaimed a fast, and everyone, great and small, put on sackcloth. . . .

¹⁰When God saw what they did, how they turned from their evil ways, God changed his mind about the calamity that he had said he would bring upon them; and he did not do it.

## Theological Perspective

Like the magi whose journey to pay tribute to the infant Jesus we remember during this season of the Epiphany, Jonah heeded God's summons to go to a foreign city. But unlike the magi from the East, Jonah initially resisted and then rebelled against God's call to go to the Assyrian city of Nineveh. Spared from certain death in the stormy sea by divine intervention (1:17), Jonah reluctantly and perfunctorily completed his mission by announcing to the Ninevites that in forty days the city would be overthrown (v. 4).

*Jonah as Prophet.* Jonah is a distinctive prophetic book because it is primarily a narrative about a prophet's adventures rather than a collection of prophetic utterances, like Hosea and the prophets known as Isaiah. The story portrays the human response to the call of God rather than focusing on the causes for the call. Like Jeremiah and Moses, Jonah initially tries to deflect God's call to deliver the prophetic message. Yet eventually Jonah consents to deliver God's message to the people, and his oracle lies at the heart of today's text (v. 4). Unlike other prophets, who issue a call for Israel to repent and to return to righteousness, Jonah delivers the uncompromising oracle of impending destruction to the Gentile Ninevites.

## Pastoral Perspective

Jonah had a sense of urgency about time. He felt something big was about to happen. He said to himself, in essence, "I don't have much time left. I need to act now." He understood the community organizer's mantra: thought does not create action, action creates thought. Ironically we are often short term when it comes to our anxiety, and long term when it comes to our hopes. Hope is for later. Anxiety is for now.

Some days I believe Jonah when he says that I have forty days before I am overthrown, and other days I think Jonah is nuts. I repent not—because I do not really think I have sinned. If I do not know where I am headed with my life and do not have distinct goals, I will probably be quite comfortable not knowing if the prophet is right in telling me where I have gone wrong.

It is very different to be poor or about to be deported than it is to be well-off and comfortable. The well-off and comfortable do not know what urgency is! Luckily we have prophets like Jonah to remind us that someone is about to be deported, someone is about to be laid off. If we cannot manage our own obsession with the self, then we can use a well-polished prophetic trick. Imagine yourself in the place of someone who is oppressed, or poor, or in trouble. That will focus our attention.

## Exegetical Perspective

The book of Jonah is difficult to classify. Is it fable or farce? Serious history or salacious satire? Or is it—with its combination of life-saving fish, misplaced psalms, and repentant cows—a little of all these things? And what is this one passage doing plopped down toward the end of Epiphany? Upon whom is the light of God's revelation shining brightest: the Gentiles, the Jews, or the character of God Godself?

At the heart of this passage is the question in verse 9: "Who knows?" Who knows the true character of this strange God who rules over the waves and the creatures over and under these waves; who inspires sacred songs even on the lips of those running from his presence; who worries over desert bushes and over great cities and over those sent to be stewards and witnesses to both? One way to exegete this passage is by asking this question for each of its primary characters: the residents of Nineveh, Jonah, and the Lord.

*The Ninevites.* One of the favorite jokes of the Scriptures is the unexpected faithfulness of the outsider, the other, the enemy. Anyone who knows the stories of Balaam, Ruth, and the good Samaritan should recognize in the residents of Nineveh a stock character. In contrast to the insider, Jonah, who hears God's word and repeatedly disobeys, the

## Homiletical Perspective

In 2005, the *New York Times* reported the death of the joke. Under the headline "Seriously, the Joke Is Dead," the *Times* explained:

> In case you missed its obituary, the joke died recently after a long illness, of, oh, 30 years. Its passing was barely noticed, drowned out, perhaps, by the din of ironic one-liners, snark and detached bons mots that pass for humor these days.
>
> The joke died a lonely death. There was no next of kin to notify, the comedy skit, the hand-buzzer and Bob Newhart's imaginary telephone monologues having passed on long before.[1]

As America's greatest humorist once said of himself, reports of such a demise are greatly exaggerated. The joke is as timeless as Jonah.

The book of Jonah finds out what kind of readers we are—whether literalists or lovers of a tall tale. In this story, literalists lose a lot. They must justify this wildly funny, improbable, subversive story as history; so while they may not miss its point, they may well miss its pleasures.

The book of Jonah is structured like a joke, starting with an outrageous premise (Jonah's impossible assignment) and an outlandish response (he runs in

[1]Warren St. John, "Seriously, the Joke Is Dead," *New York Times*, May 22, 2005.

# Jonah 3:1-5, 10

## Theological Perspective

Jonah's story features a number of reversals and contrasts between human actions and the divine will: After trying to save his own life by fleeing to Tarshish, Jonah volunteers to be tossed into the stormy sea—the very waters of chaos and destruction—to save the lives of the Gentile crew. Jonah prefers the seeming certainty of his own death (and thus avoiding the completion of his mission to Nineveh) to the probable destruction of the entire ship. Another contrast in the story is that, after defying God's directions, God's will persists and prevails over the prophet's protest. More significantly, following the Ninevites' expressions of contrition, God rescinds the judgment on Nineveh that has been prophesied. Reversing the expectation of divine judgment, the story depicts the graciousness of God in contrast to the vindictive attitude of the prophet. Thinking that his word no longer would carry binding authority, Jonah begrudges the Ninevites' reprieve and yearns to die. The culminating contrast in the story is a parable about a leafy plant springing forth to provide shade for Jonah before being eaten by a worm. While Jonah bemoans the death of the plant, he fails to feel compassion for the Ninevites whose destruction had been forestalled by God (4:10–11). The reversals underscore the contrast between human desires and God's will, between human sin and God's mercy.

Amid these narrative turns, several theological themes emerge, especially out of this focal passage. The most significant ones are related to the character of God: the persistence of God, the responsiveness of God, and the universality of God.

*God's Persistence.* Repeatedly the story portrays God as persistent. After being rebuffed by Jonah and then watching him board a ship to take him in the opposite direction of the divine will, God persists, intervening in ever new ways to bring Jonah to repent and to fulfill the divine command to deliver the prophecy to the Ninevites (v. 3). The story shows that God's will cannot be circumvented or thwarted. Yet while God persists in faithfulness, God also interacts in ways unanticipated by the prophet, expressing mercy where judgment had been promised. As the story unfolds, God changes the promise of punishment to Nineveh—much to the regret of Jonah—and extends forgiveness to the repentant people. Throughout this process God persists in requiring and rewarding righteousness.

*God's Responsiveness.* Jonah's declaration of God's impending judgment on Nineveh is unwavering. It

## Pastoral Perspective

Once, when I told a friend that I was feeling a bit burnt out, she caught me up short by responding, "You ain't even been lit." That phrase brought me to my Nineveh. It brought me to a place where I could say, "I have forty days to get this life and God thing together."

Prophets focus our attention on getting lit. They bring us into the present and the immediate: from there prophetic energy derives.

Serendipity, what you find that you are not looking for, is a magnificent experience. Sometimes wonderful things find me. Nevertheless, serendipity also can get in the way of purpose. The wonderful things that happen while we sort of bop along are sometimes the enemy of prophecy. They get in the way too of art, the play we should be writing, the song we should be singing, the change we should be making, the church we should be being. Strategy is good—and to behave strategically, we need to give ourselves over to something like a creed. A creed is a statement of belief, within or outside of a religious context. We need a Nicaea or a personal mission statement or a personal map. We need a destination. We need to focus our attention.

Most of us have a rug under the living-room furniture. We do not look at it much, but it is there. Most of us have invisible creeds too. I love the way the Masai people in East Nigeria rewrote the Gem Na creed in 1960 at their own council, called the Congregation of the Holy Ghost.

> We Believe in One High God, who out of love created the beautiful world. We believe that God made good his promise by sending his Son, Jesus Christ, a man in the flesh, a Jew by tribe, born poor in a little village, who left his home and was always on safari doing good, curing people by the power of God, teaching about God and man, and showing that the meaning of religion is love. He was rejected by his own people, tortured and nailed hands and feet to a cross, and died. He was buried in the grave, but the hyenas did not touch him, and on the third day he rose from the grave.

Why is it important to have some kind of creed at the center of our life? Because knowing what we believe and why we believe it is important to how we behave, whether we matter, whether we live in the world we make or the world others make for us. Absent our creedal thinking, which I mean in the broadest and most strategic of senses, others will be happy to do our thinking for us.

Ninevites hear a one-sentence sermon with no mention of God ("Forty days more, and Nineveh shall be overthrown!"), and repent—king, people, and cattle. Surely all through Scripture, the key to faithfulness is responsiveness: Abram and Sarai hear a call and go; some fishermen receive an invitation and follow. Here it is not the insider (who can recite Israel's sacred songs by heart, 2:1–9) who truly "knows" the heart of the Lord. No, it is the Ninevites, the foreigners and enemies, who hear God's voice and believe and, even more, put their belief into action. Though they stand outside the special revelation available to God's people Israel (note how the Ninevites think and talk about "God" while Jonah receives the word of "the Lord," God's personal name), they act the part of the *faithful*, those who should know what kind of God they worship and serve.

*Jonah.* Jonah is the best player of the role of "unfaithful insider" since Israel in the wilderness. Though it becomes quite clear in the next chapter ("I knew that you are a gracious God and merciful, slow to anger, and abounding in steadfast love, and ready to relent from punishing," 4:2) that Jonah is familiar with the heart of the Lord's revelation to Israel (cf. Exod. 34:6–7), he continually acts as if he does not: he attempts to flee from a God who is inescapable (cf. Ps. 139); he preaches destruction unattached to God's justice or mercy (compare with even the bleakest of prophets, such as Amos); he celebrates deliverance as belonging to the Lord in one instance (2:9) but resents it in another (with regard to Nineveh). The one who knows the Lord, acts as if he doesn't; the ones who don't know the Lord, act as if they do. Is this fable or farce? Serious history or salacious satire? Or perhaps could it be deeply profound revelation as well?

*YHWH, or the* Lord. Constantly running through Scripture is a threat: if God's special people fail to trust the promises of the Lord, God may pass over them and choose some other. God threatens to start over again with Moses after the incident of the golden calf (Exod. 32). Jesus observes that God can make even stones shout at his arrival if God's people will not (Luke 19:40). When the first list of guests makes excuses for the master's banquet, a second group of revelers is quickly invited in (Luke 14:15–24). If it is difficult for the Lord to forgive the Ninevites, how much more costly is it for him to forgive God's own people, like Jonah?

the opposite direction, as if to hide from God). A disaster at sea is played for laughs. Jonah has such an unintentionally saving effect that even hardened sailors repent because of him. But Jonah himself may not be saved. Hoping to rescue their ship, the sailors lighten their load of every last bit of cargo, and finally throw him overboard. Just when things could hardly get any worse, he winds up in the belly of a great fish. So Jonah prays. He prays that the very God from whom he fled now will hear him calling from the depths of the sea. As prayers go, it is not terribly sincere—he alternates between pleading and blaming God for the situation. God answers the prayer, as the fish unceremoniously vomits Jonah onto dry land. Now this Jew who thought he was too good for Nineveh is *treyf,* unclean.

All this sets up the laughs of our lectionary reading. "The word of the Lord came to Jonah a *second* time." You can hear the mirth of an ancient Hebrew audience as God tells Jonah almost word for word what God told him the first time: "Get up, go to Nineveh, that great city, and proclaim to it the message that I tell you." Professional comedians call this effect a callback.

Nineveh, we should note, holds no appeal for Jonah. It is fantastically vile and, in this telling, preposterously huge—a three days' walk, or about sixty miles across. Clearly the task is impossible for one reluctant man.

And he says hardly anything. All he says, according to the story, is, "Forty days more, and Nineveh shall be overthrown!" There is not a word of hope in his preaching. He holds out no promise at all; if anything, he announces an antigospel. Jonah (in Hebrew his name is Noah's turned inside out) seems to expect something like the flood, when the people did not repent and God wiped them out in forty days.

But amazingly, Nineveh *does* repent. The entire city repents. Even the pagan king calls for fasting in sackcloth. The only one who suffers a flood is Jonah, who has spent time in the belly of that fish.

Apparently God's purposes can be accomplished with a minimum of faithfulness; and such faithfulness turns out to be a matter of not merely what one feels, but what one does.

Confronted with his astounding success, Jonah stomps off to sulk. "I *knew* that you are a gracious God and merciful, slow to anger, and abounding in steadfast love," he cries, turning the Hebrews' ancient praise of God into a complaint. Melodramatically he asks God to put him out of his misery. (David Plotz

# Jonah 3:1-5, 10

## Theological Perspective

includes no condition for possible reprieve. Yet when the people fast and don sackcloth, the king joins them, recognizing the Lord God's rule over the city and decreeing that even the animals would be subject to penitent acts (vv. 5–6). The Ninevites' immediate response in repentance stands in stark contrast to Jonah's initial refusal to follow God's command. And the repentance of the city signifies "the answer to social sin," as Jacques Ellul insisted, because it combines "the conversion of an entire population *and* its government."[1] Moved by this comprehensive act of contrition, God renounces the city's impending destruction. The merciful response of God to the Ninevites is anticipated earlier in the story when God responds to the Gentile sailors' acts of obedience, quieting the stormy seas and saving them from terror and destruction (1:15–16).

*God's Universality.* A third major theological theme is that God's power and mercy are not reserved for the Israelites alone; they are universal. God's rule and grace extend to the Gentile Ninevites who probably do not understand Hebrew, Jonah's language. Earlier in Jonah's travels, God exercises control over nature and saves the Gentile sailors who had been guiding the ship toward Tarshish. Even after they had appealed to their gods to intervene, the storm raged more fiercely. As a final act of desperation the sailors reluctantly tossed Jonah into the tempestuous sea; they then observed the immediate stilling of the storm and made vows to the Lord. Thus to Gentiles in distress or penitence, the story of Jonah suggests, God offers salvation.

*Conclusion.* The story of Jonah affirms the character of God as persevering, responsive, and merciful to all who repent. While the Assyrian city of Nineveh is being portrayed as the focus of the prophecy, the nation of Israel, which is exemplified in the postures and responses of Jonah, is being warned that its "narrow and bitter attitude . . . is a rejection of the God of their fathers."[2] As the chosen people who should be the light to the nations, they should rejoice with its mission, not merely out of self-interest but out of fulfillment of the divine command.

JOSEPH L. PRICE

## Pastoral Perspective

Surely some people—I think of many foundations and most school testing—take the notion of measurement way too far; contrarily, many of us take it not far enough. How would we measure if our church were a successful congregation for the next period of time? How would we know? If we felt good? If we made our own choices? Or if we had a driving vocation to matter to someone else besides ourselves? The creed matters here: Jesus mattered to someone besides himself. How would we know if our own lives, however long or short, measured up to goals we had set for ourselves? One goal could be to maximize serendipity. Another would be to leave a legacy of beauty or excellence or good jokes. A third would be to be a good parent or good school board member. Knowing our destination is a matter of creed. It is a matter of shade: under which tree do we stand and think and sift and strategize.

Nevertheless, whatever goals we may establish for ourselves, by whatever creeds we live, wherever we think we are headed, this story reminds us that we should not be surprised by a sudden change of direction. Jonah heads out for Tarshish and ends up in Nineveh. The once proud and powerful king takes off the royal robe and puts on sackcloth. Even God changes God's own mind about the fate of the city. Everyone in the story repents, including God. Everyone experiences a surprising change of direction. This passage brings to mind the Jewish proverb: "Whenever someone says, 'I have a plan,' God laughs."

DONNA SCHAPER

---

[1] Jacques Ellul, *The Meaning of the City*, trans. Dennis Pardee (Grand Rapids: William B. Eerdmans Publishing Co., 1970), 69.

[2] James D. Smart, "Jonah: Introduction and Exegesis," in *Interpreter's Bible*, vol. 6 (Nashville: Abingdon Press, 1956), 873.

## Exegetical Perspective

And yet, right here, the "who knows" of the king of Nineveh becomes an ongoing question in the very heart of God. How far can God's love and mercy extend? God has first had mercy on Jonah by setting him free from the belly of the fish in chapters 1 and 2. God is a God of deliverance, even toward his rebellious children. God next shows mercy toward Jonah by speaking to him a second time at the beginning of chapter 3: "The word of the LORD came to Jonah a second time, saying . . ." The God of the Scriptures is a God of second chances. God speaks once, then speaks again. Finally, in chapter 4, the Lord will provide Jonah a third word, an enacted parable, which should help Jonah see how the Lord is concerned with (the Hebrew word is *hus*, better translated "has compassion") not only desert shrubs and Ninevites, but a reluctant witness such as himself.

Maybe the main joke and gospel in this strange book of Jonah is the sense that not even the Lord knows how far divine mercy and compassion can go, especially when it comes to sticking with this particular people God has chosen. Unlike Jonah with regard to this desert shrub, Israel *is* a plant that the Lord has grown and for which the Lord labored (cf. Isa. 5). No one could question the Lord's decision to raze this garden—or leave Jonah in the fish's belly, appoint another prophet, or let him stew in his anger. But here is the one place that the Lord does *not* change God's mind. The God of the Scriptures sticks with those God is stuck with—like Jonah and Israel, like the elder brother in Jesus' parable, and like the early church. Why? "For I am God and no mortal, the Holy One in your midst, and I will not come in wrath" (Hos. 11:9).

Yes, Jonah is a difficult book to classify. But so is the gospel. Fable or farce? Serious history or salacious satire? Maybe this is not so bad a passage for Epiphany after all.

RICHARD BOYCE

## Homiletical Perspective

suggests: "This is a distinctively Jewish form of complaint. The kill-me-now joke is one of the great foundations of modern Jewish humor—the mother who sticks her head in the oven when her son drops out of medical school or dates a Christian girl, for example, or the entire oeuvre of Woody Allen.")[2]

Comics speak of "the rule of three," which means that a joke gets its greatest laughs when the situation comes round a third time. But when God addresses Jonah for a third time, the laughs are deeper, not greater, as we begin to see that Jonah embodies our own grudges.

Originally the fairly pointed message was that Israel, which had once seen itself as "a light to the nations," had grown ever more defensive after years of military losses and diplomatic concessions to foreign idols. Nineveh, the Assyrian capital, represented the enemy camp at its most powerful and wicked. No Jew would have wanted to lift a finger for the Ninevites. Likewise, nothing in the historical record suggests that the Assyrian king and all his people turned to the Hebrew God. This belongs to the realm of fantasy. But the point of the message remains: if God really intends salvation for all the peoples, then in all seriousness, we must at least talk to our enemies.

It is a timeless message that could be drawn from today's headlines. It so happens that as these words are written, there is fierce fighting in Mosul—modern-day Nineveh. American soldiers, who really don't want to be there, are contending with Iraqis who really don't want them there either. It looks like a fool's errand. No soldier is on a mission from God, the army is not there to prophesy, and the circumstances of power are totally reversed from those in Jonah's story. But modern suspicions and animosities match the ancient story perfectly. In this deadly serious mess, the only way to avert total catastrophe is to talk.

More current headlines may occur to you, but none more current than Jonah. This is not just a tall tale about ancient feuds. No, the joke, if it is a joke, is on us.

LAWRENCE WOOD

[2]David Plotz, "Blogging the Bible: In Which I Discover the Source of All Jewish Comedy," *Slate*, July 27, 2006.

# Psalm 62:5-12

5For God alone my soul waits in silence,
    for my hope is from him.
6He alone is my rock and my salvation,
    my fortress; I shall not be shaken.
7On God rests my deliverance and my honor;
    my mighty rock, my refuge is in God.

8Trust in him at all times, O people;
    pour out your heart before him;
God is a refuge for us.
                 *Selah*

9Those of low estate are but a breath,
    those of high estate are a delusion;

## Theological Perspective

In the opening paragraph of his *Confessions*, Augustine declares that humans are made for God and, therefore, "our hearts are restless until we find our rest in you."[1] The spirit of Psalm 62 is very much the same, professing that the only peace available to mortals is found in the bosom of the Divine. "For God alone my soul waits in silence, for my hope is from him" (v. 5). This psalm confronts the theological issues of finding meaning in the midst of finitude and the corresponding temptation for mortals to place their trust in something less than God. In other words, it describes the nature of true faith and human sin. Throughout, it asserts that because we are made by and for God, to place our hope anywhere else is self-defeating.

Today, when people use the term "faith," they tend to use it as a synonym for beliefs to which they offer intellectual assent. Certainly faith includes beliefs about ourselves, the world, and the ultimate conditions of existence. Also, many of these beliefs cannot be justified easily. Nevertheless, faith is not simply a set of beliefs, a function of the mind. Fundamentally, it is a condition of trust or confidence located in the heart or soul that orients one in the world through certain persistent dispositions and affections.

[1]Augustine, *The Confessions of Saint Augustine*, trans. Rex Warner (New York: Penguin Books, 1963), 17.

## Pastoral Perspective

As Hebrew is read from right to left, so Psalm 62 can be read "backward," from the end to the beginning. In the final verse the psalmist addresses God for the first time as "you." Throughout the rest of the psalm God is spoken of in the third person and described through traditional metaphors of security—rock, salvation, and fortress. But the psalm ends on a note of personal trust and commitment to God. "Power belongs to God, and steadfast love belongs to you, O Lord. For you repay to all according to their work" (v. 11b–12).

Trusting the assured judgment of the God to whom power and steadfast love belong, the psalmist declares twice his quiet repose in God. "For God alone my soul waits in silence." The psalmist's waiting in silence is not wordless passivity. It is, as James Mays, retired professor of Old Testament, says, "a quietness of soul, an inner stillness that comes with yielding all fears and anxieties and insecurities to God in an act of trust."[1]

Every pastor knows how easily such an assurance can sound like merely wishful thinking to ones who feel assaulted by forces beyond their control. That is why it is so important to make clear that the psalmist's trust in God does not come from a naive

[1]James L. Mays, *Psalms*, Interpretation Series (Louisville, KY: John Knox Press, 1994), 216.

in the balances they go up;
 they are together lighter than a breath.
<sup>10</sup>Put no confidence in extortion,
 and set no vain hopes on robbery;
 if riches increase, do not set your heart on them.

<sup>11</sup>Once God has spoken;
 twice have I heard this:
 that power belongs to God,
<sup>12</sup>and steadfast love belongs to you, O Lord.
 For you repay to all
 according to their work.

## Exegetical Perspective

Psalm 62 is a confession of trust in God alone. One might think of the psalm as a "personal testimony" given in the midst of the worshiping community. First, the individual shares his or her own experience of trusting in God (vv. 1–4). Then he or she encourages the congregation to learn from that experience and apply it to their own lives (vv. 5–10). Finally, the testimony concludes with the individual's revelation about why God is worthy of trust (vv. 11–12).

The lectionary reading omits the "personal testimony" of the psalmist in verses 1–4. While the psalmist's confession of trust in God alone (vv. 1–2) is repeated and expanded in verses 5–7, what is lost is the personal predicament that led to a crisis in the individual's life and faith (vv. 3–4). Apparently, the psalmist is the victim of persecution and deception by enemies masquerading as friends. This situation has led (as it often does) to a struggle between despair and trust. No longer able to trust other people, even friends, the psalmist ultimately comes to realize that God alone is worthy of trust—*and* that trust in God creates a peace in the soul more powerful and hopeful than any distress caused by human beings. This revelation about God is, of course, not new. It echoes throughout the Old Testament witness of the people of God. Yet here the individual's personal experience confirms the

## Homiletical Perspective

As a psalm of trust, this psalm offers an important opportunity for the preacher to explore what it means to trust God and how trust looks in daily living. This psalm sets up a contrast between trusting in that which is perceived by the senses and trusting in the unseen God who is the ultimate reality. The contrast is highlighted by the repetition of the word "only" or "alone" (NRSV; NIV). Six times in this psalm that word is used, five times with the sense of a restrictive force (vv. 1, 2, 4, 5, 6). The restrictive force emphasizes the exclusive nature of trusting God. We might say it like this: "Say what you will, I'm putting my trust in God," or, "Regardless of the objections, I'm trusting God," or "No matter what happens . . ." The psalmist underscores the contrast between the competing objects of our trust by using the word "alone."

The psalmist has been under heavy attack from enemies (vv. 3–4). Yet she does not succumb to their assaults. Clinton McCann proposes that since the enemies are never specifically identified in the psalms, the preacher should take responsibility for naming the evil forces in the world today. McCann singles out greed and materialism as the "enemy" that assaults us relentlessly.[1] Especially in light of

<hr>

[1] J. Clinton McCann, "Greed, Grace, and Gratitude: An Approach to Preaching the Psalms," in *Performing the Psalms*, ed. Dave Bland and David Fleer (St. Louis: Chalice Press, 2005), 51–65.

# Psalm 62:5-12

## Theological Perspective

The Protestant Reformers shared this richer understanding of faith. Luther writes, "Faith is a living and unshakable confidence, a belief in the grace of God so assured that a man would die a thousands deaths for its sake. This kind of confidence in God's grace, this sort of knowledge of it, makes us joyful, high-spirited, and eager in our relations with all mankind."[2]

According to Calvin, "piety [is] that reverence joined with love of God which the knowledge of his benefits induces. For until men recognize that they owe everything to God, that they are nourished by his fatherly care, that he is the Author of their every good, that they should seek nothing beyond him—they will never yield him willing service."[3] For both Luther and Calvin, faith or piety is a fundamental life orientation built upon trust or confidence. The fundamental question of faith is not "What do you believe?" but "Whom do you trust?"

In Psalm 62, the psalmist confesses and exhorts trust in God as the only sensible way of orienting one's life. God is unshakable and immovable, like a rock or a fortress. The intersection of ultimate power and undying love, God alone is worthy of absolute trust and the foundation of persistent hope. By comparison, all other things are weak as reeds and erratic as the wind. Every human effort, finite cause, and mortal relationship is an unsuitable object for our absolute trust and final hope. The career that shows such promise, the children that seem so exceptional, the nation that appears so strong: they are like shifting sand, which offers no security, no permanent purchase (Matt. 7:24–27). This is the message of Augustine's *Confessions*, foreshadowed in its opening paragraph. There is no resting place for our hearts, no trustworthy object of hope and meaning, other than God, who is all in all. Only in the light of this fundamental orientation toward God do these other commitments become valuable. Apart from it, family, work, nation, even church are simply "delusions," according to the psalmist (v. 9), or "vanity," in the words of Ecclesiastes.

Today sin is most often conceived as an act of willful disobedience. Traditionally, however, Christians have understood sin as a condition, not simply an event. Jesus said, "Each tree is known by its own fruit" (Luke 6:44a). Sinful acts are merely symptoms of a heart that is disordered, sick,

## Pastoral Perspective

refusal to look reality in the face. There is nothing escapist in the trust of the psalmist. There are indeed enemies among us who assail and batter their victims, both the vulnerable (symbolized by a "leaning wall . . . tottering fence") and the seemingly strong and prominent. At one time or another, that includes all of us. We are often the most vulnerable when we think of ourselves as the most secure.

Because the psalmist's trust is anchored in God "my rock and my salvation, my fortress," he is able to declare, not in arrogance, but in quiet trust, "I shall never be shaken." A similar image is found in Psalm 46. Just as the "city of God . . . shall not be moved [shaken]" (Ps. 46:4–5) amid the raging chaos of nature and history, so the psalmist is not shaken by the assaults of nameless others. A clear recognition of the threats to a secure trust in God saves the metaphors of rock, salvation, and fortress from becoming empty clichés.

Thus it would seem that the lectionary reading which begins with verse 5 does not do justice to the way in which the psalmist moves back and forth between quiet trust in God and honest recognition of the threatening forces around him. The strength that comes from relying on the power and steadfast love of God is not given once for all. It must continually be reclaimed by the psalmist and the community of faith to whom he speaks. Leaving out verses 1–4 lessens the dramatic tension in the psalm as it alternates between secure trust and very real threats.

At the heart of the psalm is a call to place one's trust in "one God alone, to whom alone we must cleave, whom alone we must serve, whom only we must worship, and in whom alone we put our trust."[2] Nothing else can secure our lives without enslaving us to our would-be liberators.

Using the image of balance scales with two pans suspended from a crossbar, the psalmist insists that all human beings are weighed, judged, by God—rich and poor, powerful and powerless alike. The "heavyweights" of the world—the movers and shakers, the rich and famous—have no weight, no gravitas. Their self-importance is a delusion. Their end of the balance scales goes up instead of down. But the same is true for the weak and vulnerable, the poor and defenseless, the victims of injustice. They also have no weight, no substance. Neither rich nor poor, neither powerful nor powerless, are able to secure their own lives. Both are "lighter than a breath" (v. 9).

---

[2]Martin Luther, "Preface to Romans," *Martin Luther: Selections from His Readings*, ed. John Dillenberger (New York: Anchor Books, 1962), 24.

[3]John Calvin, *Institutes of the Christian Religion*, 2 vols., ed. John T. McNeill, trans. Ford Lewis Battles, LCC (Philadelphia: Westminster Press, 1960), 1.1.1.

[2]The Scots Confession, in *The Book of Confessions*, Presbyterian Church (U.S.A.) (Louisville, KY: Office of the General Assembly, 1999), 11.

## Exegetical Perspective

community's long-standing affirmations about God, giving more power to the psalmist's exhortation in the verses that follow.

*Verses 5–7.* In the midst of a difficult personal situation, the psalmist has focused attention on God rather than on his own problems, and so has discovered an inner stillness, a calmness of soul. Because the psalmist places hope and trust in God, the anxiety and distress caused by other people have lost their power. Why? Because, unlike human beings, God is like a "rock" (vv. 2, 6, 7), solid and dependable, a sure foundation on which to build one's life. God is like a "fortress" (vv. 2, 6), where one is safe and secure from all enemies. God is both deliverer ("my salvation," vv. 1, 6; "my deliverance," v. 7) and "refuge" (vv. 7, 8) from anyone and anything that threatens our well-being.

*Verses 8–10.* Because God is our refuge, we—the people of God—are urged to trust in God. We are invited to pour out our hearts to God in prayer, seeking God's help in whatever situation of distress we may find ourselves. God alone is worthy of our trust. In contrast, human beings are nothing— lighter than air. No matter how weighty their social standing or influence, we cannot depend on other people to provide security or stability in our lives. Nor can we rely on our own power or wealth to create safety or happiness in life—especially if it is used or gained in ways contrary to God's will (such as extortion or robbery, v. 10).

*Verses 11–12.* The psalm concludes with a statement of what God has revealed to the psalmist in the midst of his personal crisis. That revelation is both simple and profound, and provides the reason for trust in God. What God has revealed to the psalmist is the two essential aspects of God's character: "power" (v. 11) and "steadfast love" (v. 12). Power belongs to God, not to other people who may seek to destroy our lives (as did the psalmist's enemies, vv. 3–4), or on whom we may hope to depend (v. 9), and not to ourselves, should we try to provide our own security in life (v. 10).

Yet God's power is not by itself sufficient reason to trust in God. God's power is combined with steadfast love—love for us that is constant and eternal, in contrast to the affection of the people who pretend to be the psalmist's friends, but secretly plot his downfall (v. 4). God is worthy of our trust precisely because God's power is united with and

## Homiletical Perspective

verse 10, a sermon could name materialism as the enemy of the church today.

The two subjects in this psalm that compete for our trust are humans and God. On the one hand, we tend to trust in human power (v. 9). We seek security in the material goods of this world (v. 10). However, when all is said and done, humans—whether rich or poor—are transient and insignificant. And efforts to secure life through materialism—whether legitimate or by violence—are futile (vv. 9–10). The temptation to rely on wealth, social prestige, military power, intellectual achievement, or personal skill will inevitably fall short.

On the other hand, the psalmist, because of personal experience, exhorts the congregation to trust in God at all times (v. 8). Though unseen, God is more real and more reliable than that which we can experience with our senses. The psalmist strives to persuade the worshipers to trust in the unseen God of the universe. The psalmist's perspective defies human reason. His or her admonition to depend *only* on what cannot be perceived makes little sense in our society. So the preacher must take on the task of nurturing the congregation in such a way as to equip them to trust in what they cannot see and rely on the countercultural belief that trusting in the tangible leads only to destruction. That's the challenge of the psalm.

The movie *The Matrix* provides a helpful analogy for getting a better handle on the real versus the unreal. In the film, reality was a lie. A computer-driven conspiracy was created to deceive humans into trusting their sensory perceptions, while concealing the truth from them. The psalm teaches that what we perceive to be real and therefore worthy of our trust is not as certain as the unseen truth. God alone is real, dependable, and trustworthy. It is futile to trust in human strength. Do not depend on humanity; humanity is only breath.

The one who trusts in God will receive a blessing of inner peace and strength. We gain confidence knowing that in whatever the circumstances we find ourselves—whether in want or plenty, whether in life or death—God is present and we are richly blessed.

A preacher can take the opportunity this psalm affords to explore more deeply the quality of trust. Trust is an essential part of life. An environment of trust is necessary in order for mental, emotional, and spiritual development to occur. When I encounter mistrust, I withdraw to myself. As Jürgen Moltmann observes, "Fish need water in which to swim, birds need air in which to fly, and we human beings need

# Psalm 62:5-12

## Theological Perspective

misshapen. The heart's disease may be understood as *hamartia*, misorientation. Rather than orienting itself toward God, the heart aims itself at something less than God, producing fruit that is less than godly. Something in the human condition tempts us to idolatry—ignoring God and orienting ourselves to something else, a mere creature of God, as though it were God.

Reinhold Niebuhr offers an explanation (though not a justification) for the human tendency toward misorientation. "Since [humanity] is involved in the contingencies and necessities of the natural process on the one hand, and since, on the other, he stands outside them and foresees their caprices and perils, he is anxious. In his anxiety, he seeks to transmute his finiteness into infinity, his weakness into strength, his dependence into independence."[4]

The psalmist also points to the finite and passing nature of mortal existence. Rich and poor, powerful and weak face a common end shared by all mortals (v. 9). This realization produces anxiety, which in turn generates the temptation to preserve one's finite existence at any cost (v. 10). Oriented toward self rather than God and neighbor, the constricted heart falls away from its true peace into the restless and ultimately fruitless quest for immortality—to be like God. And so individuals and nations, ethnic and class groups, religious communities and political parties betray God's orderly and good creation in a self-deluded attempt at self-preservation that finally produces destruction and disorder.

Realizing all this, the psalmist exhorts us to place our trust in God alone. God is the only source of hope and peace for mortals. If life has any significance, it will be found in God. If our families, communities, nations, and churches have any worth, it will be located in God. This is the meaning of the final, problematic verse in Psalm 62, "For you repay to all according to their work." The psalmist is not claiming that people get what they deserve but that orienting one's life toward God is the only way to find hope, peace, and salvation.

TIMOTHY A. BEACH-VERHEY

## Pastoral Perspective

So the psalmist turns to the community of faith around him and exhorts, "Put no confidence in extortion, and set no vain hopes on robbery; if riches increase, do not set your heart on them" (v. 10). One can hear here echoes of Ecclesiastes . . . and Jesus. Nothing we have and hold, nothing we gain legally or illegally, no "securities" in the portfolio of our lives, can offer the ultimate security that comes only from the God of powerful, loyal love. The rich cannot secure their lives by the things they amass. The poor cannot secure their lives by getting what the rich and powerful have. Both are equally vulnerable. Both are equally fleeting. "Take care!" says Jesus. "Be on your guard against all kinds of greed; for one's life does not consist in the abundance of possessions. . . . Strive for [God's] kingdom, and these things will be given to you as well" (Luke 12:15, 31).

Psalm 62 offers the pastor the opportunity to explore what it means to trust God in a risky, precarious world in which such expressions of trust can easily appear out of touch with reality. Faith does not shut its eyes to the assaults that beset us. It does not place its trust in those who seem to be the "winners" in the game of life. Faith clings to and relies on the living God alone. Authentic trust is not engendered by our own efforts at self-assurance. It comes from God's own self-revelation and clings to the assurance that "power belongs to God, and steadfast love belongs to you, O Lord. For you repay to all according to their work."

That is the "good news of judgment" which enables people of faith to "wait in the Lord," not in passive resignation to the powers that be, but in eager expectation of every fresh epiphany of the "kingdom, power, and glory" of the vulnerable One who alone is our "rock and salvation."

ALLEN C. MCSWEEN JR.

---

[4]Reinhold Niebuhr, *The Nature and Destiny of Man*, 2 vols. (New York: Charles Scribner's Sons, 1964), 1:251.

## Exegetical Perspective

tempered by God's steadfast love for us. Therefore, we can trust that God's power will always be used for our good. Whatever our predicament or distress, we can trust that God both is *able* to deliver us and *desires* to do so.

The final line of the psalm states the consequences of God's power and steadfast love for human beings: "For you repay to all according to their work" (v. 12b). This statement can be construed by the worshiping congregation as both hope and warning: hope that those who put their trust in God will ultimately experience deliverance, and warning that those who put their trust elsewhere and/or use their power to harm others will ultimately be defeated.

*Relationship of Psalm 62 to the Other Lectionary Texts.* In the context of Psalm 62, that final statement in verse 12b emphasizes hope for those who trust in God despite their human predicament. The underlying warning of the possibility of God's judgment is muted. In other lectionary readings for the day, the urgent warning of judgment is the primary note sounded.

In the Old Testament reading, Jonah 3:1–5, 10, the prophet Jonah reluctantly proclaims God's message to the people of Nineveh: "Forty days more, and Nineveh shall be overthrown!" (v. 4). Because the people of Nineveh believe and repent of their evil ways, God's mind is changed about destroying the city.

In the Gospel reading, Mark 1:14–20, Jesus proclaims, "The time is fulfilled, and the kingdom of God has come near; repent, and believe in the good news" (v.15). With the beginning of Jesus' earthly ministry, there is a new urgency about the message of repentance and faith in God. In him, the kingdom of God has come near, and a decision about where to put one's trust must be made. The rest of the passage describes Jesus' call of his first disciples, Simon and Andrew and James and John. Both sets of brothers "immediately" respond to Jesus' call, leaving behind livelihood and family to follow him—an obvious expression of trust.

MARSHA M. WILFONG

## Homiletical Perspective

trust in order to develop our humanity. Trust is the basic element in which human life exists." In addition Moltmann remarks, "Trust is always a mutual affair, and this is true of trust in God too: We trust in God because God trusts in us."[2] God's love for humans generates trust.

God is the one on whom and in whom we can depend; God is most worthy of our trust. God practices steadfast love toward us (v. 12). God bears our burdens, shares our grief, forgives our sins, and endures our unfaithfulness. God's sharing, forgiving, and enduring qualities are most poignantly demonstrated in the suffering of Christ on the cross. Experience and history and the cross teach us that we can trust God.

Trust in God is exemplified in the life of Abraham and Sarah, who left their homeland, their familiar surroundings, and wandered as strangers in order to follow God's promise (Gen. 12:2, 3). This trust caused them to take risks, but it also gave them confidence in taking the risks. Confidence involves stepping out from what is comfortable, familiar, and safe and being open to the unknown future. Again in Moltmann's words, "Here trust has the future as its lodestone, and is a power that can face the challenges of the future creatively, with joy in the adventure and experiment. Here, trust in God means the courage to risk."[3] Later he continues, "In biblical faith, trust in God does not mean the comfortable protection and safekeeping of our mother's womb. It means the risky freedom of the wide spaces and ever-new coming of God."[4] One might compare the trust a child has toward its mother. That trust grows out of the mother's love, commitment, and care. Such trust will weather difficult storms even when the mother turns away from the child for a time. "The child acquires a trust in life stronger than its fear and mistrust of what is strange. We might say that a capacity for trust develops that can even stand up to justifiable mistrust."[5] If a child develops that kind of trust in a mortal being, how much more can we bond in trust with God who will never turn away from us!

DAVE BLAND

[2] Jürgen Moltmann, "Control Is Good—Trust Is Better: Freedom and Security in a Free World," *Theology Today* 62, no. 4 (January 2006): 473.
[3] Ibid.
[4] Ibid., 474.
[5] Ibid., 467.

# 1 Corinthians 7:29-31

<sup>29</sup>I mean, brothers and sisters, the appointed time has grown short; from now on, let even those who have wives be as though they had none, <sup>30</sup>and those who mourn as though they were not mourning, and those who rejoice as though they were not rejoicing, and those who buy as though they had no possessions, <sup>31</sup>and those who deal with the world as though they had no dealings with it. For the present form of this world is passing away.

## Theological Perspective

This passage is set within the same wide-ranging instructions as 1 Corinthians 6:12–20, one of last Sunday's readings, and the theological comments on both passages should be read together. Interestingly, neither passage operates primarily at the level of instructions about specific relationships, institutions, and activities. Both rise to make a general point about the appropriate attitude or stance for faithful living. Unlike 6:12–20, however, 7:29–31 presents a *single* argument whose fundamental premise is *resolutely eschatological.*

The time has grown short and the form of this world is passing away (premise). Therefore, let
— those who have wives be as though they had none,
— those who mourn be as though they were not mourning,
— those who rejoice be as though they were not rejoicing,
— those who buy as though they had no possessions,
— those who deal with the world as though they had no dealings with it.
Presumably, were the time longer, wives, mourning, rejoicing, possessions, and society might be differently regarded. As things stand, says Paul, they provoke anxieties that may hinder devotion to the

## Pastoral Perspective

Paul's eschatological expectation frames the entirety of his first letter to the Corinthians. He reminds the Corinthians at the outset of the letter that God's grace in Christ has been given them to strengthen them and keep them blameless as they await the day of the Lord (1 Cor. 1:7–8). At the end of the letter he discusses at length the promised resurrection of the body that will take place at the return of Christ. Paul was clearly expecting the Parousia, the return of Christ and the day of judgment, as an imminent event that would occur in the lifetimes of those to whom he was writing. Paul lived in a state of urgent anticipation of this event, with a vivid sense that "the time has grown short" (v. 29), and felt this urgency ought to shape all aspects of Christian life, including the ones mentioned in today's passage.

At first glance, the theological framework of Paul's teachings to the Corinthians in this passage is foreign to us, such that it might seem difficult to apply these teachings to the pastoral needs of contemporary Christian communities. Now, more than 1,900 years after Paul's letter, we know that his expectation of Christ's return was not met in the way that Paul expected. Nevertheless, this text challenges us to recognize that as Christians our lives too are framed by eschatological expectation, and this ought to shape our way of living in the world,

## Exegetical Perspective

In 1 Corinthians 7:1–15:58 Paul addresses the questions that the Corinthian church asked him in writing. The first issue taken up in chapter 7 is marriage and celibacy. It is impossible to reconstruct precisely what the question from the Corinthian church was about. Perhaps some married women in the Corinthian church declared celibacy, believing that sexual abstinence was necessary for purity of soul. That would have resulted in disruption in the patriarchal order of their household, in which sex and childbearing were part of the mechanism for domesticating women.

Whatever the exact scope and nature of the original question was, Paul begins by stating his general principle that abstinence is better, but marriage is also recommended to avoid sexual immorality (vv. 1–8). Then he moves on to provide specific pastoral advice to various groups of people: to the unmarried and the widows (vv. 8–9); to the married (vv. 10–11), especially to those married to an unbeliever (vv. 12–16); to the virgins (vv. 25–26); and to the engaged (vv. 36–38). For all these different pieces of admonition, the recurring theme Paul repeatedly cites is, "Remain as you are" (v. 20). Then our passage (vv. 29–31) lays out the underlying reason for the kind of theological position on which Paul is operating in his pastoral advice: the

## Homiletical Perspective

How on earth do you preach on a passage of Scripture that seems to have proved dead wrong? "The present form of this world is passing away" (v. 31). Not yet it has not—and we are two thousand years on the other side of Paul's assertion.

This could not have been one of Paul's easiest sections of writing. More than once in this extended discourse on the conduct Christians should practice in light of what he saw as the "last days" rapidly drawing to a close, he has interrupted himself to say, "Now, I don't have this from the Lord, it's just me talking here" (7:12, 25—an interesting statement that the great theologian-apostle can make, but one that is rarely found on the lips of lesser preachers of the Bible). In other words, Paul is crossing new territory for the gospel, uncharted terrain, with no road map from the Lord, and he is seeking to guide the first generation of Christians across it.

With the exception of chiliastic groups and those who are persuaded by bumper-sticker theology, few Christians today are sitting up nights trying to decide if they really should marry their fiancées because Jesus might return before they can cut the wedding cake. "The impending crisis" (v. 26), at least the one Paul meant, is simply not on our minds. If it is coming at all, it is still pending.

*1 Corinthians 7:29–31*     279

# 1 Corinthians 7:29-31

## Theological Perspective

Lord, and it is better to be anxious not about worldly affairs but about being holy (7:32–35).

Paul makes concessions to worldly expectations and human desires. For example, "If anyone thinks that he is not behaving properly toward his fiancée, if his passions are strong, and so it has to be, let him marry as he wishes; it is no sin" (7:36). Thus, it seems that wives, mourning, rejoicing, and possessions are not, in and of themselves, the basic point of our passage. The purpose is to recommend a general attitude, a manner of dwelling in the world *as though not*.

Would it make sense to speak as Paul does here even if we *were* convinced that the end will soon arrive? After a fashion, this question is taken up by a TV series called *Three Moons over Milford*, in which the moon, having been blown into three pieces, now threatens to destroy the earth, although no one knows exactly when. How do people in the town of Milford, Vermont, respond? One sells more real estate. A judge becomes unsure whether to impose long sentences. An executive leaves both family and business to climb the world's highest mountains, an activity he otherwise would forgo because it damages long-term relationships and possibilities. By contrast, his youngish wife resolves to uphold responsibilities to her children. Not many Milfordians heed Paul's recommendation. But then this *is* commercial American television, and we also recall that the apostle did not simply think our world was hurtling toward extinction. He believed that we belong to God, that "flesh and blood cannot inherit the kingdom," and that those united with Christ will be raised with imperishable spiritual bodies (1 Cor. 15:50–51). So we are not surprised that he saw things differently.

Does 7:29–31 make sense if we don't believe the end is coming soon? The twentieth-century Bible scholar and theologian Rudolf Bultmann thought so. Bultmann recognized that here Paul presents an attitude or stance of living in the world *as though not*, and that this attitude is authorized partly by Paul's eschatological expectation. But Bultmann insisted that the key point, for Paul as for Jesus, is simply that we belong completely to God. A person who recognizes this—a person of faith—obeys the radical demand of the Creator and Judge who stands beyond this world, and such a person is therefore freed from worldly claims.[1] But this is the attitude that appropriately accompanies faith in every age. So, if Bultmann is correct, our passage does not

[1] *Existence and Faith: Shorter Writings of Rudolf Bultmann*, trans. Schubert M. Ogden (London: Collins, 1964), 229–30.

## Pastoral Perspective

just as Paul recommends that it should shape the Corinthian community. As the Nicene Creed states it, "we look for the resurrection of the dead, and the life of the world to come." Although we may not expect the return of Christ to happen in our lifetimes, as Paul did, as Christians we nonetheless do not simply resign ourselves to the givenness of the world, for we have planted within us a great hope that God's kingdom will come on earth as in heaven. This means that we are a people who look to the future in trust and hope, confident that God is working God's purposes out and that God's realm is even now breaking into our world. Moreover, Paul's teaching reminds us that our expectation of God's inbreaking kingdom ought to have an urgency to it that puts all other aspects of our lives into their proper perspective.

Although the coming reign of God is much larger than the trajectory of our own personal lives, a sense of eschatological urgency is available to us whenever we reflect on our own mortality and realize that we too live in a situation in which "the time has grown short." As humans our lives are compressed into a limited span of life, and time can seem very short, especially as we grow older. We can seek to deny this fact of our mortality, but Paul's teaching suggests that it is salutary to awaken to the truth of the limitedness of our lives. Benedict said, "A monk should have death always before his eyes."

The value of this eschatological awareness is that it can give to our lives both a sense of freedom and a sense of urgency. Once we recognize, with Paul, that "the present form of this world is passing away" (v. 31), we can see that the structures of our lives— our human relationships, even the closest ones, the experiences that cause us grief and joy, our possessions, indeed all our dealings with the world—are among those things that are passing away. They are not ultimate or permanent. This recognition of the transience of all earthly things need not drive us to despair, nor should it induce the kind of detachment practiced by Stoics of Paul's time, who withdrew from their circumstances to an inner world where they could be resigned to the laws of fate. Rather, according to Paul, the recognition that the structures of this world are passing away changes our relationship to the things of this world, allowing us to live with them "as though not." We can remain involved in all the elements of our daily lives, yet have an inner freedom in relation to these things, recognizing their impermanence. This inner freedom allows us to live more graciously with the vicissitudes of

designated eschatological time (*ho kairos*) is drawing very near.

The introductory remark in verse 29—"I mean" or "I say this"—has two critical functions. First, it alerts the readers that what follows is an important statement. Second, as an exact parallel to "I give my opinion" in verse 25, it makes crystal clear that it is not the Lord but Paul himself who says the following instruction. That is, in the same ethos as verse 25, what Paul has to say about the nearness of the eschaton (v. 29) and the impending nature of the dissolution of the present order (v. 31) is no more and no less than Paul's own opinion (*gnōmē*).

The ensuing eschatological statement that the time has been drawn up in verse 29a could be a maxim that was shared by early Christians who were of apocalyptic persuasion. It is very similar to a saying attributed to Jesus in Mark 1:15a, "The time has been fulfilled" (*peplērōtai ho kairos*), which, by the way, is edited out in Matthew 4:17. That means, at least, the author of the earliest Gospel, Mark—if not those of the later ones like Matthew and Luke—seems to agree with Paul on the imminent Parousia eschatology.

Even though it is most natural to interpret "the time" (*ho kairos*) as a reference to *the* last moment in history in apocalyptic terms, it is possible to take it as one of the moments designated by God for a direct intervention, not necessarily on a cosmic scale. The ambiguities are inherent in the text and should not be done away with by exegetical presumptions.

There are two different ways to construe the syntax of verses 29–31a. The first option is to take verse 29a and verse 29b as two separate sentences. That is how NRSV and most other English versions take it. In this case, the series of five instructions in verses 29b–31a is construed elliptically. It is preceded by an adverbial phrase, which can be translated either as "from now on" or "as for the rest." Then the remaining part of the sentence is led by a conjunction *hina* and contains five conjugated verbs in the subjunctive mood. The whole clause is presented without a main verb. Considering that it is an exhortation, one might supply such a word as *paraineō* (I exhort, I advise) as the main verb. Then the subordinate clause is identified as a noun clause functioning as the direct object of the main verb. The problem with this option is that it goes against the general principle of "Remain as you are."

The other option is to take the statement, "The time has been drawn up" (NRSV: "appointed time") as the main clause and the *hina* clause (vv. 29b–31a)

This whole matter raises many interesting questions for modern-day Christians, many more than anyone could possibly pursue in one sermon. These complex issues of hermeneutics are perhaps best explored in a series of studies where congregants are free to pose those questions that would inevitably arise (not to mention Paul's specific admonitions to slaves, wives, husbands, etc., that themselves open whole carloads of ethical issues). That leaves us with the basic question that faces every preacher, every Sunday. What word is here that God wants said? And more specifically, said by me here, now, to these people? That primary question is followed by its corollary. What difference would it make if we all heard this word? Let us take each of those questions in turn.

*What word is here that God wants said?* "For the present form of this world is passing away." This verse is clearly the thrust of all Paul will say in this context. Christians invariably take one of two approaches to this text—and for that matter, most texts. Reading these words as a news bulletin handed to their personal anchor desk, they either attempt to prove them literally true or ignore them as a relic of a worldview no longer possible. No doubt, Paul certainly meant that the end of the age was drawing near and therefore Christians could no longer pursue business as usual. Given the intensification of pressure on Christians by imperial Rome, particularly in Asia Minor, where cities vied for the honor—and the financial gain—of building a temple for emperor worship, that statement was by no means unreasonable. Nevertheless, the return of the Lord did not occur, and countless such statements by preachers since the time of Paul have likewise proved inaccurate.

In the early 1950s, the forerunners of the Branch Davidians assembled on a hilltop to the west of Waco, Texas, to wait for the coming of the Lord. They were certain that Jesus would descend into their midst at precisely 2:00 p.m. on a particular Tuesday. But just to be sure they did not miss him, they gathered a few days early and sang hymns and rejoiced, their eyes on the central Texas sky. In their spare time they answered questions from reporters eager for the story. When Jesus somehow misunderstood the schedule, they waited anxiously a few more days and then returned sadly to their compound east of town.

So, who is more foolish? The Davidians and others who can think of nothing but the soon return of the Lord, or we who think of nothing but our own time and place as if it were eternal?

# 1 Corinthians 7:29-31

## Theological Perspective

present a stance that is fitting only for an interim period before the end; it presents the perennially genuine attitude and resolve of true faith. We are to live in complete obedience to God and therefore to be in the world but not of it, or in the world *as though not.*

This does not mean that I *must* remain unmarried, as Paul's instructions about mutual conjugal rights and his concession that some singles should marry clearly show. (Much less does it mean that I should leave my spouse if I am married already.) Instead, it means that my fundamental vocation is defined by God's claim upon me, rather than by the many worldly claims made on me by my wife, my possessions, and so on. Perhaps we should go further and say, somewhat as we did with reference to 6:12–20, that God's radical claim relativizes these other claims and puts them in their place. Perhaps we should conclude that responsibilities to wife and family continue to make claims, but these must be adjusted to and fitted with the ultimate claim that God makes. Perhaps we should even join Paul's negative in 7:29 with a positive: Discharge obligations and responsibilities to your spouse in a manner that is consistent with your ultimate devotion to God.

Perhaps, although difficulties remain. After all, in 7:29 Paul does *not* say, "Don't put too much stock in marriage." He does not say, "Don't overestimate the claim that your spouse makes upon you," or "Don't elevate your spouse into an idol." He says, "Let those who have wives be as though they had *none.*" That's a strong negative. So even if his statements here are rhetorical, the rhetoric is not especially balanced, and the attitude expressed may not be either. It seems too conventional, sensible, and domestic to conclude that Paul is really only saying that the mundane claims upon us should be balanced by or seen in the context of God's claim. My conclusion? In 7:29–31 anyway, Paul finally fails to recognize with sufficient seriousness that *God's* good world appropriately *does* make claims upon us. In the end, I just can't shake the sense that the mother in *Three Moons over Milford* who continues to care and worry over her children probably got it right.

DOUGLAS F. OTTATI

## Pastoral Perspective

life, recognizing that our identity is not determined by them.

This inner freedom serves a larger purpose than helping us cope with life, however; this inner freedom helps us fulfill our calling as Christians. Paul reminds the Corinthians that their calling as Christ's followers is to glorify God and build up the Christian community of which they are a part. Paul notes, directly after this passage, that those who are married have divided loyalties in regard to this mission, since they must please their spouses, while those who are unmarried can devote themselves wholeheartedly to the Lord. However, the advice Paul gives in today's passage suggests that living in eschatological expectation can give even those who are married a freedom that allows them to fulfill the calling of ordering all aspects of their lives to the greater glory of God and to service of the community.

In relation to this calling, the inner freedom of Paul's eschatological perspective also gives a sense of urgency. The time has grown short for us to do that to which we were called, which is to proclaim Jesus Christ, and him crucified, and to devote our lives to Christian love, *agapē*. This urgency can give us a healthy dissatisfaction with those structures of the world that hinder God's coming reign, and spur us to devote ourselves wholeheartedly to changing those structures as part of our participation in God's work in the world. All the other aspects of our lives—relationships, possessions, or any and all other dealings with the world—must be ordered toward the mission of God. This radical devotion to God can be practiced only when we grasp the urgency of Paul's eschatological message and understand both the shortness of the time we have and the greatness of the hope to which God has called us.

RUTHANNA B. HOOKE

as its subordinate adverbial clause indicating the result of the main clause. If this is the case, the five subjunctive verbs in the subordinate clause are not exhortations but statements for virtual reality. Then the translation of the whole section will be as follows: "I say this, brothers and sisters. The time has already been drawn up short with the result that from now on those who have wives would be just as those who have not, and those who are weeping just as those who are not weeping, and those who are rejoicing just as those who are not rejoicing, and those who buy things just as those who have no possessions, and those who deal with the world just as those who do not deal with it." The idea is that in this critical eschatological time there is no meaningful difference between any binary oppositions regarding one's status and therefore it is good to remain as you are. This interpretation coheres with the flow of argument in the entire chapter 7.

The final remark in verse 31b, "For the scheme of this world is passing" (my translation), is a corollary to the beginning statement in verse 29a, and both function as the basis for what goes in between. The noun *schēma* is derived from the second aorist infinitive *schein* of the verb *echō*. So the closest etymological meaning of *schēma* is "the way things are." Then the phrase *to schēma tou kosmou toutou* can be interpreted as "the configuration of the current world," and as such it comprehensively connotes all the social, historical, cultural, economic, and political order of the then-contemporary world. The image of the Roman Empire, the dominant superpower that defined the order of the lands inhabited by all the people in the Mediterranean world, looms large in the background. Then it is remarkable that Paul's eschatological hope envisions God's direct intervention that would bring about a radical reconfiguration of such an order, however unchangeable and invincible it may sound.

EUGENE EUNG-CHUN PARK

Look again at the text. Is Paul wrong, or is it not ever true today, as it was then, that the present form of this world is passing away? Like many of the prophets of ancient Israel whose words were intended one way but were fulfilled in another, Paul told Christians exactly what they needed to hear. Though no one could see it, imperial Rome was sick unto death. The subversive words of the Galilean were undercutting their monolithic world, cracking apart its foundation like a seed bursting through the smallest crack in the stone. Therefore, Paul tells them to give utmost priority to the cause of Christ. Is that not exactly what Christians need to do today, in this world whose present form is likewise passing away? In our interpretation for preaching we must move from principle to principle, not from word to word. Only in this way can we avoid unwarranted literalism or skepticism.

*What difference would it make if we all heard this word?* Chiliastic groups are criticized theologically for ignoring this present world by focusing exclusively on a world to come. Yet in some ways, not focusing on a world to come is a failure of the mainline church. Why do we do what we do? How do we do it? With what motivation, to what ends? When we become preoccupied with social work and good deeds merely in the name of our organization, we run several risks. First, we lose the opportunity to transform others—and ourselves—in the name of Christ and become nothing more than a religious Rotary Club (without as good attendance!). Furthermore, offering all that we do out of love for Jesus—the redeemer of society as well as the individual—leads other Christians to similar commitment. Next, doing so will witness more plainly to the world than all our promotions and church-growth movement strategies. Finally, attentiveness to the ultimate purposes of God will point us to a new horizon of optimism and alleviate our weariness in the task.

Remember, Jesus said: "Be of good cheer, I have overcome the world!" (John 16:33 RSV). "For the present form of this world is passing away" (1 Cor. 7:31).

CLYDE FANT

# Mark 1:14-20

¹⁴Now after John was arrested, Jesus came to Galilee, proclaiming the good news of God, ¹⁵and saying, "The time is fulfilled, and the kingdom of God has come near; repent, and believe in the good news."

¹⁶As Jesus passed along the Sea of Galilee, he saw Simon and his brother Andrew casting a net into the sea—for they were fishermen. ¹⁷And Jesus said to them, "Follow me and I will make you fish for people." ¹⁸And immediately they left their nets and followed him. ¹⁹As he went a little farther, he saw James son of Zebedee and his brother John, who were in their boat mending the nets. ²⁰Immediately he called them; and they left their father Zebedee in the boat with the hired men, and followed him.

## Theological Perspective

Mark's brief account of the beginnings of Jesus' Galilean ministry links Jesus' proclamation of the gospel with his calling of a band of disciples. These activities are by no means unrelated. Jesus' proclamation is not just a solo recitation of informative words but is an efficacious action that creates community and is taken up and continued by that community. Consequently, these few verses have had wide-ranging implications for the doctrines of the church and its proclamation, the Christian life, and even the person and work of Christ.

Jesus' message, aptly characterized as "good news," is a declaration of God's victory, an announcement of a wondrously new state of affairs breaking into the present. Mark's Gospel will proceed to illustrate how liberation, restoration, and reconciliation are already happening in Jesus' healing miracles, his casting out of demons, and his teaching. The trajectory initiated by Jesus' proclamation and ministry is promised to eventuate in the final consummation of God's purposes for humanity when the Son of Man returns in glory.

The indicative concerning the inbreaking of God's kingdom is followed by an imperative: repent and believe in the good news. Ever since Luther stressed the priority of grace and faith over human works, Protestant interpreters have drawn attention

## Pastoral Perspective

Jesus begins his public ministry proclaiming that "the time is fulfilled." "Fulfilled" would seem to suggest that something is accomplished, finished, brought to completion. And yet the gospel story is just beginning. How do we strike a balance between Epiphany (when we proclaim that God's kingdom is near and fulfilled) and Advent (when we proclaim that we are to wait and pray for God's coming)? Both themes are true: yes, "This is the day"; but also "When that day appears." God's promised future is both now and, at the same time, not yet. Pastorally, we comfort the distressed with assurances that the divine help they hope for is already present; because we trust that God will make everything right at the end, everything is right already. In the mystery of time from God's perspective, the past, the present, and the future are collapsed. We who are bound by space and time have a relationship with the eternal and unbound God—so no wonder the language of faith relies on ambiguity and paradox!

Along those lines, we have here another case of instant decisions for Christ: Simon, Andrew, James, and John drop everything and become disciples, just like that, "immediately." But, again, this is not the end of the story. This is just the beginning of "the beginning" (v. 1). Ahead, for them and for us, there is much to learn, much stumbling,

## Exegetical Perspective

Jesus returned to Galilee following his forty days in the wilderness (1:12–13), ready to begin his mission to proclaim the "good news." He announced that the moment has finally come for God to retake control over the world that God has created. Because the time (*kairos*) was right, Jesus' ministry could begin.

Jesus used a metaphor that appears sixty-six times in the New Testament, "the kingdom of God," to announce the beginning of his ministry. The Matthean equivalent, "the kingdom of heaven," occurs an additional thirty-two times. In the Old Testament the expression "the kingdom of YHWH" occurs only twice (1 Chr. 28:5; 2 Chr. 13:8), and "kingdom of God" occurs never. Still, the idea that God rules as king over Israel, the nations, and the cosmos certainly does occur, for example, in the "enthronement psalms" (Pss. 47, 93, 96–99). Of course, there are many Old Testament texts that call God "king." Similarly, the expression "the kingdom of God" appears in only one intertestamental text (*Ps. Sol.* 17:3), though several such texts speak of God as king.

One reason Jesus used this metaphor is because he sought to contrast the goals of his mission with the goals of the Herodian dynasty. Herod the Great ruled as king because he was placed on the throne by the Roman Senate as a reward for his support during the

## Homiletical Perspective

The Gospel lesson for this day is just seven verses long, but it dreams of many sermons. Mark's style is both simple and superconcentrated. Whole sermons might grow out of short phrases, even single words. A preacher might find herself and her congregation grasped by fragments like "now after John was arrested," "the time is fulfilled," "repent and believe," "they left their father," or even just "immediately." She might see the text dividing into two stories and choose to preach only on Jesus' proclamation of good news (vv. 14–15) or only on his call of the first disciples (vv. 16–20). Or she might bring the pieces together into a glorious meal of small, intensely flavored tastings. Whatever their scope, the best sermons will grow out of close attention to each of these words and some sense of their connection to one another.

Attending to the words involves attending to the time of the Gospel. Mark begins like an alarm clock, persistently declaring the time and demanding some response. Markers of time fill the early verses: this is the time when the prophets' words are fulfilled (vv. 2–3); the time of the new Elijah (vv. 4–8); the time when the heavens are torn open, the Spirit descends, and a voice sounds from heaven (vv. 9–11); and the time when both the Spirit and the Adversary are at work in the world with new intensity (vv. 12–13).

# Mark 1:14-20

## Theological Perspective

to the precedence of the indicative to the imperative in this text. The imperative to repent and believe, turning away from prior trusts and loyalties, is a response to the indicative claim that the kingdom is at hand, that God is graciously at work.

The story of the calling of the disciples follows the synopsis of Jesus' proclamation of God's kingdom in order to demonstrate what this kingdom involves. Right away Jesus not only talks about the reign of God but enacts it. The ultimate religious authority that he would later exercise over winds, waves, and demons is immediately evident in his calling of the disciples. In the narrative Jesus is the sole catalyst of the action. He calls the disciples categorically, compellingly. The only words reported are Jesus' words; the disciples say nothing. Drawn only by his summons, they follow Jesus before he has performed any spectacular miracles that could serve as validating credentials. As Karl Barth has noted, they are elected to discipleship simply through the fact that Jesus claims them.[1] When Jesus declares that now they shall be fishers of people, their new status is anchored in the fact that Jesus has fished for them; Jesus is the ultimate fisher, and they are the netted fish. In the obedient responses of the two sets of brothers the reign of God is actualized in the present.

For theologians through the centuries this connection of message and call has had critical consequences. Jesus' own action is the inbreaking of the proclaimed kingdom, the fulfillment of the promise. As Rudolf Bultmann noted, wherever Jesus was active, the time was fulfilled and the kingdom was present. Whenever the gospel is preached, the reign of God draws near to the hearers, calling for a decision.[2] But Bultmann may have underestimated the equally important future orientation of Jesus' proclamation. Although the kingdom is inbreaking in the present, it remains hidden; the full manifestation of the newly inaugurated era awaits the future. Theologians have described this new era variously, elaborating it according to the hopes of their specific cultures and personalities. For some it has been seen as a new situation of unconditional acceptance of sinful humanity. For others it has been seen as a time of unprecedented spiritual vitality displacing an era of stagnation. For yet others it has been seen as a new age of peace and justice healing the old order of oppression and hostility. But

[1] Karl Barth, *Church Dogmatics*, IV/3, trans. G. W. Bromiley (Edinburgh: T. & T. Clark, 1962), 588–92.
[2] Rudolf Bultmann, *History and Eschatology* (Edinburgh: University Press, 1957), 256–58.

## Pastoral Perspective

misunderstanding, and backsliding. Becoming a faithful Christian disciple takes both a moment and a lifetime.

In Mark's Gospel we see how this early decision needs to be reaffirmed and even corrected time and again. At Caesarea Philippi, Simon affirms his faith in Jesus, but not his faith in Jesus as the suffering Messiah—that will take a lifetime (8:27–33). On the mount of transfiguration Peter knows how good it is to be with Jesus but forgets that the real task is to follow Jesus—for a lifetime (9:2–8). In the courtyard, warming himself before the fire, Peter threatens to give up a lifetime of fidelity for a moment of fear (14:66–72). At the very end, when Jesus is on the cross, Peter, Andrew, James, and John are nowhere to be found. Even then God does not count that moment as the final word: now Jesus will go before them—for a lifetime (15:40–41; 16:7–8).

Some of our churches so stress the moment of decision for Jesus that we fail to nurture the long-standing commitment. Decision is to be lived out in fidelity, service, even sacrifice. Some of our churches are so good at nurturing that we forget that even "cradle Christians" sometimes need to decide for fidelity, service, even sacrifice. Christianity is always both for now and for the long haul; both a moment and a lifetime.

Still, stories like these instant conversions give legitimacy to spontaneity, acting on impulse, trusting in the prompting of the Holy Spirit. We remember and prize those rare moments when, in the midst of life's prevalent ambiguities, choices suddenly became clear.

Furthermore, sometimes in the more ordinary days we find courage for the drudgery or the dread by remembering those moments when we did know the call and did say, "Yes." In quite another context Paul tells the Roman Christians that "the gifts and the calling of God are irrevocable" (Rom. 11:29). When we feel most like revoking our own discipleship, we remember the call.

James and John "immediately" left Zebedee, which probably pained him. But did they dishonor their father? I would like to think not. I would like to think that this parent taught his children to strike out onto the unpredictable seas—and so he could not fault them for going their own way.

The recent movie *Billy Elliot* tells the story of a young boy growing up in a working-class neighborhood in northern England. Quite unexpectedly (quite suddenly almost) he discovers that he loves classical dance and that he dances well.

Parthian invasion of Roman Palestine. Herod was anxious to show both his Roman patrons and his Jewish subjects that he was worthy of the title king. He rebuilt the temple of Jerusalem because temple building was a royal prerogative. Herod constructed an impressive building over the tombs of the patriarchs and their wives in Hebron to show his subjects that he honored Jewish tradition. Herod built the cities of Caesarea Maritima and Sebaste to impress and honor Augustus Caesar, his imperial patron. Herod's son Antipas rebuilt the city of Sepphoris, which was just three miles from Nazareth, the village where Jesus grew up. This beautiful city, described as the "ornament of Galilee," served as Antipas's capital until he built Tiberias along the western shore of the Sea of Galilee to honor Tiberius Caesar. The New Testament does not record that Jesus ever entered these cities, which stood as testaments to the royal power and prestige of the Herodian dynasty.

The kingdom of God that Jesus proclaimed was not bolstered by the construction of monumental buildings and great cities. God's kingdom is manifest in the human embrace of God's rule through repentance and faith. Jesus' mission was to call people to repentance, that is, a total reorientation of their lives so that they will be in a position to accept God's sovereign rule authentically. The Gospel of Mark recounts the resistance that Jesus experienced to his mission. This resistance eventually led to his death and—ironically—to the recognition of Jesus' true identity by the Roman centurion (Mark 15:39). The comment in verse 14a, that Jesus' ministry began following the arrest of John the Baptist, hints that the Baptist's fate was to foreshadow that of Jesus, for example, Mark 9:31.

Jesus' mission was not a solitary one. The church remembers that there were some people who were associated with Jesus from the very beginning. Jesus calls four men—two sets of brothers—to follow him. Later he would commission them and eight others to preach and to drive out demons (3:13–19). Peter and Andrew, James and John provide the reader with a striking example of what a response of repentance and faith means. Their response to Jesus' invitation is immediate and complete. The Old Testament lesson (Jonah 3:1–5, 10) highlights the response of Nineveh to the message of judgment that Jonah proclaimed. Their response prompted God to withdraw the judgment that God commissioned the prophet to announce.

The name of Andrew stands out from those of the other four disciples. It is a Greek name with no

Then in verse 14 we are propelled into a time when John has already been arrested—the time of Elijah's preparation passed before we even knew what it meant!—and finally the one around whom all this activity has been swirling speaks: "The time is fulfilled, and the kingdom of God has come near" (v. 15). Jesus does not just announce the time. He fulfills it, in word and in flesh.

And he calls people to respond. Because the time is fulfilled, Jesus calls us to "repent, and believe in the good news" (v. 15). And because the kingdom of God has drawn near, Jesus calls disciples to follow him and be made into fishers for people (v. 17). These are not all-purpose ethical imperatives, always in season, but responses to the fullness of time made present in Jesus Christ. Repenting, believing, following, fishing—these are actions that keep time with this great tempo change in the music of redemption.

A preacher might think with a congregation about this temporal order. It runs counter to the order implicit in so many church programs and personal devotions. We do not repent in order to usher in the time of redemption, but because that time is already at hand. We do not become fishers in order to meet the quota that will summon up the reign of God, but because that reign has already come near. And we do not follow Jesus with the hopes that one day we might find him, but because he has already come to us and called us. As Mark tells the time, God takes the initiative. The reign of God is not the product of discipleship, but the precondition of it. What would be the shape of church programs and individual lives with that sense of time?

A preacher might also consider the difficulties created by Mark's sense of time. If the time is fulfilled, how come history still seems like one disaster after another? If the reign of God is at hand, why bother taking care of anything—or anyone—in this age? And how are we supposed to keep time with a redemption that is both already present and still on the way? These questions have been with the church for centuries. They are especially acute in our own time, when talk of the end floods popular culture, politics, and social movements.

The call of the first disciples (vv. 16–20) grows out of Jesus' announcement of the time. In calling the Galilean fishermen to discipleship, Jesus does not just ask them to add one more task to their busy lives. He calls them into new ways of being. When Simon and Andrew leave their nets, they leave a way of life. This is even clearer with James and John, who leave not only their nets but also their father. These

# Mark 1:14-20

## Theological Perspective

however the reign of God has been envisioned, it consistently involves God's satisfaction of the deepest human yearnings and the accomplishment of God's purposes.

Recent theologians have concluded that Jesus' message and Jesus the messenger mutually reinforce and define each other. The message, the delivery of the message, and messenger merge into one phenomenon. This observation has served as a counterargument to those Christians who claim to detect a sharp distinction between the authentic message of Jesus and the church's allegedly distorted proclamation concerning the identity of the messenger. Whenever that juxtaposition of message and messenger has been proposed, the purpose has been to valorize some interpretation of Jesus' ethical teachings, cultural attitudes, or exemplary spiritual life, and to disparage the church's focus on Jesus as the historical enactment of God's reconciling and liberating purposes. But the symbiosis of message and messenger in this passage indicates that Jesus is more than a model teacher, spiritual guide, or activist; Jesus is the presence of the transformative power of God.

John Calvin helped popularize this passage as a paradigm of the calling of all Christians. We the readers, in whatever culture or century, are they. According to Calvin, God called "rough mechanics" like Simon, Andrew, James, and John in order to show that none of are are called by virtue of his or her own talents or excellences.[3] Like those disciples who misunderstood and failed Jesus at every turn, we too are sinners in need of forgiveness for our multiple betrayals. Like them, we sinners, despite our failings, are slowly being transmuted into followers of Christ. Like them we are called not to the enjoyment of a private salvation but to a public vocation. Like them, and like Abraham, we are summoned by God to leave our parents' house, abandoning self-interest, security, and social approbation. Like them, we can find our inadequate attempts at ministry transformed by grace into extensions of Jesus' proclamatory activity. Just as it did for the disciples, the command "Follow me" points to the way of the cross for us. Just as it did for the disciples, the ominous reference to the arrest of John the Baptist warns that we too are called to a life of risk, insecurity, and self-abnegation.

LEE BARRETT

## Pastoral Perspective

Then, over the long weeks and years, his father has to learn to entrust his son to a world he can barely understand. But at the end of the movie we watch the old man come to London to watch Billy Elliot leap and turn and dance with beauty and with joy. And in the old man's face: sheer pride and true joy.

Our eldest son followed the Spirit's leadings into Orthodox Judaism and is now a cantor! I am proud of him and feel honored that he learned at home to follow his heart. Don't we have to affirm the Holy Spirit's freedom to call our children in directions we didn't expect?

In northern Minnesota, the opening day of fishing season is practically a holy day! Sermons on fishing texts, therefore, are well received. The problem is that our kind of fishing—using lures or live bait—is predicated on trickery. But the biblical casting of nets is different—straightforward, totally encompassing, without artifice. Yes, evangelism aims to take human fish where they did not plan to go, but we should seek to convert without resorting to "bait and switch."

Given that Jesus introduces the analogy of catching fish and catching people, can we make something of the reminder here that fishing involves more than the act of casting nets and pulling in the haul? There are also the preparations, the mending of nets, repairing the tools that are bound to be damaged and worn in the rough-and-tumble between the hunter and the hunted and the ever-changing environment in which the drama is played out. You can't always be fishing, even if that's your favorite part.

This passage begins with an ominous note: John was arrested. Mark's audience needed no further elaboration—they knew the story, they knew the risks involved with giving yourself over to a new vision that challenges the status quo. To repent, to begin a new life, to be led by the Spirit, takes not just faith but also courage.

ELTON W. BROWN

---

[3]John Calvin, *Commentary on a Harmony of the Evangelists, Matthew, Mark, and Luke*, vol. 1, trans. William Pringle (Edinburgh: Edinburgh Printing Co., 1845), 242–44.

## Exegetical Perspective

Semitic equivalent. While the New Testament shows little interest in Andrew, his Greek name is a harbinger of the extent of Jesus' mission as carried on by the disciples. They would carry his proclamation of the good news beyond the Jewish community to the Gentile world.

Jesus and the four disciples are active agents in leading people to experience the presence of the kingdom of God. The disciples, in particular, are not passive recipients of God's favor. Jesus called them in order that they might join him in proclaiming the coming of God's reign on earth. Like Jesus, the disciples will experience opposition that will eventually claim their lives (see 13:3–13). But the end of Mark's Gospel shows that death's victory over Jesus—and therefore over the disciples—is only temporary. God raised Jesus from the dead and God will raise the disciples as well. It is significant that in Mark the risen Jesus chose to meet his disciples in Galilee (16:7), the place where his ministry began. This underscores the connection between Jesus' ministry on earth and the hope for the complete and final revelation of the kingdom of God.

The kingdom of God then is an eschatological image. The mission of Jesus begins at the right time (*kairos*), that is, when God signals the divine intention finally and definitively to take control of this world from the powers of evil. The second lesson (1 Cor. 7:29–31) reflects the early Christian belief that this was on the verge of happening. Jesus' words proclaim this, and his works make it possible for people to experience the power of God's kingdom in tangible ways. The rest of Mark's Gospel, then, offers a testimony to the inbreaking of the kingdom of God through Jesus' powerful words and mighty deeds. This testimony serves to support the faith of those who await the full and final revelation of the kingdom upon Jesus' return (13:24–27).

The preacher can call believers to examine their response to the church's proclamation of the gospel. Has their response been as immediate and complete as that of the four disciples? What is it that keeps people today from responding to God's invitation as the Ninevites and the disciples did?

LESLIE J. HOPPE

## Homiletical Perspective

disciples leave behind a whole matrix of work, family, and place—all the stuff of a new identity.

The best translation of verse 17 will reflect this new identity. The NRSV has Jesus say, "Follow me and I will make you fish for people." This makes it sound as if fishing for people were a *task*. The better translation receives fishing for people as a new *identity*. A literal translation might read, "Follow me, and I will make you to become fishers for people." There is a world of difference between "I will make you fish" and "I will make you to become fishers." "I will make you fish" gives us one more activity to work into our datebooks. ("Right, Jesus, fish for people. How about every fourth Monday? Can anyone else do fourth Mondays?") But "I will make you to become fishers"? That promises a whole new life.

Congregations and preachers might reason together about the difference between discipleship as a task and discipleship as an identity. And they might try to imagine what it means to be made "fishers for people." If that is a statement about identity, then it must involve something other than participation in church growth programs in the narrow sense. The rest of Mark begins to suggest a richer picture. If we can take Jesus at his word—that if the disciples follow him, he will make them fishers—then the story of the disciples shows what fishers' lives look like. They find themselves astounded at Jesus' teaching. They witness the rebuking of unclean spirits, the healing of sick people, and the cleansing of lepers. They lose track of Jesus and must search for him again. They know that their lives unfold in the shadow of the arrest and execution of John. And this is only chapter 1.

TED A. SMITH

# Deuteronomy 18:15-20

¹⁵The LORD your God will raise up for you a prophet like me from among your own people; you shall heed such a prophet. ¹⁶This is what you requested of the LORD your God at Horeb on the day of the assembly when you said: "If I hear the voice of the LORD my God any more, or ever again see this great fire, I will die." ¹⁷Then the LORD replied to me: "They are right in what they have said. ¹⁸I will raise up for them a prophet like you from among their own people; I will put my words in the mouth of the prophet, who shall speak to them everything that I command. ¹⁹Anyone who does not heed the words that the prophet shall speak in my name, I myself will hold accountable. ²⁰But any prophet who speaks in the name of other gods, or who presumes to speak in my name a word that I have not commanded the prophet to speak—that prophet shall die."

## Theological Perspective

The last chapter of Deuteronomy tells of Moses' death and describes the incredible magnitude of his role as prophet: "Never since has there arisen a prophet in Israel like Moses, whom the LORD knew face to face" (34:10). Not only did Moses perform great signs and wonders in Egypt in securing the liberation of the Hebrews; he also served regularly as the mediator between YHWH and the people. A notable mediation was at Horeb, where Moses told the people, "At that time I was standing between the LORD and you to declare to you the words of the LORD; for you were afraid because of the fire and did not go up the mountain" (5:5). As a prophet, Moses was unequaled, because of all the terrifying displays of power he performed in the sight of all Israel (34:11–12).

Earlier, in Deuteronomy 18:15–20, though, we learn that YHWH will not leave the people without a prophet after Moses. In fact, YHWH would raise up a prophet like Moses, who would speak to Israel (v. 15, 18). At Horeb, the assembly asked for a mediator, since they would surely die if they again met YHWH face to face, and YHWH agreed. Consequently, the vital role of prophet in the life of Israel did not end with Moses' death.

The meaning of the Hebrew root for *prophet* is uncertain but is most likely "one who is called" or

## Pastoral Perspective

Where have all the prophets gone? Where is this century's Martin Luther King Jr.? Where are the great prophets and preachers of old who challenged the establishment and called the people to faithfulness? Why must we reach back forty years to find the voice crying in the wilderness that changed the world? I'm not talking about well-known megachurch pastors, many of whom are certainly doing good works. The ministries of Rick Warren's Saddleback Church, Bill Hybels's Willow Creek Church, and Brian McLaren's Emergent Movement are making significant waves in American public life, reshaping ministry and church life for thousands of people. I'm talking about prophets who labor outside the glare of cameras and who do not count success by worship attendance. "There ain't no prophet in the written record who is pastor of a megachurch," said Jeremiah Wright of Trinity United Church of Christ, Chicago, at a recent denominational meeting. Prophets aren't usually that popular.

Perhaps we cannot find the prophets among us because we have forgotten what prophetic ministry is about. Moses's announcement to the Israelites that God will raise up for them a prophet, like Moses himself, is an opportunity for preachers to address the prophetic ministry for and with their congregations today. There are many directions a preacher

## Exegetical Perspective

The divine promise of Deuteronomy 18:15–20 stands in stark contrast to the grasping practices of verses 9–14 that immediately precede it. The earlier verses seek connection with the gods through practices like divination, child sacrifice, soothsaying, and sorcery—practices that focus on human efforts rather than on the action of God. The text explicitly says that these practices are "abhorrent" (v. 9) and declares those who practice them to be disloyal to YHWH (v. 12–13). In the case of the prophet in Israel described in verses 15–20, it is the action of YHWH rather than practices initiated by Israel that will convey the divine will and direction. The responsibility of the people in the face of this prophetic voice is to listen and to hear.

The question of prophecy in Israel—its origins and development—is a complex one. Our text represents the paradigmatic canonical text for the authorization of that prophecy. In the canonical sequence, all prophetic power, even the understanding of what a prophet does, flows from this Mosaic authorization. According to the text, the prophet will be "like" Moses, and a look at the canonical picture of the prophets confirms that their call and vocation is shaped on the Mosaic model (cf. Jer. 4–10). The prophet is to be "from among your own people" (v. 15), that is, the prophetic voice is to

## Homiletical Perspective

Whenever a pastor starts making noises about leaving, it stirs up anxiety within the congregation. When is he/she moving on? When is the next pastor coming? Who will the next one be? How can we ever get a pastor as good as this one has been? Think how long it is going to take to break in the new one.

Moses practically reads the people's minds, anticipating their dilemma, when he says, "The LORD your God will raise up for you a prophet like me from among your own people" (v. 15). In other words, quit worrying so much about the future. God will provide, and the choice will come from within. Often we have to go outside to find the right match. But Moses hints that one within their ranks will be tapped on the shoulder and nudged into service. That's a message for churches and their search committees to hear when they start worrying about where their future leadership is going to come from. God is the one who will do the calling, just as God does through his servant Samuel when the search is on for a new king. Samuel is the search committee on behalf of God. Of course, the choice of the runny-nosed kid from the field, the ruddy-faced boy named David, with nothing but a slingshot and a lot of heart, is a surprise to everyone, including David himself. But Samuel is sure because God has told him.

# Deuteronomy 18:15-20

## Theological Perspective

"one who calls." The combination of "called" and "calls," though, is helpful in understanding the prophet's twofold role. First, the prophet is the moral and ethical agent who summons the people to repentance; second, the prophet anticipates what YHWH will do in the covenant. The prophet, who is called by YHWH, calls the community back to the covenant. YHWH's prophet represents the single, legitimate mediator of divine participation and purpose, whose ultimate word is one of hope and promise for the people.

Deuteronomy 18:15–20 presents four theological reflections about YHWH, the prophet, and the people. First, divine revelation does not finish with the encounter at Horeb when YHWH spoke out of the fire (4:12). While the theophany at Horeb (5:1–21) is fundamental to ordering Israel's life together (and ours), it is not the last word from YHWH. Repeatedly, YHWH moves and speaks to Israel about the divine-human relationship (including directly to individuals) through the prophets. YHWH's continued interactions with Israel and all YHWH's actions through Jesus Christ are acts of justice and mercy.

A second reflection is that YHWH accommodates us in our weakness. YHWH's word, even when it is painful, is for our well-being (4:40). We hunger for the word (unless we have somehow convinced ourselves that we do not need bread). In our weakness, though, we ask to receive this word through a mediator, not directly (v. 17). We want a prophet to go and have a deeply personal and fervent experience with YHWH and then to come back and verbally and/or physically express YHWH's word to us. With the prophets, YHWH accommodates us in this request.

A third reflection is that the prophet is a member of the community and, therefore, is firmly rooted in Israel's covenant history. Having grown up in the tradition, the prophet understands through personal experience the longings and brokenness of the people. Thus, the prophet is not so detached from the community that he or she only offers vague platitudes. But neither is the prophet co-opted by the community's current cultural situation, because YHWH's fiery presence cleanses all sin (cf. Isa. 6:7). Consequently, the prophet is called out from the people to announce to the people YHWH's word—a word that creates justice, brings hope, and brings the promise to fruition.

A final reflection is that YHWH holds us accountable to the prophetic words. Coupled with

## Pastoral Perspective

could go with a sermon on prophetic ministry, but not all of them are advisable. A basic question to consider: What is the nature of prophetic ministry? (Often dangerous and lonely, but pure and true.) Who can be a prophet? (Anyone whom God calls.) How will the people know a particular person is a prophet from God? (The prophet's words will come true, according to v. 22.) What does "coming true" mean? Is prophetic ministry about predicting the future, or is it more, and what is that "more"?

The sermon could be an opportunity to demonstrate to the congregation that the preacher is himself or herself a prophet of God, one who stands between God and the people, bringing the word of God to the faithful. We might glean criteria from today's text that a congregation could use to be sure their preacher is a prophet: Is the preacher/prophet like Moses? Does he or she talk to God routinely, resisting most of what God asks, needing signs like burning bushes and blistering heat waves to incite action? Is the preacher/prophet as humble as Moses, who was never terribly fond of his chats with God or the duties God gave him to do? Does what the preacher/prophet says actually come true? Is it strange and confusing at first, its purpose only becoming clear later? Is the preacher an embodied sermon, and is the sermon embodied by the preacher and the congregation?

Then there is the Christian claim that Moses's prophecy in this text refers to the coming of Jesus Christ; that the only one who could be like Moses is the Son of God himself. Those are big shoes to fill. More criteria: Is the preacher/prophet like Jesus himself? Of course, the very act of trying to convince a congregation that their preacher is a prophet of God like Moses, or like Jesus, would actually prevent the preacher from meeting the above criteria. Humility is one of those prophetic characteristics that is so difficult to find these days. This would be an unadvisable sermon direction.

A more helpful sermon direction may be to explore the ways in which prophets minister from places other than the pulpit. What about the prophets sitting in the pews? Those who give their lives in public service, advocating for the poor, calling neighbors and communities to accountability through their deeds as well as words. The prophet Moses conveyed God's wisdom and love through more than proclamations and sermons. He organized the nomadic community in the wilderness. He established God's laws and judged disputes. He even fed the people and pastored their

be one of you, one who has shared the history and the struggle, one who knows the history of YHWH with Israel.

However, the historical relationship between this sixth-century Deuteronomic text and the appearance of prophets in Israel, at least as early as the eighth century, is uncertain. In which direction do the lines of influence run? How much did the earlier appearance of prophets affect the shaping of the Deuteronomic text? How much did the existing Deuteronomic tradition determine the behavior and reports of earlier prophetic activity? The constant is that prophetic activity, while clustering around the crises of history that tested Israel's faith, has been in Israel from the early days of the people.

What is clear is that the Deuteronomic answer to the crisis of the sixth-century exile is the promise of YHWH's presence through the dependable word uttered in the mouth of the prophet. In comparison to other figures of power in Israel—kings, priests, and judges—the power of the prophet is not bound by the existence of political and religious structures that were destroyed in the chaos of the exile. Rather, the authority of the prophet is grounded in the true utterance of the divine word, a word not dependent on temple or army, but one that finds its voice even in a foreign land. Therefore, the charismatic power of the prophet is an antidote for the hopelessness and despair of a people who have lost the historic, concrete moorings of their nation (palace and army) and their faith (temple and priesthood).

The prophet is an intermediary, one who stands between the people and divine power, just as Moses stood before YHWH and brought the law to the people at Horeb when the people shrank back from the voice and presence of their God (v. 16). Ironically, the problem of the sixth-century people is the opposite of the overwhelming theophany at the holy mountain. The question of the people in exile is not how to survive a confrontation with the power of their God. Rather, the question is where to find the presence of that God who seems absent—where and who is the God who let this happen to us? The answer of this text is that God is to be found in the word uttered by the prophet.

But will everyone who claims to be a prophet actually have YHWH's word? Deuteronomy has already addressed the question of prophets who purport to bring a divine word and call people to follow gods other than YHWH. They shall be put to death (13:1–5). In today's passage, the text reiterates that command and adds to it the prophet who

The same is true for Moses. He knows his time is coming. He will not be their leader forever. It isn't that he has done all he can do with them, as some pastors have a tendency to say. It isn't that he is burned out or that he knows they are finishing his sentences in his sermons. No, God has told him it's time for a transition, and you need to announce your retirement. "Just let them know that I will provide, so they won't worry about it."

Not only will God provide the new pastor/leader, but God will provide the words for that leader to say. "I will put my words in the mouth of the prophet, who shall speak to them everything I command" (v. 18). Preachers who understand what's really occurring as they stand in their pulpits on Sunday mornings know that it is God speaking through them. Their goal is to be the window through which the light of God shines. Through the power of the Holy Spirit, it is God who gives them the words to say week after week, day after day. So, not only should the people not worry about the future, but the preacher God calls shouldn't worry about the words she or he will say. God will provide.

One of the greatest honors a pastor has is to hold the hand of someone who is dying and pray that person into heaven. Pastors are like ushers at the performance hall where a grand opera is about to be performed. Ushers are not the point; the great spectacle on the stage that is about to happen is the point. So also, pastors are ushering people into the presence of the Almighty, not only when they are dying, but when they come to worship. Preachers are not the point; Christ is. Our job is to get out of the way and allow the glory of God to shine through. The same is true for laity who witness on behalf of God in the world. Don't worry about what you are going to say. Open yourself to the Scripture, and allow God to speak through you to those who need to hear God's word.

So, first, God provides by calling the new pastor/leader. Second, God provides the words that new leader will say. But, finally, we have to listen to what the new leader says. Public speaking doesn't happen unless there is a public present and paying attention. It's the Shema all over again: "Hear, O Israel: The Lord is our God, the Lord alone" (Deut. 6:4). Of course, hearing in ancient Israel also meant heeding. It is good to have an ambassador, one who will help interpret the divine word for the people. Part of the reason for that is that people who take seriously coming into the presence of God know that they have no right to be there on their own. "If I

# Deuteronomy 18:15-20

## Theological Perspective

the sending of a mediator comes the command to pay careful attention and act accordingly. We are to heed the prophet's words because they are YHWH's words; "I will put my words in the mouth of the prophet, who shall speak to them everything that I command" (v. 18b). And if we do not, YHWH holds us accountable (v. 19). This single route of communication, though, places a great burden on the prophet. First, the prophet must speak the word that YHWH provides *in* YHWH's name. The prophet shall not utter the truth to the community in anyone else's name, under penalty of death. Also, the prophet shall not announce a word that YHWH has not provided, again under the penalty of death. No wonder none of the Old Testament prophets ever wanted the job! Prophets do not make applications; they are raised up solely by YHWH.

Today, we do not have the office of prophet, even though we are just as hungry for both a word from YHWH and a mediator. In the New Testament period, the increase of false prophets seemingly overwhelmed the community's ability to discern who was speaking for YHWH and who was not. Some today, though, recognize modern-day prophets such as Dietrich Bonhoeffer, Mother Teresa, Rabbi Abraham Heschel, and Martin Luther King Jr. As of old, YHWH has raised up these and others to announce where we are in breach of the divine-human relationship, particularly regarding violence. And like all YHWH's prophets, they provide us a vision of what YHWH is going to do. As King prophesied,

> I have a dream today. I have a dream that one day, down in Alabama . . . black boys and black girls will be able to join hands with little white boys and white girls as sisters and brothers. I have a dream today. I have a dream that one day every valley shall be exalted, every hill and mountain shall be made low, the rough places will be made plain, and the crooked places will be made straight, and the glory of the Lord shall be revealed, and all flesh shall see it together.[1]

DAVID FORNEY

## Pastoral Perspective

insecurities and concerns. What are the ways in which deeds are as prophetic as words?

Where have all the prophets gone? Perhaps they are in the streets and soup kitchens, in the halls of justice and government. Perhaps they labor unrecognized by a world they are changing every day.

A preacher may be tempted to use this text as an opportunity to comment upon the validity of other identified modern-day prophets. After all, the verses following the text set for this Sunday (vv. 21–22) acknowledge that some prophets may speak presumptuously, not for God. We are tempted to decry some of the prominent preachers in American public life today, who claim to be prophets, but whose actions and words are far removed from anything the God we know in Jesus Christ would say or do. Is that a responsibility a preacher has to his or her congregation? To the larger community? To the common good? Should a preacher judge the prophetic ministry of other preachers?

Where have all the prophets gone? Perhaps they are reluctant to judge others, lest they be wrong or impolite.

Many pastors worry about prophetic preaching. They are concerned about preaching a message that challenges the beliefs and worldviews of people in the congregation. They fear that it may prevent their ability to pastor the congregation. At worst, they might be fired from the pulpit. Equally troubling would be the loss of church membership. But the most pertinent concern is one of alienation—parishioners feeling unable to trust their pastor because he or she believes something diametrically opposed to what the parishioners believe. How do preachers overcome this?

Where have all the prophets gone? Perhaps they are afraid to preach. Is this fear, this tension, worth a sermon?

Finally, the preacher may feel the call of God to give a prophetic word to his or her congregation about the pressing concerns and needs of the world on this day. Whether it be a sermon about poverty, war in the Middle East, culture wars in America, greed, abuse, globalization, violence, God has given a word—many words—that need to be heard.

VERITY A. JONES

---

[1] Martin Luther King Jr., "I Have a Dream," in *A Testament of Hope: The Essential Writings of Martin Luther King, Jr.*, ed. James Melvin Washington (San Francisco: Harper & Row, 1986), 219.

## Exegetical Perspective

claims to speak in the name of YHWH, but who in fact brings a word not commanded by YHWH. That prophet also shall be put to death (18:20). The simple test added here for the people to test the truth of the prophetic word is whether that word comes true (v. 22). This text stands in tension with that of the previous passage (13:1–5), where the listeners are cautioned not necessarily to trust a word, even it comes true. In that earlier passage, the test is whether the prophet calls on the people to follow other gods; if so, then even if the word the prophet utters comes to pass, it is not a true word, and the prophet should be killed.

The crucial task of Israel in response to the word given by the prophet is to heed (*shema'*) that word. The verb *shema'* appears three times in this passage (vv. 15, 16, and 19) and connotes not only hearing, but responding or "paying attention." Listening to the prophet and obeying YHWH's word communicated through that prophet is so important that—unlike many other violations of the law—punishment will not be by the community through burning or stoning offenders; YHWH reserves the right to punish (v. 19). As a people in exile, without priest or king, it is the acts of listening and obeying that create and shape the community. Failure to listen is also disloyalty to YHWH and bears the serious consequence of divine punishment.

Our text therefore promises to the people that God's ongoing care for them is found, not in spectacle or splendor, but in the simple fact of God's word. That word validates the prophets, and the prophets have authority precisely because they are those who convey the word. The role of faithful people is to listen—not simply to hear, but to listen thoughtfully and courageously. By learning to recognize and trust God's true word, the people learn to trust God's own self.

RICHARD A. PUCKETT

## Homiletical Perspective

hear the voice of the Lord my God any more, or ever again see this great fire, I will die" (18:16). Why do they say this? They say it because they haven't lived lives worthy of God. They have hurt or ignored the poor. They have cheated and lied, and it is a scary thing to come into God's presence when you know how you have been living.

Thus, we see the need for a vessel, no matter how earthen, through which God speaks and communicates the blessed message of love. But if the people do not hear and heed, then nothing has been gained by the entry of this new pastor/leader into the community, no matter how effectively that preacher preaches. One Sunday morning, a pastor preached an eloquent sermon, both brilliant and scintillating. The people were deeply moved by it and said it was the best sermon they had ever heard. The next week that pastor preached the same sermon, and again the people were excited to hear it. But when that pastor preached the very sermon, word for word, the third week in a row, people began to wonder. Finally, one of the congregants shaking the pastor's hand at the door with a small crowd gathered around him said, "Preacher, that was a great sermon, thoughtful, insightful, even inspiring. But some of us wanted to know why you keep preaching the same sermon again and again." The pastor smiled and replied, "Because I haven't seen anyone do anything about what I said."

God provides the leader and the words spoken. We need to hear and heed.

WILLIAM J. CARL III

# Psalm 111

¹Praise the LORD!
  I will give thanks to the LORD with my whole heart,
    in the company of the upright, in the congregation.
²Great are the works of the LORD,
    studied by all who delight in them.
³Full of honor and majesty is his work,
    and his righteousness endures forever.
⁴He has gained renown by his wonderful deeds;
    the LORD is gracious and merciful.
⁵He provides food for those who fear him;
    he is ever mindful of his covenant.

## Theological Perspective

We human creatures seem to be born to wonder, to love, and to praise. We are born for other things as well, of course. We work, we speak, we create, and we make and keep covenants together. All these things are found in all human communities we know about, and they take central place in our lives as well. But wonder, love, and praise seem different somehow. They are expressions of our deepest being and deepest longing. No matter what happens to us or what we achieve, they point us to something greater, something better that surrounds our lives and makes us glad.

I now live on a country road, surrounded by very tall trees and dense undergrowth that flowers in season, beside a flowing stream that provides background music. I lived for years in a large city, surrounded by tall buildings and densely populated streets, near an expressway that provided a continual background sound as well. As one emerges from the trees or comes around the corner, a beautiful sunset can suddenly capture one's attention and reframe the whole moment in an instant. It is a touch of eternity in time, for many such moments merge in our awareness of the beauty and awesome grandeur of our life here and now.

Lost in wonder, we are opened up to praise the divine Source of all things. For a moment we are

## Pastoral Perspective

In verse 1, "Praise the LORD!" is a translation of the Hebrew superscription *hallelu yah*. A simple hallelujah it isn't. The praise is like that coming from a young child who takes a simple refrain of "Halle Halle Hallelujah" and crafts his or her own praise lyrics incorporating total confidence in God's love. Strapped in the backseat of the minivan, he or she sings a familiar tune with new lyrics. "God is holding me, yes! Yes! Yes! God is talking to me, in my head! God is holding onto the whole earth! Hallelujah, Hallelujah!"

The psalmist sings praise that rises from the inner seat of courage and passion, of appetites and emotions, praise uttered deep from her heart. Praising with clarity and brilliance, like that of a full moon's reflection on a still evening lake, abundant joy resounds. In Christmastide, children sing with joy "Go Tell It on the Mountain" before God and before the gathered congregation. They sing with reckless abandon and joy before the Lord and the congregation. Sitting upon cushioned pews, members listen and absorb the joy of the children whom they promised to nurture in baptismal promises. Just as each child stands on the chancel steps and shares gifts for ministry in song, the psalmist gives thanks, confessing the Lord's great deeds singing, "I will give thanks to the LORD with my whole heart!"

⁶He has shown his people the power of his works,
in giving them the heritage of the nations.
⁷The works of his hands are faithful and just;
all his precepts are trustworthy.
⁸They are established forever and ever,
to be performed with faithfulness and uprightness.
⁹He sent redemption to his people;
he has commanded his covenant forever.
Holy and awesome is his name.
¹⁰The fear of the LORD is the beginning of wisdom;
all those who practice it have a good understanding.
His praise endures forever.

## Exegetical Perspective

The lectionary locates this song of praise on the fourth Sunday after Epiphany, deep in the days of Ordinary Time. Perhaps the hope is that the psalmist's call to "praise the LORD" (v. 1) and intent to do so publicly will summon us in the bustle of our everyday lives to do the same—to offer with our "whole hearts" communal thanksgiving for the works of God. The psalm is an alphabetic acrostic: each line begins with the next letter of the Hebrew alphabet (see also Psalm 112). This literary framework signals that the psalm is a comprehensive, or A-to-Z, celebration of God's works. Indeed, following the invitation (v. 1) and reasons for praise (vv. 2–3), the psalmist recalls God's work on behalf of Israel, from exodus and entry into the land (vv. 4–6) to Sinai and the giving of the law (vv. 7–10). This prompts some interpreters to regard Psalm 111 as a condensed version of longer recitals of God's salvation history (e.g., Pss. 105; 106; 136),[1] perhaps for use by the postexilic community.

The psalmist opens with an invitation to praise (v. 1a) followed by a statement of her intent to do so with her "whole heart" in the presence of the congregation (v. 1bc). The term "heart" (*leb*) refers

[1] So M. Dahood, *Psalms III: 101–150*, Anchor Bible, vol. 17A (Garden City, NY: Doubleday, 1970), 122.

## Homiletical Perspective

The season following the Epiphany gives space to reflect on the nature of God in community, without the temptation to translate this into a congregational call for watchfulness (Advent) or penitence (Lent). There is an invitation for the preacher to explore what we often find to be the paradoxical qualities of God's immanence and transcendence. Psalm 111 gives the congregation a rendering of God's character that is both immanent and transcendent. The rhythm of this text allows us an opportunity to reflect on these traits both in majesty and in our immediate experience. This then allows us to be open to a broader reflection on how that movement between immanence and transcendence translates into a framework for relationship within our communities. The same God who is both above and within is also named as a God palpably present and engaged within the faith community.

The transcendent qualities are more immediately noticeable in the listing of God's powerful deeds and the attending principles of compassion, faithfulness, and justice (vv. 2, 3, 4, and 9). The God described here is so powerful and present that one must be drawn to study, reflect, and celebrate as a community. The presence of the Divine is obvious, and one we cannot but give witness to. It is worth noting that the unquestioned assumption of a God

# Psalm 111

**Theological Perspective**

aware of a wider reality: "My God, look at that!" This is no empty speech. It is the most proper use of that word.

The last lines of our psalm couple together the praise of the Lord with a life of developed wisdom and understanding:

> The fear of the LORD is the beginning of wisdom;
> all those who practice it have a good understanding.
> His praise endures forever.

Those who revere ("fear") God live in a larger world, because they allow themselves to be open to something greater, something better, that lies deeply within even the most ordinary experiences. It is all too easy to be overfocused and miss the full range of reality in what we live through. It is so easy to let our lives be defined by the little world we have created through habits of mind and body that do not allow anything that may lie beyond to be registered in our awareness.

Psalm 111 can stand as a table of contents for the entire Psalter. If we ask, "Why should we praise God?" the answer is surely because it is the door to a life of mature spiritual wisdom. The eternal God, the Source of all, does not need our praise, as some divine figures need to be fed human goods or flattery. To gain a healthy spiritual self-understanding, *we* need to remember that our lives are set in the midst of an unimaginable greatness and goodness.

What then shall we render to the Lord, if not to receive the things of our lives thankfully, to receive the divine blessings gladly and unselfishly, and to live loyally before God (Ps. 116)? It really is all about cultivating a sense of the presence of God. To live as if there were no God is to live in a space too small for our souls to grow and flourish. Praise the Lord then, for the works of God are great, and there is great delight in studying them in the company of the faithful (v. 2).

What works of God does the psalmist have in mind? Many scholars believe that the fifth book of Psalms (Pss. 107–50) is a reflection of the experiences of the Jewish people in their long exile in Babylon and their joy at the prospective return. If this is so, then the background reference is God's work preserving the people in their extremity (v. 5: "He provides food for those who fear him; he is ever mindful of his covenant") and in leading their victorious return (v. 6: "He has shown his people the power of his works, in giving them the heritage of the nations").

**Pastoral Perspective**

How often do we, as God's gathered folk, take the time to trample back through time and "study" the Lord's great works or tread within the unfolding of each day to discern the Spirit of a living Lord ? How is it that we come to sing God's praise with reckless abandon and deep joy, beginning with God's activity in our own lives and turning to God's activity in the world? What might help us to come to the place where we shout hallelujah?

Travel with a group of nine-year-olds into an extended care facility to lead worship and celebrate the sacrament of the Lord's Supper. What unfolds is the clear vision of young and old alike gathered to give praise. Singing "God Is So Good" and "Jesus Loves Me" with a certain heartfelt longing, the Spirit reveals the perpetuity of the Lord's steadfast and enduring love to God's gathered children. Indeed, God is "gracious and merciful" and the "[the LORD's] righteousness endures forever."

During this worship, speak the gospel question at the invitation to the Lord's Table, "Do you wish to see Jesus?" This question has a different impact when delivered in an intentional community of God's people in the late stages of life, people who know the reality of death through the sting of death's knock in the loss of lifetime partners and longtime friends. Like a favorite pendant passed through the generations, God's grace (v. 4) is known in the deep recesses of an octogenarian's memory. At the same time, a new memory of God's grace is crafted in a fourth-grader's emerging identity. The Lord is "gracious and merciful," and in worship and the celebration of the sacrament a brilliant hallelujah chorus raises.

Serve in urban mission with college students and youth in various stages of defining their Christian identity. With them, sit down at table with the working poor and the homeless, and listen. As you eat at table together, listen for foundation-shaking stories of God's abandonment where it seems as if all human dignity has been stripped. Listen for parallels. College students and youth sometimes perceive their lives in tandem with those living on the streets. "I feel lonely." "I don't like it when people judge me." In the midst of those stories, listen for a recollection of the Lord providing in needy times (v. 5).

After the meal, worship together. If, during the course of your service with the Lord, a man stands up and lifts a prayer before God, "I pray for the rich who have thousands, yet can't spare a quarter for my life on the streets." Then ask those gathered, "So do we wish to see Jesus?" Hear the man's blessing,

metaphorically to the inner self, the source of a person's thoughts and feelings. The "heart" is the seat of reason, understanding, and imagination (e.g., 1 Kgs. 3:9; Ezek. 13:2). It is the conscience (e.g., 1 Sam. 25:31; 2 Sam. 24:10) and wellspring of emotions (e.g., Exod. 4:14; Isa. 35:4). The psalmist's praise thus involves her completely; it is testimony—deeply personal and, because it takes place in the congregation, utterly public.

As verses 2–3 indicate, the psalmist is moved to praise by "the works of the LORD," an expression that can refer to God's work in creation (Ps. 104:24) but most frequently, as here, recalls God's work for the sake of God's people (e.g., Ps. 107:24; Exod. 34:10; Deut. 11:7; Judg. 2:7; Jer. 51:10). Skillful use of repetition keeps God's work on center stage throughout the psalm. The Hebrew root 'asah ("to do, make") occurs four times with God as the subject, three times as a noun ("works," vv. 2, 6, 7), and once as a verb (NRSV "gained," v. 4a). Third masculine singular suffixes abound—[God's] righteousness, [God's] wonderful deeds, [God's] covenant, [God's] people, [God's] name—while 'olam ("eternity, forever," vv. 5b, 8a, 9b) and 'ad ("forever, perpetuity," vv. 3b, 8a, 10c) underscore the permanence of it all. For the psalmist, delight in God's work prompts such tenacious attention (v. 2; e.g., Ps. 119:2, 10). The psalmist first celebrates God's work for all people as revealed in the history of Israel (vv. 4–6). Her words stir up memories of the exodus, wilderness wanderings, and entry into the promised land. The expression "wonderful deeds" (v. 4a) often refers to the exodus event (e.g., Exod. 3:20; 34:10; Judg. 6:13; Ps. 77:11, 14). God as "gracious and merciful" (v. 4b) echoes God's self-description after the episode with the golden calf (Exod. 34:6). God's provision of food (v. 5) recalls quails and dewy manna in the wilderness (Exod. 16, Num. 11), and God's giving an "inheritance of nations" to God's people (v. 6b) evokes descriptions of Canaan as Israel's "inheritance" (e.g., Deut. 4:21; 15:4; 20:16; 26:1; Judg. 20:6; Jer. 12:14). In just a few short verses, the psalmist sweeps through time and space, reminding the community of all that God has done for us.

At verse 7, the psalmist turns to God's work in the Torah (vv. 8–10), a rhetorical move that is suggestive of the chronological story, namely, Sinai follows the exodus. In doing so, the psalmist reminds the congregation that God's "faithful and just" work (v. 7a) precedes God's gift of the law—that which makes it possible for God's people to be "faithful and upright" (v. 8b). God's faithfulness summons our

who is active in history is generally difficult for postmodern congregations. This text gives the preacher a natural entry into that conversation. Do we still think God's deeds are "renowned" (v. 4) or that the "power of his works" (v. 6) is clear to us? Is this meant to be an individual sense of the Divine or something that can be discernibly testified to as a community? Where do we see those signs even in our postmodern context?

Some images that easily resonate are from nature and other experiences of beauty. The experiences of beauty that call us to stop or take notice might be indicators to those signs of the Divine we fear are no longer present. The same tree we have seen come into bud every spring still garners our attention. Last season's blooms do not diminish its power in subsequent blooming. Many resonate with the majesty of God's creation in nature as an entry point for acknowledging that which is beyond our human finitude. That recognition of something outside of individual experience is often the launching point for reflection on the God who transcends.

Community praise of the transcendent can be imaged in the echoes from recently full churches during the season of Christmas. It can be a concrete exemplification of the desire to join together in corporate praise. The preacher may wish to reflect with the community about the difficulty of sustaining that impulse that draws us to community. We know why we come, but how do we sustain and translate that spark into an ongoing journey of faith exploration? Are there particular prayer practices or spiritual disciplines that help take the burden away from sustaining a particular emotional state of praise and instead create a deeper reservoir of joy?

The concluding verse, which encourages us to see fear as the beginning of wisdom, particularly points us toward a sense of awe and reverence that can help us name the transcendent qualities of God. However, in all likelihood, the textual use of the word "fear" will require some attention by the preacher. Rather than imagining terror as being connected to wisdom, it is important for contemporary communities to hear "fear" in the more traditional Hebrew sense of awe and reverence. Examples, such as an astronaut's experience of seeing the earth from a previously unseen and unimagined vantage point, reinforce the transcendence that can open us to deeper relationship with God.

The immanent qualities might initially be less obvious. The shift in verse 5 reminds us that the faith community not only comes together to reflect

# Psalm 111

## Theological Perspective

The redemption of the people ransomed from captivity is accompanied by a new reverence for the precepts of Torah and a new obligation to perform them (vv. 8–9). While each individual is personally responsible to God for a life of loyalty and righteousness, God's faithfulness to Israel is known and praised in the gathering of the people. "I" who praise am "I" who is a part of the company in congregation (v. 1). In exile it was difficult to gather together and remember Zion (Ps. 137). To return to the land, the city, the temple and praise God in their own tongue and way, is the greatest work of God. All the works of God deserve study and bring joy to the faithful, for they are "full of honor and majesty," of enduring righteousness (v. 3), but this is the supreme good work.

The redemption is fulfilled in keeping covenant. The relation is so close that the two ideas can be connected in a poetic couplet (v. 9). The prophets had taught that the defeat and exile of the people were a result of their sins. If righteousness exalts a people and sin defeats them, redemption is established by righteous covenant keeping. It is the greatest wisdom to fear the Lord in awe and reverence, to practice the ways of the covenant (v. 10). What sensible Jew would doubt this, now that the people are brought back to their land by a mighty act of God? If the act of redemption was an act of divine grace, the response to that grace is surely faithfulness. It is a "good understanding" when the Lord is praised in this vitally alive way.

Christians who read this psalm together as part of their common worship join with their spiritual ancestors and present-day Jewish brothers and sisters in a common song of praise. Such Christians know that there is an intimate connection between God's unfathomable gift of love in Jesus Christ and their response of faithfulness. Faith in Christ means letting our lives be shaped by taking God's love to heart. We receive love by becoming loving, just as we receive grace by becoming gracious.

THOMAS D. PARKER

## Pastoral Perspective

"Thank you, God, for taking care of me. Thank you, God, for feeding me, when I can't feed myself." Remember with college students and the working poor and homeless the unleashed Word at work in the world. Call forward the lasting works of God's hand, as "the works of his hands are faithful and just" (v. 7). Perhaps another sound of praise, a broken, yet mended hallelujah, may be heard.

The beginning of wisdom begins with fear of the Lord—not fear in the sense of outright paralyzing terror closing in from all sides, but fear in the sense of reverence. Fear in the sense of awe for the Lord's amazing deeds. This fear and awe allowed Shiprah and Puah, the Egyptian midwives, to seek life for infant Hebrew children. This fear and awe created a path for Noah to craft an ark to seek continued life for God's good creation.

The church is called to be the visible and witnessing community of the gospel of Jesus Christ. The essential structure of God's gathered people is to be an unfolding narrative, rather than a rigid institutional system. We see patterns for such a story when we are sent into places where we can sing hallelujahs and live the good news of the gospel, while at the same time we listen with the Spirit and discern God at work.

Perhaps, a prophetic word from this psalm will come in the form of a question. How are we trampling through the past, treading in the present, and looking for the future coming of our Lord? Are we gathering together and listening and discerning God at work through us? In the world, are we crafting and singing awe-filled hallelujah songs?

We gather to sing hallelujahs and to be swaddled in the holy and awesome melody of God's abundance. As we receive God's call to serve, whether making up lyrics from the backseat of a minivan or sitting down with strangers, at table together, we practice praise and live into God's promise. Like the psalmist, we gather and trust that "[the LORD's] praise endures forever."

ANNE H. K. APPLE

own. God's work ('*asah*) inspires our work. God's people "do" ('*asah*') God's precepts (v. 8b; cf. v. 10b).

In the end, then, the psalmist's praise of God's work reminds the congregation to get back to our work, namely, to "fear of the Lord" (v. 10; cf. v. 5a). "Fear of the Lord" is a way of life, a posture in the world that acknowledges God's sovereignty and the place of humanity (our capacities and limitations) before God and creation. For the psalmist as for the ancient sages, such a posture is the "beginning" (*re'shith*) of wisdom (v. 10a; cf. Prov. 1:7; 9:10). The term *re'shith* has a range of meaning. On the one hand, it can be interpreted temporally as "beginning or starting point" (e.g., Gen. 10:10; Jer. 26:1), suggesting that "fear of the Lord" is the prerequisite, the foundation for wisdom. On the other, it may be read qualitatively, as "first, best, or epitome" (e.g., Amos 6:6; Jer. 2:3; Ezek. 48:14), in which case "fear of the Lord" is the quintessential expression of wisdom. The psalmist thus designates "fear of the Lord" as the beginning and end of wisdom. Knowledge begins and ends with praise. And so she summons the people of God onward: "[God's] praise endures forever" (v. 10c).

The rich range of the acrostic form therefore helps the psalmist affirm the rich variety of ways in which God relates to humankind and humankind to God. We come to God as individuals and in the assembly. We come to God with fear and praise. We come to God with reverence and wisdom.

God comes to us in the remarkable works God has done with God's people, but also in the precepts that call us to obedience. History and law are inseparable. Finally God's praise lasts from A to Z—from before the beginning of time until forever.

CHRISTINE ROY YODER

on the presence of the God of awe and transcendence, but actually receives individual food and sustenance. The image of food and sustenance is delightfully tangible and makes the shift to that which is immediately obvious as an immanent experience. To taste and be nourished by God is an experience of intimacy that cannot be considered detached or unrelated to our lives. The preacher has opportunities to name those things that nourish us in our journey with God. For liturgical and sacramental communities, there is an opportunity to link the experience of Holy Communion to a tangible experience of the unobtainable mystery of God. The bread we eat at our kitchen countertop for breakfast becomes transformed in a liturgical setting that reminds us that this nourishment is also the body of Christ.

The use of "fear" in verse 5 also makes a linkage between the immanent and the transcendent. Not only does one have an experience of awe in the presence of God; that very experience is what leads us into the relationship that intimately nourishes us. The covenant that has constituted the community creates an embodied reminder of the relationship between God and God's people.

The experience of a God who is both immanent and transcendent evokes a deep sense of a dynamic and multifaceted relationship. This might give the preacher an opportunity then to reflect on the nature of the faith community that is created by such a God. This community is inwardly focused to be sustainable, but it also goes beyond its wall to evidence signs of God's character in the world. What are the signs that the preacher's congregation may not have noticed? Is the congregation known in the community in ways that reflect the character of God? Is there a good balance of renewal and service? Is there time given to reflection, discernment, and praise? Are these activities designed in a way that evokes reverence and awe?

The season following the Epiphany gives the preacher a chance to reflect on the character of God and the community. Psalm 111 in particular provides a good lens to look in a new way for manifestations of God's living presence both in the world and in individuals and communities.

ELIZABETH C. KNOWLTON

# 1 Corinthians 8:1-13

[1]Now concerning food sacrificed to idols: we know that "all of us possess knowledge." Knowledge puffs up, but love builds up. [2]Anyone who claims to know something does not yet have the necessary knowledge; [3]but anyone who loves God is known by him.

[4]Hence, as to the eating of food offered to idols, we know that "no idol in the world really exists," and that "there is no God but one." [5]Indeed, even though there may be so-called gods in heaven or on earth—as in fact there are many gods and many lords—[6]yet for us there is one God, the Father, from whom are all things and for whom we exist, and one Lord, Jesus Christ, through whom are all things and through whom we exist.

## Theological Perspective

*Worshiping Idols (v. 1a).* This passage begins with the theological issue of idolatry, namely, worshiping foreign gods. The theologian Paul Tillich was deeply concerned about idolatry in modern Christianity. For him, Christians unknowingly devote themselves to cultural beliefs and practices fashionable during their own time. In his words, "Idolatry is the elevation of a preliminary concern to ultimacy."[1] People show more devotion to "gods" in their surrounding society and culture than to God, who created the world and sent Jesus Christ into it.

*We Know that All of Us Possess Knowledge (v. 1b–2).* An amazing aspect of v. 1 is the manner in which Paul moves immediately from idolatry to knowledge. This is a move from worship theology to philosophical theology. Such a move might seem surprising, until one remembers that Greek philosophy had deeply influenced the minds of the people to whom Paul was writing. Paul presents the issue as knowing God in a manner that enables a person to distinguish what is truly God from what is simply an idol. But how can a person truly know God?

From a theological perspective, sin keeps humans from knowing God. Most apocalyptic literature at

[1]P. Phillips, "The Toppling of Idols: Tillich's Account of Ultimate Concern," *Theology* 99 (1996): 27–33.

## Pastoral Perspective

In all my years of listening to sermons, including my own, I don't believe that I have ever heard one based on this text. Perhaps that reflects the fact that, on the surface of it, eating meat sacrificed to idols hardly seems like an earthshaking issue for twenty-first-century Christians. But the text, it turns out, is about much more than that!

The occasion for Paul's comment is that the Corinthian church has a strong faction of well-educated, well-to-do, relatively sophisticated members who believe that Christians should be free to eat meat offered to idols. The reason is very simple. Idols do not exist and, therefore, have no power, since there is no God but one, as proclaimed in the Shema of Israel. For such people, this is obvious to all those "in the know." Perhaps it was even from Paul himself that these people had also learned that as Christians they were free from the Law, and therefore they could not be bound by rules and regulations. The only reality to which they were bound was the experience of being "in Christ."

It appears that the social life of the upper classes in Corinth revolved around frequent feasts, banquets, celebrations, and public events held in dining spaces related to temples and that the well-to-do patronized the meat markets connected with the temples for the meat used in their own households.

⁷It is not everyone, however, who has this knowledge. Since some have become so accustomed to idols until now, they still think of the food they eat as food offered to an idol; and their conscience, being weak, is defiled. ⁸"Food will not bring us close to God." We are no worse off if we do not eat, and no better off if we do. ⁹But take care that this liberty of yours does not somehow become a stumbling block to the weak. ¹⁰For if others see you, who possess knowledge, eating in the temple of an idol, might they not, since their conscience is weak, be encouraged to the point of eating food sacrificed to idols? ¹¹So by your knowledge those weak believers for whom Christ died are destroyed. ¹²But when you thus sin against members of your family, and wound their conscience when it is weak, you sin against Christ. ¹³Therefore, if food is a cause of their falling, I will never eat meat, so that I may not cause one of them to fall.

## Exegetical Perspective

This passage opens a deliberation of the relationship between individual freedom and responsibility for a community's overall health (8:1–11:1), instigated by questions over eating idol meat. Paul devotes three chapters (8–10) to these issues, demonstrating their importance for the letter. His argument is structured in an A-B-A pattern, with the Corinthians' questions about eating idol food (chaps. 8 and 10) surrounding an example drawn from Paul's conduct (chap. 9). The argument is divided into three sections: (1) the contrast between knowledge and love (vv. 1–3); (2) the Corinthians' theological reasoning (vv. 4–6); and (3) an ethical argument setting the issues in a broader context (vv. 7–12). The passage concludes with Paul's declaration that "if food is a cause for the fellow member's falling, then I (Paul) will not eat meat at all" (v. 13).

Claims by some of the Corinthians to have a deeper spiritual knowledge than their fellow believers permeate this letter (cf. 1:5, 21; 2:11–14; 3:18–21; 12:8; 13:2), but they are especially evident in here (8:1, 2, 3, 7, 10, 11). Although these "elites" wished to discuss the *logical* implications of their "knowledge," Paul focuses on the *ethical* implications. In verse 1, he shifts the focus and insists that the real question is not whether one has a deeper knowledge, which "puffs up" (*physioō*, i.e., inflates

## Homiletical Perspective

I can easily see seven themes for sermons emerging from this text. Each could become the focus for a separate sermon, or some of the themes might be combined.

As a first theme, many congregations find themselves in analogous situations to the one in Corinth, in which one group of members think the attitudes, feelings, or behaviors of other members are theologically offensive. A segment of the congregation that views its perceptions as progressive may consider the proclivities of another group as repressive. A group of traditionalists may think the ideas of a less traditional group are unfaithful. For instance, in a congregation I knew when I was growing up, one group thought they were free to use alcohol, while another group believed that the use of alcohol was sub-Christian. On a trip to the Holy Land taken by members of both groups, adherents of the second viewpoint refused to sit at the supper table with members of the drinking group. Those who permitted the use of alcohol could easily have limited their partaking for the sake of the others. Do preachers notice comparable issues in their own congregations?

However, second, a congregation may find itself in a position in which the mission of the church is immobilized by one group's limiting its freedom for

# 1 Corinthians 8:1-13

## Theological Perspective

the time of Paul asserted that sexual desire (covetousness) was the origin of all sin, and thus the origin of ignorance of God. While Paul probably did not disagree with this, he overmapped it with a view that arrogance or pride, being "puffed up" with one's own knowledge, was as great a problem as sexual desire. People who obsessively devote themselves to their own knowledge turn their devotion away from God, and in so doing they do not acquire true knowledge of God.

*Being Known by God (v. 3).* The answer to arrogance that leads to sin, in Paul's view, is loving God. Paul gets this naturally from the Shema ("Hear, O Israel"), which Jews say in their worship of God: "You shall love the LORD your God with all your heart, and with all your soul, and with all your might" (Deut. 6:5). Paul clearly accepts the Christianized version of the Shema that talks about loving God through a triad of heart, soul, and mind,[2] rather than heart, soul, and might. Paul's view was that the major avenue toward knowledge of God was through a mind that directed its love toward God. Once the mind directs its "love knowledge" toward God, the result is "being known by God." Since the nature of God's wisdom is love, loving God takes a person into God's wisdom, and the eye of God's wisdom "sees" and knows the one who loves (cf. Prov. 5:21; 15:31; 22:12).

*One God and One Lord Jesus Christ (vv. 4–6).* A primary theological issue for knowing God concerns the relation of creation wisdom to soteriological ("saving" or "savior") knowledge. Can a person know God through God the Creator, namely, through one's perception of order and beauty in God's creation (general revelation)? Or must one have knowledge through Christ, namely, through an unexpected "gospel" message (special revelation)? Paul's answer is carefully balanced. A person knows God, and is known by God, through knowing "both" God the Creator and Jesus Christ the "agent" of God's power in creation and the "agent" through whom we exist (v. 6). Neither one alone is sufficient, since both God and Christ are intimately related to creation, and we are created beings. This knowledge clarifies that no idol humans create really exists. Rather, there is one God who creates through the Lord Jesus Christ for the sake of our existence in God's creation.

## Pastoral Perspective

If one had scruples against eating meat offered to idols, it would have virtually excluded one from participation in the social life of Corinthian society.

Also present in the Corinthian church were more ordinary working people whose incomes and habits allowed for very little meat in their diets. For these people, who didn't "know any better," eating meat offered to idols threatened faith by drawing them back to the idolatrous cultures from which they had only recently been converted to the Christian faith.

Paul's own convictions are similar to those "in the know." Food, as such, has nothing to do with salvation, idols have no existence of their own, and Christians are free from the Law. Yet Paul does not take sides favoring the strong (those who eat idol meat) against the weak (those who refrain). Instead, Paul makes the point that knowledge without love "puffs up," while wise and knowing love "builds up" the community.

At the heart of Paul's message is a peculiar understanding of Christian freedom. Freedom is not the right to choose to do as one wishes. It is not simply a lack of restrictions or a negation of the Law or of other requirements. Christian freedom is grounded in love, God's love for us in Jesus Christ. If love is a matter of knowledge, it is God's knowing of us. As Martin Luther was to learn from Paul, "[A] Christian is a perfectly free lord of all, subject to none. A Christian is a perfectly dutiful servant of all, subject to all."[1] Freedom is slavery to Christ, so that in the Christian life we become responsible for one another. That is central to what it means to be "in Christ." For that reason, in any conflict, relationships are as important an element in decision making and behavior as are the facts of the case. Paul comes down very hard on those who justify their behavior on the basis of theological arguments, even arguments with which he agrees. He himself will, if necessary, become a vegetarian for the rest of his life rather than harm those who would be hurt by his eating idol meat.

This brief account raises many questions for our own congregational life. What are the appropriate relationships between the church and its surrounding cultures? What practices should the church condone or condemn in relation to the cultures of secularism, materialism, and nationalism? How can the church act prophetically in society and at the same time maintain appropriate pastoral relations with its divided membership? How does the church

[2] Cf. Deut. 6:5 with Matt. 22:37; Mark 12:30, 33; Luke 10:27.

[1] Martin Luther, *The Freedom of a Christian*, trans. W. A. Lambert, rev. Harold Grimm, in *Three Treatises* (Philadelphia: Fortress Press, 1970), 277.

the self), but that one exhibits love which "builds up" (*oikodomeō*). He thus starts with the question of how one's behavior affects the faith of a fellow believer, and this serves as the foundational question for all that follows.

Paul underscores this by contrasting not only "knowledge" (*gnōsis*) with love (*agapē*) (v. 1b) but "apparent knowledge" with "real knowledge," that is, knowledge that results from a proper understanding of God (v. 3). The mark of such knowledge is not special privileges restricted to a few, but a love for God that demonstrates concern for one's fellow believers.

Verses 4–6 contain Paul's paraphrases of the elites' claim that Christians were free to eat idol foods because they "possessed the knowledge" that idols have no spiritual reality. Paul agrees with their claim, but not with their conclusions. He grants that idols are only "so-called gods" (v. 5), but not that they are without influence in the world. In fact, he maintains that these gods and lords—both seen and unseen—constantly affect humans.

Such gods are, however, subordinate to the "one God." Paul's language recalls the Shema of Israel (see Deut. 6:4–9), but it is drawn from an early Christian hymn rooted in Hellenistic Judaism (e.g., Wis. 8:1, 6). The hymn proclaims God's actions in creation ("from whom all things") but also attributes to Christ a role in those acts ("through whom all things"), forming the background for the claims about food in 8:8 (cf. also 10:26). The final phrase, "we through him [Christ] exist," is parallel to the statement "we to him [God] exist," showing that in Christ a new relationship with God exists. This is the basis for Paul's statements that insisting on one's freedom to eat idol food not only harms others, but actually is a sin against Christ (vv. 11 and 12).

A few Corinthians still considered eating this food a form of idol worship that "defiles their conscience." Eating the idol food, even if it is not impure, causes them to return to the culture of their prior commitments and so abandon their allegiance to Christ. Ironically, it was not that the "weak" were careless about food or dining partners, but that they were bothered too deeply by these things. They were defiled not by *what* they ate, but *because* they ate.

The spiritual elites argued that despite their fellow believers' qualms, idol food could not cause impurity because idols were ineffectual. Paul allows that if all the church's members had recognized this, then the elites' conclusions would stand. However,

the sake of another. I think of issues such as attitudes toward biblical authority, supporting war, termination of pregnancy, and same-gender relationships. Tensions around such issues occur not only within congregations, but between congregations, denominations, and movements. Groups sometimes believe that their integrity is at stake and that silence is complicity with evil. At such times, ministers can seek to bring dissonant voices into conversation (in sermons as well as in other settings). I do not say this casually, but if no resolution is possible, the groups in the congregation (or in different congregations or movements) may need to separate in distinct communities and trust that the God through whom all things exist (1 Cor. 8:6) can ultimately bring about eschatological resolution. Even so, all participants should treat one another with respect in both public and private settings.

A third theme has to do with the relationship between social status and power in the congregation. A number of scholars think the tensions in Corinth were between upper-class/typically well-educated people (those who perceived themselves free to eat food offered to idols) and lower-class/typically not-so-well-educated people. The former group expressed their freedom while rolling over the latter group, with the result that the congregation lost its eschatological witness. A preacher can reflect on the degree to which similar dynamics may be at work in the church today.

Fourth, the preacher could explore what the congregation believes about supernatural beings such as the "so-called gods in heaven or on earth" (v. 5). Some people today do not know what to make of such notions (along with demons, principalities, powers, thrones, dominions, and even angels). Must the congregation believe the world is populated by personal beings of this kind who exert direct agency over individuals and communities? Or can the preacher offer a more social and systemic interpretation of the principalities and powers as transpersonal forces, such as racism, sexism, and colonialism? If so, the insistence of the group at Corinth on their right to eat food offered to idols is similar to today's ideology of radical individualism that undermines community. Self-limitation for the good of community is thus an act of resistance to a latter day "so-called god" of individualism.

In a fifth approach, the preacher might use the situation at Corinth as a case study in the importance of critical thinking. Groups in Corinth summarized their perspectives through slogans. "All

# 1 Corinthians 8:1-13

## Theological Perspective

*Using Knowledge of God and Christ to Avoid Sin (vv. 7–13).* It is encouraging that Paul does not turn away from rigorous, careful theological reasoning. In fact, Paul requires that leaders in the church engage in serious theological reasoning and then accept the responsibilities that come along with it. Paul claims that proper theological knowledge can lead us away from sinning against others, against Christ, against God, and against ourselves.

Paul warns those who have acquired reputable theological knowledge not to become so accustomed to it that they forget how to use it in the context of the church. In other words, having started with worship theology (vv. 1–6), Paul ends with church theology (ecclesiology). Here Paul is guided by the Christian addition to the Shema, "and love your neighbor as yourself" (Matt 22:39; Mark 12:31, 33; Luke 10:27). Paul applies the concept of neighbor to fellow members of one's church, whom he considers to be members of one's family (v. 12). Eating food or not eating food in the temple of an idol may not, theologically, mean a person is engaged in the worship of idols, if a person knows that idols do not really exist. But eating such food may lead a person away from loving one's neighbor, which is the additional part of being known by God (v. 3). People who are known by God also know their neighbors, and love them. And perhaps Paul might also be willing to say that a person who shows that kind of love is also known and loved by that neighbor!

By the end of his argument, Paul has moved from knowledge about God (theology), Jesus Christ (Christology), the creation (general revelation), and the church (ecclesiology) to sinning against Christ. How can this be? Surely it is idolatry to confess that Christ is "one Lord, Jesus Christ, through whom are all things and through whom we exist" (v. 6) and at the same time, to cause a member of one's family under God to fall, isn't it? This would be worshiping Christ simply as an idol, someone who does not really exist in the world, rather than worshiping one Lord Jesus Christ, who has an intimate relation to one God, "from whom are all things and for whom we exist" (v. 6).

VERNON K. ROBBINS

## Pastoral Perspective

relate to the pluralistic environment in which it finds itself? The range of issues is immense, from whether the American flag should be displayed in the sanctuary, to poverty in our society, to whether gay and lesbian Christians may hold positions of leadership in congregations. At the heart of it all is whether the church views Christ as one who teaches us to build fortresses to protect Christian community or as one who is himself the bridge to neighbors of other faiths and traditions.

Paul wants his Corinthian friends and all of us to know that being certain of what is right or wrong, appropriate or inappropriate, is not sufficient, even if one's position is correct. Love is greater than knowledge! This is particularly true in connection with the "weaker" ones among us.

Does this require, then, refraining from any behavior or position that is disapproved, because of the sometimes narrow-minded consciences and outlooks of the weaker minority in a congregation? That would make prophetic witness on the part of individuals or congregations nearly impossible, and it is not what Paul intends, as illustrated in 1 Corinthians 10:29–30.

Paul's point is that when we hurt others, we hurt Christ himself because we cause pain in his body, the church. To hurt those for whom Christ died is to commit sin. Above all else, we are called to show reconciling love in the church, and that has a direct bearing on what we do and how we do it.

As I read this text, Paul's principal concern is to guard the integrity of the church and to do so in such a way that "weaker" members will be protected form the destructive temptations of the surrounding culture, which would lure them away from faith in Christ. In the final analysis, this is about loyalty to Christ himself, which has to be expressed by sometimes costly sensitivity toward weaker fellow Christians.

Knowledge without love puffs up, but knowledgeable love builds up the community.

V. BRUCE RIGDON

because this was not the case, an ethical dimension must be added to the advocates' deliberations (v. 7).

Paul imagines that the "strong" Corinthians will counter with the claim that "food is of no consequence" in terms of one's status before God (v. 8). Paul agrees food is of no consequence, but the issue is not really food. Thus he warns the Corinthians that insisting on their "authority" (*exousia*: NRSV has "liberty," but this obscures the repetition of the term in 9:4, 5, 6, 12, 18) to eat these foods will result in the destruction of their weaker brothers and sisters. The behavior of the elite becomes a stumbling block to the others (cf. Rom. 14:13). Paul is not referring to those who might object to a particular behavior, but those whose existence and standing in Christ are threatened by the example of someone else. For the sake of these weaker ones, the strong must forgo their individual freedoms. With this, Paul has come to his main point. Believers who have sufficient "liberty" or "authority" to eat any food also have the responsibility to refrain from that food if exercising their freedom will ruin the beliefs of others. Moreover, to insist on their "right" to eat such foods undercuts the basis of the community's existence: Christ's sacrificial actions on behalf of the world. When the "strong" insist on exercising the freedom that they "know to be theirs," they do not make the community stronger, but tear it down. At the beginning of the discussion, Paul noted that love "builds up" (*oikodomeō*); here, the term is used ironically to show that the strong "will build" the weak into a state of destruction.

Paul's language is familiar, shifting matters from an incidental argument about freedoms to one of ethics and commitments. (The NRSV translates *adelphos* ["brother"] with the more inclusive plural term "believers" [v. 11]; however, this does not capture the family language Paul deliberately employed.) Church members are related as parts of an organic family. The question is not therefore one's freedom to eat, but how one should freely act towards one's spiritual family. Paul notes this larger sense of community by insisting that stressing one's individual freedoms goes beyond straining human relations. It is, in fact, a sin against Christ (v. 12). In effect, though one may possess knowledge, such knowledge requires an ethic of love and self-sacrifice.

STEVEN J. KRAFTCHICK

of us possess knowledge." "No idol in the world really exists." "There is no God but one." While Paul agreed that such slogans contained germs of truth, the congregation needed to think critically about the relationship of the slogan to larger patterns of Christian thought and to the effects of behavior shaped by such slogans. In North America today, advertising, and political and religious leaders, increasingly rely on images and jingles and bumper-sticker phrases to shape public opinion. The preacher can help a congregation recognize the inadequacy of such approaches to Christian thinking, and the preacher can stress the need to reflect more deeply about such matters, as does Paul in 1 Corinthians 8.

Many members of long-established congregations today are a little unsure of what to believe about Jesus Christ. A sixth message could use this text as the springboard for a doctrinal sermon on Christology.[1] In a doctrinal message, the pastor moves from a single text to the church's broader conviction regarding the issue introduced by the text, a conviction that usually transcends the teaching of the one text. Such an approach is suggested by 1 Corinthians 8:6, which is probably a pre-Pauline affirmation. The preacher could listen to the witness of this text regarding the relationship of God, Jesus, creation, and providence, and could bring into the conversation other voices from other places in the Bible and Christian tradition and theology.

Clergy conferences often take place in January, and many congregations install new lay leadership during the same month. For ministers preaching on such occasions, a seventh possibility might ponder Paul's behavior as a leader in the dispute at Corinth as a possible model for a minister's approach to leadership in the congregation. The apostle seeks for the congregation to come together as eschatological community. Yet Paul does not give a finger-pointing lecture to the group whose exercise of freedom challenges the solidarity of that community; rather, he identifies with those very people. When Paul comes to the clinching moment in the discussion (8:13), the apostle turns to autobiography ("I will never eat meat . . ."), so that his prior suggestions to the Corinthians are now illustrated and backed up by his own life and integrity. How might ministers and other officers in congregations lead similarly?

RONALD J. ALLEN

[1] On doctrinal preaching, see Ronald J. Allen, *Preaching Is Believing: The Sermon as Theological Reflection* (Louisville, KY: Westminster John Knox Press, 2002).

# Mark 1:21-28

²¹They went to Capernaum; and when the sabbath came, he entered the synagogue and taught. ²²They were astounded at his teaching, for he taught them as one having authority, and not as the scribes. ²³Just then there was in their synagogue a man with an unclean spirit, ²⁴and he cried out, "What have you to do with us, Jesus of Nazareth? Have you come to destroy us? I know who you are, the Holy One of God." ²⁵But Jesus rebuked him, saying, "Be silent, and come out of him!" ²⁶And the unclean spirit, convulsing him and crying with a loud voice, came out of him. ²⁷They were all amazed, and they kept on asking one another, "What is this? A new teaching—with authority! He commands even the unclean spirits, and they obey him." ²⁸At once his fame began to spread throughout the surrounding region of Galilee.

## Theological Perspective

Jesus' invitation to the kingdom is radical and overwhelms the vital space of those he encounters. Accompanied by the four fishermen, Jesus begins his "kingdom campaign," inviting the neediest. He doesn't notice the great ones, nor does he call those who pose as the great ones or important ones. He comes to the desolate places, and there he summons for the kingdom those who are far away from the several kingdoms of this world.

So that is how Mark's stories are told. They are short stories that Mark has wanted to present as a model of the gospel. Separately and together, they offer the most beautiful invitation to the kingdom. The first three are progressively structured, in function of the places: from the Jewish synagogue (1:21–28), through the Christian house (1:29–34), to the villages or towns of the regions where the gospel should be proclaimed. The three following texts are linked by desolation: the leper (1:40–45), the paralyzed man /sinner (2:1–12), and the publican (2:13–17) are outcasts from society.

So Mark distributes Jesus' activity with a precise plan. It is an organized space.

The space is divided in three sectors: synagogue, house, house door. Therefore, we take the synagogue as a place of public prayer; the house as a place of private life; and the door, that is to say, the external

## Pastoral Perspective

It is not ordinarily a good idea to introduce the subject of "faith healing" at proper dinner parties, unless one wants to run the risk of not being invited back. Pictures of faith-healing practitioners run the gamut from "charlatan," "fraud," "huckster" to "anointed," "Spirit-filled," "angelic messengers of God." While many contemporaries, religious or not, have no interest in the subject at all, preferring simply "not to go there," for those for whom the issue is important, it is exceedingly important. For the most extreme, a belief in the ability of faith to heal becomes a criterion, indeed a litmus test, for true faith.

Most of us, I suspect, find ourselves most comfortable occupying the middle ground, recognizing that (1) Mark's words were written a least a half century following the birth of Jesus and are primarily based on oral tradition; (2) the worldview of the people in Mark's time was quite different from our contemporary worldview, in that divine intervention into human life was a common belief in Hellenistic religions, while post-Enlightenment advances in medicine and health care have in our time shed new understanding on the causes and remedies of illness, both physical and emotional; (3) the faith journey of most of us has taught us that what we do not know about God is

## Exegetical Perspective

A goal of a good translation is to render words from one language faithfully into words of another. Given the complexity, nuances, idioms, and particularities of any language, it is almost inevitable that certain words are lost in translation. Translating the Gospel of Mark is no exception. In the interest of cleaning up Mark's redundant use of certain words and phrases and his repetitious themes and stories, translators have often tried to smooth a rather jagged stone. Unfortunately, by so doing they have lost much of Mark's distinct voice and theological emphasis. Today's text is a clear example.

In 1:21–28, Mark uses repetition to advance the story and to set expectations for listeners. One of Mark's favorite words is the adverb *euthys* ("immediately, at once, right away"), which he uses as an aural drumbeat both to emphasize the moment at hand and to move the audience along to more momentous moments ahead. In today's brief text, *euthys* sounds like a Markan rhythm calling us to pay attention to a theme that begins in this text and continues throughout his Gospel. Yet in most English translations *euthys* disappears altogether in the first verse of the story and is translated with different English words—"then" and "at once"—in its remaining uses. In an attempt to honor the conventions of good English and to make Mark more readable, most

## Homiletical Perspective

Mark describes the teaching of Jesus in the synagogue as resulting in astonishment on the part of those present (v. 22). No doubt, we hope for similar results come Sunday, although such a comparison probably alarms most of us. The alarm is due in part to our uneasiness with the sermon being a performance. More than that, most preachers cringe at the notion of being compared to Jesus. Still, there is the textual distinction made between the teaching of the scribes and that of Jesus. His teaching has authority, according to Mark; the repetition (vv. 22, 27) indicates that this is one of the key tenets of the text. So how shall we preach this week? What should we hope for? And what shall be the focus of our proclamation?

The dilemma of finding something to preach on results not from too few choices but too many. This story in Mark's Gospel, like all the others, overflows with sermon possibilities. But we know that sermons, unlike scholarly commentaries, must be focused. Perhaps one way to go about this selection task is to consider all the possible misdirections. There are some definite pitfalls to be avoided in this brief text.

For starters, there exists the ever-present temptation of subtle anti-Semitism—bashing the synagogue and scribes, and thus indirectly bashing

# Mark 1:21-28

## Theological Perspective

space—we say the square—as a place of public life. The spaces are quite evident: Mark places the whole imaginable, religious and profane, private and public space together. It shows that Jesus' action is of interest to the human being as a whole, in all the dimensions of life. Christ's activity is not limited to the religious space, but rather enters into the sphere of friendship and goes out, directed to contacting the multitude, to those excluded and impoverished.

The whole space of the encounters is organized in a relationship to city and desert, elements that stand at the beginning and the end of the narrations, the city as a meeting place and the desert as a place of solitude and also a call to that activity of prayer so necessary for the missionary day. "At dawn, when it was still very dark, he got up and left to a solitary place, where he began to pray" (1:35).

In the synagogue, the religious space, the kingdom is embodied in Jesus' communication skills—word and much more—and power over spirits. "They entered into Capernaum" (1:21). They have left the bank of the sea that is a fishing and calling place of the messengers of the kingdom, and they come to the space of security and tradition, where the old religious teachings are transmitted. There Jesus is, in the synagogue, and in that space of the synagogue he deploys a new power. He takes advantage of the Sabbath, the day the faithful ones meet, to teach them, as a trustworthy Jew who has a word for the people. Jesus' communication skill creates vitality: "he taught them as one having authority, and not as the scribes."

But when Jesus arrives there, he suddenly finds the unexpected; there, inside the synagogue, is an "impure" man. Certainly those in the synagogue are not aware of him because he breaks all the outlines of dogmatic sanctity. When reading the text, we remember many situations in our local churches where we find it difficult to discover those who are there every Sunday, but who suffer ailments and have sufferings that demand a healing approach of solidarity.

The man is possessed by a devil or unclean spirit (1:23). In biblical language, "impure" means, simply, contrary to the sacred. All that is against the sanctity of God is considered impure. Jesus' teaching liberates the oppressed man in the synagogue. He doesn't name the illness of the oppressed one (blindness, paralysis, etc.). It is simply called "impure": it is dominated by an antihuman spirit, which Jesus discovers, and he makes it speak. This word ("new teaching—with authority," 1:27) defines Jesus. He

## Pastoral Perspective

infinitely more than what we do know; and (4) life experience teaches that it is exceedingly difficult and usually unproductive to argue with another's experience. I am sure that if I had a child diagnosed with an incurable disease, for whom the good people at our church had prayed incessantly for weeks, and one day the physician declared her completely cured (even whispering the word "miracle"), I would be the first in line at the next healing service.

So what is one in our time to make of these ancient accounts of Jesus' healing the afflicted, sick, deranged? First of all, one must note with seriousness the prominence of healing in Jesus' ministry. Mark, more than any other Gospel writer, emphasizes Jesus' miraculous power to heal and to exorcise. Of the eighteen miracles recorded in Mark, thirteen have to do with healing, and four of the thirteen are exorcisms. If nothing else, the early introduction of Jesus' healing power and the dominance of healing among the miracle stories suggest again what the Scriptures had been hinting all along; that is, the intractable relation between religion and health.

The text for today, often referred to as the exorcism at Capernaum, occurs chronologically immediately following Jesus' baptism, his forty-day retreat into the wilderness, his announcement that the "kingdom of God is at hand," and his calling of the disciples. It is virtually at the inception of his ministry that Jesus, in Capernaum, goes to the synagogue to teach. There a man "with an unclean spirit" interrupts to challenge Jesus as one who has come "to destroy." Then Jesus calls the spirit out of the man, and all who are present are amazed at his authority.

I was asked one time to perform an exorcism of a sort. It was, I suppose, about midway in my ministry. I was serving a historic old church in downtown Atlanta. About ten days before Christmas, the secretary buzzed the intercom to say, "There is a young man here to see you. He says he wants to bless him. . . . No, he is not a member of the church. . . . Says he just wants you to bless him." Well, I knew what that meant. He wanted money. They all do, especially at Christmas. Any excuse to get a foot in the door. But the emergency relief office was closed for the day, and so I said, "Sure, show him in." He was not what I had expected. He was neatly dressed, clean-shaven, late twenties, I imagined. There was an air of dignity about him, no glassy look in the eye, none of the usual signs of having "been on the street," as we say.

translators obscure this signature of Mark's storytelling and dampen this insistent gospel drumbeat that sounds with urgency until Jesus steps foot into Jerusalem.

Two other characteristics of language that are difficult to translate and thus are often lost in translation are humor and irony. In today's text, readers enjoy a surreal laugh as they listen to a bizarre Sabbath exchange in the synagogue. Mark intercalates a teaching story of Jesus with an exorcism story. Each story interprets the other, reminding readers that Jesus entered the synagogue not to be instructed by others, but to teach (didaskō), and that his teaching has obvious power (exousia), as contrasted with the apparent lack of power (exousia) of the synagogue's scribes.

Like the synagogue spectators, most modern readers are "amazed" (thambeomai, 1:27) by this story or story within a story; but they are "amazed" not by Jesus' "powerful" teaching. In fact, most modern readers would argue that Jesus does not "teach" at all in this text, at least not in any traditional understanding of the term. Instead, readers today are "amazed" by the interior story of the exchange between an anonymous and mute man and a noisy gang of demons who reinforce what Mark first tells readers as his Gospel begins (see 1:1): Jesus is the "Holy One of God" (v. 24).

For characters in this story, this face-to-face meeting with demons in the synagogue is all about teaching—teaching that all things demonic are on their way out, including the demonic hold on religious life sanctioned by synagogue and temple (see 13:1). While some readers may respond to this story by asking, "Are there really such things as demons?" the characters in Mark's story do not focus on demons, or on what they have to say, or how Jesus effectively exorcises them. The characters are amazed by this new teacher whose words carry with them power to make the unclean, clean. Like the servant of the Lord in Isaiah 50:4, Jesus is a teacher, but in Mark the emphasis is on what the teacher does, more than on any carefully worded lecture or sermon.

In 1:21–28, Jesus the teacher is interrupted by a demon-possessed man in the synagogue on the Sabbath. The arrival of this tortured man offers a profound teaching moment for Jesus and later by Mark. The exorcism story drips with irony as Jesus, a man possessed by the Spirit of God (see 1:10), faces off with a man possessed by the demonic. This battle proves to be no contest for the demonic contingent

Judaism. Such a temptation is subtle, because none of us ever intends to disparage other traditions, but its subtlety does not diminish the possible damage. The new teaching of Jesus (v. 27) is indeed totally different from what the people are accustomed to, but in no way is the comparison meant to indict Judaism as a whole. The teaching of the scribes involves handing on the traditions that have been passed down for generations. The teaching of Jesus differs.[1] No need to attack the scribes.

Of course, with any exorcism story in the New Testament there is always the temptation to conjure up images from Hollywood movies. This text says nothing about the man's head spinning around and spitting up blood. For that matter, it says nothing about sexual orgies, rock 'n' roll, and drinking cat's blood, either. Exorcism stories in the New Testament are more about the story that gets told than the details of the exorcism itself.

Closely related to this misunderstanding of exorcism is the temptation to debate miracles. Granted, there will be more spectacular displays later in Mark's Gospel (walking on top of stormy waters, feeding folks with very little bread), but this is a miracle story nonetheless. Focusing on the details of Jesus' teaching with authority will yield more fruitful possibilities than debating the authenticity of such miracles. Miracle stories are more often about the story told than the miracle itself. As John Dominic Crossan notes in his study of early Christian art, "the essential Jesus was known primarily for his feeding people and healing them."[2] This miracle story, however, unlike others to come in the early chapters of Mark, appears to be less about the compassion of Jesus (Mark 1:41) or Sabbath keeping (Mark 3:1–6)—although clearly he cares about these things—than about how his teaching had authority.

Perhaps the most devastating temptation is to assume the story is about someone else, rather than about the organized religion of which most of us partake. Like it or not, we are the scribes who profit from the scholarly work of others and bring forth our teachings in an assembly we call church. And like it or not, we are just as likely to miss the marginalized before us.

This story takes place in Capernaum of Galilee, not Jerusalem. This story posits before us, right in the middle of the story, an unnamed man suffering

[1] Richard J. Dillon, "'As One Having Authority' (Mark 1:22): The Controversial Distinction of Jesus' Teaching," Catholic Biblical Quarterly 57 (January 1995): 92–113.

[2] John Dominic Crossan, The Essential Jesus: Original Sayings and Earliest Images (Edison, NJ: Castle Books, 1998), 12–14.

# Mark 1:21-28

## Theological Perspective

goes to the synagogue to teach by healing. His gospel is a healing word and action. The Jesus of Mark's Gospel has offered, inside the very synagogue, his teaching of freedom, a word and act that heals the human being.

The forces of evil know of the healing power of Jesus' word; they are not submissive or indifferent. Jesus' powerful teaching not only is fresh to the ears of the faithful, but it also disrupts the undisturbed presence of evil. Evil discovers that it is running its course.

We are struck by Jesus' word in response to the forces of evil that dominate the impure one—"Be silent" (v. 25). The verb literally demands an action like putting on a muzzle. And here is where the main idea of the narration centers. Mark wants to demonstrate that Jesus' word is effective, powerful. His word is action, and his action is embedded in his word. The authority is not only in the teaching, but also in the action. The term "authority"—*exousia*—is understood in the strong sense of the "divine power." And this divine power is the one that Christ will transmit to the Twelve to send them to preach and cast out demons (3:14–15).

And people are amazed, and even perplexed (v. 27) in the face of this authority power. God is present and acts in the world through the teaching and through the word that provides healing. What is this? A new doctrine, set forth with authority (v. 27)! Amid so many voices, one voice finally resounds. There are so many words, but that one is the expected word. Novelty is in the fact that it is word that produces healing actions. That word liberates the earth from the forces of evil and makes our world habitable for the human being; that word guides the church to create spaces of freedom and places of healing and communion.

OFELIA ORTEGA

## Pastoral Perspective

"Sorry to take up your time," he said, "but I just want your blessing." He went on to explain in a rather articulate, if un-Presbyterian, way that he had this "devil on his back" that he could not shake. As much as he had tried, he could not get rid of it, and he thought that if he could just find a minister who would "bless him," the devil would go away. He did not seem depressed or overly desperate, in fact, he appeared in pretty good spirits, very much in control, I thought. So I made some feeble attempt to explain that Presbyterians were not usually in the practice of casting out devils or conferring blessings on people. In a bumbling kind of way, I tried to explain that we really have not been given that kind of power to heal, though somehow none of that seemed appropriate at the moment. He had not come for a lesson in ecclesiology.

"All I want," he repeated, "is your blessing."

Well, it was Christmas. So I said, "Then tell me your name."

"Andy," he said, and with that Andy knelt down on the carpet while I had a prayer, which was not so much a blessing, at least not in the traditional sense, but a rather traditional Presbyterian prayer of thanksgiving for God's presence in Andy's life: an acknowledgment of the way God had already blessed him; then affirmation of God's continuing concern and purpose for him; and the request that God would take away this "devil" that was preventing Andy from being the kind of person God intended him to be. With the "Amen," Andy stood, smiled, shook my hand and said, "Thanks." Then he left. Not a word about money or a meal or a place to stay. "All I want is your blessing," he said.

I have often wondered about Andy, and whether my feeble little effort at exorcism worked. I wonder too if Jesus ever did follow-ups on his miracle work.

P. C. ENNISS

## Exegetical Perspective

making residence in the man. They name what the readers know about Jesus, while everyone else in the synagogue stays strangely silent. A child of God is delivered from his bondage, and there are no shouts for joy or spontaneous prayers of thanksgiving. Isaiah 58:6 echoes in the background—"Is not this the fast that I choose: to loose the bonds of injustice, to undo the thongs of the yoke, to let the oppressed go free, and to break every yoke?"—and yet no one notices that what Mark signaled in Jesus' baptism (the heavens are "torn apart"—*schizō*, 1:10) is happening now before their eyes.

From the onset of his Gospel, Mark signals that no oppressive boundary will stand or withstand the *exousia* of Jesus. All that is demonic within and beyond the religious structures of the synagogue will not survive in the face of the demon-tossing, Spirit-possessed Son of God. While the synagogue crowd is awed by his "teaching," readers are perplexed at how no one (except the demons) understands that the boundary between heaven and earth has been pierced and the reign of God is "at hand" (*engizō*, 1:15).

As the characters in the story maintain a safe distance from Jesus, speculating among themselves about this new powerful teacher, readers of Mark are invited to follow Jesus into a whole new world, says New Testament scholar Brian Blount, into "Mark's world of Jesus walking around possessed by the power of the Spirit of God. In such a world you either go with the man and help him create the holy chaos he's creating or you find a way to do everything you can to stop him so you can get your people back in line."[1]

Careful readers of Mark's Gospel are put on notice from chapter 1 that the boundary-breaking, demon-dashing, law-transcending Son of God has arrived in the person of Jesus, and he expects of his followers far more than "amazement."

GARY W. CHARLES

## Homiletical Perspective

from disease. We preachers and churchgoers alike are capable of discussing this story ad nauseam, never giving thought to the man's condition. Is it possible we do the same thing on Sundays? And what about on Mondays?

In Matthew's reworking of the early chapters of Mark, we *hear* the teachings of Jesus in the Sermon on the Mount; in Mark we *see* the teachings of Jesus. His care for the poor in spirit and mournful is demonstrated. The authority here in Mark is not power, a different Greek word altogether, but a willingness or right that has everything to do with seeing justice served. This is what Jesus' ministry is about.

The unnamed man is sick. Unclean spirits are amoral in Mark's Gospel—and all of the New Testament, for that matter. The man is ill, in need of help. As Howard Clark Kee observes, neither medicine nor magic is the cure. We moderns, of course, think of the former; a diagnosis is needed, treatments and the like. Some ancients thought of the latter; a curse has been pronounced, one that needs to be broken. But as Kee rightly notes, the ministry of Jesus posits another possibility—miracle.[3]

Such a miracle comes here in the form of Jesus' teaching, his speaking. The healing word Jesus speaks, like the words he has spoken in the synagogue, cause things to happen. This is what people find so astonishing about Jesus' words. They are powerful and performative. We want the same thing, come Sunday. We do not desire simply to provide more information about this text. We do not desire to add to all the other words ever uttered from pulpits, just because that's what preachers do on Sunday mornings. No, we hope that our words, infused with the power of the One who speaks through us and on whose behalf we speak, will cause something to happen.

What is this? they asked. It is a new teaching, a new preaching. Not just information, but transformation.

MIKE GRAVES

---

[1]Brian K. Blount and Gary W. Charles, *Preaching Mark in Two Voices* (Louisville, KY: Westminster John Knox Press, 2003), 33.

[3]Howard Clark Kee, *Medicine, Miracle, and Magic in New Testament Times* (Cambridge: Cambridge University Press, 1986), 2–3.

# Isaiah 40:21-31

²¹Have you not known? Have you not heard?
    Has it not been told you from the beginning?
    Have you not understood from the foundations of the earth?
²²It is he who sits above the circle of the earth,
    and its inhabitants are like grasshoppers;
who stretches out the heavens like a curtain,
    and spreads them like a tent to live in;
²³who brings princes to naught,
    and makes the rulers of the earth as nothing.

²⁴Scarcely are they planted, scarcely sown,
    scarcely has their stem taken root in the earth,
when he blows upon them, and they wither,
    and the tempest carries them off like stubble.

²⁵To whom then will you compare me,
    or who is my equal? says the Holy One.
²⁶Lift up your eyes on high and see:
    Who created these?

## Theological Perspective

The opening chapters of Second Isaiah are poignant poetry, and in Isaiah 40 we are invited to contemplate God in relation to humanity—the magnitude of God's power and humanity's unqualified powerlessness. Isaiah repeatedly weaves with vivid threads a poetic tapestry of the all-powerful Lord God, who "marked off the heavens" and "enclosed the dust of the earth in a measure" (v. 12). We see that the Lord God comes with might, with arms of strength, and that there is no other being who gives this Lord counsel or instruction. Moreover, when earthly realms are compared to God's power, they are like "a drop from a bucket" or "fine dust on the scales" (v. 15). Before the Lord God, nations are less than nothing, less than emptiness (v. 17). Theologically, this poem draws a clear distinction between the One who sits above the circle of the earth and those who inhabit the earth, who are "like grasshoppers" (v. 22). Isaiah again and again points to God's preeminence and timelessness and our insignificance. And this God-in-relation-to-humanity comparison is central in understanding the poem's word of hope. Only when we grasp God's power and our powerlessness does a word of hope emerge—namely, that "those who wait for the LORD shall renew their strength" (v. 31).

At first glance, we might want to stand up and cheer for this powerful Lord God, especially if the

## Pastoral Perspective

Even Annie Dillard is at a loss for words. The writer who composed *Holy the Firm* and *Pilgrim at Tinker Creek*—works that portray faith with piercing eloquence—settles on abstractions to describe the phenomenon of a solar eclipse. "The meaning of the sight overwhelmed its fascination. It obliterated meaning itself," Dillard writes in her essay "Total Eclipse."[1] Comparing herself to a fellow observer who described the vision as a "Life Saver up in the sky," Dillard writes, "I myself had at that time no access to such a word. He could write a sentence, and I could not."[2] Though cosmic events may be explained scientifically, their full beauty and meaning are often unavailable, indescribable.

It is to such heavenly sights that Isaiah calls our attention as proof of God's almighty and benevolent power. "Have you not known? Have you not heard? Has it not been told you from the beginning? Have you not understood . . . ? It is [God] who sits above the circle of the earth . . . who stretches out the heavens like a curtain, and spreads them like a tent to live in" (vv. 21–22). It is none other than the "Creator of the ends of the earth" who "does not faint or grow weary" (v. 28). This mighty God also

[1] Annie Dillard, "Total Eclipse," in *Teaching a Stone to Talk* (New York: HarperCollins, 1982), 19.
[2] Ibid., 23.

He who brings out their host and numbers them,
> calling them all by name;
because he is great in strength,
> mighty in power,
> not one is missing.

27Why do you say, O Jacob,
> and speak, O Israel,
"My way is hidden from the Lord,
> and my right is disregarded by my God"?
28Have you not known? Have you not heard?
> The Lord is the everlasting God,
> the Creator of the ends of the earth.
He does not faint or grow weary;
> his understanding is unsearchable.
29He gives power to the faint,
> and strengthens the powerless.
30Even youths will faint and be weary,
> and the young will fall exhausted;
31but those who wait for the Lord shall renew their strength,
> they shall mount up with wings like eagles,
they shall run and not be weary,
> they shall walk and not faint.

## Exegetical Perspective

The passage for today from Second Isaiah builds on an assumption that lies at the core of Israel's testimony—the assumption that faith begins with memory. Where memory fails, the faith of the community is threatened. Many things can threaten the faithful memory of the community: political and social threats; enticements of ease and comfort; the lure of other, competing gods. Here, in the sixth-century time of the prophet, destruction and exile have generated despair and chaos in the people of Israel. Doubts about YHWH's attention to Israel's future and YHWH's power to control and direct that future threaten the constitution of the community. The passage is structured by questions that call for Israel to remember: "Have you not known? Have you not heard? Has it not been told you from the beginning? Have you not understood from the foundations of the earth?" (v. 21).

The passage consists of two units, linked in verse 27 by an explicit statement of Israel's complaint. The first unit (vv. 21–26) focuses on Israel's God as creator of the earth, who creates and controls the nations as part of that creation. The second unit (vv. 28–31) reiterates the testimony to God as creator, but moves quickly to describe the promise of this untiring, attentive God to the renewal and restoration of Israel. Both units are set up by

## Homiletical Perspective

One cannot read this passage without seeing Eric Liddell, that famous Olympic runner in the movie *Chariots of Fire*, standing in the pulpit of that Paris church reading these words with grace and beauty, his soft, gentle Scottish brogue filling the sanctuary. One also hears hints of that popular contemporary song "On Eagle's Wings," lilting in the background with Michael Joncas's haunting refrain: "And He will raise you up on eagle's wings."

Three things come to mind as we look at this text: (1) we are theological amnesiacs; (2) the psalmist reminds us that God really is in charge; and (3) only when we feel weak and helpless, whether young or old, are we vulnerable enough to experience the power and grace of a God who "raises us up on eagle's wings." So, this text is about us, about God and what God does with us when all we seem to be is down.

First of all, we are amnesiacs. Notice how selective our memory is. We remember what we want to. If we are constantly self-critical, we remember only the awful things we have done in our lives. If we think we are perfect, we remember only the good things.

Theological amnesia is the kind of problem that causes us to fall apart every time crisis comes. It is what happens when you hear the dreaded "cancer" word or the doctor tells you they found a spot on

*Isaiah 40:21–31*

315

# Isaiah 40:21-31

## Theological Perspective

world moves as we might wish. If our world is relatively pleasant, peaceful, or filled with riches, then we would surely applaud this powerful God because, by implication, God must be with us. Or, at the least, we might come to believe that we are blessed by this Lord, who counts us as courtiers. Yet the powerful are not the ones for whom this poem is spoken. The first hearers of this poem were those in exile in Babylon. In either case, though, we hear that we are *all* like the grass—courtier and exile alike—whose "constancy is like the flower of the field" (v. 6).

For the exiles, captivity in Babylon was a painful reality (in varying degrees). They were forced from their homes, scattered as the temple was laid to waste, and became refugees from the very land that held promise. They are a people who longed for Jerusalem and wept by the rivers of Babylon (Ps. 137:1); they are the faint and powerless and even observe their youths grow weary and fall exhausted (Isa. 40:29–30). From this condition, each Israelite concludes, "My way is hidden from the LORD, and my right is disregarded by my God" (v. 27). They could have concluded that the gods of Babylon were stronger than their God or that God really does not exist at all. But their conclusion is that they are simply "disregarded" by the One who sits above the circle of the earth.

With God located at this remote and powerful distance, we may conclude that God is only transcendent—beyond all of humanity's care and struggles. The twentieth-century theologian Karl Barth bluntly states that if we believe God "can and must be only the 'Wholly Other' . . . such beliefs are shown to be quite untenable, and corrupt and pagan,"[1] because God is equally immanent (existing close and within). As Isaiah recites, the Lord God who sits above the circle of the earth is, at the very same time, the Shepherd who gently claims, gathers, and carries us (vv. 10–11). When the poet bids us to lift up our eyes on high, we see that the One who is Wholly Other is also the One who numbers and names us all because, in sovereignty, not one thing in creation is missing or lost. The Lord God "can be God and act as God in an absolute way and also a relative, in an infinite and also a finite, in an exalted and also a lowly, in an active and also a passive, in a transcendent and also an immanent, and finally, in a divine and also a human."[2] God does and is this because sovereignty is transcendence *and* immanence.[3]

[1] Karl Barth, *Church Dogmatics*, IV/1, ed. G. W. Bromiley and T. F. Torrance (Edinburgh: T. & T. Clark, 1957), 186.
[2] Ibid., 187.
[3] Karl Barth also states that in sovereignty God "embraces the opposites of these concepts even while He is superior to them" (ibid.).

## Pastoral Perspective

cares for the people and will "renew their strength" so that "they shall mount up with wings like eagles" (v. 31).

Isaiah makes it sound so obvious and good: The God who creates all of this, who is greater even than rulers, can certainly take care of the smallest among us! Nice sermon, so far: Awesome creation, powerful God, throw your cares away. But what about those modern hearers of this word who don't think they understand much of anything about the universe or divine omnipotence ("Have you not understood?" can sound like a reproachful Sunday school teacher, after all)? Or those parishioners who are skeptical about God if the current state of the world is any indication of how almighty God actually is, or how much God really cares? Don't take for granted that appeals to heavenly grandeur work with everyone. Despite knowing that in Second Isaiah the prophet is proclaiming an end to the Babylonian exile, modern hearers of this text may not readily assent with Isaiah's audience to the idea that God's beautiful creation explains everything we need to know about God and life.

The meaning of life is not often revealed atop a mountain on a starry night. I've climbed a few, and though they are beautiful and I feel close to God, certain questions about life and faith persist, I must admit. If Annie Dillard cannot fully get around the meaning of a solar eclipse as a sign of God's power and love, how are we mere mortals to understand what the heavens reveal to us about God? Dillard writes, "One turns at last even from glory itself with a sigh of relief. From the depths of mystery, and even from the heights of splendor, we bounce back and hurry for the latitudes of home."[3] It is all too much.

Perhaps that is the point. We are mere "grasshoppers" to the God who "sits above the circle of the earth" (v. 22). We scuttle home, confused. Perhaps our lack of understanding is precisely what Isaiah hopes will overwhelm us into feeling comforted by the God who cares for us despite our limitations. The logic would then be this: God created all of these wondrous things we cannot even begin to fathom fully, but we ought to be thankful that this God, who exists beyond our imagining, still cares for each one, "calling them all by name" (v. 26).

Human development experts have identified how important receiving recognition is to a healthy psyche—not just recognition for outstanding achievements, though those should be celebrated,

[3] Ibid., 28.

questions that provide the rhetorical basis for the testimony which follows.

In the first unit the prophet proclaims that Israel's God is also the creator of the universe and the God of all the nations. The prophet's questions in the opening verse (v. 21) make it clear that Israel's knowledge is not new information or recently acquired. It is knowledge that had been known from "the beginning" and from the "foundations of the earth." It is the knowledge of YHWH's work in history and in the life of the people. And it is knowledge that is relevant for the contemporary crisis. The real problem consists of Israel's having forgotten what it once knew very clearly. Babylon may seem strong and threatening, but Israel's forgetfulness represents the real threat to the community.

In the magnificent language of creation theology, the prophet testifies to the power and awesomeness of God (v. 22). The human beings who inhabit the earth are like insects in the face of that power. Creation itself represents the dwelling of God and can be manipulated by divine power and will. The description here picks up the imagery of earlier in the chapter (v. 12), imagery typical of Israel's understanding of the cosmos. Like Job's encounter with God, the emphasis is on the incomparability of divine power and the implied impossibility of humans to compete with or threaten that power.

The prophet moves easily from describing God's power over creation to describing that same awesome power exercised in the affairs of nations (v. 23). The nations and princes are like stubble or chaff before divine power. The apparent power of the nations and their rulers is temporal and inconsequential compared to the power of the one who created the universe itself. This incomparability of God is made explicit in verse 25, where it is also made clear that the creator is the Holy One. This is the same one that calls forth the host of heaven, numbers them, and calls them each by name (v. 26). The implication here is that the God who can do this will not forget Israel.

Now, in verse 27, the prophet himself presents Israel's complaint as part of his attempt to persuade and cajole Israel from doubt into confidence. The voice of Israel is heard explicitly only in this verse, and even here it is in a reference by the prophet, addressing the people directly. In verses 21–26, the prophet has already reminded his listeners of the nature of God as creator and ruler of nations. In the face of these reminders, the prophet questions how the people can say that God ignores and disregards them. The implied statement here is that the

your lung. Some of us whine. Others of us worry in desperate silence. Like the returning exiles, we wonder whether God hasn't gone off and left us altogether.

The real problem is that we have forgotten who we are. There is a kind of theological identity crisis in the church today. We do not know who we are as Christians anymore. We do not remember what we believe or why we believe it. No wonder we feel lost and alone. No wonder we have no idea how to talk with the world about our faith.

Theological amnesia is especially troubling when life goes well. How easily we forget God when everything is on track in our lives! We forget that God loves us and wants the best for us. We forget to praise and thank God for the blessings we receive every day. This was Israel's perennial problem. No wonder the Deuteronomist and the prophets kept reminding Israel who God was and is.

What happens when we forget the God who is Creator and Sustainer, Redeemer and Friend? The moment we confront trouble we collapse with anxiety and stress. Too many people are "stressed out" these days because of their lack of trust in God. Think of Elijah hiding in a cave, scared to death of Jezebel in 1 Kings 19. The word of the Lord comes to him, saying, "What are you doing here, Elijah?" In other words, "Why are you so stressed out? Get up and get moving again! Have you forgotten what I have done for you throughout your life? Have you forgotten that I was with you when you came face to face with the Baal prophets? Why do you keep forgetting me?"

In many ways, this Isaiah text represents the same kind of theological slap in the face that reminds us how God really does reign over all nature and history, the one "who brings princes to naught, and makes the rulers of the earth as nothing" (v. 23). Isaiah is trying to cure the world's amnesia. God has not forgotten you. Why are you forgetting God? We worry because we don't trust God. Trust God more and you will cure your worry problems.

There is a woman in Tennessee who understands. Her name is Margaret Stevenson. She is in her nineties. She used to hike ten or fifteen miles every day. She is a legend in the Smokies. It was always a joy to hike with Margaret, because she knew every turn and every trail and every plant and tree by its Latin and colloquial name. My first trip up Mt. LeConte was her seventy-fifth, and my second was her hundred twenty-fifth. My third was her five-hundredth trip. When she finally stopped hiking, she had climbed Mt. LeConte more than 700 times. Her

# Isaiah 40:21-31

## Theological Perspective

In chapter 40, Isaiah poetically illustrates this seemingly paradoxical, foreign other and intimate present God and then twice asks us, "Have you not known? Have you not heard?" (vv. 21, 28). Standing in front of the tapestry that Isaiah weaves, these questions are nearly laughable, except that, in the absorption of our own suffering, we can forget who God is. Isaiah renders for us that which we have forgotten or mistaken. You might mistake your current captor (or any other nation or human construct) as sovereign. The truth, though, is that the Lord God "brings princes to naught, and makes the rulers of the earth as nothing. Scarcely are they planted, scarcely sown, scarcely has their stem taken root in the earth, when he blows upon them, and they wither, and the tempest carries them off like stubble" (vv. 23, 24). Moreover, this sovereign God is not only supremely powerful, sitting "above the circle of the earth" (v. 22), but is also the One who calls us all by name without one missing (v. 26). So again Isaiah asks, "Have you not known? Have you not heard?" and answers, unequivocally, "The LORD is the everlasting God, the Creator of the ends of the earth" (v. 28).

God's transcendence and immanence are, at the end of the poem, the word of hope for all who believe their plight to be hidden and disregarded (v. 27). In Isaiah's contemplation of God in relation to humanity, we see a tapestry of good news that shows the way the exhausted, faint, powerless, and weary renew their strength, mount up with wings like eagles, run without growing weary, walk without fainting (v. 31). The way, the poet says, is to *wait* (v. 31) for the Creator who gathers the lambs and does not faint or grow weary in doing so.

DAVID FORNEY

## Pastoral Perspective

but the simple recognition of one's very existence. Neglected, ignored children often have difficulty as adults making meaningful connections because they did not receive sufficient recognition of their mere personhood as a child. That a grand and wonderful God calls even the smallest forgotten child by name is pretty awesome!

A liturgist planning worship for this Sunday might want to avoid an overemphasis on the grandeur of the Creator and the creation as the answer to all our questions, though it would set an appropriate stage for exploring how God's love is also revealed in the smallest act of calling each of us by name. What about that group of parishioners who may look at the current state of the world and wonder how God can be powerful and benevolent, if wars still plague the earth, if poverty still cuts life short, if suffering continues unabated? How is the preacher to address the incredulity sure to be present in the room? The preacher might take the opportunity to explore the question of theodicy, the centuries-old problem of defending the goodness and omnipotence of God in the face of an evil world. The question goes like this: If God is good and all-powerful, then why does evil persist? It is a relevant subject for congregations today, as the digital information age shrinks the global community and increases our awareness of suffering both far and near.

Recognizing the truth of a skeptic's complaint, rather than discounting it or even trying to resolve it, is a good first step. God's understanding is "unsearchable," Isaiah tells us (v. 28); we will never fully understand how God works in the world, why suffering continues and evil reigns in so many places. And God's understanding is not likely to be revealed to us instantaneously on a mountaintop or during a solar eclipse. Instead, we come to know how God works in the world through years of living with God and God's people. Years of exploring, seeking, reflecting, and acting with God. Over time, through Bible study, worship, practices of faith like hospitality and forgiveness, stewardship and service, we come to a place of knowing God's ways, even if we cannot sufficiently put words to it.

VERITY A. JONES

problem does not lie with God, but with Israel itself. Given the evidence of Israel's own history and the evidence contained in creation itself, how can the people question the attention and care of God?

Finally, the prophet affirms that the God who creates not only gave life at the beginning but gives new life in the present (vv. 28–31). Immediately following this statement of Israel's complaint in verse 27, the prophet moves to reiterate his point by returning to the questions that he originally addressed to Israel in verse 21: "Have you not known? Have you not heard?" He returns to the theme of God as creator, but adds the acknowledgment that this God is eternal and tireless and understands far more than they know. Where Israel questions and doubts, the prophet reassures them that God will never fail.

The crisis of the Babylonian exile has caused the people to forget their own story, the story of God's attentiveness and dependability, the story of God's love for Israel. Because they have forgotten, they are questioning the presence and power of this God. But those who remember their history and believe in the God who fulfills promises will be able to receive new strength and life from their relationship with this God. The ones who need help the most are the ones who will receive it from the Creator, from the Holy One, from the one whom they know as YHWH. The faint and the powerless will receive new strength and power. Times are so difficult and the challenges so severe that even the young will faint and grow weary. Hope may be hard to sustain, but if they depend on God and wait and trust in their own story, they will receive the ability to meet the challenges and, indeed, to rise above them.

RICHARD A. PUCKETT

husband rarely went, even before he got cancer. Once when we were hiking together, we came upon what Margaret described as the most unrelenting two-mile ridge in the whole area—two miles up with no break, and this after a hard six miles on a very hot day. I like to hike in spurts, so I said, "See you later, Margaret," and took off in my usual fashion and got way ahead of her. At some point, I found myself lying flat on my back in half delirium. A blurred Margaret passed at her steady pace. I can still hear the click-click of her cane and with no pity at all in her voice, "One more mile to go, Bill. I'll see you at the top!" And so she did, arriving well ahead of me without stopping once.

Not long after that, her husband finally died of cancer, but because of her daily walk with God their last few hours were spent not in sadness or remorse, but in joy and celebration. For when Margaret says, "I'll see you at the top!" she means it, for her face is fixed on Christ, her step is steady and sure, and she knows the meaning of Isaiah's words:

> Even youths will faint and be weary,
>     and the young will fall exhausted;
> but those who wait for the LORD shall renew
>     their strength,
>     they shall mount up with wings as eagles,
> they shall run and not be weary,
>     they shall walk and not faint.

WILLIAM J. CARL III

# Psalm 147:1-11, 20

> [1]Praise the LORD!
>  How good it is to sing praises to our God;
>      for he is gracious, and a song of praise is fitting.
> [2]The LORD builds up Jerusalem;
>      he gathers the outcasts of Israel.
> [3]He heals the brokenhearted,
>      and binds up their wounds.
> [4]He determines the number of the stars;
>      he gives to all of them their names.
> [5]Great is our Lord, and abundant in power;
>      his understanding is beyond measure.
> [6]The LORD lifts up the downtrodden;
>      he casts the wicked to the ground.

## Theological Perspective

When the first pictures of the earth from space were flashed back to the earth, our sense of our world was forever altered. A shimmering blue-green, white-flecked ball spinning against the dense blackness of space! A world in which everything is related to everything else became visible for the first time. We live on the surface of that shimmering globe, smaller than small, invisible to any eye but the eye of God.

From the ground we stand on, the earth seems to extend outward until our sight fails at the horizon. The horizon moves as we walk. Looking at ground we stand on, each particular thing appears unique. From a few feet away, something else would be seen. Looking around, we encounter objects and people within our range at this time and place. It is hard to get a sense of the whole. Humans swim in a sea of particular things that make up their world. It takes a view from elsewhere to remind us of our limits as well as the privileges of our place.

In a culture built on differences and organized distinctions, a view from beyond us, unconfined by our smallness and nearsightedness, provides a much needed correction. It reframes everything, pointing out the great continuities and connections on which we daily depend without much thought. To see the world whole and see it steadily is to feel that we belong in a "place just right." We are at home in the

## Pastoral Perspective

Few times are more rewarding than late on a Saturday afternoon. A long day in the yard satisfies us with the accomplishment of taming our patch of nature. It doesn't matter if it is July or November, whether we mowed grass, pulled errant weeds, or raked leaves. It doesn't matter if we smelled the scent of a burning pile, got too much sun on the bridge of our noses, or scratched behind the dog's ears. It doesn't matter whether we dug holes and planted seeds or harvested a basket of homegrown tomatoes from the earth found on our one-third acre, our patio, or our "back 40" . . . by whatever measure, it felt good!

We may have restocked the bird feeder or run the sprinkler and spread compost. Regardless, after putting away the tools and wiping the sweat from our brow, we paused on the back steps or settled into the porch rocker and said, "It is good." How silly we are! Captivated with our own creativity and control, we frequently become oblivious to our capacity to become agents of God's grace and peace in this world. Consumed with our own creativity and control, we forget that it was God who after crafting, perused the created order and said, "It is good." In our own foolishness, we rush to the front of the line to take a turn at playing God.

What a gracious reminder Psalm 147 gives us! Our Lord, provider of all, doesn't boast like a proud

<sup>7</sup>Sing to the L<small>ORD</small> with thanksgiving;
    make melody to our God on the lyre.
<sup>8</sup>He covers the heavens with clouds,
    prepares rain for the earth,
    makes grass grow on the hills.
<sup>9</sup>He gives to the animals their food,
    and to the young ravens when they cry.
<sup>10</sup>His delight is not in the strength of the horse,
    nor his pleasure in the speed of a runner;
<sup>11</sup>but the L<small>ORD</small> takes pleasure in those who fear him,
    in those who hope in his steadfast love. . . .

. . . . . . . . . . . . . . . . . . . . . . . . . . . . . . . . . . . . . . . .

<sup>20</sup>He has not dealt thus with any other nation;
    they do not know his ordinances.
    Praise the L<small>ORD</small>!

## Exegetical Perspective

This psalm, like the others in the final section of the Psalter (Pss. 146–50), begins and ends with praise (*hallelu-yah*, vv. 1a, 20c). Each of its three main units (vv. 1–6, 7–11, 12–20) opens with an imperative—Praise! Sing! Praise!—and interweaves descriptions of God's creative power with God's abundant provision for God's people. Thematic and linguistic similarities with various exilic and postexilic texts, particularly Isaiah 40–66 (from which comes the other Old Testament lectionary text for this Sunday, Isa. 40:21–31), suggest the psalm was likely crafted during the early postexilic period; the Septuagint, in fact, associates it with Haggai and Zechariah (520–518 BCE). If so, the psalmist heralds the sovereignty of God for a ragtag and conflicted community composed of returnees, those who had been left behind to till and keep the land (e.g., 2 Kgs. 24:14), and others, who were struggling in the aftermath of the exile to rebuild as a small colony on the fringe of the new world empire, that of the Persians. Perhaps to encourage accord and embolden their efforts, the psalmist paints a vibrant portrait of "our God" (vv. 1b, 5a, 7b; cf. 12b) as the one whose power and graciousness embraces everyone and everything—from the downtrodden to the baby raven to the fiery stars high above. Her brushstrokes, which are thick and long, sweep attention from earth

## Homiletical Perspective

The season following the Epiphany invites us to think about God made manifest. As the days begin to lengthen, we have in nature an increasing presence of light, which points us toward that awareness. As we have more light, there is a possibility for greater revelation and recognition of God's presence. Psalm 147 is laden with images that help support our search for those signs and symbols. It also reminds us that a deepening awareness of God's presence often results in a joyful song of praise. The text concludes with a reminder that this praise is but a first step toward our recognition of our deep connection to God. Graced with abundant signs that cause us to praise, we can be moved to reverence and awe such that we give the Lord pleasure.

The preacher has an opportunity to build on the rich imagery of this psalm and use it as an entrée to a larger reflection on the presence of God. Rich in many of the monastic disciplines is a focus on attentiveness. Attention to the presence of God in each moment helps us trust in God's presence in the absence of affective emotions. We are then able to engage the world with new eyes and perceive the richness that creation and human relationships can offer us.

We hope that one outcome from increasing attentiveness to God's presence is the awareness of

# Psalm 147:1-11, 20

## Theological Perspective

universe after all, not just strangers in a strange place. However much wrong we do to each other, there is really nothing wrong about the world God made and called "good."

Psalm 147 sees the world whole, with a deep steadiness at the heart of things. It is a view from beyond, from "the strange new world within the Bible," in the words of Karl Barth.[1] The reader may hear overtones of the great nature and history psalms (103–7) in the praise of God, who is the source and sustainer of everything. Whether one thinks of the great round of life, the starry heavens, the creative and destructive forces of nature, or the gentle care of the needy and wounded, it is the Lord who creates and governs them all. It is the same Lord who builds up Jerusalem and takes pleasure in those who reverence God and keep the statutes and ordinances that constitute them as a people in covenant with God.

The special history of Israel with God belongs within the big picture of God's universal care. Christians often have distinguished God's general providence, which governs all things, from God's special providence, which governs the history of Israel and the church and God's relation to individuals. The regularities of nature obey natural law according to the wisdom and power of God. The unique events of our lives obey the special dispensations of God toward us according to the wisdom and justice of God operating through our freedom. The psalm runs them together, because the Lord is to be praised for his watch care over all things according to their nature and needs. Everything is related to everything else.

In the Sermon on the Mount, Jesus reminds his listeners that God makes no distinction between the just and the unjust in his providential care (Matt. 5:43–48). The sun shines and the rain rains on both without partiality. Those who heard him were invited to model the Father's generosity in their willingness to love enemies as well as friends. Further on, he appeals to God's care of the most insignificant weed to invite the listeners to trust God for the necessities of their own lives. They need not let anxiety about the future distract them from serving the righteous reign of God (Matt. 6). The great regularities of nature and the cause of God in the world (reign of God) are indissolubly interconnected by the sweeping movement of divine grace.

[1] Karl Barth, *The Word of God and the Word of Man*, trans. Douglas Horton (New York: Harper & Row, 1957), 28.

## Pastoral Perspective

farmer at the state-fair competition, standing beside his heirloom 712-pound pumpkin, saying, "Pounds talk, everything else walks." No, the Lord grins with those who receive, revel in, and care for the deep mysteries of the Creator's created order. The Lord's pleasure rests with those who see through the competition of a dog-eat-dog world and with singular focus put their hope in the Lord's steadfast love and enduring peace (vv. 10–11). They sing a song of praise and wait patiently upon the Lord.

Early in the day that the Lord made the first covenant with Abram, Abram has a vision in which he is instructed to lift up his eyes to the heavens and to count the stars. He is then told that his deepest longing will be fulfilled. The Lord will bind up Abram's wound of having no offspring and give to him descendants, named descendants, more than the stars in the sky. Abram is given hope and waits in that hope, which is fulfilled in the birth of Isaac through Sarah's womb and Jacob through Rebekah's womb.

Each day, human understanding dresses up in what is measurable. We plan worship with a measurable time, which ultimately limits praise offered through song, prayer, and proclamation of the word. It's likely that if we were to stand in Abram's sandals, we'd want a measurable accounting and report of the names of the stars. Our sinful nature is to bundle God's mysteries into neatly wrapped packages tied tightly with rigid doctrine and time constraints.

The Creator's milieu reveals remarkable and indescribable mysteries from small wonders to unfathomable depths. God's delight is not in the strength of a horse, but in the horse, the creature with all of its creature features. God's delight is not in the strength of a runner, but in the runner himself or herself, in all of his or her unique human features (vv. 10–11). With this knowledge, the whole of creation sings praise and delights in the Lord.

As we grow in faith and come before the Lord in acts of worship, how do we take and make the time for delight in the Lord ? How do we listen for the work of the Holy Spirit, as creation continues in each day, with newfound attentiveness as newborn raconteurs for the ongoing story of God's good creation?

It's easier to live at the surface, going day to day, moving along, doing what it takes to get by, saying what it takes to get by, and living in the shallow end of things, living out of popular piety. Piety nursed in the intensity of the Lord's creation begins by not co-opting our lives to the hegemony of inattentive

## Exegetical Perspective

to heaven and back again, offering an expansive yet deeply intimate worldview.

After the opening *hallelu-yah* (v. 1a), the psalmist commends praise but, as a comparison of modern translations indicates, her words are somewhat ambiguous (v. 1bc). While songs of praise are "fitting, beautiful" (*na'vah*), it is less clear whether the adjective "pleasant, delightful" (*na'im*) describes the act of praise (so, e.g., NJPS, NIV) or God (so NRSV). If the former, it emphasizes the beauty and joy of worship. If the latter, the adjective roots the goodness of praise (v. 1a; cf. Ps. 92:1) in the character of God (e.g., Ps. 27:4): we sing as an appropriate response to God's graciousness. Perhaps both possibilities are intended; similar ambiguity is elsewhere (e.g., Ps. 135:3).

In the first unit (vv. 2–6), the psalmist moves outward, from God's particular care of God's people to God's cosmic purview. With a cascade of active participles and imperfects—"(re)builds," "gathers," "heals," "binds up"—the psalmist describes God's restoration of God's people as comprehensive and ongoing. God brings an end to adversity. God bandages and mends. The psalmist's words recall prophetic descriptions of the exiles as the "outcasts of Israel" (e.g., Isa. 56:8) and "the brokenhearted" (Isa. 61:1) whom God gathers (e.g., Isa. 56:8; Neh. 1:9), "heals" (e.g., Isa. 57:18–19; Jer. 30:17), and "binds up" (Isa. 61:1). Then, without missing a beat, the psalmist points skyward (vv. 4–5), celebrating God's power and unsearchable wisdom: God determines the "number" (*mispar*) and names the stars (v. 4a; cf. Isa. 40:26) even as God's understanding is without "number" (*mispar*, v. 5b; cf. Ps. 139:18).

After a second summons to praise (v. 7), the psalmist moves inward, from God's command of the heavens to God's delight in God's people (vv. 8–11). She proceeds methodically, each line anticipating the next—clouds the skies (Ezek. 32:7; Hab. 3:3), readies the rain, makes the grass to grow (Gen. 2:9; Ps. 104:14; Job 38:27)—while, with definite articles, the psalmist emphasizes that God is "the one who . . . the one who . . . the one who" (v. 8, my translation). The psalmist turns then from fertile fields to beasts and birds (v. 9). The relative clause in v. 9b affords three possible interpretations, each of which highlights an aspect of divine care: God feeds the young ravens (a) "which cry" (so, e.g., NASB, RSV)—God's provision is universal; (b) "when they cry" (so, e.g., NRSV, cf. NIV)—God's provision is timely; (c) "what they cry for" (so, e.g., NJPS, NAB)—God's provision is responsive. Perhaps the

## Homiletical Perspective

God's abundance. The more we look and bring things into the light, the more we see God in the most ordinary of circumstances. God is not only in mountaintop moments, but around every corner and daily human encounter.

The fruits of such attentiveness invariably include joy. Praise then becomes a natural outgrowth of that joy. Through the centuries, song has been a primary way to find expression of that feeling. Like the creation it celebrates, to sing is good and "a song of praise is fitting" (v. 1). While contemporary congregations may feel detached from hymnody of these texts, Psalm 147 provides a wonderful opportunity to remind us of the added depth that can come when texts are joined with music to express prayer.

Another connection the preacher can offer in this text is to help flesh out the assertions that the text makes about God. What is the equivalent of God "build[ing] up Jerusalem" (v. 2) today? Who are the "outcasts" that God is embracing and bringing as the Israel of today (v. 2)? How is the faith community meant to function as holy city (Jerusalem) that shines as a beacon to the larger world of God's people (Israel)? The preacher has the opportunity to offer concrete analogies from the local faith community and the broader world. Pointing to God's presence in the community that offers hospitality to the stranger or financial assistance to the needy is part of that gathering together of the outcast.

In areas where refugee populations are increasing, we can ask how God calls us to be present and participate in the binding of their wounds (v. 3). The preacher can use this text to make the connection that our service is not only moral obligation but an outgrowth of our praise and joy. This can connect concepts of mission and worship, rather than uphold a false separation. The ability to sustain mission is often directly related to the health and quality of a community's worship. Service given from a place of gratitude and praise is experienced as qualitatively different from grudging service that comes from a sense of burden or obligation.

The psalm also offers hope in the face of our shortcomings. When we are struck with grief over the lack of response to the outcast, we can take comfort in the knowledge that these people are still loved and treasured by God. There is an eschatological element that reminds us that ultimately the Lord will "[lift] up the downtrodden; . . . and [cast] the wicked to the ground" (v. 6). This imagery is overwhelmingly

# Psalm 147:1-11, 20

## Theological Perspective

Yet each one has a unique relation to God. Jesus reminded his listeners that God takes account of human differences. Deeds have consequences that affect our relationship with God and our neighbors. God's watch care in our lives takes account of our intentions and responses. "If you forgive others their trespasses, your heavenly Father will also forgive you" (Matt. 6:14), Jesus teaches. But if not, then not. Indeed, God is patient lest any should perish, to the end that "all . . . come to repentance" (2 Pet. 3:10). God acts differently toward different objects of care to realize the same purpose. God is free to engage our freedom in ways that take us seriously in our circumstances and choices to bring about the salvation of the world.

Everything is related to everything else. "Grace perfects nature; it does not destroy it" is the way classic Christian orthodoxy puts it. God's work in the realm of nature and God's work the realm of human history are not two but one. The world is made for the gifts of grace bestowed in it, while the grace of God in the history of human salvation fulfills the purpose of God for all creation.

By reminding us that God's redemptive Word was present and active in creation, John 1 affirms that the God who creates and the God who saves are the one God—intending and working our redemption from the beginning of time:

"In the beginning was the Word, and the Word was with God, and the Word was God. . . . All things came to being through him and without him not one thing came into being" (John 1:1–3).

Christians should never forget that there is nothing ungracious about nature or unnatural about grace. "Praise the LORD! How good it is to sing praises to our God; for [God] is gracious, and a song of praise is fitting" (v. 1).

THOMAS D. PARKER

## Pastoral Perspective

living in the creation; and continues as it is nurtured by the Spirit with growing disciplines of listening and praying through the Bible, reading the confessions, and listening attentively to the world around us.

When we recognize in our lives together the despair of exile and the hope of God's restoration, our worship liturgy and our lives together begin to be framed in a manner that makes melody before the Lord for our gratefulness in creation. We participate with the psalmist who knows that the Lord alone builds up and gathers the outcasts (v. 2). With the Holy Spirit, we recognize and remember that *every* day is a day to live our lives out in service with God in creation. That every day is a day, for us as young ravens, to hope in God's love and abundant power, not our own (vv. 5–11).

Instead of hunkering down in self-protective places, we lift our eyes and join our voices together and with confidence confess, "I believe in God the Father Almighty, Maker of heaven and earth, and in Jesus Christ his only Son our Lord." We labor with our hands for the sake of God's good creation. We live and worship knowing we are the recipients of God's statutes and ordinances (v. 19). When we stop and think about how the words we speak and the actions we will perform will affect one another and the Lord's ongoing creation, we glorify God. When we direct all of our words and deeds in the spirit of God's peace, faithfulness, and steadfast love . . . the Lord delights.

Praise the LORD!

ANNE H. K. APPLE

## Exegetical Perspective

psalmist is familiar with the only other mention of the ravens' young in the OT, namely, when God asks Job from out of the whirlwind, "Who provides for the raven its prey, when its young ones cry to God, and wander about for lack of food?" (Job 38:41; cf. Ps. 104:21; Luke 12:24).

That God so tends to the most fragile of creatures prompts the psalmist's conclusion that what delights God is neither strength nor speed, qualities idolized in our culture today, but reverence (vv. 10–11; cf. Ps. 33:16–18). Those who "fear the Lord" acknowledge God's sovereignty and strive to live humbly and fully, mindful of their capacities and limitations as creatures of God. The psalmist associates this posture in the world with "waiting" (NRSV "hope") for God's steadfast love (*hesed*, v. 11b). Such waiting, for the psalmist, is not idle fancy (e.g., Pss. 31:25; 119:74; 114; 130:7; 131:3). In view of God's immeasurable power and repeated, reliable acts of generous provision, it is deep wisdom. So the lectionary reading ends as it began—in praise (*hallelu-yah*, v. 20c).

The last unit of the psalm (vv. 12–20b) is not included in the lectionary reading. Its movement roughly parallels that of the first unit (vv. 2–6), elaborating initially on God's provision for God's people of security (v. 13) and prosperity (v. 14) before turning to God's control of natural forces (vv. 16–17, 18b). But the psalmist weaves in a new and important theme, God's word (vv. 15, 18a, 19–20b), which she describes as racing across the earth to accomplish God's purposes (vv. 15, 18a) and as ultimately addressed to Israel (vv. 19–20). Thus it is not surprising that this portion of the psalm appears often in lectionary readings during Christmas, the season that heralds the incarnation of God's word (see the Second Sunday after Christmas Day, Year B).

In a remarkable way the whole psalm calls upon God's people to praise the Lord, both for God's providential care for all creation and for God's special love for Jerusalem. Appropriately for the season of Epiphany, the psalm reminds us both of God's ongoing sustenance of the cosmos and of the special and particular ways in which God visits God's creation and blesses God's creatures.

CHRISTINE ROY YODER

## Homiletical Perspective

positive and hopeful, and reminds us that the accountability of the divine is something that is worthy of our praise. We must understand our obligation to act in the world, but we ultimately are limited and rely on God's providence.

That providence provides much of the psalm's imagery drawn from the natural world. Psalm 147 uses many images, such as the stars, the rain, and the growing grass, to open our eyes to the many ways in which God is present in the natural world (vv. 4, 8, 10). God's creating and numbering and naming the stars (v. 4) is a wonderful reminder that while our acts can be numbered, the divine is beyond that type of accounting. The preacher may lift those up or offer additional images that lead toward a sense of the tangible symbols with which God surrounds us. Again, the litany of such images is meant to draw the congregation toward images of abundance and joy that result in attending praise.

But, the preacher should also notice the caution contained within the concluding verses (vv. 10, 11). While we are created to look and praise these signs and symbols of God, we are not meant to stop there. We are not to imagine that even the great gifts of our physical bodies (v. 10) are the totality of God's glory. They are markers to be integrated with our very souls. We are meant to approach God with reverence and awe (fear) and hope in God's love. God's love and grandeur may best be communicated to us through the grandeur of nature, but it is a relationship that God ultimately desires. Our praise is best sung when it is linked to our awareness that in the act of praise, we are enacting our connection and relationship with the Divine.

The ultimate fruit of the spirit that comes from such connection is that of hope. This is not hope in the sense of a shallow confidence that everything will work out as we expect, or even well. It is the deep hope born out of a confidence in God's care for each one of us and throughout the created order.

ELIZABETH C. KNOWLTON

# 1 Corinthians 9:16-23

[16]If I proclaim the gospel, this gives me no ground for boasting, for an obligation is laid on me, and woe to me if I do not proclaim the gospel! [17]For if I do this of my own will, I have a reward; but if not of my own will, I am entrusted with a commission. [18]What then is my reward? Just this: that in my proclamation I may make the gospel free of charge, so as not to make full use of my rights in the gospel.

[19]For though I am free with respect to all, I have made myself a slave to all, so that I might win more of them. [20]To the Jews I became as a Jew, in order to win Jews. To those under the law I became as one under the law (though I myself am not under the law) so that I might win those under the law. [21]To those outside the law I became as one outside the law (though I am not free from God's law but am under Christ's law) so that I might win those outside the law. [22]To the weak I became weak, so that I might win the weak. I have become all things to all people, that I might by all means save some. [23]I do it all for the sake of the gospel, so that I may share in its blessings.

## Theological Perspective

*Performing a God-Given Task Is No Basis for Boasting (v. 16).* Paul begins by presenting theological reasoning in the form of prophetic theology. The prophetic reasoning contains three statements: an opening assertion about proclaiming a message of good news and two rationales beginning with "for" (*gar*; the second rationale begins with "and" in the NRSV). The reasoning has the form of a logical argument, but it presents theological rather than philosophical reasoning.

Paul begins his reasoning with a theological principle, which functions as a major premise: there is no basis for boasting when a person proclaims good news. The verb "to proclaim the gospel" is language from the Hebrew prophets about delivering a message of good news.[1] Just as the Hebrew prophets had no basis for arrogance or pride for delivering a message of good news, so Paul also has none. This is simply a presupposition or premise for being a prophet.

Paul supports his premise first with a rationale that delivering the message is simply the prophet's task and obligation. This statement is the minor premise, which applies the major premise to a particular person. Paul has an obligation to deliver a

[1]Cf. Isa. 40:9; 52:7; 60:6; 61:1; Jer. 20:15.

## Pastoral Perspective

Why does Paul find it necessary to enter into a somewhat complex discussion of his apostleship with his friends in the church in Corinth? The answer is that he is continuing the conversation that he began in chapter 8, without which his subsequent points lose much of their impact and cogency.

When Paul takes up the issue of "idol meat" in chapter 8, he grants the "strong," that is, those who eat this meat, the validity of their convictions. They are theologically correct. Because there is but one God, the idols are nothing. But immediately he appeals to the strong to be in solidarity with the weak. The brother or sister in Christ is far more important than anyone's right to anything. Indeed, in something of an outburst, Paul exclaims that if eating meat is the cause of a fellow Christian's falling, he, Paul, will eat no meat to all eternity.

In chapter 9, Paul first asserts his right as an apostle, a right that includes salary and benefits. Immediately, however, he renounces the use of these rights. He is making an example of himself in terms of what it means to be truly free of all and simultaneously the slave of all. The reason for this, obviously, is the way of Christ's cross. Paul identifies himself with the weak so thoroughly that he renounces privilege and honor, and like the poor he supports himself by manual labor and refuses to eat meat.

## Exegetical Perspective

In this passage, Paul describes the central principle for his practices of proclamation and communal care: every aspect of the Christian life, from its initial announcement through the daily practices of faith, must be shaped by Christ's death on behalf of others.

In the first fourteen verses of chapter 9, Paul has established that, by the Corinthians' logic, he should be free to exercise personal privilege and eat or drink whatever he pleases. He has established this, not only by their logic, but also by analogy to societal norms (vv. 7–8), the authority of Scripture (vv. 8–12), and a commandment of the Lord (v. 14). Yet, having argued his case, he declares emphatically that he will not exercise this freedom; not simply as a matter of personal choice, but as a necessity of his allegiance to the gospel (vv. 12b and 15).

In verses 16–17, Paul provides his warrant for this decision: Paul did not opt to become an apostle of the gospel; it was a divine commission. That is, while his freedom in Christ is release from the bondage of prior existence, it is also lived under the lordship of Christ. Paul repeats the linking word "for" (*gar*) four times in order to demonstrate the implications of his claim. This is particularly clear in the phrases "for an obligation has been laid on me" and "woe to me if I do not preach the gospel" (v. 16, all quotes my translation). Even though he is "entitled" to a reward

## Homiletical Perspective

I follow the scholars who think that 1 Corinthians 9 continues the discussion in 1 Corinthians 8:1–13 (Fourth Sunday after the Epiphany, Year B), in which Paul urges one group in the congregation to limit their freedom for the sake of helping the congregation that embodies qualities of eschatological community in the present. This umbrella of thought shelters several possibilities for sermons.

Today's reading has a highly autobiographical quality. Paul illustrates the principle of self-limitation from 1 Corinthians 8 with his own thoughts and behavior as an apostle: Paul limits his rights as an apostle for the good of the community and its witness. A preacher could take a cue from this autobiographical illustration to tell a story from the preacher's own life that puts into practice self-limitation for the good of community. Of course, pastors who follow this sermonic path must be careful to speak about their lives in ways that demonstrate their shared humanity with the congregation, especially the complexity and struggles that accompany such a practice. The congregation may be turned off if the sermon comes across with tones that are self-congratulatory, condescending, or holier than thou. The preacher might also tell stories from individuals or groups in the congregation (or persons with whom the congregation can identify)

# 1 Corinthians 9:16-23

## Theological Perspective

message of good news, just as a person who works for the postal service has an obligation to deliver a letter. In prophetic theology, this task has been laid on a person by God. The task is not a reason for arrogance or pride, but a reason for faithfully delivering the message.

The second rationale has the form of a curse, "Woe to me if I do not proclaim the gospel!" This rationale is the conclusion that follows the major and minor premise. The conclusion comes out of the theological dynamics of prophetic reasoning. Fulfilling the obligations that accompany God's commands brings blessings, but violating the obligations brings curses. Paul talks here only of the curse. We will see below his statements about blessings.

*My Will or God's Will (v. 17).* Theologically, Paul's statement is a reformulation of Jesus' statement to God, "Nevertheless, not my will but yours be done" (Mark 14:36; Matt. 26:42; Luke 22:42; my translation). Rather than exploring the possibility that God might be willing to remove the task of proclaiming the gospel, Paul explores the nature of reward and stewardship in the context of the task. Paul's reasoning is a creative reworking of the theological principle of reward and punishment.

Once Paul introduced the curse on himself in verse 16, it would have been natural for him to say, "If I do this, I will be rewarded with a blessing; if I do not do this, I will be punished with a curse." But he does not say this. Instead, he correlates language of a laborer who receives wages (NRSV, "reward") with language of a householder entrusted with a particular responsibility (NRSV, "a commission"). His argument in the end will be a description of God's grace.

*Receiving a Wage No Matter What (v. 18).* Paul admits that he receives something like a wage, even though he refuses to understand his duties and responsibilities in the domain of a regular worker or laborer. Paul describes a blessing that is the other side of the curse he described earlier. The "wage" Paul receives for performing his task is the authority to exercise his duties in a manner he chooses, namely, without charging people for the service he performs. The issue, then, is not punishment and reward, but receiving a wage or a freedom.

*Responsible Freedom (vv. 19–22).* Next, Paul raises the theological issue if a prophet must live under God's

## Pastoral Perspective

It is important to note that this decision is not the result of applying general principles or rules of behavior. It is about relationships. Freedom in Christ means precisely the radical freedom to identify with "others" in their otherness, Jews and Greeks, the strong and the weak. But it should be noted that the identification with the weak is consistent with the way of the cross and with the gospel's preferential option for the poor. For Paul, his vocation as an apostle involves the recapitulation of Christ's own sacrifice in giving his life for the poor and the weak. Nor is this calling and pattern unique to apostles. It is the calling and vocation of all who are baptized into Christ. The church is, therefore, not a community of volunteers, but is itself a part of the gospel, the good news. By living out this pattern of self-giving, the church is an eschatological sign of what God is bringing about for the whole cosmos, the new creation.

What a jolt this must have been to the strong in Corinth who believed that they were right on the issue of idol meat and that they had been given the freedom to do as they pleased! This self-absorption made it unthinkable for the strong to identify with anyone else, most of all, the weak.

For Paul, how the community orders its life and how members relate to each other are part and parcel of the proclamation of God's reconciliation of the world. The church is a community that God calls into existence to incarnate, live out, and proclaim this new reality. But this requires that in Christ people find the radical freedom to identify fully with others, to become as they are, and thus to experience a genuine transformation of the self. This is what Paul means when he describes his own freedom to be a Jew among Jews, to be a Gentile among Gentiles, to be weak among the weak, in short, to be all things to all people.

It is time to ask again, as we did in comments on chapter 8, whether or not Paul has offered us insights to live more faithfully in situations of conflict. The obvious question to ask is whether Paul's position simply requires the strong, in any conflict, to surrender to those perceived as the weak. Does Paul's strategy subject the strong to the inevitable tyranny of the weak? The answer appears to be no. In 10:29–30, Paul speaks for the strong: "For what good does it do for my freedom to be subjected to the judgment of another's conscience? If I partake with thankfulness, why should I be denounced for that for which I give thanks?" (my translation). If chapter 8 expresses the responsibility

for his preaching, he does not accept one. Instead, he will provide the gospel without charge, because only in this way can he fully preach the gospel (v. 18).

Paul's position reflects his understanding of existence in Christ, something his audience has not fully grasped, either about Paul or themselves. Though he is "free from all" (cf. 6:12), he has voluntarily "enslaved himself to all" (v. 19). Paul uses the servant of Christ metaphor elsewhere (e.g., Rom. 1:1; Gal. 1:10; Phil. 1:1), but here he emphasizes that he is indentured to *all people*. The two forms of servitude are actually corollary, because enslavement to Christ is borne out through ministry to others.

In verses 20–23, Paul makes his claim more specific. The passage is ordered by parallel clauses ("became as . . . so that I might" . . . ) that culminate with the phrase "to the weak, I became weak." Verses 19b and 22b frame the section, beginning with the idea that Paul has become a slave to "gain many" (used five times here) and ending with the same idea, "I have become all things so that I might surely save some" (here the term is "save" [*sōzō*], but it is used synonymously with gain).

In verse 20, Paul states that he became "as a Jew," which sounds odd since by birth, he was already a Jew. Another claim is made here, namely, that though he is not "under the law," he willingly submits himself to its prescriptions in order to allow the gospel to be heard among Jews. In verse 21, he describes the same pattern for his behavior among Gentiles, that is, those "outside the law." To bring them the gospel, Paul lives as a Gentile, that is, "outside the law." This point is qualified with the phrase "not being without law towards God." Though "outside the law," this does not mean that he is without obligations. He expresses his intent with a wordplay using the terms "lawless" (*anomos*) and "under the law of Christ" (*ennomos Christou*, cf. Gal. 6:2). The "law of Christ" does not refer to another set of rules, but to the pattern of Christ's sacrifice on behalf of others, which becomes the standard by which Paul understands and evaluates all aspects of his life. It is a law in the sense that it is the determining element for existence in Christ. This is his guide regardless of whom he encounters: Jew or Gentile.

These examples serve Paul's main concern, the treatment of the "weak." With the first three examples, Paul counterbalanced Jew with Gentile and those "under the law" with those "outside the law." Now, instead of juxtaposing "strong" and "weak," he focuses solely on the latter. Again

to illustrate the principle of self-limitation for the good of community.

In 1 Corinthians 9:8, Paul names authority as an issue underlying the entire passage. Few matters vex the contemporary church as much as that of authority. Whom can the congregation regard as authoritative voices when seeking to come to Christian interpretations of life?

Paul seeks to persuade the Corinthians to accept his interpretation of the rights of the apostle and also his reasoning for not acting on those rights. Paul draws on the practice of other apostles (1 Cor. 9:5), on analogy with customs in military service, farming, and shepherding (9:6–7), on a particular interpretation of texts from the First Testament (9:8–10), on the employment procedures of the temple (9:13), and on the command of Jesus (9:14). At the risk of anachronism, we might say that Paul draws on the Bible, experience, tradition, and reason.

The preacher could take Paul's approach to authority as a case study to initiate a sermon to help the congregation consider the resources to which they can turn in search of an adequate theological interpretation of such things as the purpose of life, relationships among peoples of different ethnicities, distribution of wealth, the death penalty, or whether the church should open its building to nonreligious groups. How could the congregation draw on the Bible, tradition, experience, and reason in seeking to interpret such phenomena?

The notion of apostleship itself could spark a sermon. What was the nature and work of apostles, according to Paul? To others in the formative generations that wrote what we sometimes call the Second Testament? (How, for instance, does Paul's perception of apostleship differ from that of Luke?) While few of the long-established churches in North America continue the office of apostle, how do congregations today share in the continuing apostolic ministry?

In 1 Corinthians 9:16b, Paul is so gripped by the call to be an apostle that he says, "An obligation [*anankē*, "necessity"—a powerful concept] is laid on me, and woe to me if I do not proclaim the gospel!" This motif could provide the preacher with an opportunity to discuss the minister's perception of the preaching vocation and the broader ministerial calling. Such a sermon could not only help laity develop a better understanding of the ministry but could prompt reflection on their life works. Most people today have the sense that the jobs by which they support themselves are utilitarian. Could the

# 1 Corinthians 9:16-23

## Theological Perspective

commands simply as an obedient slave, or if God's commands can be understood in some other way. Paul has the freedom to be a slave, a Jew, a person under the law, a person outside the law, even a person who is weak (*asthenēs*, which can mean "sick"!), and, indeed, "all things to all people." The key lies in the repetitive texture in the verses: Paul takes all of these roles "to win" a wide variety of people.

Underlying the multiple roles are both a theological issue and an ethical issue. How can God and how can a prophet move people to do things that are in their best self-interest to do? Is it theologically acceptable to force people simply by command? Having introduced the image of wages and managing a household, Paul repeats the Greek word *kerdainō* ("win"), which means to experience "a gain." The word regularly applies to profit that occurs, and Paul surely is thinking of a win-win situation.

Paul wins the goal of responsibly fulfilling his God-given task in a situation where a wide variety of people "win" new blessings in their life. This is the nature of God's grace. The repetition of "to win" moves progressively to its goal in "to save" in verse 22b. This is a natural conclusion, once Paul has mentioned the weak (which can mean "sick"), since the verb "to save" can also mean "to heal." It is also Paul's greater goal to bring people into an experience of God's blessings through a message about Christ that brings healing, restoration, and well-being to their lives.[2]

*The Blessing for Paul (v. 23).* Paul ends by returning to the theological issue of blessing. In Christian theological terms, blessing refers to receiving God's grace in a context of "freely" performing the tasks God commands. This paradoxical dynamic lies at the heart of Christology. In verse 21, Paul asserts that he is not free from God's law, but under Christ's law. Paul's Christology presupposes that God's wisdom is human foolishness and God's power is human weakness. In verse 23 Paul is saying that the responsibilities entrusted to him by God, which have the human form of a curse and slavery, are actually a way of receiving remarkable blessings from God in and through the gospel.

VERNON K. ROBBINS

## Pastoral Perspective

of the strong for the weak, this passage insists on the responsibility of the weak for the strong. Paul clearly does not expect everyone to agree. Instead, he asks something of both groups, which he hopes will make it possible for all of them to move forward together. What he asks is that those on each side identify with those on the other side, in order to become *as if* they were the ones with whom they disagreed. This will not involve a change in conviction, at least not at first, but it means that they are to recognize what it would mean to act in behalf of those to whom they are opposed.

What an intriguing strategy for people in conflict, the more so because it is grounded in Paul's understanding of what God is doing in the world. What would happen if congregations were to attempt this in the pastoral life of the church? Perhaps it would help to set new terms for the conflict itself. Unimagined possibilities might appear, creating greater flexibility and new diversity in place of the increasing hardening of positions. People might learn new ways to speak and listen to one another, thus changing the character of the conflict. Indeed, such an experience might help American Christians in particular, given our culture of individualism, to rediscover Paul's point that the gospel envisions freedom as the right of individuals, not to do as they choose, but rather to relinquish their rights for the sake of others. True Christian freedom therefore expresses itself in service.

One final word. In a world as conflicted and violent as ours, if the church were to be a place where Christians learned to identify with their opponents and to experience God's power to bring about transformation, the church would realize its calling to be a sign of hope and a witness to God's offer of life to the world.

V. BRUCE RIGDON

---

[2] 1 Cor. 1:18, 21; 3:15; 5:5; 7:16; 10:33; 15:2.

## Exegetical Perspective

diverging from the earlier examples, Paul does not say that he has become *like the weak,* but that he has "*become weak.*" More than simply accommodating himself to their behavior, he becomes one of them, choosing not to eat sacrificial food and to suffer the social difficulties this could entail. Why? So he would ensure that none would suffer destruction through Paul's refusal to restrict his own behavior (v. 22).

The passage concludes with the statement that Paul does it "all" (i.e., becoming like his different audiences) for the sake of the gospel "in order that he might become a fellow partaker in it [the gospel]." The verse repeats the final clause of verse 22 ("becoming all things that I might by all means save some") and recalls the initial statement in verse 19 ("being free from all, I have made myself a slave to all") and thus follows Paul's earlier argument. However, with the phrase "that I might become a fellow partaker," it appears that Paul contradicts himself. Having argued that he does not act for personal gain, he now appears to say that everything was done in order to share in the gospel's salvation.

The reason behind this apparent contradiction is that Paul is arguing that those who relish their own "freedom" over the needs of their fellow believers do not attend to responsibility of the gift of the gospel. Unlike his readers, Paul recognizes that it is possible to be unworthy of the gospel (v. 27) through ignoring community members. In other words, while Paul fully understands that salvation is God's gift and that he cannot achieve it through his own effort, he also knows that those who fail to live out the pattern of Christ's death can forfeit the blessings of salvation. Thus he "becomes all things," not to gain salvation for himself, but as a means of embodying the release of self for the well-being of the other. In this way, he becomes a fellow sharer in the gospel.

STEVEN J. KRAFTCHICK

## Homiletical Perspective

preacher help the congregants name points in their lives at which they do feel a passion, and reflect on the degree to which such passions may partake of calling? I know scout leaders, coaches, volunteers in food pantries, workers in women's shelters, antiracism trainers, and many others who feel called.

In 1 Corinthians 9:19–23 the apostle articulates a theology of ministry that can apply both to the minister and to the congregation itself. Paul tries to relate to people where they are, not giving up his own integrity, but respecting the otherness of the Jewish community, Gentiles, the weak, indeed "all people," in order to help them become receptive to the gospel. Paul seeks to help them recognize *from their own perspectives* how the gospel offers hope. How can the preacher adopt such a perspective when developing sermons and in other aspects of ministry? How can the congregation operate in this way when thinking about ministry with people who live in the neighborhood and other arenas of congregational service?

The apostle's declarations in 1 Corinthians 9:3–12 suggest a sermon on equitable compensation for workers. Paul affirms that an apostle has "the right to food and drink," that is, to material support to carry on the apostle's life work. The reasons Paul gives (summarized above) imply that all workers are entitled to support adequate for a life of security with respect to material concerns such as food, clothing, and housing. (Indeed, in the eschaton, such things will be abundant for all.) In today's world, in which so many workers (including many in North America) are paid poorly, this passage is an implicit mandate for wages that are sufficient to provide blessing for all.

The fact that the apostle actively defends his ministry as an apostle against those who discredit him suggests that the preacher could do something of the same. I have known too many preachers who, when confronted with challenges to their ministries, become defensive, dismissive, hostile, or silent. A preacher might respond to critics by taking Paul's approach of making a case that is theologically thoughtful and winsomely presented. The preacher might also adopt Paul's approach when people question the *congregation's* ministry. The preacher could follow Paul's lead in explaining why the congregation believes and acts as it does.

RONALD J. ALLEN

# Mark 1:29-39

²⁹As soon as they left the synagogue, they entered the house of Simon and Andrew, with James and John. ³⁰Now Simon's mother-in-law was in bed with a fever, and they told him about her at once. ³¹He came and took her by the hand and lifted her up. Then the fever left her, and she began to serve them.

³²That evening, at sundown, they brought to him all who were sick or possessed with demons. ³³And the whole city was gathered around the door. ³⁴And he cured many who were sick with various diseases, and cast out many demons; and he would not permit the demons to speak, because they knew him.

³⁵In the morning, while it was still very dark, he got up and went out to a deserted place, and there he prayed. ³⁶And Simon and his companions hunted for him. ³⁷When they found him, they said to him, "Everyone is searching for you." ³⁸He answered, "Let us go on to the neighboring towns, so that I may proclaim the message there also; for that is what I came out to do." ³⁹And he went throughout Galilee, proclaiming the message in their synagogues and casting out demons.

## Theological Perspective

From the synagogue through the house (normal space of the Christian community). Jesus leaves with his four disciples, carriers of the eschatological hope, to the house of Simon, whose mother-in-law is sick. It is not said that she has an impure spirit, like the man of the synagogue (1:23), but simply fever (*pyressousa*, 1:30), a fever that prevents her from working. She seems impotent; nobody helps her. But Jesus grabs her hand firmly, to raise her up, in expression and word of paschal evocation.

This act completes the first pair of healings in Mark's Gospel: the demon-possessed man of the synagogue and the woman with fever in a house that is invaded by males. The woman is prostrated, and Jesus raises her up, carrying out a true humane work, which should come at the end of the Jewish Sabbath.

We have to point out that in the mentality of those who were present, a demonic force was attributed to fever (for that reason it is said "it left her" [v. 31] as if it were a person). The term is derived from a verb that means "to burn, to light." The rabbis spoke of the fever as a "game of bones." The following text of Leviticus is significant: "I will bring terror on you; consumption and fever that waste the eyes and cause life to pine away" (Lev. 26:16). As on other occasions, the healing done by

## Pastoral Perspective

Note the sequence of Jesus' healing miracles in Mark's Gospel. The first miracle takes place in the synagogue, where Jesus is teaching. Remember, this is at the very beginning of Jesus' public ministry. In Mark's account, it is Jesus' first exorcism. When a man, possessed by "an unclean spirit," rudely interrupts, Jesus casts the demon from the man. The crowd exclaims, "What is this? A new teaching—with authority! He commands even the unclean spirits, and they obey him" (Mark 1:27). Mark writes, "Immediately he left the synagogue and entered the house of Simon" (1:29, my translation), whose mother-in-law lay sick with a fever. "He came and took her by the hand and lifted her up. Then the fever left her." Jesus' "teaching" ministries and "healing" ministries are a part of the same ministry. Within the same week that he called the disciples to follow him, announcing that the "kingdom of God is at hand" and launching his public ministry, Jesus had already established the pattern for his future ministry. There was no discrepancy between what he preached and what he practiced. In fact, those who study the ancient languages draw a close parallel between "healing" and "salvation." The last verse of our passage makes clear the connection between preaching and healing: "And he went throughout Galilee, proclaiming the message in their synagogues and casting out demons" (1:39).

## Exegetical Perspective

Go to the movies today and you will wait to see the feature attraction. While you wait, you will see previews of coming attractions. Go to the first chapter of Mark and you will see no previews of coming attractions, no genealogies, no charming birth stories, no tales of teen Jesus stumping the rabbis after going AWOL.

Mark's feature attraction is introduced in large capitals in the opening sentence of the Gospel, "The beginning of the gospel of Jesus Christ, Son of God" (1:1). Jesus arrives on the scene with heaven-splitting force (1:10), deals with Satan in the wilderness (1:12–13), announces the impending reign of God on earth (1:15), chooses his first disciples (1:16–20), and shows his power over a demon (1:21–28) before you can blink an eye.

In one way, though, chapter 1 of Mark is more like previews of coming attractions than any in-depth viewing of the feature attraction. Mark moves through the material at the opening of his Gospel with the speed of one who is afraid to let anyone think that they can know Jesus only by a quick preview. Fueled by his favorite word, "immediately/at once" (*euthys*), Mark races you through a day in the life of Jesus as a reporter might race a candidate through a day of political appearances.

## Homiletical Perspective

When you stop to think about it, dividing the Gospels into units that we now know as texts or pericopes is a rather strange practice. We are quite accustomed to it, but still it is an odd thing to do, as at least a few scholars have noted.[1] We do nothing of the sort with most pieces of literature, books like John Steinbeck's *The Grapes of Wrath* or Marilynne Robinson's *Gilead*. But with the Bible, yes. This is an especially poignant observation when it comes to the first chapter of Mark and this week's section in particular. It begins, "As soon as they left the synagogue" (v. 29), implying a connection with what has gone before. Even the first reference to Jesus in this text (v. 30) simply employs the pronoun "him." It might be good, even when we have preached from the Gospel text the week prior, to preface our public reading of Scripture with some reminder of the bigger picture.

But this connectedness with what has gone before also has implications for us as we struggle to find a focus for this week's sermon. Four scenes are laid out before us in Mark 1:29–39: the healing of Simon's mother-in-law; the healing of many sick and

---

[1]David Buttrick, *A Captive Voice: The Liberation of Preaching* (Louisville, KY: Westminster John Knox, 1994), 5–32; and Edward Farley, *Practicing Gospel: Unconventional Thoughts on the Church's Ministry* (Louisville, KY: Westminster John Knox, 2003), 71–82.

# Mark 1:29-39

## Theological Perspective

Christ shows his intervention in the field dominated by evil, death, and illness. It is the messianic victory over the forces of evil, the radical invitation to the kingdom of God.

The house (*oikia*, 1:29), our second vital space, is a meeting space for family and relatives, a privileged place of the community. We are at the house of Simon and Andrew, where Jesus comes with his four disciples. The expression of healing is surprising, and it can almost be seen as a paschal announcement, because it uses the verb *egeirō*, "to get up," that is used for Jesus' resurrection in 16:6. But as important as Jesus' expression, in this case, is the response of the mother-in-law; she began to serve them. Service is a key topic in the call and pursuit of Jesus. This woman gets up and turns the Sabbath into a paschal day of service to others. Jesus does not command her. She is the one that assumes the initiative and awaits the consequences, discovering the value of mutual service above the sacredness of the Sabbath. She served them (1:31). Simon's mother-in-law interprets the gift that she has received; her service cannot be understood as a woman's menial work under the domination of lazy males, but as a true messianic ministry, creator of Jesus' new family. For that reason, this woman is Jesus' first servant and joins him in the radical announcement, in action, of the kingdom of God, his first deacon.

The healed mother-in-law and Jesus share the same liturgy. Nobody has taught her what she has to do. She has been well aware when receiving Jesus' help and when responding to him precisely on the Sabbath. Her diaconal work is the beginning and announcement of the gospel. Simon and the other disciples won't understand it until Easter. They will not want to become servants of each other (9:35; 10:43). They did not perceive that the Son of God came to serve and to give his life for all (10:45). She, on the other hand, knows it. She has overcome all the selfishness and restrictive teachings and has been close to Jesus; deep down she is already Christian, *diakonisa*, a servant of the church gathered in her son-in-law's house.

This healing event is beautiful because it happens in the house and almost certainly reflects the earliest Christian communities, which were house churches. These meetings in homes made the life of the community possible; they were missionary platforms, a welcome place for the itinerant preachers, and they provided economic support for the growing movement. Christianity began being affirmed socially, not in a sacred space, but rather in daily life, in small

## Pastoral Perspective

Jesus, like the author of Job before him, rejected the tendency to consider sickness as God's punishment for sin. On the contrary, Jesus' understanding seems compatible with our contemporary understanding of illness as un-wholeness, and of healing as the bringing about of wholeness. After all, what is the function of medicine, of psychotherapy, or of religion, for that matter, if it is not to restore intended wholeness? When Jesus said to the woman who pushed her way through the crowd, simply to touch the hem of his garment, "Daughter, your faith has made you well ["whole"]" (5:34), it was to reclaim the health in her that had been "broken" or somehow "lost."

One cannot dismiss as insignificant the number of times the Scriptures refer to touching. In the text, Jesus came and took Peter's mother-in-law by the hand and lifted her up and the fever left her. Throughout both testaments—the angel who touches the hollow of Jacob's thigh; Jairus's daughter; the blind man whom Jesus "touched," and so forth—there is one incident after another pointing to the power of touch. It might even be said that in Scripture touch is a metaphor for intimacy, for presence, for relationship. Some theologians even suggest that to be "created in the image of God" means that we are created for relationship, for "it is not right that human beings should be alone" (cf. Gen. 2:18). Similarly, scientists and psychologists have conducted tests on primates, as well as on infant children, that were deprived at an early age of human touch, with the results showing devastating effects on developmental skills and sociability. One recent experiment was designed to test the efficacy of prayer on patients suffering from comparable illnesses. The members of one group, located on the east coast, were each assigned the name of an ill person on the west coast with whom they were not acquainted and instructed to pray every day for the person's health. The members of the other group were each given the name of an ill person whom they knew personally and who was a member of their own church. Similar instructions were given, to pray for the ill people every day. The patients who had no intimate relationship with their prayer partner showed no significant difference in improvement from the general public, whereas members of the group who had developed a social relationship with their prayer partners indicated a decided difference in improvement and quality of life.

Gerald May, a medical doctor who practices psychotherapy in Washington, DC, writes of the importance of community in the healing process:

## Exegetical Perspective

The race continues in the text for the fifth Sunday after the Epiphany with Mark moving you through a day in the life of Jesus with more speed than depth. In 1:29–39, Mark introduces the first deacon in the New Testament, Simon's mother-in-law. She is healed by Jesus and responds to restored health by serving those gathered in her house. Just as Jesus was served (*diakoneō*) by the angels in the wilderness (1:13), so now Simon's mother-in-law serves (*diakoneō*) Jesus and his friends. In just a few verses, Simon will see it as Jesus' job to serve up some more healing to an anxious crowd rather than to serve them himself. If only he had learned from the example of his mother-in-law. This is no woman bowing to cultural convention and keeping in her restricted place as a servant; this is a disciple who quietly demonstrates the high honor of service for those who follow Jesus (10:44–45).

This first healing in Mark's Gospel follows on the heels of the first exorcism. Early on in this Gospel, we learn that Jesus will not shy from broken bodies or demonic spirits. In fact, in typical Markan hyperbole "all" the city comes knocking on Simon's mother-in-law's door looking for exorcism and/or healing.

In addition, in these opening verses from Mark, we are introduced to a most important character in his story—"the crowd" (*ochlos*). "The crowd" grows in fascination over Jesus, a theme that will take a traitorous twist in chapter 15. In the opening reel of the feature attraction, Jesus doesn't try to draw a crowd; in fact, he tries to escape them.

Another prominent Markan theme that surfaces first in this chapter is the motif of secrecy. Though Jesus often insists on keeping his identity secret, especially after a healing or exorcism, he is often disobeyed. As for the reader, there is no secrecy. From Mark 1:1, there is not a reader unaware of the identity of Jesus. Within the Gospel, though, only demons name Jesus for who he is, but no one in the story seems to hear them or pay them any attention. Mark's Jesus insists on secrecy because no one will know his true identity by viewing only the previews.

Before dawn, and presumably while the crowd is sleeping, Jesus steals out into the darkness to pray. Prayer is not as dominant a theme in Mark as in Luke, but it is an important theme. From the opening chapter of his Gospel, though, Mark introduces us to Jesus who is both a faithful Jew and a faithful Jew at prayer. Jesus is one who makes time and seeks a place to pray. For Mark, prayer is not peripheral to the identity of Jesus, and by

## Homiletical Perspective

possessed later in the evening; Jesus departing to a lonely place; and a summary of sorts that will result in Jesus leaving that area. But the Sabbath day that comes to a close with sunset in verse 32 begins back in verse 21. This day in the life of Jesus is not biography, however, but theology.

In 1:21–28, the new teaching of Jesus and his power to heal are one. This theme continues here. As the summary in verse 39 notes, Jesus goes forth "proclaiming the message in their synagogues and casting out demons." Preaching and healing. Healing and preaching. This represents the ministry of Jesus in a nutshell, and it represents still the ministry of those who follow him.

But even when we observe a narrative thread holding the text's multiple segments together, there exist so many possibilities. Scholars note a wide range of options that might serve the focus of our sermon. If we were leading a Bible study on this passage, complete with doughnuts and discussion, there might be any number of times when we would add, "Another interesting thing about this passage," and make an abrupt transition. But in our preaching, we do well to find the one focus for the sermon. Several options, then, are available. We could preach the whole passage or any of its constituent segments. Obviously, the ideal is to preach the good news contained within these segments.

The healing of Simon's mother-in-law offers several possibilities. Readers sensitive to the treatment of women in both ancient and contemporary society will perhaps chafe at her being restored to health only then to serve the men (v. 31). There is another possible reading, however, one in which her positive behavior is contrasted with that of Simon. We know, of course, how later in Mark's Gospel the disciples will be portrayed as blind, even when those who are really blind can see (10:32–52). But there appear to be hints of that even this early in the story. In addition to readers who know Jesus' true identity (1:1), already the evil spirits do (1:23–24). Do the disciples?

After Simon's mother-in-law is restored to health, she serves. This is how Jesus himself will live and what all of his followers will be called to do (10:45). By way of contrast, Simon, who stands for all of the disciples, does nothing in this text other than to request, or perhaps compel, Jesus to come back from his time of praying so that more healing may take place. The motives of Jesus and Peter are not entirely clear, although Jesus clearly has another agenda (1:36–39).

## Theological Perspective

communities, and there, in that basic social structure, this woman's figure appears, a mystic revelation of what true Christian discipleship means.

Then the healings at nightfall continue. At sunset, when Sabbath rest is over, people of the region come bringing before the house of Simon their sick people so that Jesus may heal them (1:32–34) because there are many people oppressed by evil. This ecclesiastical paradigm is important. To Jesus, neither the temple, nor the synagogue, nor the house can be closed. The characteristic of Jesus is the open message; the mission of the kingdom that he offers his church is of open doors, of missionary extension. It is not necessary to wait until the Sabbath is over for healing. God's gift, Jesus' grace, transcends all the limits imposed by the dogma of religion. He does not want to settle down at Simon's home. Simon needs Jesus to stay (1:36), but Jesus rejects the proposal; if he stayed at Simon's, it would transform his movement into a matter of miracles to those who are far off and come as an expression of hope and to those who are near and seek to satisfy their selfish desires (1:36–37).

In the middle of the night, he has escaped to pray in solitude. God has sent him to offer the kerygma to the needy, not to stay with them founding another spiritual center of healing like other existent centers in the world. Jesus doesn't want to be locked into a sacred structure. Here he is, for this he has come: "Let us go on to the neighboring towns" (1:38). The missionary work is extended; the disciples are those on the road, the outpost of the kingdom of love and justice.

OFELIA ORTEGA

## Pastoral Perspective

God's grace through community involves something far greater than other people's support and perspective. The power of grace is nowhere as brilliant nor as mystical as in communities of faith. Its power includes not just love that comes from people and through people but love that pours forth among people, as if through the very spaces between one person and next. Just to be in such an atmosphere is to be bathed in healing power.[1]

Jesus "came and took her by the hand and lifted her up. Then the fever left her." The power of touch, of intimacy, of nearness, to make whole: Jesus must have understood that which we are too often too slow to comprehend. Love not expressed, love not felt, is difficult to trust. Theologically speaking, that is the reason for incarnation. God knew the human need for nearness. Jesus is the incarnation of God's love, which makes it all the more demanding (if frightening) to realize that for some people, we are the only Jesus they will ever meet.

Another physician, Richard Selzer, has written of the miracle of touch:

> I stand by the bed where a young woman lies, her face post-operative, her mouth twisted—palsy, clownish. A tiny twig of the facial nerve, the one to the muscles of her mouth, has been severed . . . to remove the tumor in her cheek, I had cut the little nerve. The young husband is in the room. He stands on the opposite side of the bed, and together they seem to dwell in the evening lamplight, isolated from me, private. . . . "Will my mouth always be like this?" she asks. "Yes," I say, "it will. It is because the nerve was cut." She nods and is silent. But the young man smiles. "I like it," he says. "It is kind of cute." He bends to kiss her crooked mouth, and I am so close that I can see how he twists his own lips to accommodate her, to show her that their kiss still works. . . . I hold my breath and let the wonder in.[2]

P. C. ENNISS

---

[1] Gerald G. May, *Addiction and Grace* (San Francisco: Harper & Row), 173.
[2] Richard Selzer, *Moral Lessons: Notes on the Art of Surgery* (New York: Simon & Schuster, 1974), 45–46.

implication, not peripheral for those who follow him.

Jesus retreats to a "desert place," a "deserted place," a "solitary place" to pray. Echoes of 1:9 of Jesus in the *erēmos* occur here and will occur again in chapter 8 when Jesus tries to retreat with his disciples for rest and prayer. Then he is confronted by the persistence of a needy crowd; now he is confronted by the persistence of needy disciples.

Most translators are gentle with Peter and friends by rendering *katadiōkō* as "hunted" or "searched for" or "went after," missing the implicit strong, hostile sense of this verb. Peter and his friends are astonished at the behavior of Jesus and come to restore him to his senses. This is the first instance in Mark of Simon Peter correcting Jesus (implicit here); it will not be the last (8:32). Simon knows what Jesus should be doing, and it is *not* sitting in solitude and prayer. Anxious crowds await his "immediate" attention.

Simon and his friends find Jesus as if he is lost and has forgotten his task. In typical Markan irony, Jesus points out that he is not lost and that his task is not simply to respond to the incessant cries of a crowd. He has come to "preach" (1:15) and will not be constricted to one locale and confined to the expectations of anxious disciples. This is the first time in Mark that the disciples want Jesus to do something different from his own desire; it will not be the last (6:36).

The pericope ends with another summary statement from Mark. In case you have missed it so far, Mark tells us that the feature attraction consists of a Jew who has come not to draw a crowd or perform stunning miracles or rewrite Jewish history and tradition. He has come to preach and to cast out the demonic in people and in systems that diminish or distort that gracious reign of God. Mark invites you to pay attention to the rest of the story, because the feature attraction has only begun.

GARY W. CHARLES

This focus on Simon's mother-in-law over against the lead disciple himself might make for an interesting sermon. In fact, we might even play with the two possible interpretations of this one incident, focusing initially on the marginalizing of women so rampant in Christian history, both past and present. Then, in a reversal of sorts, ask, "Or is there another way to read this story?" and explore her model of discipleship over against what we will encounter with the male disciples.

Another sermon possibility is to focus on Jesus' time of prayer. Preachers have always discovered homiletical fodder in verses that describe his getting away for quiet time. The hermeneutical results are simple in such cases: Jesus did x; so should we. The Gospels do indeed portray a Jesus who prays regularly, but we may be domesticating what Mark clearly sees as anything but a quiet time. The time frame is described as "dark," a loaded phrase in Mark's Gospel. It is later used when the religious leaders hand Jesus over to Pilate (15:1) and to describe the women coming to the tomb where Jesus has been buried (16:2).

The location where Jesus prays is described as "deserted" (v. 35). Already in Mark's Gospel we have heard this same description for where John the Baptist appears (1:4) and where Jesus is tempted (1:12–13). This description of Jesus at prayer does not seem to be a "precious moments" image, suitable for framing. Rather, the disciples seem to have discovered Jesus in a time of his own searching, even as the disciples inform him, "Everyone is searching for you" (v. 37). According to scholars, it is not entirely clear whether the temptation is to choose between healing and preaching, or continuing to do both, albeit elsewhere. If the latter, it seems for Mark that the preaching of Jesus and the extinguishing of evil are two sides of the same coin. Preaching exists that evil might not.

MIKE GRAVES

# 2 Kings 5:1-14

[1]Naaman, commander of the army of the king of Aram, was a great man and in high favor with his master, because by him the Lord had given victory to Aram. The man, though a mighty warrior, suffered from leprosy. [2]Now the Arameans on one of their raids had taken a young girl captive from the land of Israel, and she served Naaman's wife. [3]She said to her mistress, "If only my lord were with the prophet who is in Samaria! He would cure him of his leprosy." [4]So Naaman went in and told his lord just what the girl from the land of Israel had said. [5]And the king of Aram said, "Go then, and I will send along a letter to the king of Israel."

He went, taking with him ten talents of silver, six thousand shekels of gold, and ten sets of garments. [6]He brought the letter to the king of Israel, which read, "When this letter reaches you, know that I have sent to you my servant Naaman, that you may cure him of his leprosy." [7]When the king of Israel read the letter, he tore his clothes and said, "Am I God, to give death or life, that this man sends word to me to cure a man of his leprosy? Just look and see how he is trying to pick a quarrel with me."

## Theological Perspective

Humanity's struggle with suffering is grueling. It taxes us when we learn of pain and suffering in the world, it exhausts us to witness the suffering of another, and it is acute when we suffer personally. And when we suffer over an extended period of time, relief becomes our sole desire. In 2 Kings 5, we learn about the strong Syrian man's suffering from leprosy. General Naaman is afflicted with the eruptive skin disease to such a point that he solicits his master, the king of Aram, to help him travel abroad for healing. Understandably, when we experience continual suffering, we will try every possible remedy that might bring comfort. Ideally, we would like to control when and in what ways relief comes, yet true healing lies in God's providence and not in our schemes.

While the presence of suffering in the world is beyond question, *miraculous* healings are unsettling. Nevertheless, the healing power of God through "the prophet who is in Samaria" (v. 3) is the topic of this passage. One fundamental reason we are disturbed about miraculous, or extraordinary, healings is that they diverge from what we believe is normative. In the modern world, we *know* that for every action, there is an opposite and equal reaction (from Newton's Third Law). Comprehensible and repeatable cause-and-effect cures are the norm.

## Pastoral Perspective

Pastors are sometimes the worst offenders, though they should not be held totally responsible, for it is part of their job description.

They enter the lives of parishioners during times of crisis. They minister to them in the immediate aftermath of calamity, death, job loss, injury, depression. They are there in the living rooms, at the funeral parlors, holding hands, offering comfort, making a difference in the lives of people they serve. Then, when the crisis is over, they move on. They leave the grieving, suffering individuals patched up, able to stand perhaps, but that's about it. The spotlight is turned off and they leave. Pastors usually do this because another crisis has arisen, another family is in trouble, another memorial service needs attention, another hospital has called. They do not choose to do it this way; many serve churches as the only pastor, and people are hurting these days. But others in the church also leave soon after a crisis is over. After the casserole dish has been returned by the widow, after the teenager has been assigned to a counselor, after the initial shock of the pink slip has abated, others move on as well. They have lives to attend to, children to get to school. They have jobs, hopes, dreams.

We all long for the quick and glamorous version of healing, though none of us really thinks it works. We

⁸But when Elisha the man of God heard that the king of Israel had torn his clothes, he sent a message to the king, "Why have you torn your clothes? Let him come to me, that he may learn that there is a prophet in Israel." ⁹So Naaman came with his horses and chariots, and halted at the entrance of Elisha's house. ¹⁰Elisha sent a messenger to him, saying, "Go, wash in the Jordan seven times, and your flesh shall be restored and you shall be clean." ¹¹But Naaman became angry and went away, saying, "I thought that for me he would surely come out, and stand and call on the name of the LORD his God, and would wave his hand over the spot, and cure the leprosy! ¹²Are not Abana and Pharpar, the rivers of Damascus, better than all the waters of Israel? Could I not wash in them, and be clean?" He turned and went away in a rage. ¹³But his servants approached and said to him, "Father, if the prophet had commanded you to do something difficult, would you not have done it? How much more, when all he said to you was, 'Wash, and be clean'?" ¹⁴So he went down and immersed himself seven times in the Jordan, according to the word of the man of God; his flesh was restored like the flesh of a young boy, and he was clean.

## Exegetical Perspective

The description of the healing of Naaman in 2 Kings 5:1–14 is at once a straightforward miracle story and the basis of a more complicated series of narratives, including Naaman's conversion (vv. 15–19a) and Gehazi's curse (vv. 19b–27). The miracle itself evokes a range of human responses from grateful confession (v. 15) to greedy plotting (v. 20), while the story demonstrates the developing universalism in Israel that sees people and nations as tools for accomplishing YHWH's will.

The narrative begins with a glowing description of Naaman as a "great man" and a "mighty warrior," one who is a commander of the army of Aram and in high favor with his master. But even this elevated position is due to the will of YHWH (v. 1b). Though successful and recognized, Naaman suffers from leprosy, the common name in ancient Israel for any of a number of diseases of the skin.

The initiator of action in the narrative is a young girl of Israel taken by the Arameans in a raid. She serves Naaman's wife. Seeing the affliction of her master and wanting to be helpful, she speaks, alluding to a prophet of Samaria who has the power to cure the disease. Naaman takes this news to his master the king, repeating what the girl has said. The king, valuing his faithful servant, tells Naaman to go to Israel seeking the prophet and promises to send

## Homiletical Perspective

This passage is about the breaking down of barriers and the beginning of new life. One of the oldest story lines in literature is "a stranger comes to town." In this case, the stranger is Naaman, a powerful commander in the Syrian army. Naaman makes a good protagonist because he is rich and famous and has access to the best health care that money can buy. But, the health-care system in his country just is not good enough to heal him of his leprosy. Think how many people you know who have something inside that is just eating them away: greed, lust, envy, revenge, regret for previous actions, you name it. But before we allegorize Naaman's leprosy into some sort of metaphorical sin, we will just say he was hurting, and whatever it was hurt badly. It also would not go away. That is the thing about sin—once scratched, it always itches.

Which bring us to the first point of this text— when you are really hurting, you will go anywhere for help, even outside your own nation or community. Imagine an Afrikaner in South Africa who even after the end of apartheid still finds racism gnawing at his soul. One day his young son is hurt badly in an accident and has to be operated on by a black female surgeon. The black surgeon is the only one around, and the Afrikaner knows the surgeon can help his son. So he consents, hoping for the best.

# 2 Kings 5:1-14

## Theological Perspective

Where we can examine, recognize, analyze, and define, we can control. And when it comes to human suffering, control is exactly what we want. In the narrative, General Naaman's world is all about command and control. But human command and control are antithetical to providence, and Naaman almost misses (twice) the healing power of God. The near misses come when Naaman travels to the king of Israel to purchase the healing, rather than to the prophet (v. 6), and again when he turns and storms away in rage, declaring: "Are not Abana and Pharpar, the rivers of Damascus, better than all the waters of Israel? Could I not wash in them, and be clean?" (v. 12). Naaman's expectation of his healing journey vastly differs from God's providential care. And we are not unlike Naaman.

Karl Barth, the Swiss Reformed theologian, challenges our view about how the world works providentially. First, Barth distinguishes God's providence in two spheres—*providentia generalis* (general history, or what we believe ought, should, and does take place) and *providentia specialis* (the particular activities of God in the history of the covenant and salvation, which includes but is not limited to healings). Through general history we believe the rational, predictable, and observable is the norm. "In fact, the general with its recognisable laws has been treated as if it were the norm, and the particular (this particular) as if it were only a single application, or from a different angle, a single infringement of the norm."[1] But Barth argues that, from a biblical perspective, we have it backwards: *providentia specialis* is "the centre" and *providentia generalis* is "the circumference." In other words, God's active care is "the controlling original," and our understanding of the world is really "the subservient copy"; the particular works of God are normative for the general.[2] Therefore, with this reversal of what is normal, what constitutes the center and the circumference in the healing of Naaman?

The center is constituted by God's particular care to a non-Israelite through the wise but anonymous voices of the lowly and the simple act of a healing wash. First, God's providential care is not limited to the chosen people. Even the enemies of Israel receive *providentia specialis*, for the Arameans have "taken a young girl captive from the land of Israel" who serves Naaman's wife (v. 2). Powerfully, through

[1] Karl Barth, *Church Dogmatics*, III/3, ed. G. W. Bromiley and T. F. Torrance (Edinburgh: T. & T. Clark, 1957), 185.
[2] Ibid.

## Pastoral Perspective

secretly long for the fast cure-all remedy for suffering. Perhaps such a remedy would ease our guilt for moving on to the next crisis so quickly. We are like Naaman, the Aramean who suffered from a painful skin disease. We want relief, and we want it now.

Maybe we are not looking for grandeur and obeisance, as was Naaman when he traveled from Aram to Israel with a full entourage of horses and chariots, silver and gold, hoping to be cured of his disease. Naaman was a famous military hero who had won many battles, a powerful man in the ancient Near East. He expected a certain reception from the king of Israel and Israel's prophet, Elisha. Maybe we are not looking for honor and glory, but we would like the same kind of quick and glamorous healing that Naaman thought he deserved: "I thought that for me he would surely come out, and stand and call on the name of the LORD his God, and would wave his wand over the spot, and cure the leprosy" (v. 11). Instead, Elisha gave him the tedious task of bathing in the Jordan River seven times.

We all want to be cured by the wave of a wand over the spot of affliction. We all want to be able to cure like this. Both caregivers and care receivers in congregations would prefer this kind of healing, no doubt. But the long road to healing is neither quick nor glamorous; it can be as tedious as bathing in the Jordan seven times.

In recent years, I have watched a friend deal with a broken spirit after suffering some of life's cruelest injustices. For her, the healing process has been anything but quick. It has taken many dips in the Jordan for her battered sense of self-worth to slowly, gradually begin to mend. And it will probably take many more before her healing is complete. A parent who grieves the death of a child is never fully healed, and even getting to a place of relative functionality can take months, even years. It is a long road, and it is a humbling experience, like that of Naaman, who was told to wash in the muddy Jordan River. Grief can send even the most devout believer back to the basic humbling questions about the faith: Is God good? Where is hope? Am I loved?

Recognizing how long healing actually takes might transform a congregation and the lives of its caregivers and care receivers, including the pastors, into a robust, thriving community of faithful believers. The default setting of most churches' care system is crisis care only. Studies and anecdotal evidence bear out the fact that people of faith respond generously to neighbors who experience sudden loss, or shock, or trauma. For example, the response of

*Sixth Sunday after the Epiphany*

along a letter to petition the king of Israel for his help. Along with the letter, the king of Aram sends an impressive array of gifts—silver, gold, and clothing. The giving of gifts was a common practice when requesting a service or favor by letter.

At least some of the words of the letter are recounted in the text, and there is no reference in them to the prophet. Because of the confusing wording of the letter, the king of Israel mistakes the intent of the letter; thinking the letter is calling on the king himself to cure Naaman, he tears his clothes and breaks into confession, pointing to YHWH as the only one who "gives death or life." The king believes that the letter is a trick, with the king of Aram trying to provoke a quarrel with him.

Here the prophet Elisha enters the narrative directly. It is notable that the prophet stands primarily in the background of the general narrative in verses 1–14. Although the narrative alludes to him throughout, only in verses 8–10 does he appear by name and speak, his words clarifying the muddle between the two kings. Otherwise, the narrative points to him only indirectly with the appellations "the prophet who is in Samaria" (v. 3), "the prophet" (v. 13), and "the man of God" (v. 14). His appearance in verses 8–10 and the flow of the larger story demonstrate that while human intentions and actions may go awry and become tangled, as they do here, it is the messenger of YHWH who sets the action back on the creative and productive path.

Naaman, who from the beginning of the story benefited from the will and power of YHWH, will now come to understand that YHWH is the initiator and director of all things in human affairs, including the healing of disease. The discovery will come because he will understand that "there is a prophet in Israel" (v. 8).

But the action required of Naaman is not a spectacular feat of bravery or wisdom; nor is it an arduous journey or a lengthy process. The healing power of God is manifested here in the simplest of actions—washing in the river Jordan. In fact, the action is so simple that it is offensive to the Aramean. He expects more. Naaman has two objections to the requirement. First, he objects that Elisha has acted offensively in not meeting Naaman at the door, but in sending a messenger. Surely, the visitor thinks, the prophet should come forth, utter appropriate magical or cultic words, and make some mysterious, magical motions over the diseased skin. The second objection is that there are rivers at least as good—in fact, better—in Aram. Why come to

Here in this biblical story Naaman is ready to try anything. He has already gotten second and third opinions from his own doctors in his own country. But no one has been able to help. So he heads to Israel a little chagrined, hat in hand, begging for some help.

Naaman even brings gifts to show how serious he is about getting help. But, when the stranger comes to town, all he spells is trouble for the poor king of Israel. The king's physicians and advisers don't know any more than Syria's. Nervous that Naaman's displeasure might spell doom for him, the king of Israel tears his clothes in a pitiful Academy Award performance of overacting.

Enter the prophet Elisha stage left to save the day. Notice he doesn't have the courtesy to speak to Naaman himself, but instead sends an emissary to speak on his behalf, which drives the impetuous Naaman up the wall. This health-care runaround is wearing thin. No more HMOs for him; no more forms to fill out. He just wants the treatment. But when he hears what it is, he nearly freaks out. "Wash in the Jordan? You have to be kidding! I could have splashed around in our rivers back home, if I had known that's all it took. How could this Israelite water be any better than ours?" A little national pride rears its ugly head here.

Which brings us to the second point of this text: when you are really hurting, you will listen to anyone with a good suggestion—even those at the bottom of the food chain. Remember how Naaman got to Israel in the first place? The young female servant to Naaman's wife suggested he go find the prophet for help. And he went on the advice of this girl who was a prisoner! Imagine that. But now, later in the story, he is going to do the same thing again. Just as he is getting himself all worked up over having to bathe in the Jordan, one of his own servants, again at the bottom of the hierarchical food chain, says, "Why not give it a try? What can it hurt?" Again, wisely he listens and takes heed. Both of these little vignettes remind me of the new practices in business of listening carefully to people down at the bottom, people who are closest to the action. So Naaman listens to the young slave girl and his own indentured servant and heads for the river to take a plunge.

Which brings us to the final point of this text: sometimes God asks you to do something too, especially to help bring about your salvation and cleansing. Do not worry; this is not salvation by works. God is still the one doing the saving and the

# 2 Kings 5:1-14

## Theological Perspective

providence, this young girl witnesses to the center. "If only my Lord were with the prophet who is in Samaria! He would cure him of his leprosy" (v. 3).

The circumference of the narrative is constituted by the complexities of human authority, politics, money, and perceived remedies. After Naaman learns of the Samarian prophet, he does not set out to find Elisha, but rather moves to the political power base, the kings. The straightforward, wise words of the young woman are ignored in his attention to the perceived normative. Then, adding to the confusion is Naaman's powerful display of his entourage (v. 5); for Naaman, the center is all but obscured, as it is for the king of Israel, who tears his clothes, swearing, "Am I God, to give death or life, that this man sends word to me to cure a man of his leprosy? Just look and see how he is trying to pick a quarrel with me" (v. 7). When viewed from a general history, the king's assessment makes reasonable sense; from the center, though, it is dismaying.

Yet the center is always near, no matter how far out we draw the circumference. Hence, Elisha tells the king to let Naaman "come to me, that he may learn that there is a prophet in Israel" (v. 8). God's providence breaks forth, returns, and comes again. So Naaman, with entourage in tow, comes to Elisha to receive personally his healing. But contrary to expectation, he is greeted rather by an unnamed messenger who gives him simple instructions for healing. But for Naaman, this is not how it is done. A proper healing has the prophet personally attend to him, call upon the name of the Lord "his" God, wave his hand over the spot, and cure him (v. 11). But the center is not located with kings, wealth, protocols, and well-known rivers. God's particular providence comes by the suggestion of a young slave girl, the words of a lowly prophet, the encouragement of servants, and the complete washing in the Jordan. We would like to be in control but, fortunately for Naaman and all of us, God's providence constitutes the center of life, wholeness and, ultimately, all healing.[3]

DAVID FORNEY

## Pastoral Perspective

religious communities to those displaced by Hurricane Katrina outstripped that of secular agencies. My own denominational relief office has had to reorganize in order to disburse all the funds given for hurricane relief efforts. We do emergencies well.

Pastors, particularly those in small and medium-size churches, are continually pulled from one emergency to another. They do emergencies well too. But if pastors and congregations do not step back and establish better systems for longer-term care of parishioners in need, pastors will continue to burn out at much too high a rate.

Might this text be an opportunity for a preacher to present a vision for a system of long-term care for parishioners who go through crises? The vision would include church members who take responsibility for individuals who have recently suffered trauma. Perhaps those church members need to be trained to offer appropriate care and to recommend professional care when necessary. Church leaders or elders might organize the effort. Perhaps additional clergy ought to be called to serve, but a strong system of long-term care will rely on lay leadership, most likely. The pastor's job description should improve with this kind of effort so that he or she is no longer the worst offender. Perhaps the congregation can become a long-term pastoral-care agent, rather than an emergency relief institution. This nourishes a missional identity for the people of God.

Transforming a congregational care system for the sake of better long-term care must be intentional, because crisis care will always demand attention. But creating a healthier care environment for both clergy and laity will help the whole church thrive.

VERITY A. JONES

---

[3]See Karl Barth, *Church Dogmatics*, IV/3.2, ed. G. W. Bromiley and T. F. Torrance (Edinburgh: T. & T. Clark, 1957), 886.

## Exegetical Perspective

Israel if all he has to do was bathe? Naaman makes ready to leave angrily.

As the young captive girl of Israel did earlier (vv. 2–3), it is once again less powerful, subordinate characters that put things back into proper perspective and set the action back on a productive path. The servants of Naaman dare to confront him with the truth. He had expected to be required to do something difficult and perhaps dangerous. He would not have hesitated to perform such an action or actions. Why refuse to do the required action just because it is easier? In response, Naaman proceeds to follow the instructions of the prophet. As a result, he is healed of his disease.

The overall effect of verses 1–14 is threefold. First, it reinforces the working of YHWH through human agents, and there are many in this brief story: the young girl of Israel who serves her Aramean master by pointing him on the path to healing; the kings of Aram and Israel who, though they stumble and take needless offense, move the action forward toward resolution; Elisha himself, who confidently mediates the power of YHWH to heal; the servants of Naaman who call him back from his human anger to participation in his own healing; and finally, Naaman himself, who begins as a powerful but flawed protagonist and ends as the recipient of YHWH's grace and healing.

Second, the narrative provides the basis for the interplay of human response to divine action in the narratives in the remainder of the chapter. Some human beings respond to God's grace with thankfulness and praise; others demonstrate the ability of human beings to pervert and use God's grace for selfish goals. Regardless of the human response, YHWH's will ultimately has its way in human affairs.

Finally, the scope of the story testifies to the universal power of YHWH to use the nations and their inhabitants to serve the will and ways of divine purpose.

RICHARD A. PUCKETT

## Homiletical Perspective

cleaning. But we still have to step forward and admit we need it; in other words, we still have to repent. We still have to step forward and ask for baptism, and then receive it by going under or having the water splashed over our heads. Either way, we are called to meet God, if not halfway, somewhere along the way. No wonder Paul says in Philippians 2:12, "Work out your own salvation with fear and trembling."

Naaman works out his salvation with fear and trembling, as he takes a dive into the river. Interestingly, the word for salvation in Greek, *sōtēria*, means *complete*, *whole*, in *harmony* and *peace* and is a synonym for *shalom* in Hebrew. In other words, salvation in the Christian tradition means the whole person—not just the Greek idea of soul, but all of who you are, as in the Hebrew word for soul, *nephesh*.

Do you see the powerful baptismal symbol working here? It reminds me of Jonah being spewed up out of the mouth of the fish onto the shore in another baptismal experience. If you are looking carefully, you will see this image in many movies where someone goes into the water and comes up a different person. Think about Russell Crowe's character, the hard-driving stockbroker Max Skinner, submerged in a swimming pool on his uncle's estate in the movie *A Good Year*, or Luke Skywalker, who nearly drowns under the water as the walls close in on him in *Star Wars*. Each time they emerge new persons altogether. That is exactly what happened to Naaman. He was thoroughly cleansed and redeemed that day.

Why? Because he went to a place he had never been before, listened to subordinates who knew better than he did where he could get the help he really needed, and agreed to do what God asked him to do to allow God to cleanse him completely. Now, if that isn't good news, I don't know what is.

WILLIAM J. CARL III

# Psalm 30

¹I will extol you, O LORD, for you have drawn me up,
   and did not let my foes rejoice over me.
²O LORD my God, I cried to you for help,
   and you have healed me.
³O LORD, you brought up my soul from Sheol,
   restored me to life from among those gone down to the Pit.

⁴Sing praises to the LORD, O you his faithful ones,
   and give thanks to his holy name.
⁵For his anger is but for a moment;
   his favor is for a lifetime.
 Weeping may linger for the night,
   but joy comes with the morning.

⁶As for me, I said in my prosperity,
   "I shall never be moved."
⁷By your favor, O LORD,
   you had established me as a strong mountain;

## Theological Perspective

Throughout the long millennia of human habitation on earth, sages and singers have left us their musings on Job's questions: Why did I not die at birth? (Job 3) What are human beings that you (God) are mindful of them . . . and test them every moment? (Job 7) Mortals are born to trouble as the sparks fly upward (Job 5). Why was I (were we) born? What is my (our) life for? Or am I (are we) just an insignificant speck in a meaningless whole?

As long as life moves along familiar patterns, these questions do not arise sharply, as they do in Job's story. Our life world supports our way of life. We know the script and we can live it out. Things fit together well enough for us to get along without raising really big questions. We can even get used to handicaps and setbacks, if they are not too severe. But let normal life be interrupted with misfortune, loss of loved ones, and pain, as Job's life was, and the questions quickly come. It seems they were always just under the surface, swimming in a sea of resentment, boredom, and diminished joy. All we noticed was a nagging sense that there must be something more to life.

Any of us may be asking the question, "Is that all there is?" without being aware of it. Interrupted by pain, however, the question bursts forth powerfully and, with the question, the possibility of a faithful

## Pastoral Perspective

Early in the book of Exodus, the hands of seven working sisters dangled a cord and drew water from a well to nurture the flock under their care. Chased away, the daughters faced fearful displacement. But fear was not the end of their story. These women testified before their family about a miraculous rescue at the edge of a well: a rescue by Moses, who had been pulled out of the water himself. Moses discerned a need, stepped forward for the sisters in justice, and satisfied the thirst of their flock (Exod. 2:16–18).

Moses stood before a burning bush and knew the contour of God's creation on the soles of his feet and God's claim on his servant life. These rescues at the water's edge point to the Lord's liberation of displaced people in troubled times and to the Lord's restoration of wholeness to all of humanity.

As in Exodus, the psalmist begins with words of rescue, "you have drawn me up." Displaced by fears, God's children sometimes complain. They cry out for rescue from the depths of life. Sometimes, the cries linger for more than a night, while at other times fear constricts weeping. Eyes drip from hearts that have witnessed the despair of laboring in a violent world. Young and old alike know pain, suffering, and sorrow. Bad things do happen to good people.

you hid your face;
  I was dismayed.

[8] To you, O Lord, I cried,
    and to the Lord I made supplication:
[9] "What profit is there in my death,
    if I go down to the Pit?
  Will the dust praise you?
    Will it tell of your faithfulness?
[10] Hear, O Lord, and be gracious to me!
    O Lord, be my helper!"

[11] You have turned my mourning into dancing;
    you have taken off my sackcloth
    and clothed me with joy,
[12] so that my soul may praise you and not be silent.
    O Lord my God, I will give thanks to you forever.

## Exegetical Perspective

It is easy to imagine Psalm 30 on the lips of the leper in Mark 1:40–45, the Gospel reading assigned by the lectionary for this Sunday. Psalm 30 is a first-person prayer of thanksgiving for God's deliverance, possibly after just such a devastating illness; its language and imagery call to mind Hezekiah's prayer on his sickbed (Isa. 38:9–20) and Psalm 6, a prayer for help. Moreover, even as the leper cannot refrain from sharing with others the good news of his healing by Jesus (Mark 1:45), Psalm 30 interweaves personal testimony and communal thanksgiving. The psalmist invites the faithful to join her in praise (vv. 4–5), and the psalm's superscription (not printed here), "a song at the dedication of the house" (NRSV "temple"), suggests it may have been used at a communal occasion. The Talmud associates Psalm 30 with the festival of dedication inaugurated by Judas Maccabeus in 164 BCE to celebrate the restoration and purification of the temple after its desecration by Antiochus IV Epiphanes (1 Macc. 4:36–59; 2 Macc. 10:1–9; John 10:22). The psalm may have been used earlier as well, perhaps at the dedication of the second temple (Ezra 6:13–18). Whatever its original context, the psalm gives personal and public voice to gratitude for God's abiding presence and restorative power.

The psalmist opens (vv. 1–3) with a synopsis of her suffering, prayer, and God's deliverance that

## Homiletical Perspective

It is particularly appropriate in the season following the Epiphany to note the ending of one liturgical season and the approach of the next. The joyful time of expectation and rejoicing in the incarnation and birth of Jesus, Advent and Christmas, will yield a different type of reflection in the more penitential overtones of Lent. Often in these times of transition we are able to reflect on where we have been and where we are going.

Our individual and corporate experiences do not always follow such a neat pattern in the calendar. They are undeniably cyclical. As we enter into phases of transition, major and minor, we often find ourselves called to reflection and discernment. One crucible for this type of reflection is the aftermath of a serious illness or disruption in our lives. Psalm 30 gives a particularly strong rendering of those cycles of transition and the way in which this alters our experience and images for God.

The psalm commences with a thanksgiving for a change in situation. The psalmist is no longer in despair, but has been healed and lifted up (vv. 1, 3). Given the lack of specificity of the psalmist's condition, there is an opportunity for the preacher to reflect on the universality of suffering. Some may encounter illness or tragic loss. Others may mainly experience loss through unmet expectations. When

# Psalm 30

## Theological Perspective

answer. Many things can suddenly break open protective shells of self-sufficiency. Psalm 30 mentions two of them: foes and ills. Foes threaten the peace anyone needs to attend to the daily business of living. Ills threaten the prosperity and health anyone needs to have resources and energy to work and to love gladly. The singer thanks God for deliverance and help and praises God as the deliverer and helper.

In the setting of Book I of the Psalms (1–41), the crisis of defeat and exile of God's people is always near to hand. Laments and prayers for help reflect the dreams of an ideal Davidic realm dashed to pieces in a history of defeat and exile. All the major elements of that dream were destroyed: monarchy, land, and temple. The jagged contradiction between dream and historical destiny cries out for a way of understanding how life in covenant with the Lord, who had saved the people from slavery in Egypt and established them as a nation in the land of promise, had come to this.

In between the laments and questions are praises to God, reflecting the steady background of the divine faithfulness in the natural and human worlds (esp. Pss. 8, 15, 19, 24, 29, 33, and 37). The interruptions of foes and ills are engaged faithfully when placed inside the larger picture of the divine creative power and wisdom. As the singer in Psalm 42 tells us, the life of faith is lived between memory (of praising God in the temple) and hope (of praising God yet again). In the present, the person of faith must live in the contradiction of loyalty to God and the absence of divine vindication. God is praised as the source of deliverance and healing even while the promised redemption has not yet happened.

Psalm 30 celebrates the saving action of God in the present. Even though we still await the hoped-for fulfillment, the present is not empty. There have been experiences of deliverance (v. 1) and healing (v. 2) that prompt grateful praise. In these extremities, God's anger stands forth along with human pain and puzzlement. Yet weeping that lingers for the night is swallowed up by joy in the morning (v. 5), for God's anger is momentary, whereas God's favor is lifelong. The secret of faith is placing the negations of life within the bigger picture of God's creative goodwill.

Looking back to moments of restoration and recovery, the singer bears testimony to God's saving activity (vv. 6–9). To the extent that the individual "I" is each member of the community together, each one is asked to remember such moments in their life and the life of the nation. In moments of prosperity,

## Pastoral Perspective

Yet even so, burdened by grief and despair, Sunday by Sunday, God's faithful people gather in sanctuaries and lift prayers before God: "For whom and for what shall we pray?" In some congregations, the prayers are voiced from members. In other congregations, the prayers are woven voices of the saints who have gone before. In prayer, the congregation sings praises to the Lord and gives thanks for God's holy name.

Daily, God's people labor before kitchen sinks; with diapers and textbooks; behind enemy lines and cash registers; beside bedsides and street signs. Sometimes, in the midst of such work, God's people cry before their Savior repeatedly, seeking help in navigating the day, the hour, the moment, "I will extol you, O Lord, for you have drawn me up." At other times, despair is so raw, so close to the surface, that it is hard to cry. Such despair is the swallowed sob of a mother who outlives her child and says to God, "you hid your face; I was dismayed" (v. 7). Despair can make faithful people manipulators who weave their life story with threads of sarcasm, anger, and cynical niceties instead of threads of hope. In that despair, pride can settle into the soul and chase away the need for a Savior.

At Sunday lunches and meals for the homeless hosted in fellowship halls, despair can hover under a veil of shallowness. "Hi!" "How are you?" "Fine." Despair can even paralyze one's ability to cry to the Lord. The Lord alone, who crafted us in our mothers' womb, knows the language of repeated cries but also the nature of humanity to live numbly, afraid to cry. In despair, we are empowered by the psalmist to cry, "O Lord, be my helper!" (v. 10). The church is called by God and empowered by the Holy Spirit to make a way for God's people to dare and cry to the Lord, "What profit is there in my death? . . . Will the dust praise you?" (v. 9).

The psalmist models the restorative power of prayer, of crying out and being drawn up by the God who turns our mourning into dancing and clothes us with joy. The model of prayer sculpted in Psalm 30 reveals the imaginative power of communal testimony to the Lord's salvific work in the world. The psalmist issues a warning against the entrapment of self-aggrandizing ways, which reek of emergent toddler independence, "I can do it *all* by myself."

When we've wept through the night, unable to breathe through our noses or see through swollen eyes, with a piercing glimpse of the Divine, we long for the joy that comes in the morning. As God's

anticipates the longer account she provides in verses 6–12. Her praise mirrors her experience. She "extols" God, literally "lifts up" God (e.g., Isa. 25:1; Pss. 99:5, 9; 107:32; 118:28) because God "drew [her] up" (*dalah*), a verb used elsewhere for drawing water from a well (Exod. 2:16, 19; cf. Prov. 20:5). The psalmist develops this imagery further in verse 3: God "brought up my soul from Sheol," the Pit. The Israelites, like many ancients, believed the underworld was a gated, dark, and dusty place to which the dead descended (e.g., Num. 16:30; Job 17:13–16). Imprisoned with no hope of escape (e.g., Job 7:9; Isa. 38:10–11), the shades—"those gone down to the Pit" (v. 3)—pass their days in a reclined stupor, stirring only to welcome new arrivals (e.g., Isa. 14:9–10, 19). When the psalmist cried out to God from even such depths, however, God revived and healed her (v. 3). And by doing so, much to the psalmist's delight, God also squelched any happiness her enemies might derive at her expense (v. 1b), whether because they either were somehow responsible for her suffering or were merely savoring schadenfreude, enjoyment of another's troubles.

The psalmist interrupts her story to summon the whole community to join her in thanksgiving (vv. 4–5). Her experience shapes her theology. She testifies, first, to God's character; God's anger is "a moment," God's favor a "lifetime" (v. 5a; cf. Isa. 54:7–8). Then, in light of that theology, she reinterprets human suffering: as surely as daylight shatters the darkness, weeping will give way to rejoicing (v. 5b). The psalmist has the newfound conviction that God's presence is perpetual and God's predilection is for life.

With a simple first-person pronoun ("as for me"), the psalmist begins her story again, moving more slowly this time, lingering over details (vv. 6–12). She describes her life before she got sick (vv. 6–7a). It was a time of "prosperity" (*shalwah*, "ease, quiet"; Ps. 122:7; Ezek. 16:49; Prov. 17:1), and the psalmist enjoyed a sense of profound security, even invulnerability ("in *my* prosperity . . . *I* shall not be shaken *forever*," v. 6, my translation), which she attributed to God's favor ("you established me," v. 7a; cf. Ps 16:8). But pain and suffering rattled the psalmist's rock-solid confidence—"I was 'horrified'" (*nivhal*, v. 7b; NRSV translates the same word as "shaking with terror" in Ps 6:2; cf. Pss. 48:6; 104:29)—and she could interpret the pain only in terms of God's absence ("you hid your face," v. 7b; cf. Deut. 31:16–18). Desperate to survive, the psalmist cried out for God's mercy. Her prayer (vv.

we come face to face with our limits, our reaction is often suffering. Regardless of how we become aware of this, we find ourselves confronting loss and often turn to God in response. This text gives the preacher an opportunity to invite the congregation to reflect on our response to the cycle of suffering. How has it changed us? Were there gifts that we received during times of illness or other grief? How did our faith communities choose to respond? Were we the faithful? Or did we fall into the trap appearing as the foe in the face of suffering (vv. 1, 4)?

One issue that often arises during illness or suffering is the unveiling of previously unconscious theologies. Intellectually one may believe that illness is random and not related to a particular person's worth or goodness. We might feel our faith is broad enough to tolerate the randomness of the created order. However, when pain and suffering strikes in unanticipated ways, we can find ourselves outraged that this suffering has come to us or to those we love. Following that initial reaction, we can then become consumed with guilt over our own lack of faith and confidence. Texts like Psalm 30 provide a wonderful homiletical and pastoral resource. The preacher can invite the congregation to remember that we have canonized the questions and feelings of despair that emerge during crisis. The very strength of our connection with God is oftentimes most obvious when we feel it has been severed. If there were no connection in the first place, we would have no cause to lament when we feel that God "hid your face" (v. 7).

As the psalmist is so willing to articulate, we find ourselves crying out and even experience ourselves near death (vv. 2, 3). Rather than succumbing to guilt over the fact that we have had these strong reactions, we can find in a text like this echoes that validate our own shock and dismay (vv. 5–10).We can be invited by the psalmist to realize that our previous view of our own prosperity might have discounted the role God had played in less challenging times (vv. 6, 7). The real need we have to maintain that relationship through praise may become evident only when we stumble (vv. 9, 10). The suffering might in fact serve as a conversion call to lead a life more focused on praise and an awareness of God's presence. The cycle from unreflective prosperity to difficulty to self-aware prosperity might indeed be converting. As we come into new awareness of God's role in all of our experiences, we find we are no longer silent (v. 12).

Suffering is not the only theme of universality in this psalm. The preacher might return to the

# Psalm 30

## Theological Perspective

when life is stable, what is more natural than to assume it will always be so? When things turn negative, we are devastated. Our destruction serves no good end. Resentment can grow and choke out a sense of God's presence. In these circumstances, it is easy to slip into Satan's theology (Job 1–2): the faithful Job praises God because of the obvious blessings in his affluent life, but will curse God if his fortunes are reversed. The praise of God depends on a bribe.

It may seem that Psalm 30 supports this view. The faithful cry unto the Lord, and they are helped (vv. 8–10). How are they helped? Destruction does not reach its end! They are not saved from trouble but saved through trouble. They are brought through a critical passage out into a spacious new life. The pain of loss, damage, sickness, and failure must still be suffered, but the resources to deal with them are actively engaged by those who know that the struggle is worthwhile. Perhaps the sense that God is with them in the crises is more penetrating than the sense of God's presence when there is no crisis. Laments arise from faith, not from unbelief.

The psalm concludes with a heightened sense of joy and a ready tongue to praise God (vv. 11–12): "O Lord my God, I will give thanks to you forever." The crisis generated by the collapse of the nation is in direct opposition to the sacred reality of the Davidic establishment. Nothing can more surely undermine the struggle for something better than a sense of hopeless futility when we are alone with our fate. To remember God's mercy and help is to exchange mourning for joy and silence for praise (vv. 11–12), even in the midst of crises before they are resolved.

THOMAS D. PARKER

## Pastoral Perspective

people we resist worldly ways through prayer, listening for the small voice that first cried out from the poverty of a manger.

We pray together and remember wise ones who followed a star and how they were overtaken with joy. We remember their act of prayer and response to the joy that consumed their hearts and minds. We are witnesses to what they saw and their discernment to go home by another way not defined by the power of the day.

In the Reformed tradition of the church, three notes of the church are the true preaching of the Word of God, the right administration of the sacraments, and ecclesiastical discipline uprightly ministered. The third note of the church includes the disciplined life of prayer. Prayer is at the heart of Christian worship.

Having been brought up from the depths, like those sisters rescued by Moses at the well's edge, God's people claimed at the baptismal font and fed at the Lord's Table, are called to worship and pray, and are sent into the world to pluck loudly the heartstrings of Truth. We are to sing praise to God for how we have seen glimpses of God's healing, justice, and restoration at work.

In the church, we are equipped to pray, through the power of the Holy Spirit, that when we find ourselves at our most prosperous places, even in despair, we might not end up terrified and spiraling out of control, unable to cry for rescue. We are equipped to pray with bold proclamation that although weeping may linger for a night, joy comes in the morning, a morning that the Lord alone brings. Like the joyful wise ones who saw the Christ child and believed, the church is sent by the Holy Spirit to pray and to proclaim that God alone can turn mourning into dancing and replace covert despair with indescribable joy.

ANNE H. K. APPLE

## Exegetical Perspective

8–10), like many laments, appealed to God's self-interest, juxtaposing the silence of dust in Sheol (cf. Pss. 6:5; 88:5, 11–12; Isa. 38:18) with sounds of life as the psalmist envisions it: "*praise* you, *tell* of your faithfulness. . . . *Hear*, O Lord!" (vv. 9–10). The psalmist's plea entwines her life with praise of God.

Recalling the imagery in verse 4, the psalmist professes that God indeed turned her weeping into joy, her mourning into dancing (v. 11). With intimate language—"you took off my sackcloth and clothed me with joy" (v. 11b)—the psalmist describes her physical recovery and transformed understanding of God as present even in the midst of her suffering (e.g., Ps. 23:4). Whereas before, in the hush of prosperity, the psalmist prayed not to be shaken "forever" (*'olam*, v. 6b), in the wake of suffering and God's provision, she cannot contain herself. She will not be silent. She will praise God "forever" (*'olam*, v. 12b).

CHRISTINE ROY YODER

## Homiletical Perspective

universal experience of community. Even the most isolated individuals usually have some connection with outside community. One role of the faith community is to participate actively with individuals who have or are suffering. Psalm 30 clearly contains a call to community participation (v. 4). It is not only the individual who has been healed that should be called forth in praise and thanksgiving, but the entire community. The community functions as a corporate witness to both the suffering and healing. Foes are not allowed to have the final word (v. 1) and the faithful are meant to affirm the healing that has been received (v. 4). The eventual emergence of the psalmist following the healing then provides a new witness and voice to the faith community (v. 12). The preacher could lift up those who have suffered in the community who later become powerful catalysts for support of those in grief later. In fact, their intimate acquaintance with the depths of suffering allows them to be present to those experiences in ways that others are not able to engender.

The imagery of the psalm provides many helpful examples of the cycle of suffering and healing. The fleeting nature of anger, the weeping that yields to joy in the morning, and the mourning that turns to dancing (vv. 5, 11) are natural sermon illustrations to support the rhythm of human experience. This need not be offered as a platitude to those who are currently in pain, but rather as a significant witness to the hope of God's presence and redemption even in our darkest moments. The natural tension created within the text allows for praise to be set within a context that recognizes the depth of suffering and the pinnacles of joy. It celebrates the new awareness and gratitude that can come from suffering, without idealizing pain. By lifting up the role of the community in its support of the individual, there is also the hopeful reminder that suffering can be supported by others when we find ourselves in the abyss.

ELIZABETH C. KNOWLTON

# 1 Corinthians 9:24-27

[24]Do you not know that in a race the runners all compete, but only one receives the prize? Run in such a way that you may win it. [25]Athletes exercise self-control in all things; they do it to receive a perishable wreath, but we an imperishable one. [26]So I do not run aimlessly, nor do I box as though beating the air; [27]but I punish my body and enslave it, so that after proclaiming to others I myself should not be disqualified.

## Theological Perspective

In this passage, Paul raises the issue whether doing theology can in any way be like playing a game. In technical language, this means asking whether good Christian theology can be "ludic theology," from *homo ludens*, human the game player. John Dominic Crossan reaches this conclusion: "To be human is to play. Our supreme play is the creation of world and the totality of played world is termed reality. This reality is the interlaced and interwoven fabric of our play. It is layer upon layer of solid and substantial play and on this play we live, move, and have our being."[1]

*Receiving a Trophy vs. Grace (v. 24).* Paul raises the theological issue of humans as game players when he formulates the goal of life as a prize to be won. Does such a formulation endanger a Christian view of grace, or does God's grace come in the midst of serious play on behalf of humans? Or, to raise even a deeper question, is God's way of relating both to humans and to the world a form of game playing?

Paul asserts that we should run the race of life in such a way that we may receive the "one" prize that is given. Does it not seem theologically problematic to have such an individualistic emphasis on receiving

[1]John Dominic Crossan, *Raid on the Articulate* (New York: Harper & Row, 1976), 27.

## Pastoral Perspective

Christianity is not a series of ideas to be held in the mind, analyzed in the classroom, or defended in the marketplace. Christianity is, above all else, a life to be lived.

As a pastor and teacher, I have often wondered if in our towns and cities we could gather congregations alongside all those who never darken the door of a church and be able to tell the difference in any discernible way. I am not in this instance thinking of doctrines or beliefs, institutional brands or labels. I am thinking instead about the shape and substance of a distinctive life that manifests genuine discipleship to Jesus Christ. I am thinking about the life of the church lived out by its members day by day and generation after generation.

Most of my Jewish friends have, at one point or another in their lives, had to decide whether to live as religiously observant Jews or to engage in secular lives involving varying degrees of Jewish culture. It is a lifestyle about which they decide, one that profoundly influences what they eat, what they remember, when they celebrate, when they rest and when they work, and how they make moral and ethical decisions.

There have been times in American history when one could describe the special characteristics of a Roman Catholic life or the features of various

## Exegetical Perspective

These verses conclude the argument Paul has been making based on his conduct as an apostle of Christ. His overriding concern has been to help the Corinthians recognize their responsibility to protect against any behavior that could render the gospel ineffective (9:17–19) or worse, cause the destruction of a fellow believer (8:9, 11–13). Now Paul exhorts them to test the effectiveness of their behavior in maintaining the church's communal health. The remarks follow nicely the claim that his efforts are always made in light of sharing in the gospel (9:23).

From Paul's understanding, the converts have misconceived Christian life and think that, having accepted the reality of the Christian message, they have achieved a spiritual state that transcends this mundane world. This is made explicit in the next chapter: "So if you think you are standing, watch out that you do not fall" (10:12 and also 10:1–5). To counter this misunderstanding Paul insists that the Corinthians must constantly test the validity of their thought and actions, lest they fail to attain the real freedom God has created.

Paul employs two examples from the world of athletics to make his points: every successful athlete competes to win, and no athlete wins without proper training. His analogy is clear: just as winning athletes require both proper training and total commitment

## Homiletical Perspective

One approach to the sermon for today is inspired by the literary context that begins in 1 Corinthians 8:1–13, where Paul suggests that a group in the congregation in Corinth that is free to eat food offered to idols refrain from doing so, in order not to destroy others whose consciences are defiled by such eating. In 1 Corinthians 9:1–23, Paul uses his life as an apostle to exemplify the practice of limiting freedom for the good of community. Some commentators think that the references to the "body" in this passage directly echo the apostle's notion of the community as the "body of Christ," so that Paul's admonitions here are not just to individuals, but to the congregation as community.

In 9:24–27, the apostle places this issue in an apocalyptic frame of reference. The apocalyptic worldview assumes that history is divided into two ages—the present evil one that is passing away and the coming realm of God in which all things will take place according to God's purposes of love and justice. Paul believes that the apocalypse itself will occur soon. In 9:24–27 the apostle compares the congregation, moving towards the apocalypse, to a runner in a race. For the members of the community to receive the prize (a place in the coming realm of God), they need to win the race (practice self-limitation of their freedom). The athlete is a model

# 1 Corinthians 9:24-27

## Theological Perspective

God's grace and perceiving grace as to be received by beating everyone else in a race? Russell B. Sisson reminds us that athletic games had a strong religious dimension in antiquity, with athletes offering prayers and offerings before the games and often perceiving the outcome of their contests to be the results of decisions by the gods. In addition, moral philosophers regularly used athletic games to describe the challenges and achievements of living a moral life.[2] Paul's view, then, appears to be a natural way for him to describe both the way in which a person experiences life under God in Christ in the world and the way in which God brings the gift of grace into people's lives. But is this really an acceptable way to understand both God and humans theologically?

*Theological Asceticism (v. 25).* When Paul introduces the concept of self-control, he raises the theological issue of asceticism. For many early Christians, devotion to God required playing a serious game of self-control throughout one's life. Living in the world was a contest in which not only other humans, but also natural instincts of survival functioned like the opposing team over which a person had to be victorious in order to receive God's grace.

The word "ascetic" derives from the Greek word *askēsis*. Instead of using this word, Paul and other NT writers used words containing the root *enkrat-*, from which comes the theological word "encratite," which refers to a second-century group of Christians who considered it immoral to marry, drink wine, or eat meat. Early Christians debated vigorously among themselves concerning what kind of self-control God might require of a believer, and the topic is still alive today. Paul exhorts self-control "in all things," and he refers to an "imperishable" garland or crown if one is successful in the race.

In the context of vigorous debate about an ascetic way of approaching life, a recent work asserts: "A certain measure of ascetic self-denial is a necessary element in all that we undertake, whether in athletics or in politics, in scholarly research or in prayer. Without this ascetic concentration of effort we are at the mercy of exterior forces, or of our own emotions and moods; we are reacting rather than acting. Only the ascetic is inwardly free."[3] Is an ascetic way of life,

## Pastoral Perspective

Protestant forms of Christian life. Today that is much more difficult. It seems almost as if we have lost our life in the midst of powerful cultural influences such as secularism, materialism, individualism, and nationalism, which demand a style of life quite alien to the ethos and traditions of the Christian church.

On the other hand, we witness many immigrant churches who struggle to live the gospel in a prophetic way, living the Christian life on a day-to-day experience and claiming their lives to be under Christ's lordship. As they struggle to become part of the American society, they also find deep conflicts between the ways their faith was embodied in their countries of origins and the ways in which "being American" challenges their Christian commitments and mission. In many ways, some of these immigrant churches provide a window to see many of the conflicts between our faithfulness to the gospel and the accommodations to our cultural patterns. This is a refreshing, and yet troubling, witness to many of us mainstream Christians and to the way in which our faith relates to our culture.

In his letter to the church in Corinth, Paul addresses a congregation living in a culture that is essentially foreign to the gospel, and he speaks to a Christian community beset with significant divisions. How Christians relate to and interact with this culture is one of the causes of these divisions. Whether or not to eat meat sacrificed to idols is one of those issues (8:1–13). Paul calls upon Christians in Corinth to do what must have seemed impossible. Instead of seeking to win their battles over and against one another, Paul calls upon them to seek to identify with one another, to stay together in community, and to be open to God's transforming the outcomes of their struggles to be faithful to the gospel. This is clearly not an easy assignment. It has to nurture patience, compromise, communication, tolerance, and mutual reflection. Above all, it requires love, which is both a gift of God and a response to God, a demanding discipline for the whole community.

Paul compares this discipline to the vigorous training of an athlete. Without sacrifice and dedication, one cannot live the Christian life. It is one thing to talk about Christian ideas; it is quite another to carry out the demands of being and living as a Christian, a disciple of Christ. For Paul, the devotion and hard work of Olympic athletes is a powerful metaphor that suggests the energy and dedication necessary for living the Christian life.

---

[2] Russell B. Sisson, "Authorial *Ethos* in Philippians: The *Agon* in Paul and Hellenistic Moralists," in T. H. Olbricht and A. Eriksson, eds., *Rhetoric, Ethic, and Moral Persuasion in Biblical Discourse*, Emory Studies in Early Christianity 11 (New York: T. & T. Clark, 2005), 238–54.

[3] Kallistos Ware, "The Way of the Ascetics: Negative or Affirmative?" in Vincent L. Wimbush and Richard Valantasis, eds., *Asceticism* (New York: Oxford University Press, 2002), 3.

to compete, so too the Christian must discipline him or herself to live in a manner consonant with the goal of salvation.

The metaphor of striving for excellence in athletics (the *agōn* motif) was a stock image in Greek and Roman (e.g., Epictetus and Seneca) philosophical instruction, especially with regard to achieving a mastery of the internal self. The terms used here—such as "prize," "competitor," "crown," "box," and "flail at the air"—are specific to the metaphor's athletic context. The language is atypical for Paul, but the ideas are not, and the athletic image would have been particularly apt since Corinth was the site of the famous Isthmian games.

As elsewhere in the letter, a rhetorical question is used to engage the readers. "Don't you know that in a race all the runners run, but only one wins the prize?" (v. 24, my translation). Paul poses it in order to focus on the necessity of exercising self-discipline, because the "spiritual race" is exceedingly more important than any human physical competition. The audience is exhorted to "run to win," and by using the present imperative form of the verb "to run," Paul underscores the importance of continual attention to the realities of the Christian life.

However, the Christian race has more than one victor, and its trophies are of everlasting significance. These points are critical because the Corinthians had differentiated themselves according to levels of maturity of faith and spiritual status. Paul insists that there is no room for this stratification and questions both the categories and their bases.

Typically at the Greek games the winner of a footrace received a laurel or pine wreath. But both the victory and its rewards were fleeting and destined to fade away. In contrast, the Christian runner receives "an imperishable award" (v. 25), one fitting the reality of life in Christ. Given the ultimate value of this goal, it was natural to exhort the Corinthians to make efforts commensurate with the salvation they have received (cf. 9:10; 9:23). Though the question is different here, the language of perishable and imperishable foreshadows Paul's remarks in chapter 15, where the perishable physical body is contrasted to the imperishable resurrection body (15:50).

Expanding the imagery, Paul turns to the self-control all athletes must display in training and competition. Paul is the only NT writer to use the verb "self-control" (*enkrateuomai*), but the word is typical of Greek moral exhortation. He used this verb at 7:9 with reference to sexual continence; here

for the Corinthian community, for "Athletes exercise *self-control* in all things" (9:25, emphasis added).

Some Christians today believe that we are living close to the end time. Others accept a permutation of the apocalyptic worldview, believing that while we may not be living in the end time, God will one day end history as we know it and bring about a new age. Others think that the apocalyptic perspective is no longer intellectually tenable, but that God continues to work in history to attempt to lure human beings and elements of nature to cooperate with the divine purposes of love and justice. Regardless of the specific orientations to eschatology present in the congregation, the preacher can help the congregation recognize that the moment-by-moment decisions they make, such as whether to eat food offered to idols, have life-shaping power. The way in which we respond to other people—particularly the ways in which we limit our freedoms—determines the kinds of communities in which the human family lives now and will live in the future.

Given the widespread curiosity about the end time prompted by the *Left Behind* books and movies, as well as other contemporary irruptions of apocalyptic fervor, the preacher might use the apocalyptic aspect of this text as the occasion to help the congregation reflect on what they most deeply believe to be true of the future, and why. How is the race similar and how is it different for followers of different eschatologies?

The preacher might develop a sermon that compares the congregation (and its members) to an athlete preparing for a race and running in it. With the help of Bible dictionaries, the preacher could describe the Isthmian games held just outside of Corinth and the ways in which athletes trained for the races and competed in them. Preachers who run (or who engage in other efforts toward physical fitness) might draw on their own experiences. For the sake of people who are not into physical fitness (and who are weary of sports stories in sermons or wary of the contemporary athletic culture), the preacher should also include examples from the arts or other arenas of life for activities that require discipline.

A runner needs good nutrition, adequate rest, and practice, beginning at the runner's present stage of ability and progressing to increase endurance and speed. During the race, runners need to monitor their bodies and behavior, keep hydrated, and pace themselves to have optimum energy at the key

# 1 Corinthians 9:24-27

**Theological Perspective**

then, the truest way to live as people who have been created in the image of God?

*Preparing without Rigor (v. 26).* As a result of the story in Genesis about God's creation of humans, it seems natural to reason theologically about the necessity for humans to work strenuously and diligently for their food and for women to suffer pain as they bear children to be raised up into God's household. But can there be serious theological reasoning about humans and God on the basis of footracers and boxing? Paul focuses on people in the context of their own bodies, which again leads to questions about ascetic theology as an appropriate way to reason about the relation of humans to the divine. He emphasizes running in a disciplined manner on an actual racetrack and boxing with an actual opponent or a solid object to build strength for the actual race or boxing match.

*Being Disqualified (v. 27).* In his final comment, Paul changes the image from winning a prize to being disqualified. One of the most shameful things for athletes, according to Sisson, was to be disqualified from the athletic competition because one had not trained properly. One thinks today of disqualification as a result of taking substances that give a person an unfair advantage over others who have trained just as rigorously.

It is noticeable that the words "God" and "Christ" never occur in these verses. Nevertheless, the challenges of living according to God's ways and of perceiving oneself under the watchful eye of God hover close to the imagery in the passage. If God became flesh and dwelt among us, perhaps serious thought about living in the flesh with self-control and carefully organized discipline can be a theologically serious way of living in the context of the great game of life God has invited us to play.

VERNON K. ROBBINS

**Pastoral Perspective**

However, the games known to Paul (Olympian and Isthmian) were all individual competitions. One can imagine what Paul might have done with this metaphor, had he known about the special challenges and demands of team sports. And Paul seeks to impress on his readers that much more is at stake in the Christian life than winning a crown of laurels (or wilted celery leaves, as one source suggests). Because the church is itself part and parcel of the good news, it matters very much how Christians live the Christian life with one another.

If this is true, then it matters very much whether the church deals with conflict in a way that is distinctly different from other social organizations. In a society as deeply divided as ours, is there any indication that the church deals better or more effectively than—or even differently from—any other organization? How do we nurture, educate, equip, and inspire church members to take Paul's challenge seriously? What kind of liturgy, sermons, classes, encounters, and experiences would help people discover how to listen to, identify with, advocate for, and learn from those who are different from themselves or those with whom they disagree? How do we learn, as Paul suggests, that love is more powerful than self-centered knowledge, that love builds up the community, while boastful knowledge simply puffs up those who think they know it all?

To live with heated controversy, to maintain the bonds of love, and to seek a new way forward are not an easy task. No one, of course, has claimed that the Christian life is easy. That is why Paul suggests that we must stay in shape, work hard at our tasks, and keep our eyes on the ultimate goal.

V. BRUCE RIGDON

he uses it for controlling one's emotions and desires. As the athlete disciplines the body, wasting no effort, so too the Christian is exhorted to discipline himself or herself so that nothing interferes with participating in the life of Christ.

In the last verses of the passage, Paul offers himself as an example. Like an athlete he is intent upon the goal and "runs accordingly" not "aimlessly" (*adēlos*—"with hesitation"), but with purpose. Seeing the goal and striving for it, the apostle dedicates all his energies to imitating Christ's existence (cf. Phil. 3).

In the next part of the example Paul shifts the image from running to boxing. The terms for "boxing," "flail at the air," and "subjugate" are found only here in the NT. The imagery refers to real fighters, those who punch with purpose and who intend to defeat their opponents. Unlike the fighter who punches wildly, Paul's efforts are direct, focused, efficient, and therefore effective. Despite this, Paul recognizes that he could "fail to qualify" as an apostle. The term he uses here (*adokimos*) means "worthless" or "unqualified" (see 2 Cor. 13:5–7, where this term is used to warn the Corinthians of their own failure). Paul's argument has been directed toward those who prided themselves on "knowledge," but who really knew nothing, due to their failure to understand the nature of Christ's actions (8:1–13). Unfortunately, in their zeal for spiritual growth these members had ignored the needs of the full body of believers. Paul wants to guard against such disastrous estimates either by him or by those who claim that their knowledge provides them special spiritual insight.

The final comments are shaped by the arguments Paul has provided in verses 19–23. The gospel is not preached at people; it is preached for them. Thus Paul's ministry takes on the form of Christ's self-emptying; otherwise it would be counterfeit, no matter how attractive. Here he advises the Corinthians that the announcement of the gospel is genuine only when it is delivered in ways that make Christ's death manifest. Indeed, Paul himself could fail without self-vigilance to ensure that his efforts match the content of the gospel. Hence his preaching of the Christ event must be applied to himself as well as to others. Otherwise, even if others respond to the message, it will have been worthless to Paul himself.

STEVEN J. KRAFTCHICK

moments. In the heat of the race, the runner must push the body to the limit ("punish my body") and keep it focused on the one goal ("enslave it"). The preacher could help the congregation think about people developing in the body of Christ in similar ways. People new to the eschatological community typically need to begin thinking about the Bible and theological matters and to engage in Christian practices and mission, at basic levels, and gradually work toward depth and detail. Perhaps a preacher can point to opportunities in the life of the congregation (and in the wider church) that encourage such growth.

Most congregations in the long-established denominations have educational programs and practices that are age appropriate for children and youth, but few congregations are prepared to help *adults* who come to God through Christ grow systematically into the life of discipleship. Congregations often take people from the waters of baptism and put them in groups where other participants already know the in-house vocabulary, or even make them committee chairs, Bible school teachers, and mission leaders, with the result that they feel as if they are stumbling through the race. The preacher could help the congregation think creatively about how to provide opportunities for growth in Christ for adults.

The athletic imagery in this passage might prompt a preacher to reflect with the congregation on the athletic culture in contemporary North America. On the one hand, increasing participation in athletics by children, young people, and adults promotes healthy lifestyles that help people run the race of discipleship. On the other hand, professional and collegiate athletics tie up incredible amounts of money that could be used to enhance quality of life for many more people. Athletic culture can reinforce unhealthy polarization regarding winning and losing and can encourage the idea that life itself is competition, in which one either wins or loses. Fascination with athletics can distract people from engaging issues that are more fundamental to human community than yards per carry. Indeed, per 1 Corinthians 9, athletics can become an idol that breaks apart human community. The preacher could propose that the congregation sponsor opportunities for intense physical activity without such negative effects.

RONALD J. ALLEN

# Mark 1:40‑45

40A leper came to him begging him, and kneeling he said to him, "If you choose, you can make me clean." 41Moved with pity, Jesus stretched out his hand and touched him, and said to him, "I do choose. Be made clean!" 42Immediately the leprosy left him, and he was made clean. 43After sternly warning him he sent him away at once, 44saying to him, "See that you say nothing to anyone; but go, show yourself to the priest, and offer for your cleansing what Moses commanded, as a testimony to them." 45But he went out and began to proclaim it freely, and to spread the word, so that Jesus could no longer go into a town openly, but stayed out in the country; and people came to him from every quarter.

## Theological Perspective

This passage represents a paradigm of purity. It also places the power of Jesus' radical invitation to the kingdom at the public space. Mark has steadily moved us from the religious space through the house/private space to the public space, strongly illustrating the overwhelming power of God's kingdom in all human spaces, announcing with unique authority and liberative acts God's option for the marginalized.

From the synagogue, going by the house, we have arrived to the open field, where the impure ones wander, those who cannot be integrated into the city. With them Jesus begins a series of signs to outcasts (later the paralytic and the publican will come). The lepers suffer from a social illness: they are impure, unclean; they are a source of danger and contamination for the family. For that reason, when the priest discovers their impurity, he must expel them from the civil and religious society, according to his sacred code (Lev. 13–14). They could not pray in the temple or go to the synagogue, or share with their healthy relatives their tables and beds. Their illness converted them into solitary persons, a separated species.

One could wonder how the experience in a "deserted place" triggered Jesus' movement outside of Capernaum "on to the neighboring towns,"

## Pastoral Perspective

Even as these words are being written, Brian Friel's *Faith Healer* is playing to sold-out audiences at the Booth Theatre on Broadway. Aside from Friel's extraordinary ability to tell a story, the popularity of the production indicates a persistent public curiosity concerning the phenomenon of faith healing. While the post-Enlightenment mind has difficulty believing in the healing miracles, the pre-Enlightenment mind cannot quite let go of the possibility that "there just might be something there." Thus the dilemma of Frank Hardy—"Fantastic Francis Hardy"—the Irish faith healer in Friel's play, who is continually ravaged by the realization that his "performances" work only part of the time. The plot is the unraveling of the life of the faith healer, who questions his unusual "gift." Friel has given us the contemporary dramatization of the perennial debate among Christians over the healing stories of Jesus, as in the text before us of Jesus' healing encounter with the leper. Our questions about faith healing become even more complicated by the scriptural references to those occasions when Jesus himself seemed powerless to perform his "mighty works." ("And he could do no mighty works there, except that he laid his hands upon a few sick people and healed them" [Mark 6:5 RSV]). It makes one wonder if Jesus, who our creeds contend was human even as we are ("Jesus

## Exegetical Perspective

The game is on.

By the close of chapter 1, Mark has established Jesus' identity as the "Son of God" (1:1), as one who heals, preaches, exorcises, and teaches with authority in and out of the synagogue. It should surprise no reader that chapter 2 will hinge not on highlighting another healing by Jesus but on the question by the apparent religious authorities about who has the authority to heal and to forgive sin. The answer is not in doubt in the minds of the boys from Jerusalem, and the answer is clearly not "Jesus."

The first chapter of Mark closes with a story that can easily be reduced to just another healing by Jesus. Echoes of Naaman from 2 Kings 5 ring in the reader's ear when an unnamed leper comes to seek healing from Jesus. The echoes cease, though, when Jesus not only listens to the leper but touches him.

Why would Jesus risk his own health and ensure that he would become ritually unclean by touching this leper? Mark precedes his touch by telling the reader something essential about Jesus. This is the first of three instances in which Mark uses the word *splanchnizomai* to describe the disposition of Jesus. English translations do not serve us well when rendering this word. The NRSV renders it "moved with pity"; the NIV says "filled with compassion"; and arguably the worst translation comes when the

## Homiletical Perspective

Pastors are typically viewed as being in the answer business, providing answers to people's religious questions. Some of those questions come from the culture around us: "So what do you think about the situation in the Middle East?" Other questions arise from a study of Scripture: "Why does Mark's Gospel portray Jesus speaking in parables in order to confuse folks?" Rarely, if ever, does a Bible study class invite the pastor to make an appearance in order that she/he might ask them a question or two. Inevitably, this notion of pastors providing answers influences the way we preach, namely with periods and exclamation points. But what if we were to conceive of sermons as asking questions, and not just rhetorical ones? What might that look like?

This line of thinking seems even more pertinent in light of the Gospel text before us. On the surface, we see a leprous man with a measure of faith approach Jesus. Jesus, moved with pity, restores the man with a touch. While a few chapters later a hemorrhaging woman touches Jesus (5:27), here Jesus chooses to touch an unclean leper. What an act of compassion! The man will also be restored to community once he goes to the priest. It is a particularly poignant story, one which we are likely to conclude with a period, followed by a maxim. "Jesus cares for the outcast. So should we." Period.

# Mark 1:40-45

## Theological Perspective

extending his proclamation beyond his immediate space (1:38–39). Was it a discovery of the extension of the public space? Was it a sudden recognition of the character of God's kingdom? Evidently, it is not an accidental movement, for proclaiming the kingdom "is what I came out to do" (v. 38).

Jesus' radical proclamation disrupts the social order by breaking the boundaries of social space. Jesus extends his hand and touches them (1:41a). He does not have to grab them, as he did to Simon's mother-in-law. Now, he simply touches and caresses (*haptomai*), offering personal presence (healing contact) to that which was condemned, devoid of any contact. Jesus' hand is the supreme expression of mercy that transcends the laws of the purity of religious dogma. This hand is sign of mercy and shared life, hence a sign that disrupts social and spatial order and liberation and reconciliation.

The leper could not come to Simon's house. He finds Jesus in the uninhabited place. He is aware of his illness and requests healing. Jesus touches him and Jesus speaks, offering him purity and requesting of him silence and legal obedience, which the man does not accept. Jesus says, "I do choose. Be made clean!" (1:41b). His voice supports the communication of expression. It is a creative word, *thelō—I do choose!*—that defines the new reality of the gospel. In that merciful desire of Jesus, a new family of disciples is founded, the church of the sick and the outcasts.

Simon's mother-in-law responded to the "miracle" by beginning to serve others on the Sabbath, overcoming in this way an aspect of the sacred day of rest. Now the leper does it in a direct and programmed way, influencing the later strategy of the gospel. It is as if Jesus himself had to learn: he has started a movement of the kingdom, and he has to wait for the reactions. Jesus has asked the former leper to accept the law—you show yourself to the priest! But the healed man can no longer obey Jesus, because he has discovered a way of liberation and kingdom that overcomes the control of the priests. And so the leper becomes a preacher. He begins to proclaim with insistence (*kēryssein polla*) and to reveal the word (*rhēma, logos*), that is to say, victory over the law of the leper's exclusion (1:45a). Their expressions take us to the heart of the gospel: the leper's healing (touched and loved by Jesus) is made kerygma and word. This is the messianic logos that Jesus himself proclaims and sows. Jesus can no longer go into town openly, but stays out in the country (1:45b).

## Pastoral Perspective

was what we are"),[1] ever had self-doubt regarding his own miraculous power. Thus the questions remain.

However, the centuries since Jesus' days on earth do seem to have produced some consensus on which most modern, as well as ancient, minds agree. For example, there exists a real, though not yet fully understood, relationship between mind and body—belief and health, the spiritual and the physical. The old dichotomies between body and spirit are questioned, if not challenged. The healing of the leper in the text is instructive in the way it reveals the human side of Jesus. The NRSV suggests that Jesus' motivation was that he was "moved with pity," while other credible ancient manuscripts prefer the more harsh translation that Jesus was moved by anger—"he snorted at him and pushed him out."[2] Jon Walton, preaching on this story at the First Presbyterian Church in New York City, declares:

> This is a healing story with passion in it. It is not just any healing story. Jesus is frustrated and upset when he heals the man; and in the process of healing him, Jesus breaks down walls that have been carefully built and scrupulously preserved by well-meaning religious types, when he touches the leper. He dares to do the unconventional, in fact, the unlawful, so that he may accomplish the unlikely.[3]

While Jesus surely was moved by pity for the leper, it is perfectly human that his act of healing was also motivated partially by anger at a social system that demonized and excluded an entire group of human beings guilty of nothing more than being "different." After all, we ourselves, do we not, grow indignant at the way our culture stigmatizes the "different" among us: the diseased and disfigured, the immigrant, the very poor, the slow to learn, the social misfit of every sort. As modern human beings, we may, in our time, become more sophisticated in divorcing our human deficiencies from our individual sins, but there remains much still to learn about the "demons" that haunt our culture, both personally and institutionally, and that continue to inflict pain and death upon countless brothers and sisters both near and far. Jon Walton, again, tells of a friend who, after leaving the doctor's office upon hearing his positive diagnosis for HIV, walked down Madison Avenue in a daze; the only word he could

[1] *Declaration of Faith* (Louisville, KY: Office of the General Assembly, Presbyterian Church (U.S.A.), 1977).
[2] Lamar Williamson Jr., *Mark*, Interpretation Series (Atlanta: John Knox Press, 1983), 59.
[3] "Jesus Iconoclast," a sermon by Jon M. Walton, First Presbyterian Church, New York, NY, February 12, 2006.

## Exegetical Perspective

New Jerusalem Bible renders the verb "feeling sorry for him."

In our book *Preaching Mark in Two Voices* Brian Blount and I make this argument about *splanchnizomai*:

"*Splanchnizomai* identifies a profoundly intense emotional response that viscerally propels one feeling compassion into action on behalf of others."[1] The compassion that Jesus feels for the crowd is more than a casual and gentle sentiment that eventually passes with time. Drawing again on the Hebrew prophetic tradition, especially that of Ezekiel 34, Mark explains that Jesus had compassion on the crowd [here referring to the verb's use in Mark 6] because they were like a sheep without a shepherd. Such pastoral and emotive language may tempt modern readers to miss the stark religio-political intent in Mark's Greek. In Ezekiel 34, the prophet tells a parable that challenges a system in which the ruling class acts more like wolves than shepherds. By having "compassion" on the crowd, who are like sheep without a shepherd, Jesus addresses more than a personal and spiritual dilemma. He condemns social and religious practices that contribute to the misery of those in the greatest need.

Mark presses his readers to see the compassion of Jesus, not merely as a matter of temperament, but also as a discipleship orientation. Disciples of Jesus are called to break down all barriers—religious, social, economic, political—between human need and God's liberating mercy.[2]

The compassion of Jesus is no sentimental pity for this poor man. His compassion compels Jesus to reach across the boundary of disease to touch an untouchable, violating Jewish law (see Lev. 13 and 14), and in the process to make himself an untouchable, ritually unclean. Lest the reader miss the issue at hand, Mark repeats the theme verb *katharizein* three times in this story, and once in its nominal form, *tou katharismou*. In a perilous act of solidarity, instead of confirming the man's exclusion by shunning him, Jesus reaches out and symbolically draws him in. He shatters the traditional boundaries of purity and in the process rewrites the book on the nature of God's beloved community.

Mark uses his favorite word *euthys* again in this pericope to describe the immediate consequence of

---

[1]Fred Lyon, "*Splanchnizomai* and the Correspondence between Compassion and the Coming Reign of God" (doctoral study paper, Rehoboth Project Office), quoted in Brian K. Blount and Gary W. Charles, *Preaching Mark in Two Voices* (Louisville, KY: Westminster John Knox Press, 2003), 101–2.
[2]Brian K. Blount and Gary W. Charles, *Preaching Mark in Two Voices*, 102.

## Homiletical Perspective

Sure, there would be more to explain and stories to add from our own day, but it is a rather clear-cut approach to the text. Period.

But for those who have studied the story closely, there are so many questions. And as Fred Craddock observed back in the early 1970s, sometimes the questions we wrestle with in the study ought to be carried into the pulpit.[1] Among the many significant questions we might ask, let us explore three key ones.

For starters, what should we make of the fact that this represents the third healing story in Mark's Gospel? Only forty-five verses into chapter 1 and already readers have encountered three accounts of healing. And what do we make of the differences among these accounts? The first occurs in the synagogue when a man with an evil spirit cries out (1:21–28). No petition on the man's part, no evidence of faith involved. The second healing occurs in the home of Simon, whose mother-in-law has a fever (1:29–39). Others approach Jesus on her behalf (1:30). No further details are supplied. She is restored. The third healing story, here in verses 40–45, has radical differences from the first two.

Consider that the man has leprosy, making him unclean according to Levitical law (Lev. 13–14). He seeks out Jesus, "begging" and "kneeling" (v. 40). He evidences a degree of faith, "If you choose, you can make me clean" (v. 40). What do we do with these differences? Depending on whether we have been preaching from Mark in previous weeks and whether we have addressed healing in general the past few Sundays, here might be a place to say something by way of contrast/comparison using all three stories. There are certainly enough TV preachers willing to express varied views of healing. Surely we preachers should not ignore the subject in light of its overexposure elsewhere.

A second question, more controversial, relates to a textual variant. Instead of Jesus being "moved with pity" (v. 41), some manuscripts read "moved with anger." Arguing that the so-called harder reading is usually preferred, and noting the stern warning Jesus issues in verse 43, some prefer the latter translation. Questions most definitely arise in the light of this possibility: Is Jesus angry with the man? With being interrupted once again? Angry with the disease itself, which separates people from society? Angry with the interpretation of the law that requires a statement of cleanness?

---

[1]Fred B. Craddock, *As One without Authority* (Nashville: Abingdon, 1971), 162.

# Mark 1:40-45

## Theological Perspective

Because they look for him too much? Because he wants to visit the people? No! Because he has become himself impure. He has touched the leper. He is polluted, he is an unclean man, according to the sacral vision of priests and scribes. There has been a reversal of religious conditions: the leper is clean; Jesus is unclean. Jesus seems to be thrown into a warp zone, with the only religious choice of isolation. Jesus doesn't go to people, but people come to Jesus. The social order is disrupted, and the people challenge the social and spatial order. Jesus has begun a process of new social relationships. The disciples still don't understand, but the leper understands perfectly; so did Simon's mother-in-law (1:31), and the Syrophoenician woman will also understand (7:24–30).

In disobeying Jesus' command, the leper has obeyed the truth and thus opens a way of hope in the process of oppression of our world. To Mark, Jesus' challenge consists of forming a new human group (church) beginning with the outcasts (lepers, widows, the impure), thus overcoming the exclusion system that reigned in the religious atmosphere of the time. Jesus' radical invitation to the kingdom of God invades all social order and changes the spatial configuration that the order demands. Perhaps Jesus rediscovers his own ministry as his power breaks and reconstitutes relationships in all human spaces—from the religious synagogue to the very public space outside of the familiar community boundaries. In our story, the leper has become a messianic preacher. As a result of Jesus' radical invitation to the kingdom, and the manifestation of his disruptive, but liberative power, the leper is the first of the evangelists, that is to say, the first of those who devote their lives to the service of the new liberating action of Jesus. This is truly the result of the power of the kingdom overwhelming all human space, and the unique development of the people's participation in this new era of good news from God.

OFELIA ORTEGA

## Pastoral Perspective

think of was "unclean." Jon comments, "It was bad enough to know he was ill, but quite another to feel the social ostracism he might suffer, not only from people who didn't understand his illness, but also from his friends who he believed would now look down on him."[4]

Historian and professor of religion at Florida State University Amanda Porterfield has written a comprehensive history and theological analysis of "faith healing." No writer I know has summarized better the ancient sources and the contemporary challenge that this perplexing phenomenon continues to present to thinking people.

> Contributing both to the development of modern science and to the emergence of a modern sense of self, Christian healing has exerted enormous influence in human history and affected the behavior and thinking of billions of people. The linkage between suffering and sin prompts Christians to action, both to combat evil and seek forgiveness of sin within themselves, and to press for change in other people and in the world around them. In the modern era the advent of science and scientific technologies increases the power of Christians to fight against people and forces they perceive to be evil. It also opens new opportunities to Christians for relieving suffering in the world and for understanding its material causes, giving people a sense of being at home in the universe, with the assurance that human suffering matters.[5]

Healing stories become healing ministries, and the pastoral and congregational challenge is to discover the liberating action that comes out of healing. The cleaned leper could not hold himself—though Jesus instructed him, "See that you say nothing to anyone"—and became a witness for the healing power of God, "But he went out and began to proclaim it freely, and to spread the word, . . . and people came to him from every quarter." Perhaps people will come seeking to be healed and restored by God's love and mercy.

P. C. ENNISS

---

4 Jon Walton, ibid.
5 Amanda Porterfield, *Healing in the History of Christianity* (New York: Oxford University Press, 2005), 185.

## Exegetical Perspective

Jesus touching the diseased man. Since Mark has already told the reader that the Son of God is afoot in the person of Jesus (1:1), he puts little focus on the miracle of healing in this story. The question that this story anticipates is, by whose authority does Jesus act? (2:10), a question that is never a question for the narrator (and by implication, the reader), but one that will fuel Mark's Gospel until the end.

Upon healing the leper, Mark describes Jesus not as jumping for joy at the leper's new situation, but as being *angry* (*orgistheis*, 1:41; NRSV: "pity"). Jesus literally "snorting with indignation" (*embrimēsamenos*) sends the man *back* to the priests. In *Binding the Strong Man*, Ched Myers explains the source of Jesus' rage:

> They [Jesus' instructions that the leper go back to the priests and undergo ritual cleansing] only make sense if the man had *already been to the priests,* who for some reason had rejected his petition. Deciding to make an issue out of it, Jesus sternly gives the leper these orders:
>
> > See that you say nothing to anyone! Rather, go back and show yourself to the priest and make the offering prescribed by Moses for your cleansing as a witness against them [1:44].
>
> The cleansed leper's task is not to publicize a miracle but to help confront an ideological system: . . . He is to make the offering for the purpose of "witnessing against them" (*eis marturion autois*). This is a technical phrase in the Gospel for testimony before hostile audiences (6:11; 13:9).[3]

Told to be silent, the newly healed man cannot comply. This theme will continue until its ultimate irony at the close of Mark's Gospel, when in 16:8, the women are charged to speak and they fall mute. As chapter 1 closes, Jesus, now himself ritually unclean, has sent the cleansed leper "back" to the priests not as any nice, obedient Jewish boy would do, but as a sign of holy defiance. He sends the healed man *back* to demonstrate that cleanliness now happens not by adhering to any codes or laws, but by being in touch with Jesus, who is now ritually unclean but who has authority to make even a leper clean.

The game is on!

GARY W. CHARLES

## Homiletical Perspective

The final question relates to that mind-boggling piece of instruction Jesus gives the man, as well as others in Mark's Gospel: the so-called "messianic secret," which can be summed up in the phrase, Don't tell! At a variety of points in Mark's Gospel, just when we think Jesus would be encouraging people to declare his good works, instead he enjoins them to keep quiet. At the very heart of Christianity, there has always been a missionary impulse, a desire to tell others about the good news. Why does Jesus indicate otherwise? Why did the man not keep Jesus' request to keep silent? Was it God's plan to let Jesus be known? Even in Mark's Gospel, the women who go to the tomb and learn of Jesus' resurrection are told to tell his disciples, even if what they do instead is tell no one for fear (16:7–8). So while Mark ends with a commission to tell, given to followers who don't tell (what might be called "the great omission"), the Gospel begins with a leper who is warned not to tell but does. That should provide enough questions to last a lifetime. Why would he forbid the man from telling? is one obvious choice, but there are alternative questions as well. For instance, is it a good thing Jesus can no longer show himself openly? What about the possibility that while healing is good, making a show of it is not?[2] What does that say to some of today's churches? The messianic secret offers lots of sermon possibilities.

But as anyone who has studied this dilemma and others in Mark will tell you, there are no easy answers. Inductive styles of preaching usually treat questions more as rhetorical devices than open-ended queries. Following Mark's lead, we might envision this week's sermon as an opportunity for asking more honest questions, even ones for which we do not have the answers.

MIKE GRAVES

---

[3]Ched Myers, *Binding the Strong Man: A Political Reading of Mark's Story of Jesus* (Maryknoll, NY: Orbis, 1988), 153.

[2]See Lamar Williamson Jr., *Mark,* Interpretation Series (Louisville, KY: John Knox Press, 1983).

# Isaiah 43:18-25

<sup>18</sup>Do not remember the former things,
  or consider the things of old.
<sup>19</sup>I am about to do a new thing;
  now it springs forth, do you not perceive it?
  I will make a way in the wilderness
  and rivers in the desert.
<sup>20</sup>The wild animals will honor me,
  the jackals and the ostriches;
  for I give water in the wilderness,
  rivers in the desert,
  to give drink to my chosen people,
<sup>21</sup>  the people whom I formed for myself
  so that they might declare my praise.

## Theological Perspective

This text is part of the book of Isaiah (chaps. 40–55) that is referred to as Deutero-Isaiah or Second Isaiah. Second Isaiah is addressed to a community of exiles in Babylon during the sixth century BCE. This text invites us to consider the nature of God and God's purposes for an exilic community and the role of memory in such a community. Two questions in particular are the focus of this theological reflection: (1) Who is the God of exile? (2) How does exile impact a community's self-understanding, and what is required of an exilic community? Answers to these questions will make sense only when presented in light of the doctrine of God (the character and actions of God) and the understanding of election (the idea that God has chosen a particular people as God's own) found within this passage and the context of Second Isaiah overall.

*Who is the God of Exile?* There are three intertwined themes that earmark the nature and activity of God in Second Isaiah and in these particular verses: God is compassionate, just, and forgiving. The opening oracle of Second Isaiah, 40:1–11, begins by proclaiming the compassion of God; God speaks thus: "Comfort, O comfort my people." This theme of God's compassion is reframed in the opening words of this passage: "Do not remember the former

## Pastoral Perspective

This text invites the community to see beyond the obvious; to see what God creates anew. New, refreshing experiences of faith are the reason for a community to praise God. Faith is restored as we see differently. The world is never as we perceive it: God's creative power, always active in the world, becomes a source of hope: "I will make a way in the wilderness and rivers in the desert" (v. 19b). This verse invites a foretaste of the fruits of "something new," something beyond the obvious, something beyond what we have been programmed to see.

Two religious experiences come to my mind. First, some Buddhist schools teach their followers to trust goodness despite the experiences of violence and oppression. This teaching seems to be similar to the Judeo-Christian eschatology grounded in God's power to destroy evil and restore creation. Buddhists are trained, through meditation and disciplined study, to see and name the cosmic progression of goodness in a suffering world. It is a training of the imagination interplaying with daily life behavior. This way of seeing demands a different way of being in the world. Correct religious perception returns the devotee to the right path toward liberation, toward nirvana.

Second, many mainline religious groups lament their decline in membership and power. In spite of methods and strategies to revitalize old, established

²²Yet you did not call upon me, O Jacob;
    but you have been weary of me, O Israel!
²³You have not brought me your sheep for burnt offerings,
    or honored me with your sacrifices.
I have not burdened you with offerings,
    or wearied you with frankincense.
²⁴You have not bought me sweet cane with money,
    or satisfied me with the fat of your sacrifices.
But you have burdened me with your sins;
    you have wearied me with your iniquities.

²⁵I, I am He
    who blots out your transgressions for my own sake,
    and I will not remember your sins.

## Exegetical Perspective

The lectionary reading for today begins abruptly: "Do not remember the former things, or consider the things of old" (43:18). Starting here, a reader might think that the prophet is calling upon the community to lay aside painful memories of sin or failure. But in context, the reference is to Isaiah 43:16–17, a poetic description of the Lord's miraculous deliverance at the Red Sea! Why would the prophet call for his community to forget such a joyous event?

Then again, our most joyous memories may also be our most painful ones. The recollection of lost loved ones can bring fresh loneliness and grief. The memory of past success, contrasted with present failure, can drive us to despair. The point, for the prophet, is that the community must not cling to its past, either in resignation or in nostalgia, but must instead turn toward God's future. The Lord is "about to do a new thing" (43:19).

The anonymous prophet of Isaiah 40–55, commonly called Second Isaiah, announces God's "new thing" to a people in Babylon, exiled far from home (45:13), while Jerusalem and the temple lie in ruins (44:26–28). But the prophet declares their time of suffering and isolation to be nearly over. Soon the exiles would return home (43:1–15); soon Jerusalem and the temple would be restored (44:26–28). In

## Homiletical Perspective

"Do not remember the former things," the prophet tells the people who are being held in captivity in Babylon, "or consider the things of old. I am about to do a new thing" (43:18–19a). In this verse we have the first of the two themes around which the preacher this Sunday can form a sermon.

The "former things" were the hidden operations of the Creator of Israel in bringing the people from captivity in Egypt to freedom. Scholars date the exodus to roughly the thirteenth century BCE. This was a God of revolution, who inspired an oppressed people to break away from oppression and make their long and hazardous journey to the promised land. The liberation and the journey were Israel's national epic and absolutely central to its faith.

The first exodus belonged to the distant past. Now the Israelites are captives again. Babylon is Egypt recapitulated. But even this present time, if only the people will learn, the Holy One will prepare a way in the wilderness and "make straight in the desert a highway" (40:3). There will be another break from oppression, another long journey home. The task before Israel now is to turn to a new future. This journey will be no less arduous than the first. Once again they will endure heat, desert dangers, hunger, and thirst. But the Creator of Israel will make a way for them through another wilderness and across other rivers.

# Isaiah 43:18-25

## Theological Perspective

things, or consider the things of old; . . . I will make a way in the wilderness and rivers in the desert" (vv. 18; 19b). Here the God of exile acknowledges that the people have much to remember that is painful, and in the midst of their current exilic pain God promises another exodus.

This promise of another exodus does not, however, overlook the failures of the people. In verses 22 through 24, God chastises the people for their failure to worship properly: "You have not brought me your sheep for burnt offerings, or honored me with your sacrifices" (v. 23). The people languish in exile because God's justice requires that the people recognize God's sovereignty; they must be reminded that their role in human history is one that God has chosen for them—"for I give water in the wilderness, rivers in the desert, to give drink to my chosen people, the people whom I formed for myself so that they might declare my praise" (vv. 20b–21). This text thus reflects an emphasis throughout Second Isaiah upon the redemptive role of Israel in God's plan for the salvation of all creation (cf. Isa. 48:1–22).

The third theme of who God is and what God does now comes to the fore: God is forgiving. God's compassion and justice culminate in God's forgiveness. "I, I am He who blots out your transgressions for my own sake, and I will not remember your sins" (v. 25). As this verse makes clear, it is God's nature to be forgiving, and Israel does not do anything to provoke or deserve such divine forgiveness. Equally important, perhaps, is this lesson for people of God: God's discipline (such as the exile in Babylon) is not a sign of God's abandonment. In sum, the God of exile is the same God who liberated the people from bondage in the past.

*How Does Exile Impact a Community's Self-Understanding?* The community exiled in Babylon is described by biblical scholars as a group of upper- and middle-class members of Judean society. Given their social status before exile, an immediate impact on their self-understanding is a newfound diminished social status, or even a sense of powerlessness. Although there may be resistance to their captor's way of life among the Babylonian exiles, their resistance is conflicted. The exilic community wants to return to their homeland and status, but they must survive in the present. As survival becomes a key characteristic of the exilic community's self-understanding, the community in effect loses their identity as they forget the God who liberated them. Unlike God's admonition not to remember the

## Pastoral Perspective

communities, the common result falls short of the institutional expectations to bring again to life the established patterns and practices that have shaped religious communities for a number of generations. Yet these same mainline groups rarely see the vitality of *their* religious traditions in different social and human locations and embodiments. The traditions have not vanished or gone to oblivion; they are incarnated in communities we rarely recognize as legitimate bearers of our faith and traditions. Recovery groups, support groups, and social action coalitions often embody much of the gospel without doing so explicitly. We are blindsided by our own despair and our inability to see anew God's gracious activity in the world and very, very close to us.

Congregations have a natural tendency not to see what is new, not to see what God is doing anew. The energy, curiosity, unfiltered and freely asked questions of children and youth are located at the margins of our worship and decision-making processes. The "itchy" presence of strangers and aliens—some who became a source of blessing for us in our last short-term mission trip—disrupts our organized and structured ways of seeing and understanding our world. Our rituals and spatial configurations are so rigid that we rarely discover the faith afresh, renewed. Faith—and as a regrettable byproduct, faith communities—become more about stability, about that which is familiar, common and certain.

God invites the community to see anew God's creation and redemption. However, this invitation is not about "newness" for the sake of keeping things rolling, or some sort of ministerial programming for entertainment and growth. Pastorally, it is an invitation to see anew what is in our communities that points to the reconciling and life-giving action of God. The text invites a visual imagination: "The wild animals will honor me, the jackals and the ostriches; for I give water in the wilderness, rivers in the desert, to give drink to my chosen people . . . whom I formed for myself so that they might declare my praise" (vv. 20–21). To have a visual imagination of God's work is to see the life of God where there is death; not to be entertained, amused, or temporarily happy. The former is redeeming eschatological vision; the latter is a deceiving immediate vision.

With this in mind, verse 18 makes sense: "Do not remember the former things, or consider the things of old." Perhaps many, shaped by our modern mind-set, might look at this verse as contempt toward history, a demand to forget the past in order to see what is new. Old and new are polarized, and the

Second Isaiah this restoration is described as a new exodus, far surpassing the first exodus from Egypt. While in the first exodus God guided Israel through the trackless waste, in this new exodus God "will make a way in the wilderness" (43:19), "a highway for our God" (40:3–4). The wilderness itself, with all its dangers, will be transformed into a garden (55:13). The threatening beasts of the wild places will join Israel's procession of praise and celebration (43:20). In this new exodus the Lord will provide "rivers in the desert, to give drink to my chosen people" (43:19–20). God's election of Israel, demonstrated, as in the first exodus, by deliverance out of bondage, is given a particular focus in Isaiah 43:21: Israel is "the people whom I formed for myself so that they might declare my praise." As the Westminster Catechism has it, our "chief end" is "to glorify God and to enjoy [God] forever." In worship God's people find their purpose and become most fully themselves.

However, the community is unmoved by Second Isaiah's promises of imminent deliverance. Though they are a people formed to give praise to God, they no longer seek the Lord at all (43:22). The Hebrew verb translated "weary" in Isaiah 43:22–24 appears more often in Second Isaiah than anywhere else in the Hebrew Scripture (see 40:28–31; 47:12–15; 49:4). The exilic community is worn out; they don't have the energy to hope or to believe anymore. The chiding references to missed sacrifices in Isaiah 43:23–24 are intended to be ironic. True, no sacrifices have been offered—but none could be, with the people in exile and the temple in ruins! Indeed, the Lord declares, "I have not burdened you with offerings, or wearied you with frankincense" (43:23). It would be a mistake to read this statement as a rejection of the temple or its liturgy, particularly after the affirmation of worship in Isaiah 43:21. Rather, these words are permissive: under the present circumstances, the Lord does not require offerings (cf. Ps. 51:15–19).

Still, the Lord says, while sacrifices have not been (and for now, need not be) offered, "you have burdened me with your sins; you have wearied me with your iniquities" (43:24). As the NRSV makes clear, the same verbs appear here and in Isaiah 43:23. Though the loss of the temple excuses the exiles from offering sacrifices, the human needs addressed by the sacrificial liturgy still remain—in particular, the need for propitiation. Perhaps the exiles are weary of God and no longer call upon or praise the Lord because they fear that God is weary of them

Every human story starts ultimately with God. And on this Sunday the text before the preacher affords the opportunity of affirming that the life of this nation (indeed of all nations) is a working out in political ways of what it perceives as its ultimate values. This then can be the theme for the preacher: to connect the mystery of the God, the Holy One, with the nation's future. This is not a July 4 occasion, not a day to make especial claims about America's past, its exceptional position, its sense of having a providential mission from God, or its conviction that it is destined to lead the way for humanity. It is a Sunday when the preacher can help direct the mind of the congregation to consider what another future might be for the nation out of the present struggles in which it is mired.

To this end, the preacher has the task of facing openly the question: Is there an active and purposeful love by which the whole created order came into being? Is there a Holy One who not only sustains this cosmic order, but also has a caring and involved relationship to a particular people? Is there a God who liberates from oppression?

It is not an easy time to speak about a God who is involved in history. The idea of supernatural intervention is problematic. It is one thing to point to the exodus or the Sinai experience as two of the mighty acts of God. Was the destruction of the firstborn in the land of Egypt (Exod. 11:5) also an act of God? C. H. Spurgeon of London expressed the hope in a sermon in 1859 that God "will again stretch forth his potent hand and his holy arm, and repeat those mighty acts he performed in ancient days." But the idea of God acting in history has become untenable in the centuries that produced the Holocaust, the tsunamis, and the bloodletting of the Middle East. If Jesus is the Messiah, a survivor of the Holocaust might ask a Christian, where are the signs of the messianic age?

Whatever they may feel about supernatural intervention, people in the Sunday congregation still have more than a hunch that every human story starts ultimately with God and that the life of their nation is a working out of what they perceive as ultimate values, values somehow related to God. If today's preacher steers away from divine acts in history, the better way may be to affirm that the whole created order indeed has its origin in the mystery of God's creation and that that order (at least on planet earth) is marked by life, loving-kindness, and community. These may not be God's direct creation, but they do provide a lens for

# Isaiah 43:18-25

## Theological Perspective

former things, so as not to become mired in the pain of the past and miss God's future, the exilic community's forgetting lulls them into seeking a place within Babylon. They do not worship appropriately their God, and perhaps they even begin to worship the captor's gods. The exilic community's self-understanding is one marked by yearning for a former way of life and self-preservation that is rooted in forgetfulness about the God who has delivered them in the past. Consequently, the exilic community's self-understanding is earmarked by a disavowal of God's presence among them and agency on their behalf both historically and presently.

*What is Required of an Exiled Community?* Seeking an answer to this question is the crux of what this text means for us in the church today. We in the church often have a self-understanding like that of the exiled community in Babylon. We fail to acknowledge the ways in which we disavow God's presence in our midst and God's agency on our behalf. We yearn for a former time when the church was the moral conscience of society and clergy were respected. We blame our exilic condition on the secularization of the world, rather than accept responsibility for the ways in which we make the church into a place acceptable to the world. One author describes this phenomenon as "the McDonaldization of the church."[1] The church whose self-understanding is like that of the exiled community in Babylon is a church that does not hear the voice of a compassionate, just, forgiving God; and such a church will therefore not be a place of compassion, justice, and forgiveness.

An exiled community, the exilic church, is thus required to break its complicity with self-affirming and self-serving practices of worship. This means remembering that the purpose of worship is to praise God, and praise of God happens most fully when we are not captive to traditional forms of worship simply because they are traditional, or distracted by contemporary forms of worship that may fill pews but not truly nourish souls.

MARCIA Y. RIGGS

[1] John Drane, *The McDonaldization of the Church: Consumer Culture and the Church's Future* (Macon, GA: Smyth & Helwys, 2001), 32. McDonaldization refers to the process by which the principles of the fast-food restaurant have come to dominate most sectors of society. An example of this process in the church is the giving of one's offering through direct bank drafts.

## Pastoral Perspective

modern human being is too well accustomed to progress and prosperity at the expense of history and tradition. Yet this is not necessarily true about the text. Jaroslav Pelikan, the late distinguished church historian, provides a liberating insight to the confused modern consciousness: "Traditionalism is the dead memory of the living; tradition is the living memory of the dead."

A living memory is eschatological: it generates continuity while discovering afresh God's creative actions. For instance, in the Christian tradition the Lord's communion breaks the immediate notions of time and space. In its multilayered celebration, Christians remember the Jewish Passover, the ministry, death, and resurrection of Jesus, the immediate restoring presence of the Holy Spirit, and the foretaste of the reign of God. There is a deep biblical and theological interplay—a freely configured sense of continuity with Scripture and different historical and theological perspectives—with a rediscovery of the gospel to be embodied today as a witness to God's future for creation. As religious leaders, do our ritual celebrations overwhelm our communities with this eschatological movement of time and space? Do our official and unofficial ritual celebrations dislocate our stoically glued—traditionalism—religious experience so as to discover God's fresh activity in the world?

Verses 23–24 name the absence of people's faithfulness despite God's fresh and renewing activity in the world. Is it because in the actions and celebrations in verses 22–24b that people discover God's renewed actions in the world, which threaten the accepted comfort of Israel? Why live in a constant expectation of "a new thing," when "how things are now" is fine? If we are to discover God's renewing action in creation through our religious celebrations, could we be undermining our own source of renewal by domesticating our celebrations? If in fact we domesticate our liberating rites—the religious space to rediscover God's renewal actions in the world—what results is burdening God with our sins, wearing God with our iniquities (vv. 24b).

Can our religious celebrations make us see God's renewing and fresh actions in the world? Whom would we need to include to see, hear, and touch God's renewing action in the world? What new words need to be uttered and what new gestures dramatized for our communities to experience God's new thing? What obstructs our perception, what blurs our vision?

CARLOS F. CARDOZA-ORLANDI

and does not hear. How can they believe the prophet's extraordinary good news about God's future when they know full well that they have burdened the Lord with their sins and iniquities? In the absence of sacrifice, altar, priest, and temple, can this burden be lifted?

The Lord's gracious response concludes today's lectionary reading: "I, I am He who blots out your transgressions for my own sake, and I will not remember your sins" (43:25). The God who calls upon Israel to no longer "remember the former things, or consider the things of old" (43:18) also stands ready to let the past go. In context, this verse opens God's lawsuit against the exiles, in which the justice of God's conduct (that is, the exile and the destruction of Jerusalem) is vindicated (43:25–28). God's forgiveness does not condone the community's conduct: they are held accountable for failing to heed the prophet's word (see also 42:18–25). Still, God's forgiveness does not depend upon Israel's worthiness or upon its penitential offerings. God promises forgiveness "for my own sake." We are forgiven, not because of who we are, but because of who God is. Our repentance is always a response to what God has done. God's word of acceptance and forgiveness comes first.

In today's Gospel reading (Mark 2:1–12), the forgiveness of sins in Jesus' ministry builds on the character of God as revealed in Second Isaiah. Like the Lord in Isaiah 43:25, Jesus acts out of his own identity and authority, not in response to any claim of worthiness. Jesus is able to forgive for the same reason he is able to heal: because of who he is (Mark 2:9–11). No wonder the startled onlookers at the healing of the paralytic exclaim, "We have never seen anything like this!" (Mark 2:12). Like Second Isaiah, Jesus announces a new beginning and an unexpected future. God's "new thing" eclipses all that has gone before and makes all things new.

STEVEN S. TUELL

interpreting the text and preparing the sermon. The sheer fecundity of the earth, the love that constantly finds new forms and is endlessly expansive, and the kind of bonding where the whole is always greater than its parts—to these at least the preacher can point as the ground mysteries out of which human history arises.

Here is the second task in getting the sermon on its way. The people of this nation, like Isaiah's people, are to hope, pray, and plan that they can come out of their present brokenness to a richer way of living and enjoying the fruits of creation and of their own labor and creativity, neither despoiling nor exploiting the environment. The preacher can help people ponder on what the good life, the blessing of God, can mean for the American people. Life first, then loving-kindness. What will it mean for these people also to be part of creating a society marked by human and political compassion? Finally, against the divisive forces that seem to be both pervasive and irresistible, the sermon can show how these people can bring about social structures that support the multiple forms of human community against all threats to divide these communities.

The one absolute condition for this blessing of freedom is repentance on the part of the nation. Repentance is the gospel call not only for individuals but also for nations. It is a personal and national ethic marked by a willingness to turn in another direction, to reorder both policies and patterns of living. So the preacher can show what it means for a nation like ours to *repent*. Repentance is an interior conversion that finds expression in social justice.

ROSS MACKENZIE

# Psalm 41

¹Happy are those who consider the poor;
  the LORD delivers them in the day of trouble.
²The LORD protects them and keeps them alive;
  they are called happy in the land.
  You do not give them up to the will of their enemies.
³The LORD sustains them on their sickbed;
  in their illness you heal all their infirmities.

⁴As for me, I said, "O LORD, be gracious to me;
  heal me, for I have sinned against you."
⁵My enemies wonder in malice
  when I will die, and my name perish.
⁶And when they come to see me, they utter empty words,
  while their hearts gather mischief;
  when they go out, they tell it abroad.

## Theological Perspective

*"Israel Is Not 'God-Intoxicated.'"* Old Testament theologian Walter Brueggemann points out that injustice drives Israel to tell of the Lord's restoring work.

> Israel is not "God-intoxicated." Israel is not excessively preoccupied with God. Rather, Israel's daily appetite is that the world should be equitable. This concern for Israel, however, is not a departure from its foundational religious concerns. Rather, Israel's faith is a radical reorientation of religion, for Israel knows from its hour of historical birth in the exodus that Yahweh has cared decisively for the public questions of justice long before Israel cared about them.[1]

*"Happy Are Those Who Consider the Poor" (v. 1).* This prayer of the psalmist connects the poor's claim for equity and justice with the religious spirit of those formed in the image of a beneficent and caring YHWH. Only those who consider the poor can be truly happy. It is not Israel's deliverance *from* the sorrow and plight of the poor that causes happiness, but rather the deliverance *of* the poor in their "day of trouble" (v. 1). Only this can be the cause of Israel's joy. There is no complex analysis here, no weighing

## Pastoral Perspective

Despite the unloveliness of the disheveled, the frequent ingratitude of the poor, the incorrigible circumstances of the lowly, the church will always be drawn to them (vv. 1–3). This is not because of our churning guilt or genteel discomfiture at their state, wanting to "fix" it. It is because we are but one step removed from being the lowly ourselves. More important, it is because our fate is tied up with theirs. Psalm 41 reminds us that we are all in "this" together, the gift of life, which God gives.

The psalmist does not idly speculate here. He testifies to personal reality. For after he affirms the connection between those mindful of the poor and the poor themselves (vv. 1–3), we learn of his own lowliness in a season of attack and distress in which he lives (vv. 4–10). The poverty of his own fear and abandonment has led him to remark at and extol those who stand by the rejected. Happiness, prosperity, and protection must surely be God's rewards for them, as he pronounces, foreshadowing Jesus' Beatitudes.

As we connect across our chasms in fortune, aside from the caprice of our estate in this world, we enter into a God-intended state of blessedness and favor. We can look to one another as the seasons of life shift and our fortunes with them, finding a steady center that buffers the extremes of individual

[1]Walter Brueggemann, *The Psalms and the Life of Faith*, ed. Patrick D. Miller (Minneapolis: Fortress Press, 1995), 61.

<sup>7</sup>All who hate me whisper together about me;
    they imagine the worst for me.

<sup>8</sup>They think that a deadly thing has fastened on me,
    that I will not rise again from where I lie.
<sup>9</sup>Even my bosom friend in whom I trusted,
    who ate of my bread, has lifted the heel against me.
<sup>10</sup>But you, O LORD, be gracious to me,
    and raise me up, that I may repay them.

<sup>11</sup>By this I know that you are pleased with me;
    because my enemy has not triumphed over me.
<sup>12</sup>But you have upheld me because of my integrity,
    and set me in your presence forever.

<sup>13</sup>Blessed be the LORD, the God of Israel,
    from everlasting to everlasting. Amen and Amen.

## Exegetical Perspective

*Assurance of God's Help to Those in Need.* Like many of the Psalms, Psalm 41 uses several literary genres to make its point. The combination of these genres testifies to the complex literary history of the psalm, but even more important, the mixed literary types reveal Israel's struggles to understand the theological point that the psalmist wants to make. In this case, the whole psalm affirms God's care for those in trouble, but the nature of God's grace and concern is not always easy to understand, and the psalm raises as many theological questions as it answers.

*God's Concern for the Poor and Weak (vv. 1–3).* The psalm begins by instructing Israel in a general theological principle. Those who are concerned for the poor or weak are happy, and it is the faith of the psalmist that God will deliver and preserve the lives of those who remember the poor, protecting them from their enemies (vv. 1–2). This general description of God's goodness toward those who care becomes more specific in verse 3. God will also sustain them when they are sick and will heal their illnesses.

The psalmist does not indicate the source of this faith that God will repay concern for the poor with divine care. Does the psalm open with the repetition of a general theological principle that the psalmist

## Homiletical Perspective

At the conclusion of a biblical exegesis class concerning how exegetes might finally fashion the fruit of their labors into a sermon, a young woman, almost certainly right out of the university, raised her hand for a question. She asked how the text should be preached differently if someone dying of cancer were present in worship. She was obviously eager for pastoral work, eager to be helpful to her parishioners, and her question was eager—and innocent. I answered that I assumed whenever the people of God gathered for worship and whenever I opened my mouth, there would be among us people living with cancer and other life-threatening illnesses or simply ravaged by life itself. "In the midst of life we are in death," begins *The Book of Common Prayer*'s intercessions at the funeral service, and continues: "to whom may we turn for comfort but to you, O Lord?"

The next time Psalm 41 rolls up on the reading roulette of the Common Lectionary is February 17, 2030, but no congregation can long postpone learning how to pray like this. The matters addressed by Psalm 41 are inevitably current and relentlessly relevant: sickness and the sense of being abandoned to mortality. This psalm, praying as it does for God's presence and healing, may be more helpful in dealing with such matters than the many healing stories of the Scriptures.

# Psalm 41

**Theological Perspective**

of cost or benefits for acting on behalf of the poor, but rather a simple proclamation of what must be done and the joy that comes with having done it. In the mind and heart of the psalmist the issue is clear and obvious; the poor are under YHWH's special protection and keep. Restoration to justice requires constant vigilance, but YHWH refuses to compromise and give the poor up to their enemies. No other need outweighs theirs. This is the heart of Israel's religion. No "God intoxication" here or spiritualization of God's presence. For the psalmist, YHWH's first presence is as redeemer and liberator. Act first to alleviate the needs and suffering of those whose faces Israel sees each day, and then and only then will their hearts be glad—not as their prime motivation for action, but as a welcome side effect, a benefit and grace, a "making well" of all who act on behalf of the poor. It is this restoration to justice that leads to joy and the psalmist's song.

*The Sin of the Psalmist.* In verses 4–7 the psalm turns from joy to lament and a cry for healing. The psalmist and the nation have sinned, and their lament can mean only that they have *not* considered and been gracious to the poor. In not imitating YHWH's concern, they have been both ungrateful and irreligious. And now in misery and irony the psalmist again cries out to YHWH to "be gracious to me" (v. 4). This unbreakable bond between justice and authentic piety leads the psalmist to a last resort—appealing to YHWH to use the now spiritually impoverished singer to show forth YHWH's goodness and power in the face of the psalmist's enemies. YHWH's power is YHWH's goodness, and YHWH's goodness is YHWH's concern, care, and compassion. So a new manifestation of YHWH's *good power* and *powerful goodness* will heal the psalmist and "repay" enemies (v. 10).

*No One Left but the Lord.* There is piety, pathos, and some pity, in the psalmist's cry (vv. 8–9). "If for no other reason, YHWH, heal me so that *our* enemies will not continue to gloat." Because the psalmist has not been concerned *even* for the poor, there is no community of support left—neither the poor nor the psalmist's former friends—and there is need for healing as restoration to a new communal life. Now YHWH, somewhat pitifully, is asked again to be gracious (vv. 10–12). This is not a prayer of a saint or someone we assume even to be very spiritually mature. This is a prayer of a sinner, a person in pain, one who is ready to try any port in a storm. This

**Pastoral Perspective**

circumstance. In this we experience that God does not abandon us, because God's own have shown up when it matters most, demonstrating spiritual solidarity through the kind of God-connectedness that makes a transforming impression upon people.

Tellingly, before describing sins against him in the form of hateful mistreatment and persecution by those who seek his demise, the psalmist confesses his own sinfulness before God (v. 4). We never go wrong in this instinct: knowing ourselves as sinners before examining the sins of others. Here we build a hedge against retribution and vengefulness that too often exceeds any initial offense. Here we mark the beginning in breaking the cycle of returning evil for evil. Awareness of our own sinfulness—leading with our confession despite how badly we have been wronged—is the fountainhead in living and showing forth forgiveness.

It is hard to imagine the hollowing desolation and deep betrayal that the psalmist describes in the attacks (vv. 5–9) unless one has experienced it. Many who know this haunting and heartbreaking brokenness in their relationships will find their way into our office. We must be prepared to hear their cry. If we have never deeply perceived the reality of evil in the world, distanced as we mostly are from terrorist attacks or city-killing hurricanes, we can start here. For the sheer maliciousness and the gratuitous destructiveness are essentially the same in nature as these vaster, more apocalyptic evils. And the numbers of those who have suffered this destructiveness are legion, at least for those of us with ears to hear.

We should consider the possibility that these attacks upon the speaker have perhaps originated from within the temple, from those who might generally be viewed as righteous. The holiness of our houses of worship is often a cover for cruel deeds of some who darken our doorways, allowing them to posture as solid citizens as they slay souls, sometimes for the sheer sport of it. These assaults—whether upon clergy or laypersons—are assiduous and unrelenting.

It should not be lost upon us that the psalmist speaks here (vv. 5–9) in a lament. We live in a world so full of complaint that it would be easy to confuse complaint and lament. Complaint is the rehashing of pain that lacks the reference point of a safe and strong place confidently to deposit our deepest struggles. Complaint is a blunt instrument, wielded indiscriminately and repeatedly in all directions because its transactions fail to elicit healing grace. It

already knew and that helped the psalmist to understand the meaning of a personal experience? Or is the reverse the case? Did the psalmist's own experience with suffering and divine healing lead to the generalizations that now begin the psalm? In either case, the theological point is clear. God responds graciously to those who share God's concern for the poor and the weak. When such concerned people are themselves weak and in need of protection and healing, God will supply what is needed, protecting them from enemies and healing illnesses.

*An Individual Petition and God's Response (vv. 4–12).* While the first section of the psalm makes a general affirmation, the second section is quite specific and personal. Using the common literary genre of the individual complaint, found frequently in this portion of the Psalter, the psalmist follows the usual two-part structure of such complaints. First, the writer describes in somewhat general terms an affliction, which is serious to the point of death, and asks God for relief (vv. 4–10). The psalmist is apparently ill and in danger of dying, and like many in the ancient and modern world, the sufferer confesses that this condition is due to personal sin against God (v. 4). Along with physical torment have come threats from enemies, who wish for the psalmist's death (vv. 5–8). Even the sufferer's friends have now become hostile (v. 9), and the psalmist is convinced that only God can supply healing and relief. In these verses the description of suffering remains vague, thus allowing the reader to identify easily with the sufferer.

The second part of the individual complaint follows the normal pattern for such psalms. Without providing an explanation for the shift of mood, the psalmist suddenly ends the complaint and expresses an absolute faith that God will react favorably to the prayer (vv. 11–12). The psalmist's very survival is understood as evidence that God has vanquished the enemies and sustained the sufferer. This divine response is attributed to the psalmist's integrity (v. 12), although, as in the case of the complaint, details are not supplied. Readers of the Psalms have often been puzzled by this sudden shift from complaint to affirmation, and scholars have suggested that when psalms of this sort were used in worship, a priest would speak a word of pardon that motivated the faithful response of the worshiper. Even if this explanation is correct, it has left no trace in the present form of the psalm. As the psalm now stands,

The psalmist turns to the Lord for comfort. No other comfort is imagined; no other help appears promising. The structure of the psalm in three movements might provide a dynamic movement for the sermon.

The psalmist begins with a confession of faith: God does not give up on the poor (NRSV), the weak (NIV), the wretched (JPS), the helpless (NEB), those who have no helper but God. That is what the psalmist has come to know by singing the first forty psalms in the worship of the people of God. Here, at the end of the first book of the psalms, the confession of faith of 41:1–3 echoes the Psalter's beginning: "Happy are those . . . [whose] delight is in the law of the LORD" (Ps. 1:1–2). From the law, the Torah, the psalmist has come to recognize God's solidarity with the suffering and the concomitant happiness of those in the human community who do not "pass by on the other side" (Luke 10:31–32) to avoid the helpless. The broad announcement of God's faithfulness to the helpless comes to a sharp focus in verse 3 with the image of a "sickbed": this person cannot rise, is confined to bed, is weak and helpless. The NEB imagines the required nursing care: God "nurses him on his sick-bed [and] . . . turns his bed when he is ill." Every pastor has stood and prayed alongside that bed; every person shudders at the thought of being confined to that bed of helplessness. The psalmist confesses God is faithful even there, even then.

This confession of faith is neither a liturgical nicety nor abstract theologizing, but a careful preparing of a foundation from which the psalmist may pray, "O LORD, be gracious to me" ("O LORD, have mercy on me" in NIV and JPS). The psalmist began with a general affirmation that "The LORD delivers them in the day of trouble," but verse 4 reveals the psalmist is the one in trouble who calls out for deliverance, protection, sustenance, and healing, but perhaps most of all, not to be given up or abandoned. The psalmist has been abandoned by enemy and friend alike: they are not the happy ones who "consider the poor"; they are unblessed, keeping their distance from human suffering and insulating themselves from the vulnerable. The circumstances of abandonment in the psalm may seem overdramatic and stylized, but people experiencing serious illness readily resonate with the awful sense of aloneness. Healthy people who take health for granted and go where they please can feel like a taunt to those who cannot leave a sickbed. Friends and neighbors carrying on conversation about a

# Psalm 41

## Theological Perspective

bargaining with God, so common in the psalms and the entire Hebrew Bible, has the air of the comedic amid the tragic. But that is precisely the point. The psalmist prays for a return to goodness—however flawed—not perfection. The axiom of "not letting the perfect be an enemy of the good" applies throughout the Psalms.

*A Remaining Question.* It is impossible to escape the connection of authentic religion and moral action that courses throughout the Psalms. The temptation to "God-intoxication" in a self-serving and "other disregarding" manner is ubiquitous, especially in so-called successfully religious societies. The "God-intoxicated" sermon that *separates* being and doing, faith and works, abounds. The Psalms remind us that while we can *distinguish* the work of YHWH and our own efforts, we ought never to *separate* them. Certainly our good works, especially in the faces of those who claim them by covenant and right, do not earn anything for us. Rather, such works enflesh, incarnate, make concrete and real the goodness that God desires and we seek.

Finally, after Psalm 41 an important theological and ethical question remains. Who do we love when we love our neighbor—when we love the poor? Do we love God *in* our neighbor, or do we love our neighbor, and *through* our neighbor, *also* love God? This question is raised by Jacques Pohier with the claim that "God does not want to be everything for love."[2] Psalm 41 does not give us a clear answer to this question, but like the Psalms in general, it brings us to the heart of the matter, which is always a matter of the heart. And with all of the psalmist's and our own indirections, circumlocutions, and self-serving prayers—all too human, to be sure—we know where the answer lies and what, *for the sake of love*, YHWH desires.

JOSEPH MONTI

## Pastoral Perspective

is the trackless wandering through pain, time and again, without the awareness of what God has done to transform and temporize it, vindicating the sufferer. It emanates from taxicabs and checkout lines and office watercoolers. Unchecked, it is the voice of despair.

Lament is different. Like complaint, lament articulates suffering that must not be buried and denied. But with lament, the voice of suffering has both direction and destination, for lament addresses not only fellow creatures with like experience, who are similarly powerless to make matters right. Lament is finally intended for the ears of our personal Creator and Redeemer, who *is* in a position to vindicate and restore across time. In the act of lamentation, the dread cycle of repetition to the point of endless reliving is broken by the ministrations of a higher reconciliation of heaven and earth. Where complaint leads to despair, lament can move us from the stuck places where we languish within our grief.

And once human grief is satisfactorily addressed, the need to respond to evil in kind with more evil is removed, as the pain of personal injustice gets absorbed into this secure and just center of our personally aware, yet transhistorical God. It means everything in the world that this God stands beyond and over the stage of human actions, adjudicating every life against a backdrop where lies and character assassination have no currency. It is the final and definitive court of appeal.

The note of gratitude is the closing echo of Psalm 41 (vv. 11–13). Gratitude is our most basic religious impulse, for the possibility of a living relationship with God apart from a foundation of thankfulness for God's blessings, even in the midst of our duress, is null and void. Here gratitude takes the form of knowledge that the psalmist's enemies cannot overcome him and that YHWH has inexhaustible goodwill toward him. The flooding and happy light of his living and breathing communion with God—intact and untouched by the deprecations of his enemies—outshines dark corners of existence where he has been forced to do so much living. It allows him to live upon another plane of existence, even as those who seek his demise imagine they have him trapped. This light frees him to celebrate the triumph of God.

DALE ROSENBERGER

---

[2]Jacques Pohier, *God in Fragments*, trans. John Bowden (New York: Seabury, 1986), 266.

## Exegetical Perspective

the shift in mood is unmotivated and is simply an expression of faith that God has acted or will act favorably because of the integrity of the petitioner. The psalmist's joy leads to the final pronouncement of a blessing on God, a blessing that provides an appropriate ending, both for the psalm and for the entire first section of the Psalter (v. 13).

Although the two main sections of the psalm appear to be different in form and intention, the general introductory section now puts the psalmist's complaint in a somewhat different light. The claim of verses 1–3 that God responds favorably to those who are concerned with the suffering of the poor gives specific content to the general reference to "integrity" in verse 12. The complaining psalmist of verses 4–10 can be assured of God's gracious response in verses 11–12 because by implication the psalmist is one concerned for the poor. The generality of the complaint and the unmotivated expression of faith in God's favorable response have been grounded in the specific theological stance of the introduction. In the process of putting the two parts of the psalm together, the psalmist has provided a powerful theological model for later generations. No longer does the emphasis of the psalm fall on personal sin as a cause for suffering, and no longer does the worshiper need to worry about whether or not God will respond positively to a sufferer's complaint. Thanks to the introductory verses, the worshiper knows from the beginning that those who care for the weak will receive God's care and healing when in need. Worshipers are assured that their own interests and responses are mirrored by those of God. Human concern for the weak is a reflection of God's own concern for the weak. As is often the case in the OT, the psalmist understands appropriate religious behavior to be modeled on God's own behavior toward Israel and the world as a whole. By observing how God has acted, the faithful can learn behavior that will ease their way through an uncertain world.

ROBERT R. WILSON

## Homiletical Perspective

patient's condition can seem an affront, and many sufferers disguise illness and keep hospitalizations secret lest others talk about them. Well-intentioned friends may come to visit, but the look of horror on their faces as they recognize the ravages of sickness only magnifies the distance. The prayer that God might "raise me up, that I may repay them" (v. 10) does not necessarily mean repay in kind, but rather borrows a form of shalom, peace, asking to be restored to the peace of valued relationships now sundered by sickness. The prayer that begins by asking for God to be gracious and heal concludes by asking for God to be gracious and restore relationships.

Unlike Gospel stories in which a healing is accomplished to general amazement (Matt. 9:32–34; Mark 1:21–28; 2:1–12), no healing is announced directly, but clearly in verse 11 something has changed: "By this I know that you are pleased with me," or you are "delighted with me," echoing the delight in the Torah from Psalm 1:2. The psalm moves from abandonment to delight, but what has happened between verse 10 and verse 11? How long is the interval between the two? A long feverish week with the flu? Eight weeks of chemotherapy? A series of seven surgeries over sixteen months to repair a broken body? We are not told, but the psalmist is utterly insistent: the Lord has accomplished something that changes everything, and the psalmist has been blessed far beyond what the prayer asked. Here some scholars imagine a priest announcing forgiveness or restoration or blessing, which is how we receive God's Word: from human lips speaking God's blessing. The psalmist hoped for deliverance "in the day of trouble" and prayed for healing and restoration, but what the psalmist has found is nothing less than God's good pleasure and a place before the *face* of the Lord *forever*. The psalm ends affirming what the Psalter has been teaching: "The LORD is righteous . . . the upright shall behold his face" (Ps. 11:7); "As for me, I shall behold your face in righteousness" (Ps. 17:15); "Your face, LORD, do I seek. Do not hide your face from me" (Ps. 27:8–9).

PATRICK J. WILLSON

# 2 Corinthians 1:18-22

<sup>18</sup>As surely as God is faithful, our word to you has not been "Yes and No." <sup>19</sup>For the Son of God, Jesus Christ, whom we proclaimed among you, Silvanus and Timothy and I, was not "Yes and No"; but in him it is always "Yes." <sup>20</sup>For in him every one of God's promises is a "Yes." For this reason it is through him that we say the "Amen," to the glory of God. <sup>21</sup>But it is God who establishes us with you in Christ and has anointed us, <sup>22</sup>by putting his seal on us and giving us his Spirit in our hearts as a first installment.

## Theological Perspective

According to some New Testament scholars, Paul wrote seven times to his beloved Corinthian church, which he visited twice after founding the house church during an eighteen-month stay around 49–50 CE. By the time Paul wrote the five letters that some scholars think have been edited together to comprise 2 Corinthians, Jewish Christian "superapostles" appeared bearing letters of recommendation from their prior ministries (2 Cor. 3:1). With the power of the Spirit, running from Moses through Jesus, their words and deeds brimmed with amazing events, corroborating their call (cf. 12:1–12).

Paul wrote the Corinthians to hold their course, but to no avail. He visited them, but matters worsened as the superapostles, especially one among them, publicly humiliated Paul. Paul left and wrote again, defending himself in the so-called "tearful letter" (chaps. 10–13), which was sent with Titus. On hearing from Titus that the Corinthian situation was better (7:5–16), Paul then wrote again, happy in the move towards reconciliation. "Our word to you," wrote Paul, "has not been 'Yes and No.' For the Son of God, Jesus Christ, whom we proclaimed among you . . . was not 'Yes and No,' but in him it is always 'Yes'" (1:18–19).

How extraordinary! If our very words and deeds are the gospel of Jesus Christ (cf. 1 Cor. 2:2), we can

## Pastoral Perspective

So God's word in Christ is always "Yes"? Really? Does that ring true to your life and the lives of those around you?

That God's word in Christ is always "Yes" sounds particularly strange coming from Paul, since Paul could get off a good rousing "No" at the drop of a hat. Jesus himself often spoke harshly to people, particularly highly religious people, and he had lots of negative things to say about the way people use money and power and, of course, the way people use other people. One of the most thrilling aspects of the life of Jesus is the way he said "No" to demonic forces and "No" to being manipulated, not to mention the truth that it is hard to see how his or anybody else's Yes could mean anything without the juxtaposition of a strong, solid No every once in a while.

Down through the centuries, Christians have sometimes lost the Yes of Jesus. There is a long and proud history of negativism in the church because saying no to people offers the leader so much more power and control than saying yes. In some faith communities, to hear the Yes of Christ is rare, and so a lot of the people who sit in congregations may be surprised to hear about this Yes-saying Christ. The belief system that they have learned is less about Yes and more about No, and God is often imprinted on their souls very early in life as a supersized version of

## Exegetical Perspective

Nobody needed to teach the apostle Paul about practical theology, or pastoral theology, either. Many of his most powerful and far-reaching theological affirmations come as part of his reflection on what seem to be exceedingly ordinary pastoral problems. The great hymn or affirmation of Philippians 2:6–11 comes in response to some kind of discord within the Philippian church. Romans 14:7–8 preaches with exceeding power in this century as in the first: "We do not live to ourselves, and we do not die to ourselves. If we live, we live to the Lord, and if we die, we die to the Lord; so then, whether we live or whether we die, we are the Lord's." The presenting issue is a dispute over vegetarianism.

Today's passage is part of Paul's extremely practical and perhaps even self-serving scramble to insist that he has followed the proper etiquette. It is clear enough that he has changed his mind, probably twice, about when he is going to revisit Corinth, and the Corinthian Christians are frustrated. The Corinthians accuse him of vacillating in his travel plans, and in his haste to justify his own apparent inconsistencies, he shifts the spotlight quickly to God, who, unlike Paul, really is consistent in dealing with humankind.

So in doing your exegesis, be sure you start with 2 Cor. 1:15, and then go on to look at 1:23–2:2,

## Homiletical Perspective

Reading someone else's mail is like overhearing a conversation: the words may be recognizable, but they are easily misconstrued if you haven't had a chance to read the earlier correspondence. So it is with trying to preach a brief text from one of Paul's letters to the church at Corinth.

As you read Paul's epistles, you recognize that his words are well-chosen rhetorical strategies that argue a broader theological issue. If we focus on one rhetorical strategy for the "kernel of truth" conveyed through it, we may lose sight of the larger situation. For this reason, the preacher must try to keep both the rhetorical strategy and the larger intention in view. It is kind of like wearing bifocals: you can see the distant horizon with clarity, and you can do close reading with ease; it's the space between the two that is hard to get into focus. That's where the preaching of this text needs to take place.

This particular letter is an attempt by Paul to convince a familiar but skeptical audience of the genuineness of the apostle's word to them. Some members of the church at Corinth seem to have been offended when Paul did not follow through with his plan to visit them. The letter suggests that they had accused him of fickleness, not honoring commitments, or choosing what was personally expedient, instead of acting out of concern for their

# 2 Corinthians 1:18-22

## Theological Perspective

be God's very voice spoken to others. The Protestant Reformers of the sixteenth century understood this well. For example, Heinrich Bullinger, successor to Huldrych Zwingli in Zurich, subdivided the first chapter of his *Second Helvetic Confession* (1566) with the phrase "the preaching of the word *is* the Word of God." Because God is a personal reality, not the unmoved mover of Greek philosophy and late medieval theology, God communicates personally. God speaks the word of grace, and this allows us, who also are personal beings, to participate in God's work, actually becoming God's voice when we speak the gospel. Paul himself suggested this when he talked about "our word to you has not been 'Yes and No.'" Paul meant both his own words and God's Word, which had come to them in and through his words.

What, then, is the character of our word that can be God's Word? Here we find something even more extraordinary. The character of the good news is not "Yes and No," but purely, absolutely, "Yes," and nothing more. Our God brings the much-needed sun and the much-needed rain on both the just and the unjust (Matt. 5:45). In the history of the Christian church, perhaps no theologians were clearer about this simple but profound gospel truth than were the great Protestant Reformers. This utter good news, which is Christianity itself, lies at the heart of the Protestant Reformation.

In the late medieval West (about 1250–1550), Christians were fearful of God, not knowing how it stood between themselves and God. In the gospel of Jesus Christ, found in apostolic testimony to Jesus (the Scriptures), the Reformers discovered that God was "pure love" (Luther), or the "font of all goodness" (Calvin), or, in the later words of Charles Wesley, "pure unbounded love." Whenever, through the prompting of the Spirit (2 Cor. 1:22; also see Rom. 5:5), our hearts trust this God, we discover the unequivocal character of God as utter goodness for us and with us, and we stand upright in life. This was what Luther understood when he clung to the idea from Paul that we are "justified by grace through faith."

Furthermore, only a God whose character is an unequivocal Yes for our well-being would be appropriate to the New Testament idea of faith. In the New Testament, "faith" primarily means trusting God with one's deepest self. To be sure, people could not trust if they did not know the character of the One whom they trusted, but that is exactly the point. A person can trust only that which is trust-worthy, and if the character of God is ultimately

## Pastoral Perspective

an angry, moralizing parent. Thus it is common for Christians to translate the graceful and trust-born gospel of Yes (or as Paul Tillich so magnificently says, "You are accepted!") into the No of conditional love and potential abandonment and disdain.

For those whose faith paradigm is an ironclad rule box cast in terms of Don'ts, this could be an enormously freeing text. It would also be holy and helpful to remind people of Paul's core message. In spite of his occasional forays into controlling negativity about wearing hats in church and women keeping silent, Paul's deepest word is a shift from the legalism of Don't, No, Stop, to the grace of Yes, Freedom, Gratitude. From Paul we hear that the greatest gifts we can give each other are not correction or condemnation but Faith, Hope, and Love (1 Cor. 13:13). The Yes of Christ is an affirmation of God's good and wonderful work in our lives. It is a discovery of a Yes full of the promises, sealed by the Holy Spirit in our hearts. Hence, at their heart Paul's writings ring with the Yes of Christ. Helping people hear the Yes in Christ was Paul's best work and deserves a new rendition at every given chance. Indeed Paul find in Christ's Yes a gift of such superlative worth that he finally says No to all the perquisites and privileges of his previous life: "Yet whatever gains I had, these I have come to regard as loss because of Christ. More than that, I regard everything as loss because of the surpassing value of knowing Christ Jesus my Lord" (Phil. 3:7–8).

However, for someone whose life is in a spiraling, out-of-control mess, it is almost obscene to hear that God always says Yes. What would it mean to someone who is going through a divorce or who has just lost their job to hear that God in Christ is always saying Yes? What would it mean to someone who is afraid of the future or remorseful of the past? What would it mean to a brokenhearted parent with an out-of-control child to hear that Yes is the most profound word in God's vocabulary? What about the poor, the sick, the old and alone?

Without plumbing the height and depth of God's Yes in a particular situation, to hear that God's word in Christ is always Yes is inane and/or cruel. Without listening for the nuances of Yes for another person, the speaker of the Yes is simply a chipper yes-man or yes-woman, and most of us have lived through enough sales presentations to be very wary of another. The power of positive thinking loses its power before the reality of human suffering and the depths of human pain.

So of course Yes must be made flesh, or it morphs into No. After all, the primal Word did not just stay

where Paul gives the Corinthians a theologically less rich, but practically persuasive reason why his visit has been delayed—the thought of a visit without reconciliation had seemed just too painful.

In our passage, as he often does, Paul works more as a poet than as a systematic theologian—he is stronger on metaphor than on propositions. Here the metaphor for the God revealed in Jesus Christ is the unshakable "Yes!"

Paul starts with the claim that the gospel that preaches the true God is always a matter of Yes, not No, and certainly not Maybe. The good news is good because it always declares God's unswerving affirmation of God's creation and of God's people. Preaching is never negation or equivocation.

Then there is a stunning conformity between the gospel and the Lord the gospel proclaims. Christ is as true as the gospel, and vice versa. It is not only that the gospel always *says* the great Yes of God's love for humankind. Jesus Christ *is* the great Yes of God's love for humankind. Paul probably does not know the hymn about the Word made flesh that begins John's Gospel, but here in his own way he affirms that one of God's great words is made present in Jesus Christ—that word is Yes.

Furthermore, here as elsewhere in Paul, God's Yes contains a vital element of eschatological hope. For Paul, Jesus is both the fulfillment of the promise found in Scripture and himself the promise to be fulfilled when God becomes all in all (1 Cor. 15:28).

And there is conformity between the God of Jesus Christ and the spiritual lives of believers. Here, as elsewhere in his writing, Paul provides a kind of empirical theology. He notes that when the Corinthian Christians worship they say, "Amen." The Amen after a benediction is the liturgical way in which Corinthian Christians say Yes to the promises of God revealed in Jesus Christ. God's Yes calls forth the response of Yes from us. The loan word "Amen" comes from the same root as the Hebrew word for truth. When God says "Truly, truly"—Amen—we respond, "Truly truly, amen," as well.

It is not altogether clear in verses 21–22, when Paul talks about God establishing, anointing, and putting his seal on "us," whether the "us" refers to Paul, Silvanus (Silas), and Timothy or, more likely, to all the Corinthian Christians. If the former, then Paul is asserting, as he will time and again in 2 Corinthians, the divine grounding and sanctioning of his apostleship. If the latter, then Paul may be alluding to the baptism of believers, with the gift of the Spirit and perhaps also with anointing. Whether

best interests. Whatever the accusations, Paul was prompted by them to respond to this community in writing.

How does one reestablish credibility with an audience when one's motives have been called into question? Do you swear on a higher authority as a witness? Do you rely on earned credentials to speak for you? Do you gather commendations and awards so people will know that others value your worth?

Paul didn't choose these options, and for good reason. When one is accused of saying one thing and doing another, more words would not readily satisfy the skeptic, especially if the words attempted to rationalize the perceived offense or defend one's good intentions. In a shame/honor culture, a person may claim honor for himself or herself, but in reality it is something that is conferred. That is why Paul is so tormented by the congregation's withdrawal of respect for him as an apostle—an honor that he believed had been conferred on him directly from God.

In this letter Paul appeals to their own faith in God's new order, in which the barriers of shame and honor had been dissolved by the resurrection of the crucified Messiah. Paul points to Jesus Christ, whose life, death, and resurrection revealed God's intentions for the cosmos. The resurrected life of Jesus revealed the glory of God, a glory not made visible by human efforts, but only through Christ. The life of a believer like Paul was not to be judged by his own ability to reproduce the same effects as Christ's resurrection, but could be understood more as a living affirmation or an Amen to all that Jesus Christ has already done. If Paul's words and actions arise as an Amen to the glory revealed in Jesus Christ, how can they be translated as "Yes and No"?

One problem for the preacher of this text is establishing the intention of the sermon. Many of us are familiar with accusations that diminish trust between pastors and their congregations. Paul's correspondence provides one strategy for addressing pastor-parish relations. Is that, however, the purpose of a sermon?

What does this text say more broadly about our human predicament? The reference to the human standards of saying "Yes, yes" and "No, no" at the same time in verse 17 seems like a good entry point into the message. For some individuals, the temptation to say what they think people want to hear leads to inconsistencies in both words and actions. An issue for many congregations, as well, is the intense desire to keep the majority of people happy and comfortable while maintaining a larger

# 2 Corinthians 1:18-22

## Theological Perspective

"mysterious," or if God is both "Yes and No," then perhaps one can surrender, or simply be obedient, as to a dictator from the ancient Near East; but one cannot trust either a mystery or a God whose character is mysterious or equivocal. In this simple correlation between a God who is utterly trust-worthy and the human self that trusts wholeheartedly, lies the foundation of Christian life. In our era, which seemingly longs for the spiritual life, where Christians seek spiritual advisors and traditional spiritual practices, where people piece together various spiritual disciplines learned from church and YMCA and other religions, the gospel holds forth a simple yet powerful vision of spiritual development.

When we are spiritually young, we pledge our lives to God hoping to avoid problems and receive blessings. We may even desire to avoid God's wrath and hell, finding God's forgiveness and heaven instead. Avoiding negative consequences and seeking positive consequences finds parallels in family and school practices, which organize childrearing and education by announcing negative and positive outcomes to certain behaviors. Outside the door to my son's sixth-grade classroom stands a chart, outlining just such policies.

Yet the ultimate goal for childrearing and education lies not with fearing punishment and receiving rewards, but in giving one's life to a greater good. We raise our children to see ever-widening communities to which they can give themselves: family, then school, then town and country, and finally the reign of God. To enable this development toward universalizing our lives within a common society and its ultimate reality, God, the Christian gospel ultimately speaks not a "Yes and No," but simply a divine "Yes." We learn to trust God, not because of what we might avoid and what we might receive, but simply because our faith has known a God so unequivocally good to us that we, out of sheer thanksgiving for such goodness, want to love God back by loving and caring for all whom God also loves, our neighbors, here and everywhere. For the Protestant Reformer John Calvin, all Christian life—and thus all theological reflection—can be summed with the phrase "grace and gratitude." To the initiating goodness of God, we are given the opportunity to respond with lives of gratitude, as we live before God and neighbor.

JOHN W. RIGGS

## Pastoral Perspective

on the page or ringing in the air. The Word did become flesh and dwells among us even to this day. And so if God's word in Christ is Yes, then helping that Yes get fleshed out in the lives of those in pain, need, or trouble is the job description for every follower of the Yes-sayer. The mark of the Yes of God in Christ and through the Holy Spirit is tangible and becomes a testimony; it is the embodied and lived promises and hope of God.

This opportunity to be the Yes of Christ in the flesh happens over and over if the follower of Jesus stands still long enough to experience the pain of another. This does not mean one dispenses cheap grace in a breezy or facile way, although the almost universal instinct is to pat down the pain, to make it *all* all right, to speak a Yes to the pain as quickly as possible. But for those of us who follow the Yes-sayer, who groaned his most powerful and deepest Yes with his arms stretched out on the hard wood of the cross, we know that God's Yes must emerge from the sometimes hidden and agonizing cruciform depths of the human condition groping for and finally touched by the grace of God. That is where the Yes of life overcomes the No of death and resounds authentically and eternally.

MARTHA STERNE

## Exegetical Perspective

the "establishing" is the establishing of the apostles or of all the faithful, there is again a strong eschatological note. The gift of the Spirit is the first installment, the down payment on the promise yet to come. It is the first Yes in a whole world of Yeses yet to be.

C. K. Barrett points out that the terms that the NRSV translates as "establish," "putting his seal," and "first installment" (vv. 21–22) all draw on a commercial metaphor. God guarantees our place in Christ, sets God's seal on us as testimony that we are what we are advertised to be, and offers the Spirit as the first part of the glory that is due.[1]

Note that in our passage Paul reminds us that "his" gospel is the gospel also preached by Silvanus and Timothy. From that day until this, the propagation of the gospel is not the unique calling of any preacher—not even the apostle to the Gentiles—but is the church's calling, proclaimed by a thousand thousand tongues.

It seems likely that our present book, 2 Corinthians, is composed of at least two and maybe more letters from Paul to the Corinthian churches. It is evident in reading I Corinthians 5:9 and 2 Corinthians 2:4 that Paul wrote letters to the Corinthians that have not survived, at least not in their original form. While it is canonically honorable to try to read 2 Corinthians as a worked-through argument, it is exegetically more plausible to see 2 Corinthians 1–9 as a letter basically grateful for the Corinthians' relationship to the apostle. In 2 Corinthians 10–13, the slight anxiety Paul has already evinced about his own apostolic status in Corinth has escalated to an extensive and angry apology for his own call and authority.

In our passage, he has to make excuse for his vacillation but does not yet have to defend his call. God's Yes is not yet challenged by the No of Paul's opponents. Paul affirms without having to argue that the word that he and Silvanus and Timothy preach is, by God, true.

DAVID L. BARTLETT

## Homiletical Perspective

sphere of influence. The desire to preserve status in the face of polarizing influences leads churches into a kind of captivity to an enduring shame/honor way of life. Persons and groups continue to compete for favor, although the criteria for judging both shame and honor may be somewhat different from those in Paul's day. The need to save face in difficult battles leads the church often to say yes and no at the same time to situations that compromise our faith commitment to the resurrected life of Jesus.

The paradox of the Christian life (the seeming inexhaustible inconsistency between faith and life) begs the question of credibility and integrity. The sermon can disclose a new vision that reframes this painful tension for people of faith. When the credibility of the church's witness is established by God's great faithfulness rather than ours, then the power of life within the church is pronounced as a clear Amen to the resurrection life of Christ. The Yes has already been proclaimed through Christ. Therefore, all honor belongs to Christ whose witness is always, and shall always be, Yes. From Christ's Yes we receive life, says Paul, and Christ's life in us becomes the Yes of our own integrity.

Today's culture is inundated with the rhetoric of "doublespeak," the art of saying yes and no at the same time in order to win the support of the masses. God's own Spirit within us steers us away from such ambivalence toward one affirmation—God's ultimate Yes in Jesus Christ is God's No to evil in all its forms. By the power of that same Spirit of Christ, we too can renounce evil in all of its forms instead of allowing it to set the agenda for us.

The revelation of God's Yes in Jesus Christ can be an epiphany for those who suffer from the disintegration of wholeness, both personally and corporately. Integrity does not emerge because of human effort, but from God's action. Christ's own Spirit alive in us confirms God's yes to life. What more can be said by those who are living in faith than "Amen!"

MARY LIN HUDSON

---

[1] C. K. Barrett, *The Second Epistle to the Corinthians* (New York: Harper & Row, 1973), 78–80.

# Mark 2:1-12

[1]When he returned to Capernaum after some days, it was reported that he was at home. [2]So many gathered around that there was no longer room for them, not even in front of the door; and he was speaking the word to them. [3]Then some people came, bringing to him a paralyzed man, carried by four of them. [4]And when they could not bring him to Jesus because of the crowd, they removed the roof above him; and after having dug through it, they let down the mat on which the paralytic lay. [5]When Jesus saw their faith, he said to the paralytic, "Son, your sins are forgiven." [6]Now some of the scribes were sitting there, questioning in their hearts, [7]"Why does this fellow speak in this way? It is blasphemy! Who can forgive sins but God alone?" [8]At once Jesus perceived in his spirit that they were discussing these questions among themselves; and he said to them, "Why do you raise such questions in your hearts? [9]Which is easier, to say to the paralytic, 'Your sins are forgiven,' or to say, 'Stand up and take your mat and walk'? [10]But so that you may know that the Son of Man has authority on earth to forgive sins"— he said to the paralytic— [11]"I say to you, stand up, take your mat and go to your home." [12]And he stood up, and immediately took the mat and went out before all of them; so that they were all amazed and glorified God, saying, "We have never seen anything like this!"

## Theological Perspective

The healing of a paralytic is a quintessentially Markan narrative: action packed, tension filled, and fairly brimming with detail. We are spectators at a drama involving Jesus, a crowd straining to see and hear him, four people bearing a paralytic, and some scribes. And this engaging drama raises as many questions as it answers. At issue are the nature of God's power, Jesus' authority to wield that power, the religious and political implications of Jesus' action, and the relation of sickness and sin.

The most obvious handle to grasp in trying to understand this story theologically is provided in the punch line: "they were all amazed and glorified God, saying, 'We have never seen anything like this'" (v. 12). Here is God, the all-powerful, intervening in the material world to heal a paralytic. Oh, if it were only that simple, in the first century or the twenty-first! While many of us have experienced what seems to be the physically healing power of such a God, we have also witnessed the apparent absence of such power in situations quite as compelling as that of the paralytic. So we are drawn more deeply into Mark's account and may be surprised to discover that Jesus' point in telling the paralytic to stand, pick up his mat, and go home is so that the scribes may know that "the Son of Man has authority on earth to forgive sins" (v. 10). What is this connection between

## Pastoral Perspective

"Let the Church in remembering Christ remember that it is conserving the most uprooting, the most revolutionary force in all human history. For it was Christ who crossed every boundary, broke down every barrier. . . . If ever there was a man who trusted his origins and had courage to emerge from them, it was Christ."[1]

Generally in Mark's Gospel the crowds are amazed by Jesus' miracles but do not respond by becoming disciples. Jesus, on the other hand, is about making disciples whose most important characteristic is devotion to God. Mark shows Jesus' followers overcoming obstacles with persistent faith.

The passage evokes a rich kaleidoscope of images and questions suitable for worship drama and liturgy. One can visualize and smell the bodies of the standing-room-only crowd packed tightly around Jesus, see the gestures and hear the voice inflections as he preaches the homecoming sermon, feel the strain of lifting the pallet—the perspiration and heavy breathing of the quartet of EMS-like stretcher bearers—and hear the sound of cascading roof debris. We can see the anxious anticipation and determined intensity on the face of the paralytic as he is lowered in front of the crowd, the scowl on the

[1]William Sloane Coffin, *Credo* (Louisville, KY: Westminster John Knox Press, 2004), 138.

## Exegetical Perspective

"Never seen anything like it." A paralyzed man is dropped next to Jesus from the rafters. A man incapable of moving his extremities, much less getting off his mat, encounters Jesus, stands up, rolls up his mat, and walks out the front door. Eyewitnesses to this healing, the scribes do not celebrate. They chastise this presumptuous healer and would-be agent of God. "Who do you think you are?" is the best they can get out of their mouths. The crowd behaves a bit better. The crowd, at least, gives thanks to God for this wondrous occurrence in their midst as they mutter in amazement, "Never seen anything like it." Though more favorable than the words of the scribes, these are hardly words of discipleship and engagement.

It does not take long until Jesus is surrounded by resistance, controversy, and amazement in Mark's Gospel. Chapter 2:1–12 is the first of five controversy stories that pepper Mark's narrative until he shifts gears in 3:7. As the second chapter opens, readers witness a scene swamped with people everywhere. No one moves, lest someone else take her place. For Mark, though, a huge crowd (*ochlos*) does not equate with faith, and persistent curiosity is not the hallmark of discipleship. This point is made by contrasting the stunning solitude of Jesus as he utters his cry of dereliction in 15:34 with the masses surrounding him here.

## Homiletical Perspective

Incurable diseases are often the most terrible causes of human agony. Beyond time and space, the individual and communal experiences of diseases have had a tremendous impact on religious life. What and how to preach from a healing story is one of the most challenging tasks for a preacher, because each healing story has its own particular theological implication emerging from a particular rhetorical context, which has its own characters and narrative plot set in a particular time and space.

The plot of the narrative in Mark 2:1–12 is intentionally designed to present Jesus as the Son of Man who has the divine authority to forgive sins, rather than as a "mere" miracle worker. The scribes who are the teachers of the law interrupt Jesus' act of healing by critically observing every deed and word of Jesus from their professional perspective, while other characters—a paralytic, the four litter bearers, and the crowd—are simply enthusiastic about Jesus' healing powers.

Like the paralytic, some congregants may be eager to experience Jesus' miraculous power of physical healing. Like the four litter bearers and the crowd, some congregants may believe Jesus is a miracle worker or a superman who has the power to solve their physical and material problems by listening to their prayers. Preachers who are sensitive to this type

# Mark 2:1-12

## Theological Perspective

sickness and sin, and how might that connection add to our understanding of the drama before us?

Apparently, Jesus' healing ministry challenged the system in Galilee whereby the urban secular and religious powers exploited the rural poor. The sick among the peasantry, often in such a state because of excessive taxation or the expropriation of their land, were said to be so because they had sinned. Sound familiar? Their only recourse was the temple, where they could remedy their sin, but only by giving up more of their meager resources, thereby increasing their poverty and the likelihood of further sickness. Put simply, the religious leaders had a stake in the economic game, just as the political leaders had a stake in the religious game. The conjunction of religious and political power here is unmistakable. If Jesus can cure sickness, and sickness is a divine punishment for sin, then Jesus can wield the divine power of forgiveness as well; he is a threat to the religious as well as the political elite.

In this context Jesus asks the scribes which is easier, to say to the paralytic, "Your sins are forgiven," or "Stand up and take your mat and walk" (v. 9). Given the materialistic reductionism that typifies our era, we are likely to say the latter is more difficult. Ironically, the scribes may have been more aware than we are of the profound interplay between the individual human body and the societal norms in which it makes its way. Is the Galilean paralytic a sinner, an individual who has chosen to forsake his God-given capacity to work the land, or is he a reflection of a social system that offers him nothing but misery for his labor? Is the young American woman with an eating disorder a sinner, an individual who simply chooses to abuse her God-given body, or is she the reflection of a society that celebrates a distorted female image and spends billions in trying to achieve it? Whether in the first century or the twenty-first, the interconnected relationships between sin and sickness, the individual and society, and religion and politics are complex. That very complexity should give us pause when we try to answer Jesus' question.

It may help to shift the focus of our theological reflection to the paralytic and the four people who bore him on a mat. Keep in mind what it would be like, not only to push through the crowd to get to the roof of the house, but then to "[dig] through it" and "let down the mat on which the paralytic lay" (v. 4). Talk about chutzpah! But Jesus sees it as faith and says to the paralytic, "Son, your sins are forgiven" (v. 5). Notice that it is the four mat-bearers

## Pastoral Perspective

scribes' faces, and the amazed, awestruck crowd parting like the Red Sea as the forgiven and healed man walks out with his mat tucked under his arm like an Appalachian Trail hiker.

Mark emphasizes the verb "take up," using it four times. Jesus uses the phrase in verses 9 and 11, and then in verse 12 the man stands, takes up the mat, and walks out. In contrast to the calling of the disciples in chapter 1, in this story the healed man is not told to follow Jesus, but to "go to his home."

Jesus fundamentally challenged the social and religious structures of Israel, demonstrating that YHWH is beyond human control. Clearly, "the Temple and the priesthood that serviced it need no longer be recognized as the way station between God and humans."[2] Jesus here is assuming not only God's prerogative, but also priestly duties.

Notice the "why" questions: "Why does this fellow speak in this way?" "Why do you raise such questions in your hearts?" To prove who he was, Jesus forgave sins. To be who he was, he healed the sick. Forgiveness did not cure the paralysis of body but of soul. Would the Pharisees have had as much trouble with Jesus if he had healed only the physical affliction and not the spiritual?

The story invites us to ponder the relationship between sin and sickness or disability. Some behaviors, such as drug abuse or promiscuity, directly lead to illnesses, but sometimes sources of illness are beyond our control. In declaring forgiveness, Jesus first restores the paralytic's relationship with God, thus disputing the common belief that sin caused the paralysis. The passage emphasizes the connection among faith, forgiveness, and healing. Can we open ourselves to God's forgiveness and to forgiving others?

Do you ever feel as if your life is paralyzed, stuck, not going anywhere, imprisoned in a body with cancer or ALS or AIDS or Alzheimer's or trapped by depression or addiction or loveless, perhaps even abusive, marriage? (Ever feel alone or frustrated, like someone has put the remote control button of your life on "permanent pause"?) Are we open to receiving the grace of acceptance or physical restoration that enables us to move forward spiritually?

U2, the popular Irish rock group, on their CD *All that You Can't Leave Behind* has a cut entitled "Stuck in a Moment You Can't Get Out of . . ."

---

[2] Brian K. Blount and Gary W. Charles, *Preaching Mark in Two Voices* (Louisville, KY: Westminster John Knox Press, 2002), 25.

## Exegetical Perspective

The crowd pressing upon Jesus in a house in Capernaum provides the dilemma that four anonymous friends of an anonymous paralyzed man must solve. Unlike the curious crowd, their faith compels them to take a radical action on behalf of their friend. Readers know nothing of the faith of the paralyzed man or the nature of his disability or society's "disability" in responding to him; they know only that this man's friends had faith in Jesus, and for Mark, faith in Jesus leads to radical action.

The temptation for readers, especially modern readers, of 2:1–12 is to focus on the healing miracle. Readers expect Jesus to touch or say something about this man's disability and then heal him. For Mark, though, this healing story is intercalated with a controversy story, and it is the controversy to which this story draws the reader's focus. When readers expect Jesus to say something about his disease, Jesus tells the man that his sins are forgiven. It is not that his sins will be forgiven only after he visits the religious authorities and completes a rite of purification; they are forgiven *now*. Jesus does not draw the conclusion that this man was ill and therefore had sinned, though such a conclusion would not have been uncommon. Mark draws the reader's eye, not to the nature of sin, but to the authority of Jesus to forgive it.

At this point the story shifts from a miracle story to a religiopolitical controversy story. If Jesus can forgive sin, then he speaks with the authority of God. If this is true, then no ruling structure is safe or can survive for long amid the impotent claims of authority. When Jesus pronounces the forgiveness of the man's sins, the scribes do not question his healing authority; they question his divine authority (*exousia*).

"While Jesus does not specifically say 'I forgive you of your sins,'" writes M. Eugene Boring, "the passive *aphientai* points to God as the actor and portrays Jesus as acting in God's stead."[1] The scribes, who do not benefit from the privileged position of the reader and do not know that Jesus is the Son of God (1:1), hear the claim of Jesus in blasphemous contradiction to Israel's claim of "one God" (Deut. 6:4–5). "He blasphemes!" (2:7) links this first controversy story to the final controversy story, in which another "blasphemy" charge against Jesus (14:64) will lead to his crucifixion. The scribes counter Jesus' authority to forgive with the complaint that only God can forgive sin (2:7). They are right, of course. They are dead wrong, though, as they fail to see the

[1] M. Eugene Boring, *Mark: A Commentary* (Louisville, KY: Westminster John Knox Press, 2006), 76.

## Homiletical Perspective

of wish from their congregants are easily tempted to bypass the christological claim that Jesus is the one who has the divine authority to forgive sins and quickly focus on the faith of the four litter bearers who made it possible for Jesus to work a miracle. Consequently, such a sermon may present the litter bearers as role models of true Christian believers.

However, the narrative plot of this passage invites the preacher to ponder the deeper meaning of healing in relation to Jesus' divine authority to forgive sins. Jesus sees the paralytic's sinful condition. It is not only a physical paralysis but also a paralysis of sociocultural and religious relations caused by a disease. By announcing the forgiveness of sins, Jesus heals the broken relationships between the sick and others in the community, as well as the paralytic's physical illness. The paralytic is no longer a sinner; instead, he restores his whole life by becoming a member of the community.

Such holistic healing happens by the power of the life-giving Spirit, who is present and works to make the human life human. Jesus is the man of the Spirit (Mark 1:8, 10–12, 24). When Jesus is with the sick, the Spirit of God is with Jesus; when Jesus heals the sick, the power of the Spirit works through Jesus. When the Spirit works through Jesus, the divine authority to forgive sins is present, so that new life is given to the sick. From the scribes' point of view, the forgiveness of sins is possible by God alone, through appropriate ritual ceremonies administered by authoritative, professionally trained priests, following the instructions in the Torah, in the holy temple. However, the radical christological claim in the text overturns the conventional knowledge of the privileged class and challenges their limited understanding of God's revelation. According to the text, the Spirit is present in the margins of society, including among stigmatized and rejected sinners. The Spirit works for holistic healing in and among our communities through those who follow the lead of the Spirit.

Like the scribes, some congregants are used to limiting the boundaries of experiencing the forgiveness of sins to their familiar areas, where the legally appropriate group of believers belong. But what if God is not in their holy places, but in unexpected areas such as the communities of the marginalized in race, gender, sexual orientation, and occupation? If we, as members of the mainline Christian church or as a privileged group of believers, limit our understanding and experience of God's revelation to our fragmented knowledge and

# Mark 2:1-12

## Theological Perspective

who have demonstrated their faith. As a result, the paralytic's sins have been forgiven, but he has yet to do anything in response. Thanks to the scribes, who serve as Jesus' foils in so many Markan dramas, the focus shifts from the forgiveness of sins to physical healing. The scribes think Jesus is blasphemous. "Who can forgive sins but God alone?" (v. 7) Perceiving their criticism "in his spirit," Jesus asks them the question we've already discussed. Then he turns to the paralytic. "I say to you, stand up, take your mat and go to your home" (v. 11). How much tension-filled time elapsed as the expectant crowd waited to see how the previously passive paralytic would respond? What was he thinking or feeling? What theological insights did he later share with his family? Mark answers none of these questions. All we know—perhaps all we need to know—is that the paralytic "stood up, and immediately took the mat and went out before all of them" (v. 12). In so doing, he became the poster child for the human capacity *actively* to tap into the forgiving, healing power of God *now*.

John Dominic Crossan distinguishes between "apocalyptic eschatology" and "sapiential eschatology." In the former, preached by John the Baptist, we wait for God to act. In the latter, preached by Jesus, God waits for us to act.[1] Like Gandhi or Martin Luther King Jr., the paralytic, in his interaction with Jesus, exhibits what we might call a *panentheistic* theology.[2] In this profoundly relational and incarnational theology, God's all-embracing transcendence is known in God's all-pervasive immanence. Today's Epiphanal reading celebrates the God revealed in Jesus *and* the paralytic.

JERRY IRISH

[1] John Dominic Crossan, *The Essential Jesus* (New York: HarperCollins, 1994), 8.
[2] For examples of panentheistic theology, see Marjorie Suchocki, *God, Christ, Church* (New York: Crossroad, 1995), and Sallie McFague, *Models of God* (Philadelphia: Fortress, 1987) and *The Body of God* (Minneapolis: Fortress, 1993).

## Pastoral Perspective

You've got to get yourself together
You've got stuck in a moment
And now you can't get out of it

Can persons with mental illness or disabilities whom many others may see as liabilities actually be welcomed and nurtured as needed assets in our faith communities? Or do we who call ourselves religious unintentionally or intentionally create barriers like the blocked doorway to Christ?

Can persons of faith honor the risk taking of the paralytic's friends and enable people with disabilities to move from the impossible to the possible? Will we be the compassionate, healing faith community that encourages active participation and integration into congregational life? Can the special needs of persons with disabilities be seen as gifts to the community that would not have been experienced otherwise? Perhaps it is the friends of the paralytic and we ourselves who need Christ's healing touch and forgiveness as much as, or more than, persons with disabilities.

The text is somewhat analogous to the integration of alternative medicine into traditional health-care settings. Healing, forgiveness, and cure are not synonymous. Modern medicine can cure (fix), but is that the same as healing? This is an easy question for a healthy person to pose, but for ALS patients, there is no present cure. Perhaps the healing is accepting the lack of cure and coming to grips with the condition; the healing may be how grace is received. Can those persons say in their deepest recesses that being accepting is enough? Can we trust healing and cure when they happen simultaneously? Jesus did not ask which is easier to do, but which is easier to say. Both forgiveness and healing are easy to say, but both are also hard to do.

Like the crowd, we seek signs, proof. We want to be healed, forgiven. We promise to do anything if God will help us. We make bargains with God, but do we repent of our sins? Can we accept healing and forgiveness as the same? Maybe the face on the pallet is our face—do we not also need our sins forgiven so we can walk in newness of life?

The crowd was ecstatic and glorified God. Jesus "blows their mind" and reveals a God of surprise. Perhaps pondering Christ's questions leads us to recover the Messiah's mysterious ways. What would it take for us to pick up our mats?

AL MASTERS

## Exegetical Perspective

dawn of God's reign (1:14–15) in Jesus as he heals the lame (Isa. 35:6).

The initial dilemma of this story is how four friends can penetrate a mob to aid an ailing friend. As the story continues, Mark confronts the scribes and the readers with one who has the power to break through the most formidable boundary of human sin. "It was only to make this point clear," writes Brian Blount, "that Jesus followed up his proclamation of sin release with the physical healing of the man who was paralyzed. He demonstrated the authority to bring physical wholeness as a sign that he had the power to bestow spiritual wholeness in the form of the forgiveness of sins. This is the boundary-breaking power that his life and ministry represent."[2]

The four friends had carried (*airō*) the paralytic to Jesus. Restored to health, the paralytic is now commanded by Jesus to carry (*aron*, the imperative form of *airō*) his own bed. "At the word of Jesus," writes Boring, "the passive victim has become an active participant in life."[3] Just as the charge of blasphemy by the scribes foreshadows the death of Jesus, so now the rising of the paralytic foreshadows a promised resurrection.

Because the reader is in on Jesus' messianic secret from the start (1:1), Mark 2:10 is another reminder to the reader that the one who is challenged by the scribes and will be hunted by scribes and Pharisees, Herodians and Sadducees, until his death is the Son of God, who speaks with the authority of God and is ushering in the reign of God. The crowd that began the story also appears at the story's end, now in total amazement. For Mark, amazement (*thaumazō*) is never a sign of discipleship, but of reverent curiosity at best. Discipleship will follow in the next pericope, but it will not be this "amazed" crowd that follows.

GARY W. CHARLES

## Homiletical Perspective

imperfect language, with pride for being experts in knowing God, we may overlook God's amazing redeeming acts of reconciliation and healing among the people in the communities that we do not belong to.

Robert was born and raised in a pious Protestant family and dreamed of becoming a pastor. When he announced that he was gay, his family rejected him. Robert also learned that he could not be ordained by his mainline denomination. Later he became infected with AIDS, which many people surrounding him consider to be God's punishment. While struggling to survive this incurable, cursed disease, Robert did not give up on his dream of becoming a pastor; instead, he enrolled in a seminary that embraces homosexuality. During his years at the seminary, he experienced holistic healing by the reconciling power of the Spirit. The faculty and his peers did not treat him as a sinner, abandoned by both God and others, but as a friend and member of a community, healed by the liberating power of the Spirit of his sinful condition, physical as well as social. Now Robert actively serves in a congregation that is diverse in its sexuality, as an ordained minister of one of the "least" denominations in the Christian church; he preaches and teaches the good news of Jesus Christ who has the divine authority to forgive sins. Robert has benefited from the advanced medical research on AIDS and has become healthy enough to fulfill God's call to ministry.

In the text, the scribes were surely included among the group of witnesses who were amazed by the unusual event that happened by the Spirit of God through Jesus. Would they continuously have charged Jesus with blasphemy, even after witnessing the presence and power of God in, with, and through Jesus? Or would they glorify God for the forgiveness of sins for the least person in the least place of society? The text does not address this question but calls the preacher to witness God's presence and reconciling work in the margins of society. Perhaps those who listen to the sermon and are challenged to open their eyes to see the presence of God beyond their boundaries may answer that question.

EUNJOO MARY KIM

---

[2]Brian K. Blount and Gary W. Charles, *Preaching Mark in Two Voices* (Louisville, KY: Westminster John Knox Press, 2003), 25.
[3]Boring, *Mark*, 78.

# Hosea 2:14-20

¹⁴Therefore, I will now allure her,
  and bring her into the wilderness,
  and speak tenderly to her.
¹⁵From there I will give her her vineyards,
  and make the Valley of Achor a door of hope.
There she shall respond as in the days of her youth,
  as at the time when she came out of the land of Egypt.
¹⁶On that day, says the LORD, you will call me, "My husband," and no longer will you call me, "My Baal." ¹⁷For I will remove the names of the Baals from her mouth, and they shall be mentioned by name no more. ¹⁸I will make for you a covenant on that day with the wild animals, the birds of the air, and the creeping things of the ground; and I will abolish the bow, the sword, and war from the land; and I will make you lie down in safety. ¹⁹And I will take you for my wife forever; I will take you for my wife in righteousness and in justice, in steadfast love, and in mercy. ²⁰I will take you for my wife in faithfulness; and you shall know the LORD.

## Theological Perspective

Reading the book of Hosea is perhaps more difficult than ever today. One of the most contested social institutions of the twenty-first century is marriage, and marriage and the betrayal of such is one of the metaphorical frames for the book of Hosea (chaps. 1–3). This theological reflection is an exploration of the interpretative challenge posed by this passage in the context of current debate about the definition of marriage. The exploration has two parts: (1) explication of the text as prophetic critique of Israel's relationship with God, as a means for understanding the theological theme of covenant; (2) discussion of the limits and possibilities of the text as prophetic witness to contemporary people of faith.

The book of Hosea opens with a command to the prophet to marry a promiscuous wife: "Go, take for yourself a wife of whoredom and have children of whoredom, for the land commits great whoredom by forsaking the LORD" (1:2). Hosea takes a prostitute, Gomer, as his wife, and thus begins a prophetic critique in which the human relationship serves as allegory for (or, perhaps, foreshadows) the divine-human relationship: God is cast as the faithful husband and Israel as the unfaithful wife. Chapter 2 details Israel's infidelity (vv. 2–8), punishment (vv. 9–13), and redemption by God (vv. 14–23). Israel's infidelity is acceptance of the

## Pastoral Perspective

As soon as I read this text, the image returns: The worship service is charismatic, and the sermon is filled with fire. The preacher reminds the congregation of God's steadfast love for Israel, as revealed in the symbolic embodiment of Hosea marrying Gomer, a promiscuous wife with a history of prostitution. As the preacher continues to describe the demand on Hosea and the character of God's love and reconciling act, the congregation becomes quiet. The preacher insists on God's loving action and the demand that this symbolic act imposes on Christian men. She juxtaposes God's reconciling act to patriarchal ways of being: "Females are expected to accept the ways of womanizing men—abuse, exploitation, rejection. But females should expect differently from Christian men. Christian men are expected to be faithful, as God is faithful to Israel. Christian men are required to sustain the covenant of God by loving and honoring their wives despite their wives' entanglements and struggles, even their sexual misbehavior."

It was a bomb! For the first time in my Christian journey I heard men in the congregation raise their voices in contempt to the spoken word: "If a man does that, he is a stupid fool! Men do not need to be humiliated in this way. This is absurd!" It became clear that the sermon was disruptive of a patriarchal

## Exegetical Perspective

Today's reading presents one of the most poignant and powerful metaphors for the divine/human relationship found in Scripture: Israel is married to YHWH. While the marriage metaphor is central to Hosea 1–3, the prophet did not invent it. In the ancient Near East, a city or nation was often personified as a woman (or identified with a goddess) and understood to be the wife of its people's patron god.[1] But so far as we know, Hosea was the first to apply this image to Israel and YHWH. The marriage metaphor can be used negatively (see Ezek. 16 and 23) or positively (see Rev. 21:9–27). However, it must never be forgotten that it is a *metaphor*! In no sense does the tormented, topsy-turvy relationship described in Hosea 1–3 represent a picture of what marriage is or ought to be. Rather, through the window of the stormiest of human passions, the text strives to give us a means to understand ourselves and our God.

Hosea was among the first of the writing prophets. With the resurgence of Assyria in the

## Homiletical Perspective

As the preacher looks at this text—having done the theological and exegetical homework—a choice has to be made.

At the heart of Hosea's message is his concern with the waywardness of Israel. In the heat of the desert, God had cared for the people and saw the rich potential that they had: "Like grapes in the wilderness, I found Israel" (9:10). But Israel had turned away from YHWH and chosen instead, the ecstasies of worshiping Baal—the fertility god, seductive lover, and lord of rain and dew.

So Hosea is commanded by YHWH to take to himself a promiscuous lover, a wife of whoredom— "certainly one of the more startling divine allocutions recorded in the Bible," as the Anchor Bible comments. The exegesis completed and the question resolved of whether the marriage was a real-life experience for the prophet or a symbolic literary creation, the preacher will ask: In what way will I shape my sermon? Will the core of my message be one that covers the large horizon—the fidelity of our own nation to God? Or will I focus rather on a more specific theme, that of the fidelity of the church to its gospel and to its Lord? For the church, like Israel, is a people of the promise, "If you obey my voice and keep my covenant, you shall be my treasured possession out of all the peoples" (Exod. 19:5). But the church has also been faithless.

---

[1] See Aloysius Fitzgerald, "The Mythological Background for the Presentation of Jerusalem as a Queen and False Worship as Adultery in the OT," *Catholic Biblical Quarterly* 34 (1972): 406–15; and Mark E. Biddle, "The Figure of Lady Jerusalem: Identification, Deification, and Personification of Cities in the Ancient Near East," in *The Biblical Canon in Comparative Perspective: Scripture in Context IV*, ed. K. Lawson Younger Jr., William W. Hallo, and Bernard F. Batto; Ancient Near Eastern Texts and Studies 11 (Lewiston, NY: Mellen, 1991), 175–79.

# Hosea 2:14-20

## Theological Perspective

worship of Baal, including, perhaps, participation in the ritual prostitution of the Baal cult. God's punishment for this infidelity is severe; God causes massive deprivation in the land, as a sign that Baal is a lesser god. This lectionary reading marks the turn from punishment to redemption.

This reading locates the turn to redemption, as does last Sunday's Isaiah text with reference to the wilderness and the exodus. In this passage, the wilderness and exodus are important symbols for recalling the place where Israel is faithful to the covenant with God. The relationship between God and Israel, celebrated at Sinai (Exod. 6:2–8; cf. 19:9–15), is built upon God's promises and contingent upon Israel's obedience. As in the Isaiah text for last Sunday (Isa. 43:18–25), the emphasis is not on the consequences of Israel's disobedience, but on the steadfastness of God in spite of human failure.

This steadfastness of God is at the heart of covenant. This is the case because when a covenant is made between God and God's people, the mutually binding agreement is made between parties who are not equals. The lack of parity between the parties pushes us to remember that redemption flows from God's grace and not from human effort. In the context of covenant, humans must never confuse faithfulness in fulfilling covenantal obligations with winning favor with God or manipulating God's love for humanity. God is the maker of the covenant, and God's covenant is inclusive and not limited to humanity. In the words of Hosea 2:18–20: "I will make for you a covenant on that day with the wild animals, the birds of the air, and the creeping things of the ground; and I will abolish the bow, the sword, and war from the land; and I will make you lie down in safety. And I will take you for my wife forever; I will take you for my wife in righteousness and in justice, in steadfast love, and in mercy. I will take you for my wife in faithfulness; and you shall know the LORD."

In these words just cited, there is an indication of how Hosea's use of marriage as a metaphor for the covenant between God and God's people may in fact be a prophetic witness needed by us in these times of contention about the definition of marriage. However, a theological interpretation of the metaphor's usefulness cannot be made without first acknowledging how it is problematic. Biblical scholar Gale A. Yee states a central problematic of this metaphor in terms of the cycle of violence portrayed in the text (2:9–13) as mirroring the cycle that accompanies real-life domestic abuse. When a reader of the text forgets that this is a metaphor, the metaphor

## Pastoral Perspective

order where males could be abusive and yet continue to enjoy the benefits of marriage and family life. The sermon reconfigured the patriarchal order—it was like a reformation of male-female relationships—critically naming the abusive character of *machista* (sexist) behavior. The sermon placed God-given actions of reconciliation on the males. It is as if God said to men: "Hey, you got power . . . let me give you real power!" The preacher framed that power play in the following way: "How is true power configured when living in God's covenantal relationship? Forgive, reconcile, redeem, and sustain the life of abused women—including your own wives and daughters!"

There is little doubt that this text needs a strong critique from a female perspective. Hosea 2:9–13 portrays a metaphor of abusive acts against women. In some Christian circles, this metaphor is interpreted literally, with real and concrete abusive acts in marriage, family circles, and even in the broader community. Dishonor, punishment, shame, and confiscation of "her" belongings—for they are the result of prostitution (bodily and spiritual)—are "justified" by the text. Consequently, the text "embodies" religiously sanctioned acts of domestic and social violence. Moreover, even when such literal interpretation is questioned or even dismissed, the text functions as an underpinning secret code to endorse subtle ways of marginalizing and abusing women. That might help explain why when confronted with the subsequent verses (2:14–20), where the metaphor changes and the text seems to demand the unreasonable from men, the literalists ignore, resist, remove, or simply deny the text. It shifts from "Word of God" to some other kind of word, but certainly not for men. Interestingly, the complete chapter provides a pastoral opportunity to engage in questions of biblical authority and interpretation in our congregations.

This pericope also provides a unique pastoral opportunity to raise critical questions about the effect of God's covenant upon marriage, family composition, power roles, and domestic violence. The symbolic act points to the historic realities of power and liberation with language of love and restoration. Hosea is required to *make room* for Gomer in the economy of marriage and family, just as God *makes room* for Israel in the economy of salvation. The text in Spanish is very radical and beautiful (my translations from the Spanish are in parentheses):

> 14. *Yo la voy a enamorar* (I am going to make her fall in love with me) . . .

middle of the eighth century and the renewed threat that power posed to Israel and to Judah (see 2 Kgs. 14:23–17:41), an explosion of prophetic activity produced the core of the first prophetic books: Amos and Hosea in the north, Micah and Isaiah in the south. Like Amos, Hosea delivers a message of unstinting condemnation and judgment: because of its faithlessness and immorality, the northern kingdom is doomed (cf. Hos. 4:1–19 and Amos 2:6–16). However, unlike his near contemporary, Hosea looks beyond that inevitable destruction, to hope and restoration.

God's judgment and forgiveness are expressed through a symbolic act: YHWH commands Hosea to wed Gomer, a prostitute (1:2–3). Their tortured marriage becomes a lived metaphor for God's relationship to Israel. Just as Gomer is unfaithful to Hosea, so Israel has been unfaithful, turning from YHWH to worship other gods. Certainly, there are legitimate grounds for divorce. Yet God desires reconciliation.

Today's lectionary reading opens after a graphic depiction of judgment (2:1–13). Because of Israel's faithlessness, YHWH will "make her like a wilderness, and turn her into a parched land" (2:3). But then the message shifts. The image of the wilderness appears again—but this time, as the wilderness through which Israel wandered after the exodus from Egypt (2:14–15). In the synagogue, Hosea 2 is read with Numbers 1:1–4:20, which recalls Israel's first journey through the wilderness. Hosea sees his own time through the lens of that journey, remembered as a time of radical dependency upon God (cf. Jer. 2:1–3). The Valley of Achor (2:15) was the route into the northern territory, which tradition said the tribes had followed during their entry into the land (Josh. 7), but it also means "valley of trouble." So when YHWH declares that the valley of trouble will become instead "a door of hope" (2:15), the point is clear. Once more, Israel is entering the valley of trouble: Assyria will come, the kingdom will fall (11:5–7). But once more the wilderness will prove to be, not a place of God-forsakenness, but the place where God's care becomes real, and through which Israel will be brought once more to the place of promise.

From first to last, the language of intimacy permeates today's text. In the NRSV of Hosea 2:14, YHWH says of Israel, "I will allure her." However, a better translation would be "I will *seduce* her" (cf. Jer. 20:7, where the same word is used)! Similarly, the connotation of "know" in Hosea 2:20 is not

The text in question, Hosea 2:14–20, bears the good news that YHWH, the true lover of Israel, is more than ready to renew the covenant with Israel, despite all its betrayal: "I will now allure her" (2:14). The false god will be pulled from its pedestal, all false religious allegiance torn from the Jewish heart. "I will make for you a covenant. . . . And I will take you for my wife for ever" (2:18–19). This is the kind of good news that a pastor will want to bring, whether the focus of the sermon is to be on nation or church.

Alert to the apostolic teaching that judgment begins with the household of God (1 Pet. 4:17), the preacher can take this as a prompt to focus this Sunday on the constancy of God's loving-kindness to the church, despite its failures to be true to what it has learned about the way to follow, the truth to affirm, and the life to share abundantly.

This, then, is the initial question: How has the church failed to be the church? How has it turned away from what it has learned about feeding the hungry, giving something to drink to the thirsty, and welcoming the stranger? Why has it forgotten that its call is to work out in practical terms the blessings of being poor in spirit, merciful, and peacemakers, being the very salt of the earth and the organizers of social justice (Matt. 5:3–10; 25:35–45)? Just as Hosea moves between the extremes of anger and tenderness in his appeal to Israel to return to its true love, the love of God, so Jesus—in rage or compassion, as occasion demanded—called for a total reorientation of life, for a return to a love of God, and for a radical restructuring of society. Greatness in the kingdom has nothing to do with wealth, prestige, or influence (Mark 10:43). It has everything to do with loving God and loving the neighbor.

In the memorable phrase of Scottish moral philosopher John Macmurray, "The final issue we shall have to face will be concerned with the economics of the Kingdom of Heaven."[1] According to Macmurray, Jesus is a special representative of God, who came, like the prophets, to proclaim the truth that when people act in ways that negate this community, they are inhibiting their full development and acting against their true nature. The commitment of the Christian, therefore, is to face the class, sexual, and economic issues that separate people in society and to seek ways of providing for a community of mutual service and support along democratic lines. Macmurray shows no mercy in

[1]John Macmurray, *Search for Reality in Religion* (London: George Allen & Unwin, 1965), 79.

# Hosea 2:14-20

## Theological Perspective

gets translated into justification for such abuse. Yee poignantly asserts this: "Certainly, the male violence embedded in the text of Hosea as it stands should make readers, both male and female, wary of an uncritical acceptance of its marriage metaphor. Moreover, the imaging of God as male/husband becomes difficult when one forgets the metaphor God is *like* a husband and insists literally that God *is* a husband and therefore always male."[1]

When the problematic of the marriage metaphor is taken into account in the context of God's inclusive covenanting, as described in verses 18–20, there is a prophetic word to twenty-first-century people of faith. Current debate about the definition of marriage is revealed as misdirected. Instead of focusing on the definition in terms of the relationship between a man and a woman, the debate might be reframed for people of faith as one concerning how marriage as a covenant requires an expansive understanding of the conditions under which healthy marriage is feasible. In other words, the debate should not be about a definition of marriage in terms of the gender of the marriage partners, but about whether or not the social context in which we are living is one that supports marriage as a covenant between partners whose relationship is part of a larger social matrix. The context of God's inclusive covenant (vv. 18–20) is one that is earmarked by a renewed sense of humanity's relatedness to all of creation, as well as a cessation of warring conflicts. If God's inclusive covenant is the larger social matrix in which healthy marriage can thrive, then the prophetic critique of the current marriage debate is not unlike Hosea's critique of Israel's involvement in the worship of Baal. When people of faith participate in the marriage debate as if preserving the social institution is a matter of salvation, then political debate about marriage is our Baal. As people of faith become captive to the political debate, faithfulness to God's inclusive covenant is subsumed, if not subverted, by the quest to influence sociopolitical life, rather than be witnesses to God's inclusive covenant of peace.

MARCIA Y. RIGGS

## Pastoral Perspective

*Y le hablaré al corazón* (and I will speak to her heart).
15. *Le devolveré sus viñas* (I will give her back her vineyards).

Notice how love is intertwined with belongings. Love is not an abstract reflection of compassion. Love is truly manifested in the restoration of Gomer's property. Love is the radical expression of justice in giving Gomer, as Israel, the fundamental embodiment of freedom: land!

Pastorally, this text also evokes restoration of relationships even in the order of creation. Betrayal is the reason for condemnation. Yet in God's covenant, despite the peoples' deviation, God heals broken relationships by loving *entrañablemente* (deep from God's soul). Such love restores and reorders honor and belongings. Such restoration has an eschatological dimension, a radical gift for creation's reordering: "I will make for you a covenant on that day with the wild animals, the birds of the air, and the creeping things of the ground; and I will abolish the bow, the sword, and war from the land; and I will make you lie down in safety" (v. 18). Hosea seems to bring earth and heaven together: the marriage restoration of Hosea and Gomer is the covenant restoration of God and Israel, with impressive cosmic consequences. The reordering of power in the microreality of marriage is an eschatological symbol/event for the reordering of creation.

Given the current debate about family and marriage, this text offers an opportunity for a multilayered discussion on these issues. The increasing number of intercultural and interreligious marriages and family configuration invites Christian communities to imagine what kind of pastoral counseling and care are needed for these new socioreligious relationships. This text also provides an opportunity for a dialogue on sexual practices and the way in which those affect married and family life. It also provides a unique window to explore with the congregation issues of power in family life and in the broader community of faith. There is no doubt in my mind that when allowing the text to be concrete and as scandalous as it is, it will create fiery discussion and dialogue—perhaps needed in order to rediscover God's wondrous acts of liberation and reconciliation.

CARLOS F. CARDOZA-ORLANDI

---

[1]Gale A. Yee, "Hosea" in *The Women's Bible Commentary*, ed. Carol A. Newsom and Sharon H. Ringe (Louisville, KY: Westminster/John Knox Press, 1992), 200.

## Exegetical Perspective

intellectual knowledge but personal intimacy. The declaration "you will call me, 'My husband [Heb. *'ishi*],' and no longer will you call me, 'My Baal [Heb. *ba'li*]'" (2:16) also speaks to the intimate character of the relationship that God desires. Both *'ishi* and *ba'li* mean "my husband" in Hebrew. However, the latter term refers to ownership and power, while the former "is the more intimate and personal term."[2] Baal, of course, is also the name of the Canaanite fertility god, so to say that YHWH is not Baal means rejecting idolatry. However, to say that YHWH *is*, rather, *'ishi* ("my husband") means discovering a new relationship with God, grounded not in fear but in love.

Hosea 2:16–20 is a marriage proposal. Like a couple repeating their vows, YHWH and Israel begin anew. The covenant with the threatening beasts of the wilderness and the abolition of the weapons of war alike represent this new beginning as a time of unprecedented peace (2:18). Just as in the ancient world a husband paid to the bride's family a bride-price (Deut. 22:29), so YHWH brings to this renewed relationship a gift: not of gold, but of righteousness, justice, steadfast love, mercy, and faithfulness.[3] Israel, transformed by this gift, can at last be a steadfast and committed spouse (cf. Jer. 31:31–34).

God's acceptance and empowerment resonate through all of today's readings. When asked why he eats with sinners and tax collectors, Jesus declares, "I have come to call not the righteous but sinners" (Mark 2:17). Paul recognizes that his identity as an apostle, and even his competency for ministry, derive not from his own worthiness and ability, but from God (2 Cor. 3:5–6). Hope and possibility are grounded in our Lord, who has chosen to relate to us not in justice, but in mercy, grace, and committed, steadfast love (Ps. 103:8).

STEVEN S. TUELL

## Homiletical Perspective

dealing with those at the top of any hierarchies: Ruling groups in every society, he insists, disguise their own self-interest and continued unequal distribution of possessions in the language of necessity or power. God's justice involves care for the victimized and the marginalized. Macmurray is a cogent interpreter of the economics of Jesus.

The churches have never been certain about how to deal with the kind of self-interest and with the continued unequal income distribution to which Macmurray refers. It will take courage on the part of the preacher, who faces the Hosea passage this week, to preach about the economics of the kingdom of God.

Israel had pledged itself to a false lord, a false husband. But repentance is possible. God will remove the Baals from their hold on unfaithful Israel. Who and what are the Baals to whom or to which the preacher may refer, the false allegiances to which the churches that claim to follow Jesus have turned, the easy accommodations with an economy that hurts the poor, the deliberate avoidance of those who are wounded and crying for help in our society? How often and how intently has the church—if not the bride of Christ, according to an earlier theology, at least the body of those who cleave to Jesus Christ as his people—proved faithless, as faithless as Hosea's bride? And how can the people of the church, chosen, as Gomer was chosen, put away their unfaithfulness and clothe the church itself "with compassion, kindness, humility, meekness, and patience" (Col. 3:12)?

The prophets are never easy to live with. Preachers often fall into the trap of preaching (in Charles Kraemer's witty phrase) "mild-mannered sermons to mild-mannered people, telling them to be more mild-mannered than they were last week." Hosea will not allow the preacher to do this.

ROSS MACKENZIE

[2]James Luther Mays, introduction and footnotes to Hosea in *The HarperCollins Study Bible*, 1st ed., ed. Wayne Meeks (San Francisco: HarperCollins, 1993), 1333.
[3]Elizabeth Achtemeier, *Minor Prophets I*, New International Bible Commentary (Peabody, MA: Hendrickson, 1996), 28–29.

# Psalm 103:1-13, 22

[1]Bless the LORD, O my soul,
and all that is within me,
bless his holy name.
[2]Bless the LORD, O my soul,
and do not forget all his benefits—
[3]who forgives all your iniquity,
who heals all your diseases,
[4]who redeems your life from the Pit,
who crowns you with steadfast love and mercy,
[5]who satisfies you with good as long as you live
so that your youth is renewed like the eagle's.

[6]The LORD works vindication
and justice for all who are oppressed.
[7]He made known his ways to Moses,
his acts to the people of Israel.

## Theological Perspective

*Praise of the God Who Is* Hesed: *The Theology of Blessing.* In this great psalm of praise, Israel effusively responds to YHWH's blessings, not just with the words of her lips, but with her whole soul—"and all that is within me" (v. 1). Amid all dangers, and there are many, the Lord has been *hesed*—faithful with "steadfast love and mercy" (v. 4). This psalm remembers, praises, and without hesitation or fear expects the Lord's *hesed* (vv. 4; 8; 11; 17). Walter Brueggemann notes that the crucial factor in *hesed* is "covenantal loyalty and solidarity and not simply an impulse to kindness."[1] And it is also crucial to know that this is the *nature* and *essence* of God *in practice*—"natures" and "essences" are really known only in practice. And this is most especially true of the divine nature. This is how God *is*—the divine *persona* revealed as God *acting* and *interacting* with us in time, place, and circumstance. There is no other God but this God, no other divine Self.

*A Practical Divinity.* Sometimes amid our "speculations" about God, and the *ways* and *will* and *rules* of God, this simple but profoundly practical truth is forgotten. We are called in the Psalms to remember, bless, and praise the *only* One who will

[1]Walter Brueggemann, *The Psalms and the Life of Faith*, ed. Patrick D. Miller (Minneapolis: Fortress Press, 1995), 275.

## Pastoral Perspective

Much as some lyrics could find full expression and make sense only when set to song, so this outpouring of thanksgiving is conceivable only as a hymn, sacred and worshipful. Psalm 103 clearly resounds as a song of thanksgiving set within the Jerusalem temple cultic community. The soul of the psalmist-hymnodist chants out beams of sunlight in awe at the grace of YHWH. "Bless the LORD, O my soul, and all that is within me, bless his holy name" (v. 1). Simply reading the psalm aloud, one can almost hear his singing, with the backing of the chorus.

Blessing the Lord as source of his blessedness (vv. 1–2), the psalmist catalogs his jubilation at God's goodness (vv. 3–5) like a lover reciting why she loves her beloved. With impressive cadences of forgiveness, redemption, and contentment, the case for YHWH's incomparability accumulates, mounts, and overflows, tapping the extravagance that good worship brings. Is it over the top? Yes, and that represents the psalm's magnificence. For even so lavishly stated, it barely scratches the surface of God's greatness. So further affirmations of God's greatness must follow, more and more, forming a staircase of praise, lifting the hearer heavenward.

This psalm is a study in the transformative power of praise within Christian community and how praise invariably strengthens and edifies all parties

$^8$The Lord is merciful and gracious,
   slow to anger and abounding in steadfast love.
$^9$He will not always accuse,
   nor will he keep his anger forever.
$^{10}$He does not deal with us according to our sins,
   nor repay us according to our iniquities.
$^{11}$For as the heavens are high above the earth,
   so great is his steadfast love toward those who fear him;
$^{12}$as far as the east is from the west,
   so far he removes our transgressions from us.
$^{13}$As a father has compassion for his children,
   so the Lord has compassion for those who fear him. . . .

. . . . . . . . . . . . . . . . . . . . . . . . . . . . . . . . . . . . . . . . . . . . . .

$^{22}$Bless the Lord, all his works,
   in all places of his dominion.
Bless the Lord, O my soul.

## Exegetical Perspective

*Praise and Thanksgiving for God's Faithful Love.* The verses that the lectionary takes from Psalm 103 are a ringing affirmation of divine forgiveness, love, and care for God's people. In this form the psalm is understood as a celebration of God's faithfulness by people who have learned of it through direct experience. The lectionary thus reminds the faithful of God's eternal presence and loving concern, gifts that are so reliable and constant that people are likely to take them for granted and overlook them entirely. The focus of the lectionary is solely on God's righteous deeds and loving care, and there are no references to the darker side of religious faith: the fears of divine abandonment and the inability of believers to experience God's healing and forgiveness.

Although the message of the lectionary is an important one to hear, it needs to be set into the larger context of the psalm as a whole. The lectionary has not included all the verses of the psalm, and when those additional verses are considered, the overall message of the psalm is somewhat different. Both messages deserve to be heard, for each speaks to a different aspect of the human condition, and each has something to contribute toward helping people to live the faithful life.

## Homiletical Perspective

Psalm 103 begins with a soliloquy: self speaks to self and to no one else. The tone seems quiet, introspective, a resolute statement barely breaking silence: "Bless the Lord, O my soul, and all that is within me . . ." Self speaks to self and to that even more interior self lurking furtively wherever selfhood may be found inside oneself: "*all* that is *within* me." This must be right from the beginning, the psalmist insists, or all else will skew off in one false direction or another. We may remember another soliloquy in Scripture: a rich man catalogs his abundant possessions, determines to build more and more barns in which to store them (Luke 12:18). The psalmist, however, catalogs "all that is within me" to check each organ, each muscle, every conviction, and every memory among the "all that is within me" to see where there might be restraint or hesitation to "Bless the Lord." A sermon might begin with such an introspective interlude, wondering where we resist blessing God or bowing before God, or simply resist God. Do we hold something against God? Are we distracted? Are we bored? Are we afraid of drawing near?

The soliloquy continues with a second, tense "Bless the Lord, O my soul," but now the psalmist's voice rises to audibility and speaks half a prayer or perhaps only an overture to prayer, "and do not

*Psalm 103:1–13, 22*

393

# Psalm 103:1-13, 22

## Theological Perspective

always and forever redeem our lives "from the Pit" and crown us "with steadfast love and mercy" (v. 4)—"the LORD" who "*works* vindication and justice for all who are oppressed" (v. 6). Brueggemann continues: "The same God who guards heaven and earth to keep them functioning is the one who also guards the hungry, the oppressed, the bowed down, and the strangers." Israel's praise "makes no distinction between Yahweh's fidelity toward stars and moon, and toward widows and prisoners. Both forms of God's fidelity are cause for wonder in our world where such fidelity is so unknown." Such praise prayer "is endlessly surprised about the character of God and endlessly grateful for life in the world that God makes possible. . . . Praise is a glad statement of 'disbelief,' an acknowledgement that there is more to the reality of Yahweh than we dared to hope and more than we could have imagined." In the end, "doxology is an *irrational act*."[2]

***Steadfast Love and the Pathos of God.*** Heartache and trouble are not denied in the Psalms, but rather overcome in the always strange and risky encounter of *hesed*, which not even the deepest human sin or most profound evil can diminish. In its praise, Israel need not linger over its inadequacy and sin: "Israel prays well beyond itself, utterly sure of God's 'Goodness' that overrides and transforms."[3] It is this God "who forgives" and "redeems," "crowns," "satisfies" (*makes enough*), and renews (vv. 3–5). Who among us would expect that the divine anger would be so "slow" and steadfast love so "abounding" (v. 8)? This is not the way of the world; this is not how things work. How naive are we being asked to be, that the Lord of the universe "will not always accuse . . . nor repay us according to our iniquities" (vv. 9–10)? In the reversal of expectations of the divine pathos, praised and blessed so exuberantly in this psalm, let us, for a change, say *hesed* also of ourselves. In the religion of the prophets—which along with the Psalms is surely the religion of Jesus—the discrepancy and distance between God and us finally gives way to relationship, reciprocity, and engagement. Abraham J. Heschel points out that "the disparity between God and the world is overcome in God, not in (us)."[4] And so this is why this psalmist of "the people of God" does not linger[5] in any place of infinite distance and bereftness from

## Pastoral Perspective

involved. Praise—whether of God or each other—is discouragingly rare in our world. What blessing that it is so firmly lodged at the center of who we are and what we do as the church. For just as someone will rightfully glow when praised at a job well done, a whole people will radiate light as the goodness of God is lifted up! Ask consistent worshipers about missing a Sunday and how that changes their whole week. The church specializes in praise, and we do well not to forget that. It is a temptation to substitute more pragmatic, efficacious, and utilitarian agendas.

Such personal and transforming praise here finds expression as thanksgiving converts darkness into light. Here realities of sin, illness, and death (vv. 6–10) become occasions of justice for the oppressed, mercy for the guilty, and a fresh start for the burdened. Here repentance is the gateway to happiness and prosperity, for our well-being is based upon no other foundation than God's removing from between us the obstacle of our sinfulness. The suffering of our separation from God becomes the stage for the drama of God's loving-kindness. Here God does for us what we cannot do for ourselves, reaffirming the "cup runneth over" (Ps. 23:5 KJV) quality of Psalm 103.

The power of the opening (vv. 1–2) is the psalmist's hunger to know God by experiencing God. This drives throughout the psalm. It is also a strikingly contemporary impulse, animating much spirituality of rising young generations. It further witnesses to the Psalms' timelessness, as eternal as the yearning of human hearts.

The psalmist's longing is full of wonder at how a Lord so elevated and mighty could also design to be the same God who is personal and accessible. The psalmist cannot quite get over that, his incredulity further fueling his wonder. In this regard, the psalm anticipates a Messiah at once fully human, fully divine. The human desire to experience God, even more than knowing about God, points us toward the gift of the suffering-victorious Messiah whom the church affirms.

The psalm also demonstrates how joy enlarges itself out of nothing to create holy space not present before. In this, worship forms a contagion of gladness inviting in all who seek God. That joy works as healing balm in a joyless world. Witness how many liturgists and pastors seize upon verse 8, "The LORD is merciful and gracious, slow to anger and abounding in steadfast love," to assure and steady the faithful following the rigors of confession.

---

[2] Ibid., 41; 50–51.
[3] Ibid., 53.
[4] Abraham J. Heschel, *The Prophets*, vol. 2 (San Francisco: Harper, 1975), 9.
[5] Brueggemann, *The Psalms and the Life of Faith*, 53.

## Exegetical Perspective

*An Exhortation to Praise God (vv. 1–5).* The psalm begins with a rather unusual self-exhortation by the psalmist (vv. 1–2). The psalmist's whole being is addressed and urged to bless the divine name and to remember everything that God provides to the community of faith. God's care is so constant that the psalmist wishes to guard against understanding it as expected and routine.

The self-exhortation is followed immediately by a succinct catalog of divine virtues (vv. 3–5), and the recitation of the catalog itself constitutes the praise called for in verses 1–2. God is one who forgives all iniquity and heals all diseases (v. 3), redeems the faithful from the underworld, faithfully supplies love and mercy (v. 4), and finally sustains members of the community as long as they live (v. 5). At this point in the psalm, the writer does not indicate the source of this profound belief in God's goodness. It may come from the general testimony of the community, or perhaps the psalmist has personally experienced God's healing and care (v. 4).

*God's Great Acts in History (vv. 6–13).* Whatever the source of the affirmations in verses 3–5, the source of the claim in verse 6 is clear. For the psalmist, communal testimony and personal experience are not adequate to reveal fully God's goodness to the community. Rather, Israel learned most profoundly about God by remembering God's gracious acts throughout its history. God vindicates the community and provides justice for the oppressed (v. 6). This central aspect of the divine character is revealed most clearly to Israel in the community's foundation narrative, the story of God's liberation of Israel from slavery in Egypt, the giving of the law to Moses at Sinai, and the leading of Israel safely through the wilderness (v. 7). During these events God showed mercy to the people and remained faithful to the covenant, even when the people rebelled and deserved punishment. God did become angry and punished disobedience, but God was also slow to anger and mercifully did not allow anger to last forever (vv. 8–9). Although Israel was punished, it received less punishment than it deserved (v. 10). Israel's experience with God in the exodus leads the psalmist to conclude that God will always remain faithful to the covenant so long as the community remains faithful, and God will always respond in love, removing the community's transgressions and showing it compassion (vv. 11–13). From the perspective of the lectionary, the memory of God's historical actions and the affirmation of God's love

## Homiletical Perspective

forget all [God's] benefits." "Benefits" is the traditional and widely employed translation (AV, NRSV, NIV, NEB), but "benefits" are what we calculate and negotiate at our place of employment; "benefits" are part of our remuneration, our repayment for doing the job; "benefits" are what we are owed according to labor contracts or company policy or state law. "Benefits" are our due, and that is precisely what the psalmist most definitely wants to say is not the case, is not the manner in which God gives to us. We are *not* given what is due us; we do *not* receive what we have earned; we get much better than that! The JPS translation, "do not forget all [God's] bounties," gets more to the point of Psalm 103, for the psalmist will go on to catalog God's bounties as an overflowing fount of "steadfast love and mercy." A torrent of verbs describes God's bounty in verses 3–5: God forgives, heals, redeems, crowns, satisfies, and renews. What does God not do that we could possibly need?

The psalmist does not "forget God's bounty," but in a bold act of remembering gets to the heart of the matter by recalling what Walter Brueggemann has called "Israel's core testimony."[1] The psalmist first remembers Israel's central mystery, the giving of the law on Mount Sinai (v. 7; Exod. 20 and 34), and then remembers the rhetoric of the Lord's self-disclosure to Moses in that place: "The LORD is merciful and gracious, slow to anger and abounding in steadfast love" (v. 8; Exod. 34:6). Lest this testimony be misunderstood, the psalmist swiftly elaborates with two verses, beginning with a negative, as if to say this (v. 7) is true, but this and that (vv. 9, 10) are not: not always accusing, not keeping anger forever, not dealing with us according to our sins, not repaying us according to our iniquities. This is the sort of negative theologizing proposed by Christopher Morse in *Not Every Spirit: A Dogmatics of Christian Disbelief,*[2] who insists that if we believe the gospel ("The LORD is merciful and gracious") we must necessarily disbelieve that which distorts that gospel (God accuses and nurses anger; God's faithful response is calculated by our faithfulness).

With a pair of dazzling parodies of measurement, the psalmist invites us to imagine the immeasurable and incalculable grace and mercy of God. The "steadfast love" of the Lord can be compared with the height of the heavens, but how high is that

[1]Walter Brueggemann, *Theology of the Old Testament: Testimony, Dispute, Advocacy* (Minneapolis: Fortress Press, 1997), 117–228.
[2]Christopher Morse, *Not Every Spirit* (Valley Forge, PA: Trinity Press International, 1994).

# Psalm 103:1-13, 22

## Theological Perspective

God for too long. Even the reminder of verse 14 (not included in this reading) that "we are dust" does nothing to temper the joy. Because God knows the extent of our weakness and our need for the "steadfast love" of the divine kindness, from our ashes will come new life.

*God's Presence Is God's Dominion.* This great psalm of praise ends where it began. The Lord is to be blessed in all of the Lord's works, and everything—*all in all*—is a work of the Lord. All places are the Lord's dominion (v. 22). No other divine power is necessary than the *hesed* of God's presence—God-with-us as the compassionate *Other*, like us and not like us at the same time. YHWH's presence is filled with security, comfort, and mercy, as well as risk, discomfort, and a "fear" that is always creative and not destructive—the anxiety and edginess that sometimes brings us to the brink of danger as a way to vitality and new creation (vv. 13, 17).

*The God Who Saves Is the God Who Risks.* Again, the irony of the *nature* and *essence* of God reveals YHWH, whose *hesed* has risked all "ordinary divinity" (see also Phil. 2:5–11) for us, now asking only that we risk a little of ourselves by giving up the "standard accounts" of world and religion for this new "sub-version."[6] Praise is always risky. *Hesed* will undoubtedly make for "costly companionship,"[7] especially for those who insist—before and after all else—on breaking bread with others (Lat. *com+panis*). Since God has taken this *hesed* chance with us, perhaps it is high time we began to take similar chances with each other.

JOSEPH MONTI

## Pastoral Perspective

This is no less true of verses 11–12, "For as the heavens are high above the earth, so great is his steadfast love toward those who fear him; as far as the east is from the west, so far he removes our transgressions from us." These familiar words echo in our ears across decades of worship. The psalmist's palpable joy is holy because it is not at anyone's expense. Just the opposite, it translates into the healing of the broken.

Psalm 103 represents worship in the purest sense in that, despite how personal it begins (v. 1, "Bless the LORD, O *my* soul, and all that is within *me* . . ."), God is ultimately praised for God's own sake. This is the force of adducing God's mighty acts (vv. 6–10) in God's saving deeds. This God is no mere projection of the self.

Awareness of YHWH's saving transcendence becomes the context within which the psalmist can properly understand his own life. This deep sense of worship—at once as personal as breathing, yet as majestically transcendent as the skies—does not just happen. It exists as a function of worshiping within a structured community with norms, beliefs, practices, rites, and shared texts ordered in a common life.

In a former day, this might go without saying. But in today's highly interiorized environment of popular inner "spirituality," with few external reference points, and without the ties that bind us in community, such balance becomes rarer. The interplay of personal participation in the divine with revelatory landmarks is the strength of the poetry, the particular individual locating him or herself in the vastness of the God whose character and intention have been known across space and time.

This unity of the intimately personal experience of God, where the psalm began, with the powerful and distinct otherness of God is also where the psalm ends. The charm and force of this thanksgiving song returns once more in verse 22 as the "works" and "dominion" of God are remembered as a blessing within *my* soul.

Along the way, the poet summons images mounting an impressive tableau, from the points of the compass to a father's compassion to the eagle's youthful vigor. The psalm is a testimony to the overwhelming greatness of God's grace, a gift against which our own offerings and contributions must necessarily pale.

DALE ROSENBERGER

---

[6] See Walter Brueggemann, "Preaching as Sub-Version," in Brueggemann, *Deep Memory, Exuberant Hope: Contested Truth in a Post-Christian World*, ed. Patrick D. Miller (Minneapolis: Fortress Press, 2000).
[7] Brueggemann, *The Psalms and the Life of Faith*, 50.

## Exegetical Perspective

and compassion motivate the final self-exhortation to praise God (v. 22), thus bringing the psalm to an end at the same point where it began.

However, the verses of the psalm not included in the lectionary supply a somewhat different message. After the psalmist's triumphant memory of God's love and fidelity during the exodus, the text next turns to a different memory, an admission of human weakness and impermanence. Illnesses are not always healed, God does not always respond favorably, and death is a regular part of the human condition. God recognizes Israel's true nature and understands that the people are dust (v. 14). They are like grass that dies and is blown away by the wind (vv. 15–16). In contrast, God is eternal and will show righteousness to future faithful generations (vv. 17–18). This too is a memory of the exodus story. The weakness of the wilderness generation led to disobedience and in turn to punishment. The rebellious Israelites died in the wilderness and were not allowed to enter the land that God had promised to their ancestors. However, the disobedience of one generation did not cause God to reject the covenant made with the people at Sinai. God remained faithful to Israel and renewed the covenant with the children of the wilderness rebels. Temporary sin and punishment do not fundamentally change God's relationship to the community. God remains both the covenant partner of Israel and indeed the ruler of the entire universe and everything in it (vv. 19–20). The obedient inhabitants of heaven praise God as the ruler of the universe (v. 21), and the faithful earthly community, now in a restored covenant relationship with God, echoes that praise (v. 22).

The overall message of the psalm, then, is that human weakness and disobedience cannot permanently destroy the family bond between God and Israel. The bond remains, waiting to be enjoyed by a future faithful community. God remains faithful and steadfast, even if a particular Israelite community does not.

ROBERT R. WILSON

## Homiletical Perspective

measured in light years? "As far as the east is from the west" sounds like a straightforward geographical equation, like the distance from Los Angeles to New York being 2,824 miles, until we recall that east and west are directions, not destinations, and there is no conceivable end to the distance between them.

Worshipers fascinated with *The Da Vinci Code* and *The Gospel of Judas* might be interested to know some gnostic groups in early Christianity described sin in terms of *amnēsia*, forgetting. They understood humans were created purely spiritual beings in communion with God, but had been so traumatized by taking on human flesh and enduring birth that they had forgotten that primal unity with God.[3] In quite a different way, the psalmist understands our separation from God in terms of forgetting. Forgetting God's bounty, we may assume an accusing and angry God bent on exacting full compensation for every sin, every slight, every failure, every stupid thing we ever did. As if aware of that dreadful characterization of the OT God as angry, vengeful, and accusing, the psalmist engages in a profound remembering: You remember the law you have broken? Remember also the character of the Lord who gave it: gracious and merciful, slow to anger. Remember God's bounty and do not forget.

The psalmist of Psalm 103 provides a fine model for preachers. Our preaching could use more of the doxological imperative that begins and concludes the psalm (vv. 1–2, 21–22). The psalmist/preacher focuses tightly on what the Lord does (vv. 3–5). What we do (and fail to do) is mentioned only within the framework provided by the text of the psalmist's sermon (v. 7). The psalmist/preacher interprets and elaborates the sermon text negatively by describing exactly what the Lord does not do with our failings, sins, and iniquities (vv. 9–10) before depicting more positively how God does treat our transgressions (vv. 11–12) and providing a stunning and evocative image from human experience to assist us in recognizing the Lord's compassion (v. 13). The song that began in soliloquy with one voice finally commands every voice in creation to sing and "Bless the Lord."

PATRICK J. WILLSON

---

[3]C. K. Barrett, *The New Testament Background*, 2nd ed. (New York: Harper and Row, 1989), 93–103.

# 2 Corinthians 3:1–6

¹Are we beginning to commend ourselves again? Surely we do not need, as some do, letters of recommendation to you or from you, do we? ²You yourselves are our letter, written on our hearts, to be known and read by all; ³and you show that you are a letter of Christ, prepared by us, written not with ink but with the Spirit of the living God, not on tablets of stone but on tablets of human hearts.

⁴Such is the confidence that we have through Christ toward God. ⁵Not that we are competent of ourselves to claim anything as coming from us; our competence is from God, ⁶who has made us competent to be ministers of a new covenant, not of letter but of spirit; for the letter kills, but the Spirit gives life.

## Theological Perspective

Letters of recommendation, introducing people and facilitating reception and care for the ones bearing such letters, were a common feature of Paul's world, known to Paul himself, who commended people to his churches (1 Cor. 16:15–18; Rom. 16:1–2; Phil. 4:2–3). The "superapostles," who came to Corinth and sparked the series of letters that together comprise 2 Corinthians, possessed such letters of recommendation (2 Cor. 3:1).

Paul responds by saying that he needs no such letters because the Corinthians themselves are his letters; even more, through Paul's missionary efforts the Corinthians are, strictly speaking, *Christ's* letters into whose very being the gracious presence of God has been brought by the Spirit (3:3). Here Paul recalls to the Corinthians their own experience of God, which came through the preaching of the gospel. He will take this same approach a few years later when writing to the churches of Galatia (Gal. 1:6–8; 3:1–5). Further, Paul contrasts this inner authority with the external authority that is written "on stone tablets," and by this contrast, Paul differentiates himself from the superapostles who have appealed to a Spirit-laden tradition, from Moses through Jesus to themselves, in which miraculous powers, including their own, have been exhibited.

## Pastoral Perspective

This passages beckons in at least two directions.

The first direction, which may be useful for pastors and teachers in churches where people are worried about numbers and growth, is the reframing of church marketing.

At first glance, the twenty-first-century seeker is an odd duck. We think we have not seen her before. She is not loyal to denominational ties and will leave the church of her childhood in a flash (if she had a church identity as a child). Instead of brand loyalty, the seeker of today is looking for and open to the gathering that fits him or her individually. He is looking for programs, services, amenities that will enrich his life and deepen his faith. She wants a singles group that will offer friendships and potentially a romantic relationship, or she is looking for an outreach program in which to volunteer. Perhaps he is looking for a church home that has already attracted the people that he wants to get to know in town.

Many seekers who are parents choose their church on the basis of the nursery and children's activities. One seeker wants contemporary music and hates the organ, while another insists on traditional music with a fabulous organ. One looks for continuity and stability in a time in the history of the world of great flux and stress. Another, raised on

## Exegetical Perspective

Whether 2 Corinthians was originally a single letter or is a composite of two or more, one theme that recurs often in our present epistle is the struggle between Paul as apostle and other "apostles," who not only claim their own authority but question his. The discussion about what counts as a valid "letter of recommendation" for an apostle is a part of this argument.

In Paul's world, letters of recommendation were as common as they are today. We write letters to help people as they apply to school or apply for new jobs. In this way, we introduce the person to the potential faculty or employer. In Paul's world, without telephone or e-mail, one might give a letter to a traveler to introduce him or her to friends at the journey's destination. Surely it would not be surprising if apostles and traveling missionaries carried letters of commendation from a church they had served to a church in an unfamiliar community. And Paul himself is perfectly capable of including a commendation of Timothy in Philippians 2:19–24 and of Phoebe in Romans 16:1.

Because much of 2 Corinthians consists of Paul's defense of his own apostleship over against that of other Christian leaders who have apparently criticized him, it may well be that in the first verses of our text, he is contrasting his own self-evident

## Homiletical Perspective

"*You* are our letter." This statement toward the beginning of the text introduces metaphorical language that breaks open conventional thinking. Preaching should find a way to do the same.

Paul's wordplay that cascades throughout this third chapter uses strong metaphorical images to shape the theological meaning of this text, but not without some confusing twists. Paul's use of "letter" zigzags through the passage like an Olympic skier racing down a slope. With every zag, the theological intention of the text seems to turn in a slightly different direction, leaving the preacher struggling to stay on course.

Pithy statements fill this text, including that famous concluding phrase, "for the letter kills, but the Spirit gives life." Preachers through the ages have found that each statement alone provides a rich subject for topical preaching, and many have opted to treat these statements separately. Each saying draws into consciousness a whole theological tradition that is worthy of proclamation. These theological worlds, however, have been blended together in rapid sequence by Paul. How do the various statements merge to form meaning here? How can preaching work with all of them within one sermon?

Verses 1 and 2 subvert conventional thinking about letters of recommendation. The old expression

# 2 Corinthians 3:1-6

## Theological Perspective

This argument should make us pause, because Paul appeals to the very experience of the Corinthians, although, to be sure, not to the merely day-to-day experiences that people commonly have. Paul appeals to the experience of God's grace when they heard his apostolic preaching. He contrasts the experience of grace in response to faithful hearing with the experience of the superapostles' miracles. This means that finally there are two broad authorities to which Christians can appeal: apostolic testimony about Jesus Christ and our experience of a gracious God, known in our hearts through the Spirit. Are these not the external and internal authorities to which Paul appeals when he reminds the Corinthians of "our word to you" (2 Cor. 1:18–19), and then later reminds them that they are Christ's letter written authoritatively on their hearts (3:2–3)?

While this relationship between external witness and internal experience might sound strange, it proves to be a commonly held way of looking at authority: Consider, first, the American law court where the judge and the defendant come together. The judge has authority over the defendant, because the law authorizes that to be so. Yet, relative to the law which authorizes the judge to have authority over the defendant, the judge and the defendant stand on equal footing, so that the defendant can appeal the judge's ruling by appealing to the law itself. This is why we have appeals courts. Or, to take another example, in the classroom the professor has authority over the arguments made by students, handing out grades. Yet, relative to the rules of scholarship that govern a particular field of study, the professor and the student stand on equal footing so that the student can appeal the professor's grade by appealing to the rules of scholarship.

To sum, Paul's comments to the Corinthians on the structure of religious authority reflect the basic nature of what it means to have authority over someone, as compared to having sheer power over them. Authority is granted by some source of authority (the law, or the rules of scholarship, or the presence of the Spirit), and relative to that authorizing source both the authority (the judge, or the professor, or the Scriptures) and that which stands under the authority (the defendant, or the student, or the Christian) stand on equal footing. Simply put, the inner, subjective experience of the Spirit forms a conversation partner with the outer, objective testimony of the Word, both authorities authorized by God. Between these two poles we must hammer out an adequate theology for our context.

## Pastoral Perspective

MTV, looks for short and entertaining spurts of information because the greatest sin of all is the sin of being boring.

At first glance, the twenty-first-century seeker truly is an odd duck. But when we look at his feathers and little webbed feet, his bill and beady eyes long enough, we see that we have seen him time and time again. He, she, they are just the plain old always and ever common human being ducks. She is hungry and stressed and often afraid, like a sheep without a flock and, even more important, without a shepherd. He wants an authentic faith community and a true home in God, and he doesn't know how even to begin to ask for what he needs. This was true from the get-go. Every human being, from the moment the umbilical cord is cut, is trying to find a way to attach and belong, while also being a separate person. One might dare to say the seekers of the day are exactly whom Jesus had in mind when he invited people to leave their mothers and fathers and journey with him in faith. Instead of church leaders moaning about the fluidity and fickleness of seekers in our day, would it be possible for us rather to imagine them as especially open to new paths of healing and forgiveness and a new heaven, new earth, new faith, just as Jesus prayed we all would over and over again? Perhaps we are asked to discover in the odd-duck seekers our own condition and rediscover the gospel in a refreshing way, to rediscover their and our own new beginning?

This brings us back to the greatest new church starter in history, Paul, and this passage. Paul understands that the best church growth program for any Christian community is the grace of Jesus Christ in the lives of the members of the body. All of the promotional materials ever produced and all the church programs ever invented can only point to the power of the risen Lord in the community of faith.

What if all the people in the congregation began to think of themselves as letters of introduction to their church? On an even more profound level, what if all of us accepted the responsibility that Jesus gave us in our baptism, which is to be a letter of recommendation to the whole world of the good news of God in Christ? We would have to stop looking for the next newest and greatest marketing ploy for church growth. Instead, we would know that we are invited to be, not just the marketing program for the church, but the healing and growth of Christ—in us, through us, and among us.

As the church of Jesus Christ and through the power of God, we are made "competent to be

apostolic status to the status of those who came to Corinth bearing letters of recommendation, and who will ask the Corinthian Christians for such letters to carry on their further journeys. These later apostles may also be the same preachers Paul identifies in 2 Corinthians 2:17 as "peddlers of God's word."

The verbal phrase in verse 3 that the NRSV translates "prepared by us" uses the Greek verb *diakoneō*, the root of the Greek (and English) for "deacon." Sometimes, this verb suggests a kind of ministry of serving (see 2 Corinthians), but sometimes a "deacon" is one who represents another in full authority. It is clear that Paul is trying very hard *not* to say that he is the author of the Corinthians' exemplary faith. He is either Christ's servant or Christ's representative in the penning of a true letter of recommendation on the Corinthians' hearts.

We have exactly the same ambiguity in the term *diakonos* in 2 Corinthians 3:6. Paul may be saying that he is the servant of a new covenant, or he may be saying that he is the representative, the ambassador of such a covenant. What is clear in either case is that his authority as apostle is always and entirely derivative from the authority of the one who sends him.

Paul's metaphor of the letter, epistle, opens up for him a contrast between two kinds of letters, messages. There is the contrast between the letter written with ink and the letter written by the Holy Spirit. And there is the contrast between letters written in stone and those written on the human heart. At the beginning of our passage, Paul contrasts Christ's true letters of recommendation with the puffery of the false apostles. Now, he contrasts Christ's letter written on the heart with Moses's commandments written on the tablets of stone. Surely Paul here recalls Jeremiah 31:33: "But this is the covenant that I will make with the house of Israel after those days, says the LORD: I will put my law within them, and I will write it on their hearts; and I will be their God, and they shall be my people" (see also Ezek. 11:19 and 36:26).

Second Corinthians 3:5 may be translated "not that we are competent of ourselves" or "not that we are adequate in ourselves" or "not that we are sufficient in ourselves." If 3:4–6 is understood as a defense of Paul's authority, if he is constructing his own version of the letter of recommendation, then competence seems the issue. Adequacy seems a bit thin for what he tries to claim. If we want to read the text more in the light of the rest of the epistle (see 4:7–12; 12:9 for different vocabulary, but a similar concern) and of Paul's argument in such passages as

"It's not what you know, but who you know," still rings true in today's world. Letters of reference are written daily by "important" people in order to commend others for placement in colleges and schools, jobs, even social clubs. Those letters are written in ink to serve as a documented testimony to be seen by the eyes of those who have the power to confer favor. Some letters are written by the very hand of a person of influence whose words, signature and seal convey the patron's own authority. What if, however, you could imagine *yourself* as a walking, talking letter of recommendation? You are written, not with ink, but with Spirit. The recommendation is written, not on the surface of your body, but on the heart that cannot be seen. You might prefer a tattoo, thinking that it can tell your story for you, but a tattoo cannot duplicate your own personal voice and action springing to life from the core of your being. Your letter is not delivered to some person of influence who bestows special favors on your behalf. You are, instead, a public document whose beating heart is recognized and known by everyone. But who wrote your letter? Wasn't Jesus Christ, the crucified and risen Messiah, the actual author of the letter, written in the familiar handwriting of those who served you in ministry? Playing with this metaphor opens up a whole new world of meaning for preaching about the nature of the church's life and witness!

A second metaphorical phrase, "not on tablets of stone but on tablets of human hearts," is introduced in verse 3. Stone tablets symbolize the theological meaning surrounding the giving and receiving of the Mosaic covenant. If a congregation is unfamiliar with this theological tradition, they may need a minicourse to bring them up to speed in order to understand the richness of that tradition. Any treatment of the theology of new covenant should not result, however, in a diminishment of the importance of the original Mosaic covenant of law. The reference to "tablets of human hearts" alludes to the prophetic vision of both Ezekiel (36:26–27) and Jeremiah (31:33), who preached from within that Mosaic covenant. Exploring the physical characteristics of the human heart in contrast to the qualities of stone may uncover some fresh insights about the theological meaning of new covenant.

The text abruptly returns to the question of sufficiency for ministry. Is the competence of those who minister responsible for the effective establishment of a new covenant in human hearts? "No," Paul says. Only the competence of God to

# 2 Corinthians 3:1-6

## Theological Perspective

Recently Gary Dorrien, in his magisterial three-volume series *The Making of American Liberal Theology*,[1] has identified the appeal to experience and reason alongside external authority as the hallmark of liberal Christianity, as it weaves a middle ground between authoritarian overbelief and atheistic underbelief. Much of the theological trajectory of the late twentieth and early twenty-first centuries has developed along just this path, hewing to the theistic side: The development of African American theology, womanist theology, feminist theology, mujerista theology, queer theology, Latin and South American liberation theology, postcolonial theology, postmodern theology, and other theological perspectives derived from contextually engaging the ancient texts, attests to a theological approach that dialogues between concrete and communally interpretive experiences of the living God and the biblical texts authorized by God's Spirit.

These many Christian voices that now come to the theological table have inspired us to discuss our old assumptions in relation to many issues such as the ordination of women; the role of GLBT (gay/lesbian/bisexual/transgendered) Christians in our churches and pulpits; the ways that Christian missionary activity has related to its context, often both suppressing indigenous experiences of God and impressing particular patriarchal theologies; and the proper role of, and interpretation of, external authorities in Christianity.

Some voices have criticized such theology as postmodern "politically correct" theology: Borrowing a phrase from the criticism that Karl Barth (1886–1968) made of older liberal Protestantism, they have called these new theological voices countercultural, "cultural Christianity." Is such criticism fair? What could be more significantly multicultural than Paul's church at Corinth, which was a rebuilt seaport city with plural religious voices? In the Corinthian church were Jews, Greeks, males, females, slaves, citizens, superapostles, and regular folk who didn't feel so super. To them Paul appeals to their experience of inner testimony by the Spirit, by which they are Christ's letters; and he also appeals to the outer apostolic witness about the Christ event. Can we do any better than working out our theology between these two poles?

JOHN W. RIGGS

## Pastoral Perspective

ministers of a new covenant" (v. 6). We are made witnesses of the grace of God in Jesus Christ, and our lives become the ultimate and most definitive market strategy for the glory of God.

The second way the passage beckons is toward a reframing of the discussion of the letter of the law versus the spirit of the law.

The new covenant is different from a contract (of course the old covenant was as well, but we seemed not to be able to grasp that). The new covenant is written in flesh and blood by the Spirit of the living God. Here is an invitation to break free of arguing about this little point and that little point, and to remember the ways that people have seen this new covenant in Christ, in the lives of those around them, and in the grace God gives each of us, if we will but accept it. God making us competent is through the power of the Spirit, and not the letter. The letter kills, because it is contingent, fragile. The Spirit gives life, because it is everlasting.

In an age that is paradoxically both biblically illiterate and addicted to proof-texting, this particular text offers a marvelous door through which people can enter a larger room of understanding in their faith. No matter what our favorite biblical fight or passage, Paul invites all of us to look for the spirit of Christ in the ways we understand Scripture and, more important, in the way we live our lives.

MARTHA STERNE

---

[1] Louisville, KY: Westminster John Knox Press, 2001–6.

## Exegetical Perspective

1 Corinthians 2:1–5, the issue seems to be one of sufficiency. Again, Paul is contrasting his limited skills with the unlimited grace that grounds them.

It is tempting to try to draft Paul for our contemporary hermeneutical wars and to argue that when he makes the distinction between letter and spirit, he is distinguishing between "literal" and more nuanced methods of biblical interpretation. But in the context of our passage, and especially in the light of the following verses, it is quite clear that Paul's distinction is between the covenant from Moses, the commandments written on stone, and the covenant from Jesus—the covenant of justification. In 2 Corinthians 3, the old covenant is not annulled, but it is outshone by the glory of the new covenant in Christ.

So too the claim that "the letter kills but the Spirit gives life" must be read in the context of 2 Corinthians 3:9. The function of the old covenant was to pronounce judgment, condemnation, and therefore death; the letter kills. The function of the new covenant is to pronounce justification, and therefore life.

As is so often the case with Paul, a remarkable number of suggestions are contained in the scope of a few verses. There is the distinction between the old covenant and the new. There is the discussion of what makes an apostle, or indeed a faithful person, sufficient for serving Christ. There is the claim that what counts in judging the authority of an apostle (and a pastor too?) is not the credentials contained in a letter of recommendation, but the credentials evident in the lives of the people the apostle (and the pastor) serves. The entire discussion serves to underline the theocentric basis of Paul's ministry and ours: our sufficiency is from God.

DAVID L. BARTLETT

## Homiletical Perspective

bring about a new order of creation makes anyone sufficient for a ministry of service. God's sufficiency honors weakness as a source of life. How can highly competitive, driven people grasp the plausibility of this claim? Preachers can assist congregations in comprehending this idea by turning away from heroic images of human accomplishment to embrace examples of ordinary, uncelebrated folk whose weaknesses make room for real change to emerge.

The final words of the text cut to the chase with their own stark contrast: "For the letter kills, but the Spirit gives life." What kind of letter is death dealing? Is it the letter of commendation written by an influential patron? Is it the letter of the law, which reveals human guilt? Is it both? Whatever the theological intention is here, it is in contrast to the life-generating power of Christ's Spirit.

An hourglass shape could allow the theological flow of the sermon to begin with the world of patronage and commendation that is alive and well today. From there, we may turn to the tablets of stone that once conveyed the presence and power of God's own life and see that they quickly became a possession to be exploited for their influence in conferring status and favor on specifically chosen people. (Of course, this interpretation takes some liberties with the intention of the text.) As a written document, the law failed to reflect the glory of God's liberating power, but cast a dark shadow across the alienation of sin that fed practices of ongoing discrimination among people and groups. Century after century, humanity lay dead while stone tablets silently pronounced its eulogy. This revelation moves the sermon to its turning point with the announcement of a new covenant written on the tablet of fleshy, human hearts—the fulfillment of God's promise made known through the prophets. This covenant is established in the realm of the interpersonal, transcending the rule of judgment. As human hearts are made alive by the Spirit of Christ, people themselves stand as living witnesses to the glory of God and commend the ones who provided the ministry of service for them to enter into this new creation. Letters no longer have power to confer favor when God's favor is alive in human hearts. Even now, *we* are the public letters of commendation toward God's great sufficiency, written by the crucified and resurrected Christ by the Spirit.

MARY LIN HUDSON

# Mark 2:13-22

[13]Jesus went out again beside the sea; the whole crowd gathered around him, and he taught them. [14]As he was walking along, he saw Levi son of Alphaeus sitting at the tax booth, and he said to him, "Follow me." And he got up and followed him.

[15]And as he sat at dinner in Levi's house, many tax collectors and sinners were also sitting with Jesus and his disciples—for there were many who followed him. [16]When the scribes of the Pharisees saw that he was eating with sinners and tax collectors, they said to his disciples, "Why does he eat with tax collectors and sinners?" [17]When Jesus heard this, he said to them, "Those who are well have no need of a physician, but those who are sick; I have come to call not the righteous but sinners."

## Theological Perspective

In this particularly appropriate reading for the season of Epiphany, Jesus' behavior, as well as his words, reveals clearly and unmistakably the nature of God and God's will for us. "And as he sat at dinner in Levi's house, many tax collectors and sinners were also sitting with Jesus and his disciples—for there were many who followed him" (v. 15). There are few things we do that are more intimate, more deeply material and spiritual, than eating with one another. Whether on the job or at home, in church or at a dinner party, table fellowship is powerfully personal and communal. It is also, for most of us, highly structured in terms of our ethnicity and socioeconomic status. We tend to eat with people like ourselves. This self-selective intimacy, no less prevalent in the first century than today, reinforces the status quo. It serves as a barrier to communication between groups—rich and poor, employer and employee, black and white, urban and rural, young and old—groups that would profit from the interaction that takes place over a meal.

Here in Mark, Jesus disrupts the social stratification of mealtime. He eats with all comers: tax collectors, sinners, his disciples, scribes. In words that many of us have heard in conjunction with the Eucharist, "Anyone, wherever they are on the journey of faith, is welcome at Jesus' table." This kind of

## Pastoral Perspective

"Without awe, people turn to doctrine.

Without reverence, people turn to rules."[1]

As in Mark 2:1–12, the "why" questions are significant. "Why does he eat with tax collectors and sinners?" "Why do John's disciples and the disciples of the Pharisees fast, but your disciples do not fast?"

The questions function rhetorically as a means of challenging opponents. Likewise, answering a question with a question is a means of opposition. A period of silence indicates that the Pharisees have no appropriate answer to Jesus' question(s). At the heart of the questions is the issue of purity. The purpose of purity laws was to represent Israel as a holy people, set apart from surrounding cultures and social practices, and to ensure proper boundaries. Israel's mission was to reflect the holiness of God in her own holiness: "For I am the LORD your God; sanctify yourselves therefore, and be holy, for I am holy" (Lev. 11:44).

Both debt and purity rules were enforced through the law (Torah) and the temple. Mark's Gospel rejects the temple but reinterprets the Torah. The law is still law, but not always in the familiar way.

There is some insecurity in the human spirit that desires and needs rules, certainty, control, principles to live by. Avoiding ambiguity and paradox in Scripture

[1]William Martin, *The Art of Pastoring* (Decatur, GA: CTS Press, 1994), 72.

<sup>18</sup>Now John's disciples and the Pharisees were fasting; and people came and said to him, "Why do John's disciples and the disciples of the Pharisees fast, but your disciples do not fast?" <sup>19</sup>Jesus said to them, "The wedding guests cannot fast while the bridegroom is with them, can they? As long as they have the bridegroom with them, they cannot fast. <sup>20</sup>The days will come when the bridegroom is taken away from them, and then they will fast on that day.

<sup>21</sup>"No one sews a piece of unshrunk cloth on an old cloak; otherwise, the patch pulls away from it, the new from the old, and a worse tear is made. <sup>22</sup>And no one puts new wine into old wineskins; otherwise, the wine will burst the skins, and the wine is lost, and so are the skins; but one puts new wine into fresh wineskins."

## Exegetical Perspective

"Be careful of the company you keep." This modern caution could well have come out the mouths of the "scribes of the Pharisees" in the first pericope of this text (vv. 13–17). When chapter 2 opens, the religious leaders are back here, as are the crowds. Once again the crowds are curious about Jesus, but Jesus is searching for more than curiosity. Once again the religious leaders are in a stir. Once again Jesus is teaching. Not only *what* he teaches, but more specifically *how* he teaches it, will present a major problem for those traditionally in charge of religious teaching.

For the reader, the teaching of Jesus begins as he walks along the sea and calls Levi—someone who was not numbered among the crowd and someone who will later be numbered among the Twelve—to follow him. Levi has not listened to Jesus and chosen to follow him. Levi is a tax collector and therefore a sinner in the Markan math. In the prior pericope, Jesus established himself as one who can forgive sins, and in this text Jesus invites a nondebatable sinner to follow him.

Levi may hold a priestly name, but his profession sets him at odds with the religious leadership of occupied Palestine. He was "sitting *epi to telōnion*, which probably refers to one of the toll booths located along main highways and at bridges and

## Homiletical Perspective

The text involves two stories of controversy. One concerns the question why Jesus eats with tax collectors and sinners (vv. 13–17), and the other concerns the question why his disciples do not fast (vv. 18–22). These two stories happen in different settings; however, since the lectionary thoughtfully combines them into one text, they make an outstanding pair by which preachers are invited to envision the church as a radically eschatological community.

Regarding the first story, imagine the dinner table in Levi's house. Levi, called by Jesus to be his disciple despite his shameful reputation as a tax collector (vv. 13–14), is so excited and grateful that he prepares a dinner table to celebrate his calling. He invites his new teacher, Jesus, and his new colleagues, the disciples of Jesus. In addition, Levi invites his old fellows—tax collectors and sinners—who live outside the law like himself, because he wants proudly to introduce Jesus and his disciples to them. For Levi, Jesus' calling is not merely his individual acceptance by God but Jesus' welcoming of all his people who are religiously and socially marginalized and have shared with him suffering and pain as well as joy and happiness in everyday life. And Levi is right. Jesus gladly shares the meal sitting at the same table with them. The dinner table prepared by Levi is

# Mark 2:13-22

## Theological Perspective

inclusive table fellowship was as subversive in the first century as it is today. Tax collectors and sinners were thought to be impure. No wonder the scribes asked Jesus' disciples, "Why does he eat with tax collectors and sinners?" (v. 16). Such barrier-breaking behavior flew in the face of the purity system's spectrum of distinctions between rich and poor, male and female, Jew and Gentile, sick and healthy. That same purity system, with its burdensome web of taxation and sacrifice, was also highly profitable for the temple and its priesthood.

If Jesus is our Epiphany, our revelation of God, then his table fellowship reveals a God who welcomes all of us without reference to our social status. Where we were born, who our parents are, our physical appearance, how many degrees we hold, how much money we make, what we have accomplished in life, how old or healthy we are—these are not criteria for receiving God's interest and compassion. All of us are welcome at God's table. *And so is everyone else.* This recognition may strike us as it struck the scribes, calling into question our own social stratification, our own covert purity system. To live in the spirit of divine compassion, as that compassion becomes tangible in Jesus' eating with tax collectors and sinners, actively challenges social structures that impede the realization of anyone's full humanity. For the early Christian communities, their open and inclusive table fellowship and their egalitarian lifestyle were at once an expression of their experience of God's love in Jesus Christ and the embodiment of a social vision in which all people are seen as God's children.

When the scribes question Jesus' table fellowship with tax collectors and sinners, Jesus responds in a remarkable way. "Those who are well have no need of a physician, but those who are sick; I have come to call not the righteous but sinners" (v. 17). At first glance, this analogy seems perfectly reasonable from a conventional point of view. Just as you would not expect a well person to be in need of a doctor, you would not expect a righteous person to be in need of Jesus' message. But surely Jesus doesn't mean to exclude those who are righteous from his company, nor would he say such people are any less the objects of God's love than the sinful. His response must be meant ironically. Indeed, in the context of this reading, it is precisely the scribes, the socially defined and self-proclaimed righteous ones, who are most in need of Jesus' message, and yet least able to hear it. By virtue of their social status, their role in the religious community, they have access to Jesus, but

## Pastoral Perspective

and religion enables us to feel comfortable in our beliefs and to have a clear sense of right and wrong.

The Pharisees and scribes wanted to take care of religious business and keep people in line; whereas Jesus demonstrated blatant disregard for ritual purity laws. Mark 2:13–22, the second and third of five conflict events in Mark 2:1–3:6, is where he is drawn to outcasts and those outside the religious establishment. Tax collectors were unclean and not allowed to attend synagogue, yet Levi invited fellow sinners to table fellowship to check Jesus out for themselves. Jesus included those who had been lawfully excluded.

Jesus made it clear that "whoever said that nobody was above the law was wrong, that *everybody* was above the law, because the law was made to serve humans, humans weren't made to serve the law."[2] The true purpose of Torah was to glorify God and bless humankind. The call of Levi, like the paralytic's healing, was an act of forgiveness and a crossing of boundaries. Even despised tax collectors were worthy of coming to the table.

Hospitality and sharing a common meal were sacrament-like experiences that encouraged or at least allowed healing and forgiveness in relationships. To have fellowship at the table implied a strong relational bond. For example, one former senior vice president of Bank of America urged believers to make a weekly commitment to have lunch with someone whose theology and lifestyle was different from their own.

Jesus is also questioned about fasting. In response, he refers to the "already" present dimension of the kingdom of God. Fasting included abstaining from sex, bathing, and eating certain foods, as a symbol of penitence, but Jesus is the bridegroom who brings joy and traps the scribes in their own metaphors. To know Jesus is to taste new wine—the call to discipleship is like a joyful wedding, a freedom to love and a freedom to die so that others might live. The joy of Christ's presence in the power of the Spirit reveals new wine and exposes the tension between the early church and the synagogue.

New life in Christ is reorientation of mind, heart, and lifestyle. Surrender and lordship do not come easily for us. We tend to follow Christ at a safe distance, maintain control, and integrate our faith into older, established patterns of thinking and behavior.

But the church that is not culturally bound finds new wineskins in every generation. The essence of

[2]Brian K. Blount and Gary W. Charles, *Preaching Mark In Two Voices* (Louisville, KY: Westminster John Knox Press, 2003), 25.

## Exegetical Perspective

waterways where customs were collected for the regime of Herod Antipas, puppet 'king' at the pleasure of Rome."[1] As a tax collector, Levi would have been ritually unclean, as he dealt with Gentiles and Gentile money. As a collaborator with Rome, Levi would also have been considered a traitor to his own people, profiting from Rome's oppressive taxation. Despite a huge crowd pressed upon him, Jesus pulls this tax collector, this sinner, into the community of disciples.

Like the fishermen disciples, Levi leaves everything at the word of Jesus, and as with Peter (1:29), Jesus joins Levi in his home. But they are not home alone. Relying on the power of repetition in aural communication, Mark describes the company Jesus keeps no less than three times—"tax collectors and sinners."

Jesus does more than keep company with Levi and his likes. Mark says, "Jesus was reclining at table in his house" (2:15, my translation). That Jesus was "reclining" (*katakeisthai*) suggests more than a quick and perfunctory visit to this sinner's house; it suggests a Roman banquet at which guests would recline around a central table. Jesus was not just visiting the house of a sinner; he was eating with him and others like him. This is the first of three controversies that arise in chapter 2 surrounding eating practices, and Mark includes it for good reason. The issue of table fellowship would become a major concern in the early Christian church (Acts 15; Gal. 2:12).

In Levi's house, Jesus does not revise the ancient purity laws; he defies them, at least as traditionally interpreted. In God's reign, God's table will feed all who hunger, regardless of class, of religious identity, of purity status. Mark is not romantic in his casting of "scribes of the Pharisees" and "tax collectors and sinners." The religious leaders are not evil, nor are the sinners saints. They are all caught up in a system that is sick unto death and will be transformed in the imminent reign of God.

Jesus responds to the objection concerning the company he keeps by first citing an old aphorism. He reminds them that the physician goes where she is needed, namely, among the sick. The Pharisees (the separated ones) maintain their "righteousness" by staying clear of contagion (embodied in "tax collectors and sinners"), while Jesus associates with contagion ("tax collectors and sinners") to bring about God's righteousness.

[1]M. Eugene Boring, *Mark, A Commentary* (Louisville, KY: Westminster John Knox Press, 2007), 80.

## Homiletical Perspective

inclusive—not for the privileged "members only," but for the whole community. At the dinner table, God's grace and mercy are offered even to tax collectors and sinners, who are often grouped together with beggars, thieves, murderers, sexually immoral people, and Gentiles. The dinner party is filled with the joyful sounds of laughter and boisterous noise.

Now the scribes of the Pharisees, who separate themselves from others by strictly observing the law, especially purity laws, are curious about what Jesus does in the house of the tax collector. They peek in the house and are surprised by the event inside the house. Jesus, who claimed to be the one who had the divine authority to forgive sins (Mark 2:1–12), eats with people of impurity! Confused, the scribes ask his disciples, "Why does he eat with tax collectors and sinners?" (v. 16). Overhearing this, Jesus says, "Those who are well have no need of a physician, but those who are sick; I have come to call not the righteous but sinners" (v. 17).

Preachers who read the text would be shocked by Jesus' radical acts and words. For Jesus, there are no boundaries between insiders and outsiders, because God's grace and mercy are not limited to insiders who are righteous, but rather are extended to outsiders marginalized as sinners in society. By freely crossing boundaries between the community and the rest of the world, Jesus reveals the presence and work of God's Spirit, who makes the human community a whole.

To the preacher, overwhelmed by this radical vision for a community, the second story affirms the power of this vision. When asked why his disciples do not fast while John's disciples and the disciples of Pharisees do, Jesus replies by making a comparison to a wedding banquet. Jesus' disciples are like the guests who are invited to a wedding to celebrate with the bridegroom and other guests (vv. 18–19). The preachers who imagined the dinner party in Levi's house (vv. 15–17) would readily picture Jesus' wedding banquet as an inclusive party to which sinners as well as the righteous are invited. Although other religious people are living an old lifestyle of "business as usual" by habitually observing such traditional religious practices as fasting, Jesus' disciples discern the times and choose to disregard the old lifestyle. For them, it is time to practice a new lifestyle with Jesus, just like the guests who are invited to an inclusive wedding banquet by the bridegroom. For them, it is time to celebrate the presence of God all together beyond the boundaries between them.

# Mark 2:13-22

## Theological Perspective

whatever satisfaction, monetary or otherwise, derived from that status blocks their capacity to hear Jesus' unconventional wisdom. From the narrow perspective of their socioeconomic position, Jesus is a threat rather than a liberator. Indeed, it is the despised and vulnerable ones, the poor and dispossessed, who flock to Jesus and his message of divine compassion. The songwriter Leonard Cohen captures this haunting irony. When Jesus "knew for certain / only drowning men could see him / he said 'All men shall be sailors then / until the sea shall free them.'"[1] These enigmatic lines tell us, as Mark does, to give up our socially constructed security and go in search of others who are in need.

In verses 18–20 Jesus is asked why John's disciples and those of the Pharisees fast, while his disciples do not. This represents yet another hostile attempt to get Jesus to identify proper religious practice. Not surprisingly, he resists endorsing one practice over another. Instead, he responds, "The wedding guests cannot fast while the bridegroom is with them, can they? As long as they have the bridegroom with them, they cannot fast" (v. 19). In other words, take pleasure in the celebration of a marriage; it is a time of feasting and joy, not fasting and sorrow. In the context of Jesus' table fellowship, the later association of Jesus with the bridegroom is less important than the endorsement of more than one way to live in the presence of God.

If the Jesus of today's reading represents our Epiphany, then God is a God of compassion for one and all. Jesus incarnates that compassion in his table fellowship. In responding to Jesus as the Christ, we are not taking on a particular set of requirements; rather, we are entering a relationship with God, a relationship that establishes and colors our relationship with all other creatures. In all likelihood, this amounts to a revolution in our lifestyle. It will not do to put the new wine of God's love into the wineskins of our old behavior.

JERRY IRISH

## Pastoral Perspective

Christianity does not change, but the cultural wrappings are always changing. For example, at a gathering of young adults reviewing a lengthy mainline denominational confessional statement, the suggestion was made to devise a new, more straightforward way of expressing similar beliefs in a format more available to all persons.

Vision: Jesus loves me this I know: Embracing the Story
Daring to share our lives: Telling our Stories
Authentic, purposeful, real: Living the Story

Mission: Embracing the story: We seek to understand what it means to be Christ-centered and rooted in the reformed tradition, recognizing that we are the beloved community of God.

Telling our stories: We seek to embody a fresh model of community that embraces our identity as young adults, energizing out of our shared stories, and is united by our common story.

Living the story: We seek to unearth new forms, new language and new approaches to reach young adults for the sake of Christ in the church and culture.[3]

Jesus came to heal the religiously sick as well as tend to physical, emotional, spiritual, and mental hurts. A fundamental problem for the Old Testament prophets as well as contemporary believers is that people "do religion" or "do church" as a substitute for doing justice and mercy. Christ did not call and invite people who thought they were righteous, but people who knew they needed God.

It is no accident that the Mark 2:15–20 text for Ash Wednesday is joined with the Isaiah 58:3–12 passage regarding fasting. Practicing the imposition of ashes can be a powerful symbol of recognizing our human sinfulness. But if it represents only our humility, then we will not experience the spiritual healing that comes from sharing our bread with the hungry. Spiritual practices are not only enacted in community; they are for the healing of those outside the community. Sometimes the old wineskins need to be reserved for old wine!

AL MASTERS

[1] Leonard Cohen, "Suzanne," *Stranger Music* (New York: Random House, 1993), 95.

[3] Statement of the Young Adult Ministry Team, Presbyterian Church (U.S.A.), 2003.

## Exegetical Perspective

The second response of Jesus involves how people understand their essential identity before God. If they consider themselves "righteous," they exclude themselves from this banquet table with Jesus, for he did not come to "save" the righteous. "Specifically, those who want to be insiders in Jesus' group must envision themselves reclining next to people whose politics and behavior they find disgusting, and eating out of the same dish with them (14:20)."[2]

Mark introduces the term "the disciples" (*tois mathētais*, v. 15) in this text as those who join with Jesus to eat with "tax collectors and sinners." Disciples are therefore those who do not try to separate themselves from sin and sinners, but acknowledge that all are sinners and yet all are welcome to recline at table with a Lord who forgives sin and transforms sinners into righteous followers.

The controversy in the second pericope in this text (vv. 18–22) is that Jesus and his disciples do not follow the traditional fast patterns. As members of renewal movements in Israel, John's disciples and the Pharisees fasted in preparation for the coming of the anointed one, the Christ. Mark's readers know that the whole basis for argument is lost on the Pharisees (and John's disciples for that matter), because they are calling for behavior consistent with the longing for God's reign, when the initiator of God's reign in standing in their midst (1:1). In his response to the Pharisees, there is a proleptic uneasiness in the words of Jesus as the reader senses the bridegroom, Jesus, will be taken away from them.

Writing about this text in its entirety, Mary Ann Tolbert argues:

> The distinct needs of human beings in every special moment in time always take precedence over the established rules, rituals, and customs dictated by tradition. Just as a physician cannot treat the sick if custom prevents his or her contact with them, so Jesus cannot fulfill his mission to preach the gospel to sinners if he does not share table fellowship with them. . . . Traditional rituals are suitable for traditional situations, but new situations require new responses.[3]

"Be careful of the company you keep." To which, the Jesus we meet in Mark would respond, "Exactly."

GARY W. CHARLES

## Homiletical Perspective

The new lifestyle based on the vision of an inclusive community is as powerful as a piece of new cloth that is not yet shrunk but sewn onto an old cloak or as powerful as new wine that has not yet fully fermented but has been put into old wineskins. When the time comes, the new cloth will pull away from the old cloak and make the tear worse; when the time comes, the new wine will burst the old wineskins and ruin them (vv. 21–22). Like the piece of new, unshrunk cloth, the new lifestyle of Jesus' followers will eventually tear apart the old, conventional, lifeless, co-opted religious beliefs and practices. Like the new wine, the new lifestyle of following the life and ministry of Jesus will eventually overturn the vicious circle of prejudiced human systems and structures. And Jesus in the Gospel of Mark proclaims that the time is fulfilled; the reign of God has come near (1:15). No one can delay God's time; no one can interrupt the transforming power of God's Spirit.

The preacher who sees the radical vision in the text of an inclusive community becomes a visionary and is called to witness the power of a new lifestyle based on this vision. The preacher is challenged to convey and preach this vision creatively in many different contexts. If a congregation regards itself as a group of insiders who are righteous before God and others, the preacher's witness to God's presence beyond their own community has the power to disrupt their exclusive way of thinking and provides implications for a new lifestyle. If a congregation regards itself as outsiders in some manner, the preacher's inductive approach to God's offering of grace and mercy to sinners as well as to the righteous has the power to liberate them from the old bondage and give them a new vision for life. If a congregation struggles to break down the dividing walls within and beyond the church surrounding race, gender, religious practices, and sexual orientation, the preacher's provocative witness to the power of the new lifestyle encourages listeners to be like new wineskins strong enough to hold the transforming power of the Spirit of the risen Christ, who continues to work to make the human community a whole.

EUNJOO MARY KIM

[2] Sharyn Dowd, *Reading Mark* (Macon, GA: Smyth and Helwys, 2000), 25.
[3] Mary Ann Tolbert, *Sowing the Gospel* (Minneapolis: Augsburg-Fortress, 1989), 135.

# Deuteronomy 5:12-15

[12]Observe the sabbath day and keep it holy, as the LORD your God commanded you. [13]Six days you shall labor and do all your work. [14]But the seventh day is a sabbath to the LORD your God; you shall not do any work—you, or your son or your daughter, or your male or female slave, or your ox or your donkey, or any of your livestock, or the resident alien in your towns, so that your male and female slave may rest as well as you. [15]Remember that you were a slave in the land of Egypt, and the LORD your God brought you out from there with a mighty hand and an outstretched arm; therefore the LORD your God commanded you to keep the sabbath day.

## Theological Perspective

How do we make time for rest in a society and world that most often rewards workaholism? A question like this is one way we often begin to reflect upon the meaning of Sabbath. Although such a question is an important point of departure for twenty-first-century people of faith to engage this lectionary text, we must also discern the meaning of rest in terms of practices of faithfulness and an understanding of work with reference to vocation.

This text in Deuteronomy highlights a third theological key for interpreting the relationship between God and Israel. In last Sunday's Isaiah text (43:18–25), God's relationship with Israel is a matter of election (God chooses a particular people as God's own). In this week's Hosea text (2:14–20), covenant (a mutually binding agreement based on God's promises and the obligations for humans) is the earmark of the relationship. Here in the Deuteronomy text, keeping a commandment or "living the way of Torah"[1] is at the center of how Israel is to be faithful. The three texts thus may be understood as a threefold commentary on the requirements of moral life for communities who seek to be faithful people of God because of the

[1]Tikva Frymer-Kensky, "Deuteronomy," in *The Women's Bible Commentary*, ed. Carol A. Newsom and Sharon H. Ringe (Louisville, KY: Westminster/John Knox, 1992), 52.

## Pastoral Perspective

This text points to a theology of work. While many have emphasized the theology of Sabbath or rest, the Sabbath is intertwined with work. Frequently we confuse income with work. We think that work is simply a matter of earning our income. Work is the embodiment of vocation nurtured by a deep calling and clarity of direction, commitment, and sacrifice. Because work is an organic function of our daily life, it is both life-giving and draining. Work as a vocation consumes and restores; it is fulfilling and frustrating.

The text is clear about the need for work: "Six days you shall labor and do all your work" (v. 13). Because work is the embodiment of a vocation, it is multifaceted. If we limit work to what we have been trained to do or to the hours we spent doing a task, we lose the divine dimension of work as vocation. Work as vocation gives meaning and transcendence to the encompassing tasks that define who we are in our daily life experience. It is the transfer of not only kinetic but also psychic and spiritual energy. The result of our tasks returns with varying degrees of satisfaction and frustration that become nutrients to continue our work, to continue our vocation.

If verse 12 demands that the Sabbath be observed and *kept holy*, does that mean that all we do during the other six days is *unholy*? Perhaps the text

## Exegetical Perspective

The Decalogue, or Ten Commandments, appears twice in Scripture, in two different versions (Exod. 20:1–17; Deut. 5:6–21). Jewish tradition holds that Exodus 20:2–6 and Deuteronomy 5:6–10, which are virtually identical in the two versions, were spoken by God to all Israel, while the later commands, which differ, were interpreted by Moses (see the Babylonian Talmud, *Makkot* 23b–24a). Clearly these two Decalogues are related; however, the nature of that relationship is difficult to discern. The Exodus Decalogue, which belongs in its present form to the final editing of the Torah, may be based on the version in Deuteronomy.[1] However, archaeologist Ron Tappy argues that the latter part of the Decalogue (Exod. 20:12–17; Deut. 5:16–21) is old family and clan law and likely predates the monarchy in Israel (though the pairing of those commandments with religious law was a later development).[2] It may be best, then, to think of these two passages as alternate forms of a common tradition. But whatever their relationship, the question of the role each version plays in its context remains.

[1] S. Dean McBride Jr., "The Essence of Orthodoxy: Deuteronomy 5:6–10 and Exodus 20:2–6," *Interpretation* 60 (2006): 136.

[2] Ron E. Tappy, "Lineage and Law in Pre-Exilic Israel," *Revue Biblique* 107 (2000): 177, 203. McBride, however, argues for a short composition history, noting that neither version "is demonstrably older than or independent from the literary stratum in which it is preserved" (McBride, "Orthodoxy," 135).

## Homiletical Perspective

*Observe the Sabbath day and keep it holy.* The preacher will likely begin studying in preparation for Sunday by asking something like this: "Will I encourage the folk who come next Sunday to return to an older way of Sunday observance, and urge them, as the catechism once commanded, to observe 'a holy resting all that day, even from such worldly employments and recreations as are lawful on other days'? That's the older discipline, enforced rigorously by the Puritans when they came to the New World, and still kept by a few. Or will I face the fact that for most of the congregation Sunday has become less and less the Lord's Day, and increasingly just another day for shopping, eating out, or attending some public entertainment? Will my sermon be one that urges people to live according to the strict way, and keep Sunday free 'from worldly employments and recreations'? Or can it somehow link the original intention of the Sabbath rest with the central emphasis of Sunday worship for Christians, namely, that on the first day of the week Jesus Christ was raised from the dead?"

How, then, can one shape a sermon that will deal with the life situation of twenty-first-century Christians?

The first task will be to inquire into what the Shabbat means in the Hebrew Scriptures. It was a

# Deuteronomy 5:12-15

## Theological Perspective

promises God makes and steadfastly fulfills. The common reference in all three texts is remembrance of the exodus.

This text (Deut. 5:12–15) is part of the Decalogue or Ten Commandments. These specific verses are the fourth commandment, the commandment to observe the Sabbath day and keep it holy. Biblical commentaries remind us that Deuteronomy's version of this fourth commandment differs in form from the one in Exodus 20:8–11. Although the intent of both versions of the commandment is that there be one day without work and set apart to the Lord, the Exodus version begins by recalling God's work of creation in six days followed by a seventh day of rest; that remembrance of creation establishes a pattern for Israel and the basis of the commandment. In Deuteronomy, it is the memory of God's redemptive work in terms of Israel's deliverance from slavery in Egypt (v. 15) that is the reason for observing the commandment; this remembrance is the reason why all persons in the community—perhaps, especially the slaves—and all animals are to rest. In sum, "in the case of Exodus, the community is called to remember and to obey out of that memory; in the Deuteronomic form, the community obeys to keep alive the memory of redemption and to bring about the provision of rest from toil for all members of the community."[2]

These two emphases, keeping alive the memory of redemption and providing rest from toil for all members of the community, are crucial because God has consecrated the day. God's consecration of the day means that Israel's obligation is to keep the day holy. The question of how to keep the day holy pushes us to ask, "What are the practices of faithfulness that embody the meaning of rest in this commandment?" "Practices" here refers to ways of being and doing that are formative to a community. Here are a few ideas regarding rest and practices of faithfulness.

First, rest is not simply the cessation of work; rest as a practice of faithfulness requires that the doing of work is replaced by the worshiping of God. A community at rest keeping the Sabbath holy is a community that is worshiping God for the purpose of thanking God for deliverance and redemption. A practice that embodies this meaning of rest is worship—worship marked by thanksgiving and rituals that evoke historical memory of the ways that God has delivered and redeemed us.

## Pastoral Perspective

provides an opportunity to discuss a theology of work or vocation that offers continuity and connection between the holiness of the Sabbath and the other six days. Exploring the continuity and connection between the Sabbath and the other days of the week might offer the following opportunities: (1) To discern the vocational and missional grounding of working committees in the community. Could you imagine the budget committee working with a missional grounding rather than exclusively exercising its administrative oversight? (2) To discover in our daily life activities—such as parenting, cooking, teaching, playing, reading, thinking, shoveling cement, sharing time with friends, accompanying an ill neighbor to the hospital, making love, debating—the divine intention and vocation of our life. (3) To differentiate our income-making tasks from work as vocation and, as a result, discover how our vocation should guide and shape our income-making tasks. (4) To create a new modus operandi that would illuminate the ways in which our personal and communal theologies of work or vocations—work as embodied vocation—inform and form our Sabbath worship experience. Seeking, thinking, and discovering the continuity and connection between work and the Sabbath can be draining. The discernment of the Holy in our vocation, of the relationship between the six days and the Sabbath in our daily life experiences, demands a time for rest, a time to be renewed. Sabbath is irrelevant without transcendence and meaning in our daily work!

The command is clear: "But the seventh day is a sabbath to the Lord your God; you shall not do any work" (v. 14a). This is God's invitation to shift energy and focus from our work—our embodied vocation and the daily wrestling that comes with and from it—to our relationship with the Creator. It is amazing: God demands time and space for us to deliberately rest. Focusing our attention and self on God prevents us from burnout and exploitation of others. While some may think that the Sabbath is a day for God, the Sabbath is commanded for our sake: to liberate us from being trapped in a loop of overanalysis and overwork in our vocation and, consequently, protect those who are intertwined with our vocation.

The Sabbath is also commanded to protect those abused and exploited by our misguided vocation and by those who do not have a vocation but have an income-oriented task totally submitted to the insatiable but mistaken values of wealth and

---

[2] Patrick D. Miller, *Deuteronomy*, Interpretation Series (Louisville, KY: John Knox Press, 1990), 80. Cf. Moshe Weinfeld, *Deuteronomy 1–11*, Anchor Bible, vol. 5 (New York: Doubleday, 1991), 302.

## Exegetical Perspective

Today's lectionary reading, the commandment concerning the Sabbath in Deuteronomy 5:12–15, marks the most significant difference between the two Decalogues. The Sabbath commandment in Exodus 20:8–11 refers back to the Priestly creation account (Gen. 1:1–2:4a), where God completes creation by resting on the seventh day (Gen. 2:1–3). In Deuteronomy, however, Sabbath refers not to the timeless story of creation, but to the history of Israel—specifically, to the exodus (Deut. 5:15). What theological purpose is served in Deuteronomy by linking Sabbath to deliverance from slavery?

A core feature of the book of Deuteronomy is a deep concern for what we today would call human rights. Indeed, Deuteronomy does for ancient Israel what the U.S. Constitution does for American democracy: it describes the polity of the society while ensuring limits on governmental power and guaranteeing the rights of individuals. No wonder S. Dean McBride Jr., who translated Deuteronomy for the NRSV and is perhaps the greatest living expert on this book, suggests that Deuteronomy is the first constitution in world history.[3] Deuteronomy's concern for the individual shows itself in numerous ways. The often abused practice of debt slavery (see Amos 2:6–8) is carefully regulated in Deuteronomy 15:1–18. No Israelite man or woman could be forced to serve as a slave for longer than six years (cf. Exod. 21:2–11, which lacks any time frame for freeing female slaves). Further, upon release, a male slave had to be provided for generously, so that the cycle of indebtedness didn't start all over again (as in the Sabbath commandment, this law is linked to the memory of Egyptian slavery; see Deut. 15:15). A special concern for the rights of women is evident in legislation regulating treatment of women taken in wartime (Deut. 21:10–14) and within the Decalogue in the framing of the commandment regarding coveting (cf. Deut. 5:21, which places the neighbor's wife first and clearly separates her from the neighbor's property, to Exod. 20:17, where the neighbor's wife is subsumed under the contents of his house). Concern for the rights of the accused is evident in the law regarding capital crimes (Deut. 17:6–7), which requires multiple witnesses for conviction and requires the witnesses to demonstrate their certitude by administering the penalty—regulations that would certainly have reduced the number of actual executions. Perhaps most remarkable are the procedures for holy war (20:5–9),

## Homiletical Perspective

festive day, to be welcomed with the lighting of candles, a day to celebrate the perfection of creation. The Creator "rested on [this] day," according to the creation story (Gen. 2:2), so it was a day also of rest and abstention from work. But even for modern Jews, "time makes ancient good uncouth," and the Shabbat is not now for most a day of rest and abstention from work. For most Christians too, Sunday is no longer controlled by blue laws and enforced social conduct.

In facing the changes forced by modernization, a modern rabbi speaks helpfully of the Sabbath as the diastole of the heart, its intent being "to counterbalance the systolic action of the weekdays. . . . It is a time to loosen the pulls and strains of ambition and to become aware of the gifts of inner tranquility."[1]

Here is a first point of reference for the preacher. The sermon can be focused on the joy of coming together with other Christians to worship the Creator who made everything good. But it remains important also for people still to regard Sunday (or, at least, some unbroken twenty-four-hour period) as a time to find sustained rest in the "one damn thing after another" of modern life, time to seek a systolic counterbalance to the activity of the days of work and duty.

A second point of reference for the preacher is that Sunday for Christians is a day to hear the God of creation calling them to celebrate the new creation. When the first Christians chose Sunday as their principal day of worship, commemorating Christ's resurrection, they laid aside the notion of enforced rest on the seventh day and stressed instead, on each first day of the week, the coming of a new age (see 2 Cor. 5:17). So the sermon this week can proclaim that every Sunday is a gift and sign that the Holy One, God the Creator, is still at work in the world, making all things new, even if we do not see the reality that "things which were cast down are being raised up."

Sunday is the place and time when we become alert to the presence of the Holy One in our midst. Rabbi Lawrence Kushner writes of the Sabbath what Christians can no less firmly say of the Sunday: "Just this is the difference between the days of the week and the Sabbath, for on the Sabbath . . . we are able to understand how the presence of the Holy One is everywhere—even when it's not immediately apparent."[2]

---

[3]S. Dean McBride Jr., "Polity of the Covenant People: The Book of Deuteronomy," *Interpretation* 41 (1987): 229–44, esp. 242–44.

[1]Harold Schulweis, *For Those Who Can't Believe: Overcoming the Obstacles to Faith* (New York: HarperCollins, 1994), 207 f.
[2]Lawrence Kushner, *The Way into Jewish Mystical Tradition* (Woodstock, VT: Jewish Lights Publishing, 2001), 154.

# Deuteronomy 5:12-15

## Theological Perspective

Second, rest interrupts the established flow of things at the same time that it opens up a space for recognizing that which may be awry in the midst of everyday living and for reaffirming members of the community, as well as expanding the community. When the commandment makes clear that all members of the community, regardless of social status and species, are to rest, the established order of hierarchy and the potential for exploitation, abuse, and objectification of those who are not the power brokers of the community are suspended. Likewise, this understanding of community is one premised upon radical inclusion. A community at rest keeping the Sabbath holy is a community that respects interpersonal and interspecies relationships. A practice that embodies this meaning of rest is hospitality, and hospitality will be manifest through acts of care, service, and justice toward those from whose labors we reap benefits or over whom we have power. For if hospitality as described is practiced over time, then hospitality that is in effect justice making will become part of the character and actions of the community all of the time.

Still, how does the twenty-first-century person of faith, prone to workaholism, keep this commandment? As suggested at the beginning of this essay, there must be a shift in how we understand work. If our work is the job whereby we earn money, and accumulating money is why we work, then work is detached from a theological understanding of vocation. Frequently today we seem to reserve discussion of calling or vocation to those who are in ordained ministry. Focusing the discussion in that way has led us away from nurturing each person to discern his or her vocation; in the words of one author, "vocation is not a profession. It is definitely not 'work' and even less a 'job.' Vocation is knowing and staying true to the deep voice."[3] The deep voice is our purpose for living, and this voice can be best discerned over time, when we observe the Sabbath day and keep it holy in communities where practices of worship and hospitality are at the heart of what it means to rest.

MARCIA Y. RIGGS

## Pastoral Perspective

prosperity typical of the global economy. The command stretches not only to family and household members but to the living things that contribute to sustain daily life—"or your ox or your donkey, or any of your livestock" (v. 14b). Moreover, the command also includes the most vulnerable—"the resident alien in your towns, so that your male and female slave may rest as well as you" (v. 14b). The Sabbath fulfills many critical functions: (a) it invites a true embodiment and continuous reflective evaluation of our theology of work or vocation; (b) it protects the believer from exhaustion given the intensity of living in and critically reflecting on our vocation; (c) it protects those who directly or indirectly participate in our vocation; and (d) it protects those who, because of their particular role and/or vulnerability in society, may fall prey to exploitation from a misguided vocation or an income-oriented taskmaster. Shifting our focus and direction to God creates justice for all.

Faith communities and pastoral ministries—ordained and laity—need to reconsider the meaning of Sabbath. Among many Protestant communities, Sabbath is about renewal and revitalization, but often it does not include the vocational and protective elements described above. Perhaps it is because there is something missing in our recovering of the Sabbath. The text's historical referent is crucial. We can ask, Why should we keep the Sabbath? The text answers: "Remember that you were a slave in the land of Egypt, and the LORD your God brought you out from there . . . therefore the LORD your God commanded you to keep the Sabbath" (v. 15).

A slave has no vocation. A slave lives in exploitation and abuse, mechanically performing offensive and humiliating tasks. Energy is consumed with no life-giving return. Life is drained. Rest is given to pursue further exploitation. A reminder of this condition will demand a different approach for the time of rest and for the experience of work. Not anymore under the control of Egypt, daily life finds God's direction in the Sabbath, for it is a time of constant discovery of vocation and protection of creation. Will our religious communities find a historical referent with the power to change our interpretation of the Sabbath?

CARLOS F. CARDOZA-ORLANDI

---

[3]John Paul Lederach, *The Moral Imagination: The Art and Soul of Building Peace* (New York: Oxford University Press, 2005), 167.

which require the officials to release from service soldiers who have just built a house, have planted a vineyard, are newly married, or simply are afraid! The Sabbath commandment in Deuteronomy 5:12–15 must be seen against this backdrop of concern for human rights.

In Deuteronomy, the Sabbath is labor legislation: absolutely *everyone* in Israel gets the day off. Deuteronomy 5:14 provides a reason for the universal prescription of rest on the seventh day: "so that your male and female slave may rest as well as you." The reference to the exodus is an invitation to empathize with the downtrodden: "Remember that you were a slave in the land of Egypt" (Deut. 5:15). Knowing what it is to be a slave and to work without rest should prevent Israel from inflicting such hardship on anyone else, even on their animals (Deut. 5:14, rather than referring generically to livestock, mentions specific beasts of burden: oxen and donkeys). However, should empathy prove insufficient, the installation of Sabbath is made a divine commandment. No one is to be deprived of the God-given right to rest.

Particularly compared to the importance Sabbath has in Priestly legislation (see esp. Exod. 31:13–17, where Sabbath is the sign of the Sinai covenant), Deuteronomy pays little attention to this institution: in fact, apart from the Decalogue, the Sabbath is not mentioned in Deuteronomy (although Deut. 16:8 does stipulate "a solemn assembly for the LORD your God, when you shall do no work" on the seventh day of Passover). However, the sabbatical principle does appear in the commandment that debts are to be forgiven (Deut. 15:1, 9; 31:10) and slaves are to be freed (Deut. 15:12) in the seventh year. In Deuteronomy, the sabbatical principle is everywhere linked to economic justice and concern for the rights of the needy. Thus, the principle of Sabbath observance followed by Jesus in today's Gospel reading (Mark 2:23–3:6), that meeting human need trumps legal scrupulosity, is a fine expression of the ideals found in Deuteronomy. For Deuteronomy as for Jesus, "The sabbath was made for humankind, and not humankind for the sabbath" (Mark 2:27).

STEVEN S. TUELL

The gift of Sunday is that it is a time to be alert to the presence of the Holy One everywhere.

> God is truly with us; sing we and adore now:
> praise the One we come before now.
> Here within this temple, here in sound and silence,
> Worship God in deepest reverence.[3]

Gerhard Tersteegen's hymn announces that, come Sunday, we are in the day beyond other days, the time beyond other times.

The gift of Sunday is that it is also the festive day on which Christ rose from the dead, opening the kingdom for which we daily pray. So the preacher's task this Sunday will be to help the people in the congregation learn that, even if that kingdom is not immediately apparent, on every day in the week they are still called to seek it. The eternal God, Genesis seems to say, never had a day as good as the seventh day of creation. This is the same Creator who made Leviathan for the sheer sport of it (Ps. 104:26). But on the first day of the week the preacher has the privilege of calling the people to be alert to an utterly new, utterly entrancing reality: the kingdom for which they pray is indeed coming into being. There may be anger or hatred around, but they will discern the presence of the Holy One when they sow love. For injury, they will offer forgiveness; in doubt, stand firm by faith; in discord, work for union; in sadness, respond with joy. When we say we believe in the resurrection—the opportunity of every Sunday—we are committing ourselves not only to face up to the suffering that is a mark of all human life, but also to develop an ethic of compassion that will be our part in bringing closer the kingdom of God.

ROSS MACKENZIE

---

[3] *The New Century Hymnal* (Cleveland: Pilgrim Press, 1995), 68.

# Psalm 81:1-10

<sup>1</sup>Sing aloud to God our strength;
    shout for joy to the God of Jacob.
<sup>2</sup>Raise a song, sound the tambourine,
    the sweet lyre with the harp.
<sup>3</sup>Blow the trumpet at the new moon,
    at the full moon, on our festal day.
<sup>4</sup>For it is a statute for Israel,
    an ordinance of the God of Jacob.
<sup>5</sup>He made it a decree in Joseph,
    when he went out over the land of Egypt.

## Theological Perspective

*The Feast of Booths and the Theology of Dwelling.*
Psalm 81 is a "hymn for the feast of booths"—a
joyous harvest festival shaded by the wanderings of
Israel in the desert and the solemn Day of Atonement, Yom Kippur. Because of Israel's lack of faith in
YHWH's promise, it wandered for forty years
without a place of permanent dwelling. The question
of dwelling, inhabitation, and place is a large part of
Israel's attempt to understand itself theologically. And
it is thematic in the Psalter. How are we to *dwell* with
God? What is our place? How are we to live as
*inhabitants* with others—those within our own
community and, most especially, with travelers,
strangers, and immigrants? The theology of dwelling
raises profound questions of identity and character.
Character is always intertwined with how we abide,
interact, and dwell with others.

*Traveling Light: Singing Statutes and Trumpeting
Ordinances.* There is both a desire for and a caution
against permanence in Israel's theology of dwelling.
The booths built for the celebration of Sukkoth are
temporary and flimsy, quick to put up and even
quicker to take down. Traveling light is best, enough
baggage for the journey and no more. Traveling light
gives us more time to celebrate and makes it easier to
dance: "Sing aloud," "shout for joy," "sound the

## Pastoral Perspective

We live in a day when the worship of the true and
living God is marginalized by the worship of idols.
They may be idols of coercion and violence, whether
in militaries of respected empires or gangs of ethnic
enclaves. They may be idols of individualism and
consumerism, where the self becomes the measure of
all things and then gets ruthlessly exploited in the
marketplace. They may be idols of sizzle in popular
culture or psychological self-actualization or
territorial expansion.

    The psalmist faced down different idols, but he
knew something about living in such a day. Psalm 81
is about the worship of the true and living God in a
culture tainted by the worship of idols. These verses
are prophetic poetry reminding us that, for the
people of God, no part of life is immune to the
culture of YHWH's lordship. While the psalm begins
on a note of celebration, the psalmist—in the style of
Moses and the prophets—will not take no for an
answer in this matter. Unlike our pluralistic
environment, where worship becomes one more
lifestyle option, YHWH's marginalization is
unthinkable for the psalmist.

    The psalm opens with affirmations of worship at
the Feast of the Tabernacles celebrating the harvest
and recognizing the new year. Here one can hardly
turn from worship (vv. 1–2) to festival (v. 3) to

I hear a voice I had not known:
<sup>6</sup>"I relieved your shoulder of the burden;
   your hands were freed from the basket.
<sup>7</sup>In distress you called, and I rescued you;
   I answered you in the secret place of thunder;
   I tested you at the waters of Meribah.
                                             *Selah*

<sup>8</sup>Hear, O my people, while I admonish you;
   O Israel, if you would but listen to me!
<sup>9</sup>There shall be no strange god among you;
   you shall not bow down to a foreign god.
<sup>10</sup>I am the LORD your God,
   who brought you up out of the land of Egypt.
   Open your mouth wide and I will fill it."

## Exegetical Perspective

*God's Word in Worship.* Readers of the Bible often think of the Psalms as a collection of human responses to God's gracious acts on behalf of the community of faith. This collection of texts contains songs of praise, petitions for divine aid, sage instruction, and professions of faith, and all of them have helped to shape communal worship. For centuries Jews and Christians have used the Psalms in public and private worship, looking to them for help in shaping personal responses to God. The Psalms have been a rich worship resource that can be used virtually unchanged by modern communities seeking to find their own words to address God.

However, at the same time, both Jews and Christians have maintained that the Psalms are Scripture. They are not simply a collection of human words but are of divine origin in some way. The Psalms are not only a human response to God; they are also God's word to the community. This latter understanding of the Psalms is particularly prominent in Psalm 81, where God's direct address to the worshiping community is stressed in the two portions of the psalm included in the lectionary: the introductory call to the people to celebrate (vv. 1–5a) and the following exhortation to ground that celebration in God's gracious acts in Israel's history (vv. 5b–10).

## Homiletical Perspective

Although the Ninth Sunday after Epiphany (Proper 4) is provided specifically for churches that celebrate the Feast of the Transfiguration on August 6 rather than the last Sunday before Lent, God's plea in Psalm 81:8—"Hear, O my people . . . O Israel, if you would but listen to me!"—echoes in the transfiguration Gospel: "This is my Son, the Beloved; listen to him!" (Mark 9:7). The poetic movement of Psalm 81 intends to bring us to a place of listening and can provide dramatic structure to a sermon.

Psalm 81 summons us to a celebration. Sing, the psalmist commands, sing songs, beat the tambourine, strum lyre and harp, sound the trumpet, and shout for joy, because we have so much to celebrate. Celebration is appropriate when "you have gathered in the produce of the land," and at the harvest it is fitting to celebrate "the festival of the LORD" (Lev. 23:39). We readily resonate with the invitation to celebrate. We receive wedding invitations to the celebration of a marriage. Bulletins at funeral services announce a celebration of a person's life. Church growth specialists counsel worship leaders to make each service a celebration, and the burgeoning nondenominational church with the six-acre parking lot at the edge of the city names itself The Cathedral of Celebration. Celebration, however,

# Psalm 81:1-10

## Theological Perspective

tambourine," "blow the trumpet" (vv. 1–5). Only when absolutely necessary ought we to make ordinances, statutes, and weighty decrees. All law and regulation is best framed, before and after, top to bottom, by music, voice, and song. Liturgist and psalmist Joseph Gelineau writes:

> A Psalm is a religious song. The very word psalm suggests a musical instrument, tambourine or sistrum, harp or primitive lyre, with which the singer accompanied his song. . . . The psalms are a series of shouts: shouts of love and hatred; shouts of suffering or rejoicing; shouts of faith or hope. Here, a man who has suffered injury demands justice (Ps. 55) or the whole defeated nation laments (Ps. 43); there, a sick man who has escaped death gives thanks (Ps. 29) or the whole people proclaim that the hand of God alone has rescued them from foreign slavery (Ps. 80).[1]

The psalmist would have understood, with agreement and assurance, Friedrich Nietzsche's proclamation that "I should only believe in a God that would know how to dance."[2]

*Seeking the Other: Atonement as Relief.* The relation of the Feast of Booths to the wanderings in the desert and the Day of Atonement continues to prompt our theological understanding. Even times of sin and the need for atonement are not, in the Psalms, without dancing and joy. Human sinfulness and guilt are not to be experienced in total desperation or nihilistic silence. In the Psalms, atonement is both relief and rescue: "I relieved your shoulder of the burden; your hands were freed. . . . In distress you called, and I rescued you" (vv. 6–7). There is irony here—dwellings that abide but are not permanent, a blessed people whose blessing is more for the stranger than for themselves, a God who is quick to forgive and a neighbor who may not be. Jewish philosopher Emmanuel Levinas muses that on the Day of Atonement we do not need to petition God for rescue and relief as desperately as we might think, since, being God, forgiveness comes with the territory. But the neighbor whom we have offended is another matter. That bit of atonement and forgiveness may, indeed, take more seeking, searching, and begging than we ever imagined—even a lifetime.[3]

[1] Joseph Gelineau, *The Psalms: A New Translation* (London: Collins Fontana Books, 1963), 5.

[2] Friedrich Nietzsche, *Thus Spake Zarathustra*, trans. Thomas Common (IndyPublishing.com: 2004), part I, chapter 7, "Reading and Writing."

[3] Emmanuel Levinas, "Toward the Other," in *Nine Talmudic Readings*, trans. Annette Aronowicz (Bloomington: Indiana University Press, 1990), 15–16; cf. 12–19.

## Pastoral Perspective

statute and ordinance (v. 4) to decree (v. 5) without being reminded of the absolute sovereignty of YHWH. Here the psalmist imbues the hearer within the seamlessness of Yahwistic culture, attempting to fill the mouths of the people with right affirmation (v. 10b). Here celebration within the covenant community becomes a testimony to the redemptive work of God. Thus God's people get pointed in the right direction.

Immersion within an extended and faithful counterculture to the threat of idolatry is perhaps the best inoculation against becoming caught up in a system of illusory divinities that promise us everything and deliver us nothing. Today our approach to idolatry—and perhaps one of our foremost idols itself—is much more individualistic. We wonder whether we live in thrall to mammon, to lust, to success, and so we seek to evaluate ourselves along these lines. But the reality of idolatry is at once much more powerfully systemic—like aquifers moving deep beneath us—and infinitely more subtle, nuanced, and undetectable. To face idolatry in our own day we can only begin, like the psalmist, considering ourselves within the context of vaster cultural crosscurrents of which we are more unaware and in which we are more complicit than we realize. We discover the truth of the adage "systems are more powerful than individuals" when we consider our suggestibility to more user-friendly alternatives to the true and living God. What we "catch" in larger systems of culture and commerce must first be faced there, not within the slippery solitude of an imagined relationship with God.

Practically speaking, the church's faithful response has to do less with individual devotions at home than with pointed litanies prominent within our worship at the watershed moments in the church year, such as at the Sunday after our national Thanksgiving, the busiest shopping days of the year. No one will thank us for doing this—no one other than God.

After this opening invitation to find oneself by locating oneself in proper context with regard to the temple and YHWH, the psalmist becomes more direct. "I hear a voice I had not known," exclaims the psalmist, speaking on behalf of the whole of God's people (v. 5b). It is the voice of the God who has been forgotten or muted while the nation has been running after the strange and foreign gods identified in verse 9. Resorting to the artifice of this voice is a dramatic convention on the part of the psalmist to attract and turn the hearer.

## Exegetical Perspective

However, as is sometimes the case, the lectionary does not include all of the verses of the psalm. When the remaining verses are considered, the message of the lectionary version is changed considerably, and the people in the community hear the psalm in a context different from the one provided by the lectionary.

*A Call to Celebration (vv. 1–5a).* The psalm begins with an introductory exhortation from the psalmist. The worshipers are to sing to God as a community and to celebrate a festival day with music. The precise identification of the occasion is not clear, but the language used to describe it suggests the Festival of Tabernacles or Booths, Israel's fall harvest celebration. However, the text makes clear that this celebration is not a human creation. It is required by God, included in the laws given by God to Israel at Sinai (Lev. 23:34), and stressed by Moses in his final exhortation to the Israelites before they crossed the Jordan and entered the promised land (Deut. 16:13, 16). By grounding the call to celebration in God's direct command, the psalmist suggests that worship and liturgy are not simply human activities. Rather, they are of divine origin. God mandates worship, provides an order for it, and in the Psalms even provides the words that are to be used in the process.

*A Divine Exhortation (vv. 5b–10).* The divine origin of the psalmist's words becomes explicit in verses 5b–10, where the direct words of the Deity are quoted. Scholars often claim that these words would originally have been spoken by a prophet or priest delivering a divine oracle. Whether this is true or not, these verses are clearly in the form of a direct address from God to the worshiping community. God reminds Israel of the oppression in Egypt and the way in which God answered the people's complaints, rescuing them from bondage, leading them safely through the wilderness, making a covenant with them at Sinai, and giving them laws to guide them in fulfilling their obligations under that covenant (vv. 5b–7). The divine speech continues by urging the worshipers to obey God's instructions, which are here summarized by referring to the first of the Ten Commandments: Israel is to worship only God and is to reject all foreign deities (Exod. 20:2–5; Deut. 5:6–9).

The effect of this divine exhortation is to change the context of the psalm's opening call to celebration. Whereas in verses 1–5a the worshipers are to celebrate the fall harvest festival because it is

## Homiletical Perspective

is not just our happy idea, but God's "statute for Israel, an ordinance of the God of Jacob," and "a decree in Joseph" (vv. 4–5; Lev. 23:33–44). "Celebrate!" is nothing less than God's command.

No sooner has the psalmist intoned God's cheerful requirement to celebrate than we begin to recognize transmission problems. An eerie, enigmatic cloud settles over verse 5c, and translation problems are evident. "I hear a voice I had not known," attempts the NRSV, but the NIV offers, "We heard a language we did not understand," and the NEB reads, "I hear an unfamiliar language." The voice of the One who delivers the people from Egypt is not only unfamiliar but slightly uncanny. We do not know this voice, this language, this meaning. The One who speaks has heard the people when they called, lifted their burden, and taken away the baskets of servitude. "In the secret place" (v. 7c) on Mount Sinai, this One answered the sound of their trumpets with thunder from heaven (Exod. 19:19) and the giving of the law (Exod. 20). Although all these actions are remembered, the voice remains a secret, just as the place is a "secret place" and even the name of the One who speaks is secret. Psalm 81 customarily is classified as part of the Elohistic Psalter. Like the other psalms attributed to Asaph, it refers to God as Elohim, and keeps the holy name of the Lord a secret until verse 10. Only after we know what we do not know—the unfamiliar voice, the unfamiliar language, the unfamiliar meaning—may we recover what we thought we knew but did not in fact *know*.

We do not know, according to Psalm 81, because we have not listened and we do not listen. In verse 8 God pleads, "If you would but listen to me!" and in verses 11 and 13, just beyond the limits of the lectionary reading, God diagnoses the people's dilemma as a failure to *listen*. "Hear, O my people," represents God's plea, echoing that primal call to hear, the Shema: "Hear, O Israel: The Lord is our God, the Lord alone. You shall love the Lord your God with all your heart, and with all your soul, and with all your might" (Deut. 6:4–5). The worship of the synagogue service still begins with that invitation to listen. That command to hear, to listen, to surrender attention must be clearly articulated from the beginning of worship, from the outset of any supposed celebration. Jewish liturgical manuals insist on meticulous pronunciation of the Hebrew words. Consonants should not be slurred. Each word must be perfectly clear. If the liturgist runs the words together, start again. If a word is inadvertently

# Psalm 81:1-10

## Theological Perspective

*"I Hear a Voice I Had Not Known" (v. 5): The Redemption of God.* Coming to understand YHWH as a God of such abundant forgiveness and joy is no small feat. And this is the chief theological accomplishment of the psalmist and why the psalms are so theologically paradigmatic. If we bracket our theological cultures and conclusions for a moment, and try to describe our more primitive and raw religious sensibilities—that *feeling* of power or presence that is greater than and so much more than we are—we find that it is not obvious or even necessary that such a "power" be in our best interests. For *the Other* to be a presence *for* us, something else must be accomplished, some other revelation and assurance given, some rescue and relief come into play. H. Richard Niebuhr describes this *other salvation* as the transformation of God *from enemy to friend.*[4] This grace-filled "accomplishment" in the faith of the psalmist and of the Scriptures—Hebrew and Christian—of the caring and merciful God is continually being destabilized among our *many gods*, and needs to be repeated again and again as the greatest work of our theology and faith.

*Sweet Honey from the Rock.* In the concluding verses of Psalm 81 (vv. 11–16, not appointed for this Sunday's reading), Israel's stubbornness and failure to listen and to trust in YHWH's deliverance are rehearsed. Perhaps it is the *rehearsal*, one we know all too well, that leads to this omission. But we should not keep the treat of verse 16 to ourselves. Yes, we are hard-hearted and stingy, hoarding as much blessing for ourselves as we can. But if we would just relent and relax, let go of our defenses and, more important, our fears, then YHWH's abundant life would be enough for all. Theologian Karl Rahner reminds us that our greatest heresy surely must be that God's grace is scarce.[5] From abundance to abundance is the better orthodoxy. Indeed not the orthodoxy of narrow doctrine or excluding law, but rather of sweet "honey from the rock" (v. 16).

JOSEPH MONTI

## Pastoral Perspective

How does this lost and mysterious voice address us? It is a voice from our past, the Lord's voice, reminding us who rescued us from the burden of our slavery, as we fashioned bricks out of baskets in the Egyptian sun to make lofty pyramids for Pharaoh (vv. 6–7). It is the Lord's voice recalling how God intervened on our behalf and challenged us to make us strong in the worst of our wilderness wanderings. It is the God of history still speaking today about the deep perils and tremendous opportunities of the moment, the voice of the true and living God.

This God is a zealous God and will not stand idly by as those whom God bought at a high price go running after false gods. We are not our own, to run hither, thither, and yon. God made us, God persevered after us, and God owns us. Here poetry stiffens into the rhetoric of binding covenantal obligation.

In verse 8 we gain a precious glimpse into the heart of God. Within the span of this one short verse, God's stern admonishment softens into tender yearning after God's wayward children. It evokes a parent's deep ambivalence after his or her own as they grow lost. This transition from reprimand to invitation happens like stormy skies morphing into blue, momentarily pulling back the cloud cover, revealing a judgment suffused in grace.

Still, this tenderness is fleeting compared with God's truthfulness and strength, an emotional half-holiday up against the rock-ribbed eternal covenant. So verses 9–10 revert to ancient covenantal affirmation, testifying to the nonnegotiable nature of the first commandment. Artur Weiser writes, "The most important prerequisite for the renewal is precisely that faithfulness to God which bars the worship of other gods besides that of Yahweh. . . . Within the covenantal relationship the promise of divine salvation is tied up with loyalty and obedience in religion; for this reason, in contrast with the Ten Commandments, God's affirmation of his faithfulness to his people follows the manifestation of God's will in the present context."[1]

Psalm 81 moves from festive call to worship, to recalling the origins and boundaries of the people's common life, to hearing the forgotten voice above all other voices, speaking in cadences clear and unequivocal. The effect is galvanizing.

DALE ROSENBERGER

[4]H. Richard Niebuhr, *The Responsible Self* (San Francisco: Harper & Row, 1963), 143; cf. 127–45.

[5]Karl Rahner, SJ, *Nature and Grace: Dilemmas in the Modern Church*, trans. Dinah Wharton (New York: Sheed & Ward, 1964), 133.

[1]Artur Weiser, *The Psalms, A Commentary*, trans. Herbert Hartwell (Philadelphia: Westminster Press, 1962), 554–55.

## Exegetical Perspective

required in God's law, in verses 5b–10 the people are to celebrate their great transition from slavery into freedom. Their celebration is not just a regular liturgical act mandated by law, but is taken to be a response to God's gracious acts toward Israel in the past. By implication, the celebration and the obedience that God demands also hold out the promise of further divine responses on Israel's behalf. It is important to note, however, that the grounding of the celebration in a historical event does not simply replace the yearly harvest festival described in verses 1–5a. Rather, both need to be taken together. In the mind of the psalmist, the regular harvest and the events in Egypt and in the wilderness are all testimonies to God's love and care for the community. The celebration is a response to both and is appropriate on any occasion when God's graciousness is experienced by the community.

The lectionary ends its treatment of the psalm on a positive note. God directly exhorts the people to fulfill their covenant obligations and promises divine support and sustenance in exchange for obedience (v. 10). In a sense the lectionary in this way identifies the worshiping community with Israel on the banks of the Jordan at the end of Deuteronomy. Israel has been purged of rebels, and the next generation of Israelites has the opportunity to make a new life for itself, a life marked by obedience to God's covenant. The remainder of Psalm 81, however, remembers the rest of the story. The Israelites who finally entered the land were not obedient, as Moses had exhorted them to be, and as a result God let them follow their own desires, a path that led to death, rather than to the life promised by God's law (vv. 11–12). Still, the psalmist reassures the community that, as was also the case in the wilderness, God has not rejected Israel. Rather, God still longs to act favorably on its behalf and hopes once again to act graciously toward the people. In contrast to the lectionary, the psalmist leaves the people on the edge of redemption, facing the challenge of being obedient so that they can again claim God's love (vv. 13–16).

ROBERT R. WILSON

## Homiletical Perspective

skipped, start over.[1] If a proper listening is not established from the beginning, then no amount of blaring trumpets or beaten tambourines or strummed lyres can conceal the cacophony of chaos among an unhearing people. Walter Brueggemann comments tersely, "The history of the covenant begins with an invitation to hear, but the course of that history is a refusal to hear."[2]

We customarily think of the proclamation of the gospel as the characteristic and defining activity of the church, but the University of Aberdeen's John Webster suggests we think of the church first as the hearing church:

> The definitive act of the church is faithful hearing of the gospel of salvation announced by the risen Christ in the Spirit's power through the service of Holy Scripture. As the *creatura verbi divini*, the creature of the divine Word, the church is the hearing church. . . .
>
> The church exists in the space which is made by the Word. Accordingly, it is not a self-generated assembly and cannot be adequately described only as a human historical trajectory or form of human culture. The church exists and continues because God is communicatively present; it is brought into being and carried by the Word.[3]

Lest Webster's definition be construed only as an appeal to listen more attentively to the sermon, note the identity of those generating the hearing that constitutes the church: "the risen Christ in the Spirit's power" and God who "is communicatively present." When worshipers gather on Sunday morning, is it in expectation that God speaks in this celebrative drama? Do they hope for a word from the One who pleads, "if you would but listen to me!" or are their hopes confined to more ordinary hopes, that the sermon will be interesting and not too long? For that matter, how many preachers prepare in expectation that God set apart and sanctify their carefully prepared words as a means of speaking God's own Word? If God will speak, then we have much to celebrate.

PATRICK J. WILLSON

[1]Lawrence A. Hoffman, ed., *My People's Prayer Book: Traditional Prayers, Modern Commentaries*, vol. 1, *The Sh'ma and Its Blessings* (Woodstock, VT: Jewish Lights Publishing, 1997), 96.

[2]Walter Brueggemann, *The Message of the Psalms*, Augsburg Old Testament Studies (Minneapolis: Augsburg, 1984), 92.

[3]John Webster, *Holy Scripture: A Dogmatic Sketch* (Cambridge: Cambridge University Press, 2003), 44.

# 2 Corinthians 4:5-12

⁵For we do not proclaim ourselves; we proclaim Jesus Christ as Lord and ourselves as your slaves for Jesus' sake. ⁶For it is the God who said, "Let light shine out of darkness," who has shone in our hearts to give the light of the knowledge of the glory of God in the face of Jesus Christ.

⁷But we have this treasure in clay jars, so that it may be made clear that this extraordinary power belongs to God and does not come from us. ⁸We are afflicted in every way, but not crushed; perplexed, but not driven to despair; ⁹persecuted, but not forsaken; struck down, but not destroyed; ¹⁰always carrying in the body the death of Jesus, so that the life of Jesus may also be made visible in our bodies. ¹¹For while we live, we are always being given up to death for Jesus' sake, so that the life of Jesus may be made visible in our mortal flesh. ¹²So death is at work in us, but life in you.

## Theological Perspective

Paul wrote to the Corinthians that the power of the gospel, which constituted authentic Christian ministry centered on Jesus (cf. 2 Cor. 11:4), cannot be found in extraordinary human feats. Rather, the power belongs to a great God, and we, in contrast, bear this power in frail, earthen vessels. Unlike glass containers, which the ancients could melt and recast, earthen vessels were fragile and, once broken, were gone. Paul here contrasts his own pedigree, suffering in and through his easily broken, mortal flesh, with the supposedly proper pedigree of the "superapostles," who bodily did wondrous works (cf. 12:1–10).

Paul's image that contrasts the great, creative power of God known in and through our mortal being has seemed familiar to readers across the millennia. We can do great and creative things, such as bear and raise children, create visual, literary, and performing arts, grow food from the earth, and build great structures. We can love and be loved. Our creativity seems almost godlike in its ability; and sadly, when used destructively, this creativity sometimes has explicitly taken godlike traits, such as breathing "intelligence" into inanimate things when we create "smart bombs." A famous cultural anthropologist, Ernest Becker, won a 1974 Pulitzer Prize, awarded two months after his own death of cancer at the age of 49, for his work *The Denial of*

## Pastoral Perspective

Martyrdom has a long and glorious history in the annals of the church and was the lifeblood of the faith as it spread across the Roman Empire and beyond in the first three centuries. The word "martyr" means "witness," and so it would follow that those who witness to the central saving act of our faith, Christ's gift of his life and death upon the cross, would offer up their lives as well. The words of Tertullian, "The blood of the martyrs is the seed of the church," continue to resonate as we read Paul's words: "We are always being given up to death for Jesus' sake, so that the life of Jesus may be made visible in our mortal flesh" (v. 11).

This is hard to understand in any day, but particularly in our day, and even more particularly for middle-class Americans and other Westerners. On a psychological level, martyrdom is frowned upon as unhealthy and manipulative. Savvy mental-health-care providers are concerned about people who hand over their lives—whether that is the parent that lives through the children, the person in a work setting who overfunctions, or the partner in a relationship who always gives in and gives away. Giving one's life for a cause or for somebody is awkward, suspicious, and questioned. For contemporary Westerners, the biblical verse should read: "Those who lose their lives will lose them."

## Exegetical Perspective

This is Paul's great apology for his apostleship—not an apology in the sense that he has something to be ashamed of, but a bold defense of the nature and function of the gospel he preaches. Whether the "we" of these verses is to be understood as referring to Paul alone, or to Paul and Timothy, or to all the apostles is less clear.

What is clear is that the shape of apostolic ministry, as Paul describes it here, corresponds strikingly to the drama of his own ministry—and indirectly to the drama of the passion and resurrection of Christ himself.

Paul is still puzzling about the appropriate role of letters of recommendation for an apostle. It seems that the Corinthians, perhaps persuaded by rival apostles, are thinking that Paul ought to be able to confirm his own apostolic authority by producing letters from others (2 Cor. 3:1).

Now he goes on to insist that when he preaches he does not recommend himself either. He always and only recommends Christ Jesus as Lord. In light of Philippians 2:6–11, we can suggest that for Paul the title "Lord" is the highest title, the name above every name, that is bestowed on Jesus. The Greek *kyrios* does not represent just a term for "sovereign," but often itself translates the Hebrew reading *adonai*—the reverential term for the deepest

## Homiletical Perspective

"But we have this treasure in clay jars." With this jewel of a statement, Paul illustrates the paradox of the resurrection life of faith. Various facets of the metaphor offer rich insights into the human experience, as well as glimpses into the nature of God's power in us.

The image of a clay jar evokes a myriad of other biblical references: the story of creation (Gen. 2:7), in which God fashions the human creature out of earthy stuff like clay; the potter at the wheel in Jeremiah's prophetic vision (Jer. 18); the broken vessel in Isaiah's prophecy (Isa. 30:14).

Clay jars are concrete objects, which can be transposed onto the canvas of the listener's imagination through sensory language within the sermon. Clay jars are crafted by careful hands of a potter from a lump of cool, thick earth into something useful that can serve the needs of people. Once formed, shaped, fired, and cooled, the malleable substance becomes hard and brittle. Jars of clay are fragile, easily broken, dispensable. So are human bodies: useful, but full of vulnerability, susceptible to injury and even death. In every nation, bodies mangled and crushed by violence testify to the fragility of physical existence. Clay jars break easily.

The kind of assault on this earthly body that Paul is talking about, however, is not from natural causes.

# 2 Corinthians 4:5-12

## Theological Perspective

*Death*, which argues that the tension between our mortality and our godlike creative gifts lies behind the production of all human culture.

Paul makes this contrast and even more. Somehow our mortal flesh, capable of suffering and death, bears a reality far beyond our human deeds themselves. How can this be? Consider that no one could be without a prior relationship to God, established by God, even if in the negative mode of sin. And so, for example, when writing to the church at Rome only a few years after his Corinthian letters, Paul holds all people fully accountable before God (Rom. 1–3), even if they close themselves to this relationship, even if they live according to sin (Rom. 3:9–20). In fact, when speaking to the Romans, Paul uses the same verb to describe God being revealed on the cross (Rom. 3:21) that he uses when describing God self-revealing to humankind (Rom. 1:19). God's revelation in and to human experience as such is a true revelation, which God gives again on the cross.

One way, then, that our mortal lives bear treasure is that they inwardly contain, in and to all our living moments, a divine revelation that is not ours to possess, any more than an earthen vessel can possess fresh water. We do not possess God. Yet our very lives, anywhere and at any moment, cannot fail to be the object of divine love. What then of the cross? The cross reclaims us who already are claimed by God. To be open to God's reclamation project is to take upon ourselves who we ultimately have always been—God's beloved ones; although to do so we must also die to all that we have proximately trusted, because God alone ultimately claims us. Such radical trust may mean we are afflicted, despairing, persecuted, and struck down; yet we are neither crushed, nor utterly desperate, nor forsaken, nor destroyed (4:8–9), because in our trust we realize that finally we belong to God.

Here also lies the second way that our mortal lives bear treasure: By taking on the cross that reclaims us, we die to the old and carry in our bodies "the death of Jesus," but we do so in order that we might also carry in our bodies "the life of Jesus," not merely for our own sake, but that life might be active in others (4:10–12). We outwardly become the good news for our neighbor. We become, as it were, God's reclamation power of the cross for others (cf. 5:14–20). Our very words and deeds, though still very much our own, somehow become the earthen vessels that bear a power incomparably greater (4:7) than we ourselves.

## Pastoral Perspective

We also do not associate martyrdom with our religious identity. Our religious identity is usually associated with stability, prestige, comfort, satisfaction, and happiness. We get up on Sunday morning and go to the church that strikes our fancy. We give money or do not give money. We vote for leaders who probably have taken a scientific poll and decided how to market their own religious identity—which may be a hot commodity in the voting booth or a liability. We are not harassed by civil authorities, and in our communities of faith we are almost never asked to sacrifice. Instead, we are wooed to join the club—oops, the church. Christian life and discipleship are frequently confused with good citizenship, appropriate decorum, and following socially acceptable norms and lifestyle. Doing good seems to be a part of doing well.

Most dramatically, however, we associate martyrdom with extreme Islamists. In this early part of the new millennium, we are entangled with an obscene distortion of martyrdom, and it would be important for the preacher or teacher to unpack both the word and our context. The martyrs we know about are not people who have passed along life to us. Instead, we have been terrorized by people who call themselves martyrs and then blow up airplanes and buildings and busses and railroads and take random and relatively innocent lives. We see "martyr" videotapes glorifying the taking of life, not the giving of life. Those images and the terror that goes along with them are our primary and overwhelmingly negative association with martyrdom. The costs have been so outrageous that we have allowed ourselves to look past any culpability our own culture has in creating this demonic situation.

In the history of the church, martyrs never sought to be martyrs; their martyrdom came upon them, and they tried to evade the situation. Once trapped, however, they would die, not because they knew the faith better than others or their death would become a source for understanding the faith, but because their lives were in God's hands. Martyrs knew that their faith was a "treasure in clay jars, so that it may be made clear that this extraordinary power belongs to God and" did not come from them (v. 7). Martyrdom is the paradox of God's sustaining power amidst affliction, persecution, and death and the faithful's sustained conviction in God's righteousness and justice.

This passage could be a powerful reclamation of the truth of martyrdom on any of the levels

## Exegetical Perspective

name of God—YHWH. (See most famously Deut. 6:4.)

There is a surprising twist in Paul's argument. We might expect him to say that he preaches Christ as Lord and then himself as Christ's slave. Instead, he preaches Christ as Lord and himself as slave to the *Corinthians*—though of course always and only for Jesus' sake. Now the Corinthian Christians are not only his letters of recommendation; they are his masters in the gospel. Here surely we have the paradox of an authority based in slavery.

In verse 6, Paul's humility is quickly qualified. Soon enough, Paul will tell the Corinthians that in Christ there is a new creation (2 Cor 5:17). Now, audaciously he suggests that he is instrument of that creation. The first words of the first creation—"let there be light"—are now echoed in the word God speaks to and through Paul: "Let light shine out of darkness!" And because the light shines in Paul's own heart, Paul can bring the light of the gospel to those who hear him. That light is manifest as knowledge. To know the gospel is to walk in the light. But now Paul qualifies his role again—the light that has shone in his heart is not his own light. It is supremely and finally the light that shines in the face of Jesus Christ.

In verse 7, Paul moves to the full measure of humility—in this tricky balance of insisting that he *brings* the light but *is* not the light. The metaphor of the clay jar is used in biblical, Hellenistic, and Jewish literature to suggest both fragility and ordinariness. While there may be no precise parallel to Paul's thought, the function of the image seems clear. The gospel itself is a treasure; the apostles, the common clay jars, are both breakable and expendable.

However, as always, for Paul the function of fragility and expendability is not to produce despair at the human condition, but to produce joy at God's superabundant power. The phrase for abundant power uses the Greek root for our word "hyperbole"—but here what Paul says of God's power is both hyperbolic and true. There is a small distinction too in the way Paul speaks of power in relationship to God and to the apostles. Translated rather woodenly, Paul says: "the extraordinary power is *of* God and not *from* us." The NRSV captures the distinction well: "this extraordinary power *belongs to God* and does not *come from* us" (emphasis added).

Verses 8–10 give a kind of catalog of suffering that illustrates just how fragile these clay pots, the apostles, really are. While Paul refers to all the apostles, he surely refers especially to himself, and

## Homiletical Perspective

The attacks that Paul suffered were in direct relation to the proclamation of Jesus Christ. Christ's own announcement of the reign of God drew criticism from Roman and religious authorities and resulted in crucifixion. Paul describes threats to his well-being as direct consequences of his own service to the gospel. Later in chapter 6, Paul testifies to the fact that his belief in the fulfillment of God's promises in Jesus Christ has put him in physical danger from his opponents. This helps the preacher make sense of Paul's words, "always carrying in the body the death of Jesus." People who shared faith in Christ shared in Christ's opposition to the structures of death within the culture. As a result, the violence and death that sought to silence Jesus were turned on them, as well. And as in the case of Jesus, the anticipated outcome of such violence was overthrown by the power of God.

Those who know the violence of oppression because of race, gender, economic class, or ethnicity listen intently to the encouragement and hope these words bring. Can you imagine how a refugee from a war-torn region might hear these words? Churches who experience condemnation and hardship because they advocate life-affirming practices of love and justice may also find hope that the assaults on their credibility cannot and will not destroy them.

Imagine a simple clay jar, beaten with a stick, kicked with a foot, dropped on a concrete patio, but never breaking. The contents inside it provide a protective stability that overrides the container's fragility. Chips, cracks, and smudges may show visible evidence of abuse, but the jar isn't shattered. It retains its usefulness as a vessel.

This passage doesn't imply that the pain of suffering should not be a part of people's faith experience. It reveals that the resurrection life of Christ that is already at work in us continues even as we suffer. That is how Paul can claim that although the experiences of violence and suffering may damage our bodies, resurrection life can be "made visible in our mortal flesh" (v. 11), even as it was made visible in Jesus' crucified body that was raised from its tomb.

One would expect the concluding sentence to read something like, "So death is at work in us, but life is, as well." That's not what the reader finds, though. Instead, there's a twist that connects with the earlier statement in verse 5, in which Paul tells the church in Corinth that his proclamation was not self-promotion, but Christ-promotion. It was, in fact, self-*de*motion, declaring himself a slave in

# 2 Corinthians 4:5-12

## Theological Perspective

In the Latin West, both Roman Catholics and Protestants, each in their own way, have understood that taking on Christ, in order to be God's presence to others, constitutes the basic ministry of the church. When Luther, for example, proclaimed that the Christian life, and the foundation of Christian ministry given at baptism, was to be "Christ to neighbor," he meant something literal by that. We are given the privilege that our lives might be Christ to neighbor, and in those moments of ministry that they do bear so great a treasure, we realize how awesome a privilege has been given us. Likewise, for the Roman Catholic Church the Second Vatican Council (1962–65) took up again the tradition that the church is fundamentally a sacrament or mystery, not an institution. In the Rite of Christian Initiation of Adults (1972) the Council affirmed that through Christian initiation believers are converted into the life of Jesus Christ and given the Holy Spirit that empowers them for the mission of the church.

As Paul put the matter, no matter who we thought we had to be, in Christ we have become "a new creation" entrusted as earthen vessels with God's very "ministry of reconciliation" (5:17–20). The church itself thus becomes the ongoing real presence of Christ in the world. The great Reformed theologian Friedrich Schleiermacher (1768–1834) said that as the body of Christ the church "is related to Christ as the outward to the inward, so that in its essential activities it must also be a reflection of the activities of Christ. And since the effects produced by it are simply the gradual realization of redemption in the world, its activities must likewise be a continuation of the activities of Christ Himself."[1] Thanks be to God.

JOHN W. RIGGS

## Pastoral Perspective

previously mentioned—psychological, civic, religious, international, really in whatever activity a human being finds himself or herself. The truth of martyrdom, which Paul lived and wrote about so beautifully, is the power of sacrificial love by the grace of our Savior Jesus Christ.

This is the truth that Jesus taught us from the cross—that life shines out of darkness. This is the glory of God in the face of Jesus Christ.

When we allow ourselves to be grasped by that power and truth, we no longer feel the need to proclaim ourselves and our agendas. We proclaim Jesus, and for the sake of that proclamation we become impassioned and free slaves to the well-being of others.

If you are looking at Jesus and passionate about the well-being of others, many things in your universe shift. You no longer worry so much about your own competence, for the "extraordinary" power comes from God, not from you. You may be tried and afflicted, but you are not crushed. You may be puzzled and perplexed at some turn of events or some strangeness or meanness in yourself or others, but you are not driven to despair. You may be persecuted, but you are not alone. You may be struck down, but you will not be destroyed.

And so you live in the confidence and peace that is given to those who follow the One who martyred himself, who gave his life away, so that others might live and then receive that life again in the glory of the resurrection. The deeper the faith pilgrim goes into the risen life of Jesus Christ, the more life swallows up death. And eternity makes a holy and life-giving circle of sacrificial love, so that the sacrifice brings life even to the sacrificed, and love wins the day.

MARTHA STERNE

---

[1] Friedrich Schleiermacher, *The Christian Faith*, ed. H. R. MacKintosh and J. S. Stewart, 2 vols. (New York: Harper & Row, 1963), 2:589–90, §127.3.

## Exegetical Perspective

the list of the disasters that confront but do not overcome him becomes a testimony to the courage and grace of his apostleship. He has already pointed toward his own suffering in 2 Corinthians 1:9–11. The second part of verse 8 contains a kind of play on words: "We are *aporoumenoi* but not *exaporoumenoi*"—perplexed but not perplexed beyond measure. Victor Furnish helpfully translates: "despairing, but not utterly desperate."[1]

By now, if they have been paying any attention to Paul's preaching and writing at all, the Corinthians will realize that his description of the apostolic life conforms closely to his description of Christ's activity among humankind. The shape of apostolicity is cruciform.

Verse 10 is not just an analogy, as the apostle participates in the story he proclaims. Paul is being given up to death for the sake of Jesus' own death; Paul's living manifests the glory of the risen Lord. Perhaps, when he speaks of "mortal flesh," Paul simply reinforces the image of the fragile clay jar with which this section began. It may be, however, that the section carries something of the connotation of "flesh" elsewhere in Paul, where "flesh" refers not only to humanity's mortality, but to humanity's sinfulness. If so, then the life of Christ is made manifest even in his mortal and temptation-prone apostles.[2]

The last verse surprises us. Until now, it has looked as though it is the mission of the apostles that conforms to Jesus' story. Being put to death, nonetheless they live. But now, while the apostles suffer the pangs of death, it is the Corinthian Christians who live in Christ's resurrection. "So death is at work in us, but life in you." We remember that at the beginning of this passage, Paul is not Christ's slave, but the slave to Christ's people. Earlier yet in this letter, it is the believers who are Paul's letter of recommendation. Now, the resurrection he proclaims he finds embodied—not so much in himself as in the church he founded. His suffering becomes vicarious: Christ's death in him becomes Christ's life in them—Christ's life in us.

DAVID L. BARTLETT

## Homiletical Perspective

service to them for the sake of Jesus Christ. Thus, the death he carries in *his* body serves *their* needs—to make them alive in Christ.

The rhetorical intent of this text serves the greater conversation about Paul's relation to the church at Corinth. Herein lies the complication for preaching. Who is the audience of this message? From Paul's pen, the proclamation is from minister to congregation in an attempt to clarify both the church's theology and its relationship to its leader. In a similar way, the sermon could awaken in the congregation a new appreciation for the service of those whose work has enabled them to participate in resurrection life. This awakening could lead to gratitude and joy in the hope that, because the suffering of others has not overcome the power of God at work in them, the listeners' own suffering will not destroy them.

An inherent danger in this approach is that it artificially places the minister in isolation from the community and sets up the preacher as a kind of martyr on their behalf. Another problem for preaching is that an attempt to compare the sacrificial suffering of the early church with the current conditions of people in the pews today may become so strained that the meaning of the text is compromised. Paul provided no easy assurances to persons who suffer from natural causes or from the consequences of their own bad choices. Paul's message brings assurance to those whose faith leads them into conflict with the old order of the day.

If the preacher positions herself, instead, within the midst of the congregation as a listener among listeners, the sermon may herald good news in a different way. People of faith may more readily identify with Paul in their vocation as ministers of Christ, commissioned at their baptism. Preaching that allows this identification may encourage the faithful to see the hand of God at work in their own ministries, even as they suffer. Death is at work in us, but resurrection life in the world served by our ministry.

MARY LIN HUDSON

---

[1] Victor Furnish, *II Corinthians*, Anchor Bible, vol. 32A (Garden City, NY: Doubleday, 1984), 254.
[2] C. K. Barrett, *The Second Epistle to the Corinthians* (New York: Harper & Row, 1973), 141.

# Mark 2:23-3:6

23One sabbath he was going through the grainfields; and as they made their way his disciples began to pluck heads of grain. 24The Pharisees said to him, "Look, why are they doing what is not lawful on the sabbath?" 25And he said to them, "Have you never read what David did when he and his companions were hungry and in need of food? 26He entered the house of God, when Abiathar was high priest, and ate the bread of the Presence, which it is not lawful for any but the priests to eat, and he gave some to his companions." 27Then he said to them, "The sabbath was made for humankind, and not humankind for the sabbath; 28so the Son of Man is lord even of the sabbath."

1Again he entered the synagogue, and a man was there who had a withered hand. 2They watched him to see whether he would cure him on the sabbath, so that they might accuse him. 3And he said to the man who had the withered hand, "Come forward." 4Then he said to them, "Is it lawful to do good or to do harm on the sabbath, to save life or to kill?" But they were silent. 5He looked around at them with anger; he was grieved at their hardness of heart and said to the man, "Stretch out your hand." He stretched it out, and his hand was restored. 6The Pharisees went out and immediately conspired with the Herodians against him, how to destroy him.

## Theological Perspective

"The sabbath was made for humankind, and not humankind for the sabbath; so the Son of Man is lord even of the sabbath" (2:27–28). In this brief statement that Mark attributes to Jesus we see at once the pitfalls and possibilities of religion as an institution intended to facilitate and enhance our relationship with God. Once again it is the Pharisees, as Mark portrays them, who provoke Jesus' words, this time by wondering how it is that Jesus' disciples can pluck heads of grain on the Sabbath. "Look, why are they doing what is not lawful on the sabbath?" (2:24). Paraphrasing Jesus' answer, "Because they are hungry." As in the time of David (2:25–26), providing basic human necessities, food in this case, trumps religious practice. As in Matthew 25, true righteousness is associated with feeding the hungry, giving drink to the thirsty, welcoming the stranger, clothing the naked, caring for the sick, and visiting the prisoner (25:35–36). The unavoidable revelation in today's reading from Mark, even more powerfully emphasized in 3:3–6, is that keeping the Sabbath may deepen our awareness of God and thus heighten our awareness of human need and our own role in meeting that need. The more fully our actions are in response to God, the more fully those actions will benefit our hungry neighbors. On the other hand, keeping the Sabbath in a legalistic manner

## Pastoral Perspective

"The Kingdom of God is a present reality that comes to us from beyond, a kingdom that precedes and judges all of our concepts and experiences of the kingdom of this world, particularly religiously derived concepts of the Kingdom of God."[1]

As in the previous two lectionary texts in Mark 2, in verses 23–28 we are confronted by the "why" question: "The Pharisees said to him, 'Look, why are they doing what is not lawful on the sabbath?'" However, in the closing section (3:1–6), the "why" questions are absent. The scribes are watching, wanting only to accuse Jesus.

Mark 2:23–28 deals with the legal violation of the Sabbath. Jesus appeals to 1 Samuel 21:1–6, where David and his followers are engaged in an important campaign. Mark likewise sees Jesus and his followers as being on an important mission. Jesus has authority not only over the debt code but also over the Sabbath.

From Mark's perspective, the Pharisees in their zeal to maintain Sabbath laws actually violated the spirit of God's original intention. Sabbath commands were not to be understood as rigid and legalistic obligations, but instead, Torah was a gracious gift to establish the covenant relationship. Regardless, the traditions of the Pharisees had

[1]William H. Willimon, *Conversations with Barth on Preaching* (Nashville: Abingdon, 2006), 11.

## Exegetical Perspective

Mark loves irony of all types. The irony in the two pericopes of this text revolves around the Sabbath. Artificially separated by chapter divisions, these two stories culminate a series of five controversies between Jesus and the religious leadership that begins in 2:1. These two stories continue to illustrate the boundary-breaking, life-transforming power of the imminent reign of God (1:14–15) and the deadly resistance arising against it.

In both stories, the religious leaders challenge Jesus' piety and his divine authority. The context for these controversies centers in perceived violations of Sabbath observance by Jesus and his disciples. These stories are not a modern slight on Sabbath observance as some sort of petty religiosity or obsession. Instituted by God at creation (Gen. 2:2) and confirmed as essential in Torah law (Exod. 20:8–11; Deut. 5:12–15), the Sabbath was intended to be a regular reminder of the liberating and generative grace of God. Keeping a faithful Sabbath was understood as a prerequisite for the coming reign of God.

The tragic irony in both stories is not only that the religious leaders do not see the Lord of the Sabbath (2:28) standing in their midst, but that on the Sabbath (a day of life) they conspire to kill (3:6) the one who has come to bring them life. Long before Jesus steps foot in Jerusalem, the passion of

## Homiletical Perspective

The text reveals a high level of tension between Jesus and the Pharisees. Controversies in previous passages over the issues of the forgiveness of sins (2:1–12), a fellowship table (2:13–17), and the practice of fasting (2:18–22) have created an uncomfortable relationship between Jesus and the Pharisees. And their relationship culminates in a most bitter and serious confrontation over the observance of Sabbath (2:23–3:6). The Pharisees, who are the authoritative lawmakers and interpreters of the law, measure Jesus' ministry based on their own practice of Sabbath observance, and Jesus persistently does not respect their "measuring stick," nor does he negotiate with them.

In response to the Pharisees' accusation that his disciples violate the Sabbath law by plucking the heads of grain from the grain fields on the Sabbath, Jesus defends his hungry disciples by reminding the Pharisees that the Sabbath was made for humankind, and not humankind for the Sabbath (2:23–27). Later, also on the Sabbath, Jesus cures a man's withered hand in the synagogue in front of the Pharisees. Jesus knows that such an act of healing violates their set code of Sabbath observance but does heal—wittingly reminding them that it is lawful to do good or save life on the Sabbath (3:1–4). Rather than gently exchanging their differing

## Theological Perspective

may inhibit that very divine-human interaction. As with any religious practice, what was meant to enhance our relation with God and neighbor can become idolatrous and inhumane.

The verses under consideration (2:27–28) are especially interesting because they exhibit something of the transition from the historical Jesus to the Jesus of early Christian tradition. In the unlikely event that the historical Jesus spoke of himself as "son of man," he would have used the phrase in the generic sense. Some sources in the earliest postcrucifixion tradition use the phrase in that sense; others, like Mark, give it a titular meaning in association with Daniel 7:13.[1] In identifying Jesus as the apocalyptic Son of Man, Mark is obviously asserting Jesus' unique revelatory significance and, by implication, committing himself to Jesus' teachings. For us, like Mark, to assert that Jesus is the Son of Man, or the Messiah, or the Christ, is to assert as well that feeding the hungry is of the utmost importance. Put another way, the theological issue here is not whether Jesus ever referred to himself as the Son of Man, but whether he reveals to us the God who wills that all human beings be adequately fed.

The remainder of today's reading is a searing indictment of the Pharisees and a window into the humanity of Jesus as one utterly responsive to God. Here again the Pharisees serve as the foil for Mark's Christian agenda, as they remain silent in the face of Jesus' question as to whether it is lawful "to do good or to do harm on the sabbath, to save life or to kill" (3:4). Their use of the Sabbath law to sustain their monopoly on religious authority and the power that comes with that authority blocks any human sympathy they might have for the man with the withered hand. When the man stretches out his hand in response to Jesus' command to do so, and his hand is restored, the Pharisees go out and conspire with the Herodians against Jesus, "how to destroy him" (3:6).

We must be clear that Mark's Pharisees are by no means representative of the Jews or even the Pharisees of their day. On the contrary, they represent the religious elite who, along with the secular authorities, lorded over the Jewish population. They mirror those religious leaders of our own day who favor the particular beliefs of their religious organization over the humane treatment of some of their neighbors. The institutional church is one of those "powers" that constitute what Walter

## Pastoral Perspective

become traditionalism—the dead faith of the living—and were not to be challenged.

Marva Dawn suggests, "Our Sabbath keeping puts us more firmly in touch again with the comprehensiveness of God's grace."[2] Sabbath practices for Christians and Jews are not only means of faithfulness and worship, but also expressions of grace. For our postdenominational, postmodern worldview, perhaps our equally legalistic but opposite tendency is not to practice Sabbath at all. We get enmeshed in the spiritual vs. religious tension where spirituality becomes individualistic and eclectic, rather than being spiritual *and* religious. Sabbath practice requires discipline and is with and for the community well-being. We do not keep Sabbath—Sabbath keeps us!

Our human need to control through rigid law keeping or through external busy-ness discourages intentional reflection and is symptomatic of our basic mistrust and lack of devotion to God. One new church development pastor admitted that a deeper relationship with God might challenge his closely managed life and force him to connect with the God of the universe in unsettling ways.

For the scribes and Pharisees, there no longer is any amazement toward Jesus, only increasing hostility. The kingdom of God brought healing and forgiveness for others but conflict and the cross for Jesus. Jesus also is fed up with their stubborn, closed minds, hardened hearts, and lack of compassion. One can almost see, feel his penetrating gaze.

Religion and nationalism were being juxtaposed, and rules took priority over reality. While the purpose of the commandment was to celebrate God's creation and redemption, the Sabbath became dehumanizing.

In Mark's version of Jesus' story, the Pharisees could not, would not mingle with the masses and become unclean. But in their zeal for the law, I wonder if they were not jealous, resentful, perhaps even lonely and too far removed from the people. Was there something about this Jesus that they in their deepest core truly desired? Even the most ambitious career climber has moments of regret at the loss of relationships sacrificed for the job, the promotion, and the power they bring. Perhaps fear is also an underlying motif. We do not know how to be fluid, nimble, open to the transforming power of the Holy Spirit.

We each find our own way to create control, erect boundaries and prejudices. We decide to whom we

---

[1] For an excellent discussion of the "Son of Man" issue, see John Dominic Crossan, *The Historical Jesus* (New York: HarperCollins, 1991), 238–59.

[2] Marva Dawn, *Keeping the Sabbath Wholly* (Grand Rapids: Eerdmans, 1989), 87.

Jesus begins in Mark's Gospel. From 3:6 on, the reader knows that the question is not whether Jesus will die, only when.

Though incorrectly identifying Abiathar (2:26) as a priest during David's time, Mark's point in this first pericope is clear. There are scriptural, humanitarian (human need), and christological (Jesus is Lord of the Sabbath) exceptions to work on the Sabbath. The ultimate issue in this story is not whether the disciples can "work" to abate hunger on the Sabbath, but who is Lord of the Sabbath. Readers know the answer (1:1) long before Mark's concluding verse (2:28).

The second pericope is set in the synagogue, which functions as a courtroom. While cast in this judicial setting, modern readers tend to focus on the miracle in this story and about the larger debate over miracles and if and how they happen. For Mark, miracles are assumed, even by the antagonists, the Pharisees. They do not question whether Jesus can heal, only whether he will profane the Sabbath to do so.

As the story opens, Jesus is confronted by a man who needs healing, and the Pharisees watch to see if Jesus will profane the Sabbath by doing this healing work. "The man is designated not by the general *tis* ('someone', 'a certain person') but by *anthrōpos* just referred to in 2:27, the 'living being' of Genesis 1 for whom the Sabbath was made. But the description of the man's present condition connotes death. In a dry land where moisture means life, *exerammenēn* ('withered') often implies 'death.'"[1]

Like the paralytic in 2:1–12, this man does not ask for healing. The Pharisees, keepers of the life-giving gift of the Sabbath, remain silent as Jesus asks his questions and grows in anger. Jesus asks the fundamental question of Torah faith, "Is it lawful on the Sabbath to do good, or to do evil?" He then speaks with ominous foreshadowing, "to save life, or to kill?" (3:4). Asked a direct question, the religious leaders remain frighteningly silent. Jesus answers his own question by restoring life to this "everyman."

For Mark, these two stories are not parochial, religious quarrels that he dutifully reports to any interested reader. These are stories that strike at the heart of what it means to follow the Lord of the Sabbath, calling readers not to deny its import but to celebrate its possibilities, not to get lost in the forest of tedious rule regulating but to find in these stories the tree of life-giving freedom. These stories do not simply look back to controversies between Jesus and

opinions on Sabbath observance, Jesus and the Pharisees are so severely tangled with emotion that Jesus is angry and deeply grieved (3:5) at the Pharisees' hardness of heart, and the Pharisees conspire to destroy Jesus after watching him violate their Sabbath law.

Jesus' anger at the Pharisees' hardness of heart is not a quick emotional reaction, but rather rises in depth from a feeling of tremendous sadness over how closed their hearts are against the will of God. Ironically, Mark locates this bitter conflict between Jesus and the Pharisees on this legal issue in the synagogue, which is supposed to be a holy place for interpreting and teaching the Law.

Preaching based on the empathic approach to Jesus' righteous anger can cultivate an environment for serious and healthy deliberation over our contemporary laws. Traditionally, Christian preaching has been understood as the ministry of interpreting and teaching the Scriptures, and the preacher as the interpreter and teacher of Scripture, of which a great portion is about the Law. Church history teaches us that in numerous cases the Christian pulpit has misused the Scriptures as proof text or as a weapon to kill people rather than saving lives, by supporting the vested interests of certain privileged groups, particularly when dealing with legal issues such as slavery, women's rights, and wars. We still witness controversies around the use of the Scriptures in relation to contemporary legal issues both within and beyond churches.

Strikingly, the judicial council of one of the largest mainline denominations in the United States recently ruled that pastors in the denomination could reject, at their sole discretion, homosexuals who seek membership in their churches. In addition, the council urged families and churches to "reject or condemn lesbian and gay members and friends" although they must be aware of what the gospel affirms regarding the life of the church, as it is clearly expressed in their book of discipline that "God's grace is available to all, and we will seek to live together in Christian community." If Jesus were to visit their churches and see persons rejected because of their sexuality, what would Jesus do at these churches? Regarding the recent changes in the immigration laws in the United States, what would Jesus do for the immigrants and say to the lawmakers, if Jesus saw immigrants losing their human rights and those of their children because of lawmakers' prejudiced, ruthless decision making?

[1] M. Eugene Boring, *Mark* (Louisville, KY: Westminster John Knox Press, 2006), 93.

# Mark 2:23–3:6

## Theological Perspective

Wink calls the "domination system." These powers are at once good "by virtue of their creation to serve the humanizing purposes of God," fallen "because they put their own interests above the interests of the whole," and redeemable "because what fell in time can be redeemed in time." Like the other powers, all interlocked in the domination system, the church has a tendency to sustain the status quo and, however passively or unwittingly, give credibility to the idea that might makes right, war brings peace, and violence saves. Wink calls this idea the myth of redemptive violence.[2] We see it in the Pharisees' determination to destroy Jesus, and we see it in the United States' determination to order the Middle East by military force.

The numbing effect of the domination system is evident in the Pharisees' insensitivity to the man with the withered hand. Ironically, it is their religious perspective that clouds their awareness of God and, in turn, their capacity to affirm the restoration of the man's hand. Their mistaken allegiance to a fallen power leads them to dehumanize others as they are themselves dehumanized. Jesus "looked around at them with anger; he was grieved at their hardness of heart" (3:5). The Pharisees could only be so callous toward a fellow human being because they had succeeded in closing off their own spiritual resources. Here, as in the healing of the paralytic, the spiritual and the material are integrally related, and the health of the individual is in some profound way a mirror and function of the prevailing cultural worldview. In both narratives, Jesus, the man, represents the human capacity to be responsive to God and thereby enter into compassionate solidarity with all human beings; likewise, in both narratives, Jesus, the Son of Man, is affirmed as the Christian's primary organizing principle and transforming power for exercising that capacity. In Jesus Christ we have our role model for loving God and neighbor and our enabler to do just that.[3]

JERRY IRISH

## Pastoral Perspective

will minister and when and how and to what degree. Whether because of the megachurch's pep-rally atmosphere or by the growing trend of home-based churches that resist polity and organization, mainline churches similarly feel threatened, react defensively, and hold tightly to traditions. Even worse, instead of emphasizing acts of missional kindness toward poverty and sustaining the earth, institutional religion debates sexuality or restructures the bureaucracy! There is some Pharisee in all of us.

Some scholars see Mark 3:1–6 as a "sign" story rather than a "conflict" story. A sign story demonstrates a "proof" of divine authority by one who is facing hostility or disbelief, in order to establish the validity that the action is of God. Within this background, Mark 3:1–6 becomes a culmination of Mark 2:1–12, where Jesus demonstrates a healing "sign" to prove divine authority when challenged. In both situations, Jesus responds to challenges to his claims, not by initiating an argument, but by making something happen.

Mark's purpose in telling the stories is not to have Jesus prove his authority by something he intends to do, that is, the healings, but to emphasize his legitimacy in terms of the questions and objections already raised by the Pharisees.

The text is justification for all of the things Jesus has done since healing the paralytic—his mingling with tax collectors and "sinners," his coming in contact with things that are unclean, his rejection of official fasting rules, and his violation of the Sabbath commandment by doing "work." Mark 3:1–6 is the literary and rhetorical ending to the beginning text in Mark 2:1–12.

In Mark 3:1–6, the narrative reaches a climax as Jesus gives a Deuteronomic ultimatum to his opponents regarding the meaning of Sabbath and then provokes the Pharisees to arrest him by a grandstanding act of civil disobedience—"Stretch out your hand."

In these acts of intentional Sabbath breaking, Jesus provides all the evidence needed for his impending crucifixion. Daniel Berrigan, in reflecting on Ched Myers's political perspective on Mark's Gospel, writes, "We breathed the bracing air of new starts, we were introduced to the way of Jesus, announced and lived out in the midst of conflicting ideologies and frenzies, the itch toward collaboration and violence"[3]—much like our world today.

AL MASTERS

[2]Walter Wink, *The Powers That Be* (New York: Doubleday, 1998), 31–36, 42–48.
[3]H. Richard Niebuhr, *The Responsible Self* (New York: Harper & Row, 1963), esp. Appendices A and B.

[3]Ched Myers, *Binding the Strong Man* (Maryknoll, NY: Orbis, 1988), xix.

## Exegetical Perspective

the religious leaders of the day; they warn the church of Mark's day and any day when it is tempted to live as if God's reign were not "at hand" (1:15).

Reflecting on all five controversy stories, Brian Blount concludes,

> Mark presses the thesis he established with his use of the verb rip, tear (*schizō*) at 1:10 to describe God's unruly behavior. God tears through the heavenly veil that separates God from humans. God runs loose through human history in the person and ministry of Jesus. And in that running God demands change. God transforms the landscape of human living and requires transformed lives in return. God breaks down walls that separate the people of Israel from God and the people of Israel from each other. And, given Jesus' charge that his disciples follow in the same transformative task, God also directs Mark's reading disciples to become players in the same boundary-breaking movement of God's imminent reign.[2]

As the reader reaches 3:6, Mark has established an atmosphere of fatal controversy. The religious leaders are not awed or inspired by Jesus. They have no intention to relinquish their cultic authority and every intention to end any claim by Jesus to divine authority. As for Jesus, these texts contend that he "is the one who makes whole, or saves, life (*psychen sosai*, 3:4). The repetition of the verb 'to rise' (*egeiro*) in these two healing stories points ahead to Jesus' own resurrection (16:6). The religious leaders plot the death of the life-bringer, whose resurrection will put an end to death forever."[3]

These two pericopes end with a deadly dose of Markan irony. Gone from the other controversy stories, Mark's favorite pre-Jerusalem word *euthys* (immediately, at once) reappears in 3:6. Jesus should not heal on the Sabbath according to these silent purists. He could not use a day set aside to refresh life to restore life, but they can use this Sabbath day to plot his death. They cannot wait. They must do it at once—even on the Sabbath. How ironic.

GARY W. CHARLES

## Homiletical Perspective

While American congregations encounter these kinds of legal issues at church and in society at large on a daily basis, people who live in different parts of the planet encounter different legal issues deeply related to their everyday lives, emerging from such issues as a globalized economy and neoliberalism, postcolonial militarism, and ecological crises. For example, vast areas of Niger and other African countries have turned into barren, dust-choked wastelands decaying into desert since Western countries began colonizing them. From colonial to contemporary neoliberal times, trees were by law regarded as property of the state, and millions of trees have been chopped down for profit, first by the colonizing countries and now by transnational corporations with complete disregard for environmental costs. In the economy of God the Creator, however, nature must be guaranteed a freedom unique to itself, which cannot be violated by human exploitation or expropriation (cf. Lev. 25). If Jesus were to hear nature groaning in pain, how would he feel about nature? Furthermore, if Jesus were to see people living in poverty because of the fruitlessness of unprotected land, or if he were to hear that starving people were being charged with violating laws that increase the profits of multibillion-dollar transnational corporations in developing countries, what would Jesus say to the accusers?

For congregations who are urgently facing similar legal issues, the text provides illumination and insight. Some preachers and congregations may choose to act indifferently to legal issues that they feel are not directly related to their interests. In the text, however, Jesus calls the preacher to help the congregation make the connection to those who are the underprivileged and the victimized by a particular law. The fundamental challenge of the text is whether both the preacher and the congregation are willing to have the same level of compassion toward the victims that Jesus had. Jesus' deep compassion for the victims of the law drove him to violate the law and eventually resulted in his death on the cross. Jesus, who is the Lord of the Sabbath (2:28), was killed by those who were faithful to the Sabbath law. This irony leads all preachers and congregations to rethink the way of discipleship.

EUNJOO MARY KIM

---

[2]Brian K. Blount and Gary W. Charles, *Preaching Mark in Two Voices* (Louisville, KY: Westminster John Knox Press, 2003), 27–28.
[3]Sharyn Dowd, *Reading Mark* (Macon, GA: Smyth & Helwys, 2000), 25.

# 2 Kings 2:1-12

<sup>1</sup>Now when the LORD was about to take Elijah up to heaven by a whirlwind, Elijah and Elisha were on their way from Gilgal. <sup>2</sup>Elijah said to Elisha, "Stay here; for the LORD has sent me as far as Bethel." But Elisha said, "As the LORD lives, and as you yourself live, I will not leave you." So they went down to Bethel. <sup>3</sup>The company of prophets who were in Bethel came out to Elisha, and said to him, "Do you know that today the LORD will take your master away from you?" And he said, "Yes, I know; keep silent."

<sup>4</sup>Elijah said to him, "Elisha, stay here; for the LORD has sent me to Jericho." But he said, "As the LORD lives, and as you yourself live, I will not leave you." So they came to Jericho. <sup>5</sup>The company of prophets who were at Jericho drew near to Elisha, and said to him, "Do you know that today the LORD will take your master away from you?" And he answered, "Yes, I know; be silent."

<sup>6</sup>Then Elijah said to him, "Stay here; for the LORD has sent me to the Jordan." But he said, "As the LORD lives, and as you yourself live, I will not leave you." So

## Theological Perspective

In this text, a gap appears in prophetic continuity as God initiates a transfer of spiritual leadership. One era is ending, but the next has not yet begun, and everyone in the story is occupied by the implications of the succession. Such in-between times give rise to several significant theological themes: the flow of time in relation to the constancy of the eternal, the dealings of infinite Spirit with finite humanity, and the nature of faithful response in the face of the unknown and the Unknowable.

First, Elijah's imminent departure raises the issue of God's eternal constancy in a world where time changes all. In the hymn "O God, Our Help in Ages Past" Isaac Watts poses the question clearly: "from everlasting thou art God, to endless years the same"; but "time, like an ever-rolling stream, bears all its [children] away." God has clearly been present in Elijah's durable ministry (see 2 Kgs. 1:1–16). The future is not so clear; the temporal instrument of God's everlasting rule is going away. The divine/human encounter is a mismatch like that between mortal Winnie and immortal Jessie in Natalie Babbitt's novel *Tuck Everlasting*. Unrelenting time threatens any lasting relationship between the Everlasting One and mortals destined to be borne away.

The end of Elijah's era is neither surprising nor secret. Verse 1 states it plainly, and it is reaffirmed

## Pastoral Perspective

The inclusion of this text on Transfiguration Sunday seems straightforward enough: Elijah makes a cameo appearance in Mark's transfiguration story. However, this is a story about Elisha more than Elijah, the latter's triumphal ascension into heaven notwithstanding. It is Elisha who is transformed, indeed *transfigured*; that is, the *figure* of Elisha is *transported* through and beyond his role as Elijah's apprentice to a completely new place. Indeed, Elisha's transfiguration can serve as a parable for our own *trans-figuration* as individuals and as communities of faith.

*Trans-figured by the Journey.* On any given map of a territory there are landmarks and features marked with small print, and others marked with bold print. On a map of Elijah and Elisha's journey, all of the stops are theological bold-print locations: Gilgal, where the Israelites camped after crossing the Jordan River; Bethel, a sacred temple site; Jericho, the location of the Israelites' famous military victory; and the Jordan itself. However, Elijah's ascension takes place beyond them all, past the Jordan—at an unnamed location where the two men walk together. In exploring this passage with the congregation, we do well to acknowledge the transformative events that occur not in A-list destinations or on

the two of them went on. ⁷Fifty men of the company of prophets also went, and stood at some distance from them, as they both were standing by the Jordan. ⁸Then Elijah took his mantle and rolled it up, and struck the water; the water was parted to the one side and to the other, until the two of them crossed on dry ground.

⁹When they had crossed, Elijah said to Elisha, "Tell me what I may do for you, before I am taken from you." Elisha said, "Please let me inherit a double share of your spirit." ¹⁰He responded, "You have asked a hard thing; yet, if you see me as I am being taken from you, it will be granted you; if not, it will not." ¹¹As they continued walking and talking, a chariot of fire and horses of fire separated the two of them, and Elijah ascended in a whirlwind into heaven. ¹²Elisha kept watching and crying out, "Father, father! The chariots of Israel and its horsemen!" But when he could no longer see him, he grasped his own clothes and tore them in two pieces.

## Exegetical Perspective

This passage is part of a larger passage that is chiastically structured.

> A Elijah and Elisha Leave Gilgal (2:1–2)
> B Elijah and Elisha at Bethel (2:3–4)
> C Elijah and Elisha at Jericho (2:5–6)
> D Elijah and Elisha cross the Jordan (2:7–8)
> E The Ascent of Elijah (2:9–12)
> D¹ Elisha Recrosses the Jordan (2:13–18)
> C¹ Elisha at Jericho (2:19–22)
> B¹ Elisha at Bethel (2:23–24)
> A¹ Elisha Returns to Samaria (2:25)

It is clear from this chiastic pattern that the ascent of Elijah in a whirlwind into heaven is the heart of the entire passage. The events in the reading for today's liturgy all prepare for and move toward this extraordinary event.

The cities mentioned in this passage are important to the story. Most scholars agree that the Gilgal referred to should not be confused with the Gilgal that played such an important role in the occupation of the land at the time of Joshua. That Gilgal was on the eastern border of Jericho (Josh. 4:19). The Gilgal in this account appears to have been located in the hill country of Samaria, north of Bethel (v. 2). Bethel, of course, enjoys a long and

## Homiletical Perspective

Scenes portraying the passing of the torch are often quite moving. This one is no exception. Drawing us deeply into the surprising intimacy among the prophets, this scene of Elisha assuming Elijah's mantle as Israel's chief prophet portrays simultaneously the passing of a generation, the poignancy of parting, and the importance of maintaining a continuity of leadership. There are few details to the narrative, but their starkness suggests the importance of paying attention to each.

Interestingly, it is not the drama or spectacle of Elijah's actual departure—complete with horses and chariots of fire—that makes the lasting impression, but rather other "relational" realities that seem more potent and more real: Elisha is discouraged from following Elijah to the end, both by the senior prophet himself and by the larger fellowship of prophets, and yet, because of his devotion to his mentor, he will not be deterred. Elisha requests a "double portion" of Elijah's spirit, not to be "twice the prophet" Elijah was, but to signify that he is Elijah's true heir (see Deut. 21:17). Elijah admonishes Elisha that he will have to rely on God for whatever portion he receives. And finally Elisha exclaims in both anguish and awe as his spiritual father is taken up into heaven, leaving him alone and yet confirmed in his status.

# 2 Kings 2:1-12

## Theological Perspective

twice before verse 6. Elijah, Elisha, and the companies of prophets all know that change is on its way. The question is whether God's spirit will keep continuity with God's people when the one identified with that spirit is borne away. Elisha calls out in grief and a sense of vulnerability at the moment of Elijah's departure (v. 12).

Augustine addressed this theological tension between time and eternity in book 11 of the *Confessions*. He asserts time is part of the created order and therefore God's activity is not bound by its flow. God's presence in history is mysterious, says Augustine, but it is not time-bound. The canonical setting of this biblical text accentuates this exceptional quality of God's acts, which are in time but not of it. Walter Brueggemann suggests the placement of the ascension of Elijah between the end of one king's reign (1:17–18) and the beginning of another's (3:1–3) places God's initiative outside normal timekeeping.[1] The calendarless character of these events is further indicated by Elijah's crossing the Jordan into territory beyond the kings' timekeepers (v. 8). God, as the saying goes, is "always right on time," but not in bondage to any clock.

The same is not true of people. People are bound by time. As Augustine noted, we are forced to act within a tiny window of time—the present—since the past is unrecoverable and the future is not yet available.[2] In a sense we act in between what was and what will be. The human necessity to act meaningfully in the existential present, disengaged from the predictable past and unattached to a known future, is found in this text. How does one stay faithful to the Unknowable in the face of the unknown on the edge of the cleft between eras?

The narrative is enigmatic. The text does not say why the Lord sends Elijah where he is sent, why Elisha calls for silence, or what is the significance of Elijah's symbolic actions. Elijah cannot say if Elisha will be granted his spirit (v. 10). They can see the end of one path and cannot see the beginning of another.

The text suggests at least two faithful responses to the crises of the in-between times: persistence and silent watchfulness. Elisha persists in accompanying Elijah. Three times Elijah pleads with his disciple to abandon him. Three times Elisha refuses, insisting on hope as long as life remains (vv. 2, 4, 6). Twice the prophets question Elisha, asking if he knows of

[1] Walter Brueggemann, *Smyth and Helwys Bible Commentary, 1 & 2 Kings* (Macon: Smyth & Helwys Publishers, 2000), 293.
[2] Augustine, *Confessions*, 11.15.18.

## Pastoral Perspective

predetermined timelines, but in the nondescript places and in the humdrum of Ordinary Time. There and then, life is disrupted in ways both glorious and disturbing.

Elijah gives Elisha three opportunities to leave, and each time Elisha says no: "As the LORD lives, and as you yourself live, I will not leave you" (vv. 2, 4, 6). Is it simple devotion to his master that motivates Elisha—a desire to accompany him in that thin place between life and the world beyond? Or is it Elisha's dogged persistence in seeking after the "double share" that keeps him tagging along?

Either alternative might resonate with a congregation. In the first place, Elisha's fidelity provides inspiration in a world of disposable relationships and transient loyalties. In the second place, we cannot help but compare Elisha's journey with Jacob's wrestling match with the angel: "I will not let you go, unless you bless me" (Gen. 32:26). Elisha may be less scrappy than Jacob, but he is just as unrelenting. Such tenacity might appear unseemly to those who are squeamish about asking boldly for what they need—for "the hard thing." Too many good-intentioned Christians seem willing to make do, to go without, to give without ceasing, while refusing the balm that they need. Whether driven by a culture of rugged individualism, an unhealthy self-denial, or a theology of scarcity, we are both convicted and inspired by Elisha's determination to follow Elijah through river and town until he receives what he knows he will need for his own ministry. Elisha's faithfulness to the process allows for his transformation. How too might we be trans-figured by such faithful perseverance in our journeys with God and one another?

*Trans-figured in Community.* The company of prophets speaks to Elisha twice. Both times, the message is the same—Elijah will be taken away—and Elisha's response is the same, "I know. Be silent." The prophets share their message, Elisha affirms it, there is a call for silence, and the journey continues, the process repeats. And though the exchange is the same, one wonders whether Elisha hears it differently in a new place down the road, from a different vantage point.

The rhythm of their interaction is catechetical: question, answer, silence; question, answer, silence. What would it look like to make this rhythm more explicit in a service of worship? We gather faithfully as a community Sunday after Sunday, though never the same as we were the week before. We talk to God

colorful tradition in the religious and political history of ancient Israel. Shortly after his entry into the land of Canaan, Abram built an altar to the Lord here (Gen. 12:8), and there Jacob saw the ladder reaching to heaven (Gen. 28:11–19). The site served as a prominent shrine during the period of the judges (Judg. 20:18), and it became one of the two major places of worship established by Jeroboam when the northern tribes seceded from Davidic rule (1 Kgs. 12:29). At the time described in this reading, it was also the home of a company of prophets.

Jericho was a strategic entry point from Transjordan into the highlands of Judah. Its proximity to the Jordan River and the wide plain within which it was situated made it an ideal launching site for Israel's foray into the land of Canaan (Josh. 4:13). After its destruction by the invading Israelites, it lay unoccupied for about four centuries until it was reinhabited during the period when Elijah and Elisha lived. At that time, it too was the home of a company of prophets (2 Kgs. 2:5). It should be noted that these prophets approached Elisha, not Elijah. This may be because they were under Elisha's leadership.

These cities are important in this passage because they serve as stations in Elijah's journey to heaven and in Elisha's rite of passage from protégé to legitimate successor of Elijah. At each step of the way, Elijah told Elisha to "stay here" (vv. 2, 4, 6,). In each instance, Elisha responded with an oath: "As the LORD lives, and as you yourself live, I will not leave you" (vv. 2, 4, 6). It is not clear why Elijah tried to dissuade his assistant. Was he perhaps testing him, to see whether he would be able to withstand the obstacles that would accompany his role as prophet? The recurrence of this exchange is not the only repetition in the passage. The companies of prophets in Bethel and in Jericho seemed to know what was about to happen to Elijah, and they both posed the same question to Elisha, inquiring into his own knowledge of this matter. His response to each company was the same: "Yes, I know; be silent" (vv. 3, 5). This repetition may be a literary device meant to mount the anticipation of and mystery surrounding the upcoming events.

The events that transpire at the Jordan River are reminiscent of Israel's crossing of the Red Sea (cf. Exod. 14:15–22). Like Moses before him, Elijah caused the waters to part; then he and Elisha crossed on dry ground (2 Kgs. 2:8). Moses accomplished that feat by means of his staff, a symbol of his office; Elijah accomplished this feat by means of his rolled-

Here is where the heart lingers, over the fragility and transience of these relationships. To be Elijah's heir, as it turns out, means far more than simply to do similar miracles; it is to go wherever the prophet goes, to bear the same burdens, to risk the same hardship, to venture into times of both solitariness and solidarity in order to receive and ultimately bear a word of the Lord.

Through this scene we learn something new about prophets, or at least have our popular conceptions of prophets thoroughly challenged. To be a prophet is *not* to be a solitary figure standing at a distance in order to predict the future or call upon the judgment of the Lord. Rather, to be a prophet is to enter deeply into the realities and relationships of the people to whom you are sent. It is for this reason, perhaps, that the prophet's message is so potent, for it is driven by the anguish of witnessing the disparity between the grand desire of God for God's people and the paucity and poverty of the reality God's people has been willing to accept. To be a prophet, finally, is to love God's people enough to tell them the truth about their condition. Elijah and Elisha are not stoics. They are bound to each other, to the larger band of prophets and their families (see 2 Kgs. 4:1–7), to Israel, and even to the surrounding nations.

Further, to be a prophet is to be completely vulnerable, absolutely dependent on God's word and mercy. This is what makes Elisha's request to receive a double portion "a hard thing." He has asked to be Elijah's heir, his spiritual son. Elijah, in turn, must admit that granting such a desire is beyond him. Rather, Elisha's fate and fortune will rest with the Lord, the God of Israel. In accepting this dependence, Elisha does indeed become Elijah's heir and so is granted a vision of his mentor's grand departure and can only cry aloud in anguished wonder.

Here, perhaps, is the strongest connection to the Gospel reading appointed for the day. While this text has most likely been chosen (a) for its portrayal of Elijah as the mightiest of prophets (the only one who does not die but is taken up into heaven), and (b) because it, like the Gospel, portrays a theophany of epic proportions; nevertheless the most striking link to the Gospel narrative is found in this theme of vulnerability. The dependence of these two prophets on the mercy of God is qualitatively similar to the vulnerability and dependence of Jesus, the beloved Son, who will come down the mountain only to be betrayed and made to suffer and die on the cross, a fate he anticipates and accepts only by his trusting completely in God's mercy.

# 2 Kings 2:1-12

## Theological Perspective

Elijah's departure. Twice Elisha answers yes, but ends discussion and continues following his master. His last request of Elijah is a "double share" of the prophet's spirit. Elijah says if Elisha sees things through to the end, maybe.

Silence is another faithful response in the in-between times. Elisha admits to the prophets that his master Elijah is about to be taken away, but he calls for silence (vv. 3, 5) or stillness (so NASB) rather than premature conclusions. Unlike Peter at the transfiguration, who in his terror at the unknown did not know what to say but spoke anyway, and spoke unwisely (Mark 9:5–6), Elisha responds with a call for something reminiscent of the "sheer silence" in which Elijah had heard God (1 Kgs. 19:12).

Elisha is rewarded by the revelation of God bridging the boundaries between time and timelessness, endings and endlessness. Soon he finds that God's spirit remains and rests on him (2 Kgs. 2:14). We worry the spirit will leave us. The truth is that the spirit stays; it is we who must go.

The history of interpretation for this text focuses on Elijah's ascension and its relation to his unended life. Since he was taken up without dying, hope arose in the Christian canon for his return, free of time's restraints. The Christian Old Testament canon ends with that expectation (Mal. 4:5–6), and the New Testament soon reveals his spirit resting with John the Baptist (Matt. 11:13–14) and present at the transfiguration. Elijah's ascension signifies the unbound, timeless presence of the spirit's continuation within history, from the era of dividers of waters—Moses (Exod. 14), Joshua (Josh. 3), Elijah, and Elisha (2 Kgs. 2:14)—to Jesus, upon whom the Spirit descended at baptism and was reaffirmed at the transfiguration. Jesus' disciples, who were promised at Jesus' ascension that if they would but wait for its timely coming, they too would be clothed in power from on high (Luke 24:48–51), were included at Pentecost, as are all who enter the waters of baptism in the flow of time.

WM. LOYD ALLEN

## Pastoral Perspective

and listen for God; we rehearse and rehear the stories of the faith; we reiterate the promises of God that are trustworthy and true; we affirm our faith; and we let the Word sink into us in prayer and silence. Worship trans-figures us and prepares us for times of adversity, when we will need those stories, prayers, and promises to be second nature.

The third time, when Elijah ascends, the silence is absolute. There are no words from the company of prophets; they simply stand nearby—witnesses, present and available, yet at a respectful distance. Words are no longer necessary. The community has helped name the experience for Elisha, and this naming is one of the most important works of the church, a key component in "re-storying" the people—but naming is no substitute. Elisha must witness Elijah's departure with his own eyes, and be brought to a new place: trans-figured by it.

*Trans-figured in Solitude.* It is unclear what Elisha expected to receive from Elijah in terms of the double portion. What he does receive is the awareness that whatever Elijah has taught him up to now will have to be enough; he must go on alone. What he receives is *grief.* The text is meticulous to point out that Elisha tears his clothes into two pieces. A play on the double portion, perhaps? Elisha will go on to do great deeds, to be sure, but for now, his mantle is one of sorrow. It is a fitting initiation for a man whose mentor looked sorrow in the face in his ministry to the widow at Zarephath (1 Kgs. 17); who himself knew vulnerability, alone in the wilderness, praying for death, straining to hear God in the "sound of sheer silence" (1 Kgs. 19).

In the topsy-turvy reign of God, strength comes from weakness, glory from despair. The loss of Elijah does not deter Elisha from what must be done: it does not *dis-figure* him for the ministry to come. In the next section, the transformed, trans-figured Elisha will pick up Elijah's mantle that has fluttered to the ground. He will strike the water with it, pass through, and journey on. It is a welcome reminder to those of us to lead, mentor, and shepherd others. It is not our ministry but God's; we cannot walk the journey for others, but we can invite them, as Elijah did, to keep their eyes open—to keep watch for evidence of God's grace and power.

MARYANN MCKIBBEN DANA

## Exegetical Perspective

up mantle, which under those circumstances resembled a rod. This mantel was the very garment Elijah had earlier thrown on the shoulders of Elisha, designating him his disciple. Through these actions Elijah is seen to be a prophet like Moses. It is interesting to note that this took place across the Jordan, outside of the land of Israel, yet another link with Moses, who saw the land but was prevented from entering it.

Having crossed the river, Elisha entreated Elijah to grant him a double portion of the prophet's spirit (v. 9). Double portion was the share of inheritance the elder son and legitimate successor received from his father in the patriarchal structure of ancient Israel (cf. Deut. 21:17). Elisha was making a bold claim, and Elijah assured him that it would be granted if he would be courageous enough to witness Elijah's departure. Here we see a final test of his courage. Would he be able to withstand an encounter with the Divine?

The passage twice states that Elijah was "taken up to heaven by a whirlwind" (vv. 1, 11). The description of this event is far more dramatic than these simple statements suggest. A fiery chariot and horses of fire appeared and separated the prophets. The fire of this theophany may have prevented Elisha from seeing everything that was happening, but he held his gaze and thereby met the final test. The text does not state whether or not he witnessed Elijah as he was swept up into the whirlwind of God. Yet, when he lost sight of his mentor, Elisha tore his clothing in a traditional act of mourning. Elijah was gone, and Elisha was left with prophetic responsibility.

While the primary theme of the passage is the ascent of Elijah, other themes are also important. First is the matter of prophetic succession. Elisha was chosen by Elijah; he did not assume that role independently. Though chosen, he had to prove his mettle, withstanding rejection, resisting inappropriate acclaim of others (the company of prophets), and standing humbly yet steadfastly in the presence of God.

DIANNE BERGANT

## Homiletical Perspective

With this homiletical trajectory in mind, we might wonder, In what ways is the preacher's congregation presently vulnerable and dependent? The first inclination in posing such a question may be to turn this into a prescription, calling the congregation to greater trust in and dependence on God's mercy. But while there may be appropriate prescriptions to discern, perhaps we might for the moment concern ourselves with the descriptive; that is, in asking in what ways the congregation is presently experiencing vulnerability, difficulty, struggle, and challenge, and to image these, not simply as obstacles to be overcome, but as points of dependence on God's mercy to embrace. Congregations (and for that matter, preachers!), like prophets, are not immune to the hardships of life, but rather are called to embrace these realities as the arenas in which God proves God's faithfulness.

To move in such a direction is, we should be aware, to challenge popular notions of strength, as we discover that to be strong in faith is to accept one's vulnerability, trusting ourselves to the "weak" word of God first uttered by all-too-human prophets and later enfleshed in the beloved Son who chose not the way of "power" but rather that of vulnerability and self-sacrificing love. To be prophetic in our context, then, is to be immersed in the challenges confronting God's people and, amid these difficulties, to throw ourselves to mercy of the God of Elijah and Elisha, the God we know most fully in the beloved Son, and so to give voice to God's vision for wholeness and life, both for us and through us for the world.

DAVID J. LOSE

# Psalm 50:1-6

[1]The mighty one, God the LORD,
    speaks and summons the earth
    from the rising of the sun to its setting.
[2]Out of Zion, the perfection of beauty,
    God shines forth.

[3]Our God comes and does not keep silence,
    before him is a devouring fire,
    and a mighty tempest all around him.
[4]He calls to the heavens above
    and to the earth, that he may judge his people:
[5]"Gather to me my faithful ones,
    who made a covenant with me by sacrifice!"
[6]The heavens declare his righteousness,
    for God himself is judge.

*Selah*

## Theological Perspective

The overarching theological message of Psalm 50 is that God alone is God. A secondary theme is a call for us to listen to God, to be faithful and merciful as creatures before God. In addition to these two explicit themes, the text carries another theological issue highlighted by its designation as the psalm for Transfiguration Sunday.

*God Is God.* Psalm 50 announces God as "The mighty one, God the LORD" (v. 1). God speaks and will speak (vv. 1 and 3). God shines and will shine forth in glory (v. 2). God comes and will come (v. 3). God judges and will judge, gathers and will gather "my faithful ones"; God's judgment will be righteous precisely because God alone knows and gathers those who are faithful and merciful (see vv. 5 and 6).[1]

The primary message of this psalm is "Let God be God." We are creatures before God; acknowledging the sovereignty of God is "the key issue" in a "rightly ordered life."[2]

[1]The Hebrew originals of the verbs Ps. 50 uses to describe God's actions may properly be translated as present or as having a more future orientation (in v. 3, for example, "comes" appears in the NRSV, while the NJB uses an ongoing tone, "is coming").

[2]Walter Brueggemann, *The Message of the Psalms: A Theological Commentary* (Minneapolis: Augsburg, 1984), 91. Other secondary sources cited in this commentary are Augustine, *Expositions of the Psalms*, part III, vol. 16, *The Works of Saint Augustine: A Translation for the 21st* Century, ed. John E. Rotelle, OSA, trans. Maria Boulding, OSB (Hyde Park, NY: New City Press, 2000); and Dietrich Bonhoeffer, *The Cost of Discipleship*, trans. Reginald Fuller (London: SCM, 1966).

## Pastoral Perspective

The fiftieth psalm begins with a glorious manifestation of God who shines forth (v. 2), does not keep silent but is seen in fire and tempest (v. 3) for the purpose of judging the people (v. 4), renewing the covenant in worship (v. 5), and declaring the righteousness of God (v. 6). With the story of the transfiguration in mind, the psalmody for today makes clear that a glorious experience of divine presence is not an end in itself, but is for the purpose of both judgment and renewal.

Preaching on this lection from a pastoral perspective offers the opportunity to address community expectations about worship in general and prayer in particular, as well as addressing divine judgment as a means of grace. A pastor will be aware that many people crave experience that they can recognize as a manifestation of God. They may devote themselves to a search for religious or spiritual experience as an end in itself. Seeking such a manifestation of God is often driven by a host of expectations of which the seeker is not really aware. These hidden expectations may include the ideas that with a magnificent experience of God doubts and questions will pass away, that the seeker will know himself or herself loved in a new way, that morally ambiguous situations will come into clear perspective, that worship in general and prayer in particular will

## Exegetical Perspective

*Expecting the Tepid, Finding the Tempestuous!* A pilgrimage to one of ancient Israel's sacred festivals was not always life-changing. All too often, in fact, pilgrims would simply practice the rites required of them and then depart, figuring God was pleased and sated (cf. vv. 12–13). They left unchanged and unsanctified (cf. v. 21). It is sometimes too easy to imagine one has God's approval.

Psalm 50 will have none of this. It holds that worship without ethical transformation is worthless and is not a real encounter with "the mighty one, God the Lord" (v. 1). It ignores that "God himself is judge" (v. 6), that God is *not* "just like yourself" (v. 21).

A visit to God's sanctuary should orient us to God's judgments. We should go home convicted about how life ought to be lived, focused on practicing justice, mercy, and steadfast discipleship. The northern Levites who penned Psalm 50 hoped it would rehabilitate Israel's festival worship. They hoped it would inspire true reverence as pilgrims renewed the Sinai covenant each fall (see Judg. 21:19; 1 Kgs. 8:2; Hos. 9:5).[1]

To live as God's people, our psalm insists, means a commitment to ethics and discipleship. It preaches

[1] For more on these Levites (the Asaphites), see Stephen L. Cook, *The Social Roots of Biblical Yahwism* (Atlanta: Society of Biblical Literature, 2004), 17, 24–25, 53–57, 130, 237–41.

## Homiletical Perspective

Transfiguration Sunday holds a precarious place in the Protestant lectionary. Thematically and chronologically, the readings all take us to the dawn before the darkness, a last breath of clarity before we plunge headfirst into the chaos of Lent. For those of us who have peeked ahead in the script and know what is to come, it can be difficult fully to trust the mountain's revelation. How does the preacher deal with such "power-full" texts when the horizon looms so dark? What can we say on Sunday's peak that we will not regret under Wednesday's ashes?

Psalm 50 begins pleasantly enough. God cries out to the heavens and the earth, "Gather my people" (v. 5) and breaks a long silence (v. 21). These verses speak of God's glory in summoning the world itself to attention—complete with "raging fire" and "furious storm" (v. 3 TEV)—but those who read past the assigned lection will find that God is calling the faithful not to blessing but to accountability.

In words that ring of Micah, God reminds the people that faith is not just a matter of rote and routine, but passion. The Almighty seems to have more than a fair share of bulls and burnt offerings; what is lacking is a people who know their own hunger. God yearns for a sacrifice of genuine praise, of dependence, not another empty religious ritual. When the smoke of theophany clears, God brings judgment.

# Psalm 50:1-6

## Theological Perspective

Many psalms represent the speech of the worshiping community, whether in lament, praise, or thanksgiving. This psalm, by contrast, is one that represents the speech of God alone. Sometimes it is necessary for us simply to remain silent before God. How else will we be or become and remain God's faithful, merciful ones (v. 5)?

It is as if God is begging and demanding of us that we stop—now, at this very moment. Stop. Pray. Listen. Reflect. Listen, again. Perhaps now we will be empowered to hear and know at some deeper level how God wills for us to respond—and to do it.

*Listen! Respond!* God's first proclamation in Psalm 50 is that God will "gather . . . my faithful ones," those who have made a covenant with God by "sacrifice" (v. 5). These faithful persons are then assured that they do not need to fear God's coming judgment, since God is in fact righteous.

Who are these "faithful ones," and what has been their "sacrifice"? God's "faithful ones" are all who enter God's love through faith *and* who make the sacrifice of being merciful to others. We listen; we respond by giving, without reservation. Saint Augustine explains: "What it costs is what you have."[3] There is no cheap grace here, only costly grace (see Bonhoeffer). At the same time, costly grace provides assurance to believers that God will not overlook them, no matter how small or insignificant their lives may seem. The real sacrifice God chooses is "mercy," not ritual, not the mere appearance of faithfulness.[4]

*Christian Interpretation of the Psalms.* Mature, vital Christian faith calls in our age for neither a sterile critical reading nor a naive appropriation.[5] How are we to do this? One resource for us who live in this rationalistic age is to consider how mature, vital Christians did it in the early church. They lived at a time when rich allusions, echoes, and harmonies were more readily heard than they are today. Virtually all such interpreters considered it essential to read the Old and New Testaments as a unity, the one Christian Bible. For example, Augustine sees God's address in Psalm 50 as the Word of God, spoken by the Word of God, who became incarnate as Jesus Christ.[6] Augustine sees a striking parallel between the very God who "shines forth" from Zion

[3] Augustine, 394.
[4] Augustine, 382; Hos. 6:6.
[5] Brueggemann, 21.
[6] Augustine, 282.

## Pastoral Perspective

cease to be dull and will become intrinsically meaningful, and that life will become less demanding with the assurance that God is real. Rarely if ever will the seeker after religious experience harbor a hidden expectation that he or she will be subject to divine judgment and called to renewed commitment in the midst of those same doubts, questions, ambiguous situations, and dull periods of worship and prayer.

Divine self-disclosure or manifestation always has the character of a gift of grace. A particularly intense experience of the presence of God is not something that can be conjured, cajoled, manipulated, or otherwise brought about. Moses did not seek out the burning bush (Exod. 3:1–6), nor did Elijah seek a manifestation of God in a sheer silence (1 Kgs. 19:11–12). Neither Amos nor Hosea sought a divine call on their lives when they were granted vocation (Amos 7:14–15; Hos. 1:1–3). Even Isaiah offered himself for service in response to a theophany, not as a way of conjuring one into being (Isa. 6:1–8). Just so, the disciples on the mount of the transfiguration found themselves granted a powerful vision of Jesus' authority in the midst of their efforts to grasp his identity (Mark 9:1–14). In each instance, and others besides, a particular experience of the presence of God was granted freely and without effort on the part of those so blessed.

We neither pray nor worship in order to create some kind of religious experience. Prayer and worship are responses to God by which we orient ourselves toward that which is of ultimate worth. In worship we open ourselves to being shaped in conformity with what truly matters for life, and shaped by the ground and source of our being. If we have a particularly intimate experience of God such as that known by the psalmist, then that experience is an unmerited, unearned, free gift of God's grace. The place to seek the effects of our prayer is not in the prayer itself but in our lives. We do not worship in order to "get something out of it," but in order that our lives may be more fully in accord with the purposes and intention of God, more fully in accord with the deepest desires of our hearts, and more fully a manifestation of the person we were created to be. A marathon runner who does not train will soon find herself short of breath. A concert pianist who does not practice will soon find his audience dwindling. A person of faith who pays no heed to worship will soon find her life overtaken by concerns that matter little in the great scheme of things.

The theophany of Psalm 50 is neither an experience *during* worship, nor a result *of* worship. It

this word with power, drawing its energy from a mystery: *awe* is a portal to *ought*. The mystery is truly profound. *Awe* before the uncanny and "other" provokes in the soul a profound sense of *ought* (morality and obligation to God).

The *numinous*—that which dwarfs and unnerves us—gives rise to ethical awareness, moral transformation, and growth in virtue. This is the wonder that drives our psalm. This is why it returns us to Sinai, to the tempestuous epiphany at the giving of the covenant.

*Mount Sinai Erupts.* God has made an entrance, verse 2 announces; God has blazed into view. The Hebrew of the verse recalls God's appearance on Sinai, the mountain of the covenant (Deut. 33:2). It was there, after the exodus, that Israel first experienced God's dizzying otherness. There, Israel shrank back in awe as the *numinous* descended to earth.

The interactive Hebrew sounds of verse 2 are magnificent. It is from a realm of *yofi* ("towering splendor") that God has *hofia'* ("blazed forth"). As we read on, pulsing images join with such sounds to bring us up short. We soon hear of a "devouring fire" and a "mighty tempest." The more we penetrate the psalm, the more we discover God's alien majesty.

Though overwhelming, God's otherness is magnetic. Drawn in to this otherness, the psalmist soon changes the verb forms. By verse 3 we hear a tone of emotional immersion. "Let our God come and not fail to act!" the spellbound psalmist cries (NJPS). The verbs's enthusiasm gives voice to Sinai's eerie pull.

When God and Israel made their covenant, Mount Sinai quaked as God came down ablaze (Exod. 19:18), a lapping, devouring fire (Deut. 5:25; Mic. 1:4; cf. Ps. 50:3). With Sinai spastic in shudders, its smoke rising as if from a kiln, God thundered God's word (Exod. 19:19; Deut. 4:33, 36; 5:22; cf. Mark 9:7); by no means did God keep silent (Ps. 50:3). Below, the people cowered, unable to cope (Exod. 19:16; 20:18; Deut. 5:26; 18:16; cf. Mark 9:6; Luke 5:8). They learned the *fear of God* (Exod. 20:20; Deut. 4:10; 5:29).

*Morality Mounts.* The jump from *awe* to *ought* is mysterious—anything but natural. Why should we instinctively embrace the Moral in the face of that which is overwhelming, haunting, and seemingly amoral? But we do. Faced with the *numinous*, we jump to embrace the *fear of God*. Maybe agnostics should take a hint, carefully considering this pointer to God.

In many of the worship services I witness on a regular basis, however, there is a disconnect between the theophany and the accountability. Most churches exhibit neither, the congregation taking most of their risks while parking the car before the service. But even among churches that do seem to wrestle with a real presence of God, there is a growing demarcation between those faith communities that want to stay on the mountain and those who want to remain solely in the valley. Rarely will a single worshiping community have the wherewithal to pack up their theological bags and make a new camp, yet this is exactly what Asaph's psalm and Transfiguration Sunday call us to do.

With all of the texts for Transfiguration Sunday, God is out in the open, speaking boldly, shining even on mortals (even church folk!). The veil is torn, the gloves come off. On this day, the lectionary will not allow for modesty or for versions of Christianity that play their cards close to the chest. On most Sundays, we can take a parable and wrestle some nonthreatening allegorical blessing from it, or tweak a proverb into some mildly therapeutic truth about raising healthy children. We can sit safely in our pews, peering into these "ancient" texts from a comfortable distance.

But today of all days, the psalmist gives a warning: "Our God is coming, but not in silence" (v. 3 TEV). This is not business as usual, and that means that every congregation that has the audacity to speak these words before one another will have to be ready to move.

For those who have become addicted to the bright clarity of the mountaintop experience, it will be a reminder that faith is more than a matter of heart alone. The unique position of Transfiguration Sunday and its beautiful theophanies declares that the mountain is never the end of the journey. God does not gather us together just for a divine fireworks display, God always has something to say, usually something to ask. Preachers who stand before congregations that want little more than a warm and fuzzy theological moment can definitively declare that every moment of clarity with God is merely an invitation to the next question, the first step on the next journey. Faith is dynamic, sometimes painfully so.

There seem to be far more churches where the opposite is true, where God has been absent for so long that the faithful have learned to live without fire and storm, much less expect them. For congregants who have grown accustomed to the silence of God, it

# Psalm 50:1-6

## Theological Perspective

to all the earth (v. 2) and Jesus' appearances in glory from the resurrection to the ascension (see Luke 24:46–47 and Acts 1:8).[7]

As long as we recognize the move we are making, interpreting the Psalms in the light of God's revelation in and through Jesus Christ, may we not still make that move today? Our text suggests the answer is, "Yes, but not too quickly." In order truly to interpret Psalm 50 in the light of Jesus' life, death, and resurrection, we must first listen—and be prepared to sacrifice. Is this not what Christ did? We are not to *speak about* the psalm so much as we are to *listen to* it. We are to hear its words of judgment and its words of promise. Primarily, we are to hear its warning against thinking that our beliefs or rituals guarantee us anything.

The issue is not whether we believe the psalmist literally intended for us to hear the transfigured, risen Christ speaking in Psalm 50. Rather, the issue is whether we listen to God and change our lives, whether we become more Christ-like. If we do not, it is because we "do not believe."[8] If we *do* hear and believe, giving God all we have—in true worship and in loving service of others—we may be confident. God does and will forgive us and love us and "gather" us in, among all God's faithful, merciful ones (v. 5).

CHARLES QUAINTANCE

## Pastoral Perspective

is a call *to* worship as YHWH cries, "Gather to me my faithful ones, who made a covenant with me by sacrifice!" The call to worship in this instance is for the purposes of God's exercise of judgment on the people of the covenant. For many people, judgment is something to be feared. Some will imagine the examination room or the courtroom. Others will find unpleasant memories of failure awoken in them. While the theology of divine judgment led to the idea of the Day of the Lord as a day to be feared in preexilic prophecy, in general the later and postexilic idea was a cause for rejoicing in Israel as the returning exiles were considered the faithful people of God. Judgment need not imply doom. Judgment can also be the occasion that brings hope in the form of renewed commitment to what really matters in life. Judgment can be the first word of salvation, just as John prepared the way for Jesus (Mark 1:1–4). Indeed, in the continuation of Psalm 50, not included in the reading for today, God lays a number of charges against the people and rebukes them for their turning away from their covenant (v. 21). In the end this judgment leads to a challenge to those who forget God, that they will remember the word of hope for "those who bring thanksgiving as their sacrifice" (v. 23). To them, YHWH cries, "I will show the salvation of God" (v. 23). A cringing response to judgment or the threat of judgment is our attempt to avoid bad feelings or other consequences of our behavior. The alternative for people of faith is to trust in the love of God and the promise that God's desire is that we should know salvation and live. As we trust God for life, we can face anything, including the consequences of our own behavior. We can mark well God's judgment, renew our commitment to following Jesus as the way of life, and see the promised salvation of God.

GEOFFREY M. ST. J. HOARE

---

[7] Augustine, 383. Augustine does not refer to the transfiguration in his exposition. However, it has been traditional for the church to see the transfiguration as a precursor to the resurrection appearances and the "departure" Jesus was about to "accomplish" from Jerusalem (see Luke 9:31 and *Interpreter's Dictionary of the Bible*, "Transfiguration").

[8] Augustine, 387.

## Exegetical Perspective

In biblical parlance, to *fear* God is to embrace integrity in relationships (Gen. 20:11; 42:18). It is to treat others with justice and kindness. The Sinai covenant legislates this way of living. It aims to reinforce and regulate the *fear of God* through statutes, such as those lying behind verses 18–20 of our psalm. From the Sinai experience onward, Israel practiced the *fear of God* by obeying the covenant (Exod. 18:21; Deut. 6:2, 24; 10:12).

Note that our psalm's call to radical obedience and discipleship has nothing to do with works righteousness. Feelings of self-satisfaction are the farthest things from our minds the minute we encounter God's tempestuous otherness. An experience of the *numinous* convicts us of our distance from right living. It overturns us, provoking a surrender to God that can hold nothing back (Gen. 22:12; cf. Matt. 10:37).

*God's Court Convenes.* Overwhelmed by need and obligation, God's worshipers receive their lord and judge with eagerness. They are all ears, convicted of God's right to "judge his people" (v. 4), to "arraign" them in court (v. 7 JPS). This is God's purpose in coming, to hold us accountable for our worship (vv. 7–15) and our conduct (vv. 16–22). To keep things fair, heaven and earth are also present (v. 4). They are the covenant's primordial witnesses (Deut. 4:26; 30:19; Mic. 6:2).

God's court convenes for judicial review, to assess Israel's progress under the covenant. The defendants are God's "covenant people" (v. 5 REV), the ongoing objects of God's faithful care (cf. Deut. 7:9, 12), the ones whom God's grace has made God's own (v. 7; cf. Exod. 20:2; Deut. 5:6). At their feasts each fall, they renew the covenant "by sacrifice" (v. 5; cf. Exod. 24:4–8; Deut. 27:2–7). Their rites are fitting, but their hearts are not in them. Their worship is tepid, just as ours often is today.

God's review and findings in Psalm 50 sound harsh, but their intent is constructive. They set our course back on God's track of obedience, molding our character to conform to our calling. Would that all worship would critique and redirect us. We could then go forth with power, on the growing edge of faith, determined to impact the world for the better.

STEPHEN L. COOK

## Homiletical Perspective

is hard to understand the passion of the psalmist, and therefore difficult to hear it as anything more than superstitious poetry. One of the most overwhelming tasks a preacher faces with this text is translating the psalm's assumptions about God for a congregation that isn't so sure anymore that God set the sun in the sky, or that Zion is the "perfection of beauty" (v. 2). Having settled for a God who rarely or never speaks, churchgoers can be downright alienated by the "otherness" of these texts. Father Kilian McDonnell, OSB, speaks for many when he prays:

> I ask no Mount Sinais, no Tabors,
> No cloud by day, no fire by night,
> Just one unambiguous touch
> lasting one beat of my heart.[1]

The careful preacher must tend not only to those who have been to the mountain, but also to those who have only heard stories—stories that become harder to believe with each passing Sunday. Preaching Transfiguration Sunday a few times now has taught me that while Peter, James, and John might be sitting out in the pews, there are a lot more disciples who were not invited to climb the mountain with Jesus. Some of them are even preachers. A faculty member who is a lifelong churchgoer came up to me after a sermon in our university chapel service and said simply, "I want so much to be a believer." She wasn't looking for affirmation or pastoral care; she just had to say it, then walked away.

The homiletical and pastoral challenge is not to let go of the inherent tension between the psalm's sweeping majesty and the plainness of Sunday morning, but to affirm that there is room for both those whose eyes have been burned with the brightness of God's glory and those whose hearts have been burned by God's absence. Faith inspires both silence and song, and awe requires patience as much as proclamation.

"Gather my people," this God says. Gather the ones who have been to the mountain and those who have set up camp in the valley.

BRIAN ERICKSON

---

[1] Fr. Kilian McDonnell, OSB, "Must You Mumble?" in *Swift, Lord, You Are Not* (Collegeville, MN: Saint John's University Press, 2003).

# 2 Corinthians 4:3-6

³And even if our gospel is veiled, it is veiled to those who are perishing. ⁴In their case the god of this world has blinded the minds of the unbelievers, to keep them from seeing the light of the gospel of the glory of Christ, who is the image of God. ⁵For we do not proclaim ourselves; we proclaim Jesus Christ as Lord and ourselves as your slaves for Jesus' sake. ⁶For it is the God who said, "Let light shine out of darkness," who has shone in our hearts to give the light of the knowledge of the glory of God in the face of Jesus Christ.

## Theological Perspective

An important theological theme in this passage is the knowledge of God. A key question for premodern and modern theology was, "How do we arrive at reliable knowledge of God?" Under the impetus of postmodernity, contemporary preachers recognize that human beings cannot have pure, objective knowledge of God (or of most other things in life), but that all human awareness has an interpretive element. So today a preacher might say that the text introduces the issue of how we can arrive at an adequate interpretation of God.

Paul established the congregation in Corinth by preaching an interpretation of God's work in the world, centered in the claim that the death and resurrection of Jesus Christ reveal that God is bringing the present evil age to an end through a violent apocalyptic catastrophe, after which God will inaugurate a new world that Paul occasionally calls God's realm. To declare Jesus as Lord is for Paul to interpret the death and resurrection of Jesus as a paradigm for how this transformation will take place: an age of suffering (the cross) followed by a new world (resurrection). The suffering results from the principalities and powers of the present age resisting God's initiative through Christ. The Corinthians need to understand that the present world (and the lives of Jesus' followers within it) will

## Pastoral Perspective

There is some scholarly debate about the structure and content of Paul's second letter to the church in Corinth. Yet, whether Second Corinthians contains two letters or ten, what really matters to the church is that the epistle captures some essential aspects of Paul's theology, and in the case of this passage, it is the good news of the glory of God in Jesus Christ.

This particular passage begins midargument, with Paul answering the charge that his gospel is difficult to understand. "And even if our gospel is veiled, it is veiled to those who are perishing. In their case the god of this world has blinded the minds of the unbelievers, to keep them from seeing the light of the gospel of the glory of Christ, who is the image of God" (vv. 3–4). This standard if–then construction, while rhetorically useful in Paul's time, is actually an impediment to preaching this passage in a contemporary setting. To modern ears, Paul sounds like the dishonest tailors in the story of "The Emperor's New Clothes": "If you don't understand the gospel, it's because you aren't among the saved." Yet many congregations are full of people who find the gospel difficult to comprehend, and it is not because they are perishing or blind.

I once took a group of inner-city students canoeing in northern Minnesota. The first night out, when the sun had set, one young woman looked up

## Exegetical Perspective

The assignment of this short text to Transfiguration Sunday veils its larger purpose in Paul's complicated correspondence with the Corinthians. The veil, in fact, is the reason the passage is here, providing both Paul and the preacher with opportunity to compare the revelation of divine glory in Moses and Jesus. Both of these towering figures encountered God on holy mountains. Both were lit with God's own *doxa*. Both led God's people to turn from the ways of death to the ways of life, chiefly by their own example. For all of these reasons, this text is a natural choice for Transfiguration Sunday, when the Gospel reading from Mark will feature Elijah and Moses talking with a transfigured Jesus on "a high mountain apart."

Moses is not mentioned by name in the verses at hand, although he figures prominently in those that lead up to it. Chapter 3 is required reading for anyone who preaches or teaches from chapter 4. There the reader will discover Paul's real interest in the literary device of the veil, which is to use it as a judgment on "the ministry of condemnation" exercised by Moses.

Making trenchant use of *syncrisis*, a rhetorical mode of comparison, Paul contrasts "the ministry of death, chiseled in letters on stone tablets," with "the ministry of the Spirit come in glory" (3:7–8). The

## Homiletical Perspective

"Can you hear me now?" That popular phrase from a cellular telephone advertisement is one that comes to mind when struggling for reception in remote or mountainous places. When reception is poor, words become lost or, as Paul might say, "veiled" (v. 3). Rather than waste words, most cell phone callers hang up and wait for more bars of reception. In terms of gospel proclamation, lost words mean lost people. That is the concern that drives this text.

The preacher of this passage will want to consider in what ways the gospel is veiled today. Who veils it? How? And from whom is it veiled? These questions pierce every congregation's life and conscience. Most churches have a preferred way of doing ministry, but if that way is no longer effective in reaching others, then it is time for a new modus operandi. Churches that practice a centuries-old or decades-old way of being church in a fast-changing and rapidly secularizing world have probably veiled the gospel, however unintentionally. The church must ask, "Have we lost reception with our hearers?" If so, it is time for a reformation of reconnection.

Then there is the question of assigning roles in this pericope. Who are the "unbelievers" (v. 4)? After disciplining a child for misbehavior, the parent is asked a frank but stunning question, "Why do you hate me?" What was intended as a necessary act of

# 2 Corinthians 4:3-6

## Theological Perspective

be characterized by suffering that will not be relieved until Jesus returns and the entire world enters into resurrection life.

However, "superapostles" came to Corinth after Paul and preached another interpretation of the gospel (2 Cor. 11:5; 12:11). They held that Paul's gospel was "veiled," that is, that the apostle had misunderstood God's purposes. The superapostles (according to some scholars) taught a gospel of glory without suffering. They likely believed that the present possession of the Spirit with dramatic ecstatic experience and esoteric visions meant that believers would not have to undergo suffering but would receive the fullness of God's purposes through a series of ups, ups, ups, and upper ups. The superapostles may have used the language of light to describe their experience, and they likely did not believe that the present age was ending and a new world coming.

In today's lection, Paul writes to the Corinthians that if his version of the gospel appears to be veiled to some in the congregation, that veiling is the result of the work of "the god of this world" (i.e., Satan). For Paul, the interpretation of God's purposes offered by the superapostles is not only mistaken but comes from Satan. Those who accept the gospel of the superapostles are "perishing," that is, they suffer diminished life now and will be condemned at the apocalypse. Paul's understanding of the gospel is so important that Paul has made himself a voluntary slave of it.

In 2 Corinthians 4:6, the apostle declares that his version of the gospel is the one that is approved by God. Indeed, just as God said, "Let light shine out of darkness," so the real light of God for the world is the message about the apocalyptic transformation of the world that God sets forth through Jesus Christ.

The congregation at Corinth faced a dilemma: Which vision of reality—the one put forward by Paul or the one by the superapostles—should they accept as better representing the knowledge of God? On what grounds does a congregation choose? Paul claimed that his version of the gospel came from a revelation that God gave directly to him (Gal. 1:1–17) and that this revelation also shone in the hearts of the community. The superapostles may have claimed similarly that their gospel was based on a revelation. How does one decide which revelation to accept?

We really do not know what the congregation in Corinth chose, but the later church sided with Paul. Whether or not the ancient church thought along

## Pastoral Perspective

at the star-filled sky and said, "Where did those come from?" I explained that the stars were always there, but in the city, there was too much light pollution to see any but the brightest stars. The same is true for contemporary Christians: we are not suffering from blindness as much as from an excess of light.

One of the brightest human-made bulbs is the light of reason. Everyone is looking for evidence these days, and data is presumed to be more persuasive than faith. Perhaps that is why some Christians champion the theory of Intelligent Design, believing that once the facts are established, then faith will logically follow. In the same way, my confirmation class is far more interested in how Jesus fed 5,000 people than why he did it. Yet raising human reason to such a lofty position is nothing short of idolatry. It is not that faith is antithetical to reason, but that faith often transcends reason. A colleague once said, "The key to being a Christian these days is to be able to think it through as far as you can but still be willing to leap."

A second "light of the gods of this world" that "blinds" us is the cult of self-actualization. Walk into any bookstore and you will find row upon row of self-help books, all designed to enable you to become the best you can be. Apparently, the road to contentment is paved with the right diet, the perfect mate, and a well-organized closet. Even popular religious writers have come to the conclusion that we (not God) are at the center of all things, and once we understand that, we can have our best life now. Unfortunately, it is hard to see the glory of God when you are standing in the spotlight.

There are other sources of light from the gods of this world that keep us from seeing or seeking God's glory. The entertainment industry, for example, is in the business of creating glitz and glam as a way of getting and holding our attention. Exposed to a constant stream of movies, music, and info-tainment, some people are too distracted even to wonder about the glory of Christ. Another bright distraction is economic success, a shiny but elusive idol after which many people chase. Every community and congregation has its own string of lights. The point is that all the bright lights of modern life have the capacity to mask the glory of God, and we become like that young woman standing in the city, fruitlessly searching the washed-out sky for stars.

So how do we escape the blinding lights of modern life? We heed Paul's words, "For we do not proclaim ourselves; we proclaim Jesus Christ as

## Exegetical Perspective

reason Moses wore a veil, Paul says, was to keep the people of Israel from seeing "the end of the glory that was being set aside" (3:13). As Paul Sampley writes in his commentary on this letter in *The New Interpreter's Bible,* Paul treats Moses's facial glory "almost like a tan that, without further and renewed exposure, fades."[1]

Only in Christ is the veil set aside, Paul goes on to say. Contrasting the greater glory of Christ's ministry of justification with the lesser glory of the ministry of condemnation, Paul speaks for those who, "with unveiled faces," see "the glory of the Lord as though reflected in a mirror" (3:18). While scholars are divided on whether Paul's comparison suggests the fading of the first covenant's glory or the annulment of it, Paul's rhetoric effectively douses any light left on Moses's face. As appropriate as this may have been for Paul's first readers, present-day preachers will distinguish between Jewish-Christian relationships in the first century and in the twenty-first.

In chapter 4 Paul tweaks the image of the veil. Here it no longer hangs over Moses's face but over the faces of those who cannot see the light of the gospel. They are blind to the glory of Christ, but this is not the true God's doing. Instead, it is "the god of this world" (or, in the NIV, "the god of this age") who has blinded the minds of unbelievers. This curious phrase appears nowhere else in the New Testament, leaving open the question of what Paul means by it. Does he mean Satan? Does he mean some other supernatural force? Or does he mean the false loyalties of the present generation, which have taken on godlike proportions for them?

Whatever Paul means, the gist of these verses seems clear. Those who cannot see the glory of God in the face of Jesus Christ are both blind and perishing. Victor Furnish points out that most interpreters "believe that the statement in v. 3 is written to counter the charge that Paul's own gospel, not the covenant of Moses, has been veiled."[2]

As is often the case with Paul's letters, the key to understanding what he writes is to understand its context. In the Corinthian correspondence we have ample opportunity to do that, tracking the relationship between Paul and this particular body of believers through quarrels, passionate reprisals, crises of confidence, and tender reconciliations. The verses at hand likely belong to Paul's fourth letter to

[1] Paul Sampley, *The New Interpreter's Bible: Second Corinthians–Philemon* (Nashville: Abingdon Press, 2000), 11:67.
[2] Victor Paul Furnish, *II Corinthians,* Anchor Bible, vol. 32A (New York: Doubleday, 1984), 247.

## Homiletical Perspective

parental love may well be understood very differently by the child at the receiving end. Good news is not good when misunderstood or misheard. As reader-response critics have been claiming, the reader's reception of the text (as the hearer's reception of the sermon) matters![1]

More questions remain. Who is "the god of this world" (v. 4)? If the function of that "god" is to blind the minds of unbelievers, then the preacher might suggest a few: love of success, accumulation of wealth, blind nationalism, hunger for power and privilege, and church tradition. How easy it is to be so stuffed with creature comforts that the good news is smothered. Lent offers a remedy to such saturation, for it is a season of cross training with disciplines that include self-denial, fasting, praying, and almsgiving.

Who are the "perishing" (v. 3)? And who are the "gospel proclaimers" (v. 5)? Beware that self-righteous hermeneutic that puts one's own congregation, political party, interest group, industry, and nation in the role of the illumined, believing, gospel-proclaiming slaves of Jesus Christ, while those others who stand in the way become the perishing blind. We know better, or should.

To be sure, Paul's language here is dualistic, and his tone is defensive. Still, the preacher of this text should exercise much caution in assigning roles of "in" and "out of" grace. Such lines of separation—like weeds and wheat—are perhaps better left alone, undefined (see Matt. 13:24–30). Only God is judge. Human vision is at best, "in a mirror, dimly" (1 Cor. 13:12), as so many lessons of church history reveal. Paul was defending his ministry against opponents, and his language reflects such anger, fear, and pain. Indeed, the experience of many seasoned clergy is that the most opposition they have faced in ministry comes not from outside the church walls but from within the fellowship. The unfortunate reality is that the church's imperfect witness simultaneously illumines and veils the gospel. It will always be so.

One approach to preaching this text is to note how Paul separates that which is essential from all else. The message of "Jesus Christ as Lord" (v. 5) is where Paul goes in his argument and is the core of Christian proclamation. When new members unite with a Presbyterian congregation, the liturgy asks them to state, "Jesus Christ is my Lord and Savior."[2]

[1] For an overview of reader-response criticism, see David L. Bartlett, *Between the Bible and the Church* (Nashville: Abingdon Press, 1999), 51–55.
[2] Presbyterian Church (U.S.A.), *Book of Common Worship* (Louisville, KY: Westminster/John Knox Press, 1993), 450.

# 2 Corinthians 4:3-6

## Theological Perspective

these lines, I would articulate the theological difference between Paul and the superapostles this way. Paul advocated what we might call a "holy discomfort" with the present status of the world. Paul's gospel calls for people to be discontent with brokenness, injustice, scarcity, exploitation, violence, and death, and to believe that God seeks to increase community, wholeness, justice, abundance, peace, love, and life. On the contrary, the superapostles believed that God's purpose was to create a religious experience that allowed one to feel good within oneself (e.g., through ecstatic emotion) without seeing the need for social change. The gospel of the superapostles provided an escape from the present social setting, whereas Paul's gospel envisioned the transformation of the world. This change, as Paul so vividly saw, can involve suffering as the principalities and powers resist transformation and as new patterns of community struggle to be born.

When deciding whether to accept Paul's interpretation or that of the superapostles as authoritative, today's congregation has an advantage over the one at Corinth. Across the centuries we have seen that escapist religion may help people feel good in the short run, but it leaves brutalizing forces intact. While the Pauline religious life involves struggle, it also offers greater promise, for it points in the direction of a world of greater blessing. Of course, the apocalypse did not occur as quickly as Paul had hoped, and, indeed, many Christians today do not think that an apocalypse as imagined by Paul will occur. Nevertheless, an underlying motif continues to be believable: God is discontent with the fractiousness of the present age and ever offers the world opportunities to become a greater sphere of blessing. Even if conditions do not immediately improve, communities are empowered to resist exploitation and brutality, and to call for a world of community, justice, abundance, peace, love, and life. One of the preacher's theological tasks is to help the congregation identify those forces in the world (e.g., religious experiences; church programs and witnesses; patterns of social relationship; political, philosophical, and economic ideas) with which it should have a holy discomfort, and those that it can commend.

RONALD J. ALLEN

## Pastoral Perspective

Lord, and ourselves as slaves for Jesus' sake" (v. 5). Moving ourselves out of the spotlight is a good first step toward comprehending the gospel and catching a glimpse of the glory of God. It is also a powerful reminder of who serves whom. Despite what some modern evangelists proclaim, God is not some cosmic butler, some omniscient Jeeves sent to cater to our every need. No, God is the one true God, the creator who said, "Let light shine out of the darkness." The creator of light is the source of glory found in the person of Jesus Christ.

Of course, in our mainline congregations, there will undoubtedly be some person who will wonder, "What's so great about the glory of God?" It is a fair question. Why do we seek this glory when we have already managed to illuminate our lives? The answer is that not all light is the same. The bright lights we have created to fend off the darkness have only the power to shine on us. In this world, we see ourselves and others by the harsh and unforgiving human-made glare that reveals only who we are on the outside. But what illuminates Paul and shines through his words is the light of the knowledge of the glory of God in the face of Jesus Christ. This light does not demand that our reasoning be sound or our lives be perfect or our faith be immovable. This light is not something that shines on us but through us. This light reveals, not so much who we are, but whose we are, and has the power to transform us. This light is the glory of God, the glory of Christ.

SHAWNTHEA MONROE-MUELLER

## Exegetical Perspective

the Corinthians, following a third, lost letter in which he called the Corinthians to task for departing from his teachings. Here he builds on the gains of that letter, hoping not only to reestablish his authority among the Corinthians but also to secure their participation in his collection for the church in Jerusalem.

Paul uses the plural pronoun "we" more in this letter than in any other. While this may serve as his acknowledgment of Timothy, whom he names in the first verse of the letter as coauthor, the royal pronoun makes Paul sound as if he speaks for many. "Our gospel," he writes, as if there were a whole cloud of apostles standing right behind him, but it is his gospel he means. "Paul, an apostle of Christ Jesus by the will of God" (1:1) declares elsewhere that the gospel he proclaims is not of human origin but has come to him straight from Jesus Christ (Gal. 1:12).

Yet Paul is careful not to lord his privilege over the Corinthians, especially since he seems to have a reputation for heavy-handedness with them. "For we do not proclaim ourselves," he assures the congregation; "we proclaim Jesus Christ as Lord and ourselves as your slaves for Jesus' sake." Later he will accuse the superapostles of trying to enslave the Corinthians for their own selfish ends (11:20). Here he confounds the expectations of his listeners by ending his sentence in an unprecedented way. He and Timothy do not proclaim themselves the slaves of God in Christ. They proclaim themselves the slaves of the Corinthians, for Jesus' sake (4:5).

Preachers who focus on this passage have a vital decision to make: either to follow Paul's lead, developing a supersessionist sermon that is anti-Jewish in its premise if not in its tone; or to rely on the ongoing glory of God to light another way through this text. Those who choose the latter will note that Paul defends more than the gospel of Christ in these verses. He also defends his own authority to proclaim this gospel. Two thousand years later, in a very different religious situation, the proclamation of Christ's light does not require the debasement of Moses's light. Those who are being transformed by God's shining presence can find far better ways to witness to what they see in Jesus' face.

BARBARA BROWN TAYLOR

## Homiletical Perspective

While in our world we often vilify those who don't agree with us, the centrality of Jesus' lordship urges us toward grace and welcome for all who belong to Christ. We don't choose our sisters and brothers in Christ. Rather, "we baptize those whom God has called."[3] Christian hospitality unveils the good news in a world that sees distinction and shows partiality.

The gospel isn't about us. It is about Jesus the Christ, "who is the image of God" (v. 4). The preacher's proclamation should keep the spotlight there. Note how in the story of Jesus' transfiguration all eyes and ears are left on him. Glory belongs there and not on our pulpits, our politics, or our current church projects. Paul preaches Jesus Christ, not Paul.

This text encourages the preacher to stick to the essentials—to that which is known for certain. The preached word should be intelligible, hearable, and focused, because the gospel is not intended to be veiled.

Preachers of this passage may appropriately share personal witness of struggles faced, experiences lived, and strength found. For as reformer John Calvin helpfully discerned, "Without knowledge of self there is no knowledge of God."[4] As they prepare, preachers may want literally to place themselves in the pews, homes, restaurants, and workplaces of their congregation in order better to enter their world, worries, interests, and questions. Words from the pulpit will find better reception when the one speaking has done careful listening.

Christian witness spoken honestly, clearly, and directly will be effective. "One thing I do know," said the man whom Jesus healed, "that though I was blind, now I see" (John 9:25). Sunday by Sunday the preacher is under an obligation to speak good news. Day by day the congregation has a heavenly opportunity to minister by word and deed to its neighbors. For Christ's sake, let us live as slaves to those who desperately need the saving word that has been revealed to us and which we are called to proclaim.

Can you hear me now?

G. OLIVER WAGNER

[3]Ibid., 404.
[4]John Calvin, *The Institutes of the Christian Religion*, 2 vols., ed. John T. McNeill, trans. Ford Lewis Battles, LCC (Philadelphia: Westminster Press, 1960), 1.1.1, 35.

# Mark 9:2-9

²Six days later, Jesus took with him Peter and James and John, and led them up a high mountain apart, by themselves. And he was transfigured before them, ³and his clothes became dazzling white, such as no one on earth could bleach them. ⁴And there appeared to them Elijah with Moses, who were talking with Jesus. ⁵Then Peter said to Jesus, "Rabbi, it is good for us to be here; let us make three dwellings, one for you, one for Moses, and one for Elijah." ⁶He did not know what to say, for they were terrified. ⁷Then a cloud overshadowed them, and from the cloud there came a voice, "This is my Son, the Beloved; listen to him!" ⁸Suddenly when they looked around, they saw no one with them any more, but only Jesus.

⁹As they were coming down the mountain, he ordered them to tell no one about what they had seen, until after the Son of Man had risen from the dead.

## Theological Perspective

Arguably, identity questions constitute the theological core of Mark's Gospel, with the pericopes in Mark 8:32–9:13 functioning as its theological hinge. Who is Jesus? Who are we? Who does Jesus say that he is? Who does Jesus say that we are? How do we answer the same questions?

Crucifixion and resurrection lie at the heart of Jesus' answers. People are speculating that Jesus is John the Baptist redivivus, maybe Elijah or one of the prophets (8:28; cf. 6:14–16). Peter confesses that Jesus is the Messiah (8:29), which is the evangelist's opinion, too (1:1). In effect, Jesus insists, Peter's answer needs to be recontextualized by the popular one, more precisely, by recognizing that Jesus Christ stands in the great tradition of prophets persecuted by the establishment (8:29). Yes, Elijah must come first to restore all things, but John the Baptist is Elijah redivivus, who has prepared the way through his antiestablishment preaching and martyrdom (6:17–29; 9:12–13). Jesus also will be rejected by the establishment and be killed (Mark 8:31; 10:33–34).

Yet crucifixion must be recontextualized by Jesus' glory. Crucifixion and resurrection go together in Mark's Gospel. It is misleading to speak simply of Jesus' "passion predictions" when all three sayings predict third-day resurrection at the same time (8:31; cf. 9:31, 10:33–34). Just because our text does

## Pastoral Perspective

In the transfiguration story, which lies at the epicenter of the Gospel of Mark, halfway between Jesus' baptism and his resurrection, a voice from heaven tells Peter (and James and John) to "Listen to him!"—that is, to believe Jesus' word (which Peter had disputed) that rejection, suffering, death, and resurrection are integral to his messianic mission, and that the way of the cross is equally integral and inescapable for all who would follow him (cf. Mark 8:34–38).

Neither God nor Jesus the Christ ever explains *why* this must be so (or, for that matter, what cross bearing entails for nonmessiahs). In the entire Gospel, the reason is never given save in a fleeting hint that Jesus' death constitutes a "ransom" (10:45), an idea Mark leaves undeveloped and unexplained. One might even surmise, from Jesus' cry on the cross (15:34), that even *he* does not know the reason. The necessity of the passion remains, in this Gospel, a mystery hidden in the mind of God.

But if the reason is hidden, its *inevitability* should be obvious from the perspective of history. Jesus' devotion to the reign of God on earth inevitably provoked "the powers"—the fear, hatred, greed, falsehood, violence, and despair that pervade and distort everything human—to make their oppressive, murderous response, even if this response also,

## Exegetical Perspective

The boundary zones between the human and the divine are both disorienting and revelatory. Between heaven and earth, the everyday cues and perspectives that tell us who we are and how the world works no longer operate, but we may glimpse a new view of reality that transforms our understanding and refashions our world. The transfiguration of Jesus confuses and terrifies his disciples, but the heavenly voice that speaks from a cloud confirms that Jesus is not only the Christ, as Peter has confessed (8:29), but God's own Beloved Son and affirms that his word of the cross is true. Everything in this episode—Jesus' transformation, the appearance of Elijah and Moses, Peter's babbling attempt to be useful—leads up to the moment when God speaks from the cloud that suddenly overshadows them, naming Jesus and commanding the disciples to "Listen to him!"

The transfiguration is an apocalyptic moment. As at Jesus' baptism, when the heavens are torn open and the divine voice first names that Jesus is God's Beloved Son (1:11), or when the "young man" announces to the women at the tomb that Jesus is risen (16:1–8), God enters the story to uncover what has been hidden from human perception or recognition. Mark locates the transfiguration within a section of the Gospel (8:22–10:52) that weaves together teaching and healings focused on sight and

## Homiletical Perspective

The preacher has visited this text many times before. It is a familiar scene, so familiar that the preacher might be tempted to sideswipe it on her way to something more "relevant." How different is the attitude of the speakers in the text! Fear and terror are everywhere! The Gospel of Mark tells us that Peter was so terrified by the transfiguration that he did not know what to say. The Gospel of Matthew (17:1–8) reports that Jesus touched the disciples because they were overcome with fear at the transfiguration. And the Gospel of Luke records that the disciples were terrified after they entered the cloud along with Jesus, Moses, and Elijah. All three Gospel accounts record the transfiguration as an experience that was not shared with anyone else for quite some time. Now the preacher is presented with at least three choices: (1) follow the lead of the evangelists, taking up a challenge similar to theirs; (2) ignore the challenge; or (3) make the event "safe" by trying to explain it away.

Mark makes it hard to ignore the scene, which lies squarely in the center of Mark's Gospel. The transfiguration draws out the careful listener's memories of other similar biblical theophanies. The high mountain and the heavenly voice from a cloud transport most readers back to the call of Moses on Mount Sinai (Exod. 24:12–18). The brightness of

# Mark 9:2-9

## Theological Perspective

not preserve original stories of the appearance of the risen Jesus, does not mean that Mark's Gospel is skeptical about resurrection. Jesus raises Jairus's daughter (5:35–42). Coming down the mount of transfiguration, Jesus forbids the inner circle of disciples to mention the vision until he has risen from the dead (9:9). The man at the tomb tells the women that the resurrected Jesus will meet them in Galilee (16:6–8), just as he had promised at the Last Supper (14:28). Jesus brings on his condemnation by telling the high priest that he will see the Son of Man coming on the clouds at the right hand of power (14:62). Earlier, Jesus warned the disciples not to make him ashamed of them when he comes in the glory of the Father with the holy angels (8:38). Crucifixion is in Jesus' future, but the Father's honor and glory and power are his as well.

Functionally speaking, Jesus self-identifies as the Messiah who will be rejected and killed by the establishment, who will rise on the third day and return in glory. And Jesus identifies his disciples as the ones who take up their cross, who love Jesus more than our lives, who are not ashamed to confess Jesus publicly, the ones whom Jesus will acknowledge before the Father upon his glorious return (8:34–38).

To Jesus' first disciples in Mark's Gospel, neither part of Jesus' answer is welcome. Their eyes are firmly fixed on human things (8:33). They are determined to make Jesus the hero of their horizontal worlds and the vehicle of their own this-worldly ambitions (9:33–37; 10:35–45). What Mark's Gospel works to drive home is how—for Jesus' first disciples—resurrection glory proved more of a scandal than crucifixion.

The existentialists may be right to say that I cannot conceive of my own nonexistence, because whenever *I* conceive of anything, *I* am still there! But everybody knows the general truth that all humans are mortal. Mortality is intelligible, and crucifixion is intelligible. Jesus' first disciples may have seen what it entails. Doctors down through the centuries have analyzed just how it kills. Death in general, other people's death at least, can be domesticated into our understanding of the natural order, of the way things can be counted on to work. The thought of crucifixion triggers not only animal but rational fear, because we understand how and why crucifixion is a ghastly way to go. Other things being equal, it is *reasonable* to flee, literally (14:27, 50, 52) and psychologically (8:32; 9:34; 10:35–37).

Three times in Mark's Gospel, disciples are confronted with Jesus' outclassing glory: when—

## Pastoral Perspective

ironically, made possible the disclosure of the triumphant power of God's nonviolent love in their very midst.

The transfiguration is therefore also a powerful word to *us* to take up our cross and follow Christ, to walk in his way that in one way or another will provoke the powers against us, but that ultimately discloses the eternal truth and trustworthiness of God's nonviolent love and justice in the midst of evil.

It is important, however, when speaking of the way of the cross, to be clear about what it does not mean. It does not mean that we should seek or regard suffering as a spiritual good in itself or as inherently saving and redemptive—as centuries of misguided Christian theology and piety have often maintained. Jesus did not die because his suffering as such could purge the world of sin and evil. He died because the powers of evil sought to destroy his witness to nonviolent love, justice, and truth. His passion revealed, not only the "evilness of evil"—its intrinsic, deadly violence—but the transforming power of divine love, a powerful, assertive love that does not dominate and defeat evil so much as challenge, expose, and seek to transform it. Such love alone ultimately carries the day; it alone is truly redemptive and saving.

Christians are therefore not called to exhibit a passive love that simply tries to be good and avoid evil. Nor is the way of the cross a private bearing of personal woes for the sake of Jesus. It is rather a vigorous, assertive pursuit of social and personal righteousness through a love that refuses to play the world's power game of domination, exploitation, greed, and deception. The transfiguration story is a call to affirm the ultimate truth of this contrary claim of God and God's way of salvation, and to begin living it with all our heart, soul, and strength in the confidence that Jesus' nonviolent way is truly the way of salvation, healing, and eternal life.

The story of the transfiguration also reveals Jesus as utterly unique, not to be equated with even the immense spiritual stature of a Moses and an Elijah. Yet his uniqueness and divinity are not on public view. Mark strongly emphasizes its hidden character (and Jesus' persistent attempt to keep it hidden). The divinity of Christ is known only to those to whom it is revealed; it is not a matter of public record.

Today noisy evangelical movements—and the mainline churches as well—often make claims for Jesus' divinity as if it were a public truth that anyone might see and grasp. However, the knowledge of Jesus as the divine Son is a matter of revelation that

blindness—especially the disciples' own "blindness" and resistance to Jesus' teaching concerning the cross that awaits him in Jerusalem. Against this canvas of blindness and misunderstanding, the transfiguration dazzles the senses with images of unearthly white clothing (9:3b), the presence of Elijah and Moses, and the overshadowing cloud that brings revelation. Mark recounts the transfiguration as an event that is for the disciples and is told through their eyes: Jesus leads Peter, James, and John up the mountain and is transfigured "before them" (9:2); Elijah and Moses "appear to them" (9:4); Mark describes their reactions and emotions (9:5–6); the cloud "overshadows them" (9:7); the voice from the cloud addresses them (9:7); and the end of the vision is described in terms of what they see when they look around (9:8). The whole scene, in other words, is addressed to any disciple struggling to see, hear, comprehend, and believe the gospel reality.

The divine voice speaks directly to the disciples: "This is my Son, the Beloved; listen to him!" (9:7). Listen to what? The voice from the cloud imparts no new, revelatory information, but directs the disciples' attention back to what they have already heard from Jesus himself, and will again hear in what follows. The revelatory content of the vision lies in Jesus' own words, actions, and destiny. The first passion prediction (8:31), an extended teaching on the necessity of "taking up the cross" and "losing life" for the sake of the gospel (8:34–38), and the provocative claim that "there are some standing here who will not taste death until they see that the kingdom of God has come with power" (9:1) immediately precede the transfiguration.

These statements invite the disciples to embrace the consequences that face those who challenge human imperial power, while they also promise that God's rule will overwhelm the powers of this world, definitively at the cross, which is at once the preeminent symbol of Roman hegemony and the climactic expression of God's liberating power. The transfiguration not only confirms Jesus' status as God's Beloved Son, but underlines, with disruptive splendor, God's affirmation of Jesus' way of the cross. As Jesus stands alongside Elijah and Moses, his word about the cross stands alongside the Law and the Prophets.

Other symbolic images and cues confirm and extend these associations. The six days, the three witnesses, the ascent of a mountain, the transfiguration itself, the cloud, and God's voice from the cloud all recall the story of Moses

Jesus' clothes recalls the resurrection of Jesus (Matt. 28:3). The voice of God brings to mind the baptism of Jesus (Luke 3:22).

Here is a way forward. The first step is to decide what you believe or do not believe about the story. The preacher will want to be aware of what is not said in the text as well as what is said in the sermon. In other words, what people do not hear from the pulpit is just as important as what they do hear.

If the preacher chooses to tell the story as nothing more than a reminder to Mark's audience, then the sermon serves as a historical bookmark for listeners to believe or disbelieve. If the preacher decides to embrace the text as a paradigm for modern-day mountaintop experience, then listeners may want to know how to recognize similar theophanies when they occur. If, on the other hand, the preacher decides that the transfiguration is simply a compilation of biblical reassurances that Jesus is the "Son of Man," then listeners will strain their ears to hear what significance that claim holds in the world they (and we) inhabit.

The second step is to consider the range of possible responses among listeners to this text. What spots in their memories, imaginations, or curiosities does this text open up? What questions does this text provoke? Allowing the text to awaken honest responses in listeners, the preacher has a better shot at bringing the claims of the text forward and helping the congregation probe the deeper meanings of such theophanies. The primary task of the preacher is to do what the text has done—to make the "hidden" identity of Jesus available to all, not just a select group of insiders.

The third step in sermon preparation is to consider the hoped-for outcome of the sermon. What does the transfiguration story want to accomplish in the life of the faith community? Does the text allow the preacher to share modern-day theophanies? Is the transfiguration pointing individuals to their own mountaintop experiences or down the mountain to the valleys of their ordinary lives? Or is the text guiding the faith community to another level in understanding about Jesus' life, death, and resurrection?

Any cursory reading of the Gospel of Mark will reveal a mixture of high and low experiences. Throughout the Gospel we hear Jesus speak about his death and resurrection, suffering and glory. One approach to the sermon is to allow the text to dictate the ebb and flow of the sermon. Indeed we all want to travel to the mountaintop and experience the

# Mark 9:2-9

## Theological Perspective

after the feeding of the 5,000—the great I AM tramples the waves and leaves no footprints (6:47–52; Ps. 77:19); when Peter, James, and John see Jesus transfigured (9:2–9); and when the women are told at the tomb that Jesus is risen from the dead (16:1–8). Each time their response is not fear of the sort that might be heroically overcome in an adventure story, but terror of the sort evoked by horror movies (6:50; 9:6; 16:8).

Jesus' outclassing glory rends the veil of their horizontal world from top to bottom, exposing it as neither permanent nor foundational. However wonderful and challenging, human cultures and social systems, their ends and aims, the projects we invent within them, require to be recontextualized within a much wider, outclassing, really Real frame. Jesus' glory on the mount of transfiguration, like his numinous chaos trampling power, like the power and the glory of Jesus risen from the dead, show up all merely human social constructions as paper tigers, wineskins too brittle and inelastic to contain the bubbling creativity of the really, really Real (2:22). The threat of Jesus' glory is not just that this or that individual will come to an end, even each of us in turn, but that the whole framework in which we have lived and moved and had our being is insubstantial.

Jesus identifies disciples, not just as those who might follow in the footsteps of persecuted prophets and suffer a gruesome death for Jesus' sake and for the sake of the gospel (8:35). Jesus recognizes as disciples those who have the courage to march open eyed into the terra incognita of Jesus' glory, to get sucked into the vortex of really Real Kingdom coming, so as never to come out on the other side.

MARILYN MCCORD ADAMS

## Pastoral Perspective

comes in God's own way and time—as a gift. It is not a possession on the basis of which we can claim spiritual status and institutional or personal power, as if to make little gods of ourselves by ruling the world in his name as many have sought to do (9:33–37!). Like Peter, we want to build tabernacles; like the quarreling disciples, we want our little egos to bask in Jesus' power and glory. But the Gospel of Mark repudiates all such Jesusology, with its underlying egoistic power grab, as idolatry. Jesus' mission was not to make a big deal of himself or to elevate his followers to positions of power, authority, and prestige through identification with him. It was rather to point through and beyond himself to God and to God's coming reign on earth, and to invite his followers to find their voice in bearing witness to this transforming, redemptive God (see 16:8).

Still less does the transfiguration story provide a warrant for disparaging or delegitimizing Jews or Judaism. While Jesus attacks abuses of the Jewish tradition in Mark 7, and Christ ends up "alone" in solitary splendor in the transfiguration (Moses and Elijah having disappeared), Mark's Gospel clearly assumes a profound spiritual continuity with the Law and the Prophets of Israelite tradition, and views Jesus not as its nemesis or successor but as its unique exemplification and fulfillment.

High on the mountain, in a moment of numinous splendor, Jesus was indeed clothed in the dazzling light of God—but only briefly, and to a select few. The heavenly mystery was unveiled, only to be veiled again on the cross—and to be *revealed* again, not in the glorious light of a resurrection appearance, but in an empty tomb with a solitary human figure announcing his resurrection and return to Galilee.

Would that we could display such reverent mystery in *our* proclamation, and such humble, nonviolent, yet assertive love and quest for social righteousness in *our* attempts to follow in his way!

RODNEY J. HUNTER

## Exegetical Perspective

ascending Mount Sinai to receive the stone tablets containing the Law (Exod. 24:9–18). Jesus' white garments recall the divine courtroom scene in Daniel, where earthly empires are put on trial (Dan. 7:9), and foreshadow the white clothing of the martyrs (cf. Rev. 3:5, 18; 4:4; 6:11; 7:9, 13), as well as the appearance of the "young man" at the tomb (Mark 16:5). Both Elijah—the forerunner (cf. 9:11–13)—and Moses beheld the glory of God on mountains during times of trial (Exod. 24; 34:29–35; 1 Kgs. 19:11–18) and, according to Jewish tradition, both ascended to heaven at their deaths, as Jesus will be raised and vindicated by God (cf. 9:9). Their presence in this scene places Jesus' mission, identity, and destiny in correlation with theirs—but his destiny will entail the conquest of death.

Peter has recently confessed that Jesus is the Christ (8:29), but here addresses him as "Rabbi" (cf. 11:21, 14:45), perhaps because he cannot yet form a congruent image of Jesus' messianic identity and his teaching about the cross. Peter's words to Jesus have the feel of words out of place. His offer to build dwellings for Jesus, Moses, and Elijah sounds as if he wants to memorialize the moment or perhaps serve as the court architect for the divine conference. In any case, his offer is a mask for the disciples' fear (9:6). Is it fear of divine presence, or fear of the cross?

Jesus commands the disciples to keep silent until after they have witnessed his death and resurrection (9:9, cf. 8:30). Just as they do not yet accept or understand the necessity or meaning of the cross, Mark notes that they do not understand what he means when he speaks about the resurrection from the dead (9:10). They have enlightenment in association with Jesus' transfiguration, but still they perceive mostly the world's darkness (cf. 2 Cor. 4:3–6). Only after Jesus is crucified and raised can the disciples comprehend that a new world is coming into being, where the threat of death no longer dominates human imagination and where God's Son liberates those who follow his path to the cross.

STANLEY P. SAUNDERS

## Homiletical Perspective

transfiguration with Jesus. Yet the text eventually moves us back down the mountain into the normal routine of life. Even if we have a mountaintop experience, we often do not know how to share it with the faith community. At the same time, the faith community may not know how to receive an experience with God on the mountaintop.

Our individual timelines between birth and death can transport us to several mountaintop theophanies. Sometimes we react just like Peter and are left speechless out of fear. Other times we do not think anyone will believe our story, even if we feel safe to share it. The thought that our experiences in life are linked with God's story unfolding in the world can be reassuring, but it can also be terrifying! We may even experience theophanies without recognizing them at first. Subsequently, we do not attach much significance to these events. Still others of us may be able to report hearing the voice of God, but, out of fear, we do not feel comfortable sharing our experience with the faith community.

The point is this: faith communities can become safe places for both members and seekers to explore the various ways that the identity of Jesus is being revealed. There is also this: not only Jesus' identity, but also his way of discipleship is being revealed. The way that the Lenten journey will follow is a way out of comfort, complacency, and self-aggrandizement, through risk, all the way to resurrection.

No matter what approach the preacher takes to the sermon, the integrity of the sermon is dependent on the authenticity of the approach. Preachers can never assume that our listeners will agree with our interpretation of Scripture. However, most listeners are willing to follow our reasoning as long as we can assure them that we have honored the biblical text.

DONALD BOOZ

# Contributors

Charles L. Aaron Jr., Pastor, First United Methodist Church, Farmersville, Texas

Marilyn McCord Adams, Regius Professor of Divinity at Oxford University and Canon of Christ Church Cathedral, Oxford, United Kingdom

Ronald J. Allen, Nettie Sweeney and Hugh Th. Miller Professor of Preaching and New Testament, Christian Theological Seminary, Indianapolis, Indiana

Wm. Loyd Allen, Sylvan Hills Baptist Professor of Church History and Spiritual Formation, McAfee School of Theology, Atlanta, Georgia

Anne H. K. Apple, Parish Associate, Idlewild Presbyterian Church, Memphis, Tennessee

Talitha Arnold, Senior Minister, The United Church of Santa Fe, Santa Fe, New Mexico

William V. Arnold, Pastor to Senior Adults, Bryn Mawr Presbyterian Church, Bryn Mawr, Pennsylvania

Scott Bader-Saye, Associate Professor of Theological Ethics, University of Scranton, Scranton, Pennsylvania

Randall C. Bailey, Andrew W. Mellon Professor of Hebrew Bible, Interdenominational Theological Center, Atlanta, Georgia

Lee Barrett, Professor of Theology, Lancaster Theological Seminary, Lancaster, Pennsylvaia

David L. Bartlett, Professor of New Testament, Columbia Theological Seminary, Decatur, Georgia

Eugene C. Bay, President, Colgate Rochester Crozer Divinity School, Rochester, New York

Timothy A. Beach-Verhey, Director of the Lilly Programs for the Theological Exploration of Vocation; Assistant Chaplain, and Adjunct Assistant Professor of Religion, Davidson College, Davidson, North Carolina

Dianne Bergant, CSA, Professor of Old Testament Studies, Catholic Theological Union, Chicago, Illinois

Dave Bland, Professor of Homiletics, Harding University Graduate School of Religion, Memphis, Tennessee

Donald Booz, District Executive, Church of the Brethren, Mid-Atlantic District, Ellicott City, Maryland

Lee W. Bowman, Senior Pastor, First Presbyterian Church, Lexington, Kentucky

Richard Boyce, Associate Professor of Preaching and Pastoral Leadership, Union Theological Seminary–Presbyterian School of Christian Education at Charlotte, North Carolina

Paul D. Brassey, Director of Music Ministries, St. Mark Lutheran Church, Lacey, Washington

William Brosend, Associate Professor of Homiletics, The School of Theology, The University of the South, Sewanee, Tennessee

Elton W. Brown, Pastor, Aurora/Hoyt Lakes United Methodist Parish, Aurora, Minnesota

Sally A. Brown, Elizabeth M. Engle Associate Professor of Preaching and Worship, Princeton Theological Seminary, Princeton, New Jersey

William P. Brown, Professor of Old Testament, Columbia Theological Seminary, Decatur, Georgia

Katherine C. Calore, Vicar, St. Stephen's Church, Mt. Vernon, Missouri

Charles L. Campbell, Peter Marshall Professor of Homiletics, Columbia Theological Seminary, Decatur, Georgia

Carlos F. Cardoza-Orlandi, Associate Professor of World Christianity, Columbia Theological Seminary, Decatur, Georgia

William J. Carl III, President and Professor of Homiletics, Pittsburgh Theological Seminary, Pittsburgh, Pennsylvania

Gary W. Charles, Pastor, Central Presbyterian Church, Atlanta, Georgia

Linda Lee Clader, Dean of Academic Affairs and Professor of Homiletics, Church Divinity School of the Pacific, Berkeley, California

Kimberly L. Clayton, Interim Director of Lifelong Learning, Columbia Theological Seminary, Decatur, Georgia

Ashley Cook Cleere, Chaplain, Piedmont College, Demorest, Georgia

Stephen L. Cook, Catherine N. McBurney Professor of Old Testament Language and Literature, Virginia Theological Seminary, Alexandria, Virginia

Shelley D. B. Copeland, Executive Director, The Capitol Region Conference of Churches, Hartford, Connecticut

Martin B. Copenhaver, Senior Pastor, Wellesley Congregational Church, Wellesley, Massachusetts

MaryAnn McKibben Dana, Associate Pastor, Burke Presbyterian Church, Springfield, Virginia

Lillian Daniel, Senior Minister, First Congregational Church, United Church of Christ, of Glen Ellyn, Illinois

Patricia E. de Jong, Senior Minister, First Congregational Church of Berkeley, Berkeley, California

Lewis R. Donelson, Professor of New Testament, Austin Presbyterian Seminary, Austin, Texas

Mark Douglas, Associate Professor of Christian Ethics, Columbia Theological Seminary, Decatur, Georgia

P. C. Enniss, Theologian in Residence, Trinity Presbyterian Church, Atlanta, Georgia

Brian Erickson, University Chaplain, University of Evansville, Evansville, Indiana

Clyde Fant, Professor Emeritus, Religious Studies, Stetson University, DeLand, Florida

Stephen Farris, Dean, St. Andrew's Hall, Vancouver, British Columbia, Canada

David Forney, Associate Dean of Faculty and Director of Institutional Research, Columbia Theological Seminary, Decatur, Georgia

Susan R. Garrett, Professor of New Testament, Louisville Presbyterian Theological Seminary, Louisville, Kentucky

Mike Graves, Professor of Homiletics and Worship, Central Baptist Theological Seminary, Kansas City, Kansas

Christopher B. Hays, Adjunct Professor of Old Testament, Candler School of Theology, Emory University, Atlanta, Georgia

William R. Herzog II, Dean of the Faculty and Professor of New Testament Interpretation, Andover Newton Theological School, Newton Centre, Massachusetts

Allen R. Hilton, Senior Minister, Plymouth Congregational Church, United Church of Christ, Seattle, Washington

Geoffrey M. St. J. Hoare, Rector, All Saints' Episcopal Church, Atlanta, Georgia

Ruthanna B. Hooke, Assistant Professor of Homiletics, Virginia Theological Seminary, Alexandria, Virginia

Paul K. Hooker, Executive Presbyter, Presbytery of St. Augustine, Presbyterian Church (U.S.A.), Jacksonville, Florida

Leslie J. Hoppe, OFM, Professor of Old Testament, Catholic Theological Union, Chicago, Illinois

James C. Howell, Senior Pastor, Myers Park United Methodist Church, Charlotte, North Carolina

Mary Lin Hudson, Professor of Homiletics and Liturgics, Memphis Theological Seminary, Memphis, Tennessee

Rodney J. Hunter, Professor of Pastoral Theology Emeritus, Candler School of Theology, Emory University, Atlanta, Georgia

Christopher R. Hutson, Associate Professor of New Testament, Hood Theological Seminary, Salisbury, North Carolina

Jerry Irish, Professor of Religious Studies, Pomona College, Claremont, California

Cynthia A. Jarvis, Minister, The Presbyterian Chuch of Chestnut Hill, Philadelphia, Pennsylvania

E. Elizabeth Johnson, J. Davidson Philips Professor of New Testament, Columbia Theological Seminary, Decatur, Georgia

Verity A. Jones, Publisher and Editor, Disciples World, Indianapolis, Indiana

Eunjoo Mary Kim, Associate Professor of Homiletics, Iliff School of Theology, Denver, Colorado

Elizabeth C. Knowlton, Canon for Prayer and Mission, The Cathedral of St. Philip, Atlanta, Georgia

Steven J. Kraftchick, Associate Professor of New Testament Interpretation, Candler School of Theology, Emory University, Atlanta, Georgia

Kimberly Bracken Long, Assistant Professor of Worship and Coordinator of Worship Resources for Congregations, Columbia Theological Seminary, Decatur, Georgia

David J. Lose, Academic Dean and Marbury E. Anderson Chair in Biblical Teaching, Luther Seminary, St. Paul, Minnesota

Dwight M. Lundgren, Reconciliation Ministries, National Ministries, American Baptist Churches, USA, Valley Forge, Pennsylvania

Ross Mackenzie, Historian Emeritus, Chautauqua Institution, Richmond, Virginia

Al Masters, Pastor, St. Andrews Presbyterian Church, Taylors, South Carolina

Allen C. McSween Jr., Pastor, Fourth Presbyterian Church, Greenville, South Carolina

James W. McTyre, Pastor, Lake Hills Presbyterian Church, Knoxville, Tennessee

Shawnthea Monroe-Mueller, Senior Pastor, Plymouth Church, United Church of Christ, Shaker Heights, Ohio

Joseph Monti, Professor of Christian Ethics and Moral Theology, The School of Theology, The University of the South, Sewanee, Tennessee

Donald W. Musser, Hal S. Marchman Professor of Civic and Social Responsibility Emeritus, Stetson University, DeLand, Florida

Andrew Nagy-Benson, Senior Minister, Spring Glen Church, United Church of Christ, Hamden, Connecticut

Kathleen M. O'Connor, William Marcellus McPheeters Professor of Old Testament, Columbia Theological Seminary, Decatur, Georgia

Ofelia Ortega, Professor of Theological Ethics, Evangelical Theological Seminary, Matanzas, Cuba

Douglas F. Ottati, Craig Family Distinguished Professorship in Reformed Theology and Justice Ministry, Davidson College, Davidson, North Carolina

Eugene Eung-Chun Park, Dana and Dave Cornsife Professor of New Testament, San Francisco Theological Seminary, San Anselmo, California

Thomas D. Parker, Professor of Theology Emeritus, McCormick Theological Seminary, Chicago, Illinois

Joseph L. Price, C. Milo Cornick Professor of Religious Studies, Whittier College, Whittier, California

Richard A. Puckett, Director of Public Relations and Development, United Methodist Children's Home, Decatur, Georgia

Andrew Purves, Hugh Thomson Kerr Professor of Pastoral Theology, Pittsburgh Theological Seminary, Pittsburgh, Pennsylvania

Charles Quaintance, Assistant Professor of Homiletics, Hanover College, Hanover, Indiana

Gail A. Ricciuti, Associate Professor of Homiletics, Colgate Rochester Crozer Divinity School, Rochester, New York

Cynthia L. Rigby, W. C. Brown Professor of Theology, Austin Presbyterian Theological Seminary, Austin, Texas

V. Bruce Rigdon, President Emeritus, Ecumenical Theological Seminary, Detroit, Michigan

John W. Riggs, Professor of Historical Theology and Church History, Eden Theological Seminary, St. Louis, Missouri

Marcia Y. Riggs, J. Erskine Love Professor of Christian Ethics, Columbia Theological Seminary, Decatur, Georgia

Luis R. Rivera, Associate Professor of Theology, McCormick Theological Seminary, Chicago, Illinois

Vernon K. Robbins, Professor of New Testament and Comparative Sacred Texts, Emory University, Atlanta, Georgia

Dale Rosenberger, Senior Pastor, Dennis Union Church United Church of Christ, Dennis, Massachusetts

Stanley P. Saunders, Associate Professor of New Testament, Columbia Theological Seminary, Decatur, Georgia

Donna Schaper, Senior Minister, Judson Memorial Church, New York, New York

Trisha Lyons Senterfitt, Associate Pastor, First Presbyterian Church, Atlanta, Georgia

Judy Yates Siker, Dean of Faculty and Associate Professor of New Testament, American Baptist Seminary of the West and The Graduate Theological Union, Berkeley, California

G. Malcolm Sinclair, Minister, Metropolitan United Church, Toronto, Ontario, Canada

Ted A. Smith, Assistant Professor of Ethics and Society, Vanderbilt University Divinity School, Nashville, Tennessee

Thomas R. Steagald, Pastor, First United Methodist Church, Stanley, North Carolina

Martha Sterne, Associate Rector, Holy Innocents' Episcopal Church, Atlanta, Georgia

George W. Stroup, J. B. Green Professor of Theology, Columbia Theological Seminary, Decatur, Georgia

Beth LaNeel Tanner, Associate Professor of Old Testament, New Brunswick Theological Seminary, New Brunswick, New Jersey

Barbara Brown Taylor, Butman Professor of Religion, Piedmont College, Demorest, Georgia; Adjunct Professor of Christian Spirituality, Columbia Theological Seminary, Decatur, Georgia

Steven S. Tuell, Associate Professor of Old Testament, Pittsburgh Theological Seminary, Pittsburgh, Pennsylvania

W. C. Turner, Associate Professor of the Practice of Homiletics, Duke University Divinity School, Durham, North Carolina

G. Oliver Wagner, Pastor, Montoursville Presbyterian Church, Montoursville, Pennsylvania

Richard F. Ward, Associate Professor of Preaching and Performance Studies, Iliff School of Theology, Denver, Colorado

Marsha M. Wilfong, Pastor, First Presbyterian Church, Bellevue, Iowa

Patrick J. Willson, Pastor, Williamsburg Presbyterian Church, Williamsburg, Virginia

Robert R. Wilson, Hoober Professor of Religious Studies and Professor of Old Testament, Yale Divinity School, New Haven, Connecticut

Charles M. Wood, Lehman Professor of Christian Doctrine, Perkins School of Theology, Southern Methodist University, Dallas, Texas

Lawrence Wood, Pastor, Fremont United Methodist Church, Fremont, Michigan

Christine Roy Yoder, Associate Professor of Old Testament, Columbia Theological Seminary, Decatur, Georgia

Catherine F. Young, Retired Pastor, Presbyterian Church (U.S.A.), Waterloo, Iowa

# Scripture Index